JUSTICE AND CIVIL PROCEDURE IN JAPAN

by
Carl F. Goodman

Oceana Publications, Inc., Dobbs Ferry, New York

Library of Congress Control Number: 2004104266

ISBN 0-379-21521-7

Manufactured in the United States of America on acid-free paper.

Dedication

To Beatrice Delphine Goodman whose advice led me to choose law as my profession, whose encouragement led me to Hiroshima University and whose understanding led me to my studies in Japan and the writing of this book.

Summary Table of Contents

Detailed Table of Contents

About the Author

Professor Carl F. Goodman is Adjunct Professor of Japan/United States Comparative Law at Georgetown University Law Center and was Professor of Anglo-American Law at Hiroshima University for three years. In private practice Professor Goodman represented various Japanese corporate interests in litigation and other aspects of American law while a partner in the International firms of Surrey and Morse and Jones Day Reavis and Pogue from which he is retired. Professor Goodman spent four months in the Spring/Summer of 2003 at Tokyo University on a Fulbright Research grant studying the civil procedure system in Japan and the effects of the 1996 Code of Civil Procedure on litigation in Japan.

Professor Goodman was in public service for 15 years. While in the government he was the United States Agent before the International Lake Ontario Claims Commission (U.S. and Canada), a senior litigator for the Justice Department, handling both domestic and transnational litigation, and left government service as the General Counsel of the United States Civil Service Commission.

He is a former member of the Council of the Administrative Law Section of the American Bar Association and a former Chairman of the Administrative Law Committee of the Association of the Bar of the City of New York. He is a Life Member of the American Law Institute. He is a member of the New York and District of Columbia Bars and is admitted to practice before various Federal Courts including the Supreme Court of the United States.

Professor Goodman is the author of two previous legal texts: A Handbook of Civil Service Law (Law Journal Seminar Press, 1978) and The Rule of Law in Japan: A Comparative Analysis (Kluwer Law International, 2001).

Professor Goodman and Beatrice Delphine Goodman his wife of 46 years reside in Bethesda Maryland and spend their summers in Becket Massachusetts.

Acknowledgments

The number of people who influenced my interest in Japan and Japanese Law is too great for me to thank them all. Special mention must be made of Professor Hiroyuki Hata formerly Dean of Hiroshima University Faculty of Law and Kinki University Faculty of Law and presently President of Kinki University. Professor Hata's mentoring of my stay in Hiroshima, his introduction of Japanese constitutional law to my frame of reference and his assistance in arranging meetings for me with Japanese scholars over the years has been invaluable to whatever understanding I have of the Japanese legal system. Special mention must also be made of Professor Yugi Saeki of Hiroshima University whose advice especially concerning litigation under the Administrative Case Litigation Law was most helpful. Finally, the Fulbright Program and the Japan-United States Educational Committee, which provided the funding for my 2003 research into the actual workings of the civil justice system in Japan, and the Northeast Asia Council of the Association for Asian Studies, which assisted in the funding of such research, are entitled to special thanks.

1

Introduction

The American legal landscape is marked by procedural requirements. American law is consumed by procedure. This obsession with procedure began early in the life of the Republic. The Constitution of the United States is basically a statement of the structure and functioning of the new government that the Framers were creating to replace the dysfunctional Confederation established by the Articles of Confederation. The populace was not convinced that this new government would not suffer from the same defects as the British Colonial system. There was concern that this new national government, located far from many of the States under its orb, would subsume powers that the British Crown had exercised under colonial rule. On the theory that local rule was more responsive to local concerns, the populous stood in danger of rejecting the new form of government created in Philadelphia. To damp the fires of rejection, the Framers promised that a Bill of Rights would be adopted as an amendment to the Constitution to protect the rights of the public.

The first ten amendments, the Bill of Rights, are today seen as a hallmark of American democracy. Yet this Bill of Rights contains precious few substantive rights. The First Amendment's statements of the rights of free speech and religious freedom are clearly substantive, as is the Fifth Amendment's requirement that just compensation be paid for a taking of private property for public use and the Eighth Amendment's prohibition against cruel and unusual punishments. But beyond these provisions the remainder of the Bill of Rights—as it has affect on today's society—is noticeably short of substantive rights. The Second Amendment grants a substantive right to bear arms (which may or may not be conditional on the existence of a militia). The extent of this right is clearly limited by the government's authority to limit the possession of weapons and the type of weapons that can be possessed. The Third Amendment's right to be free from the quartering of soldiers has little meaning in the modern world. The rights that modern American's derive from the Bill of Rights (aside from the First Amendment rights and the debate over the death penalty centered on the Eighth Amendment) are mostly procedural in nature.

Thus, the Fourth Amendment's right against unreasonable search and seizure is a procedural right. The government has the right to search and seize papers and things in pursuance of its law enforcement function, provided it follows the procedures set forth in the Amendment. A warrant must be obtained upon probable cause, supported by oath or affirmation, and particularizing the place, person or thing for which the warrant is issued. Fourth Amendment litigation today concerns itself not with whether the government has the right to search and not with whether the citizen has a right to be secure against search, but rather with whether the procedural requirements of the amendment have been met.

So too the Fifth Amendment first concerns itself with the procedures required when a person is to be charged with a capital or otherwise infamous crime. For such a charge there must generally be a Grand Jury indictment. The double jeopardy prohibition is a procedural clause, as is the famed privilege against self-incrimination. Reflecting the Bill of Rights' concern with procedure, the Fifth Amendment contains a due process clause preventing the government from depriving a person of life, liberty or property, except in accordance with due process. Note that persons are not protected against loss of life, liberty or property. Rather, such rights may be taken as long as the taking conforms to due process.

The Sixth Amendment is filled with procedure for a criminal trial. The trial must be speedy and public; the defendant is entitled to an impartial jury, informed of the charges against him/her, a right to confront accusers, and has compulsory process and assistance of counsel rights. Even the location of the trial—a procedural issue—is dealt with in the Amendment. The Seventh Amendment sets out the procedures for trial of actions at common law. Even the first amendment adopted after the Bill of Rights, the Eleventh Amendment, concerns itself with procedural matter, namely the immunity of States from certain proceedings instituted in the courts.

Of course, the Civil War Amendments (13, 14 and 15) were specifically designed to assure that those who had previously been denied any rights were now granted basic rights of citizenship. Thus slavery was abolished and the right to vote supposedly assured to those who had been denied that right because of their race or color. But even the Civil War amendments are short on substance and long on procedure. Thus while all persons are entitled to equal protection of the laws, no specific rights are granted to such persons. Perhaps the most significant of the Civil War amendment rights is the due process right contained in the Fourteenth Amendment.

Due process and its components preoccupy much of today's American law. By "incorporating" certain of the procedural rights contained in the Bill of Rights into the due process clause of the Fourteenth Amendment, the Supreme Court has extended these procedural rights to persons, whether in conflict with their State or with the Federal Government. The landmark cases of the 20th century tend to be procedural in nature. *Gidean v. Wainright* (dealing with the right to counsel) and

Miranda v. Arizona (dealing with the right to silence) are now part of the folklore of the United States.

In a sense this is as it should be. The Framers drafting the Bill of Rights were familiar with the power of the State to suppress freedom through the use of criminal law. They were aware of the procedural rights granted by the English common law to those suspected of and accused of crime. The Framers saw these procedural rights as a way of protecting the public from abuse of government power. And, it was to protect against such abuse that the promise of a Bill of Rights was made.

In the modern administrative state, the notion of procedural rights continues to dog American law. Thus, extensive powers may be delegated to governmental agencies (in accordance with the standards required by the delegation doctrine). But in exercising those powers the agencies are constrained by procedural requirements. Administrative rules and regulations having the force and effect of law can only be promulgated after notice and comment procedures; administrative adjudications can only be had when procedural rules, closely paralleling those of a judicial trial, are followed. Failure of an agency to follow the procedural rules spells rejection of its actions by the judicial review that American administrative law inevitably provides for administrative action. The judiciary may not substitute its value judgments for those of the administrators, but the judiciary may strike down the administrative action because the administrator slipped up on a procedural point. A challenger to administrative action cannot argue that the administrator "got it wrong," unless the wrong is so wrong as to be arbitrary. A challenger can argue that the administrator went about getting the answer in the wrong way—even if the answer should be, in the view of the court, correct. We do not have a right to be free of incorrect (but not arbitrary) rules arrived at through proper procedure, nor do we have a right to correct rules arrived at through wrong procedures.

Such a focus on procedural rights is appropriate for a society consumed with ideas of individual rights to be free from obtrusive government. The individual right of the accused person is seen as more important than the right of the society to be free from the antisocial conduct engaged in by the individual. The American system sees individuals and individual rights as a means of protecting the rights of all the individuals in the society. Individual rights protect the rights of society in general—even if in a specific case it may appear that society is placed at risk by letting an admitted criminal go free because of procedural error by the governmental authorities.

American ideas of procedure extend far beyond the range of domestic law. Thus in the "War against Terrorism," American society debates what procedural rules should apply to those captured on a foreign battlefield—it is acceptable to kill the enemy on the battlefield, but is it permissible to capture him and deny him a right to counsel? Are those who make war against the society entitled to procedural due process protections? If so, is this right restricted to American citizens wherever they may be located, to those caught on American territory whatever their nationality or the legality of their presence in the United States, or is it applicable to all wherever caught and wherever held?

Procedural rights are not limited to the "public law" arena. The Constitution promises that in all actions at common law seeking damages in excess of $20 the right to trial by jury is available. Parties to a civil private law lawsuit are entitled to due process of law, including notice and an opportunity to be heard. Foreign defendants can be sued in United States courts, but only if such suit is not inconsistent with ideas of fairness encompassed in due process.

After the Second World War, the American Occupation Authority in Japan was given the task of writing a constitution for Japan. To meet this challenge the Occupation drafted a document that contained both substantive and procedural rights. Some of the substantive rights came out of American statute law—thus, workers were given the right "to organize and to bargain and act collectively,"[1] clearly a reflection of the American labor law. Other substantive rights were not enshrined in American law but reflected the New Deal ideology of the Constitution's drafters and the left-leaning sympathy of the Japanese political parties that suffered in the prewar and wartime periods. Thus Japanese were given "the right to maintain the minimum standards of wholesome and cultured living"[2] as well as "the right and obligation to work."[3] Still other substantive rights were inserted in the Constitution to clearly mark a break from Japan's feudal past and to assure that the government could not infringe on the rights of citizens. Thus, the Japanese Constitution contains a litany of rights such as: the right to "choose their public

---

1 Constitution of Japan, Article 28. The Constitution of Japan was drafted in English and then translated into Japanese. The English language version is available from numerous sources (both public and private) both on the World Wide Web ("web") and elsewhere. Various Japanese laws (codes and/or statutes) cited herein are available in English translation from various sources. The Japanese government and agencies of the government have made English language translations of selected Japanese laws available through government web sites. Private organizations have also made English language translations of some Japanese laws available on the web. There are some English language web sites that have links to English language translations of some Japanese laws and the web site of the Prime Minister of Japan (English language version) has links to Ministry sites where translations of some laws may be found. The Government of Japan is considering a project to translate additional Japanese laws into English. English language translations of various Japanese laws and portions of laws are also available as appendices to books on Japanese law. Compilations of translations of some Japanese language laws as well as stand-alone versions of numerous Japanese laws are also available. The author is not aware of the current general availability of any English language translations of the 2003 amendments to the Code of Civil Procedure discussed herein or the 2004 bills dealing with judicial reform submitted by the Government of Japan to the Diet in the Spring of 2004. The author is also not aware of the current availability of any English language translations of the various judicial reform laws enacted in 2004 as a consequence of the 2004 bills mentioned above.

2 Constitution of Japan, Article 25.

3 Constitution of Japan, Article 27.

officials and to dismiss them;"[4] adults were given the right to vote;[5] girls were given the right to an education equal to that of boys;[6] children were given a right against exploitation;[7] the right to own property was made "inviolable;"[8] the right of peaceful petition was guaranteed;[9] torture was prohibited,[10] etc. To assure that the public's rights in certain areas were guaranteed by the Constitution various "freedoms" were set out in the document. Such freedoms include: "freedom of thought and conscience,"[11] "freedom of religion,"[12] "freedom of assembly and association as well as speech, press, and all other forms of expression,"[13] freedom to choose and change a residence and an occupation as well as to travel abroad,[14] and "academic freedom is guaranteed."[15]

American ideas of procedural rights were not forgotten. The Japanese Constitution appears to embody virtually all of the procedural protections contained in the American Bill of Rights. Thus, warrants are required for arrest,[16] and for search and seizure.[17] Detainees were given the "privilege of counsel immediately upon detention;"[18] accused persons "shall have the assistance of competent counsel who shall, if the accused is unable to secure the same by his own efforts, be assigned to his use by the State."[19] In all criminal cases those accused of crimes are entitled to "a speedy and public trial by an impartial tribunal,"[20] and are granted the right to compulsory process for defensive purposes.[21] Persons may not be compelled to testify against themselves, coerced confessions are not admissible against an ac-

4 Constitution of Japan, Article 15.

5 Constitution of Japan, Article 15(3).

6 Constitution of Japan, Article 26(2).

7 Constitution of Japan, Article 27(3).

8 Constitution of Japan, Article 29.

9 Constitution of Japan, Article 16.

10 Constitution of Japan, Article 36. The use of torture in civil cases was prohibited in 1872; physical torture restrictions were adopted in 1874; and physical torture was totally prohibited in 1879. Kenzo Takayanagi, A Century of Innovation: The Development of Japanese Law, 1868-1961 in LAW IN JAPAN (VON Mehren Ed. Harvard University Press, 1963) 20; Paul Heng-Chao Ch'en, THE FORMATION OF THE EARLY MEIJI LEGAL ORDER (Oxford University Press, 1981) 52; Haruo Abe, Self-incrimination—Japan and the United States, 46 Journal of Criminal Law, Criminology & Police Science 613, 614-616 (1956).

11 Constitution of Japan, Article 19.

12 Constitution of Japan, Article 20.

13 Constitution of Japan, Article 21.

14 Constitution of Japan, Article 22.

15 Constitution of Japan, Article 23.

16 Constitution of Japan, Article 34.

17 Constitution of Japan, Article 35.

18 Constitution of Japan, Article 34.

19 Constitution of Japan, Article 37.

20 Constitution of Japan, Article 37.

21 Constitution of Japan, Article 37.

cused and an accused cannot be convicted on the sole basis of his/her confession.[22] A right against double jeopardy is provided for.[23] Persons are granted a right of "access to the courts,"[24] and criminal defendants who are found not guilty have a right to sue the State for redress.[25] Unlike the American Constitution, which provides for "due process of law," the Japanese Constitution provides "[n]o person shall be deprived of life or liberty, nor shall any other criminal penalty be imposed, except according to procedure established by law."[26] This provision is significantly different from the American provision in that the American concept is that the notion of due process overrides conflicting laws and is an overarching right of the public that needs no statutory base. In Japan however there is no constitutional concept of due process, and the only process that a citizen is due is that process that is provided for in the codes and other legislative acts of the government.

But Japanese society and the legal system are not structured on the notion of individual rights that underlies the American system. Japan is more "group oriented." The greater rights of the group, i.e., the Japanese nation, subsume the rights of the individual, and accordingly virtually all individual rights must be viewed in context and balanced against competing rights. As a consequence, both the substantive and procedural rights set out in the Constitution are given a less generous construction than in the United States when applied to individuals in Japanese society. Rather, notions of the greater good of the society or the rights of the populous in general may be balanced against the individual rights that appear to be set out in the Constitution. When procedural rights stand in the way of the greater good of the society, the procedural right may have to bend to accommodate the greater societal need.

Japan is the second largest economy in the world and its citizens are necessarily drawn into disputes among themselves and/or with trading partners. Japan's biggest trading partner is the United States, which also is the source of much of Japan's post-war legal changes. Not only was the United States the principal player in the "amendment" of Japan's Constitution but it was the moving force behind Japan's post-war adoption of a kind of adversary system for litigation and the consequent "modification" of the pre-war German-based inquiry system. But like a pendulum, the notion of procedural reform is swinging back to the European model. As a consequence, Japan's litigation system is caught somewhere between the inquiry system that is seen as its heritage and the adversary system that is enshrined in its Code. Indeed the sweep of the pendulum is sufficiently broad that Japan finds itself caught somewhere between litigation and its more ancient history of conciliation, mediation and settlement as the preferred method of resolving

---

22 Constitution of Japan, Article 38.

23 Constitution of Japan, Article 39.

24 Constitution of Japan, Article 32.

25 Constitution of Japan, Article 40.

26 Constitution of Japan, Article 31.

disputes. At the moment, the pendulum is swinging back to the inquisition system and back to conciliation and away from the American style adversary system.

It is the purpose of this text to examine the question of obtaining justice through Japan's civil justice system. Civil justice is seen through American eyes and thus includes "administrative litigation," in which the citizen and State are adversary parties, and where State administrative action is at issue. Cultural and historic norms are first examined to set the "playing field," because it is that playing field that influences how the courts in Japan view and apply both the modern Constitution and statutory law. Next, the new Constitution's restructuring of the Japanese Government is considered with emphasis on the judicial system and the question of how the system has responded to the demand of city dwellers for more say in the political life of the nation. The system's response (or failure to adequately respond, as the case may be) is useful as a reminder of the ways in which procedure may be used to thwart substantive rights. Similarly, the philosophical bent of the Japanese Supreme Court is examined. Some substantive provisions of the Constitution, beginning with the Renunciation of War clause, are examined. The post-war Code revisions, including the adoption of what appears to be an adversary system, are explored. Civil litigation is examined, beginning with the filing of the Complaint, to the judgment delivered by the court of last resort. In this connection, the New Code of Civil Procedure adopted in 1996 (effective 1998 and further amended in 2001, 2003 and under review again in 2004) is analyzed in depth. The new Constitution abolished the old Administrative Court, placing review of administrative action in the civil justice system. The Occupation's assumption that the new administrative law being created would subject government action to review by the Judicial Branch is also considered. Adoption of new reforms in the system of educating lawyers (inaugurated in April 2004), designed to better educate a larger class of legal professionals and to speed up and generally improve the civil justice system, is also considered. Modern avenues of alternative dispute resolution [ADR], the preferred method of resolving disputes in Japan's feudal past as well as during the Meiji era, are considered. Finally, the nature of Justice as seen through the Japanese legal system is explored.

2

Cultural and Historic Norms as They Affect Procedure

American obsession with procedure has its roots in feudal England. Feudalism in Europe, including Norman France from whence came the English Kings, following the Battle of Hastings and the British Isles prior to the Norman Invasion, was built on the foundation of the decline of the Roman Empire. Rome had a base in the British Isles, and Roman law extended to both England and France. European feudalism was itself a law-based governmental system in which the relationships between lord and vassal, king and lord, etc. were law-based—contract-based relationships.[1] Legal rules, particularly those that related to ownership of and use and rents from land and contractual undertakings between parties, were an integral part of the societal and governmental system.

The early English Kings made great use of Royal Courts and there were also local feudal courts as well as Church courts in existence. In an era in which religion was not simply one aspect of life but was the dominant force in society, the basic rule for determining facts in the Royal Courts was a plea to the judgment of God. Such judgment could be rendered through trial by ordeal or trial by battle. Other methods of proof were also available such as the use of documents. Many early English land disputes involved the question of whether land had been given to the Church either as alms during life or upon death. Whether land was owned by the Church or whether the heirs of the original owner owned the land was a major subject of dispute. In such disputes documents created difficulties for the King and other nobles because the Church was the keeper of many archives of writings containing the land records and further because writing was a specialty of the Church. This gave the Church an advantage when the use of documents as proof was involved, as it was possible for the Church, with its ability to write, to forge documents.[2] Proof by documents could be challenged by proof by battle. Proof was also avail-

---

1 See, e.g., J.H. Baker, AN INTRODUCTION TO ENGLISH LEGAL HISTORY 257-259, 264-265 (3rd Ed. Butterworths, 1990).

2 Kamakura Japan in the 12th and 13th Centuries similarly had a document forgery problem. Jeffrey P. Mass, The Origins of Kamakura Justice, 3 Journal of Japanese Studies No. 2 (1977) 312.

able through the knowledge of the community where the property was located and panels of witnesses representing the community could be sworn to determine the truth of a matter. These "jurors" unlike the modern jury were not the deciders of facts sworn to by others but were themselves knowledgeable of the facts and in turn swore to those facts. They represented the knowledge of the local community as to the matter.

By the 12th Century trial by battle was the preferred method of proof although trial by ordeal was not completely replaced. However, the Church objected to the use of battle and ordeal as a means of resolving disputes involving Church claims to land. The Church forbade ordeal in 1215.[3] In the criminal law arena proof by battle created issues for those who were witness to crime as their accusation might have to be proved by their engaging in battle.[4] In early medieval times there was great stress placed on procedural methods for proof.

The reign of King Henry II in the 12th Century saw a great outpouring of "legislation" dealing with procedure in the Royal Courts and a shift toward greater use of assizes[5]—panels of what were to become juries. Henry had troubles with the Church and ultimately agreed that clerics would not have to wage battle. Another mechanism of proof, which reduced the potential for document forgery, was required. The Grand Assize of 1179, as well as the assizes of novel disseisin, utrum and of mort d'ancestor made proof by means of a group of laypersons from the community knowledgeable of the facts available to all tenants on the land. Heirs claiming the land in a land dispute—whether between other tenants, lords or the Church authorities—were entitled to similar procedures.[6] This placed clerics and other tenants in the same procedural posture and enhanced the use of assizes, which later became the modern jury. Assizes relied on the knowledge of the community of which the assize members were representatives who swore to decide the matter according to their knowledge of the truth. The assize represented a kind of oral testimony by its members rather than a fact finding through fact gathering function given to the modern jury.[7] The use of assizes lessened the value of documents as evidence and hence diminished the potential for forgery and the advantage held by the Church as the keeper of archives. Similarly assizes favored tenants in disputes with their landlords and thus brought into the royal court mat-

---

3 Sherman L. Cohn, THE COMMON LAW FOUNDATION OF CIVIL PROCEDURE (Lerner Law Book Publishing, 1971) 7; Shigemitsu Dando (Translated by B.J. George Jr.) JAPANESE CRIMINAL PROCEDURE (Fred B. Rothman & Co., 1965) 6.

4 Sherman L. Cohn, THE COMMON LAW FOUNDATION OF CIVIL PROCEDURE (Lerner Law Book Publishing, 1971) 7.

5 1 HOLDSWORTH'S HISTORY OF ENGLISH LAW 314 (Little, Brown and Company, 1922); For a discussion of the movement from battle by champion to assize see, J.H. Baker, AN INTRODUCTION TO ENGLISH LEGAL HISTORY 86-87, 266-268 (3rd Ed. Butterworths, 1990).

6 J.H. Baker, AN INTRODUCTION TO ENGLISH LEGAL HISTORY 69, 86, 266 (3rd Ed. Butterworths, 1990); for a discussion of the various assizes see, 1 HOLDSWORTH'S HISTORY OF ENGLISH LAW 327-330 (Little, Brown and Company, 1922).

7 See, e.g., 1 HOLDSWORTH'S HISTORY OF ENGLISH LAW 317 (Little, Brown and Company, 1922).

ters that might otherwise have been in the feudal courts. This in turn lessened the power of the nobles and correspondingly increased the power and authority of the King. Use of assizes solved an additional problem—this dealing with jurisdiction.

Both Church and Royal Courts claimed the jurisdiction to resolve disputes over whether property had been given to the Church as alms and thus belonged to the Church or whether the property was owned by laypersons. Since the Church disdained proof by battle, Church courts used other mechanisms of proof, even going so far as to allow the ecclesiastic judge to resolve the fact question by what we would today refer to as judicial notice. This authority of the cleric judge to take his own notice of the facts of ownership without other proofs obviously benefited the Clergy. Accordingly, the question of jurisdiction and the corresponding question of procedure were intimately related to the ultimate judgment in the case. The use of panels of laypersons in all cases, whether in Ecclesiastic Courts or the Royal Courts, provided a convenient answer. If the case were tried in front of an ecclesiastic judge all was not lost by the laity, as the determiner of the facts in the matter was the lay assize.

In any event, the 12th and 13th Centuries saw great ferment in the procedural law in England. When King John in the 13th Century signed the Great Charter, Magna Carta, granting the nobles a right not to be dispossessed of land except under procedure of law and then only by a determination of their peers, procedure was raised to a new level. Magna Carta did not set forth the substantive grounds on which dispossession lay, rather it was a procedural document that was designed to protect the rights of the noble class against the King. In addition to judgment by their peers, the nobles won the concession that no longer would the King's Court follow the person of the King but instead courts would be established in regular session at localities where the nobles could attend. Thus, the victors in the war against the King insisted in the Peace Treaty (Magna Carta) ending the rebellion that the King grant to them certain procedural rights and protections in what can only be characterized as civil as well as criminal litigation.

Although England had both internal and external strife, it remained a united country from the 11th Century through to modern times. In this united country both law and the procedures of the court system could mature. As it did so, the ideas of procedure as relevant to result and procedure as a protection of rights matured. Accordingly, when the American Constitution was drafted in the 18th Century, procedure as a bedrock staple of protection of civil as well as criminal rights was a well-established principle with over five centuries of history behind it. Such important aspects of modern American procedure as use of juries, preference of oral testimony to written statements and impartiality of the judge can be directly traced back to the 12th, 13th and 14th Century.[8]

---

8 For a discussion of procedure during the reign of King Henry II and the advent of trial by jury see, Mike MacNair, Vicinage and the Antecedents of the Jury, 17 Law and History Review No. 3, Fall 1999 (Forum: The Origins of the Jury); William Forsyth, HISTORY OF TRIAL BY JURY (2d Ed., Frederick D. Lynn and Co.); the requirement for a unanimous jury dates to the 14th Century. See, 1 HOLDSWORTH'S HISTORY OF ENGLISH LAW 318 (Little, Brown and Company, 1922).

A. Kamakura Japan

The Japanese system of central government based on the Chinese model, that had existed for several centuries, suffered a severe breakdown in the 12th Century when warrior groups gained dominance over the Imperial court. In 1185 the Minamoto warrior clan defeated their only real enemy, the Taira. The leader of the Minamoto, Yoritomo extending his military rule over all of Japan but did not do away with the Imperial House or the Imperial Institution. Rather, he accepted from the Imperial House the title of *Seii-tai-shogun* and set about creating his own administrative organs of government. The Minamoto Shogunate created its headquarters in Kamakura; a small community about one hour from today's Tokyo while the Imperial House remained in Kyoto. Although the shell of Imperial Government remained, the reality was that power had been transformed from the Imperial House to the Shogun.[9] Thereafter the Kamakura Shogunate ruled Japan from Kamakura and Japan entered its feudal period. By the late 12th Century the Kamakura Shogunate had solidified its position as the administrative "government" of Japan. It remained the government of Japan, and Japan thrived under its rule, until the end of the 13th Century. As a consequence of both internal stress and strains from its successful defeat of the Mongol invasion of 1281 the Shogunate collapsed.[10] The successful defense of the homeland was brought about more by the fortuitous intercession of a typhoon (the derivation of the *kamikaze*, the divine wind) that destroyed the Mongol invasion fleet than by the Shogunate's military might. Even the Shogunate's preparations in building a defensive retaining wall in the southern island of Kyushu where the Mongols landed would not have been sufficient without the effect of the divine wind.

Unlike European feudalism, which had been built on the remains of the Roman system with Roman law as an aspect of the system, the Japanese feudal system was built on the ruins of a Chinese-based Imperial system.[11] Here land ownership was entirely different from land ownership in England of the 12th Century. Japanese feudal rules of land ownership extended to all land held by the feudal class

---

9 The idea of separating ruling from governing may go back to the origins of the Japanese State. See, Yosiyuki Noda, INTRODUCTION TO JAPANESE LAW (translated and edited by Anthony H. Angelo) (University of Tokyo Press, 1976) 20-21 wherein Professor Noda notes that the Queen Himiko (considered to have unified Japan in the 3rd Century) reigned while her brother had administrative responsibility and hence he governed.

10 For a discussion of Kamakura Japan see, John K. Fairbank, Edwin O. Reischauer and Albert M. Craig, EAST ASIA TRADITION AND TRANSFORMATION 362-368 (Houghton Mifflin Company, 1973); for a discussion of law in Kamakura Japan see, Alan McFarland, Law and Custom in Japan: Some Comparative Reflections, Continuity and Change 10(3) 1995, 369, 390 (Cambridge University Press, 1995) on the web at *www.alanmacfarlane.com/TEXTS/law&custom.pdf* page 8-9.

11 See John O. Haley, AUTHORITY WITHOUT POWER: LAW AND THE JAPANESE PARADOX (Oxford University Press, 1991) 37-38 for a discussion of Western vs. Japanese feudalism; see also, Yosiyuki Noda, INTRODUCTION TO JAPANESE LAW (translated and edited by Anthony H. Angelo) (University of Tokyo Press, 1976) 27 for the position that unlike in European feudalism, in Japanese feudalism the vassal had no right to have his overlord perform his obligations while the vassal was legally bound to his overlord.

(the samurai) but the old rules of land holdings still extended to the large estates owned by the court nobles and religious institutions.[12] Moreover, the Imperial system was not based on notions of law and contract such as the Western system. Accordingly, Japanese feudalism was not law- or contract-based. Rather, it was based on more Chinese ideals of ethics and relationships. Obligation rather than reciprocal right was the dominant aspect of the relationship in Japanese feudalism. This included the obligation of the shogun to rule properly.[13]

The Kamakura shoguns did not change the "estate" system of landholdings by Shrines and royal families but it did assign its vassals to positions of authority and positions where they were entitled to rents from such various estates. It adopted rules for its stewards and vassals that some have considered as the first Japanese feudal law. However, these rules were based on ethical not legal notions and were in the nature of instructions for carrying out duties rather than in the nature of rules to be followed by the general population.[14] They do not represent what in the West would be considered as a code of law. In some senses the "law" was the house code of rules for the Minamoto family that established the Kamakura Shogunate. Disputes did arise during Kamakura times and the Kamakura government had officials to resolve such disputes. Principally such disputes involved issues over the propriety of the actions of vassals and stewards or hereditary rights issues. Kamakura officials considered both written statements by the parties to the dispute and witness testimony from persons knowledgeable about the matter. In addition to making its independent investigation into the facts, formal questionnaires as well as summonses were in use to obtain information. A form of Complaint and an opportunity to file a form of Answer was permitted. Failure to respond to a formal summons could result in loss of the dispute. Where there was no "law" in the sense that the house rules did not apply, the deciding official would use the custom of the community in rendering a just determination.[15] This system shows some similarity to early English use of writings, witnesses and customs to develop a common law.[16] Criminal and civil matters could sometimes be handled together.[17]

12 Yosiyuki Noda, INTRODUCTION TO JAPANESE LAW (translated and edited by Anthony H. Angelo) (University of Tokyo Press, 1976) 25-27.

13 John K. Fairbank, Edwin O. Reischauer and Albert M. Craig, EAST ASIA TRADITION AND TRANSFORMATION 368-369 (Houghton Mifflin Company, 1973).

14 Thomas L. Blakemore, Post-War Developments in Japanese Law, 1947 Wisconsin Law Review 632, 636.

15 See, Jeffrey P. Mass, The Origins of Kamakura Justice, 3 Journal of Japanese Studies No. 2 (1977) 299, 312-313, 320.

16 Yosiyuki Noda, INTRODUCTION TO JAPANESE LAW (translated and edited by Anthony H. Angelo) (University of Tokyo Press, 1976) 29-30 notes that a kind of "Common Law" developed during the Kamakura period.

17 Jeffrey P. Mass, The Origins of Kamakura Justice, 3 Journal of Japanese Studies No. 2 (1977) 316.

Although Kamakura lasted only about one and one half centuries, it is a very significant period of Japanese history because the Kamakura governing model became the basic model for the Tokugawa Shogunate that arose at around 1600 and ruled Japan until the mid-19th Century.

The collapse of the Kamakura Shogunate led to an unsettled period in Japanese history that eventually produced what is known as the Warring States (Sengoku) period. Although the country continued to be unified in the sense that there was an Emperor with the trappings of central authority (and during most of this period there even was an official with the title of shogun) the reality was that there was no central authority. The country was divided into several large fiefdoms each independent and not subject to any central control. The ruling lords (Daimyo) of these fiefdoms ("Han") adopted "household rules" to govern the actions of their subordinates and these rules were the closest that could be considered as legal codes at the time. Again, rather than being the equivalent of legal codes in the West, these household rules were mainly ethical rules of conduct for the subordinate officers of the Daimyo households. The rules were subject to change by the lord and only rarely did they bind the lord's conduct.[18] A centralized legal system or a centralized litigation system did not exist and the movement of the Kamakura system toward a developing common law based on custom came to an end.[19]

With the demise of the Shogunate, the land holding system completely collapsed. Where there had been large estates controlled by vassals of the court and powerful families and Temples,[20] farmers began to organize themselves into the village organizations that were to become a staple of Japan throughout the Tokugawa period. Although subject to nominal Daimyo control, these villages achieved a great deal of political autonomy and developed their own internal system for governance based on headmen, consensus rules and conciliation and mediation of disputes. These semiautonomous villages were to have great significance in the development of Japanese law and in modern Japanese attitudes toward law. No "legal system" in the sense of the European model existed. In English feudalism lords could claim ownership to their lands and pass them on from generation to generation. Similarly peasants had rights in tenancy on the lands. In Japan all land was "owned" by the local Daimyo who permitted his vassals authority over and rents (in the form of rice taxes) from the land. These vassals were, however, totally subservient to the Daimyo and held the land at the Daimyo's sufferance. In

18 Yoshiro Hiramatsu, Tokugawa Law (Translated by Dan Fenno Henderson) 14 Law in Japan 1, 4 (1981).

19 For a discussion of the Sengoku period see, John K. Fairbank, Edwin O. Reischauer and Albert M. Craig, EAST ASIA TRADITION AND TRANSFORMATION 379-381 (Houghton Mifflin Company, 1973); for a discussion of "house codes" during this period and the view that Sengoku Japan might have led to a more Western notion of law see, John O. Haley, AUTHORITY WITHOUT POWER: LAW AND THE JAPANESE PARADOX (Oxford University Press, 1991) 47-48.

20 For a discussion of the estate system see, John K. Fairbank, Edwin O. Reischauer and Albert M. Craig, EAST ASIA TRADITION AND TRANSFORMATION 348-350 (Houghton Mifflin Company, 1973).

the Japanese system there was no need for a land court to resolve disputes over land or contractual type disputes between different vassals. There was no central authority to deal with the niceties of procedural rules to govern disputes and at the village level there was no need for courts or procedural rules.

B. Tokugawa Japan

Japan was reunified by the activities of three Daimyo. Oda Nobunaga began the unification process. Toyotomi Hideyoshi completed the unification process but could not pass on to his infant heir his hard won gains. Tokugawa Ieyasu defeated the forces loyal to Hideyoshi's young heir at the battle of Sekigahara (1600) and established the Tokugawa Shogunate, which was to rule Japan for two and a half centuries.[21]

Throughout the reunification process the Imperial Court continued to exist at Kyoto, although it had no real power. Neither Oda nor Hideyoshi was given the title of shogun (although they accepted other titles) but within a few short years after his victory at Sekigahara Tokugawa was made shogun. Ieyasu resigned this post a few years later in favor of his son and this son in turn resigned the post a few years after Ieyasu's death in favor of his son. The Tokugawa family continued in power as administrative rulers of Japan, operating out of the Shogunate capital of Edo (modern Tokyo) until the late 19th Century.

From a legal vantage point there are certain characteristics of Tokugawa rule that are relevant. In one sense the government was a kind of federation in that local Daimyo rulers were virtually autonomous within their regions.[22] However, although they exercised internal authority, the reality was that all Daimyo were ultimately responsible to the Shogunate authority, which could and did transfer Daimyo to other domains either as punishment (demotion) or as reward (promotion).[23] Thus, land while held by the Daimyo houses was in fact Tokugawa land from which the Daimyo derived their income. Moreover, unlike the West where there were rights and obligations flowing between the various classes of vassals and lords, in Tokugawa Japan the obligations of the vassals flowed to their higher lords, without reciprocal rights being involved.[24] Disputes over land rights in England became the subject of litigation before the Royal Court under procedures adopted to protect the interests and rights of the parties in conflict. Certain types of

---

21 For a discussion of the unification process see, Marius B. Jansen, THE MAKING OF MODERN JAPAN (Belknap Press of Harvard University, 2000) 11-31.

22 Yosiyuki Noda, INTRODUCTION TO JAPANESE LAW (translated and edited by Anthony H. Angelo) (University of Tokyo Press, 1976) 35; Yoshiro Hiramatsu, Tokugawa Law (Translated by Dan Fenno Henderson) 14 Law in Japan 1, 18-22 (1981).

23 John K. Fairbank, Edwin O. Reischauer and Albert M. Craig, EAST ASIA TRADITION AND TRANSFORMATION 401-404 (Houghton Mifflin Company, 1973).

24 John O. Haley, AUTHORITY WITHOUT POWER: LAW AND THE JAPANESE PARADOX (Oxford University Press, 1991) 37-3 8; Yoshiro Hiramatsu, Tokugawa Law (Translated by Dan Fenno Henderson) 14 Law in Japan 1, 9 (1981); Carl F. Goodman, THE RULE OF LAW IN JAPAN: A COMPARATIVE ANALYSIS (Kluwer Law International, 2003) 213, 218.

disputes in Tokugawa Japan, especially those that required some official act to resolve the matter might be brought before a Shogunate magistrate but decision was not based on the rights of the parties but on the magistrate's view of what was an appropriate outcome.[25] Bringing such disputes to the Shogunate undercut the autonomy of the Daimyo or of the village leading to resistance to take such a step. In any event, there was no right to have a magistrate's decision and thus no right to any specific type of procedure to protect the "rights" of the parties. Moreover, before a dispute could be brought to a magistrate it was required that the parties to the dispute attempt to conciliate the matter.[26] To the extent there were procedures they were designed more to define the problem and get the parties to resolve the problem by compromise and agreement than to have a decision reached that made one party a winner and another a loser.

Similarly, the local village authorities that had grown up in the earlier period retained their semiautonomous position. As long as the village authorities maintained order and paid taxes to the Daimyo or Shogunate as applicable, village affairs were handled by the village authority. This autonomy was magnified in Japan where the local Daimyo were required to spend every other year in Edo as virtual hostage to the Shogun. This absentee status differed sharply from European or English society where the local lord lived in the manor house directly on his fief and exerted direct control. As a consequence Japanese village authority had much greater control over village affairs. And, since Japan was an agricultural country, most of the population, perhaps 80% of the population, lived in the villages.[27]

To solidify its status as "autonomous," village elders and headmen adopted procedures that shielded the village from outside influence and that carried out the Daimyo's mandate that the village itself resolve disputes rather than send them to the Daimyo's officials for resolution.[28] Thus, disputes between members of the village were settled locally by "extra legal" means such as conciliation, mediation and compromise. If villagers refused to act "reasonably" the village authority had mechanisms to compel compromise and settlement. The basic crop in Japan was and is wet rice. The cultivation of wet rice requires cooperation of the entire village as the waterways for irrigation must be maintained, crops planted at a specific time, harvested at a specific time, etc. Wet rice cultivation is not the kind of farming that can be engaged in on an individual basis. Thus, village members who balked at local resolution of a dispute might find themselves ostracized by the local community and cut off from communal assistance in their rice growing occu-

---

25 Yoshiro Hiramatsu, Tokugawa Law (Translated by Dan Fenno Henderson) 14 Law in Japan 1, 34-35, 42 (1981).

26 Wigmore, LAW AND JUSTICE IN TOKUGAWA JAPAN Vol. 1. p. 51.

27 Dan Fenno Henderson, "Contracts" in Tokugawa Japan, 1 Journal of Japanese Studies 1, 54, 60 (1974).

28 Dan Fenno Henderson, "Contracts" in Tokugawa Japan, 1 Journal of Japanese Studies 1, 59, 61, 63 (1974).

pation.[29] This was not simply social ostracism but cut to the very basic economic existence of the dissenter. In particularly difficult cases (either criminal or civil) a villager might be expelled from the village.[30] Expulsion carried additional hazards as travel was not a right in Tokugawa Japan but required the approval of the governmental authorities. Peasants could not simply leave village A to take up residence in village B. Thus a villager who was expelled from his village was in the truest sense an outcast of the society with no place to call home. These social pressures and extra legal punishments tended to get matters resolved at the local village level through informal means in accordance with local mores without the need to involve either the Daimyo or Tokugawa authorities.[31] Consensus decision making highlighting the greater good of the village group rather than individual rights was the order of the day and it was enforced by compromise resolution of disputes, even if the compromise had to be forced on one or both of the parties.[32]

Hideyoshi had begun the process of stratifying the society into social classes. Tokugawa completed the process by creating four distinct and rigidly separated social classes. The warrior or samurai class was at the top of the social ladder. The peasant or farmer class (a samurai could not be a farmer—this was a break with the earlier period where many warriors were in fact farmers) was followed by artisans. At the bottom the class ladder were the merchants. A small portion of the society was outside of these classes.[33] Although members of the same class who had a dispute might seek assistance from Daimyo or Shogunate magistrates to resolve the problem, disputes between persons of different classes could not be brought to the magistrates. Thus, if a samurai owed money to a merchant and refused to pay,

---

29 For a discussion of village life see, Marius B. Jansen, THE MAKING OF MODERN JAPAN (Belknap Press of Harvard University, 2000) 111-116.

30 Ryuichi Hirano, The Accused and Society: Some Aspects of Japanese Criminal Law in LAW IN JAPAN (VON Mehren Ed. Harvard University Press, 1963) 291; Dan Fenno Henderson, "Contracts" in Tokugawa Japan, 1 Journal of Japanese Studies 1, 66-67 (1974).

31 For a discussion of the importance of the semiautonomous village and the role of extra-judicial decision making in Tokugawa Japan see, John O. Haley, AUTHORITY WITHOUT POWER: LAW AND THE JAPANESE PARADOX (Oxford University Press, 1991) Autonomy With Dependence: The Enforced Cohesion of the Mura p. 58-65.

32 For a discussion of the roles of compromise, reconciliation and mediation in resolving disputes in feudal Japan see, Alan McFarland, Law and Custom in Japan: Some Comparative Reflections, Continuity and Change 10(3) 1995, 369, 390 (Cambridge University Press, 1995) on the web at *www.alanmacfarlane.com/TEXTS/law&custom.pdf* page 5-6. For a discussion of the attempt to use local priests as intermediaries to resolve peasant village authority conflicts in Tokugawa Japan see, Alexander M. Vesey, Entering the Temple Priests, Peasants and Village Contention in Tokugawa Japan, Japanese Journal of Religious Studies 2001 at 293-328 on the web at *www.nanzen-u.ac.jp/SHUBUNKEN/publications/jjrs.pdf/612.pdf*

33 John K. Fairbank, Edwin O. Reischauer and Albert M. Craig, EAST ASIA TRADITION AND TRANSFORMATION 406-407 (Houghton Mifflin Company, 1973). Although Tokugawa society is generally considered as a four-class society, Wigmore adds three additional classes—the Imperial or Court class, the priesthood (Buddhist and Shinto) and the outcastes. Wigmore, LAW AND JUSTICE IN TOKUGAWA JAPAN Vol. 1. p. 6. For the role of classes in the ordering of Japanese society see, John W. Hall, Rule by Status in Tokugawa Japan, 1 Journal of Japanese Studies 39 (1974).

the merchant could not bring the matter to anything that would resemble an English court. The reality was that the merchant simply had to rely on the samurai's honor for payment. Of course, honor was a significant matter and was highly valued by the samurai class so that typically such loans and obligations were in fact paid. But the point is that no procedure for requiring payment could be established and no procedure for proving what in England would be considered contractual rights and obligations could be established for these inter class disputes. Disputes between members of the same class could, in some situations, be brought to the local Daimyo's officials or the Tokugawa magistrate. Procedural rules were adopted regarding the filing and "serving" of such cases,[34] but determination by the magistrate was a matter of largess and not a matter of right[35]—making any procedural rules designed to protect rights a matter of largess as well.

Moreover, the Tokugawa government frowned on litigation as a dispute resolution mechanism. The bias against "litigation" was so great that even if a "plaintiff" had a valid case it might be denied relief because of its obstinate attitude in insisting on bringing the matter to the magistrate.[36] Magistrates reflecting the bias against "litigation" and formal procedures to resolve what in England might be viewed as legal disputes did not look with favor on having to resolve such disputes and much preferred to have the parties reach a settlement.[37] To the extent possible the procedural hurdles (including demeaning processes that required the person bringing litigation to humiliate himself in front of the court)[38] erected against litigation were designed to have the matters resolved at the village or local level and if possible by compromise and through conciliation.[39] Nor was this bias against "litigation" only a Shogunate policy but it was also followed by the Daimyo, leaving most disputes out of the legal system. As a consequence such disputes had to be handled by local dispute resolution mechanisms that were based primarily on compromise and conciliation. Thus, there were no rights to bring cases[40] and even cases that were considered as appropriate for magistrate determination when

34 Yoshiro Hiramatsu, Tokugawa Law (Translated by Dan Fenno Henderson) 14 Law in Japan 1, 36 (1981).

35 Kenzo Takayanagi, A Century of Innovation: The Development of Japanese Law, 1868-1961 in LAW IN JAPAN (VON Mehren Ed. Harvard University Press, 1963) 24; Wigmore, LAW AND JUSTICE IN TOKUGAWA JAPAN Vol. 1. p. 41; Yoshiro Hiramatsu, Tokugawa Law (Translated by Dan Fenno Henderson) 14 Law in Japan 1, 10, 28 (1981); Dan Fenno Henderson, "Contracts" in Tokugawa Japan, 1 Journal of Japanese Studies 1, 77 (1974).

36 Wigmore, LAW AND JUSTICE IN TOKUGAWA JAPAN Vol. 1. p. 41.

37 Alan McFarland, Law and Custom in Japan: Some Comparative Reflections, Continuity and Change (Cambridge University Press, 1995) on the web at *www.alanmacfarlane.com/TEXTS/law&custom.pdf* page 6, 10.

38 Wigmore, LAW AND JUSTICE IN TOKUGAWA JAPAN Vol. 1. p. 41.

39 John O. Haley, AUTHORITY WITHOUT POWER: LAW AND THE JAPANESE PARADOX (Oxford University Press, 1991) 57; Wigmore, LAW AND JUSTICE IN TOKUGAWA JAPAN Vol. 1. p. 42-43.

40 Dan Fenno Henderson, "Contracts" in Tokugawa Japan, 1 Journal of Japanese Studies 1, 68 (1947).

brought could later be withdrawn from magistrate jurisdiction.[41] The most important commercial type disputes, such as disputes involving a failure to repay money loaned at interest, were not within the magistrate's authority. These disputes known as money disputes were frowned on. Magistrates refused to deal with them on the theory that they were disputes that should be privately resolved through conciliation. Alternatively such disputes were viewed as representing an unethical type of transaction (it was considered immoral for a samurai to engage in such mundane commercial exercises as borrowing money) unworthy of magisterial involvement.[42] What in England would be considered normal money had and received disputes or contract actions were unlikely to be resolved by the magistrate.[43]

Further, it was not easy to bring cases to the magistrate. Thus, in a dispute between members of the same village the dispute would be determined through informal means by village elders, wise men, etc., as discussed above. Where a dispute involved villagers from different villages, it might be brought to the Daimyo's officials for resolution but not to the Tokugawa officials. Where the disputants came from fiefs of different Daimyo it was possible to seek resolution before the Tokugawa magistrate. However, villagers could only take this step if they received the consent of their village, (such consent was also required where the suit involved villagers from different villages in the same Daimyo's fief) as evidenced by the seal of the village headman.[44] Consent of the Daimyo, as evidenced by the seal of the appropriate Daimyo official was also required. Failure to get these consents meant no suit could be brought and filing of such a suit without the appropriate seal was considered a serious offense subjecting the petitioning party to severe punishment.[45] The village as an institution did not want to invite attention from the Daimyo or Tokugawa authorities. Elevating to these authorities matters that the authorities did not want to deal with was not looked on kindly. Consequently, the asking for consent to bring a matter to the Daimyo or Tokugawa magistrate was not lightly undertaken. Similarly, the granting of such consent was not given lightly. Even when given, the magistrate might suggest a neutral party to conciliate

---

41 Dan Fenno Henderson, "Contracts" in Tokugawa Japan, 1 Journal of Japanese Studies 1, 71 (1974).

42 Yoshiro Hiramatsu, Tokugawa Law (Translated by Dan Fenno Henderson) 14 Law in Japan 1, 35 (1981).

43 Dan Fenno Henderson, "Contracts" in Tokugawa Japan, 1 Journal of Japanese Studies 1, 68 (1947). For a comparison of the status of law in England and Japan see, John O. Haley, Sheathing the Sword of Justice in Japan: An Essay on Law without Sanctions, 8 Journal of Japanese Studies at 277 (1982).

44 Yoshiro Hiramatsu, Tokugawa Law (Translated by Dan Fenno Henderson) 14 Law in Japan 1, 36 (1981); Dan Fenno Henderson, "Contracts" in Tokugawa Japan, 1 Journal of Japanese Studies 1, 62 and fn. 25 (1947).

45 For a case study of a "suit" in Tokugawa Japan with special emphasis on the role of the Shogunate official as a conciliator see, Dan Fenno Henderson, Nuinosuke v. Chube: Conciliation in Tokugawa Civil Trials, (from CONCILIATION AND JAPANESE LAW: TOKUGAWA AND MODERN, 127-162, University of Washington Press, 1965) relevant portion reprinted in JAPANESE LAW IN CONTEXT (Milhaupt, Jr., Ramseyer, and Young ed., Harvard University Asia Center, 2001) 14-27 (See, pgs 15-16 re: permissions for a diversity suit).

the dispute rather than have the magistrate determine the matter.[46] Even in the commercial towns (typically large commercial centers such as Osaka and Tokyo were under direct Tokugawa authority) parties could not simply bring disputes to the local magistrate. Towns were divided into block organizations (a kind of village within the town) and internal block disputes were decided much as internal village disputes were, while "inter block" disputes required consent before they could be taken to the magistrate.[47] Even when such suits came before magistrates, the order of the day was to send them to conciliators to reach some kind of "amicable" resolution, even if the parties were compelled to agree to such resolution.[48]

Tokugawa authorities were concerned with regularizing the relations between the Shogunate and its vassals and between the vassals themselves. Thus, rules were promulgated much like the household rules adopted by local Daimyo during the Sengoku Warring States period. These rules while they may seem to some to be in the nature of laws sharply differ from the Western concept of law. They were based on ethical ideals of how the persons to whom they were directed should act as well as recognition of differing social status within the samurai and other classes. They were not based on the creation of rights and corresponding obligations. Next, they were not directed to the public in general. Rather, they were directions to those to whom they were addressed, namely the vassal houses.[49] As such there was no need to publish the rules to the populace, as they were not applicable to the populace. The role of the public at large was to follow orders given by administrative officials and thus there was no need for a set of laws to be published and indeed no such set of laws existed. To the extent that there were rules to be followed they were kept secret[50] except that orders to be followed by the populace were posted on public notice boards. (Even the rules that were to be used by magistrates and other officials whose role might be considered as resembling a judicial role were

---

46 Wigmore, LAW AND JUSTICE IN TOKUGAWA JAPAN Vol. 1. p. 45; Dan Fenno Henderson, "Contracts" in Tokugawa Japan, 1 Journal of Japanese Studies 1, 69 (1947). Dan Fenno Henderson, Nuinosuke v. Chube: Conciliation in Tokugawa Civil Trials, (from CONCILIATION AND JAPANESE LAW: TOKUGAWA AND MODERN, 127-162, University of Washington Press, 1965) relevant portion reprinted in JAPANESE LAW IN CONTEXT (Milhaupt, Jr., Ramseyer, and Young ed., Harvard University Asia Center, 2001) 18 endorsement requiring parties, headmen, etc. to conciliate before returning to the Shogun official. See also, Carl F. Goodman, THE RULE OF LAW IN JAPAN: A COMPARATIVE ANALYSIS (Kluwer Law International, 2003) 218, 231.

47 Yoshiro Hiramatsu, Tokugawa Law (translated by Dan Fenno Henderson), 14 Law in Japan 1, 37-38 (1981).

48 Yoshiro Hiramatsu, Tokugawa Law (Translated by Dan Fenno Henderson) 14 Law in Japan 1, 37 (1981); see Dan Fenno Henderson, Nuinosuke v. Chube: Conciliation in Tokugawa Civil Trials, (from CONCILIATION AND JAPANESE LAW: TOKUGAWA AND MODERN, 127-162, University of Washington Press, 1965) relevant portion reprinted in JAPANESE LAW IN CONTEXT (Milhaupt, Jr., Ramseyer, and Young ed., Harvard University Asia Center, 2001) 14-27 (note the Shogunate official's use of the threat of criminal proceedings / arrest because of forgery to get the defendant to agree to a compromise and the delay in proceedings with extra cost to the plaintiff to get the plaintiff to agree.)

49 Kenzo Takayanagi, A Century of Innovation: The Development of Japanese Law, 1868-1961 in LAW IN JAPAN (VON Mehren Ed. Harvard University Press, 1963) 16.

50 G.B. Sansom, THE WESTERN WORLD AND JAPAN (Vintage Books, New York, 1949) 447.

kept secret.[51]) And, like the household rules of the Daimyo, these rules did not bind the Tokugawa authorities in any way nor did they establish norms for intercourse between the general population such as was the case with European Codes or the English common law. As consideration of the case and determinations by the magistrates were a matter of largess, and as such determinations were based not so much on the merits of the position of the parties as on the circumstances of the case (which could include the social ranking of the respective parties in the same class), cases could hardly form the basis for precedent for future disputes. Social status was an important element in determining all disputes. In such an environment no generally applicable legal system and no generally applicable procedural norms to protect rights of parties were developed.[52]

Crime did, of course, exist in Tokugawa Japan. Here again no general substantive Criminal Code was adopted, but rather internal rules of conduct for Tokugawa officials formed the basis for the criminal law. Criminal responsibility was not necessarily individual in that there was also group responsibility either at the family level or at other grouping levels such as the village itself or the village headman.[53] This not only held down crime but also meant that village officials tended to deal with crime on a local level rather than involving the Shogunate or Daimyo officials. Whether conduct constituted a crime and the level of punishment applicable to the conduct was a matter of class and status within the class.[54] Crimes not resolved at the village level were prosecuted before the Shogunate magistrates. As a consequence there was a criminal procedure adopted by magistrates to deal with persons accused of crime. The criminal process involved a two-step procedure—in step one the perpetrator of the crime was identified (the investigative state) and in step two the perpetrator was "tried" before the magistrate. Step one was the basis for step two and the principle "evidence" required at the trial was the confession of the accused. Confession was obtained during the investigative stage and there were procedural rules dealing with the obtaining of confessions. Thus, torture was permitted[55] but there were procedural norms for the obtaining of confession by torture.[56]

51 Yoshiro Hiramatsu, Tokugawa Law (Translated by Dan Fenno Henderson) 14 Law in Japan 1, 12, 15, 22 (1981).

52 Procedural norms were of course developed but these norms related more to the forms of the "complaint" and the forms of service and notice than to procedures to protect the rights of parties. Thus the Answer of the defendant did not have to be served before the hearing and there was no process to obtain facts and witnesses except the discretion of the Shogunate official.

53 Alan McFarland, Law and Custom in Japan: Some Comparative Reflections, Continuity and Change 10(3) 1995, 369, 390 (Cambridge University Press, 1995) on the web at *www.alanmacfarlane.com/TEXTS/law&custom.pdf* page 3-4 of 16.

54 Kenzo Takayanagi, A Century of Innovation: The Development of Japanese Law, 1868-1961 in LAW IN JAPAN (VON Mehren Ed. Harvard University Press, 1963) 16; see, Yoshiro Hiramatsu, Tokugawa Law (Translated by Dan Fenno Henderson) 14 Law in Japan 1, 40-42 (1981).

55 Yosiyuki Noda, INTRODUCTION TO JAPANESE LAW (translated and edited by Anthony H. Angelo) (University of Tokyo Press, 1976) 37.

56 For a discussion of torture in Tokugawa Japan see, Haruo Abe, Self-incrimination—Japan and the United States, 46 Journal of Criminal Law, Criminology & Police Science 613 (1956).

For example, torture required that there be a witness present to verify that the appropriate level of torture was being utilized.[57] In addition to torture, investigative officials used other means—including the presentation to the accused of physical evidence and witness statements as well as interrogations—to obtain confessions. In addition, deals were struck between the accused and the prosecuting authorities under which, in exchange for a reduced charge the accused would confess to the lower level crime.[58] The importance of confession cannot be overstated and, without a confession no determination of guilt could be made.[59] Thus, if an accused confessed and then at the second stage hearing before the magistrate refused to acknowledge the confession, no guilty verdict could be rendered and the accused was recommitted—probably for additional torture. In such a setting, procedural rules designed to protect the rights of the accused, such as a privilege against self-incrimination or a requirement for warrants, could not and did not arise.

Of course tax and other administrative disputes between the governing authority and samurai and other classes did arise during this period. There existed an Administrative and Tax office in Tokyo to handle such disputes and these were in the nature of legal proceedings. And, towards the end of the Tokugawa regime there appears to have been the beginnings of what could be considered as a variant of Western style litigation.[60] But these embryonic legal beginnings never ripened into a Westernized legal system with procedural rules designed to protect the rights of the litigants.

The status of the samurai underwent significant change during the Tokugawa era.[61] The samurai were primarily a warrior class. Such a class was needed during the 12th Century down through the establishment of the Tokugawa Shogunate. However, the Shogunate ushered in an era of peace in Japan—there were no internal wars requiring armed warriors and there were no external wars. The warrior class in society thus had to reform itself into an entirely different function. The samurai became the bureaucrats and hereditary civil servants of the Tokugawa government. This transformation placed the highest level of society in the position of ad-

---

57 Carl F. Goodman, THE RULE OF LAW IN JAPAN: A COMPARATIVE ANALYSIS (Kluwer Law International, 2003) 274; Torture was prohibited in civil cases in 1872 and in criminal cases in 1874. Kenzo Takayanagi, A Century of Innovation: The Development of Japanese Law, 1868-1961 in LAW IN JAPAN (VON Mehren Ed. Harvard University Press, 1963) 20.

58 Yoshiro Hiramatsu, Tokugawa Law (Translated by Dan Fenno Henderson) 14 Law in Japan 1, 43-44 (1981).

59 Alan McFarland, Law and Custom in Japan: Some Comparative Reflections, Continuity and Change 10(3) 1995, 369, 390 (Cambridge University Press, 1995) on the web at *www.alanmacfarlane.com/TEXTS/law&custom.pdf*; see also, Yoshiro Hiramatsu, Tokugawa Law (translated by Dan Fenno Henderson), 14 Law in Japan 1, 31 (1981) and Yoshiro Hiramatsu, Summary of Tokugawa Criminal Justice (summarized and translated by Daniel H. Foote), 22 Law in Japan 105 (1989).

60 John O. Haley, AUTHORITY WITHOUT POWER: LAW AND THE JAPANESE PARADOX (Oxford University Press, 1991) 57; but see for a somewhat modified view, Yoshiro Hiramatsu, Tokugawa Law (Translated by Dan Fenno Henderson) 14 Law in Japan 1, 48 (1981).

61 John K. Fairbank, Edwin O. Reischauer and Albert M. Craig, EAST ASIA TRADITION AND TRANSFORMATION 410-411 (Houghton Mifflin Company, 1973).

ministering the government and consequently, whether the general population accepted it or not, the reality was that the civil servant bureaucrat was the leading class in the social structure. This also led to featherbedding and an unwarranted increase in the size of the bureaucracy, as the administration needed to absorb the members of the samurai class. By prohibiting samurai participation in the functions of merchants and artisans, the government restricted the economic prospects of the samurai class in general and many lower level samurai were at the same time both members of the highest social class and members of a very low economic class.

Like its predecessor, the Kamakura Shogunate, the Tokugawa Shogunate succumbed as a result of internal weakness and external pressure.[62] This time the external pressure was applied as a consequence of the "opening" of Japan from its isolation by the Western powers and Russia. The Tokugawa Shogunate had successfully kept Japan a relatively closed society (there was some trade with the Dutch in the southern island of Kyushu at Nagasaki) and rejected all offers made by Western nations to open Japan to trade with the West. Finally the United States took the initiative in compelling Japan (through the use of gun ships at the command of Commodore Perry) to end its isolation and accept Western trade. Unable to defend itself against the militarily more powerful imperialistic Western forces, the Shogunate was forced to agree to terms that the populace and the Imperial Court objected to. Some of the Daimyo domains saw the Shogunate's problems in dealing with the Western powers as an opportunity to overthrow the Shogun's government. Like Hideyoshi, who had accepted office and titles from the Imperial House as a means of legitimizing his rule and Tokugawa who obtained Imperial authorization for the creation of his Shogunate, the revolutionaries found in the Imperial House a source of legitimacy for their revolt. Acting in the name of the Emperor and under the banner of restoring the Emperor to power they challenged Tokugawa supremacy. Eventually this led to civil war, basically pitting four Daimyo domains from western Japan against the eastern Tokugawa house. These western domains, while still theoretically ruled by the Daimyo houses were in reality under the influence of younger samurai from more humble origins. Victory by the western forces resulted in overthrow of the feudal system and resignation of the 15th Tokugawa shogun in favor of a "restoration" of Imperial Rule.[63] The new governmental system was based on Imperial rule but actual power was exercised by a group of oligarchs. The Emperor was consulted on major issues and began to play a role in governing. Although led by samurai, the revolution threw over the feudal structure by abolishing the feudal domains and reconstituting them as prefectures of

62 For a discussion of the internal friction see, John K. Fairbank, Edwin O. Reischauer and Albert M. Craig, EAST ASIA TRADITION AND TRANSFORMATION 430-434 (Houghton Mifflin Company, 1973) and for the external pressures see Id. at 484-492.

63 John K. Fairbank, Edwin O. Reischauer and Albert M. Craig, EAST ASIA TRADITION AND TRANSFORMATION 494-502 (Houghton Mifflin Company, 1973).

the new central government.[64] The new government took up residence in Edo newly named Tokyo, where the Emperor, who had taken the era name Meiji, was installed in the old Tokugawa castle. Eventually the class system was abolished, samurai were required to give up their stipends for pensions, which were then capitalized and paid off in bonds and samurai were allowed to enter commercial occupations.[65]

By the mid 19th Century when Tokugawa rule came to an end there was little in Japan that could be considered as a legal system as understood in the West. There were some institutions that could be recognized as civil courts but not applying "legal" rules based on the rights of parties to obtain decisions. The use of torture and forced confessions made any similarity of criminal law and criminal law procedures impossible. And there were no lawyers. Matters that in the West were the subject of publicly available Codes were, in the event they had a written form, kept secret and were available only to officials of the Shogunate. Matters that were grist for the civil and criminal judicial mill of the West with its defined rules of procedure were resolved in Japan at the most local level through extra legal means such as conciliation, compromise and consensus, which required and developed no formal procedures. Criminal matters proceeded through an inquisition process that relied on confession of the accused and the mercy of the officials. Matters that were determined by the magistrates were decided on the basis of "equity" and the circumstances of the situation rather than formal legal concepts. There were no formal rights. Finally, even when there was some form of written law or customary procedure, in a system where adjudication was a matter of largess, that form or procedure could be kept while the actual determination might differ where the authorities felt the circumstances of the case required such action. It was into such a legal environment that Commodore Perry sailed his black ships, the West obtained unequal treaties and Japan lost a certain degree of its sovereignty to consular courts dispensing a Western style justice to the Westerners living in Japan.

---

64 John K. Fairbank, Edwin O. Reischauer and Albert M. Craig, EAST ASIA TRADITION AND TRANSFORMATION 505-506 (Houghton Mifflin Company, 1973); The Imperial Rescript abolishing the Han form and replacing it with prefectures (ken) was issued on August 29, 1871. An English language version of the Rescript may be found in W. W. McLaren, JAPANESE GOVERNMENT DOCUMENTS (Asiatic Society of Japan) (University Publications of America, reprint edition, 1979) Vol. 1, 32 and at Ishii Ryosuke, JAPANESE LEGISLATION IN THE MEIJI ERA (Translated and adapted by William J. Chambliss) (Kasai Publishing, Tokyo, 1958) at 717.

65 See, e.g., Rule allowing samurai to enter occupations, W. W. McLaren, JAPANESE GOVERNMENT DOCUMENTS (Asiatic Society of Japan) (University Publications of America, reprint edition, 1979) Vol. 2, 557; commutation of incomes in return for capital, page 558 and issuance of government bonds in lieu of pensions and income to samurai, page 562-566 (1876).

3
Meiji Reforms and Prewar Law

In its final years, the Tokugawa Shogunate had been compelled to enter into a series of humiliating treaties with the Western powers. Among other things, these treaties set the customs duties that the Japanese could charge on imports into Japan at such a low rate as to create financial problems for the government. More significant however were the provisions in the treaties for foreign consular jurisdiction in Japan over the activities of foreigners in Japan. Through the treaties and jurisdiction of the consular courts in territories of Japan carved out for foreign investment, trade and living, Japan lost significant amounts of its sovereignty. The "restored" Imperial system (under the new Emperor Meiji, giving the revolution the name of the Meiji Restoration) represented a more powerful central government system to replace what had basically been a federation of Daimyo domains with a great deal of internal autonomy under a loose form of central control. The ruling oligarchs were presented with a number of problems, some legal in nature. For one thing, some formal organization of the new governmental system was required. For another, the voices of reform that sought a representative assembly as well as the objections of samurai not in the government who sought some voice in the new administration needed to be co-opted through a legislative body. And finally, a legal system (acceptable to the Western powers) had to be imported so that the Western powers could be convinced to reform the unequal treaties, give up consular jurisdiction and return sovereignty to Japan. The stage was set for major legal reform that would replace the feudal system with a Westernized governmental system and legal regime.

A. Constitutional Government

To Americans the idea of a written constitutional form of government is almost axiomatic. The relations among the newly independent States and between these States and the new National Government they were creating was simply too complicated to be left to anything other than a written document. The first attempt, the Articles of Confederation, had failed and the new document, the Constitution, was a roadmap for structural organization of the government, for defining the powers of that government, and for setting out the relationship between that government and the States. There was no history or custom to rely on and the writers were creating new ground because of the situation in which they found themselves.

But a written Constitution is not an essential element of government. The Tokugawa Shogunate had survived for two and a half centuries without one and even among the Western powers England had no written Constitution. To the extent that the Dominion of Canada had a written Constitution it was an English law (the British North America Act). Moreover, a Constitution need not define the rights of citizens vis-à-vis the government created. The American Constitution had no such definition in its original form and only obtained such definition when the Constitution was amended by the Bill of Rights. So why then did the new Meiji Government opt for a written Constitution?

For one thing, the concept of a written Constitution was fashionable in the late 19th Century. If not everyone was doing it then at least most countries were doing it. If Japan wished to join the Western powers as an equal member (and she did so wish) and if the unequal treaties were to be favorably renegotiated then it was incumbent on Japan to have a written Constitution. Moreover there were great internal pressures for a Constitution. The "Restoration" had occurred because of the weakness of the eastern establishment (the Shogunate was an eastern Daimyo phenomenon, Tokugawa Ieyasu having come from the eastern part of Japan and completed his rule over all Japan by defeating the western lords at Sekigahara). Restoration represented the victory of four western domains (Choshu, Satsuma, Tosa and Hizen). Two of these domains (Choshu and Satsuma) dominated the leadership of the oligarchs who were ruling in the Emperor's name. Others in Japan, particularly other members of the former samurai class as well as bureaucrats in the new government, wanted a role in the new government and a say in the new policies and they agitated for a constitution that would provide them with such a role. Moreover, shortly after the Restoration the Emperor had promised in the Charter Oath of Five Articles (1868) that there would be deliberative assemblies and public discussion of policies.[1] It is likely that such promise was meant to include the rival feudal Houses headed by their Daimyo in some deliberative assembly rather than a national Parliament. However, once the Daimyo domains were abolished as part of the program to abolish the feudal system the assembly could only mean some form of parliamentary body.[2] Finally, a written constitution would be a useful mechanism to cement the power of the central authority and permit the oligarchs to continue to rule in the Emperor's name.

---

1 John K. Fairbank, Edwin O. Reischauer and Albert M. Craig, EAST ASIA TRADITION AND TRANSFORMATION 503, 535 (Houghton Mifflin Company, 1973); for an English language translation of the Oath see, W. W. McLaren, JAPANESE GOVERNMENT DOCUMENTS (Asiatic Society of Japan) (University Publications of America, reprint edition, 1979) Vol. 1, 8 fn. 1.

2 G.B. Sansom, THE WESTERN WORLD AND JAPAN (Vintage Books, New York, 1949) 318-320, 340.

The Meiji Restoration was virtually completed in 1868 (the final battle was fought in 1869 when the Tokugawa Navy was defeated and Hokkaido came under the authority of the new government). A new constitution was not given to the people by the Emperor until February 1889 effective November 1890. During this 20-year hiatus the Meiji oligarchs transformed Japanese society on a Western model and researched extensively in the West to find a model for the new constitution and legal system. Opinion among the oligarchs was divided as to how "democratic" the new constitution should be, delaying the creation of constitutional government. Both an "English school," favoring an English style parliamentary democracy, and a "Prussian school" favoring a more authoritarian approach developed.[3] The Prussian school was aided by Hermann Roesler, a German legal advisor who was to play a major role in Japan's tilt toward a German Constitution and Civil Code. A draft constitution was produced by as early as 1880.[4] In 1881, after an internal rebellion among the ruling oligarchs brought on by the democratic approach of one of the oligarchs (Okuma Shigenobu),[5] the Emperor postponed creation of a representative assembly until 1890.[6] Okuma was removed from the government shortly after he raised certain constitutional issues including political party government and an election by as early as 1882 with a national assembly—parliament—to be formed in 1883.[7]

3 George Akita, FOUNDATIONS OF CONSTITUTIONAL GOVERNMENT IN MODERN JAPAN (Harvard University Press, 1967) 14, 26, 27, 56; Donald Keene, EMPEROR OF JAPAN: MEIJI AND HIS WORLD, 1852-1912 (Columbia University Press, 2002) 137-139, 339.

4 George Akita, FOUNDATIONS OF CONSTITUTIONAL GOVERNMENT IN MODERN JAPAN (Harvard University Press, 1967) 11,12; Donald Keene, EMPEROR OF JAPAN: MEIJI AND HIS WORLD, 1852-1912 (Columbia University Press, 2002) 341.

5 Okuma went on to form a political party (Constitutional Progressive Party) as had Itagaki Taisuke (Liberal Party) who also had been a member of the inner circle who found himself excluded from the government as a result of an earlier internal dispute between the oligarchs. George M. Beckman, THE MAKING OF THE MEIJI CONSTITUTION (University of Kansas Press, 1957) 61-62. Hugh Borton, JAPAN'S MODERN CENTURY (The Ronald Press Company, 1955) 93-99, 103-104, 120-122, 128-129, 132-135. For an English language version of Okuma's proposal for a constitution see Beckman at Appendix VI. Itagaki's resignation from government was part of a larger resignation by leaders whose views were rejected by the group that eventually took control of the oligarchy. Saigo was one of those who resigned. He later led the Satsuma Rebellion. Itagaki fought the oligarchs with whom he was now out of favor by organizing a political party. For a discussion of the start of the political party movement started by Itagaki and strengthened by Okuma see, G.B. Sansom, THE WESTERN WORLD AND JAPAN (Vintage Books, New York, 1949) 339-353. See also, Andrew Gordon, A MODERN HISTORY OF JAPAN (Oxford University Press, 2003) 80-85.

6 See, George Akita, FOUNDATIONS OF CONSTITUTIONAL GOVERNMENT IN MODERN JAPAN (Harvard University Press, 1967) Chapter III "Ito and Okuma: The Crisis of 1881;" Donald Keene, EMPEROR OF JAPAN: MEIJI AND HIS WORLD, 1852-1912 (Columbia University Press, 2002) 353, 357,358. An English language version of the Emperor's Announcement of October 12, 1881 that a National Assembly would be established by 1890 may be found at Ishii Ryosuke, JAPANESE LEGISLATION IN THE MEIJI ERA (Translated and adapted by William J. Chambliss) (Kasai Publishing, Tokyo, 1958) at 720-721.

7 For a discussion of the 1881 internal rebellion see, George M. Beckman, THE MAKING OF THE MEIJI CONSTITUTION (University of Kansas Press, 1957) 53-60; George Akita.

Ito Hirobumi,[8] a leader of the conservative elements in the government who favored a postponement of the creation of a national assembly and who was a supporter of Imperial authoritarian government was placed in charge of the constitution writing effort. Ito led a study group to Europe (1882-1883) to study European constitutions but spent most of his time studying the Prussian Constitution and German constitutional theory, which became the basis for the new Constitution.[9] Prior to going to Europe Ito (who had previously visited Germany) already favored a German-based constitution.[10] A small group, one of whom was the German legal scholar Hermann Roesler whose influence on the Constitution was substantial, assisted Ito in the drafting process.[11] Even before the constitution was written, the oligarchs restructured both government and society in order to

---

FOUNDATIONS OF CONSTITUTIONAL GOVERNMENT IN MODERN JAPAN (Harvard University Press, 1967) 31-57; W. W. McClaren, JAPANESE GOVERNMENT DOCUMENTS (Asiatic Society of Japan) (University Publications of America, reprint edition, 1979) Introduction Vol. 1, p.lxvii-lxviii; W. W. McLaren, A POLITICAL HISTORY OF JAPAN (1916, REISSUED 1965, Russell & Russell) p. 156-160 G.B. Sansom, THE WESTERN WORLD AND JAPAN (Vintage Books, New York, 1949) 345-346.

8 Ito was a "second generation" oligarch. The first generation was dominated by Okubo Toshimichi (who was assassinated in 1878); Saigo Takamori (who, after falling out of favor with his two rivals because of his plans to attack Korea as an outlet for samurai discontent, led a rebellion of samurai protesting the abolition of the feudal system and more particularly their annuities and stipends and was killed); and Kido Takayoshi (who died of illness in 1877). George M. Beckman, THE MAKING OF THE MEIJI CONSTITUTION (University of Kansas Press, 1957) 40. For contrasting characterizations of three leaders compare John K. Fairbank, Edwin O. Reischauer and Albert M. Craig, EAST ASIA TRADITION AND TRANSFORMATION 502 (Houghton Mifflin Company, 1973) with Sterling Seagrave and Peggy Seagrave, THE YAMATO DYNASTY (Broadway Books, 1999) 37-44. Ito's great rival in this second generation was General Yamagata Aritomi. See generally George Akita, FOUNDATIONS OF CONSTITUTIONAL GOVERNMENT IN MODERN JAPAN (Harvard University Press, 1967) for a discussion of the roles of these players in the Restoration and constitutional development in Japan. For an interesting discussion of the rise and fall of Saigo Takamori, see, Ivan Morris, THE NOBILITY OF FAILURE (Holt Rinehart and Winston, 1975) 217-275. See G.B. Sansom, THE WESTERN WORLD AND JAPAN (Vintage Books, New York, 1949) 329-336 for a discussion of the Satsuma Rebellion and Saigo's role therein; Marius B. Jansen, THE MAKING OF MODERN JAPAN (Belknap Press of Harvard University, 2000) 369-370. See also, W. W. McLaren, A POLITICAL HISTORY OF JAPAN (1916, REISSUED 1965, Russell & Russell) p. 256-257 and 262-263 for the position that Ito headed up a faction of government committed to civil government and Yamagata a faction supporting military government.

9 George M. Beckman, THE MAKING OF THE MEIJI CONSTITUTION (University of Kansas Press, 1957) 70-73; Hiroshi Oda, JAPANESE LAW (Oxford University Press, 2nd Ed. 1999) 24; John K. Fairbank, Edwin O. Reischauer and Albert M. Craig, EAST ASIA TRADITION AND TRANSFORMATION 419, 540-541 (Houghton Mifflin Company, 1973); Donald Keene, EMPEROR OF JAPAN: MEIJI AND HIS WORLD, 1852-1912 (Columbia University Press, 2002) 381-382.

10 George M. Beckman, THE MAKING OF THE MEIJI CONSTITUTION (University of Kansas Press, 1957) 33; Hugh Borton, JAPAN'S MODERN CENTURY (The Ronald Press Company, 1955) 136-148 (discussing the constitution drafting and promulgation process).

11 George M. Beckman, THE MAKING OF THE MEIJI CONSTITUTION (University of Kansas Press, 1957) 78-80; George Akita, FOUNDATIONS OF CONSTITUTIONAL GOVERNMENT IN MODERN JAPAN (Harvard University Press, 1967) 63, 165-166; Hiroshi Oda, JAPANESE LAW (Oxford University Press, 2nd Ed. 1999) 24; Andrew Gordon, A MODERN HISTORY OF JAPAN (Oxford University Press, 2003) 92-93.

meet the awaited constitutional model. Thus, for example, steps towards an independent judiciary were initiated in 1875 when the Osaka Conference (which had been convened to quiet forces of the first internal rebellion within the ranks of the oligarchs) determined on a reorganization of the *dajokwan* (Council of State), which had executive, legislative and judicial authority.[12] This constituted a kind of principal of "Separation of Powers"[13] and was followed by the separation of the judicial power from the executive.[14] Prefectural assemblies were established in 1878.[15] A Peerage was created (1884)[16] in order to be available when the new constitution created a House of Peers[17] to balance and limit the power of the House of Representatives[18] that was to be created.[19] A reorganization of government along German lines was undertaken in 1885.[20] As a consequence, the Council of State was abolished and replaced by a Cabinet[21] so that a new constitutional Cabinet

12 G.B. Sansom, THE WESTERN WORLD AND JAPAN (Vintage Books, New York, 1949) 320, 341; see also, Hugh Borton, JAPAN'S MODERN CENTURY (The Ronald Press Company, 1955) 98.

13 Takaaki Hattori, The Legal Profession in Japan: Its Historical Development and Present State in LAW IN JAPAN (von Mehren Ed. 1967) 114; Yosiyuki Noda, INTRODUCTION TO JAPANESE LAW (translated and edited by Anthony H. Angelo) (University of Tokyo Press, 1976) 53.

14 George M. Beckman, THE MAKING OF THE MEIJI CONSTITUTION (University of Kansas Press, 1957) 35; Paul Heng-Chao Ch'en, THE FORMATION OF THE EARLY MEIJI LEGAL ORDER (Oxford University Press, 1981) 55. Prior to this separation, the Minister of Justice had the power to hear appeals from lower court decisions. Whether this separation actually created an "independent judiciary" is questioned. See, W. W. McLaren, JAPANESE GOVERNMENT DOCUMENTS (Asiatic Society of Japan) (University Publications of America, reprint edition, 1979) Introduction Vol. 1, p. lxxv; W.W. McLaren, A POLITICAL HISTORY OF JAPAN (1916 ,reissued 1965, Russell & Russell, Inc.) 117-119. An English language translation of the rescript establishing the Supreme Court as a separate organ (and also establishing the *Genro*) may be found at Ishii Ryosuke, JAPANESE LEGISLATION IN THE MEIJI ERA (Translated and adapted by William J. Chambliss) (Kasai Publishing, Tokyo, 1958) at 718.

15 George Akita, FOUNDATIONS OF CONSTITUTIONAL GOVERNMENT IN MODERN JAPAN (Harvard University Press, 1967) 24; George M. Beckman, THE MAKING OF THE MEIJI CONSTITUTION (University of Kansas Press, 1957) 43; Hugh Borton, JAPAN'S MODERN CENTURY (The Ronald Press Company, 1955) 105.

16 Donald Keene, EMPEROR OF JAPAN: MEIJI AND HIS WORLD, 1852-1912 (Columbia University Press, 2002) 799n.15.

17 George Akita, FOUNDATIONS OF CONSTITUTIONAL GOVERNMENT IN MODERN JAPAN (Harvard University Press, 1967) 63.

18 George M. Beckman, THE MAKING OF THE MEIJI CONSTITUTION (University of Kansas Press, 1957) 50-51, 74.

19 John K. Fairbank, Edwin O. Reischauer and Albert M. Craig, EAST ASIA TRADITION AND TRANSFORMATION 541 (Houghton Mifflin Company, 1973).

20 G.B. Sansom, THE WESTERN WORLD AND JAPAN (Vintage Books, New York, 1949) 358.

21 Hirobumi Ito, COMMENTARIES ON THE CONSTITUTION OF THE EMPIRE OF JAPAN (2d ed. Cuo-O University, 1906) 98,99; W. W. McLaren, JAPANESE GOVERNMENT DOCUMENTS (Asiatic Society of Japan) (University Publications of America, reprint edition, 1979) Vol. 1, 94.

form of government would be easily accommodated[22] and the Grand Court of Judicature was created. A Privy Council was established (1888) to assure that the oligarchs would be able to continue to assert authority under the Emperor's name.[23] At the same time, the military establishment in Japan worked diligently to create a General Staff on the German model whose authority would come directly from and whose responsibility would flow directly to the Emperor, so as to be free from constitutional restraints.[24] During this 20-year hiatus, political parties were formed in Japan and elected assemblies were formed at the prefecture level. These elected assemblies were training grounds for the political parties.[25]

The Meiji Constitution is Emperor centered. In this sense it both reflects and departs from the Prussian model. The Prussian model provided for potential authoritarian power through the throne, but the provisions regarding the throne came in the Third Chapter of the Constitution. In the Meiji Constitution it came first. This ordering reflected the views of the Meiji Constitution's authors as to the importance of the Emperor and his powers.[26] Thus, the Emperor is head of the government and also embodies the Japanese sovereignty. He exercises the legislative power (with the consent of the Diet); he orders laws to be promulgated and executed; he has the authority to dissolve the House of Representatives (the elected House of a bicameral legislature); he can issue Ordinances with the force of law when the Diet is not in session; he determines the organization of the government and hires and fires all civil servants and military officers; he is the supreme commander of the military and makes war, peace and concludes treaties. The Constitution creates a Diet with legislative and budgetary powers (if the Diet declines to pass a budget the previous year's budget remains in force). It makes Ministers of State responsible to the Emperor for their advice and requires that all laws require the signature of a Minister of State. It provides for a Privy Council.

Although the Constitution emphasized the powers of the Emperor, early Meiji legal theoreticians debated the role of the Emperor in the government. Professor

---

22 Donald Keene, EMPEROR OF JAPAN: MEIJI AND HIS WORLD, 1852-1912 (Columbia University Press, 2002) 402; John K. Fairbank, Edwin O. Reischauer and Albert M. Craig, EAST ASIA TRADITION AND TRANSFORMATION 541 (Houghton Mifflin Company, 1973); George Akita, FOUNDATIONS OF CONSTITUTIONAL GOVERNMENT IN MODERN JAPAN (Harvard University Press, 1967) 63, 68-69; George M. Beckman, THE MAKING OF THE MEIJI CONSTITUTION (University of Kansas Press, 1957) 75.

23 Donald Keene, EMPEROR OF JAPAN: MEIJI AND HIS WORLD, 1852-1912 (Columbia University Press, 2002) 418-419; John K. Fairbank, Edwin O. Reischauer and Albert M. Craig, EAST ASIA TRADITION AND TRANSFORMATION 541 (Houghton Mifflin Company, 1973).

24 John K. Fairbank, Edwin O. Reischauer and Albert M. Craig, EAST ASIA TRADITION AND TRANSFORMATION 543, 549, 711-713; see, Donald Keene, EMPEROR OF JAPAN: MEIJI AND HIS WORLD, 1852-1912 (Columbia University Press, 2002) 366-367.

25 George M. Beckman, THE MAKING OF THE MEIJI CONSTITUTION (University of Kansas Press, 1957) 44.

26 See, Yasuhiro Okudaira, Forty Years of the Constitution and its Various Influences: Japanese, American, and European in JAPANESE CONSTITUTIONAL LAW (Percy R. Luney, Jr. and Kazuyuki Takanashi Ed., University of Tokyo Press, 1993) 1, 3-4.

Yatsuka Hozumi of Tokyo University argued that the Constitution's recognition of sovereignty in the Emperor was unchangeable and that Japanese sovereignty did not reside in the "State" but in the person of the Emperor and the Imperial House. In essence this approach reflected the view that the drafters of the constitution had rejected the English and French notions that sovereignty resided in the public or at least in the nationally elected assembly—a view that was widely held prior to the drafting of the Constitution. This approach reflects the views of the drafter of the Constitution (Ito).[27] A contradictory leading theory was Professor Tatsukichi Minobe's idea to the effect that the Emperor was really just an organ of the State rather than representing the actual sovereignty of Japan and that sovereignty as such resided in the State.[28] Adoption of this view permitted a less Emperor-centered philosophy of government and supported a more democratic structure. This view held sway through the experiment in constitutional democracy that culminated in the 1920s, but was prohibited in the military dominated governments of the 1930s and the war years.[29]

In addition to the powers of the Emperor, certain features of the structure of government created by the Constitution are notable. Although the Constitution appears to embody the concept of a separation of powers it does not embody the corollary idea of checks and balances. Thus, although different bodies are created for different functions, these bodies do not check each other and do not balance the powers of each other. Although a two-house legislature was created, one House was not popularly elected. Membership in the House of Peers was composed of three classes: members of the Imperial family, some appointed and some elected representatives of the newly created nobility and persons nominated by the Emperor. Although nominated by the Emperor the last were in actuality appointed by the Privy Counsel, which at the time of the Constitution was composed of the oligarchs. This Upper House was modeled on the English House of Lords.

---

27 Hirobumi Ito, COMMENTARIES ON THE CONSTITUTION OF THE EMPIRE OF JAPAN (2d ed. Cuo-O University, 1906) 7-10.

28 Kenzo Takayanagi, A Century of Innovation: The Development of Japanese Law, 1868-1961 in LAW IN JAPAN (VON Mehren Ed. Harvard University Press, 1963) 10-11; George Akita, FOUNDATIONS OF CONSTITUTIONAL GOVERNMENT IN MODERN JAPAN (Harvard University Press, 1967) 171; John W. Dower, EMBRACING DEFEAT (W.W. Norton & Company, 1999) 355. See, Richard H. Minear, JAPANESE TRADITION AND WESTERN LAW (Harvard University Press, 1970) 6-10, 184, and 191-193 for an analysis of Hozumi's theory and a comparison with Minobe's ideas. See, Marius B. Jansen, THE MAKING OF MODERN JAPAN (Belknap Press of Harvard University, 2000) 542-544 for a discussion of the views of Minobe and Professor Yoshino Sakuzo.

29 Kenzo Takayanagi, A Century of Innovation: The Development of Japanese Law, 1868-1961 in LAW IN JAPAN (VON Mehren Ed. Harvard University Press, 1963) 11; George Akita, FOUNDATIONS OF CONSTITUTIONAL GOVERNMENT IN MODERN JAPAN (Harvard University Press, 1967) 171; John K. Fairbank, Edwin O. Reischauer and Albert M. Craig, EAST ASIA TRADITION AND TRANSFORMATION 669-670 (Houghton Mifflin Company, 1973); Herbert Bix, HIROHITO AND THE MAKING OF MODERN JAPAN (Harper Collins 2000) 287-296; Ian Buruma, INVENTING JAPAN 1853-1964 (Modern Library Chronicles, 2003) 97-98; Marius B. Jansen, THE MAKING OF MODERN JAPAN (Belknap Press of Harvard University, 2000) 612.

The Peers were to limit the powers of the elected Lower House since any permanent law required approval by both houses. The Emperor had the authority to make temporary laws when the Diet was not in session or when a State of Siege was declared. The Emperor also had the power to both disband the Diet and declare a State of Siege.

Although a Cabinet existed before the Constitution was adopted[30] and although clearly the oligarchs anticipated that the Cabinet would continue to exist and be the administrative and executive authority, the Cabinet is not mentioned in the Constitution and clearly was not made responsible to the Diet. Lacking any discussion in the Constitution, the Diet has no constitutional say in either the membership of or duration of the Cabinet. Unlike a Parliamentary democracy such as England, the Diet did not have the power to dismiss the Cabinet through a vote of no confidence.[31] On the other hand the Emperor could dismiss the Cabinet whether the Diet had confidence in the Cabinet or not. The Cabinet was composed of the Ministers of State. The Constitution failed to say how Ministers were to be selected. The Constitution also did not outline the powers of the Cabinet or Ministers. Prior to the Constitution the Emperor (with the advice of the oligarchs) appointed the Prime Minister, who in turn appointed the Ministers of State and hence the Cabinet. The power to appoint the administrative arm of the government, the Executive power, remained a prerogative of the Emperor. The same was true of the Privy Counsel. In reality, the Emperor continued to appoint the Prime Minister upon the advice of the oligarchs who, in 1875, formulated themselves into an advisory body called the *Genro*[32] (which institution lasted in one form or another until the 1930s).[33] At the beginning of constitutional government the oligarchs appointed themselves as Prime Minister and other Ministers of State.[34] The oligarchs envisioned the Cabinet as above party politics and not as a servant

30 Donald Keene, EMPEROR OF JAPAN: MEIJI AND HIS WORLD, 1852-1912 (Columbia University Press, 2002) 202-203; John K. Fairbank, Edwin O. Reischauer and Albert M. Craig, EAST ASIA TRADITION AND TRANSFORMATION 541 (Houghton Mifflin Company, 1973); George Akita, FOUNDATIONS OF CONSTITUTIONAL GOVERNMENT IN MODERN JAPAN (Harvard University Press, 1967) 68-69.

31 Hirobumi Ito, COMMENTARIES ON THE CONSTITUTION OF THE EMPIRE OF JAPAN (2d ed. Cuo-O University, 1906) 102-103; George M. Beckman, THE MAKING OF THE MEIJI CONSTITUTION (University of Kansas Press, 1957) 91.

32 Shinichi Fujii, THE ESSENTIALS OF JAPANESE CONSTITUTIONAL LAW (University Publications of America, reprint edition, 1979) 266; W. W. McLaren, JAPANESE GOVERNMENT DOCUMENTS (Asiatic Society of Japan) (University Publications of America, reprint edition, 1979) Vol. 1, 42; W. W. McLaren, JAPANESE GOVERNMENT DOCUMENTS (Asiatic Society of Japan) (University Publications of America, reprint edition, 1979) Introduction Vol. 1, p.lxxxii; W. W. McLaren, A POLITICAL HISTORY OF JAPAN (1916, REISSUED 1965, Russell & Russell p.176-177.

33 G.B. Sansom, THE WESTERN WORLD AND JAPAN (Vintage Books, New York, 1949) 364-365.

34 George M. Beckman, THE MAKING OF THE MEIJI CONSTITUTION (University of Kansas Press, 1957) 90.

of the Legislative Branch.[35] The oligarchs saw themselves as the appropriate Ministers of State and in the early years of the constitution the position of Prime Minister revolved between representatives of the Choshu and Satsuma domains. As the oligarchs began to die off, the *Genro* was replaced in many matters by an advisory body consisting of the former Prime Ministers and the Privy Seal (appointed by the Emperor). The Emperor had the power to dissolve the Diet and to issue ordinances with the force of law while the Diet was not in session or while there was a State of Siege (which the Emperor could declare). This gave the Emperor a great deal of legislative control as well as executive control. The oligarchs acting in the Emperor's name exercised both of these powers.[36]

One of the glaring shortcomings of the Constitution was its failure to provide the civilian government with authority over the military.[37] This failure was to have dramatic effects in the 1930's.[38] Not only did the military report only to the Emperor and not only did the military feel itself responsible solely to the Emperor, but Army and Navy Ministers of State were essential members of the Cabinet. Under the harmony and consensus principle of Cabinet responsibility the entire Cabinet was required to resign and be reformulated if a single Cabinet member resigned.[39] This, together with the requirement that the Army and Navy be represented in the Cabinet, meant the military could force the collapse of civilian government and could prevent the organization of a new civilian government by failing to allow its high-ranking officers to serve as Ministers.[40] As early as 1891, when the second constitutional Cabinet was formed (Prime Minister Matsukata), the military made use of this power to threaten refusal to appoint Ministers unless

35 In a speech given on May 4, 1889 dealing with the newly announced constitution, Hirobumi Ito noted that some people thought the Diet had a role to play in administrative matters but that they were wrong—the Diet's role was limited to deliberating on laws and did not extend to administering the government. See, W. W. McLaren, JAPANESE GOVERNMENT DOCUMENTS (Asiatic Society of Japan) (University Publications of America, reprint edition, 1979) Vol. 2, 619.

36 To some extent this system replicated the Shogunate where after the 3rd Tokugawa Shogun the various shoguns (with some exceptions) were themselves figureheads with an advisory body (*roju*) that appointed itself and was the effective ruler of Japan. Wigmore, LAW AND JUSTICE IN TOKUGAWA JAPAN Vol. 1. p. 4-5; G.B. Sansom, THE WESTERN WORLD AND JAPAN (Vintage Books, New York, 1949) 182-183. It is possible that the oligarchs made no provision for how the *genro* would operate after their death on the assumption that the same system that had produced effective and good leaders in the *roju* would produce new councilors for the Emperor.

37 For discussion of the theory of "direct control" and its effect in insulating the military from civilian rule see, Marius B. Jansen, THE MAKING OF MODERN JAPAN (Belknap Press of Harvard University, 2000) 398-400.

38 See, Yosiyuki Noda, INTRODUCTION TO JAPANESE LAW (translated and edited by Anthony H. Angelo) (University of Tokyo Press, 1976) 57.

39 See, e.g., Shinichi Fujii, THE ESSENTIALS OF JAPANESE CONSTITUTIONAL LAW (University Publications of America, reprint edition, 1979) 258 to the effect that the Cabinet is a unified organization and should take joint responsibility.

40 George M. Beckman, THE MAKING OF THE MEIJI CONSTITUTION (University of Kansas Press, 1957) 92.

the government would meet its requests. Indeed, Matsukata eventually resigned as Prime Minister in 1892 when the Army and Navy Ministers resigned and no high-ranking officers agreed to replace them in the government.[41]

Party politicians in the Diet used the Diet's authority over the budget to expand the power of the Diet and the political parties.[42] Although the government could continue to exist without a Diet passed budget, as the previous year's budget would remain in effect, the reality was that "continuing resolution" budgets were inadequate for the expenses of government. Clearly, as a matter of constitutional law, the Cabinet was responsible to the Emperor and not to the Diet. And the oligarchs who composed the government could utilize the Imperial power to suspend or disband the Diet. However, the oligarchs were cautious in using their power because of fear that the Western powers would view such actions unfavorably. This in turn could inhibit the government's overriding objective of revision of the unequal treaties. On the other hand, when the Diet raised objections in 1893 and again in 1894 that the government thought would stand in the way of negotiations to do away with the unequal treaties, and when Ito as Prime Minister felt challenged by the political parties, the government used the Emperor's authority as well as power to disband the Diet.[43] Nonetheless, the oligarchs' position that the Cabinet had no responsibility to the Diet was doomed to failure because as a practical matter the Cabinet needed the Diet's consent to get both its budget and its policies adopted.[44]

The first session of the Diet was opened in 1890. In April of 1896 a political party politician was appointed to the Cabinet.[45] In 1898 the government lost its request for a tax bill to resolve a budget deficit issue. By the end of June the first party

---

41 George Akita, FOUNDATIONS OF CONSTITUTIONAL GOVERNMENT IN MODERN JAPAN (Harvard University Press, 1967) 92, 102-103; Hugh Borton, JAPAN'S MODERN CENTURY (The Ronald Press Company, 1955) 200.

42 For a discussion generally of the role of parties and the development of party governments in prewar Japan see, George Akita, FOUNDATIONS OF CONSTITUTIONAL GOVERNMENT IN MODERN JAPAN (Harvard University Press, 1967) for a discussion of the first diet session and the political parties' use of the power over the budget to make demands on the government and extend their power see pages 76-89; see also, John K. Fairbank, Edwin O. Reischauer and Albert M. Craig, EAST ASIA TRADITION AND TRANSFORMATION 539-540, 546-549, 684-687 (Houghton Mifflin Company, 1973); see also, G.B. Sansom, THE WESTERN WORLD AND JAPAN (Vintage Books, New York, 1949) 490-491.

43 George Akita, FOUNDATIONS OF CONSTITUTIONAL GOVERNMENT IN MODERN JAPAN (Harvard University Press, 1967) 115-117; Hugh Borton, JAPAN'S MODERN CENTURY (The Ronald Press Company, 1955) 202.

44 Professor Fujii recognized that while the Cabinet was not responsible to the Diet in law, in reality it required Diet approval in order to carry out its programs. Shinichi Fujii, THE ESSENTIALS OF JAPANESE CONSTITUTIONAL LAW (University Publications of America, reprint edition, 1979) 275; see, G.B. Sansom, THE WESTERN WORLD AND JAPAN (Vintage Books, New York, 1949) 492.

45 John K. Fairbank, Edwin O. Reischauer and Albert M. Craig, EAST ASIA TRADITION AND TRANSFORMATION 548 (Houghton Mifflin Company, 1973).

Cabinet was in place.[46] When Ito, the principal draftsman of the Constitution and one of the leading oligarchs formed his own political party (the Seiyukai was actually a reorganization of an existing party, the Kenseito, with Ito as its nominal leader)[47] and became Prime Minister as head of the party in 1901,[48] both a political and constitutional shift had taken place in the relationship between the Diet and the Cabinet.[49] Nonetheless Ito (the drafter of the Constitution and now political party leader and party Prime Minister) continued to maintain that the Cabinet was not responsible to the Diet.[50]

By the 1920's (by which time the power of the old oligarchs had waned) Japan had entered an era where, although not required by the Constitution and indeed inconsistent with Ito's views when he was drafting the Constitution, Cabinet government in fact represented political parties in the House of Representatives and the Cabinet de facto was responsible to, although not appointed or designated by, the majority party in the Diet.[51] [This period is sometimes referred[52] to as the era of "Taisho democracy," named after the Emperor period Taisho (the son of the Meiji Emperor).] This together with the extension of voting rights from the original perhaps 1% of the population eligible to vote for the House of Representatives[53] to an ever increasing proportion of the male population (complete male suffrage came about in 1925) had the potential for creation of a true representative democracy.[54] What had not changed was the relationship of the military to the civilian government. With its power derived directly from the Emperor and its responsibility flowing directly to the Emperor and with the requirement that the military be given two seats in the Cabinet, the military was in a strong position vis-à-vis the civilian

46 Donald Keene, EMPEROR OF JAPAN: MEIJI AND HIS WORLD, 1852-1912 (Columbia University Press, 2002) 538, 541; W. W. McLaren, A POLITICAL HISTORY OF JAPAN (1916, REISSUED 1965, Russell & Russell p.252-255.

47 Donald Keene, EMPEROR OF JAPAN: MEIJI AND HIS WORLD, 1852-1912 (Columbia University Press, 2002) 562-564.

48 John K. Fairbank, Edwin O. Reischauer and Albert M. Craig, EAST ASIA TRADITION AND TRANSFORMATION 549-550 (Houghton Mifflin Company, 1973).

49 George Akita, FOUNDATIONS OF CONSTITUTIONAL GOVERNMENT IN MODERN JAPAN (Harvard University Press, 1967) Chapter X—Ito, Yamagata, and the Kenseito: Formation of the Seiyukai 137-154.

50 See, e.g., W. W. McLaren, A POLITICAL HISTORY OF JAPAN (1916, REISSUED 1965, Russell & Russell) p.263-268.

51 John K. Fairbank, Edwin O. Reischauer and Albert M. Craig, EAST ASIA TRADITION AND TRANSFORMATION 697-702 (Houghton Mifflin Company, 1973); Andrew Gordon, A MODERN HISTORY OF JAPAN (Oxford University Press, 2003) 128-130, 162-167; Hugh Borton, JAPAN'S MODERN CENTURY (The Ronald Press Company, 1955) 196.

52 See, John K. Fairbank, Edwin O. Reischauer and Albert M. Craig, EAST ASIA TRADITION AND TRANSFORMATION 705-713 (Houghton Mifflin Company, 1973).

53 Donald Keene, EMPEROR OF JAPAN: MEIJI AND HIS WORLD, 1852-1912 (Columbia University Press, 2002) 435.

54 For a chart listing the steps in expanding suffrage to males in Japan from 1889 through 1925 see, John K. Fairbank, Edwin O. Reischauer and Albert M. Craig, EAST ASIA TRADITION AND TRANSFORMATION 699 (Houghton Mifflin Company, 1973).

government. In the 1930's the military used its position as solely responsible to the Emperor and its power over two seats in the Cabinet to cause the collapse of successive Cabinets. It then prevented the establishment of a new Cabinet by refusing to name active duty senior officers to the posts of Army and Navy Minister. This tactic was a means of obtaining greater power in the government. This together with the wave of assassinations of civilian leaders and an inability of civilian government to control the Army in Manchuria eventually resulted in control of the government by the military.[55]

The Meiji Constitution in addition to having a separation of powers between the sovereignty (Emperor), the Executive (Cabinet), the Military, and the Legislature also referred to a Judicial Branch of government. The judicial power was to be exercised by the "courts of law, according to law, in the name of the Emperor."[56] The organization of the Judicial Branch was to be determined by law, except that administrative law matters were outside the authority of the ordinary courts and solely within the authority of a special Administrative Court. Although some have suggested that the Constitution protected the independence of the judiciary by providing life tenure[57] for judges, the Constitution actually provided that judges may be dismissed for criminal activity or for "disciplinary punishment," although the rules for such punishment were to be provided by law.[58] In August 1890 such a law was enacted, and judges could be disciplined for neglect of official duties as well as for conduct that brought disrepute on the court (a somewhat flexible concept). Discipline included punishments from as slight as a reprimand to removal from the bench.[59] Thus, the possibility of discharge as a punishment was recognized by the Constitution.[60] Judges were to be appointed according to law by those who had the qualifications that were to be set by law.

---

55 See, Hugh Borton, JAPAN'S MODERN CENTURY (The Ronald Press Company, 1955) 340-342; John K. Fairbank, Edwin O. Reischauer and Albert M. Craig, EAST ASIA TRADITION AND TRANSFORMATION 711-713 (Houghton Mifflin Company, 1973); see also, Herbert Bix, HIROHITO AND THE MAKING OF MODERN JAPAN (Harper Collins 2000) 252-256, 280-281.

56 Hirobumi Ito, the principle draftsman of the Constitution considered the judicial power to be a "branch of the executive power" Hirobumi Ito, COMMENTARIES ON THE CONSTITUTION OF THE EMPIRE OF JAPAN ((2d ed. Cuo-O University, 1906) 9, 114.

57 See, Shinichi Fujii, THE ESSENTIALS OF JAPANESE CONSTITUTIONAL LAW (University Publications of America, reprint edition, 1979) 299-303 questioning whether laws requiring retirement at a certain age (Law No. 101 of 1921) and a law of 1913 requiring retirement when decided on by the court of Cassation were in violation of the Constitution.

58 Takaaki Hattori, The Legal Profession in Japan: Its Historical Development and Present State in LAW IN JAPAN (von Mehren Ed. 1967) 120.

59 Ishii Ryosuke, JAPANESE LEGISLATION IN THE MEIJI ERA (Translated and adapted by William J. Chambliss) (Kasai Publishing, Tokyo, 1958) at 487.

60 It appears that Ito Hirobumi saw judicial independence as an independence from heads of various administrative offices but he nonetheless recognized that judges could be disciplined. The grounds for discipline were to be established by law. Apparently the independence of the judiciary from the administrative departments of government was seen as a corollary to the independence of the administrative departments from the judiciary. Hirobumi Ito, COMMENTARIES ON THE CONSTITUTION OF THE EMPIRE OF JAPAN (2d ed. Cuo-O University, 1906) 116, 120.

The Law on the Organization of the courts of 1890 set requirements for qualifications to become judges and prosecutors (but not to become representatives of parties before the court—eventually bengoshi). As a general matter, applicants for a judicial position had to pass two examinations. Between the first and second exams, the applicant was required to engage in a three-year practical training course at either the existing courts or at the prosecutors office. There were certain exceptions to the initial testing requirement. Principally, graduates of the Tokyo University Faculty of Law did not need to sit for the first examination—but they did need to undergo the practical training and did need to pass the second examination. (Tokyo University Faculty of Law graduates were also exempt from certain testing requirements for positions in the Executive Branch of the government. Tokyo University had already become the training ground for government officials.) Law Professors at Tokyo University with three years experience and practicing lawyers with three years experience could be appointed judge without taking either examination.[61]

Many take the position that the independence of the judiciary was established as early as 1891 in the criminal case involving the "Otsu incident."[62] In this case the issue before the court was the punishment to be meted out to a Japanese policeman who had attempted to murder a member of a foreign royal house. Such an attempt on a member of the Imperial family was punishable by death. However, the criminal code had no special provision for dealing with an attempt on a member of a foreign royal house. The normal punishment for attempted murder was a maximum of life imprisonment. The government of Japan sought to have the court apply the death penalty by analogy to an attempt on a member of the Imperial House but the court refused and instead handed up the life imprisonment penalty. Because the court refused to buckle under to the desires of the Executive Branch, the Otsu incident case is widely regarded as an example of the independence of the Japanese judiciary during the prewar years.[63]

While the court is obviously to be commended for its resistance to political pressure in the Otsu incident case, and while the case does support independence of

61 See, Ishii Ryosuke, JAPANESE LEGISLATION IN THE MEIJI ERA (Translated and adapted by William J. Chambliss) (Kasai Publishing, Tokyo, 1958) at 483-484; John O. Haley, The Japanese Judiciary: Maintaining Integrity, Autonomy and the Public Trust p. 17. On the web at: *http://law.wustl.edu/Academics/Faculty/Workingpapers/TheJapaneseJudiciary10_03.pdf*

62 For a discussion of the Otsu case and its relationship to Judicial Independence see, Kenzo Takayanagi, A Century of Innovation: The Development of Japanese Law, 1868-1961 in LAW IN JAPAN (VON Mehren Ed. Harvard University Press, 1963) 9-10; see also, Donald Keene, EMPEROR OF JAPAN: MEIJI AND HIS WORLD, 1852-1912 (Columbia University Press, 2002) 455-457and Toru Miura, Independence, Transparency and Accountability of the Judiciary in Japan, on the web at *www.unafei.or.jp/pdf/indonesia_pdf/session4.pdf* at page 30-31.

63 The Otsu Incident is also an early example of Japanese adoption of the rule that there can be no crimes by analogy.

the court, it is suggested that the case is not as supportive of an independent judiciary as it has come to be viewed.[64] It is suggested that the real issue of independence of the judiciary from the government relate to the judiciary's role in cases where the legality of government action is involved. Otsu concerned itself with a criminal case in which the court was not asked to resolve an issue against the government, such as a potential not guilty verdict in a high profile political case or the overturning of Executive action. Americans tend to view judicial independence as reflected by the court's willingness to strike down executive or legislative decisions such as through the use of the power of judicial review. The Meiji judiciary did not possess judicial review authority.[65] Moreover, the judiciary lacked the authority to overturn executive determinations since such determinations if subject to challenge at all were only subject to the jurisdiction of the Administrative Court and not the jurisdiction of the courts of law. Some in the government during the Meiji era questioned the independence of the courts.[66] The American Occupation questioned the independence of the judiciary,[67] as did post-war writers.[68] However, it does seem fair to say that of the various instrumentalities of government in Meiji Japan the judiciary was second only to the military in having independence. If the Constitution did not grant life tenure, the Court Organization Law of 1890 granted judges a life tenure[69] until retirement and placed limits on the govern-

64 See, Dan Fenno Henderson, Japanese Judicial Review of Legislation: The First Twenty Years in Dan Fenno Henderson, THE CONSTITUTION OF JAPAN: ITS FIRST TWENTY YEARS 1947-1967 (University of Washington Press, 1969) 115, 117 where Professor Henderson notes that after the Otsu case the Meiji Government did not attempt to influence specific cases but nonetheless the authority of the executive over judicial careers undoubtedly affected the judges.

65 Richard H. Minear, JAPANESE TRADITION AND WESTERN LAW (Harvard University Press, 1970) 132-133.

66 See quote by Tsuyoshi Inoue, an assistant to Ito found in Takaaki Hattori, The Legal Profession in Japan: Its Historical Development and Present State in LAW IN JAPAN (von Mehren Ed. 1967) 116; see also, Yosiyuki Noda, INTRODUCTION TO JAPANESE LAW (translated and edited by Anthony H. Angelo) (University of Tokyo Press, 1976) 123.

67 See, Charles L. Kades, The American Role in Revising Japan's Imperial Constitution, 104 Political Science Quarterly 215, 219-220 (1989).

68 See, Shigemitsu Dando (Translated by B.J. George Jr.) JAPANESE CRIMINAL PROCEDURE (Fred B. Rothman & Co., 1965) Section 5.03 for the view that courts in Meiji Japan were without sufficient judicial independence. See also, Takaaki Hattori, The Role of the Supreme Court of Japan in the Field of Judicial Administration, 60 Washington Law Review 69, 70 (1984) and Laifan Lin, Judicial Independence in Japan: A Re-investigation for China, 13 Columbia Journal of Asian Law 185, 190 (1999) for the view that prewar efforts at judicial independence in Japan were both "quite limited and weak."

69 But see, Donald Keene, EMPEROR OF JAPAN: MEIJI AND HIS WORLD, 1852-1912 (Columbia University Press, 2002) 566 relating that in 1900 some judges and magistrates protesting the failure of the budget to provide a salary increase offered resignations (not expecting them to be accepted) and/or went on strike. The Minister of Justice removed all.

ment's right to transfer judges or to reduce pay[70] (although judges were compelled to take voluntary pay cuts in the 1930s).[71]

The court of Administrative Litigation ("Administrative Court") was designed, in part, on the French Cour de Cassation[72] as an administrative court with authority to review administrative actions of the government. Such a court can, and in France such a court does, exercise its independent authority to control the excesses of the government. However, the Meiji oligarchs had no such plans for the Administrative Court in Japan. Rather, the purpose of taking administrative jurisdiction out of the courts of law and placing it in the Administrative Court was to assure that there would be no judicial interference with the plans of the oligarchs and the authority of the Executive.[73] Judges in the Administrative Court were not judicial judges but administrative officials, most of who had no judicial experience.[74] Moreover, these judges/administrators did not have security of tenure in their position.[75] Had the Administrative Court developed a tradition of judicial independence by overturning government actions, it could be convincingly argued that a tradition of judicial independence had been established prewar.

Jurisdiction of the Administrative Court was determined by the 1890 law concerning administrative litigation, drafted by the German advisor Albert Mosse. The court lacked authority to render money damages. The concept of administrative action was broadly construed as applicable to all cases that challenged government action whether or not the case sought to actually overturn the government

---

70 Law No. 6, 2/8/1890, Chapter II—The Judges Sections 73 and 78, W. W. McLaren, JAPANESE GOVERNMENT DOCUMENTS (Asiatic Society of Japan) (University Publications of America, reprint edition, 1979) Vol. 2 p. 642-643.

71 Law No. 6, 2/8/1890, Chapter II-The Judges Section 67 provided that judgeships were created by the Emperor for life. W. W. McLaren, JAPANESE GOVERNMENT DOCUMENTS (Asiatic Society of Japan) (University Publications of America, reprint edition, 1979) Vol. 2 p. 641; John O. Haley, The Japanese Judiciary: Maintaining Integrity, Autonomy and the Public Trust p. 18. On the web at: *http://law.wustl.edu/Academics/Faculty/Workingpapers/TheJapaneseJudiciary10_03.pdf*

72 Tsuyoshi Kinoshita, The Reception in Japan of the American Law and its Transformation in the Fifth Years Since the End of World War II, 26 Law in Japan 1, 7 (2000); Toshiyoshi Miyasawa, CONSTITUTIONAL LAW (REV. ED. 1962) in Hideo Tanaka, THE JAPANESE LEGAL SYSTEM (University of Tokyo Press, 1976) at 637.

73 Kiminobu Hashimoto, The Rule of Law: Some Aspects of Judicial Review of Administrative Action, LAW IN JAPAN (von Mehren Ed. Harvard University Press, 1967) 240-241; Hideo Wada, The Administrative Court Under the Meiji Constitution, 10 Law in Japan 1, 3 (1977); Hirobumi Ito, COMMENTARIES ON THE CONSTITUTION OF THE EMPIRE OF JAPAN (2d ed. Cuo-O University, 1906) 119-123.

74 Takaaki Hattori, The Legal Profession in Japan: Its Historical Development and Present State in LAW IN JAPAN (von Mehren Ed. 1967) 54; Shinichi Fujii, THE ESSENTIALS OF JAPANESE CONSTITUTIONAL LAW (University Publications of America, reprint edition, 1979) 319 noting that judges of the administrative court were appointed from among judges and high ranking administrative officials.

75 Hideo Wada, The Administrative Court Under the Meiji Constitution, 10 Law in Japan 1, 5 (1977). Professor Wada notes that although tenure might have been formally provided for, the reality was that there was no security of tenure in office. See, pages 46-47.

decision.[76] But while the concept of administrative action was broad, thereby taking most administrative action out of the jurisdiction of the ordinary civil courts, the actual ability to sue in the Administrative Court was limited. Thus, a "legal right" of a plaintiff had to be alleged to have been injured by the administrative action implicated. It was not sufficient that an "interest" of the plaintiff might be involved. For example, if the administrative officials were of the view that a railway track should be placed in a location different from the location favored by local residents such residents had no right to sue. The interest of the residents in where the rails are laid may be great but there is no legal right to have the rails placed in a different location and thus no legal right has been violated.[77] In modern parlance we would say that while these potential plaintiffs might have an interest in the location of the rails because that interest did not rise to a legal right they lacked standing to sue. Indeed, even if it could be claimed that a legal right had been violated, there was no right to sue unless there was a specific statutory grant that permitted suit.[78] The law also contained provisions dealing with exhaustion of administrative avenues of appeal and short (60 days) statute of limitations. The 1890 law was effective until the end of the Second World War.[79]

Moreover, if one were to draw an organizational chart of the prewar government, the judiciary would not be placed on the same level as the Cabinet or the Diet.[80] Instead the judiciary was responsible to the Minister of Justice[81] who had the power to appoint judges, as was the prosecutor's office[82] and the newly emerging legal profession. Throughout the period, education of judges was in the hands of the Ministry of Justice, which also had authority to transfer judges from district to district.[83] Judges were part of the government bureaucracy and few if any practic-

---

76 Shinichi Fujii, THE ESSENTIALS OF JAPANESE CONSTITUTIONAL LAW (University Publications of America, reprint edition, 1979) 318.

77 Hirobumi Ito, COMMENTARIES ON THE CONSTITUTION OF THE EMPIRE OF JAPAN (2d ed. Cuo-O University, 1906) 122-123.

78 Kiminobu Hashimoto, The Rule of Law: Some Aspects of Judicial Review of Administrative Action, in LAW IN JAPAN (VON Mehren Ed. Harvard University Press, 1963) 240; Hideo Wada, The Administrative Court Under the Meiji Constitution, 10 Law in Japan 1, 8 (1977).

79 Ishii Ryosuke, JAPANESE LEGISLATION IN THE MEIJI ERA (Translated and adapted by William J. Chambliss) (Kasai Publishing, Tokyo, 1958) at 475-477.

80 See organization chart "The Political System Under the Meiji Constitution" in John K. Fairbank, Edwin O. Reischauer and Albert M. Craig, EAST ASIA TRADITION AND TRANSFORMATION 545 (Houghton Mifflin Company, 1973).

81 See, Rules for the Conduct of Business of the Department of Justice, December 2, 1880, which gives the Minister supervisory authority over both judges including the power to appoint, dismiss, promote and demote. W. W. McLaren, JAPANESE GOVERNMENT DOCUMENTS (Asiatic Society of Japan) (University Publications of America, reprint edition, 1979) Vol. 1, 65-66.

82 Takaaki Hattori, The Legal Profession in Japan: Its Historical Development and Present State in LAW IN JAPAN (von Mehren Ed. 1967) 114-115.

83 Takaaki Hattori, The Legal Profession in Japan: Its Historical Development and Present State in LAW IN JAPAN (von Mehren Ed. 1967) 122-124.

ing lawyers became judges,[84] although under the Organization for the Courts Law of 1890 practicing lawyers with three years experience were eligible for appointment. Eventually the position of prosecutor became more powerful than that of the judge raising judicial independence issues.[85]

The basic structure of the Meiji court system was established in 1890 utilizing a four-tier structure. The Grand Court of Judicature was at the top of the judicial structure with appellate jurisdiction.[86] It heard appeals from an intermediate appellate court (Superior Court) that had jurisdiction over a prefecture (District) level court. At the bottom of the ladder were the local courts. Local courts were presided over by a single judge and had jurisdiction over small claim civil matters. In addition these courts heard lessor-lessee cases; employer-employee cases (involving employment of one-years duration or less); certain hotel/restaurant—travelers or travelers and common carrier cases; cases involving personal property possessions only and cases dealing with the fixing of real property boundaries. In addition the court had jurisdiction over certain minor crimes. The prefectural courts were collegial in nature, were structured to contain different divisions and decided matters by majority vote. Prefectural courts had what could be considered a general civil and criminal jurisdiction over first instance cases (including a general bankruptcy jurisdiction) and civil appellate jurisdiction from decisions of the local court. The intermediate appellate court was also a collegial court that sat in divisions. It had jurisdiction over appeals from first instance judgments of the prefectural court and appellate determinations of said court that were alleged to be erroneous as a matter of law. The Grand Court of Judicature was the equivalent of the Supreme Court and it heard appeals from the intermediate appeals courts as well as possessing a limited first and final instance authority over certain criminal matters involving offenses against the Imperial family. The Grand Court of Judicature sat in panels but if a panel determined that a decision should be rendered inconsistent with a previous ruling, the court met en banc to decide the case.[87] Like the old American tradition of circuit riding judges, the judges of the Superior

---

84 Takaaki Hattori, The Legal Profession in Japan: Its Historical Development and Present State in LAW IN JAPAN (von Mehren Ed. 1967) 121.

85 Hideo Tanaka, THE JAPANESE LEGAL SYSTEM (University of Tokyo Press, 1976) 52, 557; see John O. Haley, The Japanese Judiciary: Maintaining Integrity, Autonomy and the Public Trust p. 19-20 On the web at *http://law.wustl.edu/Academics/Faculty/Workingpapers/TheJapaneseJudiciary10_03.pdf.*; see also, Alfred C. Oppler, LEGAL REFORM IN OCCUPIED JAPAN (Princeton University Press, 1976) 86 noting that the prosecutors were "watchdogs" over the judges and that the power to promote and demote affected the independence of the judiciary.

86 The Law on the Organization of the Courts of 1890 reflects the rise of the German school and the decline of the French school. Boissonade had drafted an organizational law for the court system that was rejected, whereas a German drafted this law. See, Ishii Ryosuke, JAPANESE LEGISLATION IN THE MEIJI ERA (Translated and adapted by William J. Chambliss) (Kasai Publishing, Tokyo, 1958) at 479-480.

87 See, Law No. 6, 2/8/1890 in W. W. McLaren, JAPANESE GOVERNMENT DOCUMENTS (Asiatic Society of Japan) (University Publications of America, reprint edition, 1979) Vol. 2, 625-659.

Court visited the various prefectures over which they had authority.[88] There was no rule of *starie decisis* but decisions of the Grand Court of Judicature were binding on lower courts "in all proceedings in the same action."[89]

In the United States one of the great engines of judicial independence is the independence of the practicing Bar and the Bar's view of itself as a protector of liberties. This is especially true of criminal defense lawyers and lawyers who sue the government challenging government actions. At the time of the Meiji Restoration there were no lawyers in Japan. The profession simply did not exist as the Tokugawa government prohibited representation in legal matters except for certain situations involving incapacity.[90] In 1872 for the first time representation was permitted in civil cases before the new courts[91]—however while representation was permitted there were no qualifications created for the licensing of representatives (known as *daigennin*). The Ministry of Justice created such regulations in 1876. The licensing requirement for *daigennin* was different from the requirements for judges and prosecutors. Even after this regulation, persons without credentials appeared as representatives, except now they could not use the *daigennin* title. This led to unqualified persons acting as representatives and served to put the budding profession in disrepute. In any event, even licensed *daigennin* were not permitted to represent persons in the criminal courts until 1876. Even then representation was not a right, rather the request for representation was made to the Ministry of Justice, which could grant or deny the request. It was not until the Criminal Code of 1880[92] came into effect in 1882[93] that anything approaching a right to representation was available.

The Meiji government needed to create a class of lawyers to operate in the new judicial system being created. However, in creating this professional body the gov-

---

88 Paul Heng-Chao Ch'en, THE FORMATION OF THE EARLY MEIJI LEGAL ORDER (Oxford University Press, 1981) 56-57; see, Shinichi Fujii, THE ESSENTIALS OF JAPANESE CONSTITUTIONAL LAW (University Publications of America, reprint edition, 1979) 303-306 for a discussion of the organization of the court system in Meiji Japan.

89 See, Law No. 6, 2/8/1890, section 48 in W. W. McLaren, JAPANESE GOVERNMENT DOCUMENTS (Asiatic Society of Japan) (University Publications of America, reprint edition, 1979) Vol. 2, at p. 637. For a summary of the jurisdiction of the various courts and their makeup see, Ishii Ryosuke, JAPANESE LEGISLATION IN THE MEIJI ERA (Translated and adapted by William J. Chambliss) (Kasai Publishing, Tokyo, 1958) at 479-483.

90 John O. Haley, AUTHORITY WITHOUT POWER: LAW AND THE JAPANESE PARADOX (Oxford University Press, 1991) 57, 100.

91 Takaaki Hattori, The Legal Profession in Japan: Its Historical Development and Present State in LAW IN JAPAN (von Mehren Ed. 1967) 117; Kenzo Takayanagi, A Century of Innovation: The Development of Japanese Law, 1868-1961 in LAW IN JAPAN (VON Mehren Ed. Harvard University Press, 1963) 20; John O. Haley, AUTHORITY WITHOUT POWER: LAW AND THE JAPANESE PARADOX (Oxford University Press, 1991) 100.

92 Takaaki Hattori, The Legal Profession in Japan: Its Historical Development and Present State in LAW IN JAPAN (von Mehren Ed. 1967) 119; Richard Rabinowitz, The Historical Development of the Japanese Bar, 70 Harvard Law Review 61 (1956) 67.

93 Kenzo Takayanagi, A Century of Innovation: The Development of Japanese Law, 1868-1961 in LAW IN JAPAN (VON Mehren Ed. Harvard University Press, 1963) 20 fn 17.

ernment did not wish to create too strong an independent group.[94] Accordingly, education for the new profession was initially placed in the law school maintained by the Ministry of Justice[95] (expanded in the 1890's to law faculties at Imperial Universities—especially Tokyo University, whose graduates initially did not need to pass an examination to be admitted to practice).[96] Similarly, the profession was placed under the control of the Ministry of Justice. Later, graduates of Imperial Universities (particularly Tokyo University) could become licensed without taking any examination.[97] Divisiveness in the new profession was so rampant that the public prosecutor had to be called in on several occasions in the late 1890s to restore some semblance of order to the profession. Use of the prosecutor's office to resolve internal "Bar" disputes was hardly conducive to a strong independent defense Bar or a Bar challenging government action. Under the Lawyers Law of 1893 (creating the title bengoshi for practicing lawyers) control of the "Bar" was given to the prosecutor's office. Various competing Bar associations existed during this period but it was not until the 1933 revision of the Lawyers Law that such associations were recognized as juristic persons. Even then the Ministry of Justice had a great deal of control over the profession.[98] There existed no effective legislation prohibiting the unlicensed practice of law.

Chapter II of the Meiji Constitution is entitled "Rights and Duties of Subjects." Such a title is misleading in that the Constitution was not based on individual rights concepts. The American notion of "constitutional rights" is based on a belief that there are certain rights that individuals possess and which government cannot take from them. As set out in the Bill of Rights, these rights are constitutionally granted and beyond the control of the elected legislative or Executive authority. These rights override any attempt by the governing authority to take away rights whether through legislative action or otherwise. Laws inconsistent with these constitutional rights are invalid and hence not "law." The Meiji Constitution has an entirely different approach to rights.[99] The Constitution gave the subjects of the Emperor only such rights as were given to them by laws to be enacted or pro-

94 For a general discussion of the history of the Japanese bar see, Richard Rabinowitz, The Historical Development of the Japanese Bar, 70 Harvard Law Review 61 (1956).

95 The Ministry of Justice Law School was founded in 1871. See, Setsuo Miyazawa and Hiroshi Otsuka, Legal Education and the Reproduction of the Elite in Japan, 1 Asian-Pacific Law & Policy Journal (2000) pgs 3-4. The Ministry Law School was absorbed by Tokyo University in 1885.

96 Professor Tomoko Akane, Reform of the Legal Training System in Japan available on the web at *www.unafei.or.jp/pdf/indonesia_pdf/session3.pdf* p.4.

97 John O. Haley, AUTHORITY WITHOUT POWER: LAW AND THE JAPANESE PARADOX (Oxford University Press, 1991) 100; Professor Tomoko Akane, Reform of the Legal Training System in Japan available on the web at *www.unafei.or.jp/pdf/indonesia_pdf/session3.pdf* p. 4.

98 Takaaki Hattori, The Legal Profession in Japan: Its Historical Development and Present State in LAW IN JAPAN (von Mehren Ed. 1967) 128; Richard Rabinowitz, The Historical Development of the Japanese Bar, 70 Harvard Law Review 61 (1956).

99 See, e.g., B.J. George, Rights of the Criminally Accused in JAPANESE CONSTITUTIONAL LAW (Percy R. Luney, Jr. and Kazuyuki Takanashi Ed., University of Tokyo Press, 1993) at 291.

mulgated under the Constitution or that existed at the time of promulgation. As few rights were then in existence and as the conservative House of Peers and conservative oligarchs and military were unlikely to grant extensive rights the reality was that the Rights and Duties chapter was heavy on duties and light on rights.

Freedom of speech is a good example. The First Amendment to the United States Constitution prohibits the government from making any law inhibiting the freedom of speech. Thus, laws that fail to conform to the Supreme Court's definition of the rights contained in the Amendment are void and of no force—they are not law. The Meiji Constitution on the other hand provides that within the limits of the law, Japanese subjects enjoy freedom of speech. Two things immediately are apparent. First, the Meiji Constitution contains no prohibition on governmental actions. There is no provision prohibiting the Diet from making a law that inhibits freedom of speech, nor is the Emperor forbidden from issuing Ordinances during a time of siege that inhibits speech. Indeed, the extent of the right of freedom of speech is only that extent that is given to the right by law. To the extent the law grants broad freedom, broad freedom will exist. To the extent the law restricts the freedom, then the freedom will be restricted. In short there is no freedom of speech to which the public is entitled and that cannot be taken away by the government. Second, when the United States Constitution refers to the populace it refers to them as "people" or "persons." The Meiji Constitution on the other hand does not even refer to the populous as citizens but rather as subjects, indicating that they are subject to the authority of the government rather than the government being subject to the authority of the people.[100] As Ito pointed out in his Commentaries, the full enjoyment of these freedoms is granted but only to the extent that there is no abuse of that freedom to commit crime or to disturb peace and tranquility.[101]

Another useful example is the freedom of religion clause of the Meiji Constitution. Subjects may enjoy freedom of religion but only to the extent such freedom is neither prejudicial to peace and order nor inconsistent with their duties as subjects. The government is not restricted in its authority or ability to define any of these terms—"peace" or "order," duties as subjects. Accordingly, when the notion of State Shinto with the Emperor as a deity is factored into the religion equation it becomes clear that failure to adhere to State Shinto is inconsistent with the duties as subjects. Indeed, Ito Hirobumi, the principal writer of the Meiji Constitution noted that concepts of peace and order placed limitations on the expression of reli-

---

100 See, Shinichi Fujii, THE ESSENTIALS OF JAPANESE CONSTITUTIONAL LAW (University Publications of America, reprint edition, 1979) 155-156 for the view that a "subject" is obligated to obey state authority.

101 Hirobumi Ito, COMMENTARIES ON THE CONSTITUTION OF THE EMPIRE OF JAPAN (2d ed. Cuo-O University, 1906) 61. See also, Shinichi Fujii, THE ESSENTIALS OF JAPANESE CONSTITUTIONAL LAW (University Publications of America, reprint edition, 1979) 166 to the effect that the freedom of expression does not include the freedom to be unpatriotic or to express views considered harmful to safety of "national life" and persons holding such thoughts are to be considered as "feeble-minded" or of unsound mind and thus appropriately subject to restrictions by law.

gious belief that differed from the prevailing Shinto beliefs.[102] Professor Shinichi Fuji of Waseda University similarly was of the view that the Constitution granted Japanese nationals the right to "believe" in any religion they chose but that "external effects" of that belief were not covered by the constitutional grant.[103] Thus, public rituals and conversion efforts could be restricted while public rituals venerating the Emperor could be compelled under the new Constitution, although freedom of religious belief as long as it was "confined to the mind" was permitted.[104] Not only were there limitations on what one could publicly do to support other religions, but there also were requirements that subjects participate in Shinto ceremonies. Even so ancient a tradition in Japan as Buddhism was subjected to restraints.[105] Accordingly the pre-Meiji structure of religion wherein Buddhist Temples and Shinto Shrines had a single administration—typically under the control of the Buddhist Temple—was dismantled, and family registration records were transferred from Buddhist Temples to Shinto Shrines.[106] As State Shinto became a more forceful mechanism for supporting Japanese nationalism, other religions were suppressed. In 1935 the Ministry of Education directed that the schools should foster religious sentiments but not teach sectarian religious beliefs. As Shinto was viewed as part of Japanese culture, this allowed the school system to support Shinto but not other religions. The 1940 Religious Organizations Law required registration of religious organizations and limited recognition of religions to those that recognized the divinity of the Emperor, in essence subordinating all religious activity to State Shinto. The Peace Preservation Law of 1941 specifically targeted those religions that refused to adhere to the accepted notion

---

102 Michael Young, Japan and Religious Freedom: An American Perspective (talk delivered at the conference on Religious Freedom and the New Millennium, Tokyo May 23-25, 1998) (www.religiousfreedom.com) page 4.

103 Shinichi Fujii, THE ESSENTIALS OF JAPANESE CONSTITUTIONAL LAW (University Publications of America, reprint edition, 1979) 165. Professor Fujii also notes that the right to religious belief did NOT extend to foreigners in Japan, unless included in a treaty.

104 Hirobumi Ito, COMMENTARIES ON THE CONSTITUTION OF THE EMPIRE OF JAPAN (2d ed. Cuo-O University, 1906) 60.

105 G.B. Sansom, THE WESTERN WORLD AND JAPAN (Vintage Books, New York, 1949) 469-470.

106 James L. McClain, JAPAN, A MODERN HISTORY (W.W. Norton & Company, 2002) 269-270; Donald Keene, EMPEROR OF JAPAN: MEIJI AND HIS WORLD, 1852-1912 (Columbia University Press, 2002) 137-138; John K. Fairbank, Edwin O. Reischauer and Albert M. Craig, EAST ASIA TRADITION AND TRANSFORMATION 528 (Houghton Mifflin Company, 1973); Marius B. Jansen, THE MAKING OF MODERN JAPAN (Belknap Press of Harvard University, 2000) 351-354; Andrew Gordan, A MODERN HISTORY OF JAPAN (Oxford University Press, 2003) 110-112; Michael Young, Japan and Religious Freedom: An American Perspective (talk delivered at the conference on Religious Freedom and the New Millennium, Tokyo May 23-25, 1998) (www.religiousfreedom.com) page 3. See generally, James Edward Ketelaar, OF HERETICS AND MARTYRS IN MEIJI JAPAN: BUDDHISM AND ITS PERSECUTION (Princeton University press 1990) Chapters 2 and 3.

of Emperor worship.[107] In short, while subjects may have been free to have their internal beliefs about religion, in the public arena they were required to follow State Shinto, and the government was free to support State Shinto and suppress other religious organizations. All of this was constitutionally permitted as it supported peace and order and was consistent with the subject's obligations.[108]

Although the Meiji Constitution contains a litany of supposed rights, the reality is that the Constitution in fact grants no rights by itself. Instead it permits the subjects only such rights as are given to them by the law.[109] Thus all of the rights referred to in Chapter II of the Constitution are subject to legislative restriction and the law determines the extent of the right.[110] Moreover, at the time the Constitution was given to the Japanese people there were already in existence limitations on some of the rights set out in the Constitution. Thus, as early as 1882, shortly after the announcement of a representative assembly to meet in 1890, in an effort to weaken the development of political parties,[111] laws were passed that restricted the right to hold public meetings.[112] Shortly before the adoption of the Constitution, another peace preservation law was adopted in 1887. This measure was taken to stifle objection to the government's policy concerning revision of the unequal treaties.[113] It weakened the political parties by giving the police power to disrupt and disband meetings of political parties and also gave the government power to exile from Tokyo persons who were deemed a threat to security.[114] Acting under this law the authorities removed hundreds of politically active persons from the

---

107 Michael Young, Japan and Religious Freedom: An American Perspective (talk delivered at the conference on Religious Freedom and the New Millennium, Tokyo May 23-25, 1998) (www.religiousfreedom.com) page 4.

108 See, Mark R. Mullins, The Social and Legal Status of Religious Minorities in Japan, (talk delivered at the conference on Religious Freedom and the New Millennium, Tokyo May 23-25, 1998) (www.religiousfreedom.com).

109 John M. Maki, The Japanese Constitutional Style in Dan Fenno Henderson, THE CONSTITUTION OF JAPAN: ITS FIRST TWENTY YEARS 1947-1967 (University of Washington Press, 1969) 7.

110 An exception may be Article 27, the first part of which states that the right of property is inviolate. However, subpart 2 of the Article provides that the law may provide for measures needed for the public benefit. It would thus appear that while the right is inviolate, laws made in the public interest may restrict it.

111 G.B. Sansom, THE WESTERN WORLD AND JAPAN (Vintage Books, New York, 1949) 352-353.

112 John K. Fairbank, Edwin O. Reischauer and Albert M. Craig, EAST ASIA TRADITION AND TRANSFORMATION 539 (Houghton Mifflin Company, 1973). Beckman places the date for such law as two years earlier in 1880. George M. Beckman, THE MAKING OF THE MEIJI CONSTITUTION (University of Kansas Press, 1957) 45.

113 W. W. McLaren, JAPANESE GOVERNMENT DOCUMENTS (Asiatic Society of Japan) (University Publications of America, reprint edition, 1979) Introduction Vol. 1, p. lxx-lxxii; W. W. McLaren, A POLITICAL HISTORY OF JAPAN (1916, REISSUED 1965, Russell & Russell) p.168-169.

114 George M. Beckman, THE MAKING OF THE MEIJI CONSTITUTION (University of Kansas Press, 1957) 81; John K. Fairbank, Edwin O. Reischauer and Albert M. Craig, EAST ASIA TRADITION AND TRANSFORMATION 540 (Houghton Mifflin Company, 1973).

Tokyo area.[115] The Newspaper Press Law was amended in 1883 by making it stricter and giving the Minister of the Home Ministry authority to prohibit sales of newspapers and authorizing the seizure of the printing plant.[116] A press regulation law as well as a law regulating publishing activities was also adopted in 1887.[117] Under the law the police, acting on their own authority, had the power to disband meetings, and any person refusing to obey such an order could be incarcerated for not less than 3 months and not more than 3 years, as well as being fined. Books that disturbed public tranquility could be confiscated along with the publisher's plant.[118] In 1889 various government officials and students were prohibited from attending political meetings.[119] These restrictions continued after the Constitution came into effect.[120] Further, driving home the point that rights mentioned in the Constitution were subject to restriction and were to be defined in legislation ("according to law") and were limited in nature, the Constitution provides that the entire rights chapter is not applicable to the Emperor's powers in time of war or national emergency.[121] "Peace Preservation Laws" followed in 1925 (shortly after all adult males were given voting rights)[122] and again in 1941.[123]

---

115 See, Fukuzawa Yukichi, The History of the Japanese Parliament 4/6/1889 in W. W. McLaren, JAPANESE GOVERNMENT DOCUMENTS (Asiatic Society of Japan) (University Publications of America, reprint edition, 1979) Vol. 2, 577-593 at 580-581; Ishii Ryosuke, JAPANESE LEGISLATION IN THE MEIJI ERA (Translated and adapted by William J. Chambliss) (Kasai Publishing, Tokyo, 1958) 377.

116 Ishii Ryosuke, JAPANESE LEGISLATION IN THE MEIJI ERA (Translated and adapted by William J. Chambliss) (Kasai Publishing, Tokyo, 1958) 466.

117 Hideo Wada, The Administrative Court Under the Meiji Constitution, 10 Law in Japan 1 fn. 1 (1977).

118 W. W. McLaren, JAPANESE GOVERNMENT DOCUMENTS (Asiatic Society of Japan) (University Publications of America, reprint edition, 1979) Vol. 2, 502-504 (Imperial Rescript, 12/25/87). For other publication regulations see, W. W. McLaren, JAPANESE GOVERNMENT DOCUMENTS (Asiatic Society of Japan) (University Publications of America, reprint edition, 1979) Vol. 2, 529-557.

119 W. W. McLaren, JAPANESE GOVERNMENT DOCUMENTS (Asiatic Society of Japan) (University Publications of America, reprint edition, 1979) Vol. 2, 505 (Law No. 31, 12/14/89); for a discussion of laws limiting freedom of speech, press and assembly prior to adoption of the Constitution see, Ishii Ryosuke, JAPANESE LEGISLATION IN THE MEIJI ERA (Translated and adapted by William J. Chambliss) (Kasai Publishing, Tokyo, 1958) at 257-263.

120 For a discussion of restrictions on the right to publish and assemble adopted in the early years after promulgation of the Constitution see, Ishii Ryosuke, JAPANESE LEGISLATION IN THE MEIJI ERA (Translated and adapted by William J. Chambliss) (Kasai Publishing, Tokyo, 1958) 466-471, 556.

121 Constitution of Japan, Article 31.

122 Hugh Borton, JAPAN'S MODERN CENTURY (The Ronald Press Company, 1955) 309-310; Herbert Bix, HIROHITO AND THE MAKING OF MODERN JAPAN (Harper Collins 2000) 159, 187, 206.

123 Ryuichi Hirano, The Accused and Society: Some Aspects of Japanese Criminal Law in LAW IN JAPAN (VON Mehren Ed. Harvard University Press, 1963) Law No. 46 of 1925; Law No. 54 of 1941; Ryuichi Hirano, The Accused and Society: Some Aspects of Japanese Criminal Law in LAW IN JAPAN (VON Mehren Ed. Harvard University Press, 1963) 293 fn. 96.

That the Meiji Constitution was not based on rights was inevitable.[124] The Meiji oligarchs were concerned with creating an Emperor-based government in which they and their successors would exercise power.[125] It was not without reason that Ito had selected the Prussian Constitution as his model rather than the American or French Constitutions. It is true that the idea of natural rights had been introduced to Japan before the Meiji Constitution was written, but it is also true that the concept was not accepted in the Constitution.[126] When Ito went to Europe to study foreign constitutions, he concentrated on authoritarianism rather than rights.[127] Moreover, the concept of legal rights as understood in the West was an unknown idea in Meiji Japan.[128] The oligarch's views, indeed most Japanese views, of relations between the government and the people were dominated by Chinese government doctrines and Confucianism, which stressed obligations not rights. Japanese feudalism under the Tokugawa was similarly obligation-based, rather than rights-based. Accordingly the notion of rights as distinguished from obligations was a new idea.

Indeed, the entire idea of legal rights as understood in the West was so foreign to the oligarchs that the Japanese language did not have a word that could convey the Western idea of legal rights.[129] This language problem arose more sharply when the Meiji government began to translate Western Codes in its quest for a Western-

---

124 For the view that since under centuries of feudalism the Japanese populous had been denied rights granted in common law jurisdictions there was not seen to be a significant difference between the Constitution and common law natural rights philosophy see, W. W. McLaren, A POLITICAL HISTORY OF JAPAN (1916, REISSUED 1965, Russell & Russell) p. 194.

125 George Akita has suggested that the Meiji oligarchs supported the notion of power sharing and that the Constitution "imposed certain clear restrictions on the government and . . . extended certain rights to the people. . . ." Akita, Foundations of Constitutional Government in Japan, 1868-1900 at p. 3 (Harvard University Press, 1967). While it is true that the Constitution by even being written served to diminish the power of the oligarchs, it is less clear that the oligarchs as a body, as distinguished from individual members of the oligarchy, were not forced by circumstance to adopt the notion of constitutional government and it is surely not clear that they supported the idea of sharing power with an elected legislature or that the Constitution extended any meaningful rights to the general population. For a different perspective see, G.B. Sansom, THE WESTERN WORLD AND JAPAN (Vintage Books, New York, 1949) 339-351.

126 Yoshiuki Noda, Comparative Jurisprudence in Japan: Its Past and Present, in Hideo Tanaka, THE JAPANESE LEGAL SYSTEM (University of Tokyo Press, 1976) at 202 ("it is really mystifying why . . . they (Rousseau's ideas) failed to become part of our intellectual heritage." See, Richard H. Minear, JAPANESE TRADITION AND WESTERN LAW (Harvard University Press, 1970) 161-163; see also, William Noel, THE RIGHT TO LIFE IN JAPAN (Routledge, 1997) 3.

127 Hugh Barton, JAPAN'S MODERN CENTURY (The Ronald Press Company, 1955) 136-139; Ishii Ryosuke, JAPANESE LEGISLATION IN THE MEIJI ERA (Translated and adapted by William J. Chambliss) (Kasai Publishing, Tokyo, 1958) 398.

128 Kenzo Takayanagi, A Century of Innovation: The Development of Japanese Law, 1868-1961 in LAW IN JAPAN (VON Mehren Ed. Harvard University Press, 1963) 24.

129 G.B. Sansom, THE WESTERN WORLD AND JAPAN (Vintage Books, New York, 1949) 311-312, 446; Ishii Ryosuke, JAPANESE LEGISLATION IN THE MEIJI ERA (Translated and adapted by William J. Chambliss) (Kasai Publishing, Tokyo, 1958) at 578-579; See, Kenneth L. Port, The Japanese International Law "Revolution": International Human Rights Law

ized set of Codes to be utilized in its new legal system.[130] To define rights it was necessary to create an entirely new word by joining together existing Japanese characters. But even the joinder of these characters failed to encompass the Western idea as the new word was seen in Confusion rather than Western legal terms.[131] Moreover, the characters used in the most frequently used characterization of rights contained within it a Japanese character connected to the concept of authority and power—the antithesis of the Western view of rights.

Further, rights in a Western constitutional context relate to the rights of individuals who comprise society. In Western terms we speak of "individual rights." The concept of individual rights was complicated in a Japanese setting because of the role of the family or House (*Ie*) system in feudal society. Individuals belonged to family units or Houses and these Houses were the basic societal groups not the individuals who made up the Houses. Houses owned property and the Head of the House had rights over members of the house. Inheritance rules applied the House concept as well. In such a setting individuals were not seen as the basic element in society, and to the extent that the concept of rights might have had meaning in Tokugawa Japan, it would have been as House rights not individual rights.[132] Finally, to the extent that the oligarchs understood the idea of rights, it was understood in a contextual setting. Thus rights were not fixed and immutable but, rather, changed as the context or circumstance changed. This idea that context and changing circumstance work a change in basic individual rights is fundamentally at odds with the Western idea that rights can be fixed in a Constitution and that such rights do not change when it is in the interests of the government or even the State to change them.

B. Adoption of Western Codes as the Basis for Japanese Law

As part of the process of renegotiation of the unequal treaties, it was clear that Meiji Japan would require a modern, non-feudal, legal system. China, Japan's traditional cultural source clearly could not provide assistance for such a new system, as its system was not recognized by the West, which had extraterritorial

and its Impact in Japan, 28 Stanford Journal of International Law 139, 136 (1991); Kurt Steiner, The Revision of the Civil Code of Japan, 9 Far Eastern Quarterly 169, 171.

130 See, Yosiyuki Noda, INTRODUCTION TO JAPANESE LAW (translated and edited by Anthony H. Angelo) (University of Tokyo Press, 1976) 43-44 and fn. 3 for a discussion of the language difficulties encountered in translating the French Civil Code and the extraordinary steps taken to overcome the language problem.

131 See, Takeshi Ishida, Fundamental Human Rights and the Development of Legal Thought in Japan, 8 Law in Japan 39, 44-51 (Wagatsuma and Braverman translation 1975); Eric A. Feldman, THE RITUAL OF RIGHTS IN JAPAN (Cambridge University Press, 2000) 19.

132 For a discussion of the House system and its relation to ancestor worship see, G.B. Sansom, THE WESTERN WORLD AND JAPAN (Vintage Books, New York, 1949) 487-549.

consular jurisdiction in its sphere's of influence in China.[133] Accordingly, Japan would have to look to the West for guidance. The Western model provided two basic alternative approaches—the common law approach of the United States and Great Britain and the civil law approach of France and Prussia (Germany). In some ways the common law approach was more consistent with Japan's past, as feudal Japan to the extent that it had resolved matters utilizing "law" had utilized custom of the community and these customs formed a kind of common law model. The problem with adopting a common law type approach was that the law was not conducive to simple codification. To adopt a common law approach would have required more time—and perhaps was considered as requiring more adaptation—than utilizing an already existing codified version of law such as the Napoleonic Code.[134] Japan opted for the French civil law model.

In 1873 a French school of law was started in the Ministry of Justice presided over by the French jurist George Bousquet. However, there remained a strong "English school" of legal thought in Japan with which the "French school" had to deal. In the 1870s lectures were being given in Japan on English Law at the Kasei Academy (the predecessor of Tokyo University) while an academy of French law was established in 1876.[135] In using the civil law model, Japan had two alternatives—the German approach to law or the French approach to law. As a general rule, the French approach was initially adopted but relatively quickly the German approach predominated. As a consequence, prewar Japan's legal system represented a civil law system based on a French model with a German overlay. Jurisprudence, the science of legal approach and thinking, eventually was completely dominated by the German approach.[136]

---

133 For a discussion of Meiji Japan's initial efforts at codifying the criminal law based on a Chinese model see, Paul Heng-Chao Ch'en, THE FORMATION OF THE EARLY MEIJI LEGAL ORDER (Oxford University Press, 1981) 1-30. The effect of Chinese thinking as well as Japan's feudal thinking is reflected in the fact that first criminal law measures adopted by the Meiji government were directions to subordinate officials—similar to the old House Rules of feudal Japan and the Chinese model. See, Yosiyuki Noda, INTRODUCTION TO JAPANESE LAW (translated and edited by Anthony H. Angelo) (University of Tokyo Press, 1976) 46. See also, Shigemitsu Dando (Translated by B.J. George Jr.) JAPANESE CRIMINAL PROCEDURE (Fred B. Rothman & Co., 1965) Section 1.07.

134 Yosiyuki Noda, INTRODUCTION TO JAPANESE LAW (translated and edited by Anthony H. Angelo) (University of Tokyo Press, 1976) 42-43.

135 Paul Heng-Chao Ch'en, THE FORMATION OF THE EARLY MEIJI LEGAL ORDER (Oxford University Press, 1981) 72-73; see also, Yoshiuki Noda, Comparative Jurisprudence in Japan: Its Past and Present, in Hideo Tanaka, THE JAPANESE LEGAL SYSTEM (University of Tokyo Press, 1976) at 201; Kenzo Takayanagi, A Century of Innovation: The Development of Japanese Law, 1868-1961 in LAW IN JAPAN (VON Mehren Ed. Harvard University Press, 1963) 28-30.

136 Yoshiuki Noda, Comparative Jurisprudence in Japan: Its Past and Present, in Hideo Tanaka, THE JAPANESE LEGAL SYSTEM (University of Tokyo Press, 1976) at 196; Kenzo Takayanagi, A Century of Innovation: The Development of Japanese Law, 1868-1961 in LAW IN JAPAN (VON Mehren Ed. Harvard University Press, 1963) 34.

Even before Ito drafted the Constitution, work had been completed on a new Criminal Code and a new Code of Criminal Procedure. The Criminal Code was adopted in 1880 and was strongly influenced by French law and the French legal advisor to the Japanese government Emile Gustave Boissonade de Fontarabie who had come to Japan in 1873 at the invitation of Justice Minister Oki Takato.[137] The Code while influenced by the French Code was not a copy of the French Code, rather it was designed to meet the needs of the Japanese society and took account of previous Japanese efforts at writing a criminal code. It did however work a major change in Japanese Criminal Law and adopted the civil law inquisition system as Japan's criminal procedure system.

As a starting point, criminal law was no longer based on ethical notions of behavior and was not seen as a mandate to officials as to how to act. Rather, the Code was directed to the population at large and only those crimes defined as crimes were punishable.[138] The Code adopted the principle that there was no crime without a law making the act a crime *(nullum crimen, nulla poena sine lege)* and consequently banned both ex post facto laws and crime by analogy. Moreover, it worked a revolution in knowledge by making the Code available to the public. This was the antithesis of the feudal law's concept that the law should be kept secret and known only to the officials.[139] However the Code was written (as were all Meiji era laws) in a form of Japanese that was difficult for the average citizen to understand—a problem that was only cured when the 1946 Constitution was translated and published in every day Japanese.[140] Moreover the criminal law was equalitarian in nature, treating all citizens the same regardless of class or social status within classes. This was consistent with the Meiji oligarchs' actions in tearing down the Tokugawa class structure, but it was nonetheless revolutionary for Japan. Similarly, the notions of collective guilt and responsibility for actions of others were abandoned in favor of personal responsibility for one's own actions. Moreover, to be guilty of a crime, a person (as a general rule) had to have a criminal intent or *mens rea.*[141] These principles, all of which were revolutionary to Meiji Japan, remain a mainstay of Japanese law today.[142]

---

137 Shigemitsu Dando (Translated by B.J. George Jr.) JAPANESE CRIMINAL PROCEDURE (Fred B. Rothman & Co., 1965) Section 1.07.

138 See, Yosiyuki Noda, INTRODUCTION TO JAPANESE LAW (translated and edited by Anthony H. Angelo) (University of Tokyo Press, 1976) 207.

139 One of the most significant departures that the new Codes (both civil and penal) made from pre-existing practice was the publication of the Codes. G.B. Sansom, THE WESTERN WORLD AND JAPAN (Vintage Books, New York, 1949) 447.

140 Koseki Shoichi THE BIRTH OF JAPAN'S POSTWAR CONSTITUTION (Edited and translated by Ray A. Moore) (Westview Press, 1997) at 133.

141 Ryuichi Hirano, The Accused and Society: Some Aspects of Japanese Criminal Law in LAW IN JAPAN (VON Mehren Ed. Harvard University Press, 1963) 282.

142 See, Kenzo Takayanagi, A Century of Innovation: The Development of Japanese Law, 1868-1961 in LAW IN JAPAN (VON Mehren Ed. Harvard University Press, 1963) 15-16.

The new Code also contained a set of provisions defined offenses against the Imperial House. The provisions were applicable solely to offenses against the Japanese Imperial House and included a death penalty for an attempt on the life of a member of the Imperial family. It was this provision, applicable only to attempts against a member of the Imperial family that raised issues in the Otsu incident in 1891. In the Otsu case the judges following the new approach of *nullum crimen, nulla poena sine lege* and rejecting crime by analogy found that laws applicable to the Imperial House were not applicable to actions directed against a foreign royal house. Following the French approach, the Criminal Code followed the notion that the punishment should fit the crime and thus strictly defined the punishment applicable to each crime. The concept of parole was contained in the Code. The Code provided for hanging as the method of carrying out the death penalty.

Although ignorance of the law was no defense to a criminal charge, where the defendant was unaware of the seriousness of his/her actions the penalty could be moderated. In addition, insanity in the sense of not being able to distinguish right from wrong, was a defense to prosecution. Juveniles under the age of 12 were not subject to prosecution. Self-defense was also a valid defense where the defender had not initiated the conflict. The general crime of conspiracy as understood in the United States was not provided for in the Code and a conspiracy was only punishable when there was a specific provision dealing with a conspiracy to commit a specific crime. An unsuccessful attempt to commit a felony was a crime but where the criminal activity did not go beyond the planning stage there was no crime. Attempts were punished at a lesser penalty than the crime attempted.[143]

The Code was completely rewritten in 1907 (Penal Code of 1907)[144] but the basic ideas set out above, except for the strict classification of crimes and punishments, was retained.[145] By 1907 the Constitution had been put in place, representing a Germanization of the fundamental law and the new Civil Code of 1898, which represented a victory of the "German school" over the French school, had replaced the old Civil Code of 1890. As a consequence German Law and legal philosophy also influenced the Criminal Code of 1907. The most significant aspects of this influence were felt in the granting of great discretion to judges in determining the punishments to be meted out for criminal activity. As a consequence, the old Code's French law definitions of various levels of offenses with strict punishments for each detailed in the Code were abandoned in favor of more general classification of crimes. Although the principal *nullum crimen, nulla poena sine lege* was not written into the revised Code, the theory remained an essential component of Japanese law. This was based on the view that the Constitution had adopted

143 For a general discussion of the 1880 Penal Code see, Ishii Ryosuke, JAPANESE LEGISLATION IN THE MEIJI ERA (Translated and adapted by William J. Chambliss) (Kasai Publishing, Tokyo, 1958) at 528-538.

144 Law No. 45 of 1907.

145 Yosiyuki Noda, INTRODUCTION TO JAPANESE LAW (translated and edited by Anthony H. Angelo) (University of Tokyo Press, 1976) 208.

the rule in Article 23 under which arrest, trial and punishment all had to be "according to law."[146]

Other significant modifications of the old Code were that the new Code was extraterritorial and applied to Japanese citizens whether in Japan or abroad; parole was liberalized and was available after service of 1/3 of a sentence rather than ¾ under the old Code and the age at which one could be criminally responsible was raised from 12 to 14. The fundamental change made by the new Code however was the granting to the judge wide discretion in punishment.[147] The 1908 Code is the basis of the present Criminal Code, with modifications made by the Occupation as a consequence of the change in constitutional system and equality of the sexes brought on by the new Constitution.

Criminal Procedure followed the French law system and the Code of Criminal Instruction of 1880[148] was modeled after the 1808 French *Code d'Instruction Criminelle.*[149] Like the French Code, the Japanese criminal procedure system was based on an inquisitorial model.[150] Even before the adoption of the *Code d'Instruction Criminelle* Meiji Japan required some criminal procedure system. The system adopted followed the Tokugawa system in that it was inquisitorial in nature and permitted the use of torture. The criminal court procedures of 1872 adopted a four-step process. Under this procedure the accused was: a) questioned by a judge (who had been briefed by the prosecutor who had submitted the case to the court in the first instance); b) confined and then questioned on occasions again by the judge; c) the report of the questioning sessions was then prepared and read to the accused and the prosecutor by the judge and sealed by the accused to acknowledge its accuracy. In the final stage the judge sentenced the accused for the crime committed. Minor amendments to the procedure were made prior to 1875 when a major change ensued. The first stages of the above process were formalized as a preliminary examination (one can see the French law influence as the French procedure utilized a preliminary examination). These stages were separated from the later trial stage in that the judge who conducted the preliminary examination could not also preside at the trial. The examining judge, in addition to questioning the accused had authority to compel witnesses to appear for examination and could order search and seizure at the residence of the accused. If the pros-

146 Kenzo Takayanagi, A Century of Innovation: The Development of Japanese Law, 1868-1961 in LAW IN JAPAN (VON Mehren Ed. Harvard University Press, 1963) 17-18.

147 For a general discussion of the 1908 Penal Code see, Ishii Ryosuke, JAPANESE LEGISLATION IN THE MEIJI ERA (Translated and adapted by William J. Chambliss) (Kasai Publishing, Tokyo, 1958) at 562-571.

148 Great Council of State Decree No. 37 of 1880.

149 Atsushi Nagashima, The Accused and Society: The Administration of Criminal Justice in Japan, in LAW IN JAPAN (VON Mehren Ed. Harvard University Press, 1963) 297; Hiroshi Oda, JAPANESE LAW (Oxford University Press, 2nd Ed. 1999) 423.

150 Makoto Mitsui, Criminal Law, 26 Law in Japan 24 (2000); Ryuichi Hirano, The Accused and Society: Some Aspects of Japanese Criminal Law in LAW IN JAPAN (VON Mehren Ed. Harvard University Press, 1963) 274.

ecutor was dissatisfied with the preliminary examination, he could obtain a new judge and a second preliminary examination. For certain crimes the prosecutor could proceed to final trial without a preliminary examination.

As was true in Tokugawa times, in early Meiji criminal cases proceeded on the basis of confession and confession was necessary for conviction. To assure that confessions were obtained, torture was permitted—although the handicapped, the young and the elderly were exempt from torture. However, in 1876 "proof" was required for the conviction of the defendant. Among the items of proof that were available were evidence, statements of witnesses, investigation dossiers, etc. Of course, confessions were still permitted as "proof." The ability to prove a case with evidence other than confessions lessened the need for confession and lessened the necessity to use torture to compel confession from the recalcitrant guilty. By 1879 regulations permitting torture were withdrawn.[151] Tokugawa differences in treatment based on class status were abolished. Either the accused or the prosecutor was permitted to appeal. The Minister of Justice also had the right to appeal—or in some situations the right to compel the prosecutor to appeal. Although there were time limits set for appeal by the accused or the prosecutor, there was no time limit to appeal by the Justice Minister.[152]

The Criminal Procedure Code went into effect in 1882. It too was based on the inquisition model and provided for a preliminary examination by a judicial official. The Code specifically prohibited the judge conducting the preliminary examination from also being the trial judge. Similarly the preliminary examination judge was prohibited from sitting on the bench hearing an appeal of a case wherein the judge had conducted the preliminary examination (with very limited exceptions). While the preliminary examination was private, the trial stage was to be a public proceeding. Initial investigation was in the hands of the prosecutor who, after investigation leading to belief of guilt was required to submit felony cases for preliminary investigation by way of indictment and could but was not required to submit misdemeanors to such process. In rare situations, the court could proceed to preliminary examination without indictment. The general rule was that indictment by the prosecutor was required before the preliminary examination stage.

After indictment the defendant was required to appear to answer the charge. In some situations the examining judge could imprison the accused—but in such situations the family of the accused was entitled to know the place of detention. Detention was not required in all cases and a kind of bail system was permitted that allowed defendants to stay with persons accountable for his presence in court and to post money to assure his appearance. To assure that the fact-finding process

151 Torture is specifically prohibited by Constitution Article 36. Japan is a party to the UN Convention Against Torture and Other Cruel and Inhuman Treatment.

152 For a discussion of pre-1880 criminal procedure see, Ishii Ryosuke, JAPANESE LEGISLATION IN THE MEIJI ERA (Translated and adapted by William J. Chambliss) (Kasai Publishing, Tokyo, 1958) at 320-335.

was not impeded, the court had the authority to order that the defendant be held in solitary confinement and not be visited by friends, relatives or even counsel.

The preliminary examination judge was permitted to conduct a search and seizure of premises to locate evidence and the prosecutor (but not the defense) could examine such evidence. The judge (in the presence of other court officers but not the prosecutor) questioned the accused and had the authority to question witnesses under oath. If need be, the examining judge could make use of expert witnesses. The examining judge had the authority to dismiss the indictment but if the judge concluded that the defendant was guilty the matter was sent to the court for public trial. At the public trial the defendant was accorded the right to counsel—a right not previously granted. However, because of a shortage of lawyers, where the defendant did not retain counsel there were situations where no counsel was provided. Deemed an emergency measure such denial of counsel did not affect the validity of the trial. The trial itself was a public event although in the public interest some cases could be tried *in camera*. In such cases public judgment was nonetheless required. The witnesses who had appeared at the preliminary examination were reexamined and evidence presented at the preliminary examination was again presented. At the trial the defendant was entitled to be informed of the charges and was entitled to examine witnesses who appeared. The court was required to render a reasoned decision in the matter.

The original draft of the Code had contained provision for a jury to be used in criminal cases. When a jury was used there was no right to appeal. The jury provision was dropped from the Code as adopted.[153]

The subsequent revision of the Code in 1890 was more German law in structure. It made few substantive changes (aside from changes relating to the court system—such changes were required to conform to the new law dealing with court organization (The Law on the Organization of the courts of 1890). It was based on an inquisitional rather than an adversary process. To the extent that there were substantive changes, they related to the strengthened requirement that matters proceed according to indictment, that confession alone was insufficient to obtain a conviction in felony and certain serious misdemeanor cases, and provided for appeals in felony as well as misdemeanor cases, an anomaly of the old Code.[154] In 1922 a more German law based Code of Criminal Procedure was adopted. As this

153 For a discussion of the 1880 Code of Criminal Instruction, see, Ishii Ryosuke, JAPANESE LEGISLATION IN THE MEIJI ERA (Translated and adapted by William J. Chambliss) (Kasai Publishing, Tokyo, 1958) at 320-335.

154 For a discussion of the 1890 Code of Criminal Procedure, see, Ishii Ryosuke, JAPANESE LEGISLATION IN THE MEIJI ERA (Translated and adapted by William J. Chambliss) (Kasai Publishing, Tokyo, 1958) at 524-528.

was the era of Taisho Democracy this new Code provided additional protections to defendants[155] but retained the European inquisitional model.[156]

This model is significantly different from the common law, adversary system. In the common law model the prosecuting authority is viewed as a representative of one party (the "state") and the defense another (the "defendant")—the adversaries—while the judge is considered a neutral party in the process. It is the function of each party to marshal the facts to support its position and to then present those facts as best it can, while in the process seeking to show that the facts produced by the other side are either not relevant or inaccuracies. In such a system the defendant obviously has a motive not to cooperate with the representative of the State. Permitting the State an opportunity to extensively question the defendant (especially out of the presence of the defendant's counsel) places the defendant in the impossible position of both being an adverse party to the State while at the same time assisting the State in its prosecution. In an adversary system the adversary parties are responsible for presenting their evidence to a decision-maker who then has the responsibility of determining which side is correct. Accordingly the decision-maker is kept out of the evidence gathering process and must treat each party equally so as to remove advantage for one side or the other. Whether the decision-maker is a jury or a judge without a jury, the neutrality of the judge of the facts is essential to the process. So too is the equality of the representatives of the parties who, in turn must be considered as equals even if one is the supposed representative of the "people" or the "State." To assure that the "State" gains no unfair advantage, the system grants a presumption of innocence to the accused until the State proves to the contrary.

In an inquisition system the main players in the fact-finding (and fact-gathering) process are not the parties or their representatives. Rather, the fact-finding and/or fact-gathering process is in the hands of the "State" through one of its officials—be it a judicial official or a prosecutor. Adversary parties who are equals do not present facts to a neutral fact finder but the fact-finding/fact-gathering official is an official of the State. Naturally, one of the people with the most information about the accused person's role (if any) in the crime is the accused person, and in an inquisition system the accused is subject to questioning by the fact-gathering/fact-finding official. In such a system the State is deemed as having the responsibility to find and determine the facts.

European civil law criminal justice systems are, for the most part, inquisition systems. In some the fact-gathering official is a part of the judiciary—a magistrate for example—with responsibility to oversee the activities of the prosecutor; in others the prosecutor may have greater responsibility and some greater separation

155 Kenzo Takayanagi, A Century of Innovation: The Development of Japanese Law, 1868-1961 in LAW IN JAPAN (VON Mehren Ed. Harvard University Press, 1963) 21-23; A. Didrick Castberg, JAPANESE CRIMINAL JUSTICE (Praeger, 1990) 3.

156 Shigemitsu Dando, JAPANESE CRIMINAL PROCEDURE (translated by B.J. George Jr.) (Fred B. Rothman & Co., 1965) 16; Hiroshi Oda, JAPANESE LAW (Oxford University Press, 2nd Ed. 1999) 423.

from the judiciary. In inquisition systems both judges and prosecutors tend to be career officials—a part of the government bureaucracy. In common law systems both prosecutors and judges tend not to be career officials. Common law advocates have traditionally looked with disfavor on the inquisition type system as denying the accused a fair opportunity to defend him (her) self. Those who support the inquisition mode see it as a fairer model for discovering the truth and argue that the judicial role in investigation serves to protect the rights of the accused better than the adversary model.[157]

The inquisition form of criminal process has a long history and can be traced back to the Roman Empire. After the fall of Rome, Canon Law utilized the inquisition as part of its criminal process. The inquisition type procedure was in common use in Europe by the 17th century. The use of the inquisition type system was most accommodating to the growth of a strong centralized government—a necessity as the feudal period developed into a national state period with a decline in the power of local lords. As such the inquisition system found favor among societies developing royal authority to replace local authority. In France the inquisition system was retained even after the revolution. In the French law version of the system an investigating magistrate conducted the investigation. The trial of the accused was conducted before the same investigating magistrate. The effect of this pre-trial via examination by the magistrate was to severely restrict whatever presumption of innocence the accused might otherwise have had.[158] On the other hand, the French Code of 1808 provided that the defendant could have the assistance of counsel and prohibited torture. And, while the investigative stage was private, the trial stage was public.

The European civil law criminal justice model was more accommodating to the Meiji oligarchs' view of a government with a highly competent bureaucracy acting in the interests of the general public than was the British or the American adversary model. Moreover, such a system was more compatible with Japan's past than was the common law adversary model. Indeed, the system was in many respects similar to the Tokugawa two-part system of: a) investigation (on an inquisition model) followed, b) by a second phase wherein the accused admitted to his guilt by acknowledging the confession made at the inquisition investigative stage. The European system was also similar to the procedure utilized by the Meiji government before the Code was adopted. In this procedure a suspect was charged and then subjected to questioning. If the alleged crime was considered as significant, the accused was sent to a prison and subjected to further questioning. Once a

157 For an interesting view of the two models see, Richard S. Frase, Comparative Criminal Justice as a Guide to American Law Reform: How do the French Do It, How Can We Find Out, and Why Should We Care?, 78 California Law Review 540 (1990); for a Japanese view related to arbitration see, Takeo Tateishi, Inquisitional Approach in Dispute Resolution—A Japanese Way to Mete Out Justice, Wave Length JSE Bulletin No. 44, p 8 (Japan Shipping Exchange, March 2002).

158 For a discussion of the growth of the inquest system in European law see, Shigemitsu Dando, JAPANESE CRIMINAL PROCEDURE (translated by B.J. George Jr.) (Fred B. Rothman & Co., 1965) 3-12.

confession was obtained, a court official recorded the confession (not verbatim but in summary form), and the accused then applied his seal to the confession. Finally the judge meted out the punishment for the crime confessed to.[159] The similarity between the systems was not lost on Japanese commentators who have noted that the prewar (Meiji) system permitted successive interrogations of the accused by a judicial and/or prosecutorial official thus providing opportunity for the accused to make a statement, including a confession.[160] The Japanese Code of Criminal Procedure (including the more German law modeled procedure Code of 1922)[161] adopted the French model. As a consequence when the preliminary investigation process resulted in an accusation, the presumption of innocence that common law lawyers are used to was put to the side and the defendant was required to prove that the prosecutor in the preliminary stage had erred and the defendant was not guilty.[162]

The differences between the continental European approach to criminal procedure and the common law approach—especially the common lawyer's view that the European inquisition system did away with the presumption of innocence—created some difficulties for Japan in renegotiating the unequal treaties. The British raised objections to subjecting their citizens in Japan to a French/German law criminal procedure.[163] However, the new Code was a substantial advance over the Tokugawa system. For one thing torture was first limited and then outlawed[164] even before the Constitution was adopted. In addition, for the first time an accused was allowed to have a counsel represent him at the trial stage of the proceedings, although no counsel was permitted at the investigative stage. Furthermore, the proceedings were consistent with modern Western European Codes, and while not reflecting common law views these Western Codes could not be considered as inappropriate for a modern country. The British did ultimately agree to the revisions.[165]

---

159 Paul Heng-Chao Ch'en, THE FORMATION OF THE EARLY MEIJI LEGAL ORDER (Oxford University Press, 1981) 77-78.

160 Professor Hirano in Ryuichi Hirano, The Accused and Society: Some Aspects of Japanese Criminal Law in LAW IN JAPAN (VON Mehren Ed. Harvard University Press, 1963) 274-275 in addition to noting the use of the system to obtain confession notes that the inquisition system is particularly suited to a system of law that places emphasis on subjective elements in determining whether a crime has been committed (a *mens rea* based system requiring some criminal motive for the act in order for the act to be criminal) a basic element of the Japanese and German systems.

161 Yosiyuki Noda, INTRODUCTION TO JAPANESE LAW (translated and edited by Anthony H. Angelo) (University of Tokyo Press, 1976) 210.

162 A. Didrick Castberg, JAPANESE CRIMINAL JUSTICE (Praeger, 1990) 2-3.

163 Kenzo Takayanagi, A Century of Innovation: The Development of Japanese Law, 1868-1961 in LAW IN JAPAN (VON Mehren Ed. Harvard University Press, 1963) 19.

164 Physical torture was outlawed in 1879, prior to the Constitution. For a history of the limitation on and eventually abolition of torture in Japan see, Paul Heng-Chao Ch'en, THE FORMATION OF THE EARLY MEIJI LEGAL ORDER (Oxford University Press, 1981) 64-71.

165 Kenzo Takayanagi, A Century of Innovation: The Development of Japanese Law, 1868-1961 in LAW IN JAPAN (VON Mehren Ed. Harvard University Press, 1963) 19.

The adoption of a Criminal Code and a Code of Criminal Procedure required the creation of new instruments for law enforcement. There had, of course, been police units under the Tokugawa regime. Policing in Edo (now renamed Tokyo) was a Shogunate function while policing in the Han domains was generally left to the Daimyo. The new Meiji government's major concern was with reestablishing a working police force for the country and especially for Tokyo. In 1881 a new police force was created for Tokyo. A national judicial police system was created under the control of the Home Minister.[166] The function of the judicial police was to conduct criminal investigations (under the supervision of the prosecutor) including the use of search and seizure techniques, and to arrest persons who had engaged in criminal conduct. Police could make arrests without instructions from the prosecutor when it was considered that guilt was obvious. Otherwise, the arresting police required approval for arrest from the prosecutor. In 1872, in addition to the judicial police a National Police Bureau was established to maintain order throughout Japan.[167] Thus there was one police department [administrative police] whose function was to prevent crime (and thus keep a watchful eye on the populace), and another [judicial police] to investigate crimes that had been committed.

A Home Ministry was created in 1873 and by 1877 this Ministry controlled the national administrative police network as well as the Tokyo Metropolitan Police.[168] In 1886 the Tokyo Metropolitan Police,[169] already directly responsible to the Home Minister, took over administrative authority over local police forces outside Tokyo creating in effect a national police organization subject to control of the Home Minister.[170] The police became a highly centralized national police force, although prefectural officials could call upon the police for assistance.[171] The police, in addition to having criminal law investigative functions, also had the power to enforce administrative regulations of the government through arrest and detention outside the compass of the Code of Criminal Procedure.[172] Although torture had

166 George M. Beckman, THE MAKING OF THE MEIJI CONSTITUTION (University of Kansas Press, 1957) 45.

167 Ishii Ryosuke, JAPANESE LEGISLATION IN THE MEIJI ERA (Translated and adapted by William J. Chambliss) (Kasai Publishing, Tokyo, 1958) at 247-249.

168 Ishii Ryosuke, JAPANESE LEGISLATION IN THE MEIJI ERA (Translated and adapted by William J. Chambliss) (Kasai Publishing, Tokyo, 1958) at 253.

169 The Tokyo Metropolitan Police was created in 1874. W. W. McLaren, JAPANESE GOVERNMENT DOCUMENTS (Asiatic Society of Japan) (University Publications of America, reprint edition, 1979) Vol. 1, 256 and was responsible to the Home Minister. W. W. McLaren, JAPANESE GOVERNMENT DOCUMENTS (Asiatic Society of Japan) (University Publications of America, reprint edition, 1979) Vol. 2, 312.

170 George M. Beckman, THE MAKING OF THE MEIJI CONSTITUTION (University of Kansas Press, 1957) 65.

171 Yosiyuki Noda, INTRODUCTION TO JAPANESE LAW (translated and edited by Anthony H. Angelo) (University of Tokyo Press, 1976) 104, 109.

172 Bai Gao, The State and the Associational [sic] Order of the Economy (2003) on the web at *www.wz-berlin.de/mp/ism/conf/conf03/papers/gao.pdf* at page 19-20.

been statutorily and constitutionally abolished, it appears to have still been used by the police.[173]

Similarly, it was necessary to create prosecutor offices. In 1872 the public prosecutor office was created in the Justice Ministry.[174] Following the French law model, a prosecutor office was attached to each court.[175] Prosecutors were considered "judicial officers" similar to the investigating magistrate in France and had a similar investigating function.[176] The Japanese term "*Bunkan*" was applied to both judge and prosecutor at the same time.[177] In addition, prosecutors and judges were given the same test for qualification—this test differed from the test given to *daigennin*, the predecessor to today's lawyer (the bengoshi).[178] Prosecutors—like judges—had great tenure in office[179] and could not be involuntarily terminated.[180] Prosecutors had the responsibility of directing police in investigations[181] and also had the power to conduct their own investigations.[182] It was not until the 1930s that a separate bureaucracy was created in the Ministry of Justice for

---

173 Yosiyuki Noda, INTRODUCTION TO JAPANESE LAW (translated and edited by Anthony H. Angelo) (University of Tokyo Press, 1976) 149. Noda also refers to the close relationship between the police and the prosecutor in concluding that the prosecutor used such forced confession evidence even if it was suspect because they did not want the police to "lose face."

174 Shigemitsu Dando (Translated by B.J. George Jr.) JAPANESE CRIMINAL PROCEDURE (Fred B. Rothman & Co., 1965) 14.

175 See, See, Law No. 6, 2/8/1890 in W. W. McLaren, JAPANESE GOVERNMENT DOCUMENTS (Asiatic Society of Japan) (University Publications of America, reprint edition, 1979) Vol. 2, 625-659; Yosiyuki Noda, INTRODUCTION TO JAPANESE LAW (translated and edited by Anthony H. Angelo) (University of Tokyo Press, 1976) 135.

176 Kenzo Takayanagi, A Century of Innovation: The Development of Japanese Law, 1868-1961 in LAW IN JAPAN (VON Mehren Ed. Harvard University Press, 1963) 20; John O. Haley, The Japanese Judiciary: Maintaining Integrity, Autonomy and the Public Trust p. 17. On the web at *http://law.wustl.edu/Academics/Faculty/Workingpapers/TheJapaneseJudiciary10_03.pdf*; Atsushi Nagashima, The Accused and Society: The Administration of Criminal Justice in Japan, in LAW IN JAPAN (VON Mehren Ed. Harvard University Press, 1963) 299 fn. 9.

177 Professor Tomoko Akane, Reform of the Legal Training System in Japan available on the web at *www.unafei.or.jp/pdf/indonesia_pdf/session3.pdf* p. 5.

178 Professor Tomoko Akane, Reform of the Legal Training System in Japan available on the web at *www.unafei.or.jp/pdf/indonesia_pdf/session3.pdf* p. 5.

179 Shinichi Fujii, THE ESSENTIALS OF JAPANESE CONSTITUTIONAL LAW (University Publications of America, reprint edition, 1979) 306.

180 See, Law No. 6, 2/8/1890 section 80 in W. W. McLaren, JAPANESE GOVERNMENT DOCUMENTS (Asiatic Society of Japan) (University Publications of America, reprint edition, 1979) Vol. 2, p.643.

181 See, Law No. 6, 2/8/1890 section 84 in W. W. McLaren, JAPANESE GOVERNMENT DOCUMENTS (Asiatic Society of Japan) (University Publications of America, reprint edition, 1979) Vol. 2, p. 643.

182 Shinichi Fujii, THE ESSENTIALS OF JAPANESE CONSTITUTIONAL LAW (University Publications of America, reprint edition, 1979) 306.

prosecutors.[183] Nonetheless there existed a great affinity between the prosecutors and judges with some prosecutors starting their careers as judges[184] and with some judges and prosecutors spending time in the other career to get broader experience.[185] Both prosecutors and judges were part of the Ministry of Justice and under the administrative authority of the Justice Minister.[186] Similarly, judges and prosecutors received the same practical training required to enter the professions. Such training was originally not required of lawyers, and when required of bengoshi (in 1933) the training of bengoshi was separate from that of the judges and prosecutors.[187] Moreover, at criminal trial the prosecutor and judge sat at the same raised level while defense counsel sat at a lower level.[188] Because of the inquisitional nature of the criminal procedure and the role of the judicial prosecutor in investigation and pre-trial questioning of the accused, criminal trials in prewar Japan were characterized by "trial by dossier"[189] based on the preparatory trial conducted by the prosecuting authority.[190] While defendants were entitled to counsel at the trial stage, they were not entitled to counsel during the preparatory trial when the dossier on which the trial was based was prepared.[191] It has been suggested that the function of the trial was not to determine guilt or innocence but rather the defendant was presumed guilty because of the preparatory trial before a judicial official and that the trial was for determining whether the determination of the preparatory procedure was correct.[192]

During the era of Taisho Democracy in the 1920s, a jury law was enacted that permitted defendants to select trial by jury for certain offenses. Juries did not enter

183 John O. Haley, The Japanese Judiciary: Maintaining Integrity, Autonomy and the Public Trust p. 17. On the web at *http://law.wustl.edu/Academics/Faculty/Workingpapers/TheJapaneseJudiciary10_03.pdf*

184 John O. Haley, The Japanese Judiciary: Maintaining Integrity, Autonomy and the Public Trust p. 17. On the web at *http://law.wustl.edu/Academics/Faculty/Workingpapers/TheJapaneseJudiciary10_03.pdf*

185 Tomoko Akane, Reform of the Legal Training System in Japan available on the web at *www.unafei.or.jp/pdf/indonesia_pdf/session3.pdf* p.17.

186 Shigemitsu Dando (Translated by B.J. George Jr.) JAPANESE CRIMINAL PROCEDURE (Fred B. Rothman & Co., 1965) Section 5.03.

187 Tomoko Akane, Reform of the Legal Training System in Japan available on the web at *www.unafei.or.jp/pdf/indonesia_pdf/session3.pdf* p.4.

188 Kenzo Takayanagi, A Century of Innovation: The Development of Japanese Law, 1868-1961 in LAW IN JAPAN (VON Mehren Ed. Harvard University Press, 1963) 20-21.

189 Ryuichi Hirano, Diagnosis of the Current Code of Criminal Procedure (translated by Daniel H. Foote) 22 Law in Japan 129, 139 (1989)

190 Atsushi Nagashima, The Accused and Society: The Administration of Criminal Justice in Japan, in LAW IN JAPAN (VON Mehren Ed. Harvard University Press, 1963) 299 fn. 9; See also, Alfred C. Oppler, LEGAL REFORM IN OCCUPIED JAPAN (Princeton University Press, 1976) 139.

191 Kenzo Takayanagi, A Century of Innovation: The Development of Japanese Law, 1868-1961 in LAW IN JAPAN (VON Mehren Ed. Harvard University Press, 1963) 21.

192 Kenzo Takayanagi, A Century of Innovation: The Development of Japanese Law, 1868-1961 in LAW IN JAPAN (VON Mehren Ed. Harvard University Press, 1963) 21.

guilty or not guilty verdicts as in the United States but, rather, answered questions put to them by the judge. Unanimity was not required—a simple majority was sufficient. In exchange for the jury trial privilege, the accused gave up the right to appeal from the first level judgment although the prosecutor's right to appeal from an acquittal was unaffected. However, the judge was not compelled to follow the jury's determination and could, in the event of disagreement with the jury, have the case retried before another jury until the result believed correct by the court was achieved. In such a situation it is not surprising that most defendants elected not to have a jury trial. The jury trial law was suspended during the Second World War.[193]

Boissonade was also instrumental in the drafting of Japan's first Civil Code. Prior to Boissonade's effort, the Meiji government adopted a general rule for civil cases to the effect that custom should govern in the event that there was no written law on the subject—and if there was no custom then logic and reason should govern.[194] Shortly after his drafting of a Criminal Code and Code of Criminal Procedure, Boissonade in either late 1879 or early 1880 started work on a Civil Code. The project took approximately 10 years. The objective was to create a Code based on the French Civil Code, but not a translation of that Code. Rather, the new Code was to adopt French principles as they could be applied in Japan. Nonetheless the French law nature of the Code was obvious. This was not the first attempt to compile a Civil Code. Efforts had been underway to write a Civil Code since 1872. Boissonade left certain aspects of the Code to Japanese writers—although he influenced their work and thus French law ideas worked their way into these parts of the Code as well.[195] Principle among these areas was the portion of the Code dealing with family law and succession. The Code was adopted in 1890[196] and was due to come into force January 1, 1894.[197] But by 1890 the influence of

---

193 Yosiyuki Noda, INTRODUCTION TO JAPANESE LAW (translated and edited by Anthony H. Angelo) (University of Tokyo Press, 1976) 137-138; Kenzo Takayanagi, A Century of Innovation: The Development of Japanese Law, 1868-1961 in LAW IN JAPAN (VON Mehren Ed. Harvard University Press, 1963) 22; Alfred C. Oppler, LEGAL REFORM IN OCCUPIED JAPAN (Princeton University Press, 1976) 146; Hiroshi Oda, JAPANESE LAW (Oxford University Press, 2nd Ed. 1999) 73-75; A. Didrick Castberg, JAPANESE CRIMINAL JUSTICE (Praeger, 1990) 3.

194 See, Great Counsel of State Decree No. 103 discussed in Kenzo Takayanagi, A Century of Innovation: The Development of Japanese Law, 1868-1961 in LAW IN JAPAN (VON Mehren Ed. Harvard University Press, 1963) 25.

195 Ishii Ryosuke, JAPANESE LEGISLATION IN THE MEIJI ERA (Translated and adapted by William J. Chambliss) (Kasai Publishing, Tokyo, 1958) 582-583.

196 Kenzo Takayanagi, A Century of Innovation: The Development of Japanese Law, 1868-1961 in LAW IN JAPAN (VON Mehren Ed. Harvard University Press, 1963) 24. [Noda says the old Code was adopted in 1891 (Yosiyuki Noda, INTRODUCTION TO JAPANESE LAW (translated and edited by Anthony H. Angelo) (University of Tokyo Press, 1976) 46-47) but 1890 is the better date and the Code is generally known as the Civil Code of 1890.]

197 Yosiyuki Noda, INTRODUCTION TO JAPANESE LAW (translated and edited by Anthony H. Angelo) (University of Tokyo Press, 1976) 46-47; Kenzo Takayanagi, A Century of Innova-

French law was on the decline and the influence of German law was in the ascendance.[198] The Code never became effective.

The English school objected to the Code as being too "French" and failing to take into account other Western legal systems. Moreover, while French legal thought was predominant when the Criminal Code and Code of Criminal Procedure were adopted, by 1890 a German school was developing and the old French school of the Ministry of Justice had been absorbed by the new Tokyo University, which had added a German law faculty. In addition, nationalist elements that opposed the idea of adopting Western legal thought in Japan[199] joined with the English school as a means of postponing the effective date of the Code. There were strong arguments that the Code failed to adequately take into account Japanese tradition—especially in the family law, ownership of property and inheritance articles, but more generally as well. It was, of course, true that the inheritance and property ownership provisions of the Code departed from Japanese feudal practice. For example, under the *Ie* House system property of a House member was inherited by the House (i.e., the Head of the House) and not by the member's immediate family.[200] Moreover, the very idea of ownership by a House member as distinguished from ownership by the House was novel. However, when stipends paid to individual samurai were replaced by annuities and then bonds, the idea that these bonds were owned by the House seemed far-fetched. Likewise, as samurai received salaries for their work and used such salaries for business enterprise it seemed inappropriate to turn those businesses over to the Head of the House. Clearly it had become necessary to modify the ownership and succession rights to such "privately" as distinguished from House owned property from the House ("*Ie*") system of ownership and inheritance of property to a more Western system of individual ownership of property.[201] Some modification was accordingly made in the Code, although the House system was retained, placing the Code in a semi feudal semi modern world where family and succession were concerned. Nonetheless, once steps were taken to abolish feudalism a modification of ownership rules was needed both to take account of this reality and to enable Japan to compete in the modern world.

---

tion: The Development of Japanese Law, 1868-1961 in LAW IN JAPAN (VON Mehren Ed. Harvard University Press, 1963) 27.

198 Professor Noda divides the early stages of reception of European law in Japan into three parts. The first period, the period of French influence, ends in 1890 and is followed by the period of German influence. See, Yosiyuki Noda, Comparative Jurisprudence in Japan: Its Past and Present in Hideo Tanaka, THE JAPANESE LEGAL SYSTEM University of Tokyo Press, 1976) 194-208.

199 See, Shinichiro Michida (assisted by Robert Braucher) The Legal Structure for Economic Enterprise: Some Aspects of Japanese Commercial Law in LAW IN JAPAN (Arthur Taylor von Mehren, Ed. Harvard University Press, 1963) 507, 512.

200 For an interesting discussion of the *Ie* and its relationship to social structure in general see, V. Lee Hamilton and Joseph Sanders, EVERYDAY JUSTICE (Yale University Press, 1992) 28-30.

201 G.B. Sansom, THE WESTERN WORLD AND JAPAN (Vintage Books, New York, 1949) 448-450.

While phrased in terms of English law versus French law the debate evolved into an issue of values, pitting French values contained in the Code as a representative of liberal European values against so-called Japanese values. By initiating objection to the Code the English school provided a vehicle for more conservative elements to force a postponement of what was considered too much liberal French influence. The debate was hot and heavy on both sides and eventually a compromise of sorts was reached by which the Code's effectiveness was postponed until 1896.[202] Although the opponents of Western values had won the battle, they could not win the war. A Westernized Code with Western concepts was required if the unequal treaties were to be renegotiated. But, while a Westernized Code might be required, something less "liberal" then the Napoleonic ideas based on the French revolution could be found.

A drafting committee (under the authority of a government formed commission headed by Ito Hirobumi) of three Tokyo University Professors was assigned the task of writing the new Code. They examined both English and German sources, as well as other European sources and eventually decided on a structure that followed the German Civil Code. Although the form was German, and although some attention was given to Japanese customary law in the text (especially notions of family law) many of the original provisions remained. The Code both in structure and content clearly represents the ascendance of German law and German legal thinking. The first several books of the new Code were adopted in 1896. The final books dealing with family law and succession were adopted in 1898. To avoid the dispute that had preceded the old Code, the sponsors of the new Code pointed out that they had studied Japanese customs in making their revisions and they noted the need to adopt a Code to support the ongoing treaty renegotiating efforts with the Western powers.[203] The new Civil Code of 1898, with amendments made in 1926 (based on the 1895 Civil Code of Austria) and modifications in the family law and inheritance law, remained in effect until after the Second World War.[204] Although the inheritance provisions of the old family system were substantially changed, the general thrust of the samurai family law system was retained.

---

202 For interesting discussions of the debate and its political/sociological aspects see, Ishii Ryosuke, JAPANESE LEGISLATION IN THE MEIJI ERA (Translated and adapted by William J. Chambliss) (Kasai Publishing, Tokyo, 1958) at 583-589; Kenzo Takayanagi, A Century of Innovation: The Development of Japanese Law, 1868-1961 in LAW IN JAPAN (VON Mehren Ed. Harvard University Press, 1963) 27-30; Yosiyuki Noda, INTRODUCTION TO JAPANESE LAW (translated and edited by Anthony H. Angelo) (University of Tokyo Press, 1976) 47-50; John O. Haley, AUTHORITY WITHOUT POWER: LAW AND THE JAPANESE PARADOX (Oxford University Press, 1991) 75-77.

203 Ishii Ryosuke, JAPANESE LEGISLATION IN THE MEIJI ERA (Translated and adapted by William J. Chambliss) (Kasai Publishing, Tokyo, 1958) 589-592.

204 Kenzo Takayanagi, A Century of Innovation: The Development of Japanese Law, 1868-1961 in LAW IN JAPAN (VON Mehren Ed. Harvard University Press, 1963) 30-31; Yosiyuki Noda, INTRODUCTION TO JAPANESE LAW (translated and edited by Anthony H. Angelo) (University of Tokyo Press, 1976) 50-52; Hiroshi Oda, JAPANESE LAW (Oxford University Press, 2nd Ed. 1999) 393-394.

The family law provisions in the Civil Code made the family concept of the *Ie*, the feudal family law that bound samurai families, the family law for the entire society. This reversion to Japan's past was out of date when adopted. Although it was the formal law, it was not followed in all its aspects in many parts of Japan and for many of Japan's families. Nonetheless it did set a standard of formal law that had meaning in relationships of family members. Under the Civil Code the Head of the House had the right to determine who would marry into and out of the House. As a consequence House members required the approval of the Head of the House to marry and if under 30 (male) or 25 (female) also required consent of the parents. [Since the House represented an ancestral line it was far larger than a nuclear family—it resembled more a clan or tribe than family. As such, many families were part of a single House.] Moreover, Heads of Houses could enter into agreements for the marriage of House members to take effect when the members reached marriageable age. Such agreements had force and effect and failure to live up to such agreements could lead to monetary damages. The typical system for marriage under the prewar Civil Code was for the families to engage matchmakers and for the parents to determine the spouse. Children were to follow the parent's lead as a matter of loyalty and out of respect for their parents and were to agree to the matchmaker's suggestion to assure that the matchmaker does not lose face.

Primogeniture in favor of the Head of the House's eldest son was the rule for inheritance. Although with samurai having moved to the cities and taken up administrative positions many samurai were no longer associated with their former House and their salary and earnings did not become part of the House property—this remained the case in Meiji Japan. Each House had a place of residence, and events in the life of House members were recorded in the House's Family Register even if family members lived far from that location.

As the family law was concerned in great part with ancestor worship, the Code had many provisions dealing with inheritance of the ritual items used for ancestor worship and provisions for the inheritance and use of family names. The concept of primogeniture was retained so that farms, already small by Western standards, would not be further subdivided making them uneconomical.[205] The Code recognized adoption as adoption was necessary in cases where there was no male heir and hence no one to carry on the necessary ancestor worship rituals.

Women were big losers in the House or *Ie* family concept. When a woman married she typically joined her husband's *Ie* and took his family name. In feudal times the husband retained the right to divorce his wife while she had no corresponding right. Under the Civil Code a husband could divorce his wife for adultery but adultery by the husband was considered as acceptable. (Adultery by the wife was also a crime under Meiji Penal Law but adultery by the husband was not criminal). Not only was the husband's adultery permitted but if the adultery resulted in offspring the illegitimate child could be acknowledged by the husband

205 Japanese farms remain smallholdings. See, Bradley Richardson, JAPANESE DEMOCRACY—POWER, COORDINATION, AND PERFORMANCE (Yale University Press, 1997) 252.

and then was entitled to all the rights of a legitimate child. This meant that the wife had to care for the child and the child could eventually inherit and place the wife (not his legitimate mother) in a disadvantageous position. The Code enshrined the concept that the wife's role was to take care of her husband (and his family—both ancestral and children) and bear him children. The husband (or the head of his House) had the right to choose the residence location of the family and the wife was required to live with her husband. Once married a woman needed her husband's consent to enter into contractual relationships, to invest her own property, to buy and sell real estate, to make or receive gifts, etc. Wives were entitled to keep the property they owned prior to marriage but the husband was entitled to the profits and rents from such property and had the right to manage the property. In limited situations (e.g. no male heir and hence no option) a woman could be the Head of a House, but if she then married or adopted a male child the male became Head of the House.

Marriage was a matter of "contract" but to be legally effective the fact of marriage needed to be recorded in the Family Register. Thus a couple could enter into the marriage ceremony and live together as man and wife but would not be recognized as being married unless and until the marriage was formally recorded. This led to the opportunity for "trial marriages." If the trial was successful and the husband's family accepted the wife, the documents acknowledging the marriage were filed and the marriage recognized—if unsuccessful the wife could return to her family—all without the need for a formal divorce. Divorce itself was easy if the parties agreed. All that was required for a consensual divorce was the filing of the necessary papers with the Registrar and registration in the family register.[206] Although a consensual matter, the reality was that for men divorce was easy as they could compel their wives to sign (seal) the necessary documents while for women the reality was otherwise. Husbands who could not force such consent could seek a judicial divorce and in rare cases a wife could seek judicial divorce but if she did so a male relative had to appear in court with her. On divorce the husband had priority rights to custody of the children of the marriage. On divorce the wife was entitled to take back the property she had brought to the marriage. Widows did not have much in the way of inheritance rights, as male primogeniture was the rule. Widows could only inherit in situations where no lineal descendant existed. Widows could not return to their own family's House upon the death of their husband unless they received permission to do so from Head of the husband's house. Such return could be significant, as without return the widow did not have a chance to marry again unless the head of the husband's House gave his consent.

206 The same system for consensual divorce applies today. See, Family Register Law Article 76.

The House system also placed younger children at a disadvantage to older children to whom they owed loyalty obligations. All children owed loyalty obligations to parents—essentially the father until his death and then to the mother.[207]

A Code of Civil Procedure was adopted in 1890 effective 1891 based exclusively on the German Code of Civil Procedure of 1877. Indeed, the Code of Civil Procedure was virtually a Japanese translation of the German Code (with errors in translation sometimes leading to anomalous results).[208] It is possible that the decision to follow a German Code for procedure was grounded on the fact that the German Code was modern and thus represented the latest European thinking on the subject of Civil Procedure.[209] However, it is also true that previous efforts at writing a Code of Civil Procedure used a French law model and it may be that the switch to a German law model was representative of the movement towards German legal thinking in general. While Civil Procedure was based on a German law model, the judges of the time nad been trained in the French legal system and naturally they could not disassociate themselves from French legal ideas.

Both French and German civil procedure utilized the inquisition model discussed in connection with criminal procedure. The judge was seen as having the role of discovering the true facts in a case and arriving at a correct decision. To do this the judge met with the parties or their counsel to discuss the case and get an understanding of the dispute. The process, known as clarification, was aided by the non-continuous nature of civil law "trials." At each meeting the issues and the facts related to the issues became clearer. Outstanding questions or evidence related matters could be briefed by the parties and then discussed at the next meeting. This briefing (called Preliminary Documents because the briefs were preliminary to the oral meeting sessions) helped resolve questions at the next meeting by assuring that both parties and the court were aware of the positions of each side in the matter. Under the original German—Japanese adopted—procedure there was no clear break point or indeed any break point between "pre-trial" and "trial." The entire procedure was treated as the "trial" or Plenary Proceeding. The entire process was treated as a single process even though it might involve numerous sessions, separated by several months and extending over a period of years.

---

207 For a discussion of Family Law prewar see, Note, Japanese Family Law, 9 Stanford Law Review 132 (1956); Sakae Wagatsuma, Democratization of the Family Relation in Japan, 25 Washington State Bar Journal 405 (1950); Kurt Steiner, The Revision of the Civil Code of Japan, 9 Far Eastern Quarterly 169 (1950); Tomiyuki Ogawa, An Overview of the Japanese Family Law System—Focusing on A Historic Survey (1992); Ishii Ryosuke, JAPANESE LEGISLATION IN THE MEIJI ERA (Translated and adapted by William J. Chambliss) (Kasai Publishing, Tokyo, 1958) at 660-685.

208 Kenzo Takayanagi, A Century of Innovation: The Development of Japanese Law, 1868-1961 in LAW IN JAPAN (VON Mehren Ed. Harvard University Press, 1963) 32-33; Yosiyuki Noda, INTRODUCTION TO JAPANESE LAW (translated and edited by Anthony H. Angelo) (University of Tokyo Press, 1976) 54-55.

209 Hiroshi Oda, JAPANESE LAW (Oxford University Press, 2nd Ed. 1999) 393.

Since the responsibility for clarifying issues was a responsibility of the judge and since the judge was also responsible for reaching a correct decision in the matter, the process was judge centered. Judges could on their own call witnesses ("*ex officio*") and could question witnesses before the parties were permitted to examine. The parties did not have ultimate responsibility for either fact gathering and fact production or for legal contention presentation. As the judge was responsible for arriving at a "correct" decision, these matters were part of the court's responsibility. If the judge failed to properly clarify the case (i.e., if the judge failed to address legal issues that might change the decision or failed to investigate into factual matters that might change the result—even if such legal or factual matters had not been raised by the parties) the court's decision could be reversed on appeal.

The process was seen as one continuous web leading to the ultimate clarification of the case so that a correct decision could be reached. As a consequence new issues and new factual matters could be raised at any time in the process and be treated as if raised at the start of the process. This presented opportunity for delay. It took years to resolve litigation matters. Further, since the process was judge centered there appeared to be no reason for public input or participation and trials were generally private affairs held in private. Trials were not public events.

In the early 1920s Germany reformed its civil procedure and in the late 1920s Japan followed suit. The principal of the "Oral Argument" held in public was a major aspect of both the German and Japanese reform. Under the concept the parties were required to state their positions "Orally" in public rather than stating their positions privately in written briefs. The adoption of the principal of Oral Argument did not do away with Preliminary Documents or briefs but, rather, required the statement publicly of matters set forth in the briefs. The Preliminary Documents were still utilized as a means of educating the parties and the court as to the position of the parties and remained a useful device to aid the clarification process. The reform rejected the idea of a continuous hearing—retaining the separate sessions separated by long stretches of time procedure—in favor of a clearer demarcation between the "pre-trial" and "trial" aspects of the case. Thus, a Preliminary Oral Argument process was established whose purpose was to aid the clarification process and define issues and contentions and evidentiary matters so that at the "Oral Argument" (trial) stage a more continuous process could be followed. Issues not addressed at the Preliminary Oral Argument stage could theoretically be precluded from consideration at the Oral Argument that followed. The purpose of this reform was to do away with delay occasioned by the late presentation of new contentions and fact issues. However, in both Germany and Japan judges, still responsible for getting the "correct" decision allowed in new contentions and factual material for fear that failure to do so could lead to an incorrect decision. Indeed, in Japan the judge had an *obligation* to come to the correct decision and, as this required a proper clarification of the issues and facts, failure to allow such late raised issues could result in reversal on appeal for failure to properly clarify the case. The corollary reform—the continuous hearing at the

Oral Argument stage—similarly atrophied in a system that had no jury and hence no reason for a condensed trial.

In the Japanese version of the German litigation system the lawyer—the bengoshi—was a latecomer. Unlike judges and prosecutors who needed to pass an examination and for whom there were strict licensing requirements as well as the obligation to attend the Legal Research and Training Institute established to further their education, licensing for lawyers came much later in time. Judges and prosecutors looked down on lawyers who were seen as less well trained and less well educated. Most civil cases involved parties who were not represented by counsel. Judges saw it as their role (both in cases where parties were not represented and cases where parties were represented) to protect the clients or parties before them. This meant seeing that all relevant contentions and all relevant evidence were confirmed while rejecting contentions and evidence that represented a waste of time and effort. Just as the party not represented by counsel should not suffer because it had no representative so too the represented party should not suffer because the counsel was less than competent. Judges developed a paternalistic attitude toward both the lawyers and parties who appeared before the court.

Still, neither French law nor German law or legal theory was the basis for most judicial action in litigation. Rather, judges viewed conciliation—the model used in Tokugawa Japan—as the proper means of resolving disputes and favored party resolution to determination based on the law.[210] And, when confronted with a legal resolution that was inconsistent with traditional values or mores of society, the courts inevitably rejected the legal norm in favor of the traditional or customary or community norm.[211] Beginning in 1919 there was a movement to return Japanese law to its more traditional nature. This meant turning away from the Western model of litigating disputes and returning to the values of conciliation, mediation and compromise. The first step in this direction was an effort to create a family court system whose function was to conciliate family law issues. This was followed by a series of individual laws whose effect was to require conciliation of various disputes. As conciliation became the mode for resolution courts were given authority to enforce the conciliation mode of resolution even if one of the parties (or both) objected. By 1942 all civil disputes were subject to required conciliation with the courts having power to decree the conciliated resolution as the resolution of the matter. Conciliation is, in essence, a settlement type of process and relies more on abstract notions of what is fair in the circumstance of the case than on what the Code law may require of the parties. As such it was more consis-

210 Yosiyuki Noda, INTRODUCTION TO JAPANESE LAW (translated and edited by Anthony H. Angelo) (University of Tokyo Press, 1976) 55.

211 See John O. Haley, AUTHORITY WITHOUT POWER: LAW AND THE JAPANESE PARADOX (Oxford University Press, 1991) 85; see also, Yosiyuki Noda, INTRODUCTION TO JAPANESE LAW (translated and edited by Anthony H. Angelo) (University of Tokyo Press, 1976) 217-224.

tent with Japan's past than it was with a society based on rigid legal rules to govern the interaction of people and to resolve civil disputes.[212]

As noted earlier, the Meiji Constitution separated the Administrative Court from the judicial court system. In 1890 (the same year the Meiji Constitution became effective) the Administrative Appeals Law came into effect carrying out the separation of Administrative from judicial courts.[213] The "judges" of the Administrative Court were not judicial judges but, rather, high-ranking administrative officials who, while holding their administrative post could act as Administrative Court judge at the same time.[214] These "judges" naturally had a bureaucratic bias in favor of the administrative organs of government. Moreover, although technically such judges had tenure in their position as judge, the reality was otherwise.[215] There was no "general jurisdiction" provision for review of administrative action. To be within the authority of the court there needed to be a specific statute granting authority to proceed before the court.[216] As the power of the bureaucracy grew the restrictions on permitting suit before the court similarly increased. The court adopted narrow interpretations and strict standing to sue rules to deny relief. There were no district or local administrative courts but, rather, only a single court situated in Tokyo.[217] This limited access to the court and increased costs for those located far from the capital city, making it difficult to sue even if jurisdiction was allowed.[218] Moreover, neither the judicial courts nor the Administrative Court had the power of judicial review over acts of the Diet.[219] The reality was that appeal to the Administrative Court was not a realistic means of reigning in executive power

---

212 For a discussion of the rise of conciliation in prewar Japan see, John O. Haley, AUTHORITY WITHOUT POWER: LAW AND THE JAPANESE PARADOX (Oxford University Press, 1991) 85-96.

213 See John O. Haley, AUTHORITY WITHOUT POWER: LAW AND THE JAPANESE PARADOX (Oxford University Press, 1991) 70, 209 fn.13.

214 Bai Gao, The State and the Associational Order of the Economy (2003) on the web at *www.wz-berlin.de/mp/ism/conf/conf03/papers/gao.pdf* at page 19;

215 Hideo Wada, The Administrative Court Under the Meiji Constitution, 10 Law in Japan 1, 44-47 (1977).

216 Toshiyoshi Miyasawa, CONSTITUTIONAL LAW (REV. ED. 1962) in Hideo Tanaka, THE JAPANESE LEGAL SYSTEM (University of Tokyo Press, 1976) at 637; Kiminobu Hashimoto, The Rule of Law: Some Aspects of Judicial Review of Administrative Action, LAW IN JAPAN (von Mehren Ed. Harvard University Press, 1967) 240; Hideo Wada, The Administrative Court Under the Meiji Constitution, 10 Law in Japan 1, 47 (1977); Alfred C. Oppler, LEGAL REFORM IN OCCUPIED JAPAN (Princeton University Press, 1976) 100.

217 Hideo Wada, The Administrative Court Under the Meiji Constitution, 10 Law in Japan 1, 44-47 (1977); Kiminobu Hashimoto, The Rule of Law: Some Aspects of Judicial Review of Administrative Action, LAW IN JAPAN (von Mehren Ed. Harvard University Press, 1967) 240.

218 See, Thomas L. Blakemore, Post-War Development in Japanese Law, 1947 Wisconsin Law Review 632, 643.

219 Hideo Tanaka, THE JAPANESE LEGAL SYSTEM (University of Tokyo Press, 1976) at 686.

and that administrative officials were essentially outside the control of the law.[220] The inevitable consequence was that the court, rather than acting to restrict the power of the administrative arm of the State, acted to restrict the ability of aggrieved parties to obtain relief against administrative action.[221]

1890 was also the year in which the Old Commercial Code was promulgated. This Code was drafted by the German Roesler and was a mixture of German law, French law and Japanese customary law. Roesler had started work on the Code in 1881.[222] The government had made earlier efforts to combine the various commercial laws into a unified Code. The effective date for the Code was only one year later in 1891. The Commercial Code was swept up in the controversy over the Civil Code and the attempts of the traditionalists to halt the adoption of Western-based Codes. As a consequence its effective date was extended first to 1893 and then to 1896, and finally to 1898 although major portions of the Code did become effective in 1893. A new Code was drafted prior to the 1898 effective date but it did not receive Diet approval because the House of Representatives failed to act on it. Thus in 1898 the balance of the old Code went into effect. The Diet finally acted in 1899. The New Commercial Code was based on the German Commercial Code and represented yet another victory for the German school and another sign of the waning French law influence on Japanese law. The Code was amended again in 1911 and in 1938 the company law provisions were completely rewritten.[223]

C. Summary

The Meiji oligarchs were radical reformers. Not in the sense of natural law and social contract reformers or use of the term radical in modern political terminology. But their reforms were radical for the times and the society in which they lived. In a relatively short period they took Japan from a strict class structured feudal society with a central authority and semiautonomous regions governed by hereditary lords to a unitary system of government based on a central authority governing prefectures in which there were no social classes from which there was no

220 See, See, Dan Fenno Henderson, Japanese Judicial Review of Legislation: The First Twenty Years in Dan Fenno Henderson, THE CONSTITUTION OF JAPAN: ITS FIRST TWENTY YEARS 1947-1967 (University of Washington Press, 1969) 115, 117-118.

221 Bai Gao, The State and the Associational [sic] Order of the Economy (2003) on the web at *www.wz-berlin.de/mp/ism/conf/conf03/papers/gao.pdf* at page 19; Hideo Wada, The Administrative Court Under the Meiji Constitution, 10 Law in Japan 1 (1977).

222 Shinichiro Michida (assisted by Robert Braucher) The Legal Structure for Economic Enterprise: Some Aspects of Japanese Commercial Law in LAW IN JAPAN (Arthur Taylor von Mehren, Ed. Harvard University Press, 1963) 507, 512.

223 Hiroshi Oda, JAPANESE LAW (Oxford University Press, 2nd Ed. 1999) 131; Ishii Ryosuke, JAPANESE LEGISLATION IN THE MEIJI ERA (Translated and adapted by William J. Chambliss) (Kasai Publishing, Tokyo, 1958) at 592-598.

escape.[224] They not only created the administrative structure of a modern State but they created a modern economic system. They put in place the façade of a modern Western legal system complete with constitution, courts, judges, lawyers, and modern codes of civil and criminal procedure, civil law, penal law and commercial law. They achieved their major objectives of renegotiating the unequal treaties, recovering Japanese sovereignty, modernizing the economy, placing Japan as an equal with the Western powers in world political terms and retaining power for themselves during their lifetimes. All of this was achieved while they provided a model that could (but did not) produce a representative government in the future.

But the oligarchs for all their trips abroad and their study of the West were essentially products of their society—as we all are. They were members of the samurai class trained and educated in the values of that class. They believed in discipline and a strong hand by government that ruled in a benevolent but firm fashion. They had grown up and been educated in a feudal system that was based on Neo-Confucianism notions of obligation and not rights; on concepts of loyalty to ones' superior; on views of worthy rulers having ethical obligations to rule for the good of society; of a bureaucracy that played a major role in governing and ordering society; on loyalty, ethics, morality and obligations conforming to a code that predated the Napoleonic Code. The feudal system in which they were raised was one where power was wielded from behind the screen rather than by the person nominally holding authority. Thus, while the Emperor was the nominal reigning power, the Shogunate held the real power. In some situations, even the Shogun was a figurehead, with real power residing in a council of elders. The Constitution perpetuated the traditional system wherein the Emperor reigned but the oligarchs ruled. However, it made no provision for what would happen once the oligarchs passed from the scene, as they surely would. It contained no check by the civilian authority over the military's power. The military was responsible solely to the reigning but not ruling Emperor—leaving plenty of room for the military to move into a ruling role. Moreover, the borrowing of Code law from European societies while essential for the renegotiation of the unequal treaties resulted in statute law that was inconsistent with the norms of the society to which that law was to apply. The Codes were based on concepts of rights and obligations that simply did not apply to Japanese society; they were designed for a society in a different stage of development from feudalism to modernity. When the problems of conceptualizing a legal system based on concepts new to the society (and for which words had to be created just to be able to speak about the ideas) are added to the above, it becomes

224 This is not completely accurate as the Family Register system enabled a researched to discover the family village of origin. This in turn allowed for discovery of so-called "eta"—those outside the caste system of feudal Japan who were forced to live in Buraku outside of villages. This in turn aided the continued discrimination against the descendants of these class-less people. This discrimination continues until this day although there have been laws passed forbidding the selling of "Buraku lists" and there have been laws passed providing economic relief to Buraku communities in Japan. There is no law prohibiting discrimination against the so-called Burakumin nor has the Family Register system that allows for the perpetuation of this discrimination been abandoned. See, Mari Yamaguchi, "Burakumin" Descendants Still Suffering, Japan Times on Line June 5, 2004.

clear that the suit of clothes represented by the new legal system did not fit easily on the wearer.

In the crucial area of relations of the populace to the government the Constitution, Criminal Procedure Code and Administrative Court tipped the scales decidedly in favor of the government. In the two great areas of law controlling the relations of the people and their government (criminal law and administrative law) the government had the upper hand. Although the criminal law system looked very much like the French/German continental systems, the reality was that the police/prosecutor power was virtually unchecked with the prosecutor and the police they supervised having their own authority to issue warrants and pursue investigations. Although torture had been outlawed, confession remained the mainstay of the criminal process as it had in Tokugawa times and the police used their authority to obtain confessions. Although the accused was entitled to counsel at trial, counsel was not permitted at the all-important preliminary trial and investigative stage at which guilt or innocence was determined and which the trial reviewed to see if the prosecutor had gotten it right. In the administrative law arena, although the Administrative Court was modeled on the French Administrative Court, its operative law was German in nature. Unlike in France the Japanese court was designed to assure that judicial officers in an independent judiciary did not interfere with actions of the administrative arm of the government. As a consequence, jurisdiction was broadly construed in the sense that the court had exclusive authority over all challenges to government action. But failure to provide for "judicial" review of administrative actions in statutes and strict standing requirements limiting plaintiffs to those whose "legal rights" had been violated by the government, resulted in shutting out others whose interests may have been adversely affected. And, the Constitution provided no relief, as all the supposed rights contained therein were limited to the provisions of law that either gave or took away the substance of the right. There was no constitutional right that was enforceable on its own.

In the civil law arena the law was filled with provisions taken from the Napoleonic Code and structured along the lines of German legal scientific reasoning. The government in the robes of the bureaucratic judge was ultimately responsible for properly deciding cases. Individual rights were not the basis for judicial decisions just as the individual litigants did not have ultimate responsibility for their own cases. Judges tended to decide cases based on community values and norms rather than on the strict interpretation of the Codes. Moreover, in the rural areas of Japan (and for all its economic growth Japan was still very much an agricultural country) the modern Code had little affect on life. Eventually the pre-constitutional pre-code norms of conciliation began to dominate the litigation world with conciliation becoming mandatory during the war years.

Onto this constitutional/legal scene burst the American Occupation with its New Deal philosophy, notions of Jeffersonian democracy, natural law and inalienable rights, judicial review of government actions, common law adversarial justice, neutral judges and party responsibility for cases, concentrated trials, lawyer domination of the process and an obsession with procedural justice.

4

The American Occupation and Changes in the Legal System

If the Meiji Restoration represents the starting point for the Modern Japan then the American Occupation is the starting point for the "Post-Modern Japan." The Occupation represented a blend of old and new for Japan. New because it was the first time in Japan's recorded history that there had been a successful invasion of the home country. Even the Mongols had failed when confronted with the preparations of the Kamakura Shogunate and the intercession of the kamikaze divine wind. Old in the sense that Japan had once before lost a great deal of its sovereignty to the Western powers through the unequal treaties and consular jurisdiction. New because there was now a Western military general in charge of the government administration whose rules and orders had to be obeyed. Old because Japan had previously had military shoguns in charge of the administrative arms of the government, with the Imperial House in the background. The American Occupation used the presence of the Emperor and his "Imperial authority" to obtain their objectives just as the Tokugawa and Kamakura Shoguns had used the Imperial House. In this there was a commonality of interest between General MacArthur and the Emperor. Both wanted to preserve the Imperial House and the position of the Emperor and they worked both together and at cross-purpose to achieve that objective. New in the sense that the Occupation insisted on a government and legal structure that emphasized individual rights and the common law approach to various issues, most significantly common law ideas of procedural justice. Old because Japan had previously changed its governmental structure and legal system to replicate Western models in order to recover its sovereignty. Japan would once again borrow and enact new legal models to recover its sovereignty—and mold that model to fit the Japanese experience.

The war in the Pacific had been an "allied" operation just as the war in Europe had allied the United States with other powers. There were however differences between the European and Pacific wars. Primary among those differences was the role of the United States vis-à-vis the other allied powers. The Pacific War had been more of a United States undertaking. Unlike in Europe, the Soviet Union had stayed out of the Pacific War and had honored its German-sponsored neutrality agreement with Japan until the last days of the war. There was no Soviet Army on the ground in Japan as there was in Central and Eastern Europe, including the eastern part of Germany. Japan unlike Germany was not on the border of France and was not within easy distance of London as the Blitz had proven. Accordingly, although the Occupation was an allied operation on paper, it was American in reality. MacArthur was, however, not unmindful of the fact that the allies might attempt to influence his policy.

Further, Japan was viewed differently than Germany. Japan had been an ally against Germany in the First World War. It had had a period of so-called Taisho Democracy. It had not had the equivalent of a Nazi Party apparatus that had affected the entire administration of government. The problem in Japan was seen as more a problem of militarism having replaced civilian authority combined with a "military industrial complex" (in which the *zaibatsu* played a major role) that had led Japan into war and taken from her people the rights that American's viewed as "natural" in origin. The influence of Emperor worship and State Shinto was seen as another source of the Japanese turn away from democracy. A first step in breaking the power of these old institutions was to make the Emperor more human and less godlike. In this connection the famous picture of the Emperor and MacArthur—a picture that was a clear portrait of respective power—that was published widely in Japan probably did more to debunk the myth of Imperial deity than did the Emperor's statement renouncing god-like status. In any event, MacArthur and the Occupation relied more on the Japanese administrative machinery to run operations and performed less of a purge of government officials than was the case in occupied Germany.

The American Occupation found a Japan that had in place a façade of Western law in the form of a Western-looking Constitution with an elected legislature, a supposed separation of powers and a chapter on Rights and Duties of the Japanese people; and a civil law system that replicated European civil law systems complete with a Civil Code that looked very much like a European Civil Code; a Criminal Code that looked European; a Commercial Code borrowed from the Germans; a Code of Civil Procedure and a Code of Criminal Procedure. There even was an Administrative Court modeled on the French/German Administrative Court and administrative law systems. In such a setting it was possible to "pick and choose" and make adjustments and modifications in the law rather than creating an entire new system. The Constitution and the idea of individual rights would however require a wholesale re-writing and not a simple amendment.

Before the Constitution could be redrafted, there remained the question of authority to act in Japan. Of course, de facto power resided with American Occupation authority through its troops on the ground. That authority was not questioned while the Occupation was in effect and prior to the adoption of the new Constitution. However, after the Constitution was adopted issues were presented about the scope of the continuing authority of the Occupation. A Cabinet Order was issued in 1950 (after the Constitution but before the Peace Treaty returning sovereignty to Japan—1952) for the purpose of assisting the Occupation in carrying out its function. This Order made it a penal offense to interfere with the Occupation in its functions. A defendant convicted of violation of the Order after the Peace Treaty had come into effect leveled a challenge at the Cabinet Order. The Cabinet Order was designed to carry out a censorship regulation of the Occupation and provided a penal penalty for failure to comply. The Japanese Supreme Court found that the Cabinet Order was valid during the period between the adoption of the Order and the Peace Treaty even though its provisions were inconsistent with the Constitution. The reason for this finding was that the Cabinet Order carried out the Potsdam Declaration requirements that Japan assist the Occupation during the Occupation. Accordingly, even though the Order was inconsistent with the Constitution, it still had validity until the Occupation was ended. However, once the Occupation had come to an end, the obligation to continue to support the Occupation in the future similarly came to an end, and the provisions of the Constitution were fully applicable. As a consequence the defendant could not be convicted after the Occupation ended for a violation of the Cabinet Order since the Order was no longer constitutional and its force and effect had been superseded by time.[1]

A. The New Constitution and the Structure of Government

For centuries Japanese Emperors had been figureheads of Imperial Authority while actual power resided in the military leaders or shoguns. For the two and a half centuries of Tokugawa rule the Emperor was secluded in Kyoto where he was a virtual captive of the military authority. Only at the end of this period was there any thought given to Imperial power and authority. The western province Daimyo saw in the Emperor a symbol that could be used to overthrow the eastern province Tokugawa rule. Having an adolescent Emperor at their disposal made it easier for the rebellious provinces to lead the Emperor and thus use him as a symbol of national unity to carry out their own designs. In order to strengthen their hand in unifying the country under their leadership, the oligarchs raised the Emperor's position to heights that it had never had. They utilized the machinery of government that was in their possession to venerate the Emperor and then took steps to see to it that all actions that they took bore the Emperor's seal both literally and figuratively. Thus, opposition to the oligarch's policy was opposition to the Emperor and since opposition to the Emperor could not be countenanced, there could be no effective opposition to the government's policy. The rising opposition movement, led by former government insiders like Okuma and Itagaki, understood this ploy and was careful to word its opposition in terms of absolute loyalty to the Emperor. Thus, the policy seeking greater power for the Diet was not expressed as opposition to the government's policy. Instead it was expressed as support for the Emperor's policy as set out in the Charter Oath. In short, the oligarchs

1 See, Case No. A No. 2868 of 1952, Judgment Upon the Validity of Cabinet Order No. 325 of 1950, Sup. Ct. Grand Bench, 7/22/53, available in English on the website of the Supreme Court of Japan, Judgments of the Supreme Court.

created a cult of Emperor worship—State Shinto—raised the Emperor to the status of a living God and demanded absolute loyalty to the Imperial House.

The Meiji Constitution reflected and carried forward this Emperor central idea. All legislation (while it might require Diet action) was legislation given to the people by the Emperor as the Emperor had all legislative power, all rights given to subjects were a gift of the Emperor, and even judicial actions were taken "in the name of the Emperor."[2] Moreover, having been given by the Emperor to the people, the Meiji Constitution could only be amended when the Emperor requested such amendment.[3] Thus, there was a Japanese mechanism available for amendment of the Constitution. But, clearly any amendment would require substantial change in the Emperor-based system. In fact, the Occupation had received instructions from Washington to create a government structure that either abolished the Imperial House or sufficiently reformed it that it would not impede the democratic form of government that would replace the prewar form. This new government would be based on democratic principles of an executive power responsible to the public, a Legislative Branch with greater authority, and respect for individual human rights. Further, in line with American ideas that dispersal of government power to various levels of popularly elected government (i.e., national, state and local) the new government was to break the monopoly on power that resided in Tokyo.[4]

The first effort at constitutional reform was undertaken by the post-war government.[5] Former Prime Minister Konoe Fumimaro, a member of the post-war Cabinet and a confidant of the Emperor was given the go ahead to work on a new Constitution.[6] This effort was bound to fail before it even got off the ground as Konoe had been Prime Minister during some of Japan's pre-Pearl Harbor abuses and, notwithstanding his efforts to end the war in early 1945, was soon to be charged as a war criminal. Moreover, the government in which Konoe served was to resign and be replaced almost immediately after Konoe was brought into the

---

2 It is suggested that since judges acted in the name of the Emperor they could be independent of the other branches of Government.

3 Article 73 sets up the following procedure for amendment: a) an Imperial Order to the Diet for amendment, b) action by both Houses based on a 2/3 vote of the members present and requiring a quorum of 2/3 of all members.

4 John W. Dower, EMBRACING DEFEAT (W.W. Norton & Company, 1999) 348.

5 For an extensive analysis of the Constitution drafting and adoption process see, John W. Dower, EMBRACING DEFEAT (W.W. Norton & Company, 1999) 346-404; see also, James L. McClain, JAPAN, A MODERN HISTORY (W.W. Norton & Company, 2002). For an analysis of Emperor Hirohito's role and reactions to the Constitutional process (and General MacArthur's commitment to retain the Imperial Institution) see, Herbert Bix, HIROHITO AND THE MAKING OF MODERN JAPAN (Harper Collins 2000) 567-575. For a view that is somewhat different than that of Bix see, Alfred C. Oppler, LEGAL REFORM IN OCCUPIED JAPAN (Princeton University Press, 1976) 52-54.

6 Theodore McNelly, The Japanese Constitution: Child of the Cold War, 74 Political Science Quarterly 176, 178 (1959); Robert E. Ward, The Origins of the Present Japanese Constitution, 50 American Political Science Review 980, 984 (1956); Marius B. Jansen, THE MAKING OF MODERN JAPAN (Belknap Press of Harvard University, 2000) 670.

Constitution writing phase putting him and the government in an awkward position.[7] Nonetheless Konoe and Sasaki Soichi operating in their positions as Privy Councilors continued work on the constitutional revision.[8] The new Cabinet saw this as an affront and began its own work on the Constitution. Konoe drew up a set of points to be incorporated in a new Constitution while Sasaki actually drew up a draft. Both were quite conservative in approach.[9]

The Occupation then turned to the new government of Prime Minister Shidehara for a new Constitution. Shidehara had already appointed a committee headed by legal (but not constitutional) scholar Matsumoto Joji to study the issue of constitutional modification. This committee became a committee to revise the Constitution. There are indications that although undertaking the assignment, Shidehara, Matsumoto and the government did not feel that a new Constitution was required.[10] The reality is that during the 1920s Japan had entered what many Japanese considered a period of Taisho Democracy in which there were political party governments based on universal male suffrage. What the government drafters did not consider was that even during this phase there was little that would be considered by Americans as democracy. In the United States' understanding of the term more is implicated than simply broad suffrage and representative government. Democracy in United States' terms includes such ideas as individual human rights and procedural protections of the public from arbitrary action by the government. Moreover, the Potsdam Declaration by positing the issue of human rights indicated clearly that recognition of such rights was a necessary ingredient of any new Constitution. In any event, the Matsumoto Committee began with the Meiji Constitution and saw itself as simply amending that document in a way that might satisfy the Occupation, without doing too much damage to Constitution. The operating principle of the Committee would leave the Emperor's authority almost unchanged, would make the Cabinet responsible to the Diet, would somewhat expand the Diet's authority and thereby limit the Emperor's law making powers and would make it clear that the rights of the public would not be adversely affected

7 John W. Dower, EMBRACING DEFEAT (W.W. Norton & Company, 1999) 349-351; James L. McClain, JAPAN, A MODERN HISTORY (W.W. Norton & Company, 2002) 537-538. For a discussion of Konoe's conflicting roles pre-Pearl Harbor and later in urging an end to the war, see Andrew Gordon, A MODERN HISTORY OF JAPAN (Oxford University Press, 2003) 216, 223.

8 Theodore McNelly, The Japanese Constitution: Child of the Cold War, 74 Political Science Quarterly 176, 181 (1959).

9 For a discussion of the original effort by Konoe and Sasaki see, Koseki Shoichi, THE BIRTH OF JAPAN'S POSTWAR CONSTITUTION (Edited and translated by Ray A. Moore) (Westview Press, 1997) at 7-20.

10 Hugh Borton, JAPAN'S MODERN CENTURY (The Ronald Press Company, 1955) 401-402; Koseki Shoichi, THE BIRTH OF JAPAN'S POSTWAR CONSTITUTION (Edited and translated by Ray A. Moore) (Westview Press, 1997) at 55; Theodore McNelly, The Japanese Constitution: Child of the Cold War, 74 Political Science Quarterly 176, 182 (1959); Robert E. Ward, The Origins of the Present Japanese Constitution, 50 American Political Science Review 980, 985 (1956).

unless by Diet action.[11] When a draft of the amended Constitution as visualized by the Committee appeared in the press there was a great outpouring of objection from both the Japanese press and the public.[12]

The Occupation similarly objected to the draft. General Whitney sent a memorandum to General MacArthur on February 2, 1946 detailing objections to the Matsumoto Commission's draft as reported in the press. Whitney characterized the draft as "extremely conservative;"[13] noting that it left the Emperor in substantially the same position as the Meiji Constitution. Although that view is questionable as the Matsumoto proposal did increase the authority of the Diet, the reality is that the proposal did little to enhance human rights and limit the power of government through legislative action to suppress the people.[14] While there was debate as to whether the published draft was a Commission draft or simply Matsumoto's own draft, Matsumoto made it clear in a press interview that he did not see any need to change the Emperor's status.[15] (He reiterated this view in 1950 when he indicated that he thought it might be acceptable to leave the Meiji Constitution as it was).[16] It was clear to the Occupation that more drastic action was required.[17] In the three-month period that the Constitution drafting exercise had been on going little was accomplished. The period had however prepared the Japanese public for a dramatically different Constitution. The Emperor also had time to adjust to the necessity for a dramatic change in the status of the Imperial House.

The Occupation was and was to remain an American enterprise. But at the end of 1945 and early in 1946 that did not necessarily appear to be the case. An agreement of December 27, 1945 between the allies called for the creation of a Far

---

11 Koseki Shoichi, THE BIRTH OF JAPAN'S POSTWAR CONSTITUTION (Edited and translated by Ray A. Moore) (Westview Press, 1997) at 57. See pages 57-60 for a comparison of the Matsumoto committees working drafts and the Meiji Constitution.

12 Charles L. Kades, The American Role in Revising Japan's Imperial Constitution, 104 Political Science Quarterly 215, 222 (1989).

13 Charles L. Kades, The American Role in Revising Japan's Imperial Constitution, 104 Political Science Quarterly 215, 222 (1989).

14 See, e.g., Tanaka Hideo, The Conflict Between Two Legal Traditions in Making the Constitution of Japan in Robert E. Ward and Sakamoto Yoshikazu, DEMOCRATIZING JAPAN (University of Hawaii Press, 1987) 111.

15 Memorandum for the Supreme Commander from General Whitney dated 2/2/46 subject: Constitutional Reform (Matsumoto draft) found at Hideo Tanaka, THE JAPANESE LEGAL SYSTEM (University of Tokyo Press, 1976) at 668-669.

16 See quotation of Matsumoto's statement of 11/23/50 in Tanaka Hideo, The Conflict Between Two Legal Traditions in Making the Constitution of Japan in Robert E. Ward and Sakamoto Yoshikazu, DEMOCRATIZING JAPAN (University of Hawaii Press, 1987) 107.

17 This view was not universally shared. For example George Sansom, a Japan expert, was of the view that the Meiji Constitution could be used as a starting point for a new Constitution if the power of the Diet were enhanced, the House of Peers abolished and the Cabinet were made responsible to the Diet. See, Richard B. Finn, WINNERS IN PEACE, MACARTHUR, YOSHIDA, AND POSTWAR JAPAN (University of California Press, 1992) 90.

Eastern Commission of allied powers.[18] While this Commission was to have little effect on the Occupation and modest effect on the Constitution (for example, the provision in the Constitution that Ministers of State must be civilians was inspired by the Commission[19]—this provision raises interesting legal consistency questions as Article 9 prohibits Japan from having a military and thus all persons would have to be civilians), that was unknown at the time. Although General MacArthur was committed to the preservation of the Imperial House,[20] such view was not universally shared and some of the Allies had a different approach. Consequently if MacArthur's vision of a Constitution with preservation of the Emperor was to be realized quick action that would finesse the Far East Commission[21] was required.[22] General MacArthur directed Government Section to prepare a document that could be used by the Japanese Committee as a roadmap for drafting a new Constitution.[23] Government Section was given one week to prepare the document and in that week the Section produced not simply a roadmap but what was to become the actual Constitution (with some revisions made by the Japanese Government).

In delegating this function to General Whitney and Government Section, MacArthur laid down three central principals to be incorporated into the document:

18 For a discussion of the rivalry between the American Occupiers and the FEC see, Robert E. Ward, The Origins of the Present Japanese Constitution, 50 American Political Science Review 980, 987-989, 992 (1956); Hugh Borton, JAPAN'S MODERN CENTURY (The Ronald Press Company, 1955) 403-405, 409-410; William Manchester, AMERICAN CAESAR (Little, Brown and Company, 1978) 499-501.

19 Charles L. Kades, The American Role in Revising Japan's Imperial Constitution, 104 Political Science Quarterly 215, 239-241 (1989); John W. Dower, EMBRACING DEFEAT (W.W. Norton & Company, 1999) 392.

20 See, Theodore McNelly, The Japanese Constitution: Child of the Cold War, 74 Political Science Quarterly 176, 187 (1959) for the position that MacArthur was influenced by the view that without the Emperor the Occupation would need an additional 1,000,000 troops, the Emperor had played a useful role in getting Japan to surrender and had cooperated with the Occupation. See also, Marius B. Jansen, THE MAKING OF MODERN JAPAN (Belknap Press of Harvard University, 2000) 668-669.

21 See, Richard B. Finn, WINNERS IN PEACE, MACARTHUR, YOSHIDA, AND POSTWAR JAPAN (University of California Press, 1992) 89, 92, 93, 101-103; Peter J. Herzog, JAPAN'S PSEUDO-DEMOCRACY (Japan Library, 1993) 24.

22 John W. Dower, EMBRACING DEFEAT (W.W. Norton & Company, 1999) 363; Richard B. Finn, WINNERS IN PEACE, MACARTHUR, YOSHIDA, AND POSTWAR JAPAN (University of California Press, 1992) 94; see also, Herbert Bix, HIROHITO AND THE MAKING OF MODERN JAPAN (Harper Collins 2000) 568. For a discussion of the relationship between the FEC and the Far Eastern Advisory Commission and the drafting of the Constitution see, Charles L. Kades, The American Role in Revising Japan's Imperial Constitution, 104 Political Science Quarterly 215, 217-218, 220-222 (1989).

23 Theodore McNelly, The Japanese Constitution: Child of the Cold War, 74 Political Science Quarterly 176, 184-185 (1959); Robert E. Ward, The Origins of the Present Japanese Constitution, 50 American Political Science Review 980, 986 (1956); Richard B. Finn, WINNERS IN PEACE, MACARTHUR, YOSHIDA, AND POSTWAR JAPAN (University of California Press, 1992) 93; Charles L. Kades, The American Role in Revising Japan's Imperial Constitution, 104 Political Science Quarterly 215, 223 (1989).

1) the Imperial House was to be retained as a hereditary institution but it was to be a hollow institution in that it was to have no power; 2) Japan was to be demilitarized, without a military capacity for either defensive or offensive purposes; 3) the Japanese feudal system was to be abolished and the government was to have a budgetary system similar to that of Great Britain.[24] This third principle is interesting in that Tokugawa feudalism had been abolished during the Meiji regime when the Daimyo domains (Han) were abolished, prefectures established and old ties of vassalage had been done away with. On the other hand, the feudal family system had been retained (albeit modified through the Civil Code's recognition of private property rights as distinguished from property ownership by the House) and a noble class modeled after the British nobility with Princes, Viscounts, etc. had been created by the Meiji reformers when creating the House of Peers. These titles of nobility were to be abolished.[25]

Previously the State Department in Washington had given instructions concerning a new Constitution for Japan. Under these instructions the Emperor system could remain but in such case the power of the Emperor would have to be severely limited. Moreover, the new government structure should be without ancillary bodies such as the Privy Council and no House of Peers would be allowed to have veto power over legislation. A Cabinet responsible to the Diet would be the executive. The government would be responsible to the public acting through broad suffrage. The special relationship between the military and the Emperor was to be abolished and any Minister for the military would have to be a civilian.[26]

General Whitney turned the drafting process over to a Committee headed by Colonel Charles K. Kades. Although Whitney was a conservative Republican, Kades was a New Deal reformer. The draft prepared by the Committee had a definite New Deal slant. The Committee gathered and studied Constitutions from many countries (and also studied the Meiji Constitution) as well as drafts prepared in Japan by political parties and other groups. Nonetheless there is little question but that as Ito had been guided by the Prussian Constitution and German constitutional theory, Kades and his committee were guided by the United States Consti-

---

24 Koseki Shoichi, THE BIRTH OF JAPAN'S POSTWAR CONSTITUTION (Edited and translated by Ray A. Moore) (Westview Press, 1997) at 79; Charles L. Kades, The American Role in Revising Japan's Imperial Constitution, 104 Political Science Quarterly 215, 223-224 (1989) setting out General Whitney's note of the conversation with General MacArthur and the three principles; see also, Marius B. Jansen, THE MAKING OF MODERN JAPAN (Belknap Press of Harvard University, 2000) 683-684; Peter J. Herzog, JAPAN'S PSEUDO-DEMOCRACY (Japan Library, 1993) 24.

25 Instructions given to General MacArthur from Washington called for changing the government structure to do away with its feudal tendencies. See, Alfred C. Oppler, LEGAL REFORM IN OCCUPIED JAPAN (Princeton University Press, 1976).

26 Theodore McNelly, The Japanese Constitution: Child of the Cold War, 74 Political Science Quarterly 176, 179 (1959). Note that this instruction from the State Department contemplated that a Japanese Military might be permitted at a future date. For further support for the idea that the State Department anticipated that Japan might rearm in the future see, Robert E. Ward, The Origins of the Present Japanese Constitution, 50 American Political Science Review 980, 990 (1956).

tution (and various American laws), the British form of government and common law theory. The Committee was relatively small, contained no "old Japan hands" and had no constitutional law experts among its members.[27] In six days it prepared what is in substance the present Constitution of Japan.[28] Although the Shidehara government was not happy with the American draft, it was afraid that failure to accept the basic document given to them could lead to a more radical document including abolition of the Imperial House and perhaps even trial of the Emperor as a war criminal. When the draft Constitution was submitted to the Diet by the Emperor on November 3, 1946 the government accepted the draft with some changes made by the Diet and agreed to by the Occupation. The Constitution as finally agreed to in translation was translated into every day Japanese and not the more formal language previously used for laws and other official documents.[29]

The drafting committee had adopted the form and structure of the Meiji Constitution even to the point of retaining some of the chapter headings. They had however removed the text of the document and replaced it with their own text. Since the form and structure remained (with Chapter 1 for example devoted to the Emperor and Chapter 3 to Rights and Duties of the People (previously Chapter 2 Rights and Duties of Subjects—a new Chapter 2 dealt with Renunciation of War)), the new Constitution could be presented to the Diet as an Amendment to the Meiji Constitution. However this raised an issue of constitutional law under the then existing Meiji Constitution. How should the amendment be presented? The Meiji Constitution provided that a project to amend should be submitted by the Emperor to the Diet which then debated the matter and could by a 2/3 vote pass the amendment. But the Constitution made no provision for modifications or amendments to be made during the debate. Could the Diet amend the proposed Constitution or was it required to either reject or accept? The Occupation concluded that after the Emperor submitted the draft to the Diet (as he did),[30] the Diet had the right to amend it (as it did in some ways but not in fundamental ways or in ways that the Occupation did not agree to) before acceptance.[31]

The United States Constitution has no explicit clause stating wherein the sovereignty resides. It does have a Supremacy clause making the Federal Constitution,

---

27 For a description of the members of the Committee see, Charles L. Kades, The American Role in Revising Japan's Imperial Constitution, 104 Political Science Quarterly 215, 225-226 (1989).

28 For a first hand account of the activities of the Constitution drafting committee and the Japanese role in the adoption of the Constitution see, Charles L. Kades, The American Role in Revising Japan's Imperial Constitution, 104 Political Science Quarterly 215 (1989).

29 Koseki Shoichi, THE BIRTH OF JAPAN'S POSTWAR CONSTITUTION (Edited and translated by Ray A. Moore) (Westview Press, 1997) at 133; Robert E. Ward, The Origins of the Present Japanese Constitution, 50 American Political Science Review 980, 1003-1004 (1956); Marius B. Jansen, THE MAKING OF MODERN JAPAN (Belknap Press of Harvard University, 2000) 671; Richard B. Finn, WINNERS IN PEACE, MACARTHUR, YOSHIDA, AND POSTWAR JAPAN (University of California Press, 1992) 115.

30 John W. Dower, EMBRACING DEFEAT (W.W. Norton & Company, 1999) 387-388.

31 Alfred C. Oppler, LEGAL REFORM IN OCCUPIED JAPAN (Princeton University Press, 1976) 50.

Treaties entered into by the Federal Government and Federal Laws Supreme to State laws. The sovereign States have certain powers that are reserved and the Bill of Rights refers to the fact that rights are reserved to the people. Through the use of juries in criminal cases the power of the government (at all levels) to take away freedom is limited to action that has the consent of a unanimous cross section of the public. While no specific clause sets out where the ultimate sovereignty lies it seems clear that the people are the ultimate source of government power and hence of the sovereignty that government may exercise.

Because of the Meiji Constitution's placement of sovereignty in the Imperial House and the constitutional debates about that sovereignty and the entire *kokutai* debate and issue, the Constitution of Japan places sovereignty in the Japanese people. The people in turn, through universal adult suffrage[32] elect public officials. As was true of the Meiji translators' difficulties in translating the French Codes into Japanese because there were no Japanese words to encompass such legal concepts as rights as understood in the Western Codes, so too translation became an issue during the Constitution writing process. The Japanese draft translation had used the word "*shiko*" for sovereignty but such term although it might technically be used did not carry out the idea of the American draft. Eventually the term "*shuken*" was adopted. Similarly, when moving from the Meiji Constitution's reference to the Japanese as subjects to the new Constitution's use of the term "people," conflicts in translation arose. Eventually "*kokumin*" was settled on.[33] This change has affected constitutional interpretation restricting many rights granted to the people to Japanese nationals and thus excluding Koreans[34] who have resided in Japan for generations.[35]

Whereas the Meiji Constitution had been Emperor centered, the new Constitution was Diet centered. The elected Diet is to be the "highest organ of state power;" thereby displacing the Emperor from this role, and as is the case with the United States Congress it is to have the sole law making power of the central

---

32 Constitution of Japan, Article 15 (3) provides for universal adult suffrage in connection with election of public officials. This same article provides that the people have the "inalienable right" to dismiss as well as select their public officials.

33 John W. Dower, EMBRACING DEFEAT (W.W. Norton & Company, 1999) 381-382, 389; see also Koseki Shoichi, THE BIRTH OF JAPAN'S POSTWAR CONSTITUTION (Edited and translated by Ray A. Moore) (Westview Press, 1997) at 121-122, 179-181.

34 John W. Dower, EMBRACING DEFEAT (W.W. Norton & Company, 1999) 393-394; Richard B. Finn, WINNERS IN PEACE, MACARTHUR, YOSHIDA, AND POSTWAR JAPAN (University of California Press, 1992) 117.

35 For example, the English language version of the Constitution provides in Article 14 (1) that all of the people are equal under the law. However, Korean nationals residing permanently in Japan (and having done so for generations) are subjected to different requirements than Japanese citizens in many respects. See, e.g., Carl F. Goodman, THE RULE OF LAW IN JAPAN: A COMPARATIVE ANALYSIS (Kluwer Law International, 2003) 76-82; Koseki Shoichi, THE BIRTH OF JAPAN'S POSTWAR CONSTITUTION (Edited and translated by Ray A. Moore) (Westview Press, 1997) 180; Marius B. Jansen, THE MAKING OF MODERN JAPAN (Belknap Press of Harvard University, 2000) 685.

government.[36] The American draft proposed a one-house legislature but this was changed to a bicameral body at the request of the Japanese[37] but both houses needed to be popularly elected.[38] Question has been raised as to whether the phrase "highest organ of the State" grants the Diet powers beyond those specifically provided for in the Constitution and whether it establishes a hierarchy in the separation of powers that the Constitution is designed to create.[39] If it is the "highest organ" does that mean it is higher than the Supreme Court and if so what does being higher mean? It is suggested that the wording was designed to show that the Diet not the Emperor was the repository of the powers of government that were not delegated by the Constitution to other branches and not that the Diet is superior to any other branch. Indeed, a finding that the Diet is superior would be contrary to the grant of Judicial Review power to the courts in Article 81. By granting the courts the authority to review the constitutionality of legislative enactments the Constitution makes it clear that the court is not subordinate to the Diet. Further, although the Diet is the highest organ of State power, the reality is that a committee of several hundred cannot effectively operate a government. It is unlikely that the term highest organ means that the Diet is to dominate political life. That more properly is to be expected of the executive arm, the Cabinet—although the Diet has ultimate authority through its power to vote no confidence in the Cabinet and its authority to appoint the Prime Minister.[40]

The phrase that the Diet "shall be the sole law-making organ of the State" has also raised questions. The Supreme Court is given authority to adopt rules of procedure and practice and also has authority to promulgate rules "relating to attorneys" as well as prosecutors. Further the court can prescribe rules for internal court discipline and administration. Does this conflict with the law making power of the Diet? During the American Occupation, the Occupation took the position that such rule-making power was subordinate to the Diet's authority to make laws and accordingly that the court did not have the power to enact a new Code of Civil Procedure although it could fill in blanks with rules of procedure that were

36 Constitution of Japan, Article 41.

37 Marius B. Jansen, THE MAKING OF MODERN JAPAN (Belknap Press of Harvard University, 2000) 685.

38 Richard B. Finn, WINNERS IN PEACE, MACARTHUR, YOSHIDA, AND POSTWAR JAPAN (University of California Press, 1992) 100.

39 See, Alfred C. Oppler, LEGAL REFORM IN OCCUPIED JAPAN (Princeton University Press, 1976) 88.

40 For an interesting discussion of "highest organ of State power' see, John W. Maki, The Japanese Constitutional Style in Dan Fenno Henderson, THE CONSTITUTION OF JAPAN: ITS FIRST TWENTY YEARS 1947-1967 (University of Washington Press, 1969) 20-23; see also, Yosiyuki Noda, INTRODUCTION TO JAPANESE LAW (translated and edited by Anthony H. Angelo) (University of Tokyo Press, 1976) 119 recognizing the conflict between having the Diet as the supreme organ of the State and the Judicial Branch having the power of Judicial Review to declare laws made by the supreme organ invalid/unconstitutional.

consistent with and amplified the Code.[41] The extent of the Supreme Court's rule-making power may be subject to question but as the court is the final arbiter of what is permitted the issue is unlikely to be a serious question in litigation. The Supreme Court exercises its rule-making power through the "Judicial Assembly," which is composed of all 14 Supreme Court Justices and the Chief Justice of the Supreme Court.[42] Local governments also have a rule-making authority and the Cabinet may issue Cabinet orders. These forms of "law making" are not inconsistent with the Diet's authority as all such rules and Ordinances and Orders must conform to statutory provisions of laws made by the Diet.[43]

Sovereignty, which previously had resided in the Emperor, was specifically recognized as residing with the people.[44] Moreover, although the Imperial House was to remain dynastic and subject to the Imperial House Law, this new Imperial House Law was to be enacted by the Diet.[45] This was a sharp break with the Imperial House Law of the Meiji Constitution, which had been "extra constitutional"—created by and could only be modified by the Emperor.[46] Where there was a function given to the Emperor, the Constitution made it clear that the Cabinet was not only to advise the Emperor but was to be responsible for the Imperial act and further that the Emperor had no discretion but must follow the Cabinet's advice. Whereas

---

41 See, Alfred C. Oppler, LEGAL REFORM IN OCCUPIED JAPAN (Princeton University Press, 1976) 100-101.

42 Court Organization Law Article 12.

43 See, Hideo Tanaka, THE JAPANESE LEGAL SYSTEM (University of Tokyo Press, 1976) 37-38.

44 Constitution of Japan, Article 41. A sad side light of the constitutional debate is that Tatsukishi Minobe, who had been forced to resign from Tokyo University and had been persecuted during the prewar and wartime period because of his organ theory of the role of the Emperor—which theory was rejected in this period in favor of Yatsuka Hozumi's more conservative Emperor theory—argued publicly against the need to drastically change the Meiji Constitution. James L. McClain, JAPAN, A MODERN HISTORY (W.W. Norton & Company, 2002) 269-270; John W. Dower, EMBRACING DEFEAT (W.W. Norton & Company, 1999) 355; Herbert Bix, HIROHITO AND THE MAKING OF MODERN JAPAN (Harper Collins 2000) 576. It is interesting to speculate whether Minobe's position was influenced by a lack of appreciation in prewar Japanese legal circles of the importance of human rights in constitutional government. Cf., Tanaka Hideo, The Conflict Between Two Legal Traditions in Making the Constitution of Japan in Robert E. Ward and Sakamoto Yoshikazu, DEMOCRATIZING JAPAN (University of Hawaii Press, 1987) 114-116.

45 An Imperial House Law was enacted by the Diet in 1947 and followed closely (with deletions and modifications to take account of the new Constitution) the Meiji era law. Although similar to the old law the important difference was that this law was enacted by an elected legislature and could be changed by the legislature. Indeed, legislative change may be required as the law requires descent of the throne to male heirs and the present Emperor has no male grandchildren.

46 The difference between a representative democratically elected Diet passed Imperial House Law and the Meiji law was apparent to the American drafters and was a source of disagreement between the American drafting committee and the Japanese. See, Koseki Shoichi, THE BIRTH OF JAPAN'S POSTWAR CONSTITUTION (Edited and translated by Ray A. Moore) (Westview Press, 1997) at 113; see also Tanaka Hideo, The Conflict Between Two Legal Traditions in Making the Constitution of Japan in Robert E. Ward and Sakamoto Yoshikazu, DEMOCRATIZING JAPAN (University of Hawaii Press, 1987) 122 for an exchange of views between Matsumoto and representatives of the Occupation concerning the Imperial House Law and the necessity for Diet enactment.

the Meiji Constitution made the Imperial House's finances a matter totally outside the budget and other authority of the Diet, the new Constitution even forbade the Emperor from receiving gifts unless he received approval from the Diet.[47] While a figurehead and a "symbol of the State," the Emperor was removed from the actual functioning of the government (except to the extent that his position might give him some moral authority and perhaps might influence political leaders, a matter that cannot be dealt with in a Constitution that permits an Imperial institution).[48]

Although the American draft had provided for a one-house legislative body, the Diet wished to retain the two-house structure of the Meiji Constitution. The Occupation agreed to a two-house structure[49] but required that the Upper House (House of Councilors) be popularly elected on geographic and population considerations rather than a class-based or labor/management-based system as suggested by the Japanese.[50] Although a two-House structure was retained, the power of the houses is not the same. Thus, the Lower House, the House of Representatives, is far more important than the Upper House. It is the Lower House that appoints the Prime Minister (the Upper House is given a time-limited chance to approve the Lower House's choice but in the event of refusal to act or to agree the Lower House choice is appointed[51]—the same arrangement applies to the budget). Although the Upper House can reject a bill passed by the Lower House, the Lower House has the power to override an Upper House veto by a 2/3 super majority vote. Although the Upper House gets to vote on treaties, the Lower House can override an Upper House rejection by a simple majority vote.[52] The Diet is also a check on the independent judiciary through the provision allowing the establishment of an Impeachment Court to try impeachments against members of the judiciary.[53] Echoing the United States Constitution, members are not liable for statements made on the floor of the House[54] and each House is the judge of the qualifications of members.[55]

---

47 Constitution of Japan, Articles 2-8.

48 The Matsumoto Commission's draft Constitution would have changed the provisions dealing with the Emperor by changing the word sacred to supreme. Thus the Emperor would be recognized as "supreme and inviolable" rather than sacred and inviolable. Sovereignty would continue to reside in the Emperor. See, 2/12/46 Memorandum for Chief, Government Section, comment 1 found at Hideo Tanaka, THE JAPANESE LEGAL SYSTEM (University of Tokyo Press, 1976) at 670.

49 John W. Dower, EMBRACING DEFEAT (W.W. Norton & Company, 1999) 378; Robert E. Ward, The Origins of the Present Japanese Constitution, 50 American Political Science Review 980, 1001-1002 (1956).

50 Robert E. Ward, The Origins of the Present Japanese Constitution, 50 American Political Science Review 980, 1007 (1956); Yasuhiro Okudaira, Forty Years of the Constitution and its Various Influences: Japanese, American, and European in JAPANESE CONSTITUTIONAL LAW (Percy R. Luney, Jr. and Kazuyuki Takanashi Ed., University of Tokyo Press, 1993) 1, 7.

51 Constitution of Japan, Article 67(2).

52 Constitution of Japan, Articles 59, 60 and 61.

53 Constitution of Japan, Article 64.

54 Constitution of Japan, Article 51.

55 Constitution of Japan, Article 55.

The Constitution provides that there must be an ordinary session of the Diet each year and grants the Cabinet the authority to call additional meetings. In addition, members of either House can cause an extraordinary session to be held when 25% of the members of either House make such a request.[56] The only provision in the Constitution dealing with authority to dissolve the House of Representatives is Article 69 giving the Cabinet, after a vote of no confidence or rejection of a vote of confidence, the authority to dissolve the House of Representatives. Article 7 requires the Emperor to dissolve the House of Representatives when he receives the advice and approval of the Cabinet to do so. This formulation of the dissolution authority raises an interesting constitutional question. Namely, is the Cabinet's authority to advise and approve the dissolution of the House limited to situations in which there has been a vote of no confidence or rejection of a confidence motion? May the Cabinet on its own act to dissolve the House or can such action only follow House action rejecting the government?[57] This issue arose early in the new Constitution's history. In 1948 the Prime Minister indicated that he would request that the Emperor dissolve the House. The opposition parties not wanting to face a general election argued that the Cabinet lacked such power and that the House could not be dissolved without a rejection of the Cabinet. The matter was resolved when the House voted a no confidence motion and the Cabinet had the Emperor dissolve the House. But the issue did not go away. In 1951 it resurfaced when, as a consequence of public debate of Peace Treaty issues the government dissolved the House and a minority party member sued. The issue for the court was whether the dissolution was valid. However, before reaching that question the court was required to consider whether it had jurisdiction over the matter.

The new Japanese Constitution had given the Supreme Court the power of judicial review that applies to the United States Supreme Court.[58] Thus, the court has authority to declare actions of both the Legislative and Executive Branches unconstitutional when those actions are inconsistent with the Constitution. However, common law concepts of jurisdiction also require that before a court may act there must be both a real controversy between adverse parties[59] and the matter should not be one that the court in exercising its discretionary powers considers to be a political as distinguished from a legal question. Both the case or controversy (real controversy between adversary parties) and political question doctrines are well

---

56 Constitution of Japan, Article 52 and 53.

57 Professor Tanaka takes the position that the Cabinet was given authority to dissolve the House of Representatives whenever it desires to do so. See, Hideo Tanaka, THE JAPANESE LEGAL SYSTEM (University of Tokyo Press, 1976) 41.

58 See, Yasuhiro Okudaira, Forty Years of the Constitution and its Various Influences: Japanese, American, and European in JAPANESE CONSTITUTIONAL LAW (Percy R. Luney, Jr. and Kazuyuki Takanashi Ed., University of Tokyo Press, 1993) 1, 16-25 see especially 23-25 for views on "judicial negativism" in Japan.

59 The Japanese Supreme Court adopted this same case or controversy requirement for its jurisdiction in Case No. 1952 (Ma) No. 323 (Sup. Ct. Grand Bench, 10/8/52), 6 Minshu 783, available in English on the Web through the web site of the Supreme Court of Japan, Judgments of the Supreme Court.

established in United States law. In dealing with the dissolution of the House the court held that the political question doctrine applied in Japanese constitutional law and found that the action of the Cabinet in dissolving the House was a political question outside the court's authority.[60]

1) Representative Democracy and Equality of the Power of Each Vote

The Constitution has as its objective the creation of a representative democracy and for that purpose it provides for universal adult suffrage. At the same time the Constitution gives the Diet the authority to pass election laws that establish electoral districts. These ideas of truly representative government and legislative authority to determine election districts can create conflicts when, for example, electoral districts are drawn in such a way as to deprive citizens of the effective right to vote. This conflict has resulted in substantial litigation over the recent years. It should first be recognized that when the Constitution was adopted, such cases if brought in the United States would have been considered as outside the court's authority. It was only in the 1960s when the United States Supreme Court decided *Baker v. Carr*[61] and *Reynolds v. Sims*[62] that a one-person, one-vote rule became part of American law.

In Japan the dominant political party since the end of the war has been the Liberal Democratic Party (a coalition party of the former Liberal Party and the former Democratic Party). The LDP has its base of support in the rural districts of Japan. But since the end of the war Japan has become an urban society with a significant migration from rural areas to the big cities. Nonetheless the LDP-dominated Diet has either left in place early districting that favored farm areas or drawn election districts so as to favor rural districts and so as to give rural districts more representatives than city districts with the same number of voters.[63] Relying on general ideas of democratic fairness as well as the provision in Article 14 of the Constitution that "all of the people are equal under the law", city dwellers sued arguing that the electoral districts by favoring less populous rural districts deprive them of equal rights. Since the Japanese Constitution has "American roots" the theory of *Baker* and *Reynolds* was brought to the attention of the Japanese Supreme Court.

Following the *Baker* and *Reynolds* logic, and giving the language of Article 14 a broad interpretation so that the equality clause was not limited to the specific cate-

---

60 For a discussion of the case see, Alfred C. Oppler, LEGAL REFORM IN OCCUPIED JAPAN (Princeton University Press, 1976) 57 - 58; See also, Case No. 1955 (O) No. 96 (Sup. Ct. Grand Bench, 6/8/55) available on the web on the web site of the Supreme Court of Japan, Judgments of the Supreme Court, holding that the dissolution of the House of Representatives is outside the jurisdiction of the court; see also, Kisaburo Yokota, Political Questions and Judicial Review: A Comparison in Dan Fenno Henderson, THE CONSTITUTION OF JAPAN: ITS FIRST TWENTY YEARS 1947-1967 (University of Washington Press, 1969) 152-154.

61 369 U.S. 186 (1962).

62 377 U.S. 533 (1964).

63 See, Hideo Tanaka, THE JAPANESE LEGAL SYSTEM (University of Tokyo Press, 1976) 39-40.

gories set out in the clause,[64] the Supreme Court of Japan applied Article 14 to political districting. However, the court did not apply the same test as the United States Supreme Court had used in *Reynolds*. Whereas *Reynolds* had required that the districting plan come as close as possible to a one-person, one-vote identity of voting strength (a disparity of 1 to 2.92 would be unconstitutional in the United States), the Supreme Court of Japan permitted a disparity of 1 to 4.09. In other words, although the vote of a voter in the least populous district was four times as valuable as the vote of a voter in the most populous district the court found such difference to be constitutionally acceptable and not a constitutional inequality.[65] Although the *Koshiyama* case was decided against the urban voters, the court had opened the door to voter districting litigation by finding that the question of voter discrimination was NOT a political question (which would have placed it outside the judicial sphere). The court also indicated that Article 14 was applicable to voter discrimination complaints.

Ten years after the *Koshiyama* decision the Supreme Court held that the election for the Lower House held in 1972 was based on constitutionally impermissible election districts. In *Kurokawa v. Chiba Election Commission*[66] the disparity in voting power was 1 to 4.99. This disparity was found to exceed the discretion given to the Diet under Article 47 to set electoral districts. Although the plaintiffs were successful as a substantive matter, the reality of Japanese procedure was that they could not get the relief they wanted. Obviously the plaintiffs wished to have the same or at least similar voting strength as the least populous district and in the United States a court confronted with this issue would have issued an order giving plaintiffs some form of relief. The Supreme Court of Japan however found that to give plaintiffs relief as it related to the unlawfully held election would be harmful to the public in general and thus the court refused to overturn the election results or order the holding of a new election. The court did not discuss the question of whether allowing unconstitutionally elected public officials to serve in the Lower House for several years before a new election would be held was harmful to the public. Nor did the court take effective action to assure that in any new election the disparity would be corrected. In short, the plaintiffs had won a substantive vic-

64 Article 14 in addition to stating that all people are equal under the law prohibits discrimination in "political . . . relations because of race, creed, sex, social status or family origin." In the political district apportionment cases the court applied Article 14 although the discrimination in voting power was not based on any of these categories. The court did so finding that the discrimination was of the equality provision. The Supreme Court had previously given Article 14 a broad interpretation in the Hiroshima Pharmacy case, Sumiyoshi v. Governor of Hiroshima, 29 Minshu 572, Case No. 1968 (Gyo-Tsu) No. 120 (Sup. Ct. Grand Bench, 4/30/75) available on the web in English through the web site of the Supreme Court of Japan, Judgments of the Supreme Court, also in Lawrence W. Beer & Hiroshi Itoh, THE CONSTITUTIONAL CASE LAW OF JAPAN, 1970-1990 (University of Washington Press, 1996) at 188.

65 Koshiyama v. Tokyo Metropolitan Election Commission, 18 Minshu 270 (Sup. Ct. 2/5/64).

66 30 Minshu 223, case No. 1974 (Gyo-Tsu) No. 75 (Sup. Ct. Grand Bench, 4/30/76) available on the web in English through the web site of the Supreme Court of Japan, Judgments of the Supreme Court, also in Lawrence W. Beer & Hiroshi Itoh, THE CONSTITUTIONAL CASE LAW OF JAPAN, 1970-1990 (University of Washington Press, 1996) at 355.

tory but had nothing to show for it but the opinion of the court. The dominant political party had won an election victory where its majority position was arguably augmented or even obtained as a result of its own actions in establishing electoral districts that favored its candidates. Rather than grant relief, the court sent the matter to the (unlawfully elected) Diet to correct the matter by the time of the next election.

A close examination of the grounds for the court's refusal to grant the plaintiffs real relief is in order. First the court considered whether the unconstitutionality of the districting plan meant that the districting law was void *ab initio*. There was a strong textual argument for such a result as Article 98 of the Constitution provides, in part, that no law or other act of government contrary to the Constitution "shall have legal force or validity." Nonetheless the court concluded that the districting law did have force and validity in that the election held thereunder was controlling and the Diet elected in accordance therewith would sit for its entire term. This conclusion was "obvious" to the court because it saw only two alternatives available to it: a) the law was void *ab initio* and thus there was no lawfully seated Diet—and indeed no Diet to then enact a new law and also all acts already taken by the Diet would have to be declared illegal and of no effect—an event that was not contemplated by the Constitution nor in the best interests of the public; or b) allowing the unlawfully elected Diet to sit for its full term. No consideration was given to some middle measure, such as a requirement that the Diet remedy the situation within a limited period of time and that a new election under a lawful districting plan be held at that time. Indeed, the court could have ruled that the election was unconstitutional and that a new election was required but could have stayed the effective date of its order for a period of time to permit the Diet to enact a new constitutional election law.

The court also rejected the idea that it could set aside the election in the less populous district that was targeted in the suit on the ground that if it did so *and* if suit were brought in each district then the end result would be that all elections would be upset. This would lead to the same result that the court had earlier rejected in setting aside the entire election. But, of course, a) there are many election districts where the value of a vote was not distorted—the number of which was unknown to the court—and, there was no challenge in each district so that the problem envisioned by the Court was not presented.[67] Should such a problem arise in future cases, the court could deal with it in such cases. Setting aside the election in the district targeted would at least have deprived the majority party (responsible for the unlawful apportionment) of the seats in that district.

To buttress its argument that the Diet should be allowed to sit, the court reasoned from analogy based on Article 31 of the Administrative Case Litigation Law [ACLL]. The ACLL is a general statute dealing with actions to review an administrative determination. It is similar to a grant of jurisdiction for judicial review of a

67 This point could hardly have been lost on the majority, as it was a basis for the dissenting opinion of five Justices.

decision of an administrative agency in the United States.[68] The ACLL provides in part that a court may, after finding that the agency disposition is in violation of the law nonetheless permit the disposition to remain when reversal would be against the public interest.[69] For example, where an administrative agency improperly concluded that land could be expropriated to construct a dam and after the dam's construction it was determined that the agency acted improperly the court could allow the dam to remain in place because a determination to tear down the dam could have devastating affects on people living downstream from the dam.[70] Such a "circumstance decision" (i.e., because of the circumstances the court permits the result of the improper agency action to stand) may be viewed as similar to the refusal of a court of equity in the common law system to grant injunctive relief because of the harm that relief would cause to other persons. In any event, the ACLL is not directed toward resolution of matters such as an unlawfully held election, and indeed the Election Law specifically provides that it is not subject to Article 31 the ACLL. The majority appears to recognize that Article 31 of the ACLL is not applicable to the case but it nonetheless utilizes Article 31 to conclude that it is appropriate to enter a "circumstance decision" in the circumstances of this case.[71]

In 1977 there was another election for seats in the Upper House. Again a challenge was brought to the districting plan on the grounds that the difference in voting power was in excess of the constitutional limit in that in Osaka-fu vs. Kanagawa-ken the difference was 5.26 to 1.[72] The court recognized that the right to elect Councilors[73] was a fundamental right and that Article 14 of the Constitution makes relative equality in the power of each vote a constitutional imperative. But the court noted that the Constitution left the issue of establishing election districts to the Diet and that equality in the power of each vote was not the only factor in determining election districts. The Diet could consider other factors in establishing voting districts. The court noted that because the House of Councilors and the House of Representatives each has somewhat different powers and their districts are apportioned differently, the rules regarding voting power for the Houses might be different to take into account the factors other than mere numerical parity. For example, in the Upper House of Councilors each prefecture may be apportioned at least two seats and this throws off the ratio consideration. How to

---

68 The ACLL is discussed at length in Chapter 12.

69 ACLL Article 31.

70 See, e.g., Kayano v. Hokkaido Expropriation Committee (Nibutani Dam Case), 1598 Hanrei Jiho 33, 938 Hanrei Taimuzu 75, Sapporo District Court 3/27/97. For an English language version, see, 38 International Legal Materials 394.

71 All of the dissenting and dissenting in part and concurring in part opinions recognize that Article 31 is not applicable.

72 Ken is the name given to the prefectures in Japan. Thus Kanagawa prefecture is Kanagawa ken. Tokyo is referred to as Tokyo "to" and Osaka as Osaka "fu." The "to" and "fu" have similar status to the ken.

73 Members of the Upper House are called Councilors.

deal with population changes when it comes to redistricting in the Upper House is a matter for the Diet and not for the court as long as the disparity is not so great as to rise to a constitutional level. The court found that the disparity was not unconstitutional.[74]

Although the plaintiffs in *Kurokawa* did not win in the sense that the election result in the challenged district, nor in any district, was over turned, the decision in the case required that the Diet take action to correct the disparity. Redistricting in Japan is no less politically charged than redistricting in the United States. Thus, it was to be expected that the Diet would not adopt a radical change in districts and would not drastically change the balance of power in the Diet between the LDP and the minority parties. Nonetheless the Diet did act to conform to the court's determination that gross disparities in voting power were in violation of the Constitution.

In December of 1983 there was an election for the Lower House (the House of Representatives). At the time of the election, the ratio of voting power of the smallest and largest election districts were 1 to 4.40. Voters in 21 election districts sought nullification of the election on the grounds that the districting was unconstitutional and hence the election results were unconstitutional. The Court again followed its rule that under Article 14 the right to vote included an equality element but that numbers alone were not the sole factor that the Diet could use in determining election districts.[75] While numbers alone are not decisive, when the disparity is so large as to be unreasonable even when other factors are considered, the districting is unconstitutional and exceeds the Diet's discretion. The Court recognized that because of population movement the Diet might set a districting plan that was constitutional but that such plan might become unconstitutional if the Diet failed to act to correct the plan in light of population shift. In this case the

74 Case no. 1979 (Gyo-Tsu) No. 65 (Sup. Ct. Grand Bench, 4/27/83) available on the web in English through the web site of the Supreme Court of Japan. The American Occupation had wanted to do away with the Upper House and agreed to the Japanese request for a two House legislature on condition that members of the Upper House be popularly elected. In the United States the Upper House—the Senate—is popularly elected (although under the Constitution as adopted its members were appointed by the States, popular election was a result of amendment to the Constitution) but as each State is entitled to two Senators regardless of State population there exists a great disparity between the votes of voters in small and large States. Such disparity is constitutional because the Constitution specifically recognizes it as part of the Great Compromise required to get the smaller States to agree to the Constitution and join the Federal Government being created to supersede the Articles of Confederation system. The United States Senate thus represents regions and regional differences as well as population. The original idea of the Japanese "negotiators" may have been to have an Upper House to represent different classes of society but that idea was repugnant to the Occupation. Just as the United States has a "geographic history" (North vs. South) so too does Japan (East vs. West). In such circumstance a geographic representation in the Upper House should not strike American lawyers or theorists as unreasonable or unconstitutional.

75 In the United States numbers alone are decisive for the members of the House of Representatives elected in each State. Of course as each State is entitled to at least one Representative in the House of Representatives there may be a great disparity in very small State votes and other State votes.

election was held under a districting plan that was amended in 1975 and which reduced the disparity in voting power from 1 to 4.83 to 1 to 2.92. In the intervening years the voting disparity increased to 1 to 3.94 for the 1980 election and then to 1 to 4.40 for the election at issue. This 1 to 4.40 disparity was found to be unconstitutional in a House of Representatives election. Moreover, the disparity of 1 to 3.94 in 1980 was also unconstitutional. While the 1 to 2.92 disparity was permissible, the Court found that the Diet had time to make appropriate correction once the disparity widened to an unconstitutional point and the failure of the Diet to act made the election at issue unconstitutional. Once again, however, the Court applied the principle of the circumstance decision as found in Article 31 of the ACLL and although the plaintiffs were correct that the election was unconstitutional they were granted no relief and the unlawfully elected House of Representatives was allowed to serve its term.[76]

In 1985 a national census was held in Japan. Using that census as its guide, the Diet in 1986 amended the election law to provide for more equitable election districts. The voter disparity was 1 to 2.99. The 1986 districts were used for a 1986 election and at that election the voter disparity had dropped to 1 to 2.92. In 1990 there was a general election for members of the House of Representatives. The 1986 election districts were again used for this election but the voter disparity had increased to 1 to 3.18. The court upheld its previous jurisprudence but found that this disparity, even taking into account other factors that could properly be considered by the Diet, was so large as to be unconstitutional. Because the Diet had acted (in 1986) to correct the disparity in votes and because it was impossible for the Diet to know that there would be so large an increase in voter disparity and because the Diet could not be expected to continually change the election district law, the court found that although the disparity was not consistent with the Constitution there was no violation of the law.[77]

In 1992 there was an election for House of Councilors. Notwithstanding that the disparity in voting ratio was 1 to 6.59, a ratio that the court categorized as "significant inequality," the court refused to hold the election unconstitutional.[78]

In 1994 the Diet enacted a significant election reform law. The Lower House (Representatives) was reconstituted as having 500 members of whom 300 were to be elected in entirely new small single seat districts. Previously members were elected from mid-sized constituencies wherein several members were elected. The

76 Kaneo v. Hiroshima Prefecture Election Commission, 39 Minshu 1100, Case No. 1984 (Gyo-Tsu) No. 339 (Sup. Ct. Grand Bench, 7/17/85), available on the web in English through the web site of the Supreme Court of Japan; also in Lawrence W. Beer & Hiroshi Itoh, THE CONSTITUTIONAL CASE LAW OF JAPAN, 1970-1990 (University of Washington Press, 1996) at 394.

77 Kawahara v. Tokyo Prefecture Election Administration Commission, 47 Minshu 67 (Sup. Ct. Grand Bench, 1/20/93) Case No. 111 of 1991), available on the web in English through the web site of the Supreme Court of Japan.

78 Case No. 1994 (Gyo-Tsu) No. 59 (Sup. Ct. Grand Bench, 9/11/96), available on the web in English through the web site of the Supreme Court of Japan.

new single seat constituencies more closely resemble an American styled election district where members of the House of Representatives are elected from single seat districts. The former system more closely resembled some city or county elections where several at large members were elected on a county or citywide basis or where all candidates ran citywide and the candidates with the highest number of votes were elected. In addition to these 300 single seat districts, another 200 seats were allocated on a proportional representative basis. Voters cast two ballots, one for the single constituency election and the other for the proportional representative election. Proportional representative candidates were listed on the proportional representative ballot, but votes were cast for the political party and then allocated by the political party to the candidates in the order listed until all seats permitted to that political party were filled. In establishing the single member districts, each prefecture was given one seat, and thereafter an allocation was made to prefectures based on population, such that no district should have a population ration higher than 1 to 2. Because each prefecture gets one seat regardless of size, the actual disparity in votes exceeded 1 to 2.

In 1995 the first election under the new system was held. Several lawsuits resulted from this election. In two cases the challengers were independent candidates who argued that the system gave an advantage to candidates for single seat districts who were also members of established political parties. In the third case it was ar gued that as the actual difference in vote strength exceeded 1 to 2 the law was unconstitutional.

The court held that the system adopted was constitutional even though giving each prefecture one seat in addition to the population ratio led to a disparity greater than 1 to 2. The court upheld its previous rulings that population ratio alone was not decisive and that the Diet had discretion to consider other factors. In this case the Diet did so to assure prefecture representation and the court considered this as not unreasonable. The resulting disparity of 1 to 2.3 was neither unconstitutional nor so far in excess of the statutory goal of 1 to 2 as to be unlawful.[79]

A more difficult question was the effect of certain electioneering provisions made applicable to the new system. Under the law the established political parties (i.e., those with five seats in the Diet or which received 2% or more of the popular vote in the last election for either House) with candidates running in single seat districts could campaign both for their slate of proportional representative candidates and for candidates seeking single seat district election. The candidate is also permitted to campaign for single seat election. Most significantly candidates associated with an established party can take advantage of certain political broadcasting rights granted to the party whereas independents are denied such broadcasting rights. Considering the impact of radio and television broadcasting on a political campaign, such difference significantly advantaged established political party associated candidates. Independent candidates sued arguing that giving this advan-

79 Case No. 1998 (Gyo-Tsu) No. 7 (Sup. Ct. Grand Bench, 9/11/96), available on the web in English through the web site the Supreme Court of Japan.

tage to established political party candidates discriminated against them. The court rejected the challenge finding that the distinction between established party candidates and independent candidates was within the permitted discretion of the Diet.[80]

In a third challenge it was alleged that the system of proportional representation taken in conjunction with single seat districts was in violation of the Constitution. Under the system adopted a candidate of a political party could run for the single seat post and at the same time could be listed by the party as a proportional representative candidate. As a consequence such candidate might be rejected by the voters in the single seat election but then be appointed because the party received enough proportional representative votes to reach the candidate's name as listed on the party ballot. Indeed, the candidate could be listed number one on the party ballot. It was argued that this gave political party candidates an unfair advantage and also that it disparaged the voters' choice. Taken together with the advantage gained from being a political party candidate—such as the ability to use broadcast facilities unavailable to independents—this gave single seat party candidates who were also listed on the proportional representation ballot a great advantage over their opponent. The system also gave established parties a great advantage over independents. The court held that the Diet had broad discretion in choosing an election system and that the Diet had not exceeded its discretion in enacting a proportional representation/single seat system that favored established political parties.[81]

The Upper House election of 1998 similarly brought forth litigation arguing that the voter disparity ratio in that election (1 to 4.98) was unconstitutional. The court adhered to its previous rulings and noted that the disparity was less than the previous disparity of 1 to 6 for an Upper House election and that the Diet had acted to reduce the disparity to 1 to 4.79 based on the 1995 census. That the actual disparity in the 1998 election was 1 to 4.98 was not such as to make the election unconstitutional.[82]

The Upper House election in 2001 again brought forth litigation. In this election there was a proportional representation list of candidates and voters were allowed to choose to vote either by political party or by party member listed on the party's

---

80 Case No. 1999 (Gyo-Tsu) No. 35 (Sup. Ct. Grand Bench, 11/10/99), available on the web in English through the web site of the Supreme Court of Japan.

81 Case No. 1999 (Gyo-Tsu) No. 8 (Sup. Ct. Grand Bench, 11/10/99), available on the web in English through the web site of the Supreme Court of Japan.

82 Case No. 1996 (Gyo-Tsu) No. 241 54 Minshu 1997 (Sup. Ct. Grand Bench, 9/6/2000), available on the web in English through the web site of the Supreme Court of Japan. The court reaffirmed and adhered to this ruling in Case No. 2001 (Gyo-Tsu) 223, 55 Minshu 1647 (Sup. Ct. Petty Bench, 12/18/01), available on the web in English through the web site of the Supreme Court of Japan and Case No. 2001 (Gyo-Tsu) 233 (Sup. Ct. Petty Bench, 12/18/01), available on the web in English through the web site of the Supreme Court of Japan.

candidate list. This method of selection as well as the voter disparity ratio of 1 to 5.06 was challenged but the court held both to be constitutional.[83]

In sum, over the years the political parties in Japan have dealt with the electoral system so as to improve their posture in winning elections. The original mid-sized election districts were configured in such a way as to benefit the LDP and its rural constituency. The court's decisions requiring some level of voter parity caused a restructuring of that system that continued to support the party in power—and the court never upset an election although it clearly had serious questions about the constitutionality of several elections. Eventually, tinkering with the size of districts while maintaining the competitive advantage of the political parties proved to be too difficult, and a new electoral system based on both proportional representation and single member election districts was adopted. While this system had the advantage of lowering the disparity (in the House of Representatives but not significantly in the House of Councilors) it was combined with electioneering regulations that favored the established parties and disadvantaged new parties or independent candidates. Nonetheless, the Supreme Court has upheld the system. Consequently, although influenced by American decisions requiring rough parity in voting strength, the Supreme Court of Japan appears to have despaired of obtaining such rough parity. Instead it has accepted differences as high as 1 to 6 in the Upper House and 1 to 2.3 in the Lower House. At the same time the court has countenanced a system that favors the established political parties, discourages defections from the established parties, discourages the rise of new parties and reduces the voting strength of urban dwellers.

To some extent the problem facing the plaintiffs and the courts in Japan in the election redistricting cases is procedural in nature. Japanese plaintiffs and courts lack the tools available to the United States court system in dealing with election redistricting. American courts are courts of equity and have the inherent equity power to grant injunctive relief when the situation calls for it. The availability of both prohibitory injunction (to prevent an illegal election from taking place) and mandatory injunction (to require the legislative body to redistrict in accordance with the constitutional mandate) makes it possible for an American court to take action that a Japanese court has no power to undertake. Not being a general court of equity—equity is a common law concept designed in the early days of the common law to permit the system to avoid the rigidity and thus unfair aspects of early common law—Japanese courts have only such "injunction" powers as are given to them by specific legislation. There is no legislation that would give the court the power to enjoin the holding of an election. Indeed, it seems clear that even if there were a general grant of injunction power, the Japanese court system would likely hold that it did not apply to election districting disputes because of Article 47 giving the Diet (not the court) power to establish the election districts. Japanese plaintiffs are therefore without a vehicle to seek to stop an unconstitutionally districted election before it occurs. As a consequence both the court and the plain-

83 Japan Times on Line, Upper House Electoral System Upheld, 1/15/04.

tiff are left to deal with an election challenge only after the election. As a consequence the court is presented with the dilemma noted by the Supreme Court in the *Kurokawa* case.

In addition, American courts can supervise and where necessary draft new election district plans. The court's power comes from both its equity power and also its ability to retain experts to work for the court in dealing with election plans and other matters. A District Judge dealing with an election district case in her district can obtain expert assistance without going through a judicial bureaucracy in Washington or elsewhere. But Japanese judges lack this power to obtain professional assistance in areas outside the law and for the purpose of relief.[84] Even if the court system could enter injunctive relief it could not draft its own plan for action if the legislature refused to act. Associated with this problem is the additional problem of enforcing its order. An American equity court has the traditional equity enforcement measure of contempt. Failure to act in accord with an injunction is punishable by the court as contempt of the court. The contempt power is strong allowing the judge to fine the party in contempt for each day of refusal or even to have the party arrested and confined until it obeys (with no trial by jury permitted as this is a civil not a criminal contempt). Of course, it is not suggested that the court would fine or imprison the Diet, but officers of the Diet might be reachable by the contempt power if it existed and this might compel action. Under Japanese substantive law the court is not given authority to itself enforce an order requiring or forbidding activity even in cases where the court is given authority to enter such orders. Rather, the court must seek assistance from the public prosecutor to enforce its orders.[85] The public prosecutor while having certain independence is under the Minister of Justice.

2) Cabinet Government and Factional Politics

Unlike the Meiji Constitution, the Constitution of Japan makes it clear that the Cabinet is responsible to the Diet. The Diet as its first order of business selects the Prime Minister from among its members.[86] If both Houses cannot agree on the designation of the Prime Minister, then the determination of the House of Representatives shall control.[87] The Cabinet is specifically made responsible, as a collective body, to the Diet.[88] Further, the House of Representatives has the power to cause the Cabinet to dissolve by passing a resolution of no confidence or refusal

84 Recent amendments to the Patent Law give the court authority to receive expert advice from assessors as to damages for patent infringement. See, Patent Law Section 105bis. Other intellectual property laws contain similar provisions. See Chapter 10 A—Relief.

85 For example, the court may assess a non-penal fine for violation of certain orders requiring production of documents by third persons. If such order is not complied with the court may seek assistance from the public prosecutor (rarely if ever done) rather than enforce its own order.

86 Constitution of Japan, Article 67.

87 Constitution of Japan, Article 67.

88 Constitution of Japan, Article 66.

to pass a motion of confidence in the Cabinet. Although the Cabinet may postpone its own dissolution by dissolving the House in such a situation,[89] if the House is dissolved a new election must be held within 40 days of dissolution and the new Diet must be seated within 30 days thereafter.[90] When the new Diet is seated the Cabinet must resign[91] and the Diet then designates a new Prime Minister as the first order of business.

Unlike the United States where the Executive power is given to a specific individual holding a single office—the President—in Japan the Executive power resides in a collegial body, the Cabinet.[92] Although the Prime Minister must be a member of the Diet, it is not required that all of the Cabinet be Diet members, however a majority of the Cabinet must be in the Parliament.[93] Unlike the Meiji Constitution Cabinets that required military officers in the positions of Minister of the Army and Navy, the present Cabinet has no such requirement—indeed, it is required that all Cabinet members be civilians.[94] To enhance the position and power of the Prime Minister the Constitution gives the Prime Minister extensive powers in regard to the Cabinet. The Prime Minister appoints the other members of the Cabinet[95] and has the power to dismiss members of the Cabinet.[96]

The Constitution establishes the Japanese Government on the British Parliamentary model. In such system the Prime Minister owes his position to the Legislative Branch and thus lacks the "moral" or "political" authority of the directly elected

89 Constitution of Japan, Article 69.

90 Constitution of Japan, Article 54.

91 Constitution of Japan, Article 70.

92 Constitution of Japan, Article 65.

93 Constitution of Japan, Article 68. This provision was not in the Occupation draft but was added at the insistence of the Far East Commission. See, Robert E. Ward, The Origins of the Present Japanese Constitution, 50 American Political Science Review 980, 1006 (1956). The clause was put in the Constitution at the suggestion of the Chinese member of the Far East Commission in response to the Ashida amendment to Article 9 (Renunciation of War). Richard B. Finn, WINNERS IN PEACE, MACARTHUR, YOSHIDA, AND POSTWAR JAPAN (University of California Press, 1992) 118.

94 Robert E. Ward, The Origins of the Present Japanese Constitution, 50 American Political Science Review 980, 1006 (1956). Constitution of Japan, Article 66(2), although such provision might be viewed as overkill in light of the Renunciation of War Article. However the Far East Commission considered it necessary because of the amendment of Article 9 and the American's acknowledged that the Renunciation of War clause might be amended in the future. Richard B. Finn, WINNERS IN PEACE, MACARTHUR, YOSHIDA, AND POSTWAR JAPAN (University of California Press, 1992) 118. Considering the interpretation placed on Article 9 question exists as to whether through giving a non-military sounding title to a commander in the "Self Defense Force" such person would be permitted to sit in the Cabinet notwithstanding Article 66(2). In any event, it is clear that unlike the Meiji Cabinets, Cabinets under the Constitution are not captive to the military.

95 Constitution of Japan, Article 68.

96 Constitution of Japan, Article 68(2).

American President.[97] Where the Prime Minister is elected by a coalition, the Prime Minister's authority is limited by the need to compromise with coalition members and should there be several members of the coalition, the Prime Minister's policies may be compromised. On the other hand, as the leader of the major party in the Diet the Prime Minister should have great power when that party controls a majority position and need not rely on coalition members. In such case, the party headed by the Prime Minister controls both the Executive and Legislative Branches of government and unlike the American President should not have to be concerned about inter branch rivalries and political discord between the Executive and members of the legislature. Moreover, through the power of appointment and removal of Cabinet members Prime Ministers should, in theory, be able to maintain party discipline. That has not been the case in Japan.

When the Constitution was adopted, the Liberal Party was in power and the Prime Minister was Yoshida Shigeru.[98] Although denominated the Liberal Party it was in fact quite conservative in its philosophy. The various liberal political parties merged to form the Japan Socialist Party. In response the conservative political parties in 1955 merged to form the Liberal Democratic Party [LDP].[99] The LDP has been the dominant party in Japanese politics ever since[100] and is in power today, although it is part of a larger coalition with two smaller parties. Through the first several decades of government after the Constitution the LDP remained in power through a combination of pork barrel politics that satisfied its various constituency groups, money politics that gave it a huge financial advantage over the opposition in election campaigns, election district policies that favored LDP constituencies and disadvantaged opposition politicians, and a feeling by the public that there was no viable alternative party. In the 1990s the LDP, as a consequence of public reaction to a new sales tax that was roundly opposed by most of the public, was temporarily ousted from power. It formed a strange alliance with the Socialists, the main opposition party, under which the leader of the Socialists was elected Prime Minister by the Diet. The Socialists now found themselves in the anomalous position of supporting policies that they had opposed while in the opposition. While an opposition political party, the Socialists could attack the very existence of the Self Defense Force (the military that was formed at American urging at the time of the Korean War). As the governing party the Socialist Prime

97 The American President is, of course, indirectly elected through the institution of the Electoral College. However, the members of the College typically pledge to vote for a specific candidate and are directly elected by the people to cast their vote for the President. It is true that in some cases members of the College may not be pledged and in some cases members of the College may violate their pledge. Still for purposes of this discussion the public elects the American President at large whereas the Prime Minister is elected by the Diet.

98 John W. Dower, EMBRACING DEFEAT (W.W. Norton & Company, 1999) 403.

99 For a discussion of political parties in Japan see, Hideo Tanaka, THE JAPANESE LEGAL SYSTEM (University of Tokyo Press, 1976) 44-47; see also, Marius B. Jansen, THE MAKING OF MODERN JAPAN (Belknap Press of Harvard University, 2000) 718-726.

100 For a discussion of the role of the LDP in Japan's post war politics see, James L. McClain, JAPAN, A MODERN HISTORY (W.W. Norton & Company, 2002) 565-574.

Minister was compelled to support monetary requests for the support of the SDF. As a consequence of its reverse course on matters that were at the heart of its political philosophy the Socialists lost whatever credibility they had with the public and they are today a minor splinter party. Defections from the LDP formed new parties that have become the opposition.

Starting life as a coalition party, the LDP quickly became a party of factions, each of which was loyal to their faction leader and each of which had different philosophical approaches to government policy and each of which had a somewhat different constituency. Each faction raised money on its own to finance election campaigns and faction leaders were in charge of campaign funding, thereby cementing loyalty to the leader.[101] To elect a Prime Minister, the faction leaders would meet and select the Prime Minister who would then be anointed by the Diet majority. Because the policy differences between the factions were great—although all adhered to a basic conservative policy—and because each faction was jealous of the power of other factions and was concerned that other factions not become too strong, the faction leaders united in their effort to appoint a Prime Minister who could not use the position to greatly advantage his faction compared to other factions. In short, over time the Prime Minister tended to be a compromise least-common-denominator candidate who did not have great backing from the public. Moreover, for the Prime Minister to get any policy adopted by the Diet it was necessary to first get the policy approved by the faction leaders. Accordingly, legislation became a two-step process of negotiation. First, there was the internal negotiation within the LDP to arrive at a consensus political party position. Next, there was the need to negotiate with the opposition in the Diet to try to come to a consensus understanding on legislation. This two-step procedure had the effect of watering down legislation making a strong policy position difficult to enact in a law.

Complicating this factional struggle is the reality that the factions are not the sole divisive factor in party politics in Japan. In addition to factions, Diet members may belong to "study groups" dealing with policy objectives. These study groups have their own agenda as to various policy matters and members of the study group may come from different factions of the same political party or from different political parties. To get legislation passed it may be necessary to negotiate with study groups as well as factions, creating yet another layer of compromise.[102]

Although the Japanese Constitution appears to create a strong Executive Cabinet and a strong Prime Minister, especially since the LDP has held sway for almost all of the post-war period, the reality is that the Prime Minister and Cabinet are relatively weak. Because of the nature of factional politics the Prime Minister is rela-

---

101 Factions still compete with each other in raising campaign funds. See, e.g., Reiji Yoshida, Gloves Come Off as Rival LDP Factions Fight For Cash, Japan Times on Line 4/22/04.

102 For a discussion of the role of study groups in Japanese government see, Bradley Richardson, JAPANESE DEMOCRACY—POWER, COORDINATION, AND PERFORMANCE (Yale University Press, 1997) 82-84, 98, 242-244.

tively weak and lacks the power to force the other faction leaders to carry out his policy. Rather, the faction leaders typically choose a weak Prime Minister so that they can control the agenda. It is the faction leaders, with their power to enact or refuse to enact a Prime Minister's program, who are in charge rather than the Prime Minister. Indeed, it is the faction leaders who typically have the say on who will be appointed to the Cabinet. Even if a Prime Minister attempts to avoid the faction leaders by directly appointing Cabinet members it is likely that he will be unsuccessful. The party members chosen will not agree to serve unless their faction leaders approve and if the Prime Minister goes around the faction leader he is unlikely to approve if for no other reason than to demonstrate where power lies. Because Cabinet members are responsible to their respective faction leaders, the Prime Minister cannot call upon his Cabinet for support in a fight against the factions. Because faction leaders can call upon their faction to withhold support for the Prime Minister in the event of a no confidence motion and because faction leaders of the LDP have in fact withheld such support and as a consequence LDP governments have fallen,[103] it is the faction leaders rather than the Prime Minister who claim to be in control of the Executive.

In addition to dealing with factions and policy study groups (and more recently coalition partners) as well as opposition parties, the Prime Minister must also deal with an informal group of former LDP party leaders and former Prime Ministers who act as a kind of senior advisory group not unlike the *Genro* of Meiji era Japan. The opposition of this group to a policy objective can defeat the program. One of the main roles of the Prime Minister is to act as mediator/conciliator between Ministers and between Ministries and faction groups and policy study groups. This is an important function as Ministry rivalries in Japan are a fact of life. Ministers are drawn into the bureaucratic rivalry, complicating policy making.[104] This mediation/conciliation role is responsive rather than initiative and a Prime Minister is lucky if he can get the Diet to go along with one or two policy initiatives that the Prime Minister considers significant policy.

An attempt to strengthen the position of the Prime Minister was taken when the LDP in the late 1990s determined to give constituencies say in who would be party leader. Whereas in the past the party leader and thus Prime Minister was selected by the faction leaders, constituencies were given a significant (but not majority) vote in the political party caucus that selected the party leader. Constituencies in turn held elections for party leader. The faction leaders retained enough votes in their hands to determine the outcome of the selection. Prime Minister Koizumi, the leader of a relatively small faction in the LDP and a person not particularly liked by the other faction leaders, won a resounding victory in constitu-

---

103 See, e.g., Bradley Richardson, JAPANESE DEMOCRACY—POWER, COORDINATION, AND PERFORMANCE (Yale University Press, 1997) 100.

104 See, e.g., Bradley Richardson, JAPANESE DEMOCRACY—POWER, COORDINATION, AND PERFORMANCE (Yale University Press, 1997) 100-101 for discussion of the "Supreme Advisers", 105-108 for a discussion of the weakened role of the Prime Minister and his role as arbitrator/conciliator/mediator, 116-118 for a discussion of inter Ministry rivalries).

ency elections and the faction leaders felt compelled to offer him the party leadership. Nonetheless Koizumi has been dependent on factional support to get his legislative programs passed in the Diet and such support has not been forthcoming. As a consequence many Koizumi initiatives have died in party faction meetings and have not been enacted. Public opinion in turn has shifted away from Koizumi making it even more difficult for him to get factional support for his economic reform program, but he remains the most popular politician in the LDP and thus has been reelected for another term. Even efforts by Koizumi to have the LDP adopt a policy platform of a few items that all LDP politicians could run on met with negative response by the faction leaders. While the LDP under Koizumi's leadership won the latest Lower House election campaign and Koizumi was reelected party leader and hence Prime Minister, the reality is that he is weaker today then when he was first elected Prime Minister and his reform programs remain bogged down in Diet/factional negotiation.[105]

The close ties leaders of the LDP have with members of the bureaucracy complicate the lawmaking function of the Diet. In Tokugawa Japan the bureaucracy was composed of members of the samurai class—the highest social class—and thus was highly respected. Meiji Japan had relied on a strong bureaucracy to bring the country into the modern world and to develop its industry. From as early as 1885 the Japanese civil service was based on the merit system concept and civil servants had job protection rights from as early as 1899.[106] The American Occupation had left the bureaucracy in place (with some purges but as a whole the bureaucracy survived relatively in tact) and had governed with the use of the bureaucracy. The bureaucracy continued its central role after adoption of the Constitution. Many bureaucrats sought political office after retirement and these bureaucrats were the same officials who had excellent relations with large companies that could support political campaigning. Moreover, these officials had at their disposal a ready supply of junior (now senior) bureaucrats who had been loyal to them while they served in the government and remained loyal after retirement. Both the retired bureaucrats and the LDP sought to have these people join their party and take a prominent position in the party. The presence of these retired bureaucrats in high political office (many became Prime Minister) strengthened the power of the bureaucracy while it weakened the independence of the political elite. Similarly many career bureaucrats retired from government into high positions in government corporations or major companies with government relations. From these positions they continued to have influence with the bureaucrats in the Agency from which they had retired and continued to exert influence over politicians.

105 Although a reformer on economic matters, Prime Minister Koizumi is quite conservative in other areas such as the SDF, amendment of Article 9 of the Constitution, visits to the Yasukuni Shrine, etc. Whether these positions are exaggerated at times to shore up support from other conservative factions of the LDP is unknown. Such positions have drawn criticism from many of Japan's neighbors. See, e.g., Koizumi Shrine Visit Ruled Unconstitutional, Japan Times on Line 4/8/04.

106 Hideo Tanaka, THE JAPANESE LEGAL SYSTEM (University of Tokyo Press, 1976) 43.

Further, the factional nature of the political parties means that each party wishes to have as many members as possible in high Ministry positions. As a result, Cabinet Ministers tend to have relatively short tenure in order to give other faction members a chance to serve as a Minister. Consequently Cabinet Ministers do not have the time to develop an expertise in the area where appointed and must rely on the senior career officials in the Ministry for advice. Career officials know that the Minister will shortly move on and a new Minister will arrive and can organize their agenda to go around a Minister who cannot be persuaded to go along the bureaucracy's position. The economic miracle placed bureaucrats in high esteem by the public and this also has affected their position in government although in recent years the blush has come off the bureaucratic rose, as the bureaucracy has been unable to get Japan out of its economic recession. In any event, the bureaucracy exerts great influence in Japan.[107]

The Congress of the United States has a large bureaucracy of its own with members having relatively large staffs and Committees having professional staffs, many of whom remain even if power in the legislative body passes from one party to another. (The Chairmanship will pass to a member of the party in power but the minority party will be entitled to staff positions. If the ranking minority member is the former Chairman it is likely that most of the minority staff will be former members of the majority staff. The new majority staff will be former members of the previously minority staff.) The Japanese Diet on the other hand has a small staff. The consequence is that most American legislation is written in Congressional offices. Even if the Executive Branch suggests legislation—the Executive Branch cannot submit a bill to the Congress as only a member may submit a bill—the bill is redrafted (and modified) by the Congressional staff. In short, in the United States the Executive is required to get assistance from the Legislative Branch to get bills enacted into law. In Japan the Executive is composed of members of the legislative (at least a majority of the Cabinet as well as the Prime Minister must be members of the Diet) and because the Executive has the staff capacity the Executive drafts virtually all bills. Thus, while the Constitution makes the Diet the exclusive legislative body, the reality is that the Diet on its own does not legislate. Rather the Cabinet is the initiator and the drafter of most legislation. Bills submitted by the Cabinet are called Cabinet bills and almost all legislation in Japan is by way of Cabinet bill.[108]

---

107 For a discussion of the influence of the bureaucracy in Japan and restraint on the power of the Prime Minister and Cabinet see, Bradley Richardson, JAPANESE DEMOCRACY—POWER, COORDINATION, AND PERFORMANCE (Yale University Press, 1997) 95 etc.

108 John W. Maki, The Japanese Constitutional Style in Dan Fenno Henderson, THE CONSTITUTION OF JAPAN: ITS FIRST TWENTY YEARS 1947-1967 (University of Washington Press, 1969) 21. Except for the election districting cases discussed earlier, the only law enacted by the post-war Diet to be found unconstitutional was a private member bill not a Cabinet bill that became law. See, Hiroshima Pharmacy case, Sumiyoshi v. Governor of Hiroshima, 29 Minshu 572, Case No. 1968 (Gyo-Tsu) No. 120 (Sup. Ct., Grand Bench 4/30/75) available in English through the website of the Supreme Court of Japan, Judgments of the Supreme Court and in Lawrence W. Beer & Hiroshi Itoh, THE CONSTITUTIONAL CASE LAW OF JAPAN, 1970-1990 (University of Washington Press, 1996) at 188.

The Cabinet itself does not have a large staff but it does have available to it the staffs of the various Ministries since the Cabinet is composed of the various government Ministers. The Ministries, in turn, are staffed by the bureaucracy. As a consequence the reality is that most laws enacted in Japan are enacted as a consequence of drafting by the bureaucracy.[109]

Further, while the American legislating process utilizes Committees to investigate, hold hearings and generally debate and resolve policy issues over legislation before the legislation moves to the floor of the Congress for member debate and vote, the Japanese process is fundamentally different. Policy objectives may come from many different sources including the political factions in the LDP or other government parties or from the bureaucracy itself. The first step is typically to set up a study committee to consider the policy objective. Such a committee will consist of various interest groups considered as having a special interest in the legislation. For example, a consumer related policy initiative would want attendance in study committee of representatives of business, housewives, and other consumer organizations. In addition, the study committee would have on it academic representatives (selected by the government) with presumed expertise in the field and the bureaucracy would be represented through membership by bureaucrats from the Ministry (or Ministries) involved in the issue. The only "full time employee" members of such committees would be the bureaucrats and it would be these bureaucrats who would keep the minutes, set the agenda and formulate the policy papers that are circulated and considered by study committee members. In addition, study committees in Japan typically take several years to study an issue and during this time membership on the committee might change—but the constant will be the bureaucratic organization that sends the bureaucrats to sit on the committee. The function of the committee is not simply to examine the issue but to provide a forum where the competing interest groups may debate and negotiate a compromise position that can garner a consensus. Once a policy consensus is reached and the report agreed to, the job of drafting a bill that the government can submit to the Diet is turned over the bureaucrats. The faction leaders meet to decide on the party position in the matter and the policy may be modified to meet the political concerns of the factions. Then the matter is referred to policy discussion with the minority parties to try to arrive at a consensus. When agreement (or at least near agreement is reached) the bureaucrats, who have been involved in each step of the process draft a final version of the bill to be submitted to the Diet.

Although the majority party or the ruling coalition has the votes to cram down the bill notwithstanding minority party opposition, the objective is to get minority party "understanding" so that the bill is found generally acceptable to the House. Of course, if such understanding cannot be reached, the ruling majority may resort to its voting power to get the bill passed. The opposition in such case may resort to delaying tactics that serve to make the public aware of the fact that there is

109 Marius B. Jansen, THE MAKING OF MODERN JAPAN (Belknap Press of Harvard University, 2000) 726.

sharp disagreement on a policy issue. The majority will be accused of using its power improperly to force the bill through, rather than following the more appropriate process of continuing to compromise. The minority may make non-confidence motions or motions to censure a Cabinet Minister (both of which must be dealt with prior to voting on legislation) to delay the vote on legislation and may adopt the "crab walk" of slowly walking to the desk of the Speaker to cast votes on the legislation.

The process of legislation in Japan has an effect on all three branches of the government. The Judicial Branch is affected because few laws provide for a private right of action or even provide for specific rights. General language expressing policy goals and delegation to the bureaucracy to carry out those goals is the norm. Even fewer bills provide for judicial review of administrative efforts under the enactment and none provide for judicial review of agency guidance as to how the law should be carried out.[110] The Diet is affected as few Diet members have real input in the legislative process and the institution itself has little role in actually drafting policy positions or laws. The Cabinet is affected because it is captive to the bureaucracy to obtain the assistance required to draft bills and monitor policy reviews.

In any event, the end product of the Japanese process is a law that has been watered down in study committee to obtain a consensus, watered down in faction meetings to obtain a consensus, watered down in negotiations with the minority to get understanding and has been drafted by the bureaucracy—which has its own policy concerns and gives itself broad non-reviewable discretion to carry out the general policy contained in the legislation.

Among the principal issues for the bureaucracy is the question of policing or enforcing the new legislation. In Japan enforcing legislation is a government function and a responsibility of the bureaucracy. To free its hand to the greatest extent possible the bureaucracy drafts bills in a way that provides great discretion to the bureaucrats who are to enforce the law. To assure that others do not interfere with the bureaucracy's enforcement role bills do not provide the public or the segment of the public for whose benefit the law is enacted a right to sue those who violate the law (as would be common in the United States). Moreover, the law typically is worded in an indefinite way setting out policy goals and objectives rather than specific obligations and leaving interpretation and enforcement to the bureaucracy. Needless to say, the bureaucracy is unlikely to provide that determinations of administrators can be challenged by review by the Judicial Branch and thus most laws do not provide a judicial review remedy. Similarly, the bureaucracy is not likely to write legislation that has procedural rules that bind the hands of bureaucrats and provide citizens with an opportunity to challenge bureaucratic action.

110 For a discussion of Administrative Guidance see Chapter 12.

3) The Judicial Branch

Article 76 of the Constitution provides that the entire Judicial Power is vested in the Supreme Court and such inferior courts as may be created by law. Comparing the language to that of the United States Constitution discloses the effect of the American Constitution on the Japanese. While that effect is clear, the reality is that the Occupation did not attempt to recreate in Japan the American Judicial Branch. Thus, the Japanese Constitution does not provide for life tenure of judges as does the United States document nor does it provide for Executive appointment subject to legislative approval. The American idea of Senatorial approval of judges was designed to preserve State power when the States created the new Federal Government. As initially conceived and adopted the Constitution provided that the Senators were not elected but were appointed by the States and thus represented the States in Congress. Although the Occupation sought to shore up democracy in Japan through local election of Prefecture Governors and certain other local officials, the Occupation did not give the prefectures semi autonomous semi sovereign powers. Accordingly there was no House in the Diet that was to represent the prefectures and hence no reason to provide for advice and consent by any portion of the Diet.

Justices of the Supreme Court of Japan are appointed by the Cabinet.[111] The Chief Justice is appointed by the Emperor to enhance the Chief's position and make him an equal in appointment with the Prime Minister[112]—a reflection of the American high regard for the law and the Judicial Branch. As the Emperor must follow the suggestion of the Cabinet as to appointment, the reality is that the Cabinet also appoints the Chief.[113] This is similar to the American practice where the Executive appoints the judges—in the United States the Executive is the President in Japan it is the Cabinet. However, as noted above there is no advice and consent requirement as is the case in the United States.[114] Supreme Court Justices are appointed until they reach mandatory retirement age. That age is fixed by statute and presently is 70. Supreme Court Justices must be at least 40 years of age for appointment. To assure that a judicial oligarchy is not created and to emphasize the sovereignty of the people, Supreme Court Justices must be approved by the voters at the first House of Representatives election after appointment and every ten

111 Constitution of Japan, Article 79.

112 Yosiyuki Noda, INTRODUCTION TO JAPANESE LAW (translated and edited by Anthony H. Angelo) (University of Tokyo Press, 1976) 124. The male pronoun is used as all Chief Justices to date in Japan (as all Chief Justices in the United States) have been male.

113 Constitution of Japan, Article 6 (2).

114 Since Japan is a unitary State there was not the same need for advice and consent as in the United States where the State governments were attempting to protect their sovereign interests. Further, since Japan is a Parliamentary democracy there is less need for legislative approval of appointments than is the case in the United States where the Executive and Legislative are truly separate branches of government.

years thereafter.[115] Since Supreme Court Justices are typically appointed at age 60 or above, the provision for electoral review at 10-year intervals is virtually meaningless.[116]

Unlike the unwieldy Grand Court of Judicature under the Meiji Constitution, the present Supreme Court is composed of 15 Justices and generally sits in panels of five Justices called Petty Bench. When a constitutional question not previously considered by the court is presented the court sits as a Grand Bench of all 15 Justices to hear the matter and the court must act as a Grand Bench to declare a law unconstitutional.[117] Oral arguments as well as written briefs may be submitted to the court, although oral argument is not comparable to such argument in the Supreme Court of the United States. In the United States argument is generally a free wheeling give and take with the court asking questions of counsel and counsel responding. In Japan the argument is more properly described as speeches by counsel for the parties as the court does not ask questions. By statute 10 of the 15 Justices must have had previous high level experience either as lower court judges, prosecutors, *bengoshi* (practicing lawyers) or law professors. The remaining 5 Justices need not have had any legal or judicial experience.[118] It is typical for the Supreme Court to have 5 or more Justices who had careers in the judiciary, of which at least one was a previous head of the Judicial Secretariat. The Supreme Court as of the start of 2004 had 6 justices who were career judges, 3 former prosecutors, 3 practicing lawyers, 1 foreign service officer, 1 academic and 1 career bureaucrat from the Ministry of Health. (The bureaucrat is the only woman on the court, was the youngest member of the court—age 63 appointed at age 60—and is not a graduate of a Law Faculty.) Of the career Justices, all six had held high positions in the judicial Secretariat during their career. None were appointed to the court at an age younger than 60. The longest serving Justice was appointed in 1995. Two Justices, including the Chief Justice, will be compelled to retire in 2004, three in 2005, and three in 2006—giving the government an opportunity to appoint new Justices on a continuing frequent basis. The Chief Justice of Japan as of January 2004 had served in the Executive Branch of the government (as a Councilor to the Cabinet Legislative Bureau—the Bureau that advises the government on such questions as whether a proposed law is unconstitutional) while a judge. Such "lending" of judges to Executive Departments and Ministries is not considered a violation of separation of powers doctrine in Japan. The next Justice

---

115 Constitution, Article 79. See, John O. Haley, The Japanese Judiciary: Maintaining Integrity, Autonomy and the Public Trust p. 17. On the web at: *http://law.wustl.edu/Academics/Faculty/Workingpapers/TheJapaneseJudiciary10_03.pdf* at 21.

116 see, Thomas L. Blakemore, Post-War Development in Japanese Law, 1947 Wisconsin Law Review 632, 640 predicting that the provision might prove useless.

117 For a discussion of the organization of the Supreme Court and the work of its panels see, Yosiyuki Noda, INTRODUCTION TO JAPANESE LAW (translated and edited by Anthony H. Angelo) (University of Tokyo Press, 1976) 126-127.

118 Toru Miura, Independence, Transparency and Accountability of the Judiciary in Japan, on the web at *www.unafei.or.jp/pdf/indonesia_pdf/session4.pdf* at page 35; Alfred C. Oppler, LEGAL REFORM IN OCCUPIED JAPAN (Princeton University Press, 1976) 96-97;

to be appointed to replace a retiring Justice is expected to be a bureaucrat who was the head of the Cabinet Legislative Bureau.[119]

The Constitution attempts to address shortcomings of the Meiji system and rectify them. Accordingly, no extraordinary tribunals (such as the prewar Administrative Court) may be established. To assure that administrative bodies are neither the final arbiter of their own action nor in a position to replace the courts, no administrative body is given final judicial power.[120] Judges are specifically granted independence and protection against disciplinary action by the Executive Branch[121]—discipline by way of a special Impeachment Court made up of Diet members is provided for.[122] The Judicial Branch while objecting strenuously when a legislative Committee recommended reprimanding a court for a decision in a matter may and has taken disciplinary action against judges itself.[123] Such power has been used by the Supreme Court against its own members[124] and against other judges.[125] The Constitution guarantees judges' salaries from pay reduction.[126] Nonetheless in 2002 the government cut the salaries of judges by approximately 2%. The Supreme Court indicated that it would accept such pay cut on the basis that it would not affect independence or significantly affect the judges' living standards.[127] Unlike the United States where such action would result in litigation by sitting judges contesting the legislative action, no lawsuit challenging the government action was filed in Japan.

119 The Japan Times of February 17,2004 reports that the government is considering appointing the former Director General of the Cabinet Legislation Bureau as the next Justice of the court. Bureaucrat To Be Top Court Justice, Japan Times on Line 2/17/04. Such appointment was in fact made.

120 Constitution of Japan, Article 76 and 76(1).

121 Constitution of Japan, Article 78.

122 Constitution of Japan, Article 64.

123 See, e.g., discussion of the House of Councilor's abortive effort to reprimand a court and the Supreme Court's objections to the Committee's actions in Laifan Lin, Judicial Independence in Japan: A Re-investigation for China, 13 Columbia Journal of Asian Law 185, 193 (1999).

124 See, Alfred C. Oppler, LEGAL REFORM IN OCCUPIED JAPAN (Princeton University Press, 1976) 229-234.

125 Alfred C. Oppler, LEGAL REFORM IN OCCUPIED JAPAN (Princeton University Press, 1976) 94 fn.15; Laifan Lin, Judicial Independence in Japan: A Re-investigation for China, 13 Columbia Journal of Asian Law 185, 193-194 (1999).

126 Constitution of Japan, Article 79. Professor Noda notes that this provision means that judge's salaries "cannot be lowered during the term of duty . . ." Yosiyuki Noda, INTRODUCTION TO JAPANESE LAW (translated and edited by Anthony H. Angelo) (University of Tokyo Press, 1976) 155.

127 Japan Times on Line, 11/20/02 Judges, Prosecutors Face Pay Cut. Similarly, in prewar days the salaries of judges were reduced when the salaries of prosecutors was reduced even though the law prohibited a reduction in judge's salaries.

a) Separation of Powers/Independent Status of the Judicial Branch

Separation of powers doctrine is designed to completely separate one branch of government from another in order to insure the independence of the branches and in American theory to provide that each branch acts as a check to balance the power of the others. Thus, separation doctrine and independence go hand in hand. This is especially true of the separation and independence of the Judicial Branch. In a Parliamentary Democracy it is to be expected that separation of powers doctrine would be strained where the Legislative and Executive Branches are concerned. In a Presidential system where the public separately elects the Executive a sharp and clear distinction between Executive and Legislative Branches can be obtained. However, in a Parliamentary system such as Japan, the Executive (Cabinet) is composed of members of the legislature (Diet) and the Cabinet is specifically and intentionally made subordinate to and dependent on the Diet (the highest organ of the State). Nonetheless it is possible to have a complete separation between the Judicial Branch and the elected political branches of government. It seems clear that that was the intent of the Occupation—especially as it wished to correct the lack of separation under the Meiji Constitution where the judiciary was subordinate to the Executive. In addition, the Constitution grants individual judges independent status by providing that "all judges shall be independent in the exercise of their conscience. . ."

Independence may be considered from several different vantage points—there is independence from politics and from the political process; there is independence from other branches of the government and there is independence of individual judges from the bureaucracy of the Judicial Branch itself. Complete independence from politics is not possible in today's modern age where judges hear and read the news and understand what the public or at least the pundits are saying about issues that reach the court for decision. Further, there exists a strong argument that in a democracy no branch of government should be so isolated from public opinion that it fails to understand where the public stands on an issue. In the United States judges, before they became judges, had some political life, or they would not have come to the attention of the Executive nominating them (or in the case of States where judges are elected, the attention of the parties that nominated them). Moreover, to garner Senate approval most nominees have had some relationship with the Senator from their home State or at least some other figure in the government who could help steer the nomination to a successful confirmation. Many judicial nominees come to the Executive Branch's attention through referral by the Senator from their State. To deny the existence of politics in a political appointment is to blink reality. However, once appointed because of life tenure American Federal Judges are completely independent. Their views on the law may be affected by their prior political experience or feelings—conservatives elevated to the Bench can be expected to adhere to a conservative philosophy and liberals similarly elevated may be expected to adhere to liberal views in deciding cases. But that is not always the case.

In Japan, where a merit system and a judicial bureaucracy select judges,[128] politics is not a factor in initial appointments of inferior court judges. Even at the Supreme Court level there is evidence that the judicial bureaucracy is responsible for the selection of Justices. The original Court Organization Law formalized the judicial bureaucracy's role in selecting Supreme Court Justices by providing for a Committee to recommend potential Justices to the Cabinet. However, these "recommendations" took on the character of actual appointment as the Cabinet simply adopted the recommendation out of concern that the committee should not be slighted. The Committee was abolished.[129] Nonetheless, when a Supreme Court Justice retires, the government confers with the Chief Justice concerning a replacement. The views of the court are especially important when the Justice to be replaced is to be replaced by a career judge.[130] Where the Justice to be selected comes from the ranks of academia, prosecutors service, private Bar or the bureaucracy the government will also consult with the Chief Justice. Supreme Court Justices must be approved (or at least not rejected) by voters in the first Lower House election after their appointment. There is no evidence that such approval has any impact on the independent judgment of Supreme Court Justices.

Although independent judgment of Supreme Court Justices does not appear to be politically influenced, the reality is that a Supreme Court Justice with judicial review powers, whether in the United States or Japan is a political being. Justices are beholden to the government for their initial appointment and do not stray too far from the views of the government that appointed them when rendering decisions. In a society where loyalty to those responsible for advancement is part of the national character with roots going back to feudal times, it is not to be expected that a majority of the Justices of the court would disregard the known views of the political party (parties) responsible for their appointment. Moreover, it is unlikely that the court would recommend to a conservative government the elevation to the court of a majority of Justices who would disagree with basic government philosophy. This is especially true when Justices are appointed at a late age and serve for only a few years. This short tenure means that Justices do not have an opportunity to develop a judicial philosophy of their own as a judge sitting on the highest court in the land. And, if a mistake is made, it can be quickly cured as the term of the Justice is relatively short. (In a space of three years between 2000 and 2003 a total of 9 Supreme Court Justices retired and were replaced in Japan).

Supreme Court Justices appointed during and after the Occupation had received their legal education prior to the war. Indeed, since Supreme Court Justices are

128 Although the Cabinet technically appoints judges of courts below the Supreme Court the Constitution requires that such selection be made from a list given to the Cabinet by the Supreme Court, i.e., the Secretariat. Constitution of Japan, Article 80.

129 Alfred C. Oppler, LEGAL REFORM IN OCCUPIED JAPAN (Princeton University Press, 1976) 89-91.

130 Takaaki Hattori, The Role of the Supreme Court of Japan in the Field of Judicial Administration, 60 Washington Law Review 69, 75 (1984).

rarely appointed until age 60, only those Justices appointed after 1980 received a postwar legal education. Thus the original Justices had a German law orientation to their legal education as well as an authoritarian government orientation to their studies. This is not to say that the Justices were themselves authoritarian or that they rejected the liberal philosophy set out in the new Constitution but it does suggest that the Justices had a conservative approach to legal issues. This would accurately reflect the various governments either formed by or dominated by the LDP since the Occupation. Judges with a conservative judicial philosophy are likely to recommend as their replacements others with a similar conservative judicial outlook, just as conservative Presidents are prone to select judicial conservatives to sit on the Supreme Court of the United States. When appointment to the Supreme Court is viewed as the top of a career ladder, it is expected that most judges will attempt to meet the perceived expectations of the Justices sitting on the court (as transmitted through the judicial Secretariat and decisions of the court). This perpetuates the conservative philosophy of the court. Like most inbred bureaucracies this system tends to stifle originality and diversity. Caution, rather than initiative and new thinking, may be more likely to lead to advancement. Of course, in the United States because of the long tenure of Justices, Presidents may be surprised by the evolving judicial philosophy of their appointments.[131] In any event, it is to be expected that a conservative block rather than a more liberal block dominates the Supreme Court of Japan as well as the judiciary in general. And, in politically charged areas the courts' decisions contain a decided conservative bent.

Because it is a civil law-based legal system, the doctrine of *starie decisis* does not apply in Japan. A Supreme Court decision is binding on lower courts in the case in which rendered but it is not "binding" in a technical sense on other cases.[132] But, the judiciary is a bureaucracy and like all good bureaucracy it acts to compel subordinates to follow the lead of their supervisors. Before appointment all judges attend the Legal Research and Training Institute. As that body is controlled by, run by and staffed by the judicial bureaucracy (the judicial Secretariat) aspiring judges are taught the philosophical approach of the bureaucracy. In addition, all inferior court judges are appointed for a 10-year term. For the first 5-year period the new judge in training is not permitted to decide or sit on cases on her own. In the second 5-year period the judge may be given greater responsibility because of the needs of the judicial system for additional judges. This training period gives older judges a direct and personal opportunity to educate the new judges to the bureaucracy's philosophical approach to the law. The initial 10-year term is a training period and during this time the new judge sits on cases with older judges and

---

131 The case of Justice Souter presently sitting on the court and of Earl Warren appointed by President Eisenhower come to mind as instances of surprise.

132 See Chapter 11 dealing with appeal in Japan. See especially the discussion in Chapter 11 of the 1996 Amendment provisions that limit appeal to the Supreme Court of Japan and adopt a form of certiorari review that appears to be based, at least in part, on common law views as to the effect of decisions of the highest level court.

learns the craft of judging. In addition new judges during this 10-year term attend sessions of the Legal Research and Training Institute during their first, third, fourth and ninth years of appointment. Full judges who have been reappointed to further 10-year terms also attend training sessions at the Institute. These typically deal with court administration issues as well as legal topics of particular interest either because of current trends in the law, changing aspects of the law or generally considered of importance by the judicial Secretariat.[133] This continuous training of judges allows the Supreme Court, through the judicial Secretariat and the Institute to educate all judges as to the approach to the law favored by the Supreme Court and the court's bureaucracy.

In inferior courts, unlike in the Supreme Court, there is no dissenting opinion. In a typical three-judge panel containing a new "assistant" judge, a chief judge of the panel and a third full associate judge, it is to be expected that the young judge will conform to the views of the chief, except in rare cases. During this formative stage the impulse to strike out on ones own and to break with tradition and established philosophy is stifled. And, judges are called back from time to time to attend training sessions specially designed for judges at the Legal Research and Training Institute, giving the bureaucracy an opportunity to reinforce its approach to judicial philosophy. As reappointment is not automatic but requires an act that includes being placed on the list of judicial appointments prepared by the Supreme Court, the potential for control over judges by the judicial bureaucracy is heightened. These bureaucracy-oriented judges are the group from which the largest block of Supreme Court Justices are appointed. While not a direct control over the judicial system and while not interfering with the independence of the Judicial Branch, the system perpetuates a conservative judicial philosophy.[134]

In addition, the judicial system is staffed by judges with no experience (except in rare cases) representing clients. The career judicial service is separated from the practicing Bar. It has no chance to see the effect of the workings of the system through the eyes of practicing lawyers and clients. The divide between Bench and Bar is broad and the two branches lack the shared experience of common law judges and lawyers. This enforces the insular thinking of the court as to both its role and also its philosophy of law. Over the years the Bench has objected to the Bar's efforts to create a unified Bench/Bar system through requiring judges to have experience as bengoshi. The Law Reform Council recommended in 2001 that judges have more experience as lawyers and that judges be selected from lawyers in greater numbers. However, the civil service nature of the system is counter to this suggestion. Both retirement benefits for career judges as distinguished from the benefits that a lawyer recently transferring to the judiciary from private practice can expect as well as presumed salary and assignment benefits that career

133 Takaaki Hattori, The Role of the Supreme Court of Japan in the Field of Judicial Administration, 60 Washington Law Review 69, 80-82 (1984).

134 Yosiyuki Noda, INTRODUCTION TO JAPANESE LAW (translated and edited by Anthony H. Angelo) (University of Tokyo Press, 1976) 154.

judges can expect over those who recently join the career service stand in the way of greater participation in the judicial department by practicing lawyers.

The Supreme Court has rejected the idea that all judges should have a minimum of five years experience as practicing bengoshi before being appointed to the Bench. In the past the judicial Secretariat has attempted to fill the practical experience gap by assigning some judges to executive departments and the prosecutor service. The Secretariat also borrows prosecutors to sit as judges. But such experience may tilt the playing field in favor of the government when cases arise in which the government is either a party or has a position. The borrowing/lending process helps meet the Executive Branch's need for trained legal professionals. The Lawyers Law and Bar Associations prohibit bengoshi from being full time government lawyers.[135] This prohibition is based on a belief that there is a conflict of interest between bengoshi who represent individuals and are responsible for preserving civil rights in the face of government actions and full time government employees. The borrowing/lending process neither provides judges with experience representing real people with real problems nor does it enhance the standing of the judiciary as a separate and equal branch of government. The government in the spring of 2004 submitted a bill that would permit judges in their first 10-year assignment to work for bengoshi for two and in some cases three years.[136] Employment is conditioned on the bengoshi not taking advantage of having a judge on staff. Although this may seem like equal treatment with the government the two-year program is likely to do little to give judges real experience as practicing lawyers as young lawyers in their first two years are unlikely to handle major litigation or represent clients on their own while working for bengoshi. Nor would it appear that such judges could appear in court representing clients of the bengoshi

135 Lawyers Law Article 30.

136 This bill was part of a series of bills introduced by the government in the spring of 2004 with judicial reform as their aim. Most of the bills submitted were enacted by the Diet as this book was going to press and as the text of the Diet announcement is not available as the book is going to press they are discussed herein as spring 2004 bills. Among those of most interest for Civil Procedure and discussed herein the following bills were enacted into law in the spring Diet session: Law establishing Labor Tribunal, Law amending the Administrative Case Litigation Law, Law permitting young judges and prosecutors to gain experience by working in a bengoshi office, Law establishing the Intellectual Property High Court, Law amending the courts law to provide greater protection to trade secrets disclosed in litigation. All of these bills were passed late in the spring 2004 session (some in the last week of the session) and the text of the bills was not available as this work was going to press. However, as all were Government bills, were politically acceptable to all Political Parties, were endorsed by professional groups and carry out the recommendations of the Law Reform Council and were technical in nature it is unlikely that any significant change was made by the Diet in the bills as presented and as discussed in the text herein. No information currently available to the author indicates any change in the bills as enacted and sources in Japan indicate no knowledge of any change. The Diet also enacted the bill to allow for lay participation in major criminal cases. Some minor changes were made in this bill as initially presented and as passed. These changes deal with the issue of penalty that may be assessed against lay participants who disclose private personal information coming to their attention as a consequence of their service as "jurors." Privacy questions are a subject of political debate in Japan. The substance of the law as passed is consistent with the Government bill submitted and discussed herein.

for whom they are working since to do so might be construed as taking advantage of having a judge on staff. Of course, the program does nothing to solve the inherent separation of powers problem that exists when judges work for Executive Branch Ministries or Departments.

There is debate in academic circles as to whether the conservative LDP acts in a manner that adversely affects judicial independence. Some argue that the ability of the LDP to appoint Justices on a frequent basis assures that Justices follow the LDP course; the Justices then control the Secretariat (leadership of the Secretariat is a stepping stone to appointment to the court assuring both Secretariat loyalty to the court and court knowledge of the workings of the Secretariat assuring control), which through its ability to set salary of judges through appointment to positions of higher or lower salary and ability to transfer judges to better or worse locations in the country and courts that are career builders or destroyers and its ability to recommend or refuse to recommend additional 10-year appointments, controls the lower court judges. The consequence is asserted to be political control or at least the threat and thus effect of political control over the judiciary. Others reject this thesis pointing to the historical independence of the Judicial Branch as well as its competence, integrity and incorruptibility.[137] Resolution of the argument is not necessary to recognize that the bureaucratic structure of the judiciary is bound to give the court a conservative tilt, consistent with that of the government.

In addition to the potential that an inferior court judge may not be reappointed at the end of the 10-year term appointed for, judges in Japan may be impeached.[138] The Constitution provides that the Executive Branch of government may not discipline judges but explicitly recognizes the right of the Diet to impeach judges and the authority of the judiciary to remove judges. Judges may be removed if there is a judicial determination that the judge is either physically or mentally impaired so

---

137 For a discussion of these differing views see, John O. Haley, The Japanese Judiciary: Maintaining Integrity, Autonomy and the Public Trust p. 17. On the web at: *http://law.wustl.edu/Academics/Faculty/Workingpapers/TheJapaneseJudiciary10_03.pdf*; see also, Alfred C. Oppler, LEGAL REFORM IN OCCUPIED JAPAN (Princeton University Press, 1976) 93-94; John O. Haley, Judicial Independence in Japan Revisited, 25 Law in Japan 1 (1995); J. Mark Ramseyer & Frances McCall Rosenbluth, JAPAN'S POLITICAL MARKETPLACE (Harvard University Press, 1993); Setsuo Miyazawa, Administrative Control of Japanese Judges in Philip S.C. Lewis Ed., LAW AND TECHNOLOGY IN THE PACIFIC COMMUNITY 263 (1991) reprint in JAPANESE LAW IN CONTEXT (Milhaupt, Jr., Ramseyer, and Young ed., Harvard University Asia Center, 2001) 79; David M. O'Brien, TO DREAM OF DREAMS, RELIGIOUS FREEDOM AND CONSTITUTIONAL POLITICS IN POSTWAR JAPAN (University of Hawaii Press, 1996) Chapter 3 manipulating Law's Social Reality; Yosiyuki Noda, INTRODUCTION TO JAPANESE LAW (translated and edited by Anthony H. Angelo) (University of Tokyo Press, 1976) 154; Percy R. Luney, Jr., The Judiciary: Its Organization and Status in the Parliamentary System, in JAPANESE CONSTITUTIONAL LAW (Luney & Takahashi Ed., University of Tokyo Press, 1993) 123.

138 For a general discussion of the Impeachment Power and process see, Shigemitsu Dando (Translated by B.J. George Jr.) JAPANESE CRIMINAL PROCEDURE (Fred B. Rothman & Co., 1965) Section 4.12; International Commission of Jurists, ICJ Legal Resources Center Japan-Attacks on Justice 2000 (8/13/01).

as to affect the judge's performance of judicial duties.[139] Judges may also be removed via public impeachment.[140] The grounds for impeachment are: a) malfeasance or nonfeasance of official duties by the judge; or b) misconduct that seriously affects the prestige or integrity of the judge or the judicial system whether or not such conduct occurred on private or public time and whether or not related to private or public activities.[141] Although malfeasance or nonfeasance relates to performance or failure to perform official duties, loss of prestige or integrity may relate to personal non-public non-official actions of the judge. The parameters of such off the job conduct are not spelled out in the statute. As a consequence the potential for abuse of the impeachment power exists.

The impeachment process is governed by statute. It is a three-stage process: 1) Request for impeachment, 2) Diet Impeachment Committee written impeachment, and 3) Trial before the Impeachment Court. Request for impeachment may come from either of two sources. Where a Chief Judge of an inferior court believes that there is a basis for impeaching a judge under the authority of the court the Chief may report this to the Supreme Court. The Supreme Court in turn may request that impeachment proceedings be instituted.[142] Secondly, any person may make an impeachment request.[143] Once an impeachment request has been filed with the Impeachment Committee the Committee is required to undertake an investigation.[144] The requirement that investigation must be undertaken when any party makes a request for impeachment renders the impeachment process available tc any litigant unhappy with the court's decision.[145] Such party may simply file an impeachment request with the Committee setting out reasons for the request and the machinery of impeachment must be set in motion. This power is obviously subject to potential abuse. To provide some protection against false charges, the Impeachment Law makes it a crime to give false statements with the intent of causing the Impeachment Court to remove a judge from office.[146]

The Impeachment Committee is a Diet Committee consisting of 20 members—10 from each House of the Diet.[147] In addition to investigating requests for impeachment filed by the Supreme Court or other persons, the Committee may investigate

---

139 Constitution of Japan, Article 78.

140 Constitution of Japan, Article 78.

141 Law for Impeachment of Judges ("Impeachment Law") Law No. 187 of 1947 Article 2 (1) and (2). Note the similarity to the basis for disciplinary punishment of judges in Meiji Japan. See, Ishii Ryosuke, JAPANESE LEGISLATION IN THE MEIJI ERA (translated and adapted by William J. Chambliss) (Kasai Publishing, Tokyo, 1958) 487.

142 Impeachment Law Article 15 (3).

143 Impeachment Law Article 15 (1).

144 Impeachment Law Article 11.

145 See, e.g., Japan Times on Line 3/19/03 Kofu Judge's Impeachment Sought (allegedly impeachment is sought because the judge advised a party that it would likely lose a law suit).

146 Impeachment Law Article 43.

147 Impeachment Law Article 5.

on its own.[148] The Committee itself may investigate but the Committee may also utilize the services of Executive Branch agencies to assist in an investigation.[149] Either the Committee or an agency assisting the Committee may compel the attendance of witnesses and/or the production of documents as part of its investigative function.[150] Investigation does not usually lead to impeachment (especially as private parties can and have abused the process to "get even" with a judge whose decision was objected to) and the Committee has the power to suspend investigation upon concluding that impeachment is not appropriate.[151] It has been reported that the impeachment of a Tokyo High Court judge in 2001 for having sex with a minor was the first judicial impeachment in 20 years.[152] However if the Committee determines that impeachment is appropriate its decision must be based on a 2/3 vote of the Committee members present at the vote.[153] A determination to proceed with impeachment must be made in writing and sent to the Impeachment Court.[154] The written impeachment must identify the judge involved and must set forth the reasons for the proposed removal of the judge.[155] The Supreme Court must be advised of the impeachment and proposed removal.[156]

The statute of limitations for an impeachment is three years from the date of the event giving rise to the impeachment. The period may be extended if there are criminal proceedings pending against the judge or if the Diet has been disbanded before the Committee's investigation is completed.[157]

After a written impeachment is sent to the Impeachment Court the court must serve the judge against whom proceedings have been instituted.[158] The Impeachment Court is located in Tokyo and is established by and consists of 14 members of the Diet—7 from each House.[159] The court has a Presiding Judge and a Secretariat.[160] The quorum requirement for the court is 10 but there must be at least 5 members of each House represented for a quorum to be present.[161] A quorum is required for Court hearings and also must be present when judgment is announced.

---

148 Impeachment Law Article 11 (1).

149 Impeachment Law Article 11 (2).

150 Impeachment Law Article 11 (3) and Article 44 (2).

151 Impeachment Law Article 13.

152 Japan Times on Line 11/29/01.

153 Impeachment Law Article 10 (2).

154 Impeachment Law Article 14 (1).

155 Impeachment Law Article 14 (2).

156 Impeachment Law Article 14 (3).

157 Impeachment Law Article 12.

158 Impeachment Law Article 21.

159 Constitution of Japan, Article 64; Impeachment Law Articles 3 and 16.

160 Impeachment Law Articles 17 and 18.

161 Impeachment Law Article 20.

The court has no independent authority to initiate impeachment proceedings but can only act on impeachments voted by the Impeachment Committee.

The judge who is the subject of an impeachment is entitled to retain counsel to assist in the judge's defense.[162] The Impeachment Law contains no provision dealing with a situation where the charged judge is unable to afford counsel. However the Law provides that to the extent possible the criminal procedure rules shall govern[163] and the Constitution provides that a criminally accused who cannot afford counsel is entitled to counsel at the expense of the State.[164] The Impeachment Court's proceedings are based on the same concept of public Oral Hearing[165] as controls normal civil cases and which is discussed in Chapter 8. The judge may be called before the court to testify in the matter although the protections of the criminal law are available to the judge.[166] It would appear that the judge is entitled to the protection of the clause prohibiting self-incrimination but it is unlikely that a judge who pleads this constitutional right will avoid removal. If removal is avoided, it is unlikely that the judge will be reappointed at the end of the 10-year appointment period.

Unlike normal civil cases (the exception is a case brought under the Administrative Case Litigation Law discussed in Chapter 12) where the court may not on its own call witnesses or direct the production of documents, in impeachment cases the court may *ex officio* take witness testimony and examine evidence, including requiring the production of documents.[167] The court may also request that the government produce documents.[168] Unlike the Impeachment Committee where proceedings are held in secret,[169] Impeachment Court proceedings are held in public[170] but deliberations are held in private.[171] Only those Impeachment Court judges who participated in the Oral Hearings may vote on impeachment.[172] A judgment to remove a judge requires a 2/3 vote for removal.[173] While proceedings are pending, the court may in its discretion suspend a judge from performing judicial duties.[174]

---

162 Impeachment Law Article 22.

163 Impeachment Law Article 22.

164 Constitution of Japan, Article 37 (3).

165 Impeachment Law Articles 23 (Oral Hearing) and 26 (Public Trial).

166 Impeachment Law Article 28.

167 Impeachment Law Article 29. Failure to comply with the Impeachment Court's request for witness testimony or document production is subject to a small nonpenal fine. Impeachment Law Article 44.

168 Impeachment Law Article 29 (3).

169 Impeachment Law Article 10 (3).

170 Impeachment Law Articles 23 and 26.

171 Impeachment Law Article 31.

172 Impeachment Law Article 31 (2).

173 Impeachment Law Article 31 (2).

174 Impeachment Law Article 39.

The judgment of the Impeachment Court must be in writing[175] and must set out the reasons for the judgment.[176] Where a judgment of removal is rendered, the evidence supporting removal must be set out in the judgment.[177] Both the Supreme Court and the judge being tried must be served with the judgment,[178] which must be published.[179] A judge against whom a judgment of removal is entered is removed from office on the announcement of the judgment.[180]

Impeachment of judges in Japan is quite rare. Although a judge was impeached in 2001 for having sex with a minor, this was only the fifth impeachment of a judge since the end of the war.[181] What does appear clear is that earlier attempts of the political branches to involve themselves directly in the monitoring of individual judge's decisions has been thwarted by the Judicial Branch's strong action objecting to such attempts and reminding all that the judiciary is an independent branch.[182]

Just as the Executive and Legislative Branches can impact on the judiciary and just as politics (with a small p) can affect the judiciary, so too the judiciary can affect these branches and the public debate of issues. The Constitution provides that trials and judgments are public events.[183] Because of the civil law nature of the Japanese judicial system, trials are extended affairs that can last several years. All during this period the public is kept informed of trials that have national or local significance through an active press. As a consequence the public can be educated as to the issues and the court can be educated as to the feeling of the public as to the issues. Once the court rules, the political branches are placed under pressure—if the ruling is inconsistent with government policy—to make changes that take into account the court's reasoning. For example, in the election district cases discussed earlier the court relied on its moral authority to declare that the election law was inconsistent with the Constitution and required Diet action to amend. Although the Diet has been slow to act and has failed to act decisively so as to give city dwellers parity with rural districts, the courts' various rulings have somewhat altered the political landscape. Court decisions have encouraged debate about and action to reform the election laws. The courts' decisions have brought about an entirely new single constituency plus proportional representation system that may serve to make single constituency representatives more responsive to their dis-

175 Impeachment Law Article 34.

176 Impeachment Law Article 33.

177 Impeachment Law Article 33 (2).

178 Impeachment Law Article 35.

179 Impeachment Law Article 36.

180 Impeachment Law Article 37.

181 See, Impeaching Judges, Mainichi Daily News Interactive 11/30/01; Japan Times on Line 11/29/01.

182 See, John O. Haley, The Japanese Judiciary: Maintaining Integrity, Autonomy and the Public Trust p. 17. On the web at: *http://law.wustl.edu/Academics/Faculty/Workingpapers/TheJapaneseJudiciary10_03.pdf* at 22-23.

183 Constitution of Japan, Article 82.

tricts. While the changes have not been so great as to displace the LDP from its dominant position in the political landscape and while the court has upheld election laws that clearly favor the established political parties and thus support the dominance of the LDP, the redistricting decisions have given city dwellers more power than was previously the case.

Determinations by lower courts have similarly altered the position of the political branches of government and resulted in reform. The Big Four pollution cases are a prime example of judicial leadership. After the first indications of Minamata disease (a neurological disorder caused by mercury run-off ingested by fish and passed to humans through the food chain) appeared in Minamata the company responsible for the disease eschewed any responsibility. The government supported the company. The problem continued to boil at a local level with attempts to resolve it through mediation first at the Minamata level then at the prefecture level. When the same disease appeared elsewhere and was linked to mercury run off the Minamata problem heated up and litigation (as a last resort) ensued. The plaintiffs sued more out of anger and frustration than out of any belief that they could succeed since Japan's burden of proof rules at the time required that the plaintiffs in environmental pollution cases show that the mercury coming from the company's plant caused the disease. It was unlikely that plaintiffs would be able to establish this causation with scientific certainty. As the matter drew public attention and as the public sided with the Minamata disease victims the lower courts recognized the wrong that was being perpetuated on the plaintiffs. As a consequence the lower courts in the environmental pollution cases pending at the same time as the Minamata disease case moderated the burden of proof rules in plaintiff's favor.[184] At the same time the litigation threw light on the government's pro-growth economic policy that virtually disregarded ecological effects in order to raise the gross national product. Citizens groups began to form throughout Japan to support ecological change. When the court ultimately found the company and the government responsible for the injury suffered by the plaintiffs the government took decisive pro-environment action. Japan enacted some of the most restrictive environmental laws to assure that the problem would not arise again. At the same time the government established an administrative claims mechanism to resolve future Minamata disease cases. The 1972 Water Pollution Control Act established a regime for water pollution cases that was similar to strict liability. Without question

184 See, Frank K. Upham, LAW AND SOCIAL POLICY IN POSTWAR JAPAN; Frank K. Upham, Litigation and Moral Consciousness in Japan: An Interpretative Analysis of Four Japanese Pollution Suits, 10 Law and Society Review 579 (1976); Julian Gresser, Koichiro Fujikura and Akio Morishima, ENVIRONMENTAL LAW IN JAPAN (MIT Press, 1981) 42, 128-130; Hiroshi Oda, JAPANESE LAW 196 (Oxford University Press, 1999). See also, Chris Clarke, Update Comparative Legal Study (European Union, 2001) p. 92 dealing with the Big Four Pollution Cases and p. 95 noting that strict liability is the standard under the 1972 provisions of the Water Pollution Control Act.

the litigation and the role of the judges in deciding in favor of the plaintiffs was decisive in changing the national policy.[185]

Similarly, the Nibutani Dam case[186] is an illustration of the effect of court decisions on government policy. For an extended number of years (going back to the Sapporo Olympics) the Ainu, the indigenous people of Hokkaido, have sought to have the Japanese Government pass legislation protecting and recognizing their special status.[187] Their efforts were unsuccessful until the court in the Nibutani Dam case found that the Ainu were Hokkaido's indigenous peoples and found that Ainu cultural values and rights had not properly been taken into account when the expropriation commission expropriated Ainu land for the Nibutani Dam.[188] The court's decision was specifically related to the indigenous status of the Ainu and the special rights that status gave to the Ainu under a treaty signed by Japan[189] that recognizes indigenous rights. Because the dam had already been constructed and demolition was not in the public interest (and indeed might be harmful to downstream communities) the court entered a "circumstance decision" (such as had been used in the election district cases). In its decision the court found that the Ainu plaintiffs were correct but nonetheless refused to enter relief. Within two months of the decision the Diet enacted the Ainu Shinpou—an Act for the Promotion of Ainu Culture and Dissemination of Knowledge Regarding Ainu Tradition. The legislation recognized Ainu cultural values and provided education steps be taken to preserve those values. Ainu status as indigenous people was also recognized and Ainu property rights were given consideration, etc. The Act specifically repealed the Act for the Protection of the Previous Indigenous People of Hokkaido, a law that the Ainu had tried to get repealed for many years. The Act did not prohibit discrimination against the Ainu but did give Ainu leaders many of the things they had unsuccessfully lobbied for in the past. The timing of the new law makes it abundantly clear that Diet action came in response to the decision of the court in Sapporo.[190]

---

185 See, Frank K. Upham, LAW AND SOCIAL CHANGE IN POSTWAR JAPAN (1987) for an extended discussion of the Big Four Pollution cases; see also, James L. McClain, JAPAN, A MODERN HISTORY (W.W. Norton & Company, 2002) 593-594; Marius B. Jansen, THE MAKING OF MODERN JAPAN (Belknap Press of Harvard University, 2000) 744; Carl F. Goodman, The Somewhat Less Reluctant Litigant, 32 Law & Policy in International Business 769, 775-776.

186 Kayano et al v. Hokkaido Expropriation Committee, 1598 Hanrei Jiho 33, 938 Hanrei Taimuzu 75, Sapporo District Court 3/27/97. An English language translation may be found at 38 International Legal Materials 394.

187 See, James L. McClain, JAPAN, A MODERN HISTORY (W.W. Norton & Company, 2002) 625-626.

188 For a discussion of Ainu discrimination see, James L. McClain, JAPAN, A MODERN HISTORY (W.W. Norton & Company, 2002) 287-288, 384-385; Hiroyuki Hata, Go Nakagawa and Takehisa Nakagawa, JAPANESE CONSTITUTIONAL LAW (Kluwer Law International, 2001) Section 239; Carl F. Goodman, THE RULE OF LAW IN JAPAN: A COMPARATIVE ANALYSIS (Kluwer Law International, 2003) 85-88.

189 The International Covenant on Civil and Political Rights.

190 See, 18 Waseda Bulletin of Comparative Law 103 (1977).

Similarly, judicial decisions against the government and in favor of hemophiliacs who contracted HIV after receiving unheated blood resulted in legislation and government action establishing a compensation program for such victims and future victims. A court decision in favor of Hansen's disease victims and against the government for its improper treatment of those suffering from the disease brought about a change in government policy.[191] The decision even resulted in government condemnation and criminal proceedings against a resort hotel that refused to allow Hansen's disease victims to use the hotel for "fear" of the disease.[192] The judicial developments recognizing a right to the American equivalent of light, air and access in certain construction cases resulted in legislative changes requiring that such right be protected under the Building Standard Law.[193] Most recently the Tokyo District Court upheld the discriminatory provisions of the Family Register Law under which illegitimate children were registered so as to show their illegitimate status. The court found that this discrimination was constitutional and that the officials involved had simply been performing their lawful duties. For this reason the court denied the plaintiff damages. However, the District Court noted that the Family Register Law provisions involved constituted an invasion of the illegitimate child's privacy rights and condemned the practice. Shortly thereafter the Ministry of Justice announced that it was aware of the court's decision and that it would seek an amendment of the Family Register Law to do away with the discriminatory registration of illegitimate children.[194]

It thus appears clear that whatever the argument may be about a conservative Supreme Court doing the bidding of a conservative government and insisting that lower court judges do the same, at least some inferior court judges in Japan appear not to fear rendering decisions against the government. And, the government is moved in the direction of reform by these progressive decisions.

Japan has a rather small population of legal professionals who can represent parties in litigation.[195] Most legal work in major organizations such as large corporations is done in house by employees who received legal training at a University Law Faculty (*Hogakubu*) but did not go on to become licensed bengoshi. Similarly, government agencies use such *Hogakubu* graduates to do in-house work.

---

191 See, Japan Times on Line, State Must Pay Hansen's Patients; Japan Times on Line, 12/26/01 Ministers Reach Accord on Hansen's Settlement.

192 Japan Times on Line, 11/22/03 Ministry Targets Hotel that Snubbed Patients; Japan Times on Line, 1/6/04 Hotel Now Opens its Doors to Hansen's Patients.

193 Julian Gresser, Koichiro Fujikura and Akio Morishima, ENVIRONMENTAL LAW IN JAPAN 145 (MIT Press, 1981).

194 See, Discriminatory Registry of Child Upheld, Japan Times on Line 3/3/04; Justice Minister Vows Registry Revision to End Birth Records Prejudice, Japan Times on Line 3/9/04; see also, Japan Privacy Resource of *www.privacyexchange.org*

195 In addition to bengoshi, licensed lawyers who can appear in court to represent parties, Japan has other legal professionals who specialize in other aspects of the law such as Judicial Scriveners and Patent Attorneys. Neither need to pass the bengoshi exam and neither can appear in court to represent parties, although the system is changing to allow scriveners to appear in some Summary Court matters and other legal professionals to work with and under the supervision of bengoshi in court in litigation.

Lawyers can only accept full time employment in for profit companies if they obtain Bar Association permission.[196] The Bar Association looks upon employment of lawyers by corporations with disfavor. In situations where a lawyer is on the staff of a company the Bar requires in-house counsel continue to be active in providing legal assistance outside its in-house role in matters that advance both the public interest and human rights. The case for lawyers working for the government is more difficult as the Lawyers Law prohibits bengoshi from being full time government employees.[197] The Association views the lawyer as protecting the public from the government and thus lawyers working for the government have an inherent conflict of interest.[198] However, government agencies have needs for professionals with the training of lawyers and as a consequence the Executive Branch looks to the Judicial Branch (where all professional employees—i.e., judges—have received the same training as lawyers) to provide it with legal assistance. The Judicial Branch in turn provides judges who staff legal positions in Ministries, Embassies and even in prosecutors offices. While in these Executive Branch offices, the judges remain judges and remain a part of the Judicial Branch. Thus the separation of powers of the Judicial and Executive Branches becomes blurred. This blurring of lines may affect parties in litigation if the in-house Executive Branch "lawyer" (cum judge) actually represents the Executive in litigation and surely is blurred where the judge works for the prosecutor. As prosecutors may sometimes be appointed as judges for a few years, the lines are even more blurred.

By working under a Cabinet Minister a judge can hardly consider him/her self as an equal branch with that Minister. Further, subtle effects on sitting judges are understandably present when in a litigation the sitting judge is asked to pass on a matter in the case that has previously been opined on by a colleague working for the Executive. Since the Executive has a bureau that examines each piece of legislation to determine whether it is constitutional [Cabinet Legislative Bureau] every challenger to the constitutionality of a modern era law carries a burden of overcoming the already given opinion of a colleague of the judges who are to decide the case. The sitting judge must be concerned that a decision adverse to the government will cause a colleague to lose face. Judges know that only the highest regarded of the judicial corps is lent to the Executive. As many of these judges rise to senior positions in the judiciary (including senior positions in the judicial Secretariat) and some rise to the Supreme Court (such as the present Chief Justice) the sitting judge undoubtedly knows that a well-respected colleague (who may not forget a contrary opinion by the judge) has already spoken on the matter and has

196 Lawyers Law Article 30 (3).

197 Lawyers Law Article 30.

198 Toshiro Nishimura, The Code of Ethics Applicable to Bengoshi (Temple University Japan) 12/1/98 on the web at *www.tuj.ac.jp/newsite/main/law/benethics.html* (page 3-4 of 6).

done so in favor of the government position.[199] Whether or not this policy of lending judges to Executive Branch departments and agencies has an affect on sitting judges, and whether or not it creates a bias in favor of the Executive by judges who previously worked in the Executive Branch, it is bound to have an effect on litigating lawyers and parties. It undoubtedly has an effect on perception as to judicial independence. The borrowing of prosecutors to be judges for a few years taints the judicial system because prosecutors are clearly Executive department officials. Allowing Executive Branch officials to sit on cases, especially cases where the government has an interest not only creates separation of powers issues but also raises questions about impartiality of the courts.[200] As Japan enters a new era in which the goal is to achieve a Rule of Law society, the appearance as well as the reality of independent justice is a necessity. This borrowing and lending of judges to other branches is not "required" of the Judicial Branch. Because of the effect that it has on litigants as well as on independence of that branch and on separation of powers doctrine, the judiciary would do well to reconsider its "lending" policy. The Bar Association should also reconsider its policy opposing lawyer employment with the government and seek changes in the Lawyers Law. Of course a spin off benefit of eliminating the practice of sending judges to work in the Executive would be the availability of more judges to decide cases.

In the spring of 2004 the Cabinet submitted a series of judicial reform bills to the Diet for action. One of the bills would permit young judges in their first 10-year appointment training period to work for two years (in exceptional cases for three years) for a bengoshi (while retaining a position in the Judicial Branch). Permission would have to be obtained from the judicial Secretariat and after the two-year period the employee would return to the Judicial Branch. The law permits prosecutors to also spend two years working for a bengoshi firm. The bengoshi for whom the judge (or prosecutor) works would be prohibited from taking advantage of the fact that a government employee is working in the office. This law is designed to give judges and prosecutors more experience in the real world that private practitioners work in on a daily basis.[201]

---

199 For a discussion of the policy of lending judges to the Executive (and the borrowing of prosecutors from the Executive) see, Setsuo Miyazawa, Administrative Control of Japanese Judges in Philip S.C. Lewis Ed., LAW AND TECHNOLOGY IN THE PACIFIC COMMUNITY 263 (1991) reprint in JAPANESE LAW IN CONTEXT (Milhaupt, Jr., Ramseyer, and Young ed., Harvard University Asia Center, 2001) 82-83.

200 See, Peter J. Herzog, JAPAN'S PSEUDO-DEMOCRACY (Japan Library, 1993) 250.

201 The bill was enacted into law at the close of the Diet's spring session on June 11, 2004.

b) Conservative Approach of the Supreme Court

The conservative approach of the Supreme Court of Japan can be discerned in several areas affecting the powers of the political branches of the government.[202] First, the court consistently defers to the Diet in dealing with election district decisions—even when the districting is clearly unconstitutional. It is not simply a question of deferring to the Diet in the important question of resolving districting unconstitutionality. But in the more fundamental question of how to circumscribe "equality" the court after first adopting the approach of the United States Supreme Court in its one person-one vote jurisprudence then rejects the logical conclusion of that jurisprudence. Namely, that a disproportional ratio of 1 to 5 in the House of Councilors is not unequal or that a disproportional ratio of 1 to 2.9 for the House of Representatives is not unequal. Further, the districting cases are approached as if there were a contest between competing but equally valuable factors—the citizens right to equality and the Diet's right to legislate. The court appears to have adopted a balancing test to weigh these competing interests. Thus, where the Diet has not had time to change the districting plan (although it has had several years to make changes) the plan is constitutional notwithstanding that it violates the citizen's right to equality as set out in the Constitution. A less conservative approach would be to treat the Constitution as what it was intended to be, namely a check on the power of the Diet to assure that the Diet did not infringe on citizen's rights such as the right to equality in the vote. When viewed from this perspective the Diet's obligation to assure that the right to equality is protected may be equal to the Diet's obligation to not take away that equality. In no case can the Diet's administrative concerns (not enough time) override or be equated with the citizen's right to equality.

Similarly in the area of freedom of religion the court has taken a conservative approach that places majority Shinto values ahead of the values of the minority in society who are not adherents to Shinto. But the purpose of the Constitution is to protect the rights of the minority from potential abuse from the majority. By secularizing Shinto ceremonies and thereby taking them out of the "religious" realm the court is able to uphold the holding of such ceremonies as public events supported by government bodies without having to concern itself with the effect these

---

202 The Supreme Court's conservative approach to the use of its judicial powers was evident even during the American Occupation. In 1946 there was a demonstration outside the Imperial Palace a protester held a sign that was critical of the Emperor. The protester was arrested and convicted of defamation. Shortly thereafter a general amnesty was announced and he received amnesty as part of the process. Nonetheless he appealed the conviction arguing that under equality provisions of the Constitution (Article 14) the conviction was unconstitutional since it treated the Emperor differently from other Japanese. The Supreme Court turned away the appeal on the grounds that as amnesty had been granted there was no need to address the issue raised. See, Yasuhiro Okudaira, Forty Years of the Constitution and its Various Influences: Japanese, American, and European in JAPANESE CONSTITUTIONAL LAW (Percy R. Luney, Jr. and Kazuyuki Takanashi Ed., University of Tokyo Press, 1993) 1, 4-5.

ceremonies have on the minority community.[203] Thus, in the *Tsu City* case the court permitted the City to both sponsor and hold a Shinto groundbreaking ceremony and pay a Shinto priest to perform that ceremony for a public building.[204] And, by treating a Shinto ceremony as part of Japan's culture rather than as part of a religious system, the court was able to divorce the ceremony from the actions of the prewar government in utilizing Shinto to enhance the position of the Emperor and the autocratic regime. The Supreme Court's secularizing of religious ceremonies is similar to the approach taken by the Meiji oligarchs. Under the Meiji Constitution religious ceremonies that venerated the Emperor were considered as secular rites and all subjects, regardless of their religious beliefs, were required to participate in such ceremonies. Thus educators were required to bow in reverence to the Imperial prescript on education. In modern Japan the same issues that were presented in Meiji Japan are being played out in the cases brought by school teachers who refuse to sing the national anthem because of their objection to words that venerate the Emperor.

The court's use of political question and standing doctrine to avoid difficult constitutional issues such as it did in the dissolution of the Diet litigation discussed earlier is another illustration of a basic conservative bias by the court.[205] In dealing with the complicated question of the reach of Article 9 of the Constitution (Renunciation of War) the court has refused to open the courthouse door to arguments about the scope of Article 9. In the *Sunakawa* case, the defendants in a criminal proceeding attempted to argue that the activities alleged to be unlawful could not be a crime because the Agreement between Japan and the United States they were charged with disrupting was itself unconstitutional. The court found that the validity of the Agreement was a political question and therefore not justiciable.[206]

---

203 See generally, David M. O'Brien, TO DREAM OF DREAMS, RELIGIOUS FREEDOM AND CONSTITUTIONAL POLITICS IN POSTWAR JAPAN (University of Hawaii, 1996).

204 Tsu City Ground Purification Case, Kakunaga v. Sekiguchi, 31 Minshu 533 (Grand Bench, 7/13/77) Case No. 1971 (Gyo-Tsu) No. 69 available in English on the website of the Supreme Court of Japan, Judgments of the Supreme Court.

205 For a discussion of the court's conservative approach to constitutional questions see, Hiroshi Itoh, Judicial Review and Judicial Activism in Japan, 53 Law & Contemporary Problems, 169 (1990).

206 Sakata v. Japan, 13 Keishu 3225, Case No. 1959 (A) No. 710 (Sup. Ct. Grand Bench, 12/16/59) available in English on the website of the Supreme Court of Japan, Judgments of the Supreme Court; also available in English in John M. Maki, COURT AND CONSTITUTION IN JAPAN (University of Washington Press, 1964) 298. For a discussion of the Sunakawa case see, Kisaburo Yokota, Political Questions and Judicial Review: A Comparison in Dan Fenno Henderson, THE CONSTITUTION OF JAPAN: ITS FIRST TWENTY YEARS 1947-1967 (University of Washington Press, 1969) 141, 146-151.

The Supreme Court's conservative approach is perhaps best illustrated by its failure to make substantive use of its judicial review powers.[207] The court has only used its judicial review powers to find a law unconstitutional in six cases. In two, the election district cases, the court failed to take decisive action but left finding appropriate relief to the (unlawfully) elected Diet. These cases have previously been discussed. In two other cases the court found prewar Meiji era laws to be unconstitutional. In one case a law that punished patricide more severely than other forms of murder,[208] and in another a law that prohibited the owner of a less than 50% interest in a forest preserve from demanding a division of the forest. The patricide law had been based on the family law concepts of feudal and Meiji Japan (the *Ie*) and was inconsistent with both the new Constitution and modern family concepts. Nonetheless, it took two patricide cases before the court acted. In the first case the court refused to hold the law unconstitutional but indicated that the Diet should change the law.[209] When change was not forthcoming, the court belatedly acted. In one case, the *Hiroshima Pharmacy* case,[210] the court did take bold action in broadly construing the Constitution to strike down an anticompetitive law passed at the behest of the retail pharmacy industry to prevent competition by limiting the number of retail pharmacies in an area.[211] However, the court has failed to follow up on the *Pharmacy* case and the case itself concerned a relatively rare Member's bill that became law rather than a Cabinet bill supported by the ruling political party and the government. The final case was recently decided and here the court's position in holding a section of the Post Office law (originally enacted prewar) that granted immunity to the Post Office for misdelivery of certain

---

207 All courts in Japan have the power of Judicial Review. Suzuki v. Japan, 6 Minshu 783 (Sup. Ct. Grand Bench, 10/8/52) available in English in John M. Maki, COURT AND CONSTITUTION IN JAPAN (University of Washington Press, 1964); Dan Fenno Henderson, Japanese Judicial Review of Legislation: The First Twenty Years in Dan Fenno Henderson, THE CONSTITUTION OF JAPAN: ITS FIRST TWENTY YEARS 1947-1967 (University of Washington Press, 1969) 115, 123-124. Yosiyuki Noda, INTRODUCTION TO JAPANESE LAW (translated and edited by Anthony H. Angelo) (University of Tokyo Press, 1976) 120. The inferior courts are less reluctant to use the power, perhaps because they know their determination is not final but is subject to review. That review rarely finds that the lower court's use of the power was correct. As Professor Noda relates in the first 25 years of its existence the Supreme Court struck down only one law although constitutional questions had been raised in over 41,000 cases. Professor Noda concludes that the Supreme Court is "very conservative." Yosiyuki Noda, INTRODUCTION TO JAPANESE LAW (translated and edited by Anthony H. Angelo) (University of Tokyo Press, 1976) 122.

208 Aizawa v. Japan, 27 Keishu 265 (Sup. Ct. Grand Bench, 4/4/73) Case No. (A) No. 1310 of 1970 available in English on the website of the Supreme Court of Japan, Judgments of the Supreme Court.

209 Patricide case (Sup. Ct. Grand Bench 10/11/50) available in English in John M. Maki, COURT AND CONSTITUTION IN JAPAN (University of Washington Press, 1964) 129.

210 Sumiyoshi v. Governor of Hiroshima, 29 Minshu 572, Case No. 1968 (Gyo-Tsu) No. 120 (Sup. Ct., Grand Bench 4/30/75) available in English through the website of the Supreme Court of Japan, Judgments of the Supreme Court and in Lawrence W. Beer & Hiroshi Itoh, THE CONSTITUTIONAL CASE LAW OF JAPAN, 1970-1990 (University of Washington Press, 1996) at 188.

211 For a discussion of the case see, John O. Haley, The Freedom to Choose an Occupation and the Constitutional Limits of Legislative Discretion 8 Law in Japan 188 (1975).

types of mail[212] was consistent with that of Prime Minister Koizumi. The Prime Minister has urged the privatizing of the Post Office as part of his economic reform package and immunity for its activities would be inconsistent with privatization.

In the Post Office case, the constitutional provision at issue was Article 17, which provides that persons may sue "as provided by law" when redress is sought from a public entity for damage suffered as a result of an "illegal act" of a public official. The Post Office law permits such suits in general where special delivery and registered mail are involved. But, to protect the postal service's ability to charge low rates the liability is limited in amount. It was this limitation of liability provision that was challenged. The Supreme Court found that in cases of ordinary negligence such limitation of liability was permissible but that in cases of intentional dereliction of duty or gross negligence such limitation was impermissible and unconstitutional. To reach this conclusion the court noted that while the purpose of keeping rates low was served by limiting the liability of the Post Office for ordinary negligence such purpose was not served when gross negligence was involved. The reason why the purpose was not served in gross negligence situations is somewhat fuzzy but appears to be that such cases are rare and therefore they cannot have a great impact on postal costs. There is however no analysis of how rare or how frequently acts of gross negligence occur or how frequently acts of negligence occur. Instead the court found, *ex cathedra*, it beyond logic that cases of gross negligence or intentional acts could affect the cost of postal service. What was left not considered by the court was whether the constitutional language permitting a person to sue *as provided by law* meant that the Constitution specifically recognized the authority of the State to limit its liability by not providing for suit or limiting the amount of the recovery. Instead the court deals with this issue by simply assuming and stating as a given that any such limits on liability must be reasonable. Yet earlier jurisprudence of the court indicates that when the Diet acts its actions are only subject to challenge when grossly outside the discretion of the Diet or "flagrant."[213] This is clearly a more demanding standard than reasonableness.[214] Nor does the court discuss whether the provision in the Constitution making the State responsible for illegal acts applies to gross negligence. Is gross negligence the same as an illegal act? Is gross negligence in the failure to properly deliver a registered mail package a violation of a law—does it rise to the level of illegality? Does illegality in Article 17 simply mean erroneous, or grossly erroneous? This issue was neither confronted nor resolved. Perhaps most illuminating is

212 Case No. 1999 (O) No. 1767, 56 Minshu 1439 (Sup. Ct. Grand Bench, 9/11/02) available in English through the web site of the Supreme Court of Japan.

213 John M. Maki, The Japanese Constitutional Style in Dan Fenno Henderson, THE CONSTITUTION OF JAPAN: ITS FIRST TWENTY YEARS 1947-1967 (University of Washington Press, 1969) 3, 23.

214 See, e.g. Horiki case, Case No. 1976 (Gyo-Tsu) no. 30, 36 Minshu 1235 (Sup. Ct. Grand Bench 7/7/82) available in English on the web on the web site of the Supreme Court of Japan, Judgments of the Supreme Court and also in Lawrence W. Beer & Hiroshi Itoh, THE CONSTITUTIONAL CASE LAW OF JAPAN, 1970-1990 (University of Washington Press, 1996) at 323.

the decision's discussion of the permissible limits on private company liability provided by special laws. After referring to four laws that allow such limits on liability of private firms the court notes that all are limited to acts of negligence and do not permit limited liability for acts of gross negligence or intentional conduct. What the decision implicitly does is equate the Postal Service with these private entities—exactly what the Prime Minister is attempting to do through privatization.

Additional questions are raised by the Post Office decision. The Supreme Court's jurisprudence is clear in recognizing judicial deference to legislative action. In the Post Office situation the Prime Minister is recommending legislative changes to the Post Office law. In such context the Diet will soon have the opportunity to treat the Post Office as a private enterprise or to reject such treatment. Allowing the Diet to make that determination would appear to be consistent with a long line of Supreme Court authority. It is true that the Prime Minister has not been successful in achieving several of his policy objectives and some leaders of the LDP oppose his Post Office initiative. Privatization of the Post Office is a matter of some dispute in the LDP. In fact, it appears that the Prime Minister may not be able to achieve his goal of privatizing the Post Office or at least will not achieve that goal at any time in the near future. A government study group has recommended that privatization be accomplished in 2017 after a ten-year transition that will only begin in 2007.[215] Through its decision the Supreme Court has relieved the Prime Minister of the necessity to negotiate with other factions leaders on one aspect of privatization. But the court has not explained why the court should relieve the Prime Minister of this obligation. Why is the question of immunity or limits on Post Office immunity not a question for consideration by the highest organ of the State—the Diet?

Although giving less deference to the Diet in an area of relative unimportance, the Supreme Court has given the Diet almost unlimited deference in areas where rights of citizens are involved.[216] Thus in the interpretation of the social welfare clauses of the Constitution the court has stated that the discretion of Ministers

215 See, Japan Times on Line, 4/8/04 Panel Wants Japan Post Privatized in 2017 after 10-year Transition Phase.

216 See, Taisuke Kamata, Adjudication and the Governing Process: Political Question and Legislative Discretion in JAPANESE CONSTITUTIONAL LAW (Percy R. Luney, Jr. and Kazuyuki Takanashi Ed., University of Tokyo Press, 1993) 151 for the view that the Supreme Court generally applies a balancing of interests test when dealing with challenges to legislative discretion and in doing so upholds cases of arbitrary action and unreasonable legislative determinations (see pgs. 168-169). See also, Noriho Urabe Rule of Law and Due Process: A Comparative View of the United States and Japan in JAPANESE CONSTITUTIONAL LAW (Percy R. Luney, Jr. and Kazuyuki Takanashi Ed., University of Tokyo Press, 1993) 173 for criticism of the Japanese Supreme Court approach to judicial review.

must not be exercised in an unreasonable manner so as to constitute an abuse of discretion—but it has never found such exercise to be an abuse of discretion.[217]

The two most notable aspects of this jurisprudence are: a) the court has never struck down a law passed by the postwar Diet and supported by the majority party as a Government bill[218] and b) none of the cases where a plaintiff received relief as a consequence of a finding of unconstitutionality goes to the heart of democratic government or limits on government power.[219]

There are several possible explanations, aside from political considerations, for the reluctance of the Supreme Court of Japan to utilize the judicial review power specifically given to it by the Constitution. Before discussing these possible rationales it should be noted that an argument can be made that the Constitution of Japan gives the Supreme Court of Japan even greater rights to apply judicial review than is given to the American Supreme Court. Not only is judicial review in the United States a judge made rule stemming from *Marbury v. Madison* while Japan's rule is specifically stated in the text of the Constitution, but Japan has a Supremacy Clause in its Constitution that makes the Constitution the Supreme Law. It is, of course true that the United States also has a Supremacy Clause but there is this difference. In the United States a Supremacy clause is necessary to define the role of the Federal Government vis-à-vis the semi sovereign States. Without such a clause the issue of whose law controls would remain unanswered in the Constitution and since the Constitution was the product of State action it could be strongly argued that State law controlled. Japan on the other hand is a unitary State and there is no "conflict of law" between the national law and other laws—there are no other laws except those that are permitted by national legislation. Indeed, the Diet is made the sole law making authority. So what is the Constitution supreme to? It can be argued that it must be supreme to laws passed by the Diet, as no other option exists. This is consistent with the idea that an unconstitutional law should be null and void. Thus, it can be argued that in Japan there is even more authority in the Constitution for the court to exercise its judicial review power than is true in the United States.

In any event, the Supreme Court of Japan has been stingy in exercising it judicial review power. There are several potential reasons for this inaction. The initial

---

217 See, e.g., Asahi Case, Case No. 14 of 1964, 21 Minshu 1043 (Sup. Ct. Grand Bench 5/24/67) available in English on the web on the web site of the Supreme Court of Japan, Judgments of the Supreme Court; Horiki case, Case No. 1976 (Gyo-Tsu) no. 30, 36 Minshu 1235 (Sup. Ct. Grand Bench 7/7/82) available in English on the web on the web site of the Supreme Court of Japan, Judgments of the Supreme Court and also in Lawrence W. Beer & Hiroshi Itoh, THE CONSTITUTIONAL CASE LAW OF JAPAN, 1970-1990 (University of Washington Press, 1996) at 323.

218 For the significance of government bills in Japan's governing structure see, Bradley Richardson, JAPANESE DEMOCRACY—POWER, COORDINATION, AND PERFORMANCE (Yale University Press, 1997) 110-112, 129-130.

219 The election district cases do go to the heart of democratic government and the people's rights. But in these cases the Court used the circumstance decision mechanism (though not technically applicable) to avoid giving relief to the plaintiffs.

working draft of the Constitution prepared by the Occupation had a judicial review clause but that clause did not apply to all legislation enacted by the Diet. Instead judicial review by the Supreme Court was limited to laws that were inconsistent with the rights set out in Chapter 3 of the Constitution.[220] There was even a movement to give the Diet a limited authority by a 2/3 vote to overrule a Supreme Court finding of unconstitutionality.[221] The New Deal drafters of Japan's Constitution were undoubtedly aware that the Supreme Court of the United States had struck down as unconstitutional several pieces of New Deal legislation. As to other laws the Constitution made no mention except for the supreme organ of the State language referring to the Diet. Thus it might be that the Japanese Supreme Court is loath to apply the judicial review power in cases that do not implicate Chapter 3 rights because it seeks to apply the original intent (before modification) of the Occupation draft. Such rationale would not explain why the court does not fulsomely apply judicial review when it is alleged that Chapter 3 rights are involved. But it may be complimentary to other reasons for reticence.

As earlier noted, Japan's legal system is fundamentally a civil law system. In such system the judge is not a "law maker" in the sense of a common law judge. Rather, civil law judges are more law finders who then apply the law. A basic idea of the civil law is that the law is written down in the Codes—indeed the Codes (and other statutes) *are* the law. And, in today's modern era of democracy this written law is made by the duly elected representatives of the people. For a judge to exercise judicial review and hold a law unconstitutional would thus run counter to two strongly held positions: a) the judge would be usurping the power of the majority to make law[222] and b) the judge would not be finding and applying the law as contained in the Codes and statutes but would be making law. It is to be expected that judges would exercise such power only rarely. Whatever the merits of the supreme organ of the State argument, the deference shown to the Legislative Branch by the Japanese Judicial Branch may reflect a feeling that indeed the Diet is, or should be, supreme—except in the rare case where the Diet has simply acted unreasonably. In any event, as the supreme organ it may be entitled to the benefit of the doubt when a constitutional issue is raised.

Japanese judges tend to have risen to the Supreme Court through service in a bureaucracy, be it the judicial bureaucracy or some other government bureaucracy. Japan does not have a unified Bar as does the United States where judges, lawyers and prosecutors not only have the same education but usually have freely migrated between such positions during their legal careers. In Japan prosecutors tend

220 Robert E. Ward, The Origins of the Present Japanese Constitution, 50 American Political Science Review 980, 1007 (1956)

221 Richard B. Finn, WINNERS IN PEACE, MACARTHUR, YOSHIDA, AND POSTWAR JAPAN (University of California Press, 1992) 95.

222 See, Geoffrey C. Hazard, Jr., Discovery and the Role of the Judge in Civil Law Jurisdictions, 73 Notre Dame Law Review 1017, 1027 (1998) (judicial deference to the Legislative Branch is the flip side to legislative supremacy and a staple of the French Revolution's constitutional theory).

to be prosecutors for their career (and some rise to become Supreme Court Justices), judges tend to be judges and lawyers tend to be lawyers. Indeed, judges and practicing lawyers do not even belong to the same Bar Associations. Bar Associations in Japan are organized and run by bengoshi and because of the strained relations between bengoshi and the government during the prewar era bengoshi jealously guard this preserve from possible judicial or other official interference. Since most Supreme Court Justices have not been practicing lawyers, and have not participated in organizations of practicing lawyers, most Justices have not had the experience of either arguing that a law is unconstitutional or empathizing with a client challenging a law. Instead they have been brought up to look at laws as constitutional acts of the governing elite—of which they have been a part. For such a judge, having spent almost all (in some cases all) of his/her life in government service of one kind or another it would be a stretch indeed to find that actions of the supreme organ of that government, the Diet, were unlawful. Those Supreme Court Justices who rose through the judicial bureaucracy must especially feel this difficulty—and there are always a substantial number of such career judges on the court.

Because the Supreme Court, through its judicial Secretariat, lends up and coming young judges to the Executive Branch and since some of these judges have already opined that the laws passed by the Diet are constitutional,[223] a finding of unconstitutionality would be a rejection of advice received by representatives of the judiciary. This would certainly be humiliating to the judges who had given their earlier opinion that the law is valid. Just as prosecutors may look the other way to avoid causing a loss of face to the police with whom they work on a regular basis, so too judges will not want to see their colleagues lose face. Worse yet, it would be the judiciary as a corporate entity that would lose face since the judge was selected for the Executive position by the Secretariat and is considered as of the highest quality. As the judges sent to the Executive are the "cream of the crop" of judges and can anticipate elevation perhaps even to the Supreme Court it would not be in the interests of the judicial Secretariat or other judges to overturn their Executive recommendation or judgment. To avoid such a sharp clash some harmonizing method of avoiding the constitutional question may be preferable.

Further, the Constitution is a "common law" based instrument, but Japan is a German law influenced legal system with roots that grow deep in soil fertilized with respect for officialdom and government bureaucracy. Perhaps it was simply unreasonable for the Occupation to have thought that granting the court judicial review power could plow under such deep-rooted ideas. Of course, it may be that fewer unconstitutional laws are passed in Japan or it may be that judicial review is a product of time. After all, the Supreme Court of the United States made even less use of the power than has the Japanese Supreme Court in the first 50 years of the Constitution.

223 The present Chief Justice held just such a position in the Executive Branch while still serving in the Judiciary.

Recently there has been a movement in some academic circles in Japan to establish a Constitutional Court on the model of the present German Constitutional Court to deal with issues of constitutionality. Such a Court cannot be established under the present Constitution because of the prohibition against creation of "extraordinary tribunals." The idea of a European (civil law) style Constitutional Court, apparently not bound by case or controversy rules and apparently to perform the function of granting advisory opinions to the government, may reflect a more general trend in Japanese legal circles today. Namely a return to the more German law and German legal philosophy underlying law in the prewar period and a turning away from the common law notions of American law. In any event, to date this idea does not seem to have attracted sufficient political attention to make it a "front burner" political issue. However, with moves afoot to amend the Constitution in some respects (most notably Article 9—Renunciation of War) the idea may gain traction and could be considered along with other "reform" proposals. This is not the first time such an argument has been raised in academic circles. Indeed, arguments in favor of such a court were raised in the 1950s (at about the same time as arguments for a revision of Article 9 and the Constitution in general).[224] Nonetheless, as movement for a constitutional revision moves forward[225] this may become an issue. It is suggested that although the Supreme Court's jurisprudence under its judicial review power is grudging, it is better to have a Court that is essentially a law court with daily contact with legal problems in a case or controversy arena deal with the essentially legal question of whether a law (either on its face or as applied) is or is not inconsistent with the Constitution than it is to have such issues presented to a specialist group removed from the arena of everyday litigation. The interpretation of the Constitution is a legal question and one that judges dealing with general legal issues should decide based on their understanding of how law affects the lives of ordinary people. To place such a power in the hands of a group cut off from the general public and the daily issues that courts and judges face would do a disservice to the Constitution and the people.

The problem with the court's judicial review jurisprudence is not structural. The issue is not the need for a new court. If there is perceived to be a problem it is with the court's exercise or failure to exercise its judicial review power. Appointing Justices who have more regard for judicial review or appointing more practicing lawyers who may have argued that a law is unconstitutional and thus have no fear of holding a law unconstitutional, may be a more appropriate response. Creating a special Constitutional Court may give government—which has the power to appoint the judges of the special court—even greater control than it has under the present system. Specialist judges will likely be selected from the bureaucracy and from those advising the government concerning constitutionality

224 See, Dan Fenno Henderson, Japanese Judicial Review of Legislation: The First Twenty Years in Dan Fenno Henderson, THE CONSTITUTION OF JAPAN: ITS FIRST TWENTY YEARS 1947-1967 (University of Washington Press, 1969) 115, 120-123.

225 See discussion of such movement under the sponsorship of Prime Minister Koizumi in the section on Article 9—Renunciation of War.

of bills proposed by the government. While the present arrangement leaves open the possibility of the evolution of a jurisprudence of judicial review, the creation of a specialist Constitutional Court may stifle such evolution and thus be counterproductive.

B. The New Constitution and Renunciation of War

The question of who suggested that the Japanese Constitution contain a Renunciation of War clause is confusing and has a history of its own laden with political implications. If the clause had not been recommended by the Japanese then conservative forces urging a rewriting of the Japanese Constitution have an argument for their cause—"we must rewrite the Constitution to make it a Japanese initiative and not something forced on us." On the other hand, if the Article was suggested by the Japanese themselves, that argument loses its substance. As a consequence it is difficult to separate fact from fiction.[226] Nonetheless, it seems reasonable to believe that General MacArthur is responsible for the Renunciation of War clause in the Japanese Constitution, notwithstanding protestations to the contrary, based on Prime Minister Shidehara's belated claim that he first broached the subject with MacArthur and MacArthur agreed.[227] Recall that Shidehara was of the view that there was no need to drastically amend the Meiji Constitution and that his appointed Committee drafted an amendment to the Meiji Constitution that was hollow and contained not a word about restricting or narrowing the war making power.[228]

The instructions that MacArthur received from Washington left open the possibility that at a future date Japan could rearm. But MacArthur instructed his staff that a Renunciation of War clause be placed in the Constitution and further that the

---

226 See, e.g., Kenzo Takayanagi, Some Reminiscences of Japan's Commission on the Constitution in Dan Fenno Henderson, THE CONSTITUTION OF JAPAN: ITS FIRST TWENTY YEARS 1947-1967 (University of Washington Press, 1969) 82.

227 James L. McClain, JAPAN, A MODERN HISTORY (W.W. Norton & Company, 2002) 540; Richard B. Finn, WINNERS IN PEACE, MACARTHUR, YOSHIDA, AND POSTWAR JAPAN (University of California Press, 1992) 99 (quoting MacArthur as linking the preservation of the Emperor system with the renunciation of military forces) and 103 (disputing the later claim that the idea came from Prime Minister Shidehara); Koseki Shoichi THE BIRTH OF JAPAN'S POSTWAR CONSTITUTION (Edited and translated by Ray A. Moore) (Westview Press, 1997) at 82-85. See also, Kenzo Takayanagi, Some Reminiscences of Japan's Commission on the Constitution in Dan Fenno Henderson, THE CONSTITUTION OF JAPAN: ITS FIRST TWENTY YEARS 1947-1967 (University of Washington Press, 1969) 86-88; Alfred C. Oppler, LEGAL REFORM IN OCCUPIED JAPAN (Princeton University Press, 1976) 208 fn. 1; Theodore McNelly, The Japanese Constitution: Child of the Cold War, 74 Political Science Quarterly 176, 185-186 (1959).

228 Colonel Kades suggests that other potential authors of the peace constitution idea were the Emperor whose January 1946 rescript renouncing divinity noted that the new Japan would adopt peaceful ideas and that MacArthur noted this was a sound idea as well as General Whitney who Kades suggests might have suggested the idea to MacArthur. Charles L. Kades, The American Role in Revising Japan's Imperial Constitution, 104 Political Science Quarterly 215, 224 (1989).

clause be worded permanently, and that it make clear that renunciation included both a defensive as well as an offensive war capability. It appeared to the drafters of the Constitution (especially Colonel Kades) that every country had a right to defend itself when attacked and thus they amended MacArthur's instructions so as to delete the clause making clear that renunciation included defense of Japan.[229] The Japanese also proposed an amendment to Article 9 that was agreed to by the Occupation. This amendment (the Ashida Amendment) inserted the clause in Article 9 that placed renunciation in the context of an aspiration for international peace.[230] This clause was interpreted by the Americans involved in the Constitution writing process as granting Japan the right to use force for self-defense purposes[231] and has been interpreted by later Japanese governments as giving Japan the right to maintain forces for self-defense.[232] Initial Japanese interpretation however was to the effect that the clause prohibited Japan from maintaining an Army or Navy—as it was worded. In other words original interpretation was that the clause prohibiting Japan from maintaining military forces meant that Japan could not maintain military forces.

Just as war had led to the disarmament of Japan so too war led to the rearmament of Japan. The Korean conflict meant that MacArthur's troops in Japan were needed for service in Korea and that the Occupation could not rely on a United States military to police Japan. The Occupation called on Japan to create a "National police reserve " of 75,000 troops that could serve this purpose. Although denominated a police force it had typical military equipment and was in reality the start of the Japanese Army.[233] Over the years as tensions of the cold war intensified the military relationship between Japan and the United States strengthened and with it so did the Japanese military. Of course, the Constitution forbids Japan from having a military, so it was not possible to call it a military, and word games came to be the order of the day. National Police Reserve gave way to National Safety Force to National Safety Agency to Japan Defense Agency to Self Defense Force (and its present components) responsible to the National Safety Agency—the ground Self Defense Force (read as meaning Army), the Air Self Defense Force (read as meaning Air Force) and the Marine Self Defense Force (read as meaning Navy).

The interpretation of Article 9 itself has changed over the years as the military power of Japan has increased. Initially, when the military was weak, the Article permitted it because it did not have "war potential." Later when the military was

---

229 Theodore McNelly, The Japanese Constitution: Child of the Cold War, 74 Political Science Quarterly 176, 178 (1959).

230 For a discussion of the Ashida Amendment see, Charles L. Kades, The American Role in Revising Japan's Imperial Constitution, 104 Political Science Quarterly 215, 236-238 (1989).

231 Charles L. Kades, The American Role in Revising Japan's Imperial Constitution, 104 Political Science Quarterly 215, 236-237 (1989).

232 Richard B. Finn, WINNERS IN PEACE, MACARTHUR, YOSHIDA, AND POSTWAR JAPAN (University of California Press, 1992) 116-117.

233 James L. McClain, JAPAN, A MODERN HISTORY (W.W. Norton & Company, 2002) 554.

strong enough so that it could effectively counter a military strike (i.e., it had war potential) war potential was acceptable as long as the military did not have potential to be used abroad but could only be used to defend Japan against direct aggression. As Japan purchased and developed weapons to counter attacks before they reached Japanese soil war potential was acceptable as long as it was only defensive and Japan did not have aggressive war potential.

Initially Japan's defense was a matter for the Occupation. Korea made Japan a more substantial partner and mutual defense of Japan became acceptable under Article 9. But mutual can be interpreted to mean that Japan must participate in defending the United States so it became necessary to interpret mutual to mean mutual defense of Japan and it is only recently that the term has been broadened to permit Japan to assist allies. The semantic approach to Article 9 has not been without significant meaning. Those who oppose amendment of the Constitution to eliminate Article 9 can argue that Article 9 has restrained the Japanese Government in its rearmament program. While it clearly no longer prohibits Japan from having an effective military capable of either aggressive or defensive war (after all an Aegis Naval Vessel is simply hardware, whether used aggressively or defensively is not a hardware question but a command decision) it does have meaning as a restraint on use of force and is a deterrent to military ambition. In time Japan's military budget became one of the largest in the world[234] and it is even suggested that it is second only to the United States.[235] Japan's relationship with the United States and its relationship with the world community has been the driving force both of Japanese disarmament and Japanese armament. At the time of the Japan/United States Peace Treaty, Japan and the United States also entered into a Mutual Defense Treaty (the San Francisco System) under which the United States was basically responsible for Japan's defense. To accomplish this end, the United States not only maintained its bases on Okinawa (Okinawa was not returned to Japanese sovereignty until several years later) but was granted bases on the main islands of Japan. When Okinawa was later returned to Japan, the United States retained the bases that it had on the island. The United States maintains those bases today. The return agreement gives the United States extensive rights to retain such bases on Okinawa. As the cost of American defense of Japan has increased the United States asked Japan to undertake more of the role and expense of its own defense. This meant greater defense budgets, more efficient equipment and a more potent military. Japan increased its military spending and expanded its military capacity.

Peace in Cambodia's long running civil war required an outside military force to help police the peace the parties had agreed to. Japan was the logical local power to supply peacekeepers under the UN mandate. To meet its international commit-

---

234 James E. Auer, Article 9 of Japan's Constitution: From Renunciation of Armed Force "Forever" to the Third Largest Defense Budget in the World, 53 Law & Contemporary Problems 171 (1990).

235 Marius B. Jansen, THE MAKING OF MODERN JAPAN (Belknap Press of Harvard University, 2000) 757.

ments Japan enacted a Peace Keeping Operations ("PKO") law that permitted it to send troops to Cambodia once the parties had resolved their differences, had requested such peacekeepers and so long as Japan was operating under the umbrella of the United Nations. In the Gulf War Japan was asked to participate through the use of mine sweepers. Japan declined and debated whether it could send such sweepers until it was too late to be of any assistance. Japan sent money instead, arguing that Article 9 forbade its use of force.[236] Many in the United States saw this action (inaction?) as ungrateful and as taking advantage of the United States. Japan is an oil poor country that receives most of its oil supplies from the Middle East. It was a prime beneficiary of the Gulf War. Criticism of Japan's inability to make a decision until one was too late to be meaningful greatly affected Japanese political leadership.

In Afghanistan and Iraq Japan was once again asked to assist. Japan determined not to be criticized for failure to assist its main ally. Legislation was passed permitting limited use of Japanese forces abroad and in 2004 for the first time Japanese troops were sent to a foreign country, not under UN auspices and not to a region where there were no ongoing hostilities. Each step in this process was taken slowly, after great deliberation and public debate and each step was hedged with cautionary and conservative action to avoid both the reality and appearance of a re-emerging militaristic Japan. Japan's peace Constitution (i.e., Article 9) is responsible, in part, for this cautious approach to the use of the military. While the Constitution clearly does not prevent what it says it prohibits, it does have significance and meaning through counseling caution and providing a hurdle that must be overcome by the political leadership before action can be undertaken.

As Japan's positions and actions changed, opponents of the government attempted to use the Renunciation of War clause in litigation to slow down or stop the government's action. The first legal challenge sought to prevent Japan from allowing American troops and bases in Japan as part of the mutual defense arrangement. The Supreme Court of Japan applied the political question doctrine to find that it could not deal with this challenge to the enlargement of an airstrip on a United States military base in Japan. The San Francisco system made the United States the main defender of Japan and bound Japan to the United States during the Cold War. Not all Japanese agreed with the system and there was great unrest in Japan concerning the system. The Supreme Court found the system an integral part of the return of sovereignty to Japan and the end of the Occupation. As such the mutual defense treaty was a highly political determination, and review of the San Francisco system was a political rather than a legal question.

In dictum the court deftly turned plaintiffs' arguments around to be used against them. Plaintiffs argued that Article 9 prohibited war potential and that the air base

236 For a discussion of Japan's participation in a peacekeeping operation in Cambodia and its failure to participate on the ground in the Gulf War see, Marius B. Jansen, THE MAKING OF MODERN JAPAN (Belknap Press of Harvard University, 2000) 757-759; James L. McClain, JAPAN, A MODERN HISTORY (W.W. Norton & Company, 2002).

represented war potential. The court noted that without United States assistance Japan would be helpless, as Japan could not provide for its own defense, as this would mean having war potential. In such a circumstance it was permissible for Japan to utilize the United States and the American military (that did have war potential) to provide for Japanese defense.[237]

This same argument could not be used when opponents of the government sought to prevent the Japan Defense Agency from changing the status of a forest preserve as a first step towards the construction of a Nike Missile base. Nor could it be argued that a Nike Missile is not war potential. This time the court denied relief finding that plaintiffs lacked standing to bring the action, as they suffered no direct legal injury as a consequence of the clearing of the preserve. To the argument that the clearing would cause flooding and/or otherwise damage plaintiffs' property the court noted that the suit was not about the clearing of the land but was about the change in status of the land. Such change in status created no flooding or other damage. The plaintiffs thus lacked standing to sue to challenge the change in status. There are also overtones of political question jurisprudence in the decision. In any event, the constitutional question was never dealt with.[238]

When the seller of land attempted to rescind a contract to sell the land to an anti-military group that had failed to pay the purchase price, so that the land could be sold to the Self Defense Force for an Air Self Defense Force base, the defaulting purchasers sued. Plaintiffs argued that the seller could not rescind and then carry out a purpose that was in violation of Article 9. In this case the court expanded on its reasons for not permitting litigation challenging government steps to advance its military posture by holding that Article 9 does not create any rights in individual citizens on which they can rely in litigation. In other words, in Article 9 the government renounces war and undertakes not to have a military but this is a government commitment that citizens cannot base a lawsuit on. It creates no direct rights that citizens can rely on. The defaulting purchasers argued that even if it did not create any directly applicable rights, the case before the court involved a contract dispute and in such cases Article 90 of the Civil Code applied. Article 90 prohibits a party to a contract from entering into an agreement that has as its purpose matter that is against public morals or public order. The court found Arti-

---

237 Sakata v. Japan, 13 Keishu 3225, Case No. 1959 (A) No. 71(0) (Sup. Ct. Grand Bench, 12/16/59) available in English through the web site of the Supreme Court of Japan, Judgments of the Supreme Court; see also, John M. Maki, COURT AND CONSTITUTION IN JAPAN (University of Washington Press, 1964) 298; Dan Fenno Henderson, THE CONSTITUTION OF JAPAN: ITS FIRST TWENTY YEARS 1947-1967 (University of Washington Press, 1969) 147-148; Hideo Tanaka, THE JAPANESE LEGAL SYSTEM (University of Tokyo Press, 1976) 709-711.

238 Uno v. Minister of Agriculture, Forestry and Fisheries, 36 Minshu 1679 (Sup. Ct. Petty Bench, 9/19/82) for an English language translation see, Lawrence W. Beer & Hiroshi Itoh, THE CONSTITUTIONAL CASE LAW OF JAPAN, 1970-1990 (University of Washington Press, 1996) 122. See also, James E. Auer, Article 9 of Japan's Constitution: From Renunciation of Armed Force "Forever" to the Third Largest Defense Budget in the World, 53 Law & Contemporary Problems 171, 182 (1990).

cle 90 inapplicable. As an initial matter the court saw the case as involving "private law" issues and not "public law" issues. As the State was simply a purchaser of land, no public law questions were presented. Like any other private party the State had a right to purchase land. The plaintiffs could only utilize article 90 if the purchase was for immoral purposes (such as building a house of prostitution). Because it found that the Japanese public did not consider the Self Defense Force as immoral there could be no violation of Article 90.[239]

The most recent Supreme Court decision dealing with Article 9 concerned the stationing of United States troops on Okinawa. Okinawa bears the brunt (but also enjoys the greatest economic windfall) of American troops stationed in Japan. This overuse of Okinawa as a United States military base is a flashpoint for residents of the island still smarting over the American determination to return Okinawa to Japan after the war rather than granting Okinawa independent status. Okinawa is part of the Ryukyu chain that was an independent State with its own King. In 1609 the chain was subdued by Satsuma (one of the big four Han domains responsible for the Meiji Restoration) and became a vassal state of Satsuma. Until 1879 the Ryukyu's had its own King. It was only that year that the Ryukyu's became a part of greater Japan as Okinawa Prefecture. Making Okinawa a part of greater Japan and making residents of Okinawa Japanese citizens was part of Meiji Japan's effort to define its borders as a Nation State. (Just as the settlement of Hokkaido and the "integration" of the Ainu was part of the need to define the contours of the Nation State). Many in Okinawa objected to their incorporation into Japan. The battle of Okinawa was one of the bloodiest of World War 2 and many civilians as well as military died on the island. After the War the American Occupation kept a large military force on the island, and the Peace Treaty with Japan left Okinawa in American hands. When the island was "returned" to Japan, it was agreed that the American military would remain and maintain bases.

Many bases on Okinawa are situated on leased land. When the lease for a base came due the owner refused to sign a renewal and the government in Tokyo ordered the Prefectural Governor to take steps to confiscate the land and sign a lease with the United States. Japan, because it is a unitary State may take action to force governors and other local authorities to act as arms of the national government—a power denied to the federal government in the United States since the individual States are themselves sovereign entities. However, Prefectural Governors are elected by the local population and thus attempt to represent the local interest. The Governor refused to confiscate and then sign the lease and the government sued seeking mandamus to compel the Governor to act.

The *Governor of Okinawa Mandamus case* presented an anomalous fact situation for the United States. Prior to the Meiji Restoration the Han (the feudal domains) were semi autonomous. They were, of course, subject to Tokugawa rule but as

239 Ishizuka v. Japan, 43 Minshu 385 (Case No. 1982 (O) No. 164 (Sup. Ct. Petty Bench 6/20/89) available in English through the web site of the Supreme Court of Japan, Judgments of the Supreme Court.

long as the local Daimyo rules were not inconsistent with Tokugawa rules such local rules were acceptable. The villages were even more autonomous with their own governing system and headmen. When the Meiji oligarchs abolished the Han and created prefectures they also made the country a unitary State and the prefectures had no autonomy except as national laws might grant autonomy (or subsequently take it away). The virtually exclusive authority of the Tokyo government was enforced by a strong central police force under the Home Ministry. The American Occupation saw the strong central government as one of the reasons for the authoritarian nature of the prewar State and sought to support the democratic ideal by providing stronger local government support. To this end it was required that Prefecture Governors be elected.[240] However local officials were given no autonomous powers. Local officials derived their power, as did the locality from laws passed by the National Government.[241] In the Governor of Okinawa case the Governor was attempting to express the democratically expressed will of the local population against the Central Government in Tokyo. The government in Tokyo on the other hand was essentially a proxy for the United States. In essence the United States, which had sought to strengthen democracy through the election of local officials who could then check the power of the central government in Tokyo, found itself using the central government to override the will of the local population as expressed by such elected local officials.

The procedural posture of the case was such that the government in Tokyo was the moving party and the Governor was the defendant. In such a situation standing could not be an issue nor could the political question doctrine. Although the Governor refused to act, he was in a difficult position. If he argued that the defense treaty under which the bases were established was in violation of Article 9 and was successful, then *all* American bases on the island were unconstitutional. If the bases all closed, the economy of the island would collapse. Hence the Governor could not argue that the treaty was in violation of Article 9. Yet he had to find some argument to defend his refusal to act as requested by the government. He argued that the confiscation was not for a public purpose, even though the purpose was a base for troops now concededly legally assigned to the island. The court refused to relieve him of his dilemma. The court held that the housing of troops in conformity with a treaty was a public purpose and never reached the question of whether the underlying treaty was lawful, as that point had been conceded by the Governor and thus was not an issue in the case.[242]

Ever since the suit by the Governor of Okinawa private parties appear to understand that Article 9 cannot be the basis for attacking the expropriation of land, un-

240 Constitution of Japan, Article 93 (2).

241 See, Local Autonomy Law; see also, Hiroyuki Hata, Go Nakagawa and Takehisa Nakagawa, JAPANESE CONSTITUTIONAL LAW (Kluwer Law International, 2001) Part III The State and its Subdivisions.

242 Case No. 1996 (Gyo-Tsu) No. 90, 50 Minshu 1952 (Sup. Ct. Grand Bench 8/28/96) available in English through the web site of the Supreme Court of Japan, Judgments of the Supreme Court.

der the Mutual Defense Treaty, for the use of the American Armed Forces. Judicial challenges nonetheless proceed. The Supreme Court of Japan has made it clear that such taking is for a public purpose (as required by the Constitution) and thus has blunted arguments based on Article 9. Recently the Supreme Court turned away a challenge arguing that the Expropriation Committee responsible for expropriation of property was the appropriate body to make the determination of whether the land was required by the American Forces. The court noted that such a decision had political implications and thus granting the authority to make such a decision to the Prime Minister was appropriate. In doing so the court noted that among the factors to be considered were the security of Japan *and* the security of the Far East. This appears to recognize the legality of projection of military thinking and action through the Mutual Defense Treaty beyond Japan to the Far East in general.[243]

Japan's current position regarding military doctrine may be found in two complimentary statements. First, the three-point nuclear policy statement that Japan will not: a) possess, b) manufacture or c) permit on its territory nuclear weapons. Second, the five defense principles: a) exclusively offensive weapons are forbidden to Japan's military, b) as a last resort self-defense to repel an imminent act of aggression is permitted, c) unilateral deployment of troops abroad is inconsistent with the philosophy of utilizing the minimum force necessary to defend Japan, d) collective self-defense is permissible to defend Japan and e) self-defense is not considered belligerency and belligerency by Japan against another country is forbidden either unilaterally or as part of a collective effort.[244] Yet these positions are under attack. Government officials have stated that there is no constitutional limit on Japan's rejection of the three non-nuclear principles[245] and the deployment of troops to Iraq under a recent law passed to allow such deployment would seem to be counter to the five principles.[246] The deployment to Iraq has not been without opposition within the LDP.[247] In addition, there has been objection from coalition

243 Case No. 129 and 141 of 2003, 57 Minshu ____ (Sup. Ct. Petty Bench, 11/27/03) available through the web site of the Supreme Court of Japan.

244 See, Government View on Purport of Article 9 on the web in English on the Defense Ministry link accessible through the Prime Minister's page at www.Kantei.go.jp/foreign/index-e.html .

245 Japan Times on Line, April 2, 2002; Japan Times on Line 6/2/02 Koizumi Downplays Non nuclear Policy Quip.

246 Japan times on Line 1/24/04 Main ASDF Team Arrives in Kuwait; Japan Times on Line, 1/21/04 GSDF Team To Build Ties with Iraqis; Japan Times on Line 1/20/04 Blackhawks Eyed for Dispatch; Japan Times on Line 1/18/04 GSDF Troops Get to Work in Kuwait.

247 Japan Times on Line 1/23/04 ASDF Unit Leaves for Kuwait to the Sound of Cheers, Jeers; Japan Times on Line, 1/21/04 Officials Lobby LDP Rebels over SDF Dispatch; Japan Times on Line 1/19/04 51.6% Oppose SDF Dispatch to Iraq but Cabinet Support Up.

partners,[248] opposition parties, and segments of the public.[249] It has been urged that deployment is inconsistent with the Constitution (Article 9).[250]

Does Article 9 mean what the words say and what the writers of the Article and the government that adopted the Constitution said it meant? No. Does it prohibit Japan from having an Army, Navy and Air Force? No. Does it prevent Japan from engaging in activities abroad to assist either the UN or an ally such as the United States? Prevent—No; limit how Japan does this—perhaps, and if not as a matter of law at least as a matter of politics. Is it a dead letter or as some have argued has it been written out of the Constitution by the device of Constitutional Transformation?[251] It is suggested, no. Article 9 remains a vibrant statement of the aspirations of the Japanese people both for a peaceful world and for Japan to play a role in establishing such a peaceful world. As such it limits the moral authority of the government leadership and points them in a peaceful direction whenever the question of use of military force is considered. For a country with Japan's military past—both feudal and Meiji era, this may not be such a bad thing.

In any event, Prime Minister Koizumi has been advocating a constitutional change to permit direct election of the Prime Minister (effectively changing to a hybrid parliamentary/Presidential system) and especially amendment of Article 9.[252] The exact scope of the proposed amendment has not yet taken form. However, a Research Commission on the Constitution was established in January 2000 by Act of the Diet. There appears to be movement toward a constitutional convention of some sort.[253] How Article 9 would fare at such a convention remains to be seen. Previous efforts to revise the Constitution, especially those of the 1950s, started as a supposed need to revise Article 9 and spread to a more general attempt to revise the Constitution to make it more consistent with supposed Japanese values—i.e., the more conservative values of the revisionists. Those efforts failed.[254] Under the Constitution, amendment requires a 2/3 vote of all the members of each

---

248 Soka Gakkai Feels Dissent on Dispatch, Asahi Shimbun 1/12/04 on the web at asahi.com.

249 Japan Times on Line, Protesters Rally in Tokyo Against Dispatch of Troops to Iraq 1/26/04.

250 Japan times on Line, 1/22/04 Kan Tells Koizumi to Resign.

251 See, Tomosuke Kasuya, Constitutional Transformation and the Ninth Article of the Japanese Constitution, 18 Law in Japan 1 (1986) and the introductory remark thereto by Paul Stephen Taylor; on Constitutional Transformation in general see, Bruce A. Ackerman, WE THE PEOPLE: TRANSFORMATIONS (Harvard University Press, 1998); Bruce Ackerman & David Golove, Is NAFTA Constitutional? 108 Harvard Law Review 799 (1995). For rejection of the concept of Constitutional Transformation see, Lawrence H. Tribe, Taking Text and Structure Seriously: Reflections on Free Form Method in Constitutional Interpretation, 108 Harvard Law Review 1221 (1995).

252 Japan Times on Line 1/15/04 Koizumi Urges LDP-DPJ Effort to Revise Constitution.

253 The Asahi Tribune, Constitutional Revisions to take Center Stage in Politics 1/14/04 on the web at asahi.com.

254 For a discussion of efforts to revise the Constitution see, H. Fukui, Twenty Years of Revisionism in Dan Fenno Henderson, THE CONSTITUTION OF JAPAN: ITS FIRST TWENTY YEARS 1947-1967 (University of Washington Press, 1969) 41.

House of the Diet and a majority vote of all votes cast at a referendum of the people on the issue.[255]

In each of the cases to reach it in which the legality of troops and/or establishment of military facilities were involved, the Supreme Court refused to deal with the merits and refused to deal with the extent, if any, to which Article 9 binds the government. So what then is the status of Article 9? It remains a part of the Constitution and as such it inhibits expansion of Japan's military role; it sets a roadblock around which supporters of greater use of the military must steer if they wish to establish a new policy; it provides an opportunity for political opponents of military expansion or deployment to make their voices heard and provides a legally acceptable forum for debate about Japan's policy. If it does not prevent the establishment of a military or deployment of that military abroad, it does slow down government efforts to make greater use of Japan's military.

To date the Supreme Court has erected procedural barriers that opponents of Japan's military cannot scale to challenge government action that might be considered as inconsistent with Article 9. Doctrines of standing or political question have been used to insulate the government from challenges to its rearmament policy. Challengers simply cannot get into court to be heard on the scope and meaning of Article 9. Still, it remains possible that in the event the government goes beyond what the Supreme Court believes is the consensus of society as to how to use Japan's military the court will ultimately allow a suit and declare a government policy or practice regarding the military unconstitutional. In such a situation the court would probably issue a "circumstance decision" and leave it to the government to figure out how to remedy the unconstitutionality.

C. The New Constitution, Human Rights and Amendments to the Civil and Criminal Codes

The three central principles around which the Constitution of Japan was constructed were creation of a democratic government rather than sovereignty in the Emperor, Renunciation of War and protection of human rights of the people. The issue of human rights as dealt with in the Constitution can be divided into three broad categories: economic and social rights, individual rights and rights of those suspected or accused of criminal activity. In examining these rights it is well to recall that when drafted in 1946 the Japanese Constitution was significantly more liberal in approach than was the American Constitution. *Brown v. Board of Education*[256] was still a decade away and the American South with its Jim Crow laws was a tightly segregated society with rampant discrimination against African-American citizens. While the Japanese Constitution guaranteed universal suffrage, African American citizens were systematically denied that right. Whereas

255 Constitution of Japan, Article 96.

256 349 US 294 (1955).

the Japanese Constitution proclaimed the equality of all Japanese, such equality did not exist in the United States. Shortly before the enactment of the Japanese Constitution the Supreme Court of the United States in the *Hirabayashi*[257] and *Korematsu*[258] cases had held that the Constitution permitted the separation and encampment of Japanese American citizens (and the consequent loss of both freedom and their property) for no reason other than their national origin.

In considering the protections of the criminally accused it should be recalled that cases such as *Miranda*,[259] *Gidean*,[260] *Mapp*,[261] *Brady*[262] were yet to come and certainly the court did not apply the rule of those cases. Indeed, *Weeks*,[263] holding that the exclusionary rule was NOT a constitutional mandate but simply a rule of procedure applied to federal courts (and thus not applicable at the State level) was the controlling authority. Notwithstanding the Equal Protection and Due Process clauses of the Fourteenth Amendment, women in the United States were not fully entitled to its protection and suffered discrimination both on and off the job. In interpreting the meaning of the individual rights provisions of the Japanese Constitution it is well to consider the intent of the drafters and the Japanese Diet in light of the legal understanding and rules at the time of adoption. That the United States may have chosen to give its own Constitution a different meaning at a later date is no reason to assume that Japan was required to do the same. The belief that Japan has somehow "lagged" in this regard because it has failed to adopt an American interpretation may be seen as patronizing. Nonetheless, legitimate questions may be raised as to how the human rights provisions of the Constitution have been applied in Japan.

On the economic and social welfare front, the Supreme Court of Japan has made it clear that the Constitution does not grant an abstract right in and of itself to welfare benefits. Thus, the provision to the effect that all people have a right to work[264] does not obligate the government to be an employer of last resort and create a jobs program for unemployed Japanese; that every person has a right to choose his residence[265] does not mean that everyone has a right to live in the residence of their choice, regardless of their ability to pay for such residence; and the

257 Kiyoshi Hirabayashi v. United States, 320 US 81 (1943).

258 Korematsu v. United States, 323 US 214 (1944).

259 Miranda v. Arizona, 384 US 436 (1966).

260 Gidean v. Wainright, 372 US 335 (1963).

261 Mapp v. Ohio, 367 US 643 (1961).

262 Brady v. Maryland, 373 US 83 (1963).

263 Weeks v. United States, 232 US 383 (1914).

264 Constitution of Japan, Article 27.

265 Constitution of Japan, Article 22.

right to "maintain a minimum standard[s] of wholesome and cultured living"[266] does not mean that everyone has the right to see an opera at the State's expense. These social welfare provisions are hortatory and are background for the Diet pointing the direction in which the legislature should move.[267] On the social welfare front it can be stated that the Constitution does not create legally enforceable rights.[268] Rather, the Constitution stands as a goal that the government should endeavor to meet. Thus it is for the government, through the supreme organ of the State, the Diet, to put meat on the bones of these constitutional provisions. And, when the government acts in the welfare area it is required to give credence to these provisions. Only in the case where the Diet acts and delegates authority to the Cabinet, and the implementing Executive action is so unreasonable as to be an abuse of the discretion delegated, can the court step in to find the action unconstitutional. Such a case has yet to arise, although the Supreme Court of Japan has left the door open for such a possibility.[269]

It may be relevant to consider the origin of the social welfare clauses in the Constitution. While many of the freedoms and rights provisions were American in origin, the social welfare clause was not. This clause was offered in the Diet by the left leaning Socialist Party as a substitute for a government-offered proposal. Under the government proposal there was no right to a wholesome or cultured living but simply a requirement that the government consider promotion and extension of social welfare and health when proposing legislation.[270] In essence the constitutional doctrine arising from the Supreme Court's jurisprudence on this Article is an adoption of the conservative government's original proposal.

Individual rights are treated differently. Here the Constitution would seem to apply directly without any need for legislative action to enforce the right. Thus, if the government fails to take any action it would appear that the citizen is safe and

---

266 Constitution of Japan, Article 25.

267 See, Masami Ito (assisted by Nathaniel L. Nathanson), The Rule of Law: Constitutional Development in LAW IN JAPAN (VON Mehren Ed. Harvard University Press, 1963) 205, 209-210.

268 Staple Food Control Act Case, 2 Keishu 1235 (Sup. Ct. 9/29/48) available in English in John M. Maki, COURT AND CONSTITUTION IN JAPAN (University of Washington Press, 1964) 243.

269 Asahi Case, Case No. 14 of 1964, 21 Minshu 1043 (Sup. Ct. Grand Bench 5/24/67) available in English on the web on the web site of the Supreme Court of Japan, Judgments of the Supreme Court; Horiki case, Case No. 1976 (Gyo-Tsu) no. 30, 36 Minshu 1235 (Sup. Ct. Grand Bench 7/7/82) available in English on the web on the web site of the Supreme Court of Japan, Judgments of the Supreme Court and also in Lawrence W. Beer & Hiroshi Itoh, THE CONSTITUTIONAL CASE LAW OF JAPAN, 1970-1990 (University of Washington Press, 1996) at 323. Compare the approach of the Asahi case with the Supreme Court's approach in the Post Office case. Case No. 1767 of 1999, 56 Minshu 1439 (Sup. Ct. Grand Bench, 9/11/02) available in English through the web site of the Supreme Court of Japan.

270 Koseki Shoichi THE BIRTH OF JAPAN'S POSTWAR CONSTITUTION (Edited and translated by Ray A. Moore) (Westview Press, 1997) at 182; see also, Richard B. Finn, WINNERS IN PEACE, MACARTHUR, YOSHIDA, AND POSTWAR JAPAN (University of California Press, 1992) 117.

the citizen's right is protected and the government has not acted to adversely affect rights—in essence the right is similar to the command in the United States Constitution that "Congress shall pass no law. . ." infringing the citizen's right. Thus under Article 15 the people (meaning Japanese citizens) have the right to democratic elections in which they elect officials to hold office and/or turn out of office those whose policies are rejected. If the Diet were to attempt to legislate away the right to elections, it would be a violation of the Constitution and presumably the Supreme Court would step in to uphold the constitutional right. But not all rights granted by the Constitution are as clear as the language would appear.

Under Article 20 "No religious organization shall receive any privilege from the State. . ." and under Article 89 "no public money . . . shall be expended . . . for the use . . . of any religious institution or association. . . ." The language appears rather straightforward and clear. This constitutional prohibition was designed to carry forward the Occupation's goal of freedom of religion and abolishing State Shinto and Emperor worship that was seen as central to the prewar authoritarian system. Even before the Constitution was adopted the Occupation had taken steps to abolish State Shinto and, of course, the Emperor had renounced any claim to being a deity.[271] The constitutional language is a direct command to the government not to expend any public money for the use of any religious organization. So may the government expend public money for the use of a religious organization? It depends. It depends on the purpose for which the money is expended and it depends on the circumstances surrounding the expenditure. If the money is spent for the performance of a Shinto ceremony that is deemed secular—such as the blessing of the new construction of a City gymnasium—then the expenditure is permitted.[272] On the other hand if the expenditure is relatively large and notice of the public gift to the Shrine is publicly displayed, the expenditure is unconstitutional.[273] The rationale appears to be that by publicly displaying the contribution the government is seen as supporting the Shrine and its religious sect—at least where the Shrine is the Yasukuni Shrine devoted to the nation's war dead and where Class A war criminals are buried. But what if the contribution is made but not publicly displayed? The court's opinion leaves open the possibility that such a gift might be lawful—at least if it isn't too large. Still whether large or small and

---

271 See generally, Richard B. Finn, WINNERS IN PEACE, MACARTHUR, YOSHIDA, AND POSTWAR JAPAN (University of California Press, 1992) 62-65.

272 Tsu City Ground Purification case, Kakunaga v. Sekiguchi, Case No. 1971 (Gyo-Tsu) No. 69 (Sup. Ct. Grand Bench 7/13/77) available in English on the web on the web site of the Supreme Court of Japan, Judgments of the Supreme Court and also in Lawrence W. Beer & Hiroshi Itoh, THE CONSTITUTIONAL CASE LAW OF JAPAN, 1970-1990 (University of Washington Press, 1996) at 478.

273 Ehime Prefecture Case, Case No. 156 of 1992 (Sup. Ct. Grand Bench 4/2/97) available in English on the web on the web site of the Supreme Court of Japan, Judgments of the Supreme Court.

whether displayed or not it would appear to be a violation of the language and intent of the Constitution.[274]

And, what if the sums allocated to the Shrine from public monies are related to the Shrine's performance of a public/governmental or at least semi-governmental function? In such case it would appear that the payment is acceptable for the secular purpose, such as the contributions made to Shrines that performed rites in connection with the Emperor's ascension to the throne.[275] But the ascension cases raise a more fundamental question and that is whether the government has a right to involve itself in religious activity of any sort and indeed whether religious activity has a right to involve itself with the government. If the Emperor is simply an "organ" of the State rather than above the State then it would appear that Article 20 would forbid a religious ceremony as the religious organization would, at a minimum, be receiving a privilege from the State. Surely, no other religious organization would be privileged to involve itself in the Emperor's ascension—a Christian ceremony would never be considered as part of the ascension. The issue is reminiscent of the debate under the Meiji Constitution as to the role of the Emperor except that under the new Constitution it is clear that Professor Minobe's Organ theory applies to the Emperor. Neither the sovereignty that opponents of Professor Minobe[276] attributed to the Emperor under the Meiji Constitution nor some other "extra Constitutional" status can be claimed for the Emperor. Nonetheless, courts have consistently upheld contributions made by local governments

274 The "secularization" of religious gifts in Japan is not dissimilar to those in the United States who attempt to secularize religious symbols such as the Ten Commandments. The question of whether the American Pledge of Allegiance containing the phrase "one nation under God" violates the separation of Church and State doctrine has also raised the secularization question. The Supreme Court of the United States "ducked" the issue in Elk Grove Unified School District v. Newdow (6/14/04) when it held that the plaintiff lacked standing to challenge the Pledge on behalf of his minor daughter since plaintiff's divorced wife not plaintiff had custody of the daughter and the wife had no objection to the daughter saying the Pledge with the challenged term. Three Justices would have upheld the Pledge on the merits on the basis that it was secular and not religious. Five Justices were of the view that the issue in the case was a domestic relations question concerning the custody of a minor child and who has authority to speak for the child. These Justices were of the view that such issues were properly dealt with in state courts and not in the federal court where the action had been instituted.

275 Heisei Emperor Ascension case, 1673 Hanji 3, 1003 Hanta 89 (3/24/99). See, David M. O'Brien, TO DREAM OF DREAMS, RELIGIOUS FREEDOM AND CONSTITUTIONAL POLITICS IN POSTWAR JAPAN (University of Hawaii Press, 1996) 167-178.

276 Kenzo Takayanagi, A Century of Innovation: The Development of Japanese Law, 1868-1961 in LAW IN JAPAN (VON Mehren Ed. Harvard University Press, 1963) 10-11; George Akita, FOUNDATIONS OF CONSTITUTIONAL GOVERNMENT IN MODERN JAPAN (Harvard University Press, 1967) 171; John W. Dower, EMBRACING DEFEAT (W.W. Norton & Company, 1999) 355. See, Richard H. Minear, JAPANESE TRADITION AND WESTERN LAW (Harvard University Press, 1970) 6-10, 184, and 191-193 for an analysis of Hozumi's theory and a comparison with Minobe's ideas. See, Marius B. Jansen, THE MAKING OF MODERN JAPAN (Belknap Press of Harvard University, 2000) 542-544 for a discussion of the views of Minobe and Professor Yoshino Sakuzo.

to Shrines to defray the costs of the Emperor's ascension ceremonies.[277] And the Supreme Court has held that the Shinto ceremony associated with the Emperor's ascension was merely a traditional ritual and that a governor's attendance thereat was not unconstitutional but simply a social courtesy that was to be expected of public office holders.[278]

Similarly litigation has been continuous over the visits to the Yasukuni Shrine by some of Japan's Prime Ministers to honor the war dead. The Osaka and Fukuoka District Courts rendered the most recent decisions on the issue. The Osaka court in February and May 2004 rejected the claims of a large number of citizens who argued that the visits by the Prime Minister violated their constitutional religious freedom rights. In rejecting the claim the court recognized the frustration felt by the plaintiffs but held that their individual rights to freedom of religion had not been violated.[279] The Fukuoka District Court in April 2004 held that the visits were official in character and violated the constitutional separation of Church and State, although the court rejected the monetary claims made by the plaintiffs.[280] The Fukuoka decision is consistent with a previous High Court decision rendered by the Sendai High Court in 1991. The Sendai High Court's decision was appealed to the Supreme Court, which dismissed the appeal. The Osaka District Court decision (and a similar decision by the Matsuyama District Court) is pending on appeal.[281]

While the Constitution's granting of rights may apply to restrict government action, the Constitution has been determined not to apply to private conduct—similar in many ways to the American doctrine under which Government action is constitutionally forbidden but to reach private action legislation must be passed. Thus Article 14's command that "all people are equal under the law" does not mean that private discrimination is outlawed. Indeed, even the follow-on language stating that "no discrimination in political, economic or social relations because of" the various factors set out in the clause does not provide rights on which a cause of action can be predicated. So for example, Article 14 does not prohibit private discrimination against the Ainu. Private discrimination against the so-called Burakumin is also not constitutionally prohibited. To reach this discrimina-

---

277 For a discussion of the religious freedom clauses in the Constitution in general see, David Forfar, individuals against the State? The Politics of Opposition to the Re-emergence of State Shinto in Roger Goodman & Ian Neary, CASE STUDIES ON HUMAN RIGHTS IN JAPAN 245; for a criticism of the jurisprudence relating to religious freedom in Japan see, Peter J. Herzog, JAPAN'S PSEUDO-DEMOCRACY (Japan Library, 1993) Chapter 5 Freedom of Religion.

278 Case No. 1999 (Gyo-tsu) No. 93, 56 Minshu 1204 (Sup. Ct. Petty Bench, 7/11/02) available in English through the web site of the Supreme Court of Japan.

279 See, Japan Times on Line 2/28/04 Court Denies Redress for 631 Suing over Yasukuni Visit; Japan Times on Line 5/14/04 Yasukuni visits Ruled Private.

280 Koizumi Shrine Visit Ruled Unconstitutional. Japan Times on Line 4/8/04.

281 The Prime Minister has stated that he will continue to visit the Yasukuni Shrine—where Japan's war dead are enshrined along with war time Prime Minister Tojo and other Class A war criminals from the Second World War—notwithstanding the court's determination. See, Prime Minister Pledges Yasukuni Return, Japan Times on Line 4/8/04.

tion separate legislation making such discrimination unlawful is required—and no such legislation has been passed.[282]

In addition to the primacy that the Occupation placed on ending State Shinto and Emperor worship, the Occupation (through its Civil Rights Committee, the actions of Beate Sirota and the personal support of MacArthur)[283] was committed to drastically changing the system under which women were subservient to men. Several Articles in the Constitution were framed to carry out this goal. Article 14 commands that "all people are equal under the law"—this is designed to place women and men on an equal plane. In addition Article 14 prohibits discrimination in political, economic or social relations based on sex. Under Article 13 all people, including both men and women, "shall be respected as individuals." Under Article 15 all adults (and this includes women) are given rights to suffrage. Article 26 obligates parents to give equal free compulsory education (elementary school and junior high school) to both boys and girls. Article 24 squarely confronts the prewar institution of the feudal family and the subjugation of women under the *Ie*. Not only are husband and wife given equal rights but also marriage itself is to be based on mutual consent and the family is to be maintained through mutual cooperation. Laws dealing with family matters are to be enacted based on the concept of "individual dignity and the essential equality of the sexes." The Occupation went so far as to grant woman the right to vote in the April 1946 election for the Diet even before the new Constitution was approved. This election saw 39 women elected to the Lower House[284] and they used their position as Diet members to support the Constitution and changes in the Civil Code designed to undo the old House system and grant rights to women.

The various provisions of the Constitution prohibiting discrimination appear to be outright grants of equality affecting personal as well as governmental action. It is difficult to see how anything other than personal or private as distinguished from government action is implicated by the clause obliging parents to provide a basic education to girls as well as boys or the clause making marriage a mutually cooperative venture. Yet under the court's indirect applicability as distinguished from direct applicability doctrine it would appear that women derive no equality rights from the Constitution to prohibit private action unless that private action is also in-

282 For a discussion of discrimination against the Ainu and Burakumin see, Carl F. Goodman, THE RULE OF LAW IN JAPAN: A COMPARATIVE ANALYSIS (Kluwer Law International, 2003) 82-89. See also Mari Yamaguchi, "Burakumin" Descendants Still Suffering, Japan Times on Line June 5, 2004.

283 See, Susan J. Pharr, The Politics of Women's Rights in Robert E. Ward and Sakamoto Yoshikazu, DEMOCRATIZING JAPAN (University of Hawaii Press, 1987) 221 for a discussion of the role of the Occupation in the woman's rights provisions of the Constitution and the Occupation's rejection of Japanese government efforts to water down the provisions of Articles 14 and 24. See also, Andrew Gordon, A MODERN HISTORY OF JAPAN (Oxford University Press, 2003) 236; William Manchester, AMERICAN CAESAR (Little, Brown and Company, 1978) 503-504.

284 Richard B. Finn, WINNERS IN PEACE, MACARTHUR, YOSHIDA, AND POSTWAR JAPAN (University of California Press, 1992) 108.

consistent with the Civil Code or other Diet enacted legislation. To violate the Civil Code's good faith and fair dealing and good morals clauses,[285] the activity involved must be inconsistent with generally accepted norms of the society, and in determining such generally accepted norms the Constitution, while it may be considered, is apparently not controlling. Thus, while an employer's discrimination against women employees in denying them pension and retirement benefits on equal terms with male employees is a violation of the Civil Code because the constitutional provisions providing for equality show that such conduct is a violation of fair dealing,[286] the use of two-track employment systems under which women are placed in a track subordinate to men was not unlawful. Only after the Equal Employment Opportunity Act was amended to make such systems unlawful were such systems unlawful. Discrimination in hiring prior to the Act's amendment (in 1989) was not actionable.[287] Even after amendment of the EEOA Japan's courts follow a literal approach to discrimination against women and look at the face rather than the effect of employment policies and actions. In the United States the basic approach in discrimination law is to look at actual effects rather than facial neutrality to discover if an action or policy is discriminatory. This more accommodating American approach would appear to be more in line with the Japanese Constitution that has specific sexual equality provisions while the United States Constitution has only the equal protection clause of the 14th Amendment.[288]

The constitutional provisions on the equality of women required a major rewriting of those sections of the Civil Code that dealt with family law and inheritance. The extent of that rewriting was a subject of debate between liberals, conservatives and the Occupation. The Occupation's public position was that it was up to the Japanese Government to decide how and to what extent to change the Civil Code—as long as the changes conformed to the requirements of the Constitution. The reality is the Occupation played a role whether directly, indirectly or simply through its being. The need to reform the Civil Code was recognized as soon as the Occupation "roadmap" for a Constitution was presented to the Japanese Government. Clearly the House system (*Ie*) as defined by the Code was inconsistent with the draft Constitution. Moreover, liberal elements in Japan had long recog-

---

285 Civil Code Articles 1 and 90.

286 Nissan Motors Inc. v. Nakamoto, 35 Minshu 300 (Sup. Ct. Grand Bench 3/24/81) for an English language translation see, Lawrence W. Beer & Hiroshi Itoh, THE CONSTITUTIONAL CASE LAW OF JAPAN, 1970-1990 (University of Washington Press, 1996) at 179.

287 See, Sumitomo Case, See, Japan Times on Line 3/30/01 Sumitomo Women lose Wage Bias Case; Nomura Securities Case, Japan Times on Line 2/21/02 Nomura Securities Loses Discrimination Lawsuit (damages not allowed for dual-track hiring in the 1950s and 1960s because at such time such discriminatory hiring systems were not inconsistent with Japanese mores and norms). For a discussion of dual-track hiring systems see, Leo Kanowitz, Two-Track Hiring and The Japanese Equal Employment Opportunity Act: An American Perspective, LAW IN EAST AND WEST 389, 392 (Waseda University, 1988); Kaneo Suzuki, Equal Job opportunity for Whom?, Japan Quarterly (July-September 1996) 54.

288 For an example of the Japanese approach see, Taimie Bryant, For the Sake of the Country, For the Sake of the Family: The Oppressive Impact of Family Registration on Women and Minorities in Japan, 39 UCLA Law Review 109, 115-116 (1991).

nized that the Code required change—an attempt to make changes during the era of Taisho Democracy had not been successful. In addition, some of the conservatives recognized that the House system as set out in the Code was an anachronism and was simply inconsistent with modern life. Nonetheless, change did not necessarily mean complete abolition of the House system and many conservatives considered the House system as essential to the basic structure of Japanese life and society. Indeed, to some extent the Occupation shared this view—and for this reason wanted the House system dramatically changed if not completely abolished.[289]

The Japanese bureaucracy began work on possible changes in the Civil Code while the Constitution was being debated. The process of change in the Civil Code and the adoption of the constitutional provisions dealing with the family were inter-related. At first government leaders took the position in the constitutional debate that the Constitution would not require the abolition of the House system.[290] However, as work on the Civil Code amendments preceded at the bureaucratic level it became clear that a major change in the House system was in the works. Early in the process, the head of the department responsible for considering the form of the change had considered either of two approaches: a) a severe restriction on the rights of the Head of the House and major changes in the law regarding the family and inheritance but preserving the institution of the House or b) complete abolition of the House. When the possibility of approach a) was informally broached with a representative of the Occupation, the response was—unofficially of course—that such retention would violate the Constitution. A Committee was established to work on the Civil Code amendment and some committee members were women, assuring that women, the group most severely discriminated against by the old House system, would be involved in its destruction. The Occupation also had a committee that watched the Civil Code rewriting process and Lieutenant Ethel B. Weed was active in supporting the abolition of the *Ie* and enhancing women's rights.[291] The Japanese drafting committee that set to work on the Code started with the basic doctrine that the House system would be abolished and the ultimate product was the abolition of the House system. The

289 The House system promoted authoritarianism at the family level and up through the government to the Emperor. In one sense the Emperor was seen as the Head of the Japanese House with his subjects as House members who owed piety and obedience to the Emperor as an individual House member would to the Head of his/her House. This concept is not completely dead in Japan regardless of the legal changes. In Hiroshima there is a festival each spring (sponsored by a local Shrine) in which celebrants take to the street in Yukata—summer kimono and typically the nightdress of most Japanese. At one such festival, a middle-aged woman approached me and said "You must think it strange that we walk around in the streets in our night clothes—but remember we are all members of the same family so it is all right."

290 See, e.g., quote of comments made by Prime Minister Yoshida in the Diet reported in Kurt Steiner, The Occupation and the Reform of the Japanese Civil Code in Robert E. Ward and Sakamoto Yoshikazu, DEMOCRATIZING JAPAN (University of Hawaii Press, 1987) 194-195.

291 For a discussion of the internal workings of the Occupation as it related to women's rights issues see generally, Susan J. Pharr, The Politics of Women's Rights in Robert E. Ward and Sakamoto Yoshikazu, DEMOCRATIZING JAPAN (University of Hawaii Press, 1987) 221.

system did not die without a fight from some elements in the Diet and without at least an acknowledgment of the multi generation family as an aspect of society.[292] The abolition of the House system was a major victory of those who sought to raise the position of women in Japanese society and those who wanted to bring to an end the remnants of feudalism in Japan.[293] While the Occupation assisted those Japanese involved in the effort, the Japanese involved considered the changes to have been something that the Japanese themselves wanted.[294] However, not all Japanese shared these objectives. In many rural and farming districts the concept of the House had not outlived its usefulness either socially or economically and in these areas there was resistance to the changes.[295]

The Civil Code changes brought about a revolution in the legal status of both men and women in Japan.[296] For men, the abolition of the *Ie* House system gave them freedom from the House head. Men could marry without consent once they had reached the age of majority rather than having to wait till they were 30. Men could change their residence without seeking permission, they were eligible to inherit even if they were not the eldest son, etc. For women the change was even more dramatic. They now had rights to manage their own property, were entitled to equal treatment in many respects, could determine their own spouse, could inherit property and indeed had an absolute right to a percentage of the property of their spouse on death,[297] etc.

---

292 For a discussion of the process of change in the Civil Code see, Kurt Steiner, The Occupation and the Reform of the Japanese Civil Code in Robert E. Ward and Sakamoto Yoshikazu, DEMOCRATIZING JAPAN (University of Hawaii Press, 1987) 188; Kurt Steiner, The Revision of the Civil Code of Japan, 9 Far Eastern Quarterly 169 (1950); Alfred C. Oppler, LEGAL REFORM IN OCCUPIED JAPAN (Princeton University Press, 1976) 111-120; Note, Japanese Family Law, 9 Stanford Law Review 132 (1956); Sakae Wagatsuma, Democratization of the Family Relation in Japan, 25 Washington State Bar Journal 405 (1950).

293 Some aspects of the old system remained. For example under Civil Code Article 897 custom determines who will inherit such things as genealogical records, utensils for religious rites, tombs and burial grounds.

294 Richard B. Finn, WINNERS IN PEACE, MACARTHUR, YOSHIDA, AND POSTWAR JAPAN (University of California Press, 1992) 167; James L. McClain, JAPAN, A MODERN HISTORY (W.W. Norton & Company, 2002) 549-550.

295 See, Alfred C. Oppler, LEGAL REFORM IN OCCUPIED JAPAN (Princeton University Press, 1976) 115; Kurt Steiner, The Occupation and the Reform of the Japanese Civil Code in Robert E. Ward and Sakamoto Yoshikazu, DEMOCRATIZING JAPAN (University of Hawaii Press, 1987) 220 fn. 220 referring to a poll in which a majority of the population (57.9%) favored the complete abolition of the House system but only a minority (43.3%) of farming and fishing respondents favored this course.

296 For a discussion of the changes in the Civil Code brought about by the revision see, Alfred C. Oppler, LEGAL REFORM IN OCCUPIED JAPAN (Princeton University Press, 1976); Kurt Steiner, The Occupation and the Reform of the Japanese Civil Code in Robert E. Ward and Sakamoto Yoshikazu, DEMOCRATIZING JAPAN (University of Hawaii Press, 1987) 188; Kurt Steiner, The Revision of the Civil Code of Japan, 9 Far Eastern Quarterly 169 (1950).

297 Civil Code Articles 890-893.

However, the Code changes were not a panacea for women. Under the new Code a married couple may take the surname of either the husband or wife[298] (rather than the husband's family name). But reality is that the husband's surname is virtually always chosen and the wife cannot keep her surname while the husband keeps his. This places some women, especially professional and career women, at a disadvantage. Unless the parties enter into a prenuptial agreement that is registered prior to marriage,[299] property that a spouse had when entering into the marriage and property acquired in the spouse's own name during marriage belongs to that spouse.[300] While sexually neutral on its face, the reality of business and professional life in Japan is such that the husband acquires most post-marriage property placing the wife at a disadvantage.

The Code perpetuates the old discrimination against divorced women who wish to remarry shortly after divorce by providing that women must wait six months from dissolution or annulment of a previous marriage before remarrying but that a man has no such restriction.[301] The Supreme Court upheld this discrimination on the grounds that the six-month period is reasonable in protecting against paternity complaints.[302] It should be recognized that there is no "legislative history" of meaning for this provision as it is a relic of the prewar Civil Code. Moreover, in today's world of DNA testing, paternity is not a difficult question to be resolved.

The changes in the Civil Code did not completely abolish the institution of the Family Register. Under the new Family Register law, the nuclear family rather than the extended family is the subject of the Register. The Register can be used for multigenerational purposes—for example, a Japanese woman married to an American citizen residing in the United States might register her child in her Father's Family Register in order to protect the child's right to opt for Japanese citizenship at a future date.[303] The Family Register is a useful device as many "transactions" that require court supervision in the United States can be handled by simple registration in the Register in Japan (examples are marriage,[304] consen-

298 Civil Code Article 750.

299 Civil Code Articles 755, 756.

300 Civil Code Article 762 (1).

301 Civil Code Article 733.

302 1563 Hanji 81 (Sup. Ct. 12/5/95).

303 To avoid extradition to Peru, former Peruvian President Fujimuri has claimed Japanese citizenship and has had his claim to Japanese citizenship recognized by the Japanese government on the basis of his registration in his family's Family Register notwithstanding his residence in Peru and his election as Peru's President. Japanese unwillingness to extradite its citizens (at least when they are charged with crimes abroad that could benefit Japanese society at home) is demonstrated by the Tokyo High Court's recent refusal to extradite a Japanese doctor accused by the United States of stealing secrets related to genetic research into Alzheimer's Disease because the court concluded that the scientist would not be found guilty in the United States. See, Japan Times on Line, 3/30/04 Court Rejects US Request for Extradition in Industrial Spy Case.

304 Family Register Law Article 74.

sual divorce,[305] certain adoptions).[306] On the other hand, the Register system may perpetuate discrimination against women in Japan. Under the system one member of the household must be registered first in the Register as the Head of House.[307] Typically this is the husband. Many business entities provide fringe benefits to employees who are Head of House but not to other employees. As the husband is typically registered as Head of House this places women at a disadvantage in the event of separation. Separated women who must work to support themselves (and their children) are not entitled to health and other fringe benefits that are available to the Head of the House. The system while neutral on its face actually supports the male control of the family relationship and works a detriment to women in the workplace and elsewhere.[308]

Further, merely because equality is enshrined in the Constitution does not mean that the society grants women equal rights with men. As previously noted, in private relationships the Constitution is not self-executing and does not directly prohibit private discrimination. To reach the actions of private companies there needs to be some legislation to carry out the constitutional mandate. There is no general anti-discrimination legislation in Japan equivalent to the Equal Employment Opportunity Act or the Fair Housing Act in the United States. Thus, companies for many years discriminated against women through such devices as dual track (professional and non-professional) hiring and employment systems. The Supreme Court held that women *employees* of a company could not be discriminated against by their employer in certain aspects of employment (i.e., on the job and retirement benefits) because to do so would violate Article 90 of the Civil Code.[309] That ruling did not apply to *pre-employment* discrimination such as the decision

305 Family Register Law Article 76.

306 Family Register Law Article 66, 68.

307 Family Register Law Article 14.

308 See, e.g., Suzuki v. Nissan Motor Co., 1301 Hanji 71, 694 Hanta 114 (Tokyo District Court, 1/26/89) wherein the court found that there was no discrimination in a fringe benefit plan that awarded health insurance benefits to the Head of House as either women or men could be Head of House and hence the plan was not discriminatory. Completely disregarded by the court was the fact that while neutral in form the plan was actually discriminatory in practice in light of the realities of the Family Register system. For a general discussion of the Family Register system and its affect as a tool for discrimination see, Taimie Bryant, For the Sake of the Country, For the Sake of the Family: The Oppressive Impact of Family Registration on Women and Minorities in Japan, 39 UCLA Law Review 109 (1991).See also, Japan Times on Line Discriminatory Registry of Child Upheld, 3/3/04 wherein the Tokyo District Court found that the Family Register law provisions calling for separate registration of legitimate and illegitimate children violated the right of privacy of illegitimate children but that such violation was consistent with the Family Register Law and was not unconstitutional and therefore the plaintiff was not entitled to monetary relief.

309 Nissan Motors Inc. v. Nakamoto, 35 Minshu 300 (Sup. Ct. Grand Bench 3/24/81) for an English language translation see, Lawrence W. Beer & Hiroshi Itoh, THE CONSTITUTIONAL CASE LAW OF JAPAN, 1970-1990 (University of Washington Press, 1996) at 179. Under Article 90 an act that is contrary to public moral or good order is void.

to hire.[310] The original Japanese Equal Opportunity Law (applicable only to sex discrimination) followed the distinction between pre-employment and post-employment discrimination making such post-employment acts as discrimination in employee benefits and retirement [the subjects of the Nissan Motors decision] unlawful and *urging* employers not to discriminate in pre-employment determinations like hiring.[311] It was not until 1987 (effective 1989) that the Equal Employment Opportunity Law was amended to make discrimination in hiring and recruiting, promoting and assignments unlawful. The new law did not explicitly make sexual harassment on the job unlawful but it did urge employers to take steps to prevent such harassment.[312] Sexual harassment is however a tort and since passage of the amended EEOL there have been several successful private civil tort actions based on alleged sexual harassment.

The new Constitution's provisions concerning women, abolition of the *Ie* House family system and the changes made in the status of the Emperor also necessitated amendment of the Criminal Code.[313] The Criminal Code made adultery by a woman a crime both for the woman involved and her lover. Adultery by a man (unless it was with a married woman) was not a crime. The Occupation gave the Japanese authorities the option of either making adultery by a man an equal crime or of abolishing the crime entirely. The Criminal Code was amended by entirely dropping the provisions making adultery a crime.[314] Provisions dealing with the Imperial Household were changed so that special crimes against the Imperial House were deleted from the Code. (A special provision was inserted to give the Prime Minister the authority to complain—on behalf of the Imperial House—in a case of criminal libel where the Emperor or his immediate family was libeled).[315] The deletion of the *lese majeste* chapter of the Criminal Code did not come

310 Mitsubishi Jushi K.K. v. Takano, 27 Minshu 1536 Case No. 1968 (O) No. 932 (Sup. Ct. Grand Bench, 12/12/73) an English language translation see, Lawrence W. Beer & Hiroshi Itoh, THE CONSTITUTIONAL CASE LAW OF JAPAN, 1970-1990 (University of Washington Press, 1996) at 170, also available in English through the web site of the Supreme Court of Japan.

311 Loraine Parkinson, Note, Japan's Equal Employment Opportunity Law: An Alternative Approach to Social Change, 89 Columbia Law Review 604 (1989); Masako Kamiya, A Decade of the Equal Employment Opportunity Act in Japan: Has it Changed Society?, 25 Law in Japan 40 (1955); Jan M. Bergeson and Kaoru Yamamoto Oba, Japan's New Equal Employment Opportunity Law, 1986 Brigham Young University Law Review 865 (1986).

312 For a discussion of the new EEOL see, 18 Waseda Bulletin of Comparative Law 59-61 (1997); see also, Carl F. Goodman, The Somewhat Less Reluctant Litigant: Japan's Changing View Towards Civil Litigation, 32 Law and Policy in International Business 769, 774-775 (2001).

313 See generally, Alfred C. Oppler, LEGAL REFORM IN OCCUPIED JAPAN (Princeton University Press, 1976) 75, 120-129, 165-168; Howard Meyers, Revisions of the Criminal Code of Japan During the Occupation, 1949 Washington Law Review 104.

314 Ryuichi Hirano (assisted by B. J. George) The Accused and Society: Some Aspects of Japanese Criminal Law in LAW IN JAPAN (VON Mehren Ed. Harvard University Press, 1963) 274, 281; Kenzo Takayanagi, A Century of Innovation: The Development of Japanese Law, 1868-1961 in LAW IN JAPAN (VON Mehren Ed. Harvard University Press, 1963)5, 18.

315 Masami Ito (assisted by Nathaniel L. Nathanson), The Rule of Law: Constitutional Development in LAW IN JAPAN (VON Mehren Ed. Harvard University Press, 1963) 205, 225 fn. 61.

easy as the Japanese Government objected. The Occupation forced the changes through.[316] Naturally provisions in the Code that restricted freedoms in order to support the authoritarian regime were deleted as were provisions dealing with crimes that related to the Japanese military as the Renunciation of War clause was considered at the time as prohibiting Japan from having a military. Provisions in the Criminal Code that gave special rights to the family of an Accused person when the crime was against the House were changed to take into account the change in the Family Law system. However, the imposition of a more severe punishment for the murder of a lineal ascendant was not changed as the Occupation authority considered such provision as consistent with the Japanese respect for family elders.[317] This provision of the law was later found unconstitutional as a violation of Article 14's equality provision in the Patricide case of 1973.[318]

In 1947 a new Public Prosecutor Office Law was enacted that separated the prosecutor office from the court system and created a prosecutor civil service separate from the courts. Under this new system prosecutor offices are located wherever there is a District or High Court (and in Tokyo for the Supreme Court). These offices are responsible to the Prosecutor General. The Prosecutor General is in the Ministry of Justice but has career tenure and great independence from political influence.

Similarly, in 1947 a new Police Law separated the local police function from the central government and placed local policing under the Prefectural Governors. However, by 1954 cities and other local jurisdictions disbanded their police departments, and a National Police Agency was created. The Prime Minister, after declaring an emergency, has the power to effectively nationalize the prefecture police forces. Of course as Japan is a unitary country and as the central government has the power to essentially nationalize the governor function by making the governor an agency of the central government the central government can make use of prefecture police agencies.[319]

316 Yasuhiro Okudaira, Forty Years of the Constitution and its Various Influences: Japanese, American, and European in JAPANESE CONSTITUTIONAL LAW (Percy R. Luney, Jr. and Kazuyuki Takanashi Ed., University of Tokyo Press, 1993) 1, 5.

317 Howard Meyers, Revisions of the Criminal Code of Japan During the Occupation, 1949 Washington Law Review 104, 125-126.

318 Patricide case, Aizawa v. Japan, 27 Keishu 265265 (Sup. Ct. Grand Bench, 4/4/73) Case No. (A) No. 1310 of 1970 available in English on the website of the Supreme Court of Japan, Judgments of the Supreme Court.

319 For a discussion of the Police see, Andrew Gordon, A MODERN HISTORY OF JAPAN (Oxford University Press, 2003) 236-237; Shigemitsu Dando (Translated by B.J. George Jr.) JAPANESE CRIMINAL PROCEDURE (Fred B. Rothman & Co., 1965) Section 5.07; Hugh Borton, JAPAN'S MODERN CENTURY (The Ronald Press Company, 1955) 418.

Echoing the United States Constitution, the Japanese Constitution contains explicit procedural protections for the criminally accused.[320] Thus, the Constitution has two provisions dealing with the right to counsel. Under Article 34 a person arrested or detained has the "immediate privilege of counsel" while under Article 37 an accused person "shall have the assistance of counsel." A close reading of the provisions discloses a significant difference. While a detained person has a privilege and thus may hire counsel if he/she wishes to do so and has the economic resources to do so, there is no "right" to counsel and hence the State has no obligation to provide counsel for such a person. As a result there can be no obligation on the part of the police to give arrested persons a *Miranda* warning that they have a right to counsel—they do not—as all they have is a privilege. Moreover a suspect is not an accused until the person has been formally accused, i.e., until there has been an indictment. But under Japanese criminal procedure, there is no requirement that a person be immediately or even expeditiously indicted. Rather, the police have a right to hold such a person for 2 days before turning the suspect over to the prosecutor.[321] The prosecutor then has one day to either indict or obtain a court order permitting retention without indictment. Such court order allows for 10 days of retention and may be extended for an additional 10 days. Such orders are routinely granted and the accused has no right to appear and argue against further retention, and in any event most suspects have no counsel at this stage. As a practical matter between the police and the prosecutor acting together, the government may hold a suspect for 23 days without an indictment and thus without a right to counsel. During this 23-day the authorities have a right to question the suspect. Even if the suspect has exercised the privilege granted and has hired counsel, counsel has only limited access to the suspect—the prosecutor deciding the time and duration of such meetings—and may not be present when the suspect is actually being questioned. After the end of the 23-day the suspect is theoretically entitled to either release or indictment. If the prosecutor re-arrests the suspect for another crime, even a related crime, the 23-day clock begins to run again. This process, known as *bekken taiho*, is frequently employed when suspects fail to confess during the initial 23-day holding period.

The failure to provide for counsel prior to indictment as well as the inability of counsel to be present when the police/prosecutor question the "suspect" has led to problems in Japan/United States relations. Under the status of forces agreement under which American troops are located in Japan as part of the Mutual Defense Treaty between the countries, American military personnel accused of crimes in Japan must be turned over to Japanese authorities after indictment. The United States has in most cases refused to turn such personnel over to Japan prior to in-

320 For a discussion of the constitutional protections of the criminally accused and suspected in Japan see, Carl F. Goodman, THE RULE OF LAW IN JAPAN: A COMPARATIVE ANALYSIS (Kluwer Law International, 2003) 304-318.

321 For a discussion of the structure and authority of the public prosecutor office see, Shigemitsu Dando (Translated by B.J. George Jr.) JAPANESE CRIMINAL PROCEDURE (Fred B. Rothman & Co., 1965) Sections 5.04-5.08. See also, A. Didrick Castberg, JAPANESE CRIMINAL JUSTICE (Praeger Publishers, 1990) Chapter 4 Prosecution.

dictment but after they are identified as suspects because of concern that the 23-day holding period can be used to question the suspects without counsel being present—contrary to American norms and requirements. The United States has insisted that if suspects are turned over prior to indictment that such military personnel be granted rights to have counsel or other US representatives present during questioning sessions. Japan has refused arguing that to do so would be to treat American suspects differently from Japanese suspects. [The Japanese position has overtones of concern that relate back to the special treatment granted to foreigners under the unequal treaties that were entered into at the end of the Tokugawa period and whose abolition was a major objective of the Meiji oligarchs.] Recently a diplomatic breakthrough was reached under which American suspects turned over to the Japanese prior to indictment would not be allowed a right to counsel but American personnel would be present during questioning sessions as members of the investigating team.[322] How much say such American "team members" will have in the questioning process and more importantly over the terms of the questioning procedure (how many hours on end can questioning continue, under what physical conditions must the suspect be held during questioning, etc.) remains to be seen. Also to be observed is whether this change of procedure for American personnel will be used as a wedge by Japanese reformers to demand similar treatment of Japanese suspects who have not yet been indicted but who may have hired counsel under their "privilege" to retain counsel.

Under Article 38 of the Constitution no person "shall be compelled to testify against himself." However, unlike the United States Constitution's Fifth Amendment privilege against self-incrimination, Article 38 is not interpreted as granting the suspect the right to end questioning. Indeed, although a suspect cannot be compelled to testify against himself a suspect can be compelled to undergo questioning. Nor can a suspect end the questioning session by requesting a meeting with counsel—indeed, a prosecutor has a right to schedule meetings between counsel and the accused in such a way as to assure that the meeting does not interrupt questioning sessions either in process or about to begin. Questioning sessions may go on for hours on end and day after day and although physical torture is constitutionally forbidden and forced confessions and confessions obtained after "prolonged arrest or detention" are not admissible in evidence, confessions obtained after days of incessant questioning are not considered as coerced. If the suspect is lawfully in detention or under arrest, the time of such arrest or detention is not counted when determining whether a confession was obtained after "prolonged" detention. Thus, holding a suspect for 23-days (or perhaps 46 or longer if *bekken taiho* is involved) before obtaining a confession is not considered as prolonged detention as long as the holding period is lawfully authorized.

Except for the exclusionary rule prohibiting the introduction of a coerced confession (as defined above) Japan has no general exclusionary rule so that illegally obtained evidence may and typically is admitted into evidence. If the authorities are

322 See, Japan Times on Line, 3/29/04 Japan, US Agree on Troop Crime Suspects.

found to have acted in an excessively improper manner, the court may exclude the illegally obtained evidence but this happens rarely and even more rarely is a defendant who the court considers guilty allowed to go free because the evidence against him was illegally obtained. Thus in a recent case the Supreme Court found that police officers had made a search prior to obtaining a warrant and had lied to the court as to when the search was made. The police had also altered records as to when the warrant had been shown to the defendant. Based on this search the officers obtained a warrant and collected a urine sample showing that the defendant had illegal drugs in his system. The court considered such action by the officers grossly improper and excluded the evidence obtained through the search without a warrant and the urine evidence obtained under the warrant as fruits of the poisonous tree. But in the same case the prosecutor had appealed from the lower court's dismissal of a second offense that the defendant was charged with. As to this offense the court reversed the lower court. The court found that this second charge had no relationship to the improper conduct of the officers and that the evidence obtained in the lawful search involved in the second offense was admissible. In other words, the defendant was nonetheless convicted of one of the two crimes he was charged with and the defendant was not allowed to escape conviction.[323]

The Constitution also grants an accused the right to a speedy trial before an impartial tribunal. There is no right to a jury trial as the Occupation concluded that it was inappropriate to compel Japan to adopt a jury system. As a consequence, trials in Japan are not continuous affairs but, rather, are a series of hearings separated by potential extended periods of time. In such a setting the speedy trial requirement appears out of place. This is especially so as trials in highly publicized cases may go on for over a decade and in some politically charged cases may continue until the defendant dies or becomes incapacitated as a consequence of age. However, in one case where the trial was initiated and then recessed for 15 years—a period in excess of the statute of limitations for the crime involved—the Supreme Court held that dismissal of the renewed trial based on the speedy trial requirement was appropriate.

323 Case No. 2001 (A) No. 1678, 57 Keishu 121 (Sup. Ct. Petty Bench, 2/14/03) available in English through the web site of the Supreme Court of Japan. The question of what conduct rises to the level that evidence should be excluded appears to be an ad hoc determination for the court based on all the factors, including the seriousness of the crime. Thus in a case decided a few months after the above referred to case, police officers were called to a hotel because the hotel operator complained that a guest had failed to pay a bill. The police knew that the hotel guest was suspected of being a gangster belonging to a Yakusa crime family and suspected of being involved in drug trafficking. After obtaining entrance to the hotel room several officers held the defendant, who was naked, for about 30 minutes during which time his wallet was searched (without his specific consent and without a warrant) and drugs found. Taking in to considerations all the facts the court found the search permissible, although it did entertain questions about holding the defendant naked for 30 minutes. Based on these facts a warrant was obtained and a urine sample collected. The sample was admissible in evidence. Case No. 1164 of 1999, 57 Keishu 620 (Supreme Court Pretty Bench 5/26/03) available on the web through the web site of the Supreme Court of Japan.

Although jury trial in criminal cases is not a constitutional requirement and although not presently provided for in the Code of Criminal Procedure, the Japanese government in 2004 adopted legislation to create an experiment with a form of citizen participation in major criminal cases. While not a jury, the plan calls for a panel of judges composed of both lay judges (six) and professional judges (3) for cases where the penalty for conviction could be life imprisonment or the death penalty. Where a defendant admits guilt and the prosecution and defense agree, the ratio of lay judges to professional judges could be 1 lay to 4 professional. This mixed professional/lay judge system is based on the German criminal process and reflects a continuing trend to move away from American institutions and procedures and towards German law, institutions and procedures. In order to make lay/professional judge trials less burdensome for lay judges, it is likely that such cases will be tried on a fast track trial system in which taking of evidence continues on a concentrated daily basis until completed. This is similar to trials in the United States, which adopt this procedure to accommodate lay juries. Under the new law, lay judges can be excused from serving if service would severely damage their business or if they have conscience objections to service. Employers are prohibited from penalizing employees because of their absence from work because of their service as lay judges.[324] The lay judge system was part of the recommendations of the Law Reform Council.[325] The law approving the new "jury system" was passed by the Diet in May 2004 and the system is expected to go into effect in the year 2009.[326]

The Constitution also provides that defendants have a right not to be placed in double jeopardy. But the European idea of double jeopardy not the American idea is encompassed in the rule. Thus a prosecutor in Japan may appeal from a not guilty verdict rendered by the lower level court and this is not considered as a violation of the defendant's right. Indeed, if a defendant is found not guilty at the initial level trial and the prosecutor appeals, the High Court may nonetheless deny bail pending appeal. Even though found not guilty at the first level trial the defendant may thus remain incarcerated. Considering that the High Court almost invariably reverses the initial trial court's not guilty finding the system appears to not unduly harm those found innocent (except to the extent that the innocent are hardly ever found not guilty if the prosecutor believes they are guilty. After all, the normal conviction rate is approximately 99 %.)

324 See, Japan Times on Line, 3/3/04 Cabinet Oks Reform Package Boasting Lay Judges; 1/29/04 "Citizen Judge" System Close to Reality.

325 Recommendations of the Justice System Reform Counsel: For a Justice System to Support Japan in the 21st Century, 6/12/01 on the web at *www.kantei.go.jp/foreign/policy/sihou/singikai/990612_e.html.*

326 See, Reinstating a Jury System, Japan Times on Line 5/29/04.

5

The Judicial Process in Japan

A. Amendments to the Civil and Criminal Procedure Code

The American procedure system is ancient. Its roots in early common law are firmly planted. It is fundamentally unchanged from the procedural system inherited from England when the republic was formed. Of course it has seen changes and will continue to see changes. It has moved from Code pleadings to the modern system of notice of claim pleading and has moved from a system where fishing expeditions were looked on with disfavor to an open discovery system. Nonetheless the basic outline of the system has remained the same.

The American judicial system is founded on the notion of an adversary system where the course of the case is basically in the hands of the lawyers for the respective parties and the judge acts as an observer/umpire. Even in Equity—where the judge's role is greatly enhanced because he is law determiner, fact determiner and enforcer of the decision—the judge is ultimately a passive player as the ebb and flow of the case, both pretrial and at trial is in the hands of the lawyers. This fundamental character of the American system is unchanged for centuries.

The basic elements of the adversary system are to be found in the system's belief that the best way to determine both the facts of a matter and the rule of law to be applied to the matter is to place the parties and their champions—the lawyers—in charge of the process. Like the unseen hand in economics, self-interest is considered to be the moving factor of the adversary common law system. It is the parties who have the greatest interest in the matter at hand. The plaintiff wants to win for the economic value that winning brings and the defendant wants to win to retain whatever economic value the plaintiff is seeking to extract from it. In the criminal law system the same motives are at work although the stakes of the parties may be different. The prosecutor as the representative of the State wishes to win for multiple reasons. Success means properly performing his/her job. Also the prosecutor sees conviction as protecting the public. Success has positive effects on ego and career advancement. By making a name for him/herself the prosecutor can command a higher economic value when moving from the public/prosecution to the private/defender practice. The defendant and its counsel have an enormous stake in that the defendant does not wish to lose liberty and its champion, the lawyer, is there to protect that interest. The economic stake for the lawyer is clear whether in civil or criminal practice. Reputation translates into economic value and the higher the reputation for success and unswerving representation of the client's interest the higher the rents that can be extracted from the client and future clients.

Adversarial litigation is a kind of warfare—civilized in character and governed by rules that attempt to level the playing field between the two sides in the case. These rules make it easier for the protagonists, the lawyers, to discover the true facts and present them in the light most favorable to their client. Warfare is an apt analogy because the lawyers, commonly referred to as hired guns, are the modern substitute for the champion who did battle on behalf of the parties in ancient times. Moreover, the adversarial system by pitting the lawyers against each other keeps the clients at a distance and thus serves to avoid actual bloodshed. This is especially important in cases where emotions run high and where vengeance may be part of the equation. Thus, the State through the prosecutor proceeds against the accused to avoid the blood feud. The private party litigant in a wrongful death or medical malpractice case is rewarded with monetary damages (and sometimes punitive damages) so that economic value replaces "an eye for an eye."

Indispensable to the adversarial system is a large pool of highly trained expert champions for the parties, namely the lawyers. In England the body of lawyers engaged in litigation work is even divided between Solicitors (who work behind the scenes and do not actually argue the matter in court) and the Barristers who are highly trained to handle the aspects of the case that occur before the court. The Barrister's devotion to one part of the law practice, the in court advocacy of a client's position, sharpens the Barrister's ability to represent the client's interests. In the United States the roles of Barrister and Solicitor are rolled together in a unified Bar where lawyers perform both roles. Nonetheless, major law firms are structured in a way that separates those who practice in court, the litigator, from those who perform other functions such as corporate merger and acquisition specialists. Major law firms train litigators in-house by having them assist older seasoned litigators who not only receive assistance from the younger lawyer but also teach the younger lawyer the craft. Over time the younger lawyer is given increasing responsibility, under the eye of the older lawyers, until the younger lawyer is sufficiently trained to handle a case alone. In the adversary system litigating lawyers learn to become lawyers by practicing as litigating lawyers.

Similarly the education system in the United States concentrates on educating lawyers to be lawyers. It is a system based on lawyers teaching students how to become lawyers. Thus, in American law schools the professors are on the whole lawyers, members of the Bar who can and frequently either have before entering academia or do while in academia, actually practice law. The "Socratic method" of question and answer is designed to enable budding lawyers to better learn their craft by requiring them to develop argumentative skills while at the same time teaching them to parse cases so as to discern the importance of the facts and the nuance of the decision. All this is to be done while standing on their feet and defending their position. These are all characteristics necessary to adequately perform the art of advocating a client's cause.

In an adversary system the trial judge tends to be a litigator who either temporarily or permanently has moved from advocate to umpire and decision-maker. It is believed that to properly perform the job the trial judge needs to understand the practice from the point of view of the advocates before the court. Through this understanding the judge can monitor the progress of the case and make reasonable time demands of the lawyers for the parties. Trial judges having been advocates understand the "tricks of the trade." The judge understands that when the defendant says it wants to go to trial immediately it means that it wants to postpone the trial for as long as possible while not appearing as if it wants to delay. Even appellate court judges are for the most part former trial lawyers and thus can better understand the record before them and the circumstances of its creation.

The adversary system assumes that the parties (through their champions the lawyers) having the greatest interest in success in the matter will marshal all of the relevant facts and will present the facts most likely to assist their case and most likely to adversely affect the opponent's case. When it comes to the law the assumption is the same. Having adverse interests in a real dispute the parties will present the best arguments possible on the issues before the court. It is this assumption that requires that a true adversary system be a "case or controversy" system. Only when truly adverse parties with truly adverse interests at stake in a case are confronting each other can the court be assured that all of the best arguments will be brought forth to support each side.

The adversary system is lawyer dominated—the lawyers as the representatives of the adverse parties are given the responsibility of protecting their clients' interests and presenting the best possible case to the court. The judge is relatively passive, especially where a jury is involved in deciding the issues of fact in the matter. Education is based on the actual practice of the law—students even attend clinics where, under the watchful eye of lawyer professors they represent clients, as they will eventually do in practice after being admitted to the Bar.

Not only do the lawyers dominate the system but also they are held responsible for making the system work. The use of juries in the common law adversary system forced the system to develop two separate and distinguishable parts to the litigation. The first part—the pretrial—was designed so that the parties through their lawyers could find out what the relevant facts of the matter were prior to having to present those facts to the jury. The second part—the trial—required a concentrated production of the evidence before the jury so that lay jurors could make a determination. To enable the lay jurors to complete the public service they are performing as quickly as possible the pretrial had to resolve as many factual issues as possible. That could only occur if there were some means of discovering the facts at pretrial. To make this system work efficiently the lawyers were held responsible for the pretrial and trial. If the lawyer erred and the client lost the case because of such error that was not a matter for the court to consider in dealing with the ultimate decision in the case. It was not the judge's job to do justice in the matter in the sense of assuring that the party who should win does win. That was left to the lawyers. The concentrated trial of the common law adversary system only works because of the requirements that the lawyers fully prepare the case at pretrial and the parties are responsible for the professionalism of their champions.[1]

As noted earlier, prewar Japan was not an adversary system. Rather, it borrowed its civil and criminal substantive and procedural codes from the European civil law system where procedure is based on an inquisition model. The inquisition model is older than the common law adversary model. It has been suggested that the inquisition model was a natural outgrowth of the centralization of power in the monarchy that characterized the start of the modern era in Europe.[2] Clearly the inquisition model favored a strong central government that controlled the system. The great advantage of the model was that it paved the way for logic and fact-finding rather than superstition, ordeal and battle to control decision-making.

In the modern inquisition model the lawyer is far less a player and the judge a more significant player. This difference between judge and lawyer was heightened in prewar Japan by the relative reputations of the Bench and Bar and the roles each saw themselves as playing. The civil law inquisition system is more "scientific" in approach than the common law. The common law is based on experience—the experience of earlier cases creates the law to be applied to later cases and the experience of later cases is used to distinguish earlier cases and thus refine the rules of law to be applied in the future. The civil law, on the other hand, is based on scientific understanding, explanation and application of the Codes. The Codes, in turn, are the body of law the judges apply to the cases before them.

In an inquisition system the principal inquisitor is the judge who must ultimately make the decision in the matter. The judge has the responsibility of getting the question decided properly and the role of the lawyers in fact finding and presenting is secondary. The history and thrust of this system are not based on the assumption that the litigation process is a clash of adversaries, each representing a different party. Witnesses are not subjected to blistering cross-examination, which the adversary common law system views as a necessary evil to better uncover the truth. The chief inquisitor, the judge, is the active party in asking witnesses questions and understanding what the litigation is all about. The experience of earlier cases is not as significant in understanding what legal rule to apply as the court has the law before it in the Codes. The question in each case is how to apply that law to the facts in front of the judge. How other judges applied the law to other facts may be interesting but surely not controlling on the judge who is to use independent judgment in deciding how to apply the law to the instant case. Lawyers can and do help the judge in making the decision (both factual and legal). Lawyers may sug-

---

1 See, Geoffrey C. Hazard, Jr., Discovery and the Role of the Judge in Civil Law Jurisdictions, 73 Notre Dame Law Review 1017(1998); Arthur Taylor von Mehren, Some Comparative Reflections on First Instance Civil Procedure: Recent Reforms in German Civil Procedure and in the Federal Rules, 63 Notre Dame Law Review 608, 615 (1988).

2 Shigemitsu Dando (Translated by B.J. George Jr.) JAPANESE CRIMINAL PROCEDURE (Fred B. Rothman & Co., 1965) 7-8.

gest witnesses, who should be heard and in some civil law systems may help prepare the witnesses for examination by the judge. In other civil law systems such preparation may be seen as interference with the judge's role in getting the true testimony, facts and evidence in the case. Lawyers may suggest question to the judge to assist in bringing out relevant facts. Lawyers can assist by marshaling evidence that the judge should review and consider in making a decision. But lawyers are not the active, rough and tumble questioners of the adversary system. Similarly as the law is contained in the Codes, the function of the lawyer in dealing with the law is different than in the common law system. The lawyer is far more a technician employing a scientific method to help understand the Codes. In the civil law system since the law is already written down a premium is placed on scientific analysis of the Codes rather than analysis of previous cases. The opinions of professors who have spent their entire careers in analyzing the Codes are more significant than the opinions of professors in the United States. Moreover, as practical experience is not what law schools are primarily teaching professors do not need to be lawyers who have actually handled cases in the subject matter area they are teaching. Law professors tend to be career professors. And, judges tend to be career judges.

The civil law judge similarly plays a role different from that of the common law judge. The civil law judge is no passive umpire. As chief inquisitor the judge is responsible for gathering the evidence in the case—although the parties may be asked to assist through the production of files and witnesses and through answering questions put to them by the judge. As the judge, an official of the government and belonging to a governmental bureaucracy is responsible for evidence gathering, such common law devices as the deposition (Examination before Trial) taken in a lawyer's office is not possible. This private taking of testimony is inconsistent with the sovereign nature of testimony taking in the civil law system. Accordingly the production of documents is a function of judicial decree and thus a matter for judicial consideration. To properly perform her job the civil law judge must interview the parties (and counsel if the parties are represented) in order to gain an understanding of the case, its issues and factual matters relevant to resolving those issues. The court must clarify the legal contentions and the factual issues before the judge begins the process of formal evidence taking. In the clarification process the judge may require parties to produce documents and may interview parties and party employees to gain a better understanding of the case. Through such questioning and review of documents taken together with the contentions of the parties the issues in the case may change, may be modified and some may be dropped. As more information becomes available, a different view of the case may emerge from that originally set out before the court. New issues may be presented and further clarification may be required. At all stages of the case the judge, not the parties, is responsible for clarifying the contentions and issues and evidentiary matters in the case. This is necessary so that the judge can perform her ultimate obligation—determining the case in a way in which the correct decision is reached and the party who should win does win.

The civil law procedure system was "comfortable" to the Meiji oligarchs because it had many attributes in common to the immature legal system being developed in Tokugawa Japan. The criminal procedure was especially attractive. Under the Tokugawa system, as we have seen, there was a two-stage process (investigation and trial) and both were under the control of the government. The civil law criminal procedure borrowed from the French law was also two-stage with investigation under the control of a judicial official and then trial before a different judicial official. Over time, as we have seen, the preliminary trial became the true trial of the action (without input from the accused) and the second stage was a kind of appeal to determine whether the preliminary trial had gotten the defendant's guilt correct. At the trial of the action the prosecution proceeded by submitting its dossier to the trial court. This combined with the reality that the first instance magistrate judge had determined that there was enough evidence to actually try the defendant placed the accused outside the presumption of innocence. It also placed the prosecutor's case before the court before the defendant had an opportunity to respond, thereby poisoning the well of decision. As in Tokugawa times trials were essentially determined by confession. Confession was no longer obtained through the use of physical torture but the prolonged detention of the accused who was compelled to undergo rigorous questioning ultimately resulted in a confession.

The trial process itself was similar to the feudal trial in the sense that the questioning was in the hands of the government official (the Tokugawa magistrate or the Meiji judge) and lawyers played a minor role in the process. The common law system attempts to separate the fact finder and decision-maker (separate the judge and jury). It also separates the fact finder from the party that determines punishment (even in death penalty cases where a jury recommends the penalty it is the judge who makes the penalty decision—thus if the jury recommends the death penalty the judge may nonetheless give a sentence of life imprisonment). Both the Tokugawa and Japanese prewar systems placed these functions in the hands of the judge. And, in both the Tokugawa and the prewar system the accused had virtually no pretrial procedural rights. As a consequence once the decision to go to trial was made the outcome, a guilty verdict, was almost completely assured.

The American Occupation attempted to change important aspects of the system. Thus pretrial protections were given to the criminal defendant, such as a right to counsel, a privilege against self-incrimination, a reduced period of pretrial detention before indictment, etc. The Code of Criminal Procedure was amended to conform to these constitutional guarantees. These protections were viewed as essential to bring the Japanese criminal justice system into conformity with what the Occupation saw as a fair system that protected the rights of the accused as well as the rights of society. In addition the trial phase of the case was changed by amendments to the Code of Criminal Procedure. Representing the attempt to elevate the role of the defense counsel in trials both prosecutor and defense counsel were seated at the same level instead of the prewar arrangement where the prosecutor sat at a level with the judge and both sat at a higher level than the defense counsel. Seating level may appear as a relatively inconsequential matter but in a Confusion system where seating level indicates both power and obligation duties—where a party seated "above" another is literally seen as "above"—this change was significant and demonstrated that the prosecutor and defense counsel were equals. The pretrial judicial inquiry was abolished and in its place a more "Americanized" notion of prosecutor as adversary party representing the State and defense counsel being an adversary party representing the defendant was put in its place. The objective here was clearly to introduce a more adversary process and to give the defendant back the presumption of innocence. The role of the trial judge was reduced by giving the parties (prosecution and defense) the right and indeed obligation of presenting and questioning witnesses. However, the trial judge retained a residual power to ask questions of witnesses and to decide whether witnesses were needed on a specific point. In addition rules of evidence, specifically the hearsay rule, were introduced in criminal cases to attempt to make the process more reliable and to make the court more reliant on the lawyers (for prosecution and defense) who were obligated to present "admissible" and reliable evidence. As confession had been the heart of criminal cases in both prewar and Tokugawa criminal procedure, the new system required that there be corroboration of a confession and that without corroboration a defendant could not be convicted. In the view of the Occupation the new system greatly improved the rights of the defendant and was a middle of the road amendment neither completely adopting the American adversary system nor completely retaining the prewar inquisition system.[3]

Similarly in the civil litigation arena the American Occupation attempted to create a more adversarial system. This approach was adopted both because the Occupation authorities favored the adversary system approach but also out of concern that Japanese judges were too paternalistic and exercised a form of authoritarianism through their paternalistic and inquisition approach to litigation. Further, during the prewar and wartime periods virtually all civil cases were required to go to conciliation. This had the effect of diminishing the judicial system as a mechanism for resolving disputes. The Occupation wanted to reverse this policy and establish the court as the place to resolve legal disputes. [Notwithstanding, in 1951 Japan passed a comprehensive Civil Conciliation Act.]

The major change made in the Code of Civil Procedure was the removal of the Code provision that gave the judge the authority *sua sponte* to call witnesses in a case. In its place the Code adopted a more lawyer oriented, more adversary system procedure placing the responsibility for calling witnesses on the lawyers for the parties. Japan had in 1926, following the lead of German law, amended the Code of Civil Procedure to make the Preliminary Oral Argument stage of the case (pretrial) more distinct from the Oral Argument (trial) stage.[4] This reform had sought to make the Pre-Oral Argument stage act like the common law pretrial in that the evidence would be gathered in this stage and then the trial could proceed on a rel-

3 See, e.g., Alfred C. Oppler, LEGAL REFORM IN OCCUPIED JAPAN (Princeton University Press, 1976) 136-149.

4 For a discussion of the German law reform of 1924 see, Peter Gottwald, Simplified Civil Procedure in West Germany (Comment), 31 American Journal of Comparative Law 687, 688 (1983).

atively concentrated basis. In fact the 1926 amendment called for concentrated evidence taking after the Preliminary Oral Argument stage. However the reform failed in both Germany and Japan, partly because the reform failed to place responsibility for the case on the lawyers and left the judge responsible for assuring that the party in the right should win (even if the lawyer was incompetent).[5] To enable the lawyers to know what witnesses to call the prewar prohibition against interviewing witnesses before they were called to testify was abolished. In addition, efforts were made to strengthen the previous efforts towards concentrated trial so that long periods between court sessions would be eliminated and trial would more closely resemble to American system of trial testimony on a day after day basis. The category of persons who could rely on a privilege to refuse to testify was limited. The Code called for party determination of what witnesses might be called and for party examination of witnesses. However, the Code preserved the authority of the judge to determine whether party designated witnesses were needed and thus should be called to testify orally and preserved the judge's right, after party examination, to ask questions. The judge also remained in control of the calendar. Whatever the intention of the Occupation, the judge remained responsible for seeing that the party in the right won the case. To do that the judge remained the central figure in both the pre-Oral Argument stage of the case and the Oral Argument stage of the case.

In both the civil case and criminal case arena the new procedures were designed to rely more on the role of counsel and the questioning and cross-examination of witnesses. The objective was to create a kind of adversary system for both civil and criminal cases. The process of the trial in both would be substantially the same. Evidentiary rules (such as the hearsay rule and cross-examination) would serve to strengthen the rights of the parties. The role of the judge would be diminished while the role of counsel would be expanded. To a great extent the success of the Occupation amendments to the procedure Codes depended on how the court interpreted those amendments. This in turn depended to a great extent on how willing the court was to turn over the responsibility for trials to the lawyers and how prepared trial lawyers were to undertake the new responsibilities given to them by the Codes.

It is suggested that the amended Codes had minor success in changing the litigation system in Japan. As mentioned earlier the constitutional changes designed to protect the rights of the criminally accused, such as right to counsel, privilege against self-incrimination and prohibition of coerced confession have not worked as those protections have evolved in the United States. In many ways, the present system of pre-indictment investigation of suspects remains as it was prewar, with the possible exception that judges get more involved in warrant determinations than prewar, although this does not appear to greatly hamper the prosecutor or

---

5 See, Arthur Taylor von Mehren, Some Comparative Reflections on First Instance Civil Procedure: Recent Reforms in German Civil Procedure and in the Federal Rules, 63 Notre Dame Law Review 608, 615 (1988) (concentrated trial requires lawyer responsibility for gathering the evidence before hand).

provide additional protections to the suspected. Japanese courts adopted a rule under which the constitutional rights granted to criminal suspects and accused must be balanced against the constitutional obligation of the prosecutor to charge and convict those committing crime. This balancing test has watered down the rights of the accused. As a result the constitutional privilege against self-incrimination, the right to counsel and the necessity for a warrant are essentially dormant.

In the civil litigation arena the changes have had at most a modest affect on the system. Judges in Japan continue to view lawyers as either not competent in the handling of cases or as insufficiently prepared for cases. Judges remain paternalistic. The experiment with a more adversarial system has not greatly changed the trial in Japan although the outward forms and the Codes of Procedure appear to resemble an adversary system. The judge in Japan remains the central player in the trial and the lawyers remain minor players. Recent changes in the civil procedure system are moving Japan's trial system further away from the American model and closer to the modern German law model. The judge's power and authority to question witnesses has been enhanced. The judge's authority to reject witness testimony and cross-examination in favor of written testimony has been expanded. And the judge's power to attempt to bring about a conciliated settlement rather than a judgment is stronger today than it was in the immediate post-war period. That power to attempt to compel settlement is closer today to what it was in Tokugawa times than it is to what it was post-war. While asserting the valuable role of the judicial system in Japan's asserted new policy of making the Rule of Law a dynamic part of Japanese life at all levels, the reality is that with a few exceptions (such as intellectual property matters, where Japanese commercial interests are now served by having a strong protection mechanism for Japanese inventions and creations) litigation appears to be as frowned upon by the government (and judges) today as it was by the government (and magistrates) in Tokugawa times.

1) The Presumption of Innocence in Criminal Cases

Although the preliminary inquisition trial has been abolished by the Occupation amendments to the Code of Criminal Procedure, it is questionable whether the defendant today is truly given a presumption of innocence. This comes about in part: a) because the evolving role of the police and prosecutor in which each plays a quasi-judicial role in ferreting out and declining to prosecute those believed guilty of committing a crime. There is here a subtle but real distinction between the American police and prosecutor on the one hand and the Japanese institutions on the other. b) Because virtually all defendants confess prior to indictment and must then overcome the confession at trial. c) Because of evidentiary rules that permit the prosecution to put in its case in documentary form through use of the police report exception to the hearsay rule (a return to a trial by dossier model).

As a rule, in the United States the police investigate crimes and the prosecutor is the lawyer for the police and the State. Thus, if the police require a warrant for a search they will get the prosecutor's office to assist in presenting the matter to the court so that a warrant can be obtained. The police are the front line investigators whose role is to present the results of the investigation to the prosecutor. The prosecutor is the lawyer for the State in seeking a conviction of the defendant. But the prosecutor has discretion and can decide that there is not enough evidence to support a conviction and thus can decide not to prosecute. In addition because of the existence of the Grand Jury in American jurisprudence and the authority of the Grand Jury to refuse to permit a prosecution to go forward because of lack of evidence, the prosecutor may submit a case to the Grand Jury without great vigor and leave it to the Grand Jury to refuse to go forward with the prosecution. Decisions on whether to prosecute or refuse to prosecute are generally based on the prosecution's judgment as to whether it can win the case. The decision may also involve the discretionary function of determining whether the offense committed was somehow warranted by circumstances so that it would be improper or otherwise unfair to prosecute. A decision not to prosecute is virtually the same as a not guilty verdict—there is no stigma to the defendant. Moreover, a decision to prosecute is seen as and treated by judge and jury as nothing more that a partisan's determination that it thinks it can win the case. Being seen as the advocate for only one side of the case, the determination to prosecute is not seen as carrying great weight as to the guilt or innocence of the accused.

In today's media age, in cases of public notoriety it is common for the lawyers on both sides—the prosecutor and the defense counsel—to engage the media and publicly express views as to the guilt or innocence of the defendant. (The prosecutor must take care not to abuse its office in doing so and not to so poison the well of public opinion that a fair jury cannot be selected—something the defense counsel is less inhibited by). It is not uncommon for both sides to leak bits and pieces of evidence to support the position of one side or damage the position of the other. The public is thus used to the idea that the criminal trial is a contest between adversaries and neither side is seen as a neutral representing the truth in the matter. Neutrality is reserved for the judge and jury. American television programs that lionize the role of the defense counsel (such as the very popular Perry Mason show of years ago) or that demonstrate the shortcomings of the prosecutor office (the prosecutor is wrong in some television programs and loses some cases before juries in others) lead American's to view a trial as a contest on a level playing field. The defendant may or may not be guilty but it is clear that he is presumed innocent and the prosecution has the burden of establishing and proving the defendant's guilt.

The situation is different in Japan. Perhaps because of the abuses of the police in the prewar and wartime period, the prosecutors' role in Japan is seen, in part, as an intermediary between the police authority (that may not be trusted to determine guilt and innocence) and the trial where guilt or innocence is formally announced. Thus the prosecutors' investigative function is seen not as the investigation by a champion of one of two equals—the State and the defendant—with an interest in the outcome, but rather as an investigation by a non-partisan seeking to determine the ultimate right and wrong. At a symposium held at Harvard Law School in

1961 a Japanese Ministry of Justice Official referred to the public's prewar desire to have the prosecutor investigate so that criminal cases would not be initiated with insufficient evidence. Apparently under prior practice too many accused were being found not guilty by the examining magistrates (in 1916 the rate of acquittals had dropped to 7% for magistrates and only 2.5% at trial where as previously a full 30% had been acquitted). The official found it not surprising that because of the prosecutor's investigative role and the prosecutors' desire not to bring cases that can be lost the conviction rate in Japan in 1961 was 99%,[6] the same conviction rate as today.

Moreover, both the police and the prosecutor in Japan exercise a discretionary power that is akin to a quasi-judicial determination of guilt, without sentence. Thus, police have and extensively use the authority to determine not to send what are considered minor cases to the prosecutor for prosecution, even if the evidence of guilt is compelling.[7] Because the police in Japan have greater authority to use investigative techniques that are considered unconstitutional in the United States (such as greater stop and frisk authority), police in Japan have greater success in solving crime than do their American counterparts. Because of greater public assistance to police in their investigative efforts as well as a more community oriented police function (police on bicycles, close relations between police and local businesses and the local community) most crimes in Japan are solved by the police. Yet somewhere between 20 and 40 percent of all criminals identified by the police are not reported to the prosecutor for further action.[8] This quasi judicial determination that the guilty should not be prosecuted is based on the belief that handling the matter at the police level will better resolve the matter in the interest of the victim, the accused and the society in general. Whether this is accurate is not the issue, the fact is that the Judicial Branch is aware of this practice and knows that a high percent of cases that are investigated are not sent to the prosecutor and hence never reach the criminal trial stage. Weak cases and cases not calling for judicial action are thus not only washed out of the system at an early stage but the judge is aware that such weak cases have been washed out.

The prosecutor also has a quasi-judicial authority unknown to American prosecutors. This is the authority to "suspend prosecution"[9] of accused persons whom the prosecutor believes is guilty of a crime and who, if prosecuted to completion would be found guilty. Unlike the determination not to prosecute for lack of evi-

6 See, Atsushi Nagashima, The Accused and Society: The Administration of Criminal Justice in Japan, in LAW IN JAPAN (Arthur Taylor von Mehren Ed. Harvard University Press, 1963) 196, 298-304.

7 This practice, known as *bizai shobun*, is based on Article 246 of the Code of Criminal Procedure.

8 See, John O. Haley, AUTHORITY WITHOUT POWER: LAW AND THE JAPANESE PARADOX (Oxford University Press, 1991) 126 (21%); Daniel H. Foote, The Benevolent Paternalism of Japanese Criminal Justice, 80 California Law Review 317, 342 (1992) (40%).

9 See, Shigemitsu Dando (translated by B. J. George, Jr.) JAPANESE CRIMINAL PROCEDURE (Fred B. Rothman & Co., 1965) 344.

dence (a discretion that the Japanese prosecutor shares with the American prosecutor), a suspension of prosecution presumes that the accused is guilty. Although guilty the prosecutor has made a judgment not to proceed (based on various factors including the nature of the crime, factors affecting the perpetrator and the views of the victim that suspending prosecution will more likely result in rehabilitation of the accused than would a prosecution and conviction). Separate records are kept of cases in which the prosecutor has suspended prosecution and these records, which are publicly available, show that the suspension rate is quite high—28% in 1998—and further that suspension may be used in cases where the crime is considered serious.[10] Indeed in 1998 the prosecutor only instituted prosecution in 44% of cases—and this after 20 to 40% of cases had been washed out at the police level—and only declined to prosecute because of insufficient evidence in 0.9% of cases.[11]

Courts know that most criminal cases are solved and that most cases are not brought before the court for determination. Added to this is the reality that in 99% of the cases that are brought the defendant is found guilty. In such a setting it is not too far a reach to conclude that the prosecutor would not have brought the case unless the guilt of the defendant was clear. Through the use of its quasi-judicial discretionary authority to suspend prosecution the prosecutor has assumed the role that was occupied by the investigating magistrate in the prewar period. And, this includes the prewar practice under which the defendant was denied his presumption of innocence once the case was submitted for prosecution and trial.

Almost all defendants in criminal cases have confessed prior to the trial stage of the case. Just as confession was a staple of Tokugawa criminal justice, it is a staple of "post-modern" post-war criminal justice in Japan today. Torture is no longer used, but the reality is that the accused is subjected to long questioning sessions over an extended period of time. During this period the suspect (not yet accused and thus not entitled to a right to counsel) is held in a substitute jail (a police jail rather than a prison under the authority of the Ministry of Justice). At such extended questioning sessions the suspect has no counsel or other representative and no right to refuse to be subjected to questioning even if the suspect asserts that he does not want to answer any questions because answer might tend to incriminate the accused. The result of such sessions, which can go on during a 23-day holding period or longer (if *bekken taiho* is used), is that suspects invariably confess.

---

10 For a discussion of suspension of prosecution see, Shigemitsu Dando, System of Discretionary Prosecution in Japan, 18 American Journal of Comparative Law 518 (1970); Marcia E. Goodman, The Exercise and Control of Prosecutorial Discretion in Japan, 5 UCLA Pacific Basin Law Journal 16 (1986); Daniel H. Foote, Prosecutorial Discretion in Japan: A Response, 5 UCLA Pacific Basin Law Journal 96 (1986): John O. Haley, AUTHORITY WITHOUT POWER: LAW AND THE JAPANESE PARADOX, Policemen and Prosecutors, Crime Without Punishment (Oxford University Press, 1991); A. Didrick Castberg, JAPANESE CRIMINAL JUSTICE (Praeger Publishers, 1990) 59-64.

11 See information available on the Web site of the Japan Ministry of Justice under Public Prosecutor.

The reasons such sessions may last for 23-days or longer are several. First, most suspects "voluntarily" submit to police interrogation. Suspects know that police do not send on to the prosecutor a high percentage of cases even where the police know the suspect is guilty and the suspect has confessed. Indeed to get such lenient treatment from the police a suspect must show willingness to cooperate with the police and agreement to appear "voluntarily" at a police station for questioning is a first step in cooperation. Once voluntarily present it is not so easy for a suspect to leave. The police may even use a certain low level of force to compel a suspect to remain for additional questioning. Second, under Japanese criminal procedure the police have the right to hold a suspect for 2 days before turning the suspect over to the prosecutor. The prosecutor is theoretically given one day to determine whether to indict or not. However, the prosecutor may request that a court grant an additional 10-day period and then another 10-day period for investigation. Judges invariably grant such prosecutor requests. The suspect's rights are theoretically protected through the intercession of a judicial officer in the extension decision. However the reality is otherwise. The suspect has no legal counsel to plead the suspect's case before the judge, there is no right for the suspect to appear before the judge on the extension question and judges grant such requests because prosecutors make such requests. Third, if the prosecutor does not get a confession during the 23-day holding investigation period, the prosecutor can arrest the suspect for a lesser or greater crime (whether or not related to the crime for which initially arrested) and the 23-day clock begins to run again. This *bekkon taiho* process may be used over and over again to extend the holding period for 46 days or 69 days or longer. It is the truly unique suspect—whether innocent or guilty—who can survive such extended questioning under the conditions of a police lockup without effective representation by counsel.

During this investigation stage the suspect does not have a right to bail. Bail is only possible after the suspect has become an accused—after indictment. As a practical matter only when the prosecutor consents will applications for bail be granted. Accordingly it is good for an accused to be on the good side of the prosecutor. The best way to do this is to confess early. An additional advantage of early confession is that after confession and indictment the suspect/accused may apply for bail. If the prosecutor advises the court that the prosecutor is afraid that if granted bail the accused will destroy evidence, the court will typically refuse to grant bail on this ground—although it is clear in many cases that this is mere subterfuge for continued desire to hold the accused. Even when a defendant is found not guilty at the first instance trial, if the prosecutor appeals the case the High Court may refuse to allow the defendant out on bail. Bail on appeal can be denied if the appeal court finds that there is sufficient reason to believe the defendant is guilty.[12] No weight is given to the fact that the defendant has been found not guilty after a trial. It has been argued that this remedy has been used almost exclu-

12 Case No. 94 of 2000, 54 Minshu 461 (Sup. Ct. Petty Bench 6/27/2000) available in English through the web site of the Supreme Court of Japan.

sively against aliens charged with crimes who have been exonerated by the District Court.[13]

Finally, street-smart suspects know (and suspects who have exercised their privilege of counsel learn from counsel) that to get the prosecutor to exercise the suspension of prosecution option it is best to confess early in the process. Confession and contrition as well as compensation and restitution to the victim are staples of the suspension of prosecution decision-making function. The innocent defendant who continues to assert innocence is likely to be seen as obstinate and not a good subject for rehabilitation—after all, the first step in rehabilitation is acknowledgment of wrong and contrition about the wrong having been committed. Further, judges take the same attitude regarding sentencing. Namely in exercising its broad sentencing authority (including the imposition of a suspended sentence, the typical sentence in Japan) judges in Japan consider whether the defendant is contrite, has acknowledged wrongdoing, is prepared to (or has already) made restitution, and thus is a subject for rehabilitation rather than incarceration.

The entire system pushes suspects to the logical conclusion that confession is the way to go and the sooner the better. And, counsel will advise the defendant to the same effect because counsel is aware that in 99% of cases that go to trial the defendant will be convicted. So if the defendant has not confessed prior to indictment, the defendant is likely to follow the advice of counsel and confess before trial.

Criminal cases in Japan are subject to a hearsay rule. However, the Japanese version of the rule has significant exceptions for "trustworthy" information. Included in the exceptions is the police report concerning the investigation conducted by the police. This report includes witness statements. In addition the defendant's confession is admissible without need to produce a witness. Unlike American confessions the Japanese confession is neither a verbatim question and answer session nor a handwritten statement from the defendant. Rather, the confession is a summary of the interrogation sessions (perhaps 23-days or more) made by the prosecutor's office and read to and sealed (the Japanese substitute for a signature) by the defendant. Even if the defendant later recants the confession the summary confession is admissible in evidence. The defendant then has the burden of showing that the confession is "unreliable."

---

13 In September 2003 the Tokyo High Court ordered a defendant held without bail on the grounds that the defendant (who was an alien but had lived in Japan under a valid visa since he was an elementary school child) might flee the country and also that he might destroy evidence, notwithstanding that the defendant had been found not guilty at the trial court level and the prosecutor was appealing the not guilty verdict. See, Japan Times on Line, 9/10/03 Hiroshi Matsubara, Detention of Acquitted Prompts Legal Cross Fire. It seems highly improbable that a defendant who had been found not guilty by the lower court would be in a position to destroy evidence at such a late date. Presumably the prosecution would long since have obtained whatever evidence of guilt there was. The Japan Times reported that courts routinely agree with prosecutor requests to hold defendants without bail when defendants do not confess to the charges brought against them and noted that some have characterized such cases as "hostage justice."

Because of the exceptions to the hearsay rule, the prosecutor may start the State's case by submitting to the court the defendant's confession together with the police report with witness statements (and any fruits of the confession) attached. This is sufficient to make out a prima facie case and the burden then shifts to the defendant to establish innocence. In essence the old "trial by dossier" procedure continues in the modern criminal trial. Only the form of the dossier has changed. After submission of the dossier the burden shifts to the defendant to overcome the evidence of guilt and prove innocence.

Perhaps the starkest illustration of the lack of a true presumption of innocence is the fact that even after a trial in which the defendant is found not guilty, the High Court may order the defendant held in confinement pending the prosecution's appeal. The confinement order is permissible if the appeal court, upon a review of the record, finds that there is sufficient reason to believe in the guilt of the defendant—the same standard applied by the trial court for detention prior to a trial. Even a trial in which the defendant is found not guilty is not sufficient to create a presumption of innocence that requires a showing by the prosecution of probable guilt before confinement of the defendant is permitted.[14]

2) The Inequality of Prosecutor and Defense Counsel in Criminal Cases

It is true that both prosecutor and defense counsel sit at the same level in the courtroom. But equal seating does not mean that the parties are in fact equal. As an initial matter it must be remembered that both the prosecutor and the judge have a common employer, the State, and that this common employer may and in fact frequently does intermingle their functions. Thus, as noted earlier, prosecutors may temporarily be assigned to judicial duties while judges may be assigned to prosecutors offices. Lawyers in practice, the pool for defense lawyers, do not have the luxury of a constant source of salary income. Rather, lawyers are dependent on clients and cannot take a few years off from their practice to work as a judge or prosecutor and judges do not spend time working in lawyers' offices. Even the 2004 initiative permitting young judges to work for two years in a bengoshi office during the first 10-year assignment as a judge is unlikely to establish a bengoshi/judge relationship that can rival the judge/prosecutor relationship. The period is too short and comes too early in a judge's career. The judge is unlikely to handle on his/her own any significant matter for the private lawyer and likely would not be able to appear in court to represent any client since this might be considered as taking advantage of having a judge on staff at the bengoshi office. Familiarity between judges and prosecutors does not breed contempt but rather breeds understanding, respect and a distinct advantage of the prosecutor over the defense counsel in actual trials.

The law gives the prosecutor a decided advantage in obtaining evidence. The defendant in a criminal case is the primary source of evidence concerning the case,

---

14 See, dissenting opinion of Justice Mitsuo Endo in case No. 94 of 2000 (Sup. Ct. Petty Bench, 6/27/2000) available in English through the web site of the Supreme Court of Japan.

especially when the defendant has in fact committed the crime. The guilty defendant knows where the physical evidence of the crime, such as the weapon used, the fruits of the burglary, etc. is located and knows exactly what occurred at the crime scene and how the crime was planned, carried out and how the escape was undertaken. Even if not guilty of the crime, the suspect is the best source of knowledge about the potential defense—where the suspect was when the crime was committed, any relationship between the suspect and the victim, alibi evidence, etc. In short, access to the defendant at an early stage of the criminal process can lead to a treasure trove of evidence. At this early stage of the investigation the prosecutor has a distinct advantage over the defense counsel. First, the prosecutor has a long period in which to question the suspect without interference by counsel. This extended time flows from the fact that the accused has no *right* to counsel until indicted and under the Code the prosecutor and police together have a 23-day holding period before they need to indict. (This period may be extended by further 23-day periods using the *bekken taiho* subterfuge.) Even if the defendant has resources and has retained counsel (exercising the *privilege* to retain counsel) the counsel does not have the right to be present during the questioning of the client and cannot prevent the prosecution from subjecting the accused to lengthy questioning sessions. Because the prosecutor has the right to determine when and for how long the accused may meet with counsel, the prosecutor can time meetings and questioning sessions to best accommodate the need to obtain a confession. Holding suspects in "substitute prisons" (i.e., police jail cells as a substitute for Ministry of Justice run prisons) not only makes it easier for the prosecutor to question but also makes it more difficult for the suspect to hold out and refuse to cooperate.[15] By the time the indictment is handed down the defendant has invariably confessed and the confession has led the prosecutor to physical evidence that may be useful in the trial.[16] Throughout this early stage of the case the defense counsel (if there is one) has no opportunity to obtain exculpatory evidence or work with the client in a meaningful way to formulate a defense. The period of time when counsel can meet with the client is controlled by the prosecutor who can carefully limit the scheduling of meetings so as not to "interfere" with prosecutor questioning sessions and so as to limit the time available for meetings so that such meetings are relatively short.

The limited availability of an exclusionary rule means that if the prosecutor or police overstep the bounds of proper police/investigative procedure, the fruits of their unlawful action may nonetheless be available for trial.[17] While evidence illegally obtained in egregious situations may be excluded at the trial, exclusion in-

---

15 For a discussion of "substitute prisons" see, Toshikuni Murai, Pretrial Detention and the Problem of Confinement, (translated by Frank Bennet, Jr.) 23 Law in Japan 85 (1990); see also, Yuji Iwasawa, INTERNATIONAL LAW, HUMAN RIGHTS AND JAPANESE LAW (Clarendon Press, 1998) 260-270.

16 See, Daniel H. Foote, Confessions and the Right to Silence in Japan, 21 Georgia Journal of International and Comparative Law 415 (1991).

17 See, Illegally Obtained Evidence Case, Case No. 1976 (A) No. 865, 32 Keishu 1672 (Sup. Ct. Petty Bench, 9/7/78) available in English through the web site of the Supreme Court of Japan.

volves a balancing of the defendant's interests with the public interest in having the guilty convicted. The end result is unlikely to be an exclusion of evidence if that means the guilty defendant goes free although evidence will from time to time be excluded (perhaps to demonstrate that there is an exclusionary rule) when the defendant is otherwise convicted by other evidence or for other crimes.[18]

All of this gives the prosecutor a huge advantage over the defense lawyer. Typically the prosecutor has made its case by the time the indictment is filed (defense counsel in most cases is only retained after indictment). Defense counsel, even if retained early in the process, gets a late start on meaningful access to the source of most significant knowledge about the events as they affect the defendant.

The role of defense counsel in Japan is strikingly different from the role of defense counsel in the United States. Knowing that 99% of defendants are convicted at trial, the defense counsel must attempt to convince the prosecutor to suspend prosecution or failing that to convince the court not to require the defendant to serve time or at least be lenient in sentencing. Japanese judges have a reputation for leniency and for suspending sentence. To achieve these ends the defense counsel must use his/her resources to convince the accused to confess (if the accused has not already done so) and to make restitution and payment to the victim. If a confession has already been given the defense counsel must convince the defendant not to recant and challenge the confession. This is necessary as only a defendant who recognizes and admits guilt can be seen as a worthy candidate for rehabilitation—the basis for suspension of prosecution and judicial leniency.

3) Lawyer Difficulty in Obtaining Evidence for Trial

In criminal cases the prosecutor has the resources of the police as well as the prosecutor's office to assist in gathering evidence. Both the police organization and the prosecutor organization are large institutions with modern resources and government funding to assist in carrying out their law enforcement functions. Thus, it is to be expected that in a criminal case the prosecution will be able to gather substantial quantities of evidence for use at the trial. Indeed, the prosecutor in the course of its investigation will also likely gather evidence that may be of use to the defense and which the defense may not have the resources to gather. Under the old inquisition system such evidence—both for and against the defendant—was presented to the court at the initiation of the trial stage. This had both a positive

18 Compare e.g., Case No. 2001 (A) No. 1678, 57 Keishu 121 (Sup. Ct. Petty Bench, 2/14/03) (available in English through the web site of the Supreme Court of Japan) where a urine sample and other evidence was quashed when the police lied to the court and lied when obtaining a warrant and the conviction based on the urine sample was set aside, but the lower court's dismissal of a second charge was reversed and defendant was nonetheless convicted of a crime and Case No. 1999 (A) No. 1164, 57 Keishu 620 (Sup. Ct. Petty Bench, 5/26/03)(available in English through the web site of the Supreme Court of Japan) where the use of a urine sample based on a warrant obtained based on physical evidence obtained in a search of a hotel room taken while defendant was physically held down by several police officers when nude, was held acceptable and thus the conviction of defendant was upheld.

and negative effect on the defense. As a negative it meant that the trial judge was immediately given the prosecutor's dossier and this file would likely prejudice the judge in favor of the prosecution—especially as the examining judge had decided that the defendant was likely guilty and thus had authorized the trial. From a positive point of view, the giving of the file to the court meant that the file was also given to the defense counsel. As a consequence, defense counsel had an opportunity to review evidence that was both harmful and helpful to the defendant and which defense counsel did not have the resources to otherwise obtain.

Such an open file procedure was seen as appropriate in an inquisition system where the function of the court (aided by the prosecutor) was to determine for itself the facts of the matter. The prosecutor and defense counsel were not seen in classic adversary terms, as the procedure itself was not adversarial. The new post-war system however was premised on the idea that the prosecutor and defense counsel were adversaries and that each had the responsibility to present the best case for its side. In such a system there was an advantage to holding back evidence that might assist the other side. Moreover, as the prosecutor was representing one side of the case it was seen as unfair to require that side to give evidence or conduct investigation for the other side of the case. Prosecutors particularly objected because under the new system although each side was the adversary of the other, the prosecutor had to prove its case beyond a reasonable doubt while defense counsel had the supposedly easier task of a lesser burden of proof. Under the new adversarial model, the prosecutor need only turn over such evidence as it will present at the trial—not its entire dossier.[19] Because the police report may be admitted in evidence as an exception to the hearsay rule coupled with the fact that in over 90% of all criminal cases the defendant confesses and this confession may be admitted over the defendant's objection that it was coerced, the prosecutor's modified dossier is admitted in evidence at the start of the trial and the burden then shifts to the defense to prove innocence. The modified dossier contains only such evidence and material as the prosecutor wishes to introduce and unlike the prewar inquisition does not contain exculpatory evidence.

Lawyers in Japan are typically generalist litigators handling both civil and criminal cases. Most law firms are small—single practitioners or perhaps two or three lawyers who banded together to share costs. The mega law firms of the United States are unknown in Japan and only recently have a select few Japanese firms reached two or three dozen lawyers. This phenomenon is partly cultural—lawyers tend to be individualistic (probably the reason they went on to become bengoshi rather than working for a company). It is also partly a result of legislation and rules. Until the recently enacted Lawyers Law, lawyers were not permitted to hire other lawyers to work for them. Thus a lawyer could not employ associates to assist. Each lawyer in a "firm" was essentially an individual practitioner in a joint

19 For a discussion of procedure under the amended criminal procedure code and the role of defense counsel see, Atsushi Nagashima (assisted by B. J. George) The Accused and Society: The Administration of Criminal Justice in Japan in Arthur Taylor von Mehren LAW IN JAPAN (Harvard University Press, 1963) 297, 303-310.

arrangement with other individual practitioners. Further, law firms were not allowed to have "branch offices." The Bar Associations broadly construed the definition of a branch office and thus a firm could not have offices in different cities or even two or more offices in the same city and might not even be permitted to have offices on different floors of the same building. Such restrictions reduced the size of lawyer organizations.

Small law firms, as a general rule, will find it more difficult than large organizations to ferret out evidence through their own investigation. This is true in both the criminal and civil litigation arena. Lacking the resources, the lawyer is placed in the difficult position of having the responsibility to gather and present evidence as an adversary party while lacking the ability to get such evidence. Just as the prosecutor need not make discovery of its complete file to the defense counsel so too counsel in civil litigation has no authority under the Code of Civil Procedure to compel the adverse party to produce evidence either before or after litigation has been started. The 1996 Code of Civil Procedure contains a new Inquiry Procedure post-litigation filing and the 2003 amendments to the Code contain a pre-filing Inquiry Procedure modeled on the post-filing process. But neither requires the party receiving inquires to respond and neither has a sanctions mechanism to deal with either failure to respond or inaccurate responses. The civil law system of placing the judge in control of taking and obtaining evidence makes evidence gathering and production a judicial function and not a lawyer function. There is little a bengoshi can do to get a third party or an adversary to produce evidence except request a court to order production. The grounds for ordering production are limited (and within the discretion of the court) and the sanction against a third party who refuses to obey an order to produce is more limited still.

The size of the Japanese Bar has remained relatively small throughout the post-war period. It is only recently that the number of new lawyers admitted each year (some of whom become judges and prosecutors) has risen to 1,000. Japanese industry on the other hand has greatly increased in size and volume and as a consequence the need for legal services has dramatically risen. A small pool of lawyers called upon to do an increasing amount of work has limited the time available to lawyers to do the ground work that American lawyers do to prepare and present a case for trial.

B. A Non-Adversary System

1) Lawyers and the Failure of Legal Education

Under the post-war amendments, the role of the lawyer was supposedly elevated while the role of the judge was diminished. To carry out its new role as principal player in the drama of the trial the Bar needed to have the skills that have been honed by the common law litigator over a period of centuries. Those skills are taught in the graduate law schools of the United States and are absorbed by students through the case method of study, the Socratic approach to teaching law and more recently the use of clinics at law schools to give students direct experience as lawyers. Japanese law schools did not adapt to the new role of the bengoshi. The law faculties of the major universities continued to use a lecture style rather than an interactive style of teaching. Little if any time was devoted to new skills required such as effective cross-examination or investigative techniques. This was to be expected, as the faculties of these schools were not familiar with these approaches. Indeed, faculties continued to be staffed by non-bengoshi. Although highly educated and skilled legal observers, the teachers of future bengoshi had no actual experience in trial technique and thus devoted their time and lectures to what they were familiar with—the scientific approaches to the law. What the adversary system requires however is a practical approach to the law.

The immediate post-war cadre of lawyers had, of course, all been trained in the prewar system. Whatever the shortcomings of that system it had the advantage of being familiar. The law professors were similarly prewar trained and were used to training in the prewar style. Even the judges were trained before the war and when the Legal Research and Training Institute gave "practical" training to bengoshi candidates, it used judges trained and experienced in a non-adversary system to perform such training. In short, neither the immediate post-war crop of lawyers nor their successors were well educated and trained to be adversary system lawyers. As a consequence they lacked the skills required of lawyers who take control of the courtroom and run the trial with little direction from the judge—except as may be necessary to maintain order and an orderly process for getting to the end of the trial.

This shortcoming in legal education continues to the present time. The reality is that Japanese lawyers, while the brightest of the brightest, are not trained to be adversary system advocates. As a result they lack the skills needed to present a concise illuminating direct examination and do not present effective cross-examination. Lack of courtroom skills combined with the inability to obtain evidence doomed the effort to create an adversary type system.

Part of the new reforms to the Japanese legal system are the establishment of new graduate level law schools to hopefully better educate and train specialist lawyers in the practical skills of lawyering. These schools opened in April 2004 and their first class of graduates will graduate in 2006. The new law school program is designed as a three-year graduate course but students who are graduates of an undergraduate *Hogakubu* law faculty who successfully pass an examination may complete the graduate course in only two years. Organized by the old *Hogakubu* faculties and basically staffed by former *Hogakubu* professors with no practical experience of their own it remains to be seen what effect the new law schools have on the professionalism of lawyers. As in the case of the *Hogakubu*, full time faculty in the new law schools are not members of the Bar, have not passed the Bar examination and have no experience as bengoshi lawyers.

The function of the *Hogakubu* faculty has never been to produce skilled lawyers. Most *Hogakubu* students have no desire to become bengoshi. The undergraduate *Hogakubu* faculty was designed to produce and produced (and will continue to produce) generalists with a legal background who will go into business and/or the government. With only 1,000 new lawyers licensed yearly, it has been clear that the vast majority of *Hogakubu* students could not become lawyers and thus most students did not need specialized training in lawyering skills. The *Hogakubu* did not provide such training. Similarly the graduate *Hogakubu* faculties trained the next generation of law professors, not bengoshi. Practical training was only received after the student passed the Bar Examination and attended the Legal Research and Training Institute run by the Supreme Court judicial Secretariat. Such practical training as was received at the Institute was a short internship at a lawyer's office, at a prosecutor's office and in a court chamber during the term of the training program. The Institute program was originally two years but when the number of bengoshi passing the Bar Examination was increased from 500 to 1,000 the Institute program was reduced to 1-½ years. Under the new reforms approximately 3,000 new legal professionals—judges, prosecutors and lawyers—will be licensed each year. The Institute will continue in existence and all new prosecutors, judges and lawyers will need to attend the Institute but the program will be dramatically cut back to a more internship intensive program with less classroom work. Exactly what form the new training at the Institute will take remains to be determined.

The theory is that the new law schools will provide more focused more intensive and more practical training for students who wish to be lawyers. The Socratic method used in American law schools will be attempted in some classes and schools are attempting to recruit bengoshi, prosecutors and judges to act as adjunct professors so that those who possess practical experience can teach practical skills. Recruiting judges and prosecutors has proven to be relatively easy as the government has arranged for judges and prosecutors to remain judges and prosecutors while teaching full time at law schools. Recruiting lawyers as adjuncts has proven somewhat more difficult as some schools appear to want adjuncts to devote a full schedule to teaching—inconsistent with the adjunct maintaining a law practice while teaching a single course at a law school. Additional problems relate to the control that the Ministry of Education—with no lawyer experience whatsoever—has exerted over the standardized curriculum requirements. There exists the possibility that some schools will see their role as better training lawyers to present written presentations to the court rather than the skills associated with an adversary system. If this is the case then there is little reason to believe that such staples of American adversary practice such as lawyer discovery of evidence or cross-examination or aggressive oral argument will flourish.

2) The Role of the Judge in Japan

Although the initial post-war Supreme Court was composed of Justices approved by the Occupation and thus at least semi-committed to the new role of the lawyer and the diminished role of the judge, neither the inferior court judges nor the second wave of Supreme Court Justices were committed to their diminished role. The judges in Japan, as was the case with the lawyers, were a product of the legal education system and that system was not familiar with or necessarily approving of the new adversary type procedure being attempted. Japanese legal scholars who staffed the schools and the Japanese judiciary were products of the German law school of litigation, and in that school the judge was the primary player in the litigation drama.

Under the civil law system the judge is the focal point of the litigation. The judge—not the parties—is in charge of the case. Under the civil law approach it is the function of the judge to assure that all of the relevant facts come to light and that all of the relevant arguments are presented. The judge is not simply a neutral umpire between the parties who lets the parties present their case and then based on the presentations made and the evidence brought forth by the parties decides (or where there is a jury allows the jury to decide). If the parties have failed to put their best foot forward, the common law judge or jury may not have all the best evidence available to make a "correct" decision. A party in the common law system may lose because the lawyer blundered. This is not how the civil law system is supposed to work. The parties are in court to get justice and the lawyers are to help the parties and even ease the process for the judge. But it is the function of the judge to make the correct decision—to decide the case so that justice is done in the sense of the party who should win does win.[20] In prewar Japan the judge had the function of not simply determining who was right or wrong based on the evidence presented by the parties but had a more substantive justice function of assuring that the party who was correct actually won the case. This was not a Japanese invention but was consistent with the civil law role of the judge. In the civil law system the judge was given responsibility for assembling the evidence so that the judge could properly carry out the function of correctly deciding the matter.[21]

Under the German law system the role of the judge was the classic civil law role. To assure that all of the arguments that should be raised were raised and to assure that all of the facts that should be presented were presented, the judge had to meet with the parties (and/or their counsel) to get an understanding of the case. This is possible in the civil law system—and is possible in Germany and Japan—because the trial is not a continuous affair that begins on Monday and runs till Friday. Rather, the trial is made up of several sessions separated in time. This separation gives the parties time to prepare additional materials that relate to issues raised at earlier meetings with the judge. Parties also have time to prepare arguments that issues raised at a meeting with the judge are not relevant or items of evidence are not of consequence. Through this give and take between parties, lawyers and the judge the judge begins to understand the case and points the parties in the direc-

---

20 For a discussion of the role of the judge in the Civil Law system see, Geoffrey C. Hazard, Jr., Discovery and the Role of the Judge in Civil Law Jurisdictions, 73 Notre Dame Law Review 1017 (1998); see also, ALI/UNIDROIT Principles and Rules of Transnational Civil Procedure, Proposed Final Draft (3/9/04) at p.8.

21 Geoffrey C. Hazard, Jr., Discovery and the Role of the Judge in Civil Law Jurisdictions, 73 Notre Dame Law Review 1017, 1019, 1021 (1998).

tion that they should be going. It is the judge's duty to define the issues and to send the parties out to produce the necessary evidence in their possession. The judge is responsible for getting the evidence that is required to make a correct decision. Pretrial discovery controlled by lawyers or parties is unnecessary. The role that lawyer controlled pretrial discovery plays in getting evidence together so that it can be sifted to discover what evidence is necessary and what arguments should be presented is played by the judge through meetings between the judge and counsel. If evidence is required the judge orders the party or a third person to produce the evidence. Evidence can be produced during the course of the trial as the discontinuous nature of the trial presents plenty of opportunity for production. A kind of trial through consultation results, with the judge being the central player in the trial and consultations. The process is called clarification in that the judge is clarifying the issues, the contentions and the evidence that is relevant to the real (clarified) issues and contentions.

In the German law system (both prewar and today) the judge's role in the "trial" was the focus of the trial. Through meetings with the parties the judge was and is supposed to get to the nub of the problem, to advance the arguments that needed to be advanced, to get the necessary evidence presented, to question the witnesses to discover the facts and ultimately to decide the case correctly.[22] Because the judge was and is to find the facts and point the direction of the arguments to get a correct decision and as this was and is done through meetings with counsel or the parties or both, there really was no need to proceed in other than a collegial way and that could be better done in private than in public. In Germany such procedures were originally private. The principle of the Oral Argument was adopted in the 19th Century as part of an effort to make the procedure public. Under this principle the positions of the parties had to be stated orally to the court in open session. Limited party autonomy was also adopted in Germany and the court could no longer on its own seek out evidence or call witnesses although it could suggest evidentiary lines or witnesses to parties. The initial moving forward with evidence was in the hands of the parties. Nonetheless the judge was in control of the entire process. And the process itself was a series of meetings and discussions between the parties, counsel and the court until a time was reached when the court knew all it could know and could decide the case.[23]

In prewar Japan the trial process followed the German law procedure as the Code of Civil Procedure was based on the German Code. The principle of Oral Argument was also adopted as a reform but not the principle of party autonomy. The judge was not simply the central figure in the "trial" process but the judge had the authority *sua sponte* to call and examine witnesses. No party need suggest a witness

22 See, generally, Arthur Taylor von Mehren, Some Comparative Reflections on First Instance Civil Procedure: Recent Reforms in German Civil Procedure and in the Federal Rules, 63 Notre Dame Law Review 608 (1988).

23 For a discussion of the German system and the reforms in that system see, William B. Fisch, Recent Developments in West German Civil Procedure, 6 Hastings International and Comparative Law Review 221 (1983).

and no party had the right to call a witness. The matter was entirely up to the judge. After all since the judge was obligated to make a "correct" decision it was natural for the judge to be able to call witnesses on his own and examine them. In prewar Japan the role of the judge was particularly important as the judge was the face of the bureaucracy in the court and it was the bureaucracy that had the law enforcing function. Furthermore, judges had looked down on lawyers in prewar Japan and simply passing a procedure code that gave lawyers greater responsibility for the trial did not make the lawyers any more responsible in the minds of the judges.

The American idea of the trial was entirely different from the German law and civil law idea. Control was in the hands of the parties—the real parties in interest—and their champions, the lawyers, assisted them. The judge stood above the fray as a neutral in the fact gathering, argument and contention structuring process. To the American Occupation the role of the civil law judge in Japan was seen as not simply paternalistic but as involving the use of government power in a way that it should not be asserted. To the common law mind justice is best served when the judge does not get identified with a party or a position but remains neutral throughout. In this way the decision-maker stands above the fray ultimately deciding the matter on the basis of the facts and arguments presented by the parties who have the real stake in the litigation. This to the American lawyer is the essence of the case or controversy requirement. The real case has real adverse parties who, because they are the winners or losers in the trial, have the most motive to marshal the best evidence and best arguments. In a sense the bureaucratic judge of prewar Japan represented the old joke that one of the great lies is—"I'm from the government and I'm here to help you." To change the paternalistic role of the judge, the Occupation attempted to create a party-oriented system with concentrated trial as the goal. In addition the Occupation took away the power of the judge to *ex officio* call witnesses in most cases. The *ex officio* power of the court to call and examine witnesses is retained in the Administrative Case Litigation Law[24] dealing with challenges to administrative dispositions and is retained by the Impeachment Court in dealing with cases of impeaching judges.

The Occupation effort to change the balance of power in the courtroom between judges and lawyers was not successful. Whether Japanese judges retained their prewar paternalism towards the lawyers in their courtrooms and the parties before them for altruistic reasons, or because the prewar German influence was simply too strong to challenge, or because they did not want to lose their position as major player in litigation for status reasons or for a combination of reasons is subject to debate. It does seem clear that part of the reason for the judge's continued active participation in the case was the felt need to protect the litigants. A very high percentage of Japanese litigants appear without counsel. In such cases, even in an adversary system, judges tend to support the not represented at least to the extent of making sure that injustice does not result because of lack of professional assistance and unfamiliarity with the procedural rules. When lawyers who had the new responsibility of gathering the evidence pretrial and presenting it at trial appeared

24 Under Article 24 of the ACLL the court may *ex officio* examine evidence.

unable to do either (in part a result of bad training and in part because of the Code's failure to provide mechanisms for obtaining evidence from an adversary) judges (who saw themselves as government officials responsible for administering justice) stepped in to assist the process of truth finding. As a consequence the Japanese judge remains the principal player in the courtroom drama, controlling the calendar, the witness presentations and the production of evidence.[25] While the judge may not examine evidence *ex officio* (except in Administrative and Impeachment cases) the judge may determine what evidence is needed and what evidence is not relevant. The judge may also examine witnesses after the lawyers have completed their examination and under the reforms recently enacted the judge may, if it is deemed necessary, change the order of witness testimony so that the judge may examine the witness first with the lawyers following thereafter.

3) A System Incompatible with the Adversary Process

Years ago I appeared in the District Court for the Southern District of New York to argue a motion for a more definite statement of plaintiff's Complaint. I advised the judge that I could not understand the basis for Plaintiff's claim and hence could not file a sufficient answer. The judge denied my motion and admonished me pointing out that he had never granted such a motion and that he was sure I would soon figure out all I needed to know to defend the case. As for an Answer he was sure I could simply deny anything I couldn't understand and that would be fine. His point was that during the pretrial procedures I would have many opportunities to get to understand the plaintiff's case while formulating a defense. He was, of course, correct and I filed an Answer with little problem. That is not how a Japanese court would approach the issue.

One of the most important aspects of trial in Japan is the process of clarifying the issues in the case. Moreover this is seen as a function of the judge rather than as a function of the parties. Clarification of issues in Japan has a much broader meaning than that term would have to an American lawyer, and the process of and function of clarification is discussed in greater detail in Chapter 6 (2). Here it is sufficient to note that clarification by the judge is inconsistent with the idea of a lawyer-dominated procedure. It places the judge in the center of the procedure of the trial and puts the adversary parties and their representatives in the hands of a non-adversary party running a non-adversary process.

The American and British common law adversary process owes much to the use of the common law and criminal law jury. The jury puts the judge to the side and makes him an umpire ruling on technical legal points while the parties, through their lawyers, place evidence and arguments before the jury. Of necessity, the judge's role is diminished and the lawyer's role is enhanced. Common law judges must be careful not to interject themselves too strongly into the process lest the jury be swayed by the judge's feelings in the matter. As the jury is composed of lay persons who can be easily swayed by emotion or influenced by evidence that is

25 See, Masako Kamiya, Narrowing the Avenues to Japan's Supreme Court, 4 Australian Journal of Asian Law 53, 56 (2002).

not relevant to the truth but could affect the jury's determination, complicated rules of evidence are required to protect the trial process. Since medieval jurors were unable to read or write, most evidence was presented orally through the examination and cross-examination of live witnesses. Such question and answer process dominates today's trial in the United States. This procedure and the complicated rules of evidence that are required to assure that jurors do not get exposed to material that is not considered as either relevant or probative but that might prejudice a verdict or lead jurors into error, places a burden on the lawyers for the parties. The lawyers must make instantaneous determinations as to whether to object to questions before the answer is forthcoming. The judge as umpire is called upon to make instantaneous determinations when a party objects that a question asked is seeking to elicit an answer not permitted by the evidentiary rules.

The hearsay doctrine is designed to protect the right of cross-examination. Under the hearsay rule evidence that cannot be effectively cross-examined because the witness is not the source of the evidence but is simply repeating what others have said cannot be presented to the jury. Judges in the United States are prone to relax the hearsay rule when the judge is hearing the case without a jury. The reason for this liberalization of the evidentiary rules is the belief that the professional judge can determine truth without needing the protections of the formal rules of evidence. The classic statement of the judge in rejecting the hearsay objection is that the court will give the evidence such weight as it is entitled to, including no weight at all. But such a ruling cannot be made when the jury is seated in the box because the jurors do not know how much weight to give hearsay evidence and might give it more weight than it is entitled to—most of the time it is entitled to no weight.

In Japan where there is no jury, the rationale for a hearsay rule loses a great deal of its efficacy. There is no formal hearsay rule in civil cases. In criminal cases, where there is a hearsay rule, judges tend to let in evidence that is technically inadmissible because of their belief that they can later determine whether to give the evidence any weight. Such process saves time by eliminating objections at trial and also relieves the judge of having to make an instantaneous decision. It also reduces the role of the lawyer. The supposed adversaries in the case are reduced to being observers rather than active players in the testimony of witnesses. Questions do not have to be framed properly and evidentiary rules need not be observed. Having a judge decide questions of both law and fact in all cases is not hospitable to the concept of adversary proceedings. Indeed as the judge can read, the original rationale behind question and answer oral testimony loses some of its vitality. Judges in Japan prefer to read written witness testimony. This shortens the time for trials and avoids controversy and confrontation in the courtroom—both of which are seen as positive values in the American common law adversary system (because they tend to sharpen issues and are believed to lead to truth) but are seen as negatives in Japan. In Japan open conflict is not a positive value and cross-examination when done properly is confrontational. Witness testimony and cross-examination is thus to be avoided.

The Japanese judge determines the true issues in the case. The judge also ultimately decides the case (assuming it goes to judgment). The judge thus knows what facts need to be supported by evidence. Things that the judge already knows need not be proven at the trial. Evidence to establish matters that the judge considers not relevant need not be admitted. The judge decides what facts need to be proven, what evidence needs to be considered, and what facts the court can take "judicial notice" of. There is no need to make a record on any of these questions in the initial trial court as first level appeal is not based "on the record," as it would be in the United States.

The adversary process assumes a reasonable opportunity for the lawyers on both sides of the case to obtain evidence to either prove their client's cause or disprove their opponent's. An adversary system need not have the broad discovery rules of the American system and need not sanction fishing expeditions in the files and records of the opposition. But, if the lawyers are to be the gathers of the evidence that is to be submitted to the court, then the lawyers need some mechanism to compel parties and third persons to produce at least the most significant evidence. Such production needs to take place in a timely fashion to permit the trial of the action to proceed smoothly. Absent such a discovery system the judge, as the authority with the power to compel evidentiary disclosure, assumes center stage in the case, and the lawyer's role as advocate is diminished. In Japan the parties have no right to compel production of evidence by third persons or by the opposition party.

C. Old Wine in New Bottles

When all is said and done were the amendments in the procedural Codes made under the influence of the Occupation successful in changing the Japanese litigation system, both criminal and civil? Probably not much. Today's criminal trial, as was true of the prewar trial, can be viewed as a continuation of the trial by dossier system.[26] Today's dossier consists of the police report (with witness statements attached) and the defendant's confession. The early presentation of these records to the judge by the prosecutor effectively diminishes the presumption of innocence, and as a consequence today's defendant finds itself having to prove innocence rather than arguing that the prosecution has failed to make its case. The modern criminal trial is dominated by the defendant's confession—virtually all defendant's confess—and arguments as to whether it was voluntarily given or coerced. But most importantly whether the confession is reliable. Fruit of the poisoned tree is not so much evidence in chief as it is corroboration of the reliability of the confession itself. If the confession is reliable, it will invariably be permitted to influence the decision in the case. The prosecutor's determination to prosecute the criminal case takes the place of the prewar examining judge's determination that the case should go to trial.[27] Under both systems the trial court may be seen as a reviewing court. In the modern criminal case the court is determining whether the prosecutor's determination to bring the case to trial was correct. The interpreta-

26 Ryuichi Hirano, Diagnosis of the Current Code of Criminal Procedure (translated by Daniel H. Foote), 22 Law in Japan 129 (1989).

27 David A. Suess, Paternalism versus Pugnacity: The Right to Counsel in Japan and the United States, 72 Indiana Law Journal 291 (1996) for the view that the prosecutor's determination to prosecute is the equivalent of an initial stage guilty verdict.

tions of the Constitution that diminish the suspect's right to counsel and privilege against self-incrimination make the modern practice of holding suspects in "substitute prisons" (i.e., police jails) for up to 23 days for questioning (and longer under *bekkon taiho* procedures) the equivalent of prior practices that forced defendants to confess. In a system where 99.9% of criminal cases that go to trial result in conviction, the defendant is well advised to admit guilt (whether or not actually guilty), show contrition, pay recompense for the crime and throw him/her self on the mercy of either or both the prosecutor and the court. And, since in Japan both are quite merciful, this is the strategy that counsel is well advised to suggest.

In the civil case, the prewar dominance of the paternalistic judge remains the rule. The judge confirms the issues, facts and relevant evidence in the case. The judge calls witnesses and determines whether witness testimony is necessary. The judge orders parties and third persons to produce documents. The judge has the right to question witnesses and even to alter the order of witness questioning so that the judge may question first and the parties later. The parties and their counsel (when they have counsel) are not responsible for framing the issues and establishing the facts in the case but the judge is responsible for properly clarifying the case and receiving the proper evidence and ultimately in making the correct decision. The entire trial scenario takes place in the shadow of the trial judge's ultimate goal—to get the parties to conciliate the matter and reach a settlement the terms of which are agreeable to the parties and appear fair to the judge.

The challenge to an Administrative Agency disposition is similarly not much changed from the prewar situation. As discussed in Chapter 12, the stringent rules of standing to sue, the necessity that there be a disposition to challenge administrative action, the "free discretion" rule under which agencies are given great deference result in the vast majority of challenges to administrative action being rejected. In Administrative Case Litigation Law (ACLL) litigation the judge is even allowed to follow the old practice of taking evidence *ex officio*.

6

The Civil Procedure System

A. An Overview of the Civil Procedure System

1) The Practical Aspect of Litigation—Interpretation, the Judge and Settlement

As an initial matter it must be recognized that Japan is a civil law system. As a consequence the first place to look for an analysis of the civil justice system is in the Code of Civil Procedure and in the Rules of Civil Procedure promulgated by the Supreme Court under its authority under Article 77 of the Constitution. The question of the extent of the Supreme Court's authority in the rule-making area is of interest. Theoretically the Diet is the sole organ of law making in Japan but the Supreme Court is given authority to make rules. Having the Diet pass the Code of Civil Procedure and the court theoretically fill out and conform to the basic provisions of the Code finesses how far those rules can go in making "law." On its face the Code and Rules appears to replicate a system familiar to American lawyers. But as with most Japanese law, looks can be and are deceptive.

The Code of Civil Procedure is relatively new. It was rewritten and adopted in 1996 effective 1998 ("1996 Code" or "new Code"). The new Code consists of eight books. Book 1 deals with General Provisions, including such general matters as the jurisdiction of the courts, court costs, capacity of parties and general provisions concerning the trial of an action. Book 2 concerns itself with procedure in courts of first instance, including the Plenary Hearing (also known as Oral Argument) and Preliminary Plenary Hearing (also known as Preliminary Oral Argument) and Procedures Preparatory to the Plenary Hearing (also known as Preparation for Oral Argument) as well as evidentiary provisions. Book 3 deals with Appeal, etc. The Rules of Procedure similarly are divided into Books (there are nine books of Rules—the additional book dealing with miscellaneous matters). Although rewritten in 1996, the new Code is basically a compilation of the old Code of Civil Procedure rewritten into more easily understood Japanese and certain reforms to the old Code dealing primarily with trial procedures. For this reason much of the old law dealing with civil procedure is applicable to the new Code—except where the rule may have been changed by the reform legislation included in the rewrite. In addition, certain parts of the old Code were spun off into separate legislation. There is a separate law dealing with Execution of Judgments—the Civil Execution Act[1]—and a separate law dealing with provisional remedies—Civil Provisional Remedies Law (Law No. 91 of 1989). In addition, there is (and there was prior to the 1996 amendment) a separate law dealing with Administrative litigation—the Administrative Case Litigation Law.

As Japan is a civil law society, the "law" of civil procedure is to be found in the Code and Rules. But, the Code is not always self-explanatory and there may be questions as to interpretation. Under the common law, codes adopted by the legislature are viewed as only one part of a greater body of law. The cases dealing with the subject matter decided prior to the law's adoption and the cases decided after the law's adoption are part of the law. As Japan follows the civil law model, the Code (and Rules) are theoretically considered as the entirety of the "law." Opinions of experts as to the meaning of the Code are more significant in the civil law system than in the common law. In the United States part of the statutory interpretation process is an attempt to determine the intent of the legislature when it adopted the Code or statute in the context of the preexisting law. In what way did the legislature intend to change the preexisting code and/or case law (or a combination of the two)? This is important as new legislation is not seen as the totality of the law but rather the new legislation is simply another layer of law floating on the old cases. The old case law is only changed to the extent that the intent of the legislature was to change the old law. To a great extent "old law *is* good law." The judges who made the old law in the first place make the determination of how much old law remains good law. To determine the extent of the change brought about by the legislature common law courts in the United States utilize reports of Congressional Committees (both the Conference Committee Report as well as the Reports from the House and Senate Committees that considered the matter). Courts also consider the Congressional Record report of the debates on the floor of the Congress. Especially important are the explanations by and answers to questions by the legislators responsible for moving the bill through the House involved. Of course, these devices for determining legislative intent are secondary to controlling court decisions that have *starie decisis* effect. Decisions of the courts made before the statutory provision being interpreted was enacted may be relevant, as in the common law tradition the statute does not obliterate the old law, it simply changes the old law in the ways that the new law deals with the old law. To the extent that the new statute does not touch an issue, the pre-existing case law continues to control. One function of the reviewing court is to determine

1 Law No. 4 of 1979.

whether the legislature intended to change a pre-existing rule and whether its language was sufficient for the task it set out to achieve.

In the civil law system the Code is the law. The legislation does not sit on top of a layer of case law that sets out the law. The past may be prologue but it is not law. The only law is the law set out in the Code and the legislation. The question of how much of the preexisting law continues to have vitality is not presented in the same way as in the common law system. To the extent that the words of the old Code and the new Code are the same, the old law continues to exist but court interpretation and nuance may not continue to exist. These were never "law" to begin with and they remain without *starie decisis* or binding effect. The question of legislative intent is thus somewhat different in Japan from the same question in the United States. In the United States the question is: "to what extent did the legislature intend to modify, change or fine tune the existing law as contained in legislation and cases" and "to what extent do the preexisting cases continue to state the law"? In Japan the question is always "what does the Code or statutory language mean"? It is this meaning of the Code or legislation that is the law—but the court statement of this meaning does not have *starie decisis* effect and may be changed by the court without having to consider factors that would trouble an American court.

As the "law" in a civil law system is the statute law, a civil law lawyer must learn to navigate through the sea of statute law whereas the common law lawyer learns to navigate through the body of cases. Not all statute law is equal and sometimes statutes contain conflicting provisions. The general approach to the problem is that the more specific statute controls when there is a conflict with a more general statute. Thus in a commercial setting a conflict between the rule set out in the Civil Code (more general) and the Commercial Code (more specific) would be controlled by the Commercial Code. In a conflict between the Commercial Code and a more specific statute, say the Labor Law; the more specific Labor Law would govern. The need to understand the relations between different levels of statute law has impact on the Code of Civil Procedure and litigation. Substantive law statutes such as the Patent Law and other statutes may contain provisions dealing with procedural matters. For example the Patent Law (and other intellectual property laws) have recently enacted provisions easing the burden of proof, dealing with the production of documents and allowing for experts to aid the court in determining damages. These specific provisions in the more specific laws should have a controlling effect in the event of conflict with the Code of Civil Procedure.[2]

The Diet is the highest organ of the State and is the sole law-making organ of the government.[3] But that does not mean that the Diet writes the laws. Most Japanese legislation is derived from government bills submitted to the Diet by the Cabinet.

---

2 The rule that the specific statute controls over the general is somewhat inconsistent with making the Constitution (the most general law) the Supreme Law and thus controlling over the more specific statutes passed by the Diet. This philosophical conflict may have an effect on the Supreme Court of Japan's constitutional judicial review jurisprudence.

3 Constitution of Japan, Article 41.

Unlike the United States Congress the Japanese Diet does not have a large staff to assist in the process of legislation writing. Similarly the Cabinet relies on outsiders—the Ministries that comprise the Cabinet—to write Cabinet bills. In this drafting process the career bureaucracy plays a major role.[4]

The Diet has committees as does the U. S. Congress but those committees perform a different function from the Congressional Committee. The Diet's committees are a forum where the political parties can discuss issues. Rarely would such committees conduct hearing as in the American system nor would such committees prepare reports such as American Congressional Committee Reports. Most legislative groundwork is done in non-legislative study groups established to study an issue and on which various constituencies involved in legislation would have a voice. The bureaucracy is a constant factor in study groups whose membership may change over the years in which study is typically undertaken. The bureaucracy then drafts the legislation[5]—the mark up session of the Congressional Committee and the reports on mark up that constitute the Committee Reports in the United States typically do not exist in Japan. After bureaucratic drafting the political parties may make policy adjustments calling for further bureaucratic drafting.[6] The actual legislative process then proceeds through various committees of the Diet considering the bills and with Diet members and bureaucrats explaining measures to Diet members on these committees. Eventually the legislation is agreed to (or in some cases pushed forward by the ruling party without consensus) and

4 For a discussion of the legislative process in Japan see, Abe, Shindo and Kawato, THE GOVERNMENT AND POLITICS OF JAPAN (University of Tokyo Press 1994) 17-23 reprinted in part in Meryll Dean, JAPANESE LEGAL SYSTEM (Cavendish Publishing, 2002) 222-226. See also, Tetsushi Kajimoto, Lawmakers Now Looking to Make Laws, Japan Times on Line 5/11/04.

5 See, Tom Ginsburg, Dismantling the "Developmental State"? Administrative Procedure Reform in Japan and Korea, 49 American Journal of Comparative Law 585, 592-593 (2001) for the view that the bureaucracy has a virtual monopoly on legislative drafting in Japan.

6 For a discussion of the role of bureaucrats and politicians in Japan see, Michio Muramatsu and Ellis S. Krauss, Bureaucrats and Politicians in Policymaking: The Case of Japan, 78 American Political Science Review 126 (1984) Reprinted in part in Curtis J. Milhaupt, J. Mark Ramseyer, Michael K. Young, JAPANESE LAW IN CONTEXT, READINGS IN SOCIETY AND POLITICS (Harvard University Asia Center, Harvard University Press 2001) at p. 518-525; Abe, Shindo and Kawato, THE GOVERNMENT AND POLITICS OF JAPAN (University of Tokyo Press 1994) reprinted in part in Meryll Dean, JAPANESE LEGAL SYSTEM (Cavendish Publishing, 2002). The power of the bureaucracy in Japan has recently been highlighted by Prime Minister Koizumi's inability to prevent the practice of amakudari "descent from heaven." This is a practice whereby Japanese bureaucrats retire from the bureaucracy to take positions as senior executives of public or private corporations that were previously subject to their regulatory authority. Such hiring cements the bureaucracy's power to administer and cements the relationship between companies and the bureaucracy. It has been challenged both for its potential conflict of interest aspects and for its effect on strengthening bureaucratic control over the economy. As a first step the Prime Minister attempted to prevent bureaucrats from retiring to positions in semi-governmental companies such as airport or road authorities. On March 8,2004 the Prime Minister advised a Diet Committee that he would prohibit certain senior officials from accepting positions with such semi-governmental bodies. On March 11, 2004 he told reporters that he would not prevent "all" appointments of such officials. See, Koizumi Backpedals, Supports Certain Cases of 'Amakudari', Japan Times on Line 3/12/04.

brought to the floor for a vote. Throughout the process the basic policy considerations are typically those that began with the bureaucracy's draft of the legislation based on the study group report that the bureaucracy helped to draft.[7] As a consequence of this process it is not likely that a court confronted with a question of how to interpret a section of the Code—including a Section of the Code of Civil Procedure—would refer back to legislative reports or debates. More relevant for Japanese courts, which view themselves as performing a more "scientific" approach to interpretation of legislation, are the opinions of scholars in the field and bureaucratic experts (many of whom may have served on the study group that gave rise to the law). As the product being reviewed (the legislation) is likely the result of negotiated compromise between political factions and political parties not documented in reports, the court must determine for itself what the Code means. In making this judgment, the court may apply its view of what the Japanese societal norms are that relate to the law and may use those norms in assisting the legislative interpretation function.

The question of norms as applied to the Code of Civil Procedure also includes the norms of the judicial bureaucracy. The individual judge although bound by only personal conscience is likely to know what the judicial Secretariat answer is to many problems. This is because the Secretariat keeps tabs on decisions of the courts and incorporates those that represent the law, as the Secretariat understands the law, into the curriculum of the judge's section of the Legal Research and Training Institute. Judges who stray too far from the judicial system's preferred answer to a problem may find themselves in trouble with their own bureaucracy, and this can have an adverse effect on career aspirations. There is no *starie decisis* in Japan. An appellate court's holding is only binding in the case wherein rendered (a kind of the law of the case doctrine under American concepts). Nonetheless the reality is that no bureaucracy can work efficiently if members are free to disregard the opinions of superiors. In the judicial system those opinions are reflected in the appellate determinations. Moreover, failure to follow appellate determinations will lead to appeals to correct lower court errors and such appeals are a waste of judicial time and assets. The judicial Secretariat keeps up to date with whether judges are following the established judicial norms and judges are rated on their efficiency in following the Secretariat view of the norms.

Unlike Supreme Court Justices, lower court judges in Japan are appointed for 10-year terms and may (or may not) be reappointed.[8] The mandatory retirement age for District Court and High Court judges is 65 but Summary Court judges may remain until age 70. Thus both the highest and lowest court judges may stay on the Bench until age 70. This system conforms to normal business practice in

7 For a discussion of the legislative drafting process in Japan see, Mamoru Seki, The Drafting Process for Cabinet Bills, 19 Law in Japan 168 (1986).

8 Constitution of Japan, Article 80.

Japan where because of mandatory retirement policies[9] Japanese managers must either be elevated to Board status (where the mandatory retirement age is a few extra years) or demoted to a sister/subsidiary company with a higher mandatory retirement age or retired. The same policy applies in academia so that professors at *Hogakubu* faculties in national universities are required to retire at an earlier age than their counterparts at private universities. The result is that national university professors retire and then go to work for private universities.

Appointment of inferior court judges is essentially a matter for determination by the judicial bureaucracy.[10] The Supreme Court has a judicial Secretariat that manages the judicial system.[11] Unlike the United States Supreme Court, which has a small staff and does not administer the judiciary, the Secretariat is a large organization. The Secretariat has multiple functions including providing young judges to assist Supreme Court Justices in performing their duties, managing the Legal Research and Training Institute, selecting new judges, determining promotion of and relocation of judges, etc. The practice has developed for the Prime Minister to discuss appointment of Supreme Court Justices with the Chief Justice, especially when Justices are to be elevated from the civil service judicial bureaucracy.

The Secretariat's function of administering the judicial system is a direct reaction to the prewar system wherein the judiciary was under the Ministry of Justice. Through the judicial Secretariat the Supreme Court administers the judicial system. Because a member of the court—i.e. the current Chief Justice—has typically been in charge of the Secretariat at an earlier part of his career, the Supreme Court has intimate knowledge of the workings of the Secretariat. The creation of a powerful bureaucracy in the court raised concerns among the Occupation as to whether a judicial oligarchy was being created. To moderate those concerns the provision making Supreme Court Justices subject to referendum was put in the Constitution.[12] The referendum is not a part of the appointment process but rather is designed so that the voting public can, if it desires, reject a Supreme Court Justice already appointed. Accordingly, it takes an affirmative step of a majority vote

---

9 Japan has no Age Discrimination in Employment Act to prohibit mandatory retirement based on age.

10 Yosiyuki Noda, INTRODUCTION TO JAPANESE LAW (translated and edited by Anthony H. Angelo) (University of Tokyo Press, 1976) 153.

11 See, Takaaki Hattori, The Role of the Supreme Court of Japan in the Field of Judicial Administration, 60 Washington Law Review 69 (1984); Toru Miura, Independence, Transparency and Accountability of the Judiciary in Japan, on the web at *www.unafei.or.jp/pdf/indonesia_pdf/session4.pdf* at page 36-38.

12 John O. Haley, The Japanese Judiciary: Maintaining Integrity, Autonomy and the Public Trust p. 17. On the web at: *http://law.wustl.edu/Academics/Faculty/Workingpapers/TheJapaneseJudiciary10_03.pdf* at 21.

of all persons voting to effect rejection of the Justice.[13] But, as earlier noted because Justices are appointed after reaching age 60 the portion of the referendum device calling for periodic votes every ten years after appointment has been of no consequence in the post-war period. Similarly, the referendum vote at the first election of the House of Representatives following appointment has been of no consequence. No Justice has been removed from the Supreme Court as a consequence of voter rejection.

There is evidence that the Occupation's concern about a judicial oligarchy may have been justified. The Secretariat keeps close watch on the activities of inferior court judges and may take those activities into account in assignments. Assignments are important because assignment to a higher and more prestigious court is not simply rewarding but also may mean a higher salary. Lower court judges whose decisions do not conform to Secretariat views or whose decisions are regularly reversed or who do not resolve cases quickly enough for the Secretariat's statistical purposes or who do not get parties to settle a sufficient number of cases may find themselves assigned to courts that have no future prospects (in theory judges cannot be transferred without their consent but such consent is typically given if a judge hopes to have a career in the judiciary) or positions that do not lead to higher salaries, etc.[14]

The judicial selection process is related to the functions of the Legal Training and Research Institute in that all successful candidates of the bengoshi examination attend the Institute for practical training. The training course is presently 18 months having been reduced from 2 years when the number of new bengoshi passing the exam was increased in the late 1990s from 500 to 1,000. It is to be expected that the course period will be further reduced as the increasing number of new bengoshi (scheduled to reach 3,000 per year by 2011) puts strain on the Institute's resources. The new law schools (modeled after American law schools as a graduate level faculty with more practical teaching methods) are expected to pick up the slack by producing better-trained graduates. At the Institute choices are made to pursue a career either as a practicing lawyer, a prosecutor or a judge. Those who choose to be judges are then reviewed by the Secretariat and the number needed and individuals to be appointed are selected and sent to the Cabinet for appointment.

Upon appointment, new judges are typically assigned to a District Court for their first 5-years. During this time they sit on 3-judge panels where they learn the craft

13 See, Case No. 1949 (O) 332, 6 Minshu 122 (Sup. Ct. Grand Bench, 2/20/52) (available in English through the web site of the Supreme Court of Japan) upholding the National Referendum Law that counted abstaining voters as not voting for dismissal and required a majority of all voters to vote for dismissal for a Justice to be dismissed under the Referendum Law.

14 See, Setsuo Miyazawa, Administrative Control of Japanese Judges in Philip S.C. Lewis Ed., LAW AND TECHNOLOGY IN THE PACIFIC COMMUNITY 263 (1991) reprint in JAPANESE LAW IN CONTEXT (Milhaupt, Jr., Ramseyer, and Young ed., Harvard University Asia Center, 2001) 79-83.

of judging. After five years the judge is qualified to hear cases as a single judge court. The first 10-year assignment is considered as a training period. The new judge is not appointed a full judge until reappointed for a second 10-year term.

The issue of statistical record keeping by the judicial Secretariat is a significant issue when it comes to the actual functioning of the judicial system. There is great pressure on the judicial system to decide cases faster. The same political force that wants quicker "justice" is not providing the court system with sufficient additional recourses. Caught between a rock and a hard place, the Secretariat has responded by pressing judges to resolve cases more quickly through devices that may impact on how a case is tried. One casualty of the quickened pace of litigation has been the 10-year training period of new judges. New judges are considered as in training for the entire ten years of their initial appointment. During this time they learn their judicial craft by sitting on 3-judge panels, by interacting with older judges, by attending training sessions at the Legal Research and Training Institute, etc. Some young judges are sent abroad for study, some are assigned to Executive Departments. After five years some new judges may sit as single judges on matters that need not be heard by a collegial court and may perform duties that in the past were performed by judges who had completed their 10-year training assignment rather than judge trainees.[15] Further stress will be placed on the system if and when young judges take advantage of the 2004 initiative that permits young judges to work for two years (with Secretariat approval) for bengoshi.

Unlike American judges who have law clerks to assist them—each Justice of the Supreme Court of the United States is entitled to four clerks (some only use three) and Circuit Court and District Court Judges also have clerks to assist—Japanese judges do not have law clerks. Functions that American law clerks—typically the top graduates of top American law schools—perform such as research, drafting, etc. must be performed by the judge in Japan. This places a great strain on a judge's time. Mechanisms to reduce the burden on the judge are sought in Japan. Resolution of a case by settlement means that the judge does not have the obligation of writing a decision to support a ruling. In addition, if a case is settled there can be no appeal, thus freeing up time of High Court judges. The bureaucracy thus looks with favor on District Court judges who can settle cases while judges who are not as successful in bringing about settlements are seen in an unfavorable light. In fact, the statistics on bringing about settlements in cases before them is one of the factors taken into account by the Secretariat in making promotion and relocation decisions. Not only is settlement seen as assisting in solving administrative problems of the judiciary but also settlement brought about by the judge is consistent with Japanese legal history. It was, of course, the way Tokugawa magistrates tried to resolve matters and settlement is and has been an important ele-

15 For a discussion of the training program of judges see, Takaaki Hattori, The Role of the Supreme Court of Japan in the Field of Judicial Administration, 60 Washington Law Review 69, 79-82 (1984).

ment in German civil procedure[16]—from which Japanese civil procedure is derived.

Judges are aware of this "need" to settle and parties are aware of the need. As parties are aware that the judge will attempt to force a settlement of the matter, parties are more likely to look to the judge to make the initial overtures needed to get settlement negotiations moving. Moreover, all litigators, whatever the country or system, want to be on the "favorable" side of the judge. No litigator wants the decision-maker in the case to be upset with the lawyer and perhaps take that upset feeling out on the client. This puts pressure on litigators to try to structure their posture as one that is favorably disposed to settlement of the matter and places pressure on clients to settle. In the United States a trial lawyer may take positions that are seen as contrary to the expressed view of the judge and which may place him in disfavor with the judge. This is necessary a) because of a need to protect the record in the event of an appeal and b) because the ultimate decision-maker in the case may not be the judge but the jury. In Japan appeals are not taken on the basis of a record and the decision-maker in the case is the judge as there is no jury system. Accordingly there is great stress on pleasing the judge and on settling cases in Japan.

Settlement is seen as a positive good not only for statistical reasons but also for social/juridical reasons as well. One of the norms of Japanese society that the Japanese judge is trained to both understand and advance (even if it may be outdated in today's world) is harmony among the parties. A settlement results in a resolution of the matter without a clear-cut winner or clear-cut loser. Each side may take away something from the settlement and say that it achieved some success. Harmony is seen as supported by a "non-hostile" resolution of the case, i.e., a settlement (even if the circumstances leading up to the settlement were quite hostile). Settlement also means that the judge does not have to declare one party a winner and another a loser. This too is seen as a social good and a positive for the judicial system and society in general.

To bring about a settlement the judge in Japan will find him/her self in the role of conciliator trying to bring the parties together to settle their differences. The Code of Civil Procedure makes it clear that the judge may at any stage of the litigation try to bring about a compromise of the case.[17] Thus, the trial process will at various times take on the character of a conciliation proceeding. Indeed, Japanese Civil Procedure allows the court (in certain circumstances) to refer the matter for conciliation within the litigation.[18] This role of the judge as conciliator is also a comforting reflection of the role of Japanese judges in feudal times. Just as

16 See, e.g., William B. Fisch, Recent Developments in West German Civil Procedure, 6 Hastings International and Comparative Law Review 221, 257-260 (1983).

17 CCP Article 89.

18 Civil Conciliation Act (Law No. 222 of 6/9/51 as amended) Article 20.

Tokugawa magistrates tried to get the parties to settle—even using threats against the parties to bring about the settlement—so too modern Japanese judges perform a similar function. In a sense, the drive to cause the parties to settle returns the Japanese judge back to a time before the introduction of American values in the judicial system and back before European values in the judicial system to Japanese values in the judicial system. Just as conciliation was the preferred means of resolving disputes in the Japanese semi autonomous village so too it is the preferred means of resolving disputes in the modern Japanese courthouse. In debating issues of judicial reform prior to the adoption of the 1996 Code, some in the Judicial Branch recommended even greater judicial involvement in the settlement process.[19]

And, just as Mura officials would apply pressure—even compelling pressure—to bring about a supposedly voluntary settlement, so too Japanese judges apply great pressure on the parties. As the judge is the final arbiter of who wins and who loses, the judge can make known to the parties in advance what the likely decision in the matter will be. (In a jury system this is not possible as the parties and court can only speculate as to what the jury may do). The judge can, and does, use his/her position as final decision-maker at the District Court level (and appellate judges at the High Court level) to suggest settlement terms to the parties or tell the parties what (s)he will decide in the event they do not voluntarily settle.[20] At this point the calculation for the parties is fundamentally different from the calculation to be undertaken in an American litigation. While the American litigator and client must concern themselves with the question "what will the jury (or judge) decide," the Japanese client and lawyer are concerned with the question "Can I do better on appeal?" For a defendant who has been told by the court how much it will have to pay if the case goes to final decision and who decides that appeal is not going to be successful, the question becomes "can I negotiate the plaintiff down to a lower number taking into account that the plaintiff will have costs of trying to collect and costs if I decide to appeal." The winning plaintiff has the opposite calculation to make. Eventually, where the parties determine that they will not do sufficiently better on appeal, there are pressures favoring settlement. For one thing the plaintiff actually gets paid. This may be an important consideration as execution in Japan is a far more complicated procedure than in the United States and a defendant's ability to hide assets is greater than is true in the United States.[21] (There is no supplementary proceeding wherein a judgment creditor can attempt to locate assets of the judgment debtor). In addition the parties are spared

19 Takeshi Kojima, Civil Procedure Reform in Japan, 11 Michigan International Law Journal 1218, 1229-1230 (1990).

20 See, e.g., International Commercial Litigation in Japan, Masafumi & Jay Tyndall, Kitahama Law Office, on the web at *www.Masafumi Kodama & Jay Tyndall, Kitahama.or.jp/English/litigatn.htm* at page 5 of 14 (8/1/2000).

21 See, Shunko Muto, Concerning Trial Leadership in Civil Litigation: Focusing on the Judge's Inquiry and Compromise, 12 Law in Japan 23, 24 (1979).

both the time and expense of an appeal. Since Japanese lawyers receive separate fees for the initial trial and the appeal, the expenses of appeal can be substantial. Accordingly there is pressure on a plaintiff to settle—even if the court indicates that plaintiff will likely win. To the losing defendant pressure to settle also exists as, any discount it can extract from the plaintiff (in exchange for not appealing and not contesting execution of the judgment) is money saved.

This use of the judge's decision-making power to "coerce" a settlement is not viewed with disfavor in Japan. Practicing lawyers expect the court, at an appropriate time, to suggest settlement. Indeed, it is viewed by the Bar as part of the judge's function to help bring about settlement, even to the extent of using the threat of its ultimate decision making authority to make clear to the parties what settlement would be appropriate. It is typical for the court to hold settlement conferences at several times during the course of a case. Bar Associations encourage the court to assist in the settlement process and have even suggested that settlement efforts should be compulsory in all cases.[22] The idea that the court should assist the parties in finding an appropriate settlement is not unique to Japan. The ALI/UNIDROIT draft Principles and Rules of Transnational Civil Procedure[23] provides that courts "should" facilitate ADR during court proceedings and calls on parties to cooperate in attempting to resolve the matter amicably. The Principles even adopt a form of coercion by permitting the court to punish an unreasonable party in its cost award. However, the Principles also recognize that parties have a right to a judicial determination of their dispute and note that courts should not coerce parties to settle.

Conciliation, mediation and settlement are not only the judicial system's preferred methods of dealing with legal problems, they are also the preferred method of both elected officials and most Japanese. The reasons for this are contested. What is not contested is that litigation rates in Japan are low and that alternative dispute resolution mechanisms are more widely available than in the United States.[24] Among the rationales given for Japan's low litigation rates are: cultural values that reject litigation in favor of harmony;[25] social values that place law on a lower plane and make it something to be avoided, thus going to law to get a matter resolved is frowned upon;[26] the ability to predict damages in Japan, making settlement consistent with the predicted outcome a rational alternative to extended

22 See, suggestion of First Tokyo Bar Association referred to in Takeshi Kojima, Civil Procedure Reform in Japan, 11 Michigan International Law Journal 1218, 1230 (1990).

23 American Law Institute council draft 9/29/03 Principle 24 "Settlement."

24 See, for example, Joel Rosch, Institutionalizing mediation: The Evolution of the Civil Liberties Bureau in Japan, 21 Law & Society Review 243 (1987).

25 Takeyoshi Kawashima, Dispute Resolution in Contemporary Japan in von Mehren, Law in Japan (Harvard University Press, 1963) 41-72, especially 41-44.

26 Yosiyuki Noda, (Translated and edited by Anthony H. Angelo) INTRODUCTION TO JAPANESE LAW (University of Tokyo Press, 1976) 159-160; Richard B. Parker, Law, Language, and the Individual in Japan and the United States, 7 Wisconsin International Law Journal 179, 179-180 (1988).

contentious litigation;[27] institutional factors in the litigation system that tend to divert disputants to other systems for resolution;[28] the government's attempt to keep contentious issues out of the judicial realm in order to maintain bureaucratic control over the agenda for social change;[29] and a combination of these factors.[30]

In some situations parties are required to go to conciliation before they can bring their case before the court. Thus family law matters must be conciliated[31] and landlord attempts to raise residential rent if challenged must go to conciliation before suit can be filed.[32]

Clearly one factor that directs parties to alternative methods of resolving disputes is the ready availability of such methods. Thus, in Japan many issues that can only be resolved through litigation in the United States may be handled by a less contentious mechanism.[33] In the case of automobile accidents, for example, there exists a non-judicial conciliation group—funded by Japanese insurance companies—that can handle accident cases. Determinations by this body are not binding on the parties but are generally accepted by the insurance company if the victim accepts. Such process provides an inexpensive alternative to litigation and allows the victim to proceed without fear that the "deck is stacked" in the insurance company's favor. The Traffic Accident Dispute Resolution Center has branches in most major cities in Japan and resolves the vast majority of automobile accident cases. It is estimated that even though automobile accident cases account for a substantial percentage of all litigation in Japan only 1% of accidents wind up in litigation since the Center resolves most cases.[34]

---

27 J. Mark Ramseyer and Minoru Nakazato, The Rational Litigant: Settlement Amounts and Verdict Rates in Japan, 18 Journal of Legal Studies 263 (1989).

28 John O. Haley, The Myth of the Reluctant Litigant, 4 Journal of Japanese Studies 359 (1978); Nobutoshi Yamanouchi and Samuel J. Cohen, Understanding the Incidence of Litigation in Japan: A Structural Analysis, 24 International Lawyer 443 (1991); Harold See, Dispute Resolution in Japan: A Survey, 10 Florida State University Law Review 339 (1982).

29 Frank K. Upham, LAW AND SOCIAL CHANGE IN POSTWAR JAPAN (Harvard University Press, 1987).

30 Carl F. Goodman, The Somewhat Less Reluctant Litigant: Japan's Changing Views Towards Civil Litigation, 32 Law and Policy in International Business 769 (2001); J. Mark Ramseyer, The Costs of the Consensual Myth: Antitrust Enforcement and Institutional Barriers to Litigation in Japan, 94 Yale Law Journal 604, 609 (1985).

31 Law For Adjustment of Domestic Relations (Law No. 152 of 1947, as amended) Chapter III Conciliation.

32 1992 Amendment to Civil Conciliation Act Article 24-2. See, Rieko Nishikawa, Judges and ADR in Japan (Keio University) on the web at www.iadb.org/mif/v2/speeches/nishikawa.html.

33 See, Takesi Kojima and Yasuhei Taniguchi, Japanese National Report on Access to Justice Part 1 in ACCESS TO JUSTICE, A WORLD SURVEY VOLUME I (Cappelletti and Garth Ed., Sijthopff and Noordhoff, 1978) at 689, 728-733 listing various mechanisms for mediation (conciliation) by Japanese public entities.

34 Takeo Tanase, The Management of Automobile Accident Compensation in Japan, 24 Law and Society Review 651 (1990).

The availability of alternate methods of resolving disputes is ubiquitous in Japan. Not only automobile accidents but also product liability cases are subject to an administrative mechanism for resolution.[35] The government has established alternative mechanisms that can be used by parties with disputes. Thus employment discrimination claims by female employees may be referred to the Office of Women's and Young Workers Affairs of the Ministry of Labor for resolution.[36] Although the Ministry cannot order an employer to comply with the law it can advise the employer to do so and if the employer refuses it may publish the advice and refusal to comply in newspapers. While providing an administrative remedy the EEOL does not provide for a right to sue for discrimination. This does not mean that female workers who have been discriminated against cannot sue, but it discloses that the government is seeking to have such disputes resolved by the bureaucracy not the courts.[37] Where the courts have provided a remedy for a wrong that may affect a large number of people, the government may step in to provide an administrative remedy. This was done in the environmental area after the *Minamata disease cases*[38] and was done in the HIV and Hanson's Disease matters.

Even where there is no established government mechanism for resolving disputes, the government may be called upon to assist in resolving a matter short of litigation. Through its "Administrative Guidance" the governmental authorities may attempt to resolve issues that in the United States could only be resolved through litigation. Thus the government may be called on by injured parties to conciliate or mediate a dispute before litigation is instituted, as was the case in Minamata. Even where an injured party has no legal right to relief, the government may play a role as mediator to bring about a settlement that is satisfactory to all sides. For example, where builders have an absolute right to construct residential housing as long as they comply with the Building Permit law, a local government may delay issuance of the permit to allow the builder and local residents time to negotiate to try to resolve outstanding issues. This is so even though the law requires the permit to be issued in a specified time period.[39]

---

35 J. Mark Ramseyer, Products Liability Through Private Ordering: Notes on a Japanese Experiment, 144 University of Pennsylvania Law Review 1823 (1996).

36 Equal Employment Opportunity Law, Law No. 92 of 1997.

37 Suit can be based on general principles of tort law rather than on the EEOL specifically. See, e.g., Nissan Motors Inc. v. Nakamoto, 35 Minshu 300 (Sup. Ct., Petty Bench, 3/24/81) reported in English in Lawrence W. Beer and Hiroshi Itoh, THE CONSTITUTIONAL CASE LAW OF JAPAN 1970-1990 (University of Washington Press, 1996) 179. The 2000 Consumer Contracts Law designed to protect consumers from abusive contracting contains a requirement that business *endeavor* to make contracts with consumers clear and easily understandable. Consumer Contracts Law Article 3 (1).

38 See, Chris Clarke, Update Comparative Legal Study (European Union, 2001) pages 92-93 for a discussion of he administrative mechanism adopted in Japan after the Big Four pollution cases.

39 See, e.g., Nakatani v. Tokyo-to, 39 Minshu 989 (Sup. Ct., 7/16/85) discussed in Takehisa Nakagawa, Administrative Formality in Japan: Governmental Activities Outside Statutory Authorization, 52 Administrative Law Review 175 (2000).

The Japanese Copyright Act is a good illustration of legislative emphasis on mediation and conciliation rather than litigation. Thus Chapter 6 of the Act is devoted entirely to disposition of disputes by mediation.[40] Under the Act the Agency for Cultural Affairs establishes a special group of mediators who are available to mediate copyright disputes. Moreover the Act provides for arbitration decisions in such areas as broadcasting or recording.[41] In the recently active deregulation of the telecommunications industry, conciliation under the auspices of the Ministry of Posts and Telecommunications has become a significant mechanism for resolving disputes between carriers.[42] Similarly the 1999 Housing Quality Assurance Act provides for a voluntary system of quality assurance under which a Performance Evaluation Report may be made a part of a housing contract. This Report carries with it the guaranty that various safety tests have been performed on the building and its materials. The Ministry of Construction will set standards for such tests and if there is a latter dispute between the consumer (purchaser) of the home and the builder, conciliation may be had before a body appointed by the Minister of Construction.[43] Recently various Bar Associations have set up dispute resolution centers as part of the increasing availability of ADR mechanisms.[44]

Under the Japanese Labor Relations Adjustment Law[45] labor management disputes that could lead to work stoppages can be conciliated before the Labor Commission. Conciliation may be requested by either (or both) parties to the labor dispute and while if requested by only one party the other party is not required to conciliate, the reality is that conciliation is undertaken when either side requests it. Conciliation constitutes over 95% of the Labor Commission's labor dispute adjustment process and it has a more than 50% success rate.[46] In connection with individual employee claims against employers, there are counseling services maintained by various prefectures and municipalities in Japan that can be used to mediate disputes.[47] In the spring of 2004 the Cabinet approved a Bill (the Bill was passed by the Diet in the spring 2004 session) that would create a new Labor Tri-

40 Copyright Act, Law No. 48,1970 as amended, Articles 105-111.

41 Copyright Act, Law No. 48,1970 as amended, Articles 67-70.

42 See, Colin PA Jones, Japan's Telecommunications Business Dispute resolution Committee, World Telecom Report (May 2003) (BNA International Inc.).

43 JCA Newsletter No. 6 at pages 8-9 (March 2000) on the web at *www.jcaa.or.jp/e/arbitration-e/syuppan-e/newslet/news6.html* .

44 See, e.g., Norihiko Maeda, ADR in Japan (Japan Commercial Arbitration Association) on the web at *www.jcaa.or.jp/jcaa-j/jigyou/textadrinjapan.html*

45 Law No. 25 of 1946.

46 Kazuo Sugeno (translated by Leo Kanowitz), JAPANESE EMPLOYMENT AND LABOR LAW (University of Tokyo Press and Carolina Academic Press, 2002) at 679-688.

47 See, Hiroya Nakakubo, Procedures for Resolving Individual Employment Disputes on the web at *www.jil.go.jp/bulletin/year/1996/vol35-06/05.htm*. Professor Nakakubo reports that in 1994 the Tokyo city government successfully conciliated 73% of the approximately 1,100 cases referred to it.

bunal to handle employee-employer dispute cases.[48] Although entitled a court and although a judge would preside, along with two lay experts, the court would primarily be a conciliation forum for employee-employer disputes. If conciliation did not succeed and if neither party proceeded to District Court, the Tribunal would deal with the matter in accordance with the procedures of the Code of Civil Procedure, except that a determination would have to be made after no more than three Oral Argument sessions. The limitation on Oral Argument sessions is designed to speed up the decision making process. The losing party may object to the Tribunal's determination and file suit in the District Court. In such case the determination would not take effect. The creation of such a conciliation/quasi judicial body at a level below that of the traditional court system appears to be a reflection of the desire to carry out the recommendations of the Law Reform Council as they relate to strengthening the dispute resolution mechanisms for employer-employee disputes. At the same time the process retains conciliation as a preferred method for dealing with a relationship that had special recognition in feudal Japan and has special meaning in Japan today.[49]

In the environmental law area the government established Central Committees (not unlike the Labor Commissions)[50] to mediate, conciliate or arbitrate pollution disputes under the 1972 Disputes Law. This law was an offshoot of the Big Four pollution cases and the Basic Law dealing with environmental issues that followed on the heels of those cases. Like the Labor Commissions the Environmental Committees have concurrent jurisdiction with the courts. Local Commissions operate at the local level and at this level many cases are resolved without recourse to the judicial system.[51] As Japan enters the world of e-commerce, an alternative dispute resolution mechanism has arisen to deal with e-commerce disputes.[52]

The emphasis on alternative dispute resolution is echoed in the recent Report of the Judicial Reform Council. While making numerous recommendations for strengthening Japan's litigation system the Council also strongly supported

48 The Cabinet sent a series of Bills dealing with judicial procedure to the Diet in March of 2004. Most of the proposed changes are to take effect in April of 2005. The Labor Tribunal Act is to take effect within 2 years on a date determined by Cabinet Order.

49 See, Recommendations of the Justice System Reform Council: For a Justice System to Support Japan in the 21st Century, 6/12/01 on the web at *www.kantei.go.jp/foreign/policy/sihou/singikai/990612_e.html* at 22-23 of 90.

50 Kichiemon Ishikawa (assisted by Walter Gellhorn) The Regulation of the Employer—Employee Relationship: Japanese Labor-Relations Law in LAW IN JAPAN (Arthur Taylor von Mehren Ed., Harvard University Press, 1963) 439 (concerning the structure and working of Labor Commissions).

51 See, Julian Gresser, Koichiro Fujikura and Akio Morishima, ENVIRONMENTAL LAW IN JAPAN (MIT Press, 1981) Chapter 7—The Uses of Conciliation, Mediation and Arbitration in the Settlement of Environmental Disputes.

52 Takato Natsui, Online Witness—How to Prevent Fake Evidence. Professor Natsui reports that the Electronic Commerce Promotion Council of Japan has established both a mediation (conciliation) and arbitration system to deal with consumer complaints. He further reports that in a nine month period in 2003 of over 900 cases utilizing the process 88% were settled.

strengthening the mechanisms of and use of alternative dispute resolution. The Council devoted an entire subpart of its recommendations to "Reinforcement and Vitalization of Alternative Dispute Resolution (ADR) Mechanisms." Among the recommendations was a suggestion that Japan consider adopting a comprehensive ADR Basic Law to promote alternative Dispute Resolution and to coordinate ADR with trial procedures in civil litigation cases.[53] Exactly what form of reform this suggestion will engender remains to be seen.

Even after litigation has been instituted, formal conciliation may be undertaken either in or outside of the litigation itself. Thus the court may organize a conciliation commission to operate inside the judicial process. The conciliation commission has the authority to recommend a settlement (and if the parties agree in advance the commission's recommendation may be binding). If the parties fail to agree to the recommendation the commission may advise the trial judge (who may also be a member of the conciliation commission) of the reasons why settlement was not achieved and which party was recalcitrant. It is estimated that 30% of all litigation is resolved through the use of in-court mediation or conciliation or settlement.[54]

Thus, an important factor to keep in mind when considering the litigation process in Japan is the mutuality of view between the lawyers and the judge that the proper resolution of the matter should be through settlement. Sharing this view, the courtroom participants may gear their process to the best method of reaching a mutually agreeable settlement rather than finding out who is right and who is wrong. Just as judicial awards of damages provide the background for pre-litigation conciliation and settlement so too the reality that settlement is the likely end product of the litigation is the background noise of litigation in Japan. The lawyers in the case may be waiting for the judge to make the first move to get the settlement process moving and the judge may be analyzing the situation to determine when is the best time to intervene for settlement. As is true in the United States the courtroom participants may be giving and looking for subtle signs showing that the time to talk settlement has arrived. However, in Japan the judge will be much more involved and the lawyers less likely to broach the settlement question. Each side will be waiting for the judge to make the first move toward settlement and each will be looking at the signals the judge is sending in responding to settlement overtures. Indeed, the parties and their counsel may be waiting for the judge to set out a comprehensive settlement proposal for their agreement.

---

53 Recommendations of the Justice System Reform Council: For a Justice System to Support Japan in the 21st Century, 6/12/01 on the web at *www.kantei.go.jp/foreign/policy/sihou/singikai/990612_e.html*

54 Judge Tetsuya Obuchi, Role of the Court in the Process of Informal Dispute Resolution in Japan: Traditional and Modern Aspects, with Special Emphasis on In-Court Compromise, 20 Law in Japan 74 (1987).

The role of settlement in litigation is so important in Japan that it has been formalized in the Code of Civil Procedure. The Constitution requires that judicial proceedings (with limited exceptions) are to be public proceedings.[55] Trials must be held publicly and judgments in non-default cases[56] must be issued publicly[57] and served by the court in written form (not by electronic means).[58] Only where the public trial would adversely affect public order or morals may the court (by unanimous decision of the panel handling the matter) order the trial be held privately. But a public forum is not the most advantageous forum for negotiation of settlement. Settlement negotiations are typically ongoing with the active participation of the court. The court may suggest a settlement for the parties to consider. The parties may meet privately with their counsel and return to court with counter proposals presented in the presence of the judge. The judge may act the role of mediator/conciliator to try to bring the parties together to resolve the matter. The parties may then leave and have further internal discussions and then return to court for the next hearing date to engage in further negotiation. The judge may suggest a settlement and urge the parties to settle on the basis of the suggestion. The judge may even advise the parties as to what the likely outcome of the case will be absent a settlement—and may imply that the recalcitrant party might find the ultimate judgment less favorable than the settlement on terms of the tentative judgment being considered by the court. For all of this to take place in public would be to impose a restraint on the settlement negotiations and would hamper effective settlement tactics and pressure by the court. It is necessary to find a means for such in-court negotiations to be conducted in private. The new Code of Civil Procedure adopts a pre-Code mechanism of holding a "preparatory proceeding" ("Preparation for Oral Argument") that is not a formal Plenary Hearing or Oral Argument or even a Preliminary Oral Argument in the case but is deemed to be part of the preparation for such Hearing. As it is not a formal Hearing but simply part of the preparation for a formal Hearing it is not considered to be a part of the trial and thus is not required to be held in public.[59]

2) Clarification and Trial in General

Preliminary proceedings to assist in getting the case ready for trial are not unknown in the United States. Thus, many pretrial procedural hearings in the United

55 Constitution of Japan, Article 82.

56 In default cases the judge need not prepare a formal judgment but the court clerk may simply write the parties and record the judgment. CCP Article 254-255.

57 CPR Rule 155 requires that judgments be given by reading aloud the determination of the court, although the reasons for the court's decision need not be stated in the oral pronouncement.

58 Koichi Miki, Procedural Law on the Threshold of a New Millennium, World Congress on Procedural Law (1999) on the web at ruessmann.jura.uni-sb.de/grotius/english/Reports/japan.htm page 6 of 8.

59 The Preparation for Oral Argument (also called the Proceedings Preparatory for Oral Argument) procedure is discussed in Chapter 8 C.

States are conducted in the judge's chambers and not in the courtroom. These informal, but highly important hearings are not considered as a part of the trial. However, American judges typically deal with preliminary matters that may have an effect on a case by ruling on motions dealing with such matters, such as motions in limine to limit the witness testimony in a case. These rulings are a formal part of the process although not a part of the trial. The motion and the ruling are part of the public record of the proceeding. Moreover in the United States there is a clear demarcation between pretrial and trial. The trial is typically the proceeding in front of the jury or where there is no jury it is the taking of evidence before the judge. Sometimes issues may arise during the trial that require resolution based on evidence that the judge needs to hear to resolve a procedural question—for example whether an expert witness will testify to a matter that meets the *Daubert*[60] standard of being within generally accepted scientific or professional standards. The judge may hold a hearing outside the presence of the jury but such hearing is typically held in public and the transcript of the hearing is a public document.

In Japan the clear distinction between "pretrial" and "trial" in the American sense does not exist. The trial (Plenary Hearing or "Oral Argument") is started once the Complaint has been filed. There is no separate pretrial stage to the court proceedings. Thus many matters that in the United States would be considered as pretrial matters (e.g., motions in limine, or discovery motions) are part of the "trial" in Japan. In Japan the initial hearing in the case is the start of the Plenary Hearing or trial. Of course, there are some matters that must be dealt with in a "preliminary" fashion—that is to say to prepare the parties and the court to the formal taking of testimony or introduction of evidence. Thus, there are "Preliminary Proceedings" to deal with these preliminary matters[61] (not to be confused with the new Proceeding Preparatory to Oral Argument).[62]

Indeed, the nature of the trial in Japan is fundamentally different from the trial in the United States. Not only is there no jury and hence no necessity for continuous evidence gathering in a relatively compact proceeding, but the process itself has a fundamentally different function. Because there is no "line in the sand" demarcation between the taking of evidence procedure—the trial—and the events that occur in a case before the trial—the pretrial—Japan has no "pretrial" procedure. Virtually all of the things that are handled at the pretrial in the United States are dealt with in the main case in Japan. And, because the main case takes a long time to mature into a determination by the fact finder, there is time in the main case to do the sort of evidence gathering that would be performed pretrial in the United States.

60 *See* Daubert v. Merrell Dow Pharmaceuticals, 509 U.S. 579 (1993); Kumho Tire v. Carmichael, 526 U.S. 137 (1999).

61 CCP Articles 164-167.

62 CCP Articles 168-174.

In an American proceeding the first step is the filing/serving of a summons and Complaint calling on the opposing party to respond to the plaintiff's Complaint. The Complaint is (in theory) a simple statement of the contours of the basis for plaintiff's claim. The function of the Complaint is to advise the defendant that it is being sued and to provide enough information so that the defendant can begin to formulate its defense to the action. The Complaint in a notice pleading system such as the United States gets the ball rolling and is not seen as a definitive document. It likely will be amended as the case moves forward to take into account information gathered during the discovery process. While court officers (e.g. the federal Marshall) may serve the Complaint on the opposition, the court's role is simply ministerial. Indeed, in some situations there is no need to involve the court in the service of process and the complaining party or its lawyer will handle service matters.

An American trial must operate on a fast track so jurors can complete their civic duty and return to their full time jobs or other obligations. Consequently, all of the evidence gathering must be completed before the first witness is sworn in to give testimony. To accomplish this task the Federal Rules of Civil Procedure arm the lawyers with weapons to assist them in locating the facts. These weapons include the American discovery devices of interrogatories, depositions of witnesses and parties, document production etc. Along with these weapons the lawyers are given the use of the court name, stature and potential of the court's sanctioning power to assist them. Thus lawyers, as officers of the court, may prepare and serve subpoenas on witnesses whose presence is demanded at deposition and lawyers may serve third parties with subpoenas demanding that they produce books, records and other documents that may lead to admissible evidence in a case. Third persons and/or parties who object to production must make a motion to the court asking for court intervention to limit or prohibit the discovery effort. Most courts require that the lawyers for the objecting entity and the requesting party meet to attempt to resolve differences, such as by limiting the scope of the inquiry. Only after such efforts have failed will the court get involved and only when a request for court intervention has been made.

The role of the court in the American pretrial phase is mostly a monitoring role designed to expedite the process of discovery. The discovery process is fundamentally in the hands of the lawyers for the parties acting within the general rules of procedure. It is at the end of the pretrial process that the court becomes more involved. After the discovery is completed, the court will call the parties together for the purpose of drafting a pretrial Order. This Order finally defines what the trial will consider. Now that the parties (through their lawyers) have discovered all of the relevant facts and have used vehicles available under the rules to track down the witnesses who will testify, the parties (lawyers) are in a position to define the issues to be tried. The lawyers can also stipulate to the facts that are agreed to by the parties, delineate the facts that are disputed and what each party contends the true facts are, define the issues that are outstanding and state the views of the parties as to those issues. The parties can list the witnesses and evidence that each side expects to present to prove its theory of the case. It is at this stage that the judge becomes substantively involved in the case by ruling that certain issues are relevant or not relevant and that certain witnesses or evidence on certain issues may not be presented at the trial. The court may set a time limit during which the parties may present dispositive motions, such as Motions for Summary Judgment claiming that based on the agreed to or not contested facts one party is entitled to win on some or all issues. Through such dispositive motions, the true legal and factual issues in the case may be narrowed. The pre-trial Order may be viewed as a roadmap for the trial. A party who fails to list witnesses, evidence, documents or issues will likely be precluded from calling such witnesses or offering such evidence or documents or raising such issues during the trial.

In Japan the judge is involved at the very start of the case and remains involved till the decision is rendered. Once the Complaint is filed, it is reviewed by the court for adequacy, and only after such inquiry and judicial satisfaction will the court accept the Complaint and cause it to be served.[63] Thus at the very inception of the case the court becomes a major player in the case and a process of issue determination begins. After the Complaint is served (by the court)[64] the court begins the process of issue and fact "clarification". Indeed, this function has already started when the Complaint is filed with the court—even before it is served on the defendant. Clarification is the heart of the Japanese civil procedure. And the clarifying official is the judge.

To understand the civil procedure process in Japan, it is necessary to distinguish between clarification from an American perspective and clarification from a Japanese perspective. In the United States the lawyers might be asked to clarify a point by explaining it in a more understandable way. In this way issues get clarified. "When you say the defendant defrauded the plaintiff by the statement, please clarify for me what it is you claim in the statement was false?" By the time the judge asks this question—probably at the pretrial Order stage where each side is defining its issues and contentions—or the Motion for Summary Judgment stage where the defendant has moved for judgment saying that all of the not disputed facts show that there was no false statement and that the claimed statement was true—the parties have taken extensive discovery and the pretrial stage of the case is virtually over. The judge's clarifying role is either so that the judge can better understand the facts and claims so that it can rule on the motion or the judge wants to make sure the issues are framed so that the jury can better understand the evidence being presented. The judge in "clarifying" is not attempting to mold the case or determine what facts may or may not ultimately be relevant. The judge is not attempting to assist the parties in best presenting their case.

Clarification in Japan is different. The court is not attempting to clarify a statement or a contention. Rather, the court is attempting to clarify the entire case in such a way that it appears which party should win and which party should lose.

63 CCP Article 137.

64 CCP Article 138.

Clarification is thus a much broader function and in essence subsumes the trial of the action. Such a process can take place when the "clarification" stage and the trial stage are not clearly separated (as is the case in Japan) and when an inquisition system is at work where the inquiring official (the judge) is also the deciding official. To properly clarify an issue the judge may need to hear from the parties, order parties to produce documents, read documentary evidence, etc.[65] In sum, to properly clarify a matter the court may be required to do many of the things required to try the issue being clarified. But clarification is not trial. To clarify matters the judge will read the briefs of the lawyers and in sessions with them will question them about issues raised and about issues not raised but that may appear relevant to the court. The court may attempt to "clarify" an argument raised by counsel by changing it to a different argument that the court feels better meets the case at hand. Or the court may inquire as to why certain arguments not raised have not been raised and whether they should be in the case. The court may raise its own arguments and ask the lawyers to then brief those issues. Or it may raise its own issues (provided they fall within the scope of the Complaint or defense) and ask that facts be adduced at the next hearing that will bear on the issues raised by the court. To clarify, the court is permitted to question parties and bengoshi about facts and law and require them to present evidence on factual or legal issues.[66] The court may question parties or their principal employees and can obtain expert opinions as part of the clarification process.[67] In short, the process of "clarifying" is the process of molding the case as the court sees it so that the party who should win does in fact win. The court is here no mere neutral in the trial process, it is an advocate—but a fair advocate not an advocate who takes the plaintiff's side because the plaintiff has hired him to support his position. The court will be an advocate who takes plaintiff's side only after being convinced that the defendant has wronged the plaintiff. Of course to determine whether the plaintiff should win (or the defendant should win) the court needs to clarify the positions of both parties until it can see where the right and justice in the matter lies.

Clarification was the basis of "trial" in prewar Japan. It has been suggested that it was modeled on the German law procedure under which a court was *compelled* to clarify the case,[68] although the process was remarkably similar to the role played by the Tokugawa magistrate. That is not to say that the German law did not play a significant role in the clarification requirement—it did. But it is merely to point out that the clarification model of litigation can be viewed as the taking of a new (European) civil procedure and giving it an indigenous Japanese (Tokugawa) fla-

65 CCP Article 151.

66 CCP Article 149.

67 CCP Article 151.

68 Kohji Tanabe (assisted by John B. Hurlbut), The Process of Litigation: An Experiment With the Adversary System in LAW IN JAPAN (Arthur Taylor von Mehren Ed. Harvard University Press, 1963) 73, 85-86; see also, Craig P. Wagnild, Civil Law Discovery in Japan: A Comparison of Japanese and U.S. Methods of Evidence Collection in Civil Litigation, 3 Asian-Pacific Law and Policy Journal 1, 4 (2002).

vor. And, indeed in prewar Japan the clarification of the case was required of Japanese judges. Lower court rulings were regularly over ruled because the appeal court found that the judge had failed to properly or adequately perform the clarification process. The duty to clarify was not simply a procedural norm but was a positive law duty and failure to properly clarify was reversible error and could be an issue for review by the highest court, the Great Court of Judicature. Further, as the purpose of clarification was to assure that the proper party actually won the case, regardless of whether adequately represented (or represented at all), the trial court was compelled to take over the litigation from inadequate counsel (or from a party not represented by counsel). This assured that the case was tried properly, i.e., proper arguments were raised and proper evidence submitted. The prewar clarification jurisprudence requirement neutralized lawyers as strong advocates and marginalized lawyers in the eyes of the public and potential litigation clients (after all, the judge must do it anyway).

Clarification was a requirement at each level of the litigation process. Thus, appeal courts also had (and have) a clarification duty, especially as the first level appeal court could (and still can) also take new evidence in a case. The highest appeal court needed to review the record of both the trial and first level appeal court to determine whether the case had been properly clarified. As the function of clarification was to assure that substantive justice was done in a case, it was a short step to determine that where the wrong party won (in the opinion of the appeal court) the reason had to be a failure to properly clarify. As a consequence the real issue on appeal would appear to have been "did the correct party win." This made the appeal court a court of errors, not a court whose function is to decide whether the lower court has properly handled legal issues but, rather, whether the correct party won the case. Needless to say a lower court could not be criticized for doing too much clarification. Civil service judges would tend to over clarify (over try?) a case rather than under clarify it to assure that they would not be reversed on appeal. Although not as demanding as prewar, the initial trial court and the first level appeal court today considers itself bound to properly clarify the case and acts similar to the way it did prewar in clarifying the case.

At the Preliminary Proceeding or Preliminary Oral Argument stage, the court attempts to clarify the case by resolving such matters as the issues to be tried and the evidence to be adduced at the trial. Although Preliminary to the Plenary Hearing or trial, the reality is that the proceeding is an integral part of the trial since as part of the process of "clarification" the court is already deciding many of the issues that would otherwise be tried. By determining that certain issues either are in or out of the case, the court has effectively decided those issues in favor of one of the parties. Similarly by determining that evidence is not necessary on a point, either because the point is not relevant or because the court knows the answer without need for evidence, the court has decided issues in the trial. Moreover, these proceedings because they are a part of the Plenary Hearing are open to the public.

The new "Preparation for Oral Argument" provided for in the new Code is, on the other hand, a hybrid that is both part of and yet viewed as separate from the Plenary Hearing being simply "preparatory" to the hearing. Thus it is a mechanism considered as outside the trial (or Oral Argument) and takes certain procedures best conducted in private out of the formal trial to enable them to be dealt with informally. Should the informal procedures result in settlement there is no need to continue the Plenary Hearing or trial. On the other hand if settlement is not achieved, the procedure will nonetheless resolve some procedural matters. These results must be made a part of the formal record and be read out in open court to maintain the fiction of public trial and conform to the 1920s reform that embodied the concept of public Oral Argument. The procedure has its roots in a German law reform known as the Stuttgart model undertaken in the 1970s in an effort to move cases along more quickly.[69] The experiment was so successful that it was incorporated into the German Civil Code in 1976 effective 1977.[70] Unlike the Japanese version of the model, the German model does not seem to be based primarily on the theory that the process is useful to achieve settlement (although it is useful for this purpose) but rather the German model appears designed to achieve speed. The German process assumes that if a party fails to meet the deadlines set by the court, the party will be precluded from submitting arguments or facts that were not timely submitted.[71] Although the court in Germany can relax preclusion if there is a reasonable excuse or the failure will not unduly delay the case. However, in Japan the preclusion provisions of the Code are less mandatory and far more liberal than in the German law model. The reality is that while the new Code contains preclusion provisions, the failure to identify issues or facts at the Preparation for Oral Argument does not lead to preclusion in Japan.

3) Substantive Justice, Lawyers and Judges

Although the American Occupation reforms attempted to create a more adversary system, as we have seen above the reality is that the system post-war has not changed as significantly as the Occupation had intended. While the Code of Civil Procedure no longer mandates that the judge clarify a case, the reality is that the modern judge sees it as his/her duty to clarify the case. This is all the more so as Japanese law continues to move away from American concepts and back to German concepts. This places the Japanese judge in a similar inquisition procedure mode as was the case under the prewar Code (notwithstanding the modern Code may look adversarial) and makes the trial process a clarification process that ultimately leads to substantive justice in that the correct party wins. Or more accurately leads to a process where something close to substantive justice is achieved

69 Yasuhei Taniguchi, The 1996 Code of Civil Procedure of Japan—A Procedure for the Coming Century? 45 American Journal of Comparative Law 767, 771 (1997).

70 Peter Gottwald, Simplified Civil Procedure in West Germany (Comment), 31 American Journal of Comparative Law 687, 693 (1983); William B. Fisch, Recent Developments in West German Civil Procedure, 6 Hastings International and Comparative Law Review 221, 226-227 (1983).

71 Peter Gottwald, Simplified Civil Procedure in West Germany (Comment), 31 American Journal of Comparative Law 687, 698 (1983) (in the German procedure belated arguments are routinely excluded).

as the parties reach the proper settlement or if there is no settlement the proper party wins the litigation. (As will be discussed later, the winner may not win significant damages, raising a justice issue).

Substantive justice is a positive value in Japan. Procedural justice is a positive value in the United States. The American position is based on the assumption that better and more procedure leads to a better (more accurate) decision. In Japan the rule appears to be that procedure should not stand in the way of a correct (more accurate) determination. Accordingly, it is unlikely that a judge in Japan will preclude a party from submitting relevant evidence simply because the lawyer did not reveal the existence of that evidence at an appropriate time. And it is unlikely that a court will preclude a party from raising a defense or a basis for relief simply because the party failed to raise the matter at the appropriate time. This concern for getting the "correct" judgment also makes courts leery of punishing a party because either the party or its counsel has failed in a duty to the court or to the other party. Thus, sanctions that United States courts might enter for failure to make discovery are not available in Japan. The idea that sanctions are necessary to protect the procedural rule—the operating assumption of the American sanctions regime—is inconsistent with the Japanese view that sanctioning a party by preclusion deprives the court of relevant arguments or facts and may lead the court into error in deciding the case. It is, after all, the function of the court to find the accurate facts and make the correct judgment in the matter. Preclusion deprives the court of arguments, contentions and evidence. The consequence of preclusion in Japan would mean that the procedure employed might not lead to a full analysis of the facts or relevant issues—at least at the lower court level. Indeed, failure to raise an argument at the District Court does not preclude a party from raising that argument on appeal to the High Court although the Code and Rules may *appear* to require the party to jump over difficult hurdles to get such new argument—or new evidence—before the appeal court.

The prewar clarification doctrine had the effect of placing the judge and the lawyers (for both sides) in a distinctly unequal position, with judges seeing it as their duty to protect the public, including the parties in each case before them, from incompetent lawyers. This tended to make judges think of themselves as more effective, more competent and at a higher level than the lawyers in the case. Not only did the judge sit at a higher level but also he considered himself at a higher level both professionally and personally. This division between judge and lawyer that existed prewar has been moderated but nonetheless continues to have vitality today. The fact that few if any practicing lawyers—and fewer yet of successful practicing lawyers—seek to become judges or are appointed as judges highlights the judge/lawyer divide in Japan. Moreover, judges and lawyers exist in separate social and professional worlds. Judges are civil servant bureaucrats in a society where bureaucrats are held in high esteem and they see themselves as warranting that esteem, especially when they must protect parties without lawyers and parties who have lawyers from the errors their lawyers may make. Judges tend to live in government provided housing where they are surrounded by other judges or other government employees. Since judges get transferred on a regular basis, it makes no sense for a judge to try to make connection with the community where the judge sits—indeed it might be looked on with disfavor if the judge attempted to do so. After all, the judge must preserve neutrality and objectivity in all matters and therefore should not be actively involved with the local Bar or local community.

Lawyers on the other hand see judges as arrogant and either overworked or not competent to handle trials. After all, Japanese judges have little or no experience trying cases as a party representative—the only judges who get to try cases do so as judges on assignment to the Executive Branch of government. Such judges are likely to be treated differently than the lawyers who regularly appear in front of the court and are not likely to gain an understanding of what it means to represent a real live (personal as distinguished from government) client. Lawyers see judges as taking over their case rather than allowing the lawyer to handle the case as the lawyer sees fit. On the other hand, as lawyers have had little education on how to actually try a case in an adversarial way in either university or the Legal Research and Training Institute, the lawyers are probably not as competent to try cases as they think they are. Further, it is difficult for modern lawyers to disregard history. Historically it was deemed improper for a lawyer to meet with a potential witness before the witness gave a statement to the judge. Such a meeting was considered as potential witness tampering and was viewed as a violation of ethical norms. In such a setting it was difficult for lawyers to prepare, as they could not find the facts without interviewing the fact witnesses. Although today's lawyer may interview witnesses, there remains concern about how far the lawyer may go in the interview arena because of concern that the lawyer should not cross the ethical line between interview and suggestion. Although such issues also exist in the United States they have less impact on American lawyers who have a long history of witness preparation. Indeed, it would be unthinkable for an American lawyer to call a witness who has not been interviewed and most witnesses at trial have been the subjects of a deposition. This is so because the lawyer who wants to cross-examine the witness wants to know before trial what the witness his adversary is going to call has to say when called at trial. This gives time to prepare the trial cross-examination or time to obtain contradictory witnesses or evidence. As a result Japanese lawyers tend to be less prepared than American lawyers to cross-examine opposition witnesses or to directly examine friendly witnesses. This naturally leads the judge to intervene to assure that the testimony of the witness and the facts and issues that the witness may know something about are properly "clarified."

The gap between lawyers and judges in Japan is made wider by the fact that they do not even belong to the same professional groups. Again history plays a role. As lawyers were under the supervision of the Ministry of Justice (and prosecutor offices) at a time when judges were a part of the Ministry and when judges and prosecutors were placed on the same social and professional level, lawyers' organizations are jealous of the independence that came with the end of the war. Judges and prosecutors are not permitted to be members of the various Bar Associations in Japan. Only bengoshi who have been accepted by the association may be members, and as a matter of substantive law judges may not belong to such groups. Only after a judge has left the Bench, such as through retirement or resignation, may the judge be admitted to the Bar Association and placed on the list of private bengoshi. Even the idea of continuing legal education seminars in which judges are major participants is unlikely in Japan as they would be viewed by Bar Associations as a potential method by which the Judicial Branch is attempting to influence the private Bar. In the United States there is a unified Bar in two senses. First, judges, prosecutors and private practice lawyers are intermingled and most have served in a different capacity at some time in their career. The Bench and Bar are unified as judges invariably were practicing lawyers who were raised to the Bench. The practice of staffing the Bench with practicing lawyers is ancient in the common law and traces its roots to the 13th century when clerical judges were replaced by lawyer judges in the common law courts of England.[72] In Japan the Bar and Bench are divided. The concept of having a "unified legal system" in which judges are appointed from among practicing lawyers has a long but unsuccessful history in Japan. Initially proposed in 1954 by the Japan Federation of Bar Associations the idea was championed in 1961 by the Japan Jurist Association and commented on favorably by the Temporary Investigative Commission on the Judicial System in 1962.[73] Efforts by Bar Associations to create a unified Bar by requiring that all judges have some experience as practicing lawyers before becoming judges have met with objection by the judicial Secretariat as the spokesperson for the Bench.[74] Even efforts to require that judges have at least five years of practical training before ascending to the Bench have been disfavored.

As judges are trained by other judges—creating an inbred judicial system—the myths about lawyer competence and the need for judges to protect both the public and the parties become ingrained and transmitted from one generation of judges to another. As lawyers exist in a separate world from judges, myths about judicial laziness or incompetence or overbearing tend to circulate in the lawyer community and thus become ingrained. As part of its 2004 initiative the government will permit judges in training (in the first 10-year assignment) to work in a bengoshi office for two years. This may help by giving these judges a better idea of the competence of lawyers. But it is a far cry from requiring that judges of inferior courts have actually earned their living by representing clients in real disputes.

While outwardly polite to each other and while respectful, the reality is that judges and lawyers in Japan do not talk to each other but tend to talk at each other.

---

72 1 HOLDSWORTH'S HISTORY OF ENGLISH LAW 584 (Little, Brown and Company, 1922).

73 See, Takaaki Hattori, The Role of the Supreme Court of Japan in the Field of Judicial Administration, 60 Washington Law Review 69, 74 (1984).

74 Usually the disagreement between judges and lawyers is not brought into the open. However, in 1999 the dispute was brought into the open by proposals to change the system for recruiting judges. A Secretariat official was quoted in the Japan Times as stating that lawyers wanted more judges appointed from practicing bengoshi so as to better the social status of lawyers. Kanako Takahara, Calls for Overhaul of Judge System Mount Japan Times on Line 12/20/99.

This is true outside the courtroom and to some extent in the courtroom as well. In the courtroom the judge sees it as his/her duty to make sure the correct decision is reached. The right decision is the desired end product of the litigation sausage machine even if that means telling the lawyers what they should be doing and micromanaging the case. Lawyers see such actions by the judges as infringing on the attorney-client relationship and beyond the judge's duties. Nonetheless lawyers understand the reality of the situation and thus tend to leave it to the judge to handle various matters. Judges determine when it is a good time to discuss settlement; judges propose settlement terms for the parties to consider. Judges determine what evidence may be presented and which legal issues are relevant to the case. Judges decide what documents should be produced, etc. Leaving matters to the judge saves time that the lawyer can devote to other (paying) business.

The paternalistic judge of prewar Japan—a major target of the Occupation reform—has become the paternalistic judge of modern Japan. In this, the judge can be seen as playing a similar role as the paternalistic magistrate of Tokugawa Japan, whose function was not so much to decide the right and wrong of the matter based on "law" as it was to bring the parties to agreement through conciliation or if that was not possible to get a decision that was appropriate to the facts and circumstances. Not only does the modern Japanese judge display the paternalism of the Tokugawa magistrate but so too the modern judge is more concerned with the context in which the dispute either arose or is presented to the court. The context of the dispute may be more important than the legal rights that may have attached at a time prior to suit. In this regard procedure looks to the actual circumstances at the time of the case. That circumstance could be different from the circumstances that existed when the relationship between the parties that is at the heart of the suit was formed. Thus, in a contract case the circumstances at the time of an alleged breach might be more important than the circumstance that existed at the time the contract was signed. The terms of the contract governing when the parties could institute litigation, for example, may be seen as less important on the question of whether litigation is timely than the circumstance that exists when litigation is instituted. For example, if the parties have entered into a long term contract for the purchase and sale of a product made of other components at a set price and during the term of the contract world economic conditions force the price of the components dramatically higher, the contracted for price may not be given great effect by the judge. The judge may determine it is a breach of good faith or an abuse of rights for the buyer to insist on a now, under the changed circumstance, artificially low price. The legal niceties about the right to contract and the parties' ability to create their own law of contract through their agreement may have to give way to the judge's (and society's) understanding that the changed circumstance requires a modification of the agreed to price. Japanese law exists in a world of context existing at the time of the wrong or at the time of decision and not necessarily at the time of the establishment of relations. What the Japanese judge is attempting to do is to fit the changed circumstance and the facts together in a way that leads to a "correct" determination. This is a function not terribly dissimilar to the function of the Tokugawa magistrate. It is a function very different from the function of the common law judge.

Efforts are underway in Japan to bring more practicing lawyers onto the Bench. These efforts are complicated by the civil service nature of the bureaucracy. New judges—newly appointed out of the Legal Research and Training Institute—are quite subordinate to older judges. The first 10 years are considered a probationary training period and during this time salaries are accordingly lower than others in the civil service who have been in the service longer. During this 10-year probationary period it is difficult for a judge to leave the Bench to become a bengoshi. The judge is NOT a bengoshi and thus when he/she leaves the Bench the judge must apply for bengoshi status. A judge who has not completed the 10-year probationary period may find it difficult to become a bengoshi immediately. Bengoshi with more than 10-years experience need not be treated as "assistant judges" during their first 10-year assignment. However the craft of judging is different from the craft of advocating. The bengoshi turned judge needs to be trained as a judge during the first 10-year appointment. Since a judge cannot be both a judge and a bengoshi at the same time,[75] a bengoshi who elects to become a judge must give up both a lucrative profession[76] and bengoshi status.[77] But if the new judge finds that service on the Bench is not to his/her liking there may be difficulties in returning to bengoshi status and certainly there will be difficulty in rebuilding a law practice. An additional difficulty is how to deal with the lawyer's practice and ethical as well as financial questions implicated when the lawyer leaves the practice and enters the judiciary.

In the spring of 2004 the Cabinet submitted a bill to the Diet (passed June 11, 2004) that would permit young judges, during their 10-year training assignment, to work for private attorneys for a period of two and in some cases three years. While working in the bengoshi office the judge would retain status as a government employee and the bengoshi would be prohibited from taking advantage of the fact that a government employee is on the staff. After the two-year period the judge would return to the Judicial Branch.[78] The intent of the law would seem to be to give young judges training experience as practical lawyers and attempt to

---

75 The Lawyers Law Article 30 states that with certain exceptions (Prime Minister, elected officials and some senior appointed positions) a lawyer may not assume any paid public position.

76 See, Curtis J. Milhaupt and Mark D. West, Law's Dominion and the Market for Legal Elites in Japan, 34 Law & Policy in International Business 451, 477-480 (2003) for a discussion of lawyer compensation in Japan.

77 As early as 1976 Professor Noda reported that the difference in earnings between bengoshi and judges was part of the difficulty in recruiting bengoshi to become judges. Yosiyuki Noda (translated by Anthony H. Angelo) INTRODUCTION TO JAPANESE LAW (University of Tokyo Press, 1976) 155.

78 The provisions of the bill are to come into effect within one year of passage on a date to be determined by Cabinet Order. This bill was passed at the close of the Diet's spring session in June 2004.

bridge the gap between the Bench and the Bar. Under the bill young prosecutors could also work for bengoshi during their initial training period of employment after which they would return to the Ministry of Justice. The 2004 initiative seeks to equalize the lending of judges to the Executive Branch with the lending of judges to the private Bar and may be used to justify the practice of sending judges to work in the Executive Branch. Of course allowing judges to experience private practice has none of the separation of powers or checks and balances defects that are inherent in Judicial Branch employees working for a coordinate branch. Young judges just out of the Legal Research and Training Institute are unlikely to get the kind of experience that a bengoshi who has made a career in the private sector will experience.

To the extent that the parties to litigation cannot resolve their dispute by compromise and settlement, the judge will be forced to render a decision. The writing of the decision is a matter for the judge as there are no law clerks to assist through drafting a decision on the basis of points told to them by the judge. The decision is a public document and as the "face of the court" in resolving the matter should be reasoned and explain why and how the judge reached the determination. This is a time-consuming process. In cases that are followed by the press it can be expected that an active free press will pick up, parse and criticize the decision and its reasoning. Moreover, if the case involves a broad policy issue, the reasoned decision may lead the government to change its posture on a matter. This is true even if the government wins on a technical point but the judge nonetheless undertakes to discuss the issue in dicta. Accordingly the decision-writing phase of the case may take some time. The court must advise the parties (and hence the public will know in cases of public notoriety) of the date on which the decision will issue. The decision itself must be rendered in open court.

4) The Function of the Legal System

The function of the legal system may be viewed from two different perspectives: a) that of the litigant and b) that of the society as represented by the governing elite. From the perspective of the litigant, Americans are apt to think of the system as a means of asserting their rights and as a system designed to provide monetary damages for alleged wrongs. From a societal perspective the system may be seen as a means of enforcing the law by "deputizing" the public as private attorneys general to bring civil law breakers to justice through the payment of damages and if need be punitive damages. It may also be seen as a system that checks the power of government by making administrative determinations subject to court review. Americans also tend to see the system as a means of asserting political positions in opposition to the government and perhaps even as a means of embarrassing the political parties, especially the party in power through suing its elected representatives. These are in fact the traditional functions that the legal system in the United States sees itself as performing and thus there is very much a merger in perspective of the litigant and the society.

The situation is different from the perspective of the Japanese litigant. Most litigants do not run to the legal system as an initial step to receive what is viewed as compensation for a wrong. Rather, because of the ready availability of alternative methods of seeking compensation litigation is not seen as the favored alternative. Indeed, many prospective plaintiffs may see themselves as acting selfishly by bringing litigation. After all, litigation deals with my rights and me and my right to be paid compensation instead of dealing with the totality of the situation. For example, an employee suing an employer is not considering the employer's position. The suing employee does not take account of the reality that litigation may result in an injury to the company's reputation. Such injury may in turn cause the company to lose sales and this may adversely affect other employees or potential future hires by the company. An employee who brings a Complaint to the private resolution arm of the Ministry of Labor keeps the matter quiet and out of the public arena thus acting in the interest of both employee and employer. The matter is no longer a selfish act but an act that is communal in nature in that it respects the rights of the whole company community of which the employee is a part. Many potential plaintiffs may refuse to sue because they do not want to be seen as selfish or because they do not want to hurt other employees or even the offending company. Only when the employer has refused to deal with the matter reasonably—only when the employee has no place else to go—only then is litigation an act that while still selfish may be the only alternative.

From a societal prospective, the governing elite in Japan historically has not seen the litigation system as performing a law enforcement function. Law enforcement is a matter for the government bureaucracy, not for a posse of ordinary citizens bringing litigation to activist judges who are required to create law to deal with the issues presented to them which have not been the subject of legislative action. (This view has recently come under attack.[79] However, the bureaucracy has yet to adopt a change in its view.) Similarly, the system in Japan has not been historically viewed as a means of checking administrative action or of containing the activities of bureaucrats. The prewar Administrative Court was not designed to review or check governmental activities and the Occupation reforms did not significantly change the deference that the Japanese legal system gave (and continues to give) to Executive or Legislative action.

Many matters that go to litigation in the United States do not involve actual monetary damages, but the American legal system monetarizes injury because that is the only way the legal system can deal with the matter. For example, libel is a matter of reputation, not necessarily a matter of money. Many plaintiffs in libel or slander actions may be satisfied with $1 damages, as the judgment declares that the statement was false and the reputation of the plaintiff is restored. Similarly, many actions that might form the basis for a suit in Japan might be resolved ami-

79 Curtis J. Milhaupt and Mark D. West, Law's Dominion and the Market for Legal Elites in Japan, 34 Law & Policy in International Business 451 (2003).

cably if the potential defendant would simply apologize in a sincere manner for its conduct. Apology or the concomitant failure to apologize may be a reason for litigation in Japan. The role of apology in Japanese society is very different from the role of apology in the United States. And, the legal effect of apology in Japan is different from apology in the United States. Whereas American insurance companies advise their clients to never apologize if they are in an auto accident, a Japanese driver at fault is well advised to immediately apologize. Even if the parties cannot ultimately agree to the amount of damages that are appropriate, it may be possible to avoid litigation because of the apology as the potential plaintiff will likely accept less—certainly less in the way of monetary damages for physical injury. The potential plaintiff will likely be more willing to accept the amount suggested in mediation, if the other driver is seen as sincerely apologetic. On the other hand failure to apologize may be the catalyst for litigation.

Apology in Japan has a greater significance than in the United States,[80] and the law gives apology a "privileged" status that is not available in the United States. In America an apology is viewed as a statement against interest and an acknowledgment of wrong. Thus, apology is in the nature of a confession and may be introduced in evidence against the interest of the apologizing party. The Japanese view of apology is subtler. One can be seen as apologizing without necessarily admitting wrongdoing. Thus if we are in an accident I can apologize to you showing sincere regret over the incident, showing sincere regret over the injury to you or your vehicle, and at the same time the apology will not be considered as demonstrating that I am admitting to doing wrong. By taking the "legal admission" connotation out of apology, Japanese law makes it possible to use apology as a lubricant to smooth out damaged feelings, to take the "heat" out of the situation and to allow the parties to attempt to recreate a harmonious situation out of a potentially hostile situation. A sincere apology carries with it the understanding that the party making the apology is accepting not the concept of wrongdoing but the concept of accepting what that party should be doing under the circumstances. The sincere apology is acceptance of the role that one is supposed to play in the circumstance presented. When a sincere apology is accompanied by a willingness to make a payment it will be go a long way to resolving an issue and can forestall and obviate the need for litigation. Such payment need not be compensation for the injury or an acknowledgment that the paying party is in the wrong. Payment can be made out of kindness and out of recognition that socially acceptable behavior commands payment in recognition of the situation.

80 For a discussion of the role of apology in Japan see, Hiroshi Wagatsuma and Arthur Rosett, The Implications of Apology: Law and Culture in Japan and the United States, 20 Law & Society Review 461 (1986); see also Alexander M. Vesey, Entering the Temple Priests, Peasants and Village Contention in Tokugawa Japan, Japanese Journal of Religious Studies 2001 at 293-328 for a discussion of the role of apology in the context of Tokugawa village conflict where the peasant in conflict with village authority sought the assistance of local temples. On the web at *www.nanzen-u.ac.jp/SHUBUNKEN/publications/jjrs.pdf/612.pdf*.

This soothing effect of apology is a component of criminal law as well as civil law. One factor to be considered by the prosecutor in determining whether to suspend prosecution or if prosecution is undertaken in determining a sentencing recommendation, is whether the accused has made a payment to the victim. The prosecutor will consider whether the victim has agreed that prosecution is not appropriate or if appropriate that a suspended sentence or a light sentence is appropriate. What might be considered an illegal payment in the United States—a payment by an accused to the crime victim in order to assuage the victim's feelings and have the victim write a letter forgiving the accused and recommending against legal action—is considered as appropriate in Japan. Indeed, absent such action the accused can be viewed as unrepentant and can suffer greatly. Similarly in the civil law arena apology is freely given without concern that it will be used as a stick to later hit the apologizing party.

The flip side of the utility of apology is that failure to apologize can lead to litigation. Failure to apologize discloses that the other party takes no responsibility for the event that occurred and has no feelings for the suffering of the victim. Taking of responsibility is another attribute of Japanese society as it affects law in a way that is different from the United States. In the United States it is common for politicians and other leaders to publicly announce that they "take full responsibility" for an action either of their own or by their staff. Yet such *mea culpa* is rarely followed by an action that accompanies such public statement. In Japan to take responsibility for an act is to do an act showing that responsibility is in fact taken. Taking responsibility has consequences, and absent the consequence there is no taking of responsibility. Thus, after an air crash the President of the Airline Company may take responsibility for the accident by resigning from his position. Or a lower level executive may take responsibility by agreeing to be placed on leave without pay for a period or accepting a demotion. Responsibility is seen as flowing to the top so that the airline President takes responsibility even though he had nothing to do with the accident and even though it may ultimately be shown that the accident was caused by events outside his or anyone's control. The fact that the President has taken responsibility and has resigned is not an admission against the interest of the company and in litigation is not evidence against the company. What taking responsibility may do is to tell the families of the victims that the company is sorry for the accident, is understanding of their pain, and the company shows this by its Chief Executive taking responsibility by himself bearing consequences for the event. But that is not an admission of legal wrongdoing. It may however obviate the need of the families to file a lawsuit. Again, the flip side is that the failure of the President of the company to take responsibility by resigning may lead to litigation. The best way to insure that litigation will follow is for the President to deny any responsibility or to say he takes responsibility but to do nothing to show that the taking of responsibility had consequences for him personally.

The *Minamata disease* litigation is a good illustration of how these various factors run together. When the disease was first discovered (it showed up in cats before it showed up in people), the victims and their families tried to keep the existence of the disease a secret out of shame. There was no immediate outcry for litigation. When it appeared that the disease was related to the effluent from the manufacturing plant in the community, demands for compensation were made to the company. When the company refused, the victims sought mediation through local government officials. Later, prefecture officials were brought in as conciliators. An agreement was reached in which the company paid the victims a relatively small sum to recognize the difficulties suffered by the victims but not out of legal responsibility. Only after the link was made clear between the mercury run off from the plant and the disease—*and when the company refused to acknowledge its responsibility*—did a group of victims sue. To many of the plaintiffs, the failure of the company to recognize its responsibility and to take responsibility for the acts that caused injury to the victims was the basis for the decision to sue. Many victims refused to join in the litigation as they saw litigation as a selfish act seeking money when the real issue was the responsibility of the company for the injury to the victims. Had the company accepted responsibility and apologized it likely could have avoided litigation and likely would have been able to resolve the matter with a lower payment than was ultimately required.[81]

The need for apology in Japan was recently highlighted in the incident involving the accidental sinking of the Ehime Maru by an American submarine. Families of the Japanese victims could not understand why the Commander of the sub did not immediately take responsibility and apologize for the incident. The fact that the Commander did in fact eventually apologize even before the completion of the military proceedings against him likely upset his American lawyers and while it had a moderating effect on feelings in Japan it was seen as "too little too late." Bridgestone's Japanese executive's apology to American customers in connection with the failure of tires on certain Ford vehicles, at a time when Bridgestone and Ford were being sued by families of victims was obviously taken out of deep cultural values and likely in opposition to the advice of American lawyers. Such apology in the United States likely had little or no or perhaps even a negative effect on Bridgestone in negotiations with American plaintiffs—on the other hand it would have had a positive effect on negotiations in Japan. Indeed in some Japanese cases the giving of an apology by the company President is made a condition of settlement.

The use of the judicial system as a means of compelling the defendant to acknowledge responsibility or at least to have the judiciary acknowledge the justice of plaintiff's cause is part of the reason for the litigation undertaken in Japanese courts by the victims of Japan's Second World War military. These victims, such as "comfort women" or forced laborers from countries who have not yet accepted that Japan has sincerely apologized for the actions of its government and military during the war, tend to seek what are by American standards minimal damages for the injury suf-

81 See, Robert C. Christopher, THE JAPANESE MIND 166 (Simon & Schuster 1983).

fered. It seems clear that the motivation behind these suits is a psychological one—the need to have the allegedly offending party apologize sincerely and take responsibility for its acts. Likewise, Japanese defense in these cases is unlikely to be influenced by financial concerns. Rather, defense is designed to defend the honor of former soldiers, previous governments and the State in general.

Another reason why, from the plaintiff's perspective, the litigation system is not seen as a place for immediate financial relief is that damages in civil cases in Japan are notoriously low. (In the rare cases where prosecution has been undertaken but the defendant is found not guilty and thus is entitled to damages from the State the damages are also quite low). Punitive damages are not only not permitted in Japan, but they are considered as against public policy, and foreign punitive awards are not given comity in Japanese courts.[82] Actual damages awarded by the courts can take into account pain and suffering but they do not provide the "windfalls" that American juries give injured parties. Japanese judges decide on the amount of damages, and through the judicial Secretariat the judges have a reasonably good idea of what other judges are awarding for similar cases. Training sessions with the Secretariat keep judges up to date on the "going rate" for certain injuries. Damages are not seen in Japan as a tool to be used to get lawbreakers to change their ways just as litigation is not seen as a device to enforce the law. In tort cases, a winning plaintiff is entitled to include actual legal fees as a part of injury and thus to recover reasonable fees but not in excess of actual fees paid. In reality the amount of legal fees allowed in tort cases as part of the damage to the plaintiff are substantially less than legal fees actually paid.

Low damage awards became an issue in the relations between the United States and Japan in connection with American claims that patent infringement awards in Japan failed to adequately compensate American companies whose intellectual property rights were abused by Japanese firms. After a study group in Japan concluded that Japan's intellectual property laws inhibited invention in Japan (in part because of low damage awards leading to inadequate protection of inventors) the courts began to increase the size of infringement awards. This brought the court and damages in line with government policy to support invention in Japan. In 1998 the Patent Law was amended to give courts greater authority to award significant damages, although a proposal of the Patent Office to permit the award of treble damages was rejected. A 1999 amendment of the law extended the damage provisions by enabling the court to appoint appraisers who could assist in determining the amount of damages and in giving the court a greater discretion in determining the amount to be awarded. (The Patent Law provisions are incorporated into the Trademark Law and thus trademark infringement cases adopt the same

82 Case No. 1993 (O) No. 1762 (Sup. Ct. Petty Bench, 7/11/97) available in English through the web site of the Supreme Court of Japan. See also, Dan Fenno Henderson, Comparative Law in the Japanese Courts: Punitive Damages, 24 Law in Japan 98 (1991).

court appraiser damage provisions as the Patent Law.)[83] The Supreme Court of Japan in 2000 worked a change in the relationship between the court procedure and the procedures at the Japan Patent Office when an alleged infringer argued that the patent involved was invalid. As a general rule, questions of patent invalidity are for the Japan Patent Office to determine and not for the courts. Thus, when invalidity was raised, the matter was referred to the JPO and the litigation suspended. This resulted in delay in the judicial procedure while the JPO handled the administrative case. In 2000 the Supreme Court held that the court could handle the validity question when validity is clear. By making issues of invalidity a justiciable question in many cases, judicial efficiency was enhanced resulting in speeding up the handling of infringement cases.[84]

Other changes were made in the court system to permit patent cases to be tried on a fast track by courts with expert knowledge of patent matters. The High Court in Tokyo was given greater responsibility for handling appeals of Patent cases. Under a bill submitted to the Diet in the spring of 2004, a special Intellectual Property High Court will be established within the Tokyo High Court.[85] This court will have specialist judges designated by the Supreme Court to deal with patent, software program and copyright issues. (The new court is scheduled to start work in April of 2005.)[86] The court is modeled after the United States Court of Appeals for the Federal Circuit, the only United States Circuit Court with special subject matter jurisdiction rather than a broad geographic jurisdiction.[87] Not only are damages as a rule inadequately low in Japan but also collection of judgments is difficult. Indeed, the Law Reform Council specifically highlighted the difficulty of collection of judgments as an inhibiting factor in making the Rule of Law a more viable concept in Japan.[88]

83 See, Trademark Law, Law No. 127 of 1959 as amended by Law No. 220 of 12/22/99 effective 1/6/01, Article 39.

84 For a discussion of new steps being taken by Japan to strengthen its patent system, including a discussion of the effect of the 2000 Supreme Court case see, Kosaku Tamura, Japan Making Strategic Program for the Creation, Protection and Exploitation of Intellectual Property: Review of the Japanese Patent System (Center for Advanced Study and Research on Intellectual Property "CASRIP" University of Washington School of Law) CASRIP Newsletter Autumn 2003 on the web at *www.law.washington.edu/casrip/newsletter/newshome.html*

85 This bill was passed at the close of the Diet's spring session on June 11, 2004.

86 Diet Enacts Judicial Reform Laws, Japan Times on Line, June 12, 2004.

87 For a discussion of the new court see, Kosaku Tamura, Japan Making Strategic Program for the Creation, Protection and Exploitation of Intellectual Property: Review of the Japanese Patent System (Center for Advanced Study and Research on Intellectual Property "CASRIP" University of Washington School of Law) CASRIP Newsletter Autumn 2003 on the web at *www.law.washington.edu/casrip/newsletter/newshome.html*

88 Recommendations of the Justice System Reform Council: For a Justice System to Support Japan in the 21st Century, 6/12/01 on the web at *www.kantei.go.jp/foreign/policy/sihou/singikai/990612_e.html*

From the plaintiff's perspective the judicial system's function is seen more in terms of psychological factors than as a monetary damages system. It is seen as a mechanism to both require the unrepentant defendant to accept and acknowledge responsibility for its acts and as a mechanism whereby the official arm of the government (the judiciary) acknowledges the justice of the plaintiff's cause. Of course, where all else fails and money is at stake, the judicial system may be the only place to go for relief—inadequate though it may be.

From the government's point of view—and this includes the judiciary itself—the function of the judicial system is similarly a limited function. Whereas in the United States one major function of the judicial system is to enforce the law, in Japan law enforcement is seen as an executive/bureaucratic function and not a judicial function.[89] Thus, whereas the American system is characterized by low filing fees to make litigation cheap and access to the courts easy, the Japanese system is characterized by high filing fees making access both expensive and difficult. Whereas in the United States notice of claim pleadings include suing on the basis of "information and belief," in Japan fact pleading requires that the plaintiff have at least a *prima facia* case before the court will accept the Complaint. Whereas in the United States there are an excessive number of lawyers seeking clients making it relatively cheap for a plaintiff to sue (because of the availability of a contingent fee system), in Japan there are few lawyers making access to legal talent difficult and expensive for a potential plaintiff. Whereas in the United States there are a large number of trial judges available to try cases at various levels, local, State and Federal, in Japan the size of the judiciary is small. In addition, many judges are not available to try cases either because they are doing work that in the United States would be performed by law clerks or are on loan to the Executive Branch or are assigned to the Secretariat and are administering the judicial bureaucracy. Shortage of judges makes for greater difficulty in getting relief from the Judicial Branch. Whereas in the United States easy discovery rules make it easy for a plaintiff to obtain evidence to support its case, in Japan there are no effective discovery rules. In Japan restrictions on evidence gathering through broad use of privileges and exceptions to document discovery provisions make discovery of facts difficult even after litigation is started.

One of the greatest shortcomings of the system is its relative unavailability to parties claiming excess of power abuses by the Executive. Thus, while the Occupation thought that its reforms of the judicial and administrative system would result in judicial review of government administrative actions, the reality is that few administrative actions are actually subject to court review. Not only procedural roadblocks but also substantive rules such as the German law concept of "free discretion" whereby judicial officers defer to administrative officials when either

89 For a general discussion of the differences in function of the United States and Japanese civil justice systems see, Carl F. Goodman, The Somewhat Less Reluctant Litigant: Japan's Changing Views Towards Civil Litigation, 32 Law and Policy in International Business 769 (2001).

policy questions or technical issues are involved restrict review of official action. Perhaps Japanese bureaucrat judges do not see it as their function to review the actions of administrative bureaucratic officials. Or perhaps service in Executive Departments by Japanese judges makes those judges too accommodating to the Executive Branch. In any event, this is an area where the judicial reform Council has called for action to permit greater use of judicial review. Part of the government's 2004 spring initiative includes a bill to amend the Administrative Case Litigation Law. The bill would loosen the present restrictions on standing but would retain the requirement that the plaintiff suffer a "legal" injury. The bill would contain other reforms discussed in Chapter 12. The bill was passed at the close of the Diet's spring 2004 session on June 9, 2004. Whether that reform will lead to great availability of judicial review of administrative action remains to be seen.

Whether access to the judiciary is made difficult as part of a governmental policy to favor Japanese business (as suggested by at least one commentator)[90] or whether the difficulties of access are founded on a governmental belief that the agenda of society and the enforcement of laws should be left to the bureaucracy[91] or whether difficulties of access are designed to perpetuate the myth of harmony in Japan, a myth that would be shattered by high litigation rates showing the lack of harmony, or whether it is simply a perpetuation of the historic function of the Judicial Branch, the reality is that the system is not seen as performing the issue resolution, monetary damage function that the American system is seen as performing. And, as procedure follows function so the Code of Civil Procedure does not favor plaintiffs over defendants in either initiation of litigation, the process of litigation, the computation of actual damages or the execution of judgments.

The views of potential litigants, the governing elite and the judicial system as to the proper role of litigation in Japan are complimentary and self-supporting. The system's limited view of litigation leads to difficulties for plaintiffs, which in turn support the potential litigant's view that litigation is not the appropriate mechanism to resolve disputes, which in turn supports the bureaucracy's view that it is the appropriate vehicle to enforce laws in Japan. Potential plaintiffs' views that litigation is an inappropriate means for resolving disputes then supports the view (shared by the administrative and judicial bureaucracy) that most Japanese do not want to use litigation but rather prefer alternative dispute mechanisms to resolve disputes. In the end potential litigants, the judiciary and the administrators support a system that makes it difficult for plaintiffs to succeed and that measures as success a damage award that in the United States would be viewed as a plaintiff failure.

90 Sato Yasunobu, Cultural Conflict in Dispute Processing Under Globalization: International Cooperation for Legal Aid, *http://www.gsid.nagoya-u.ac.jp*.

91 See, Frank K. Upham, LAW AND SOCIAL CHANGE IN POSTWAR JAPAN (Harvard University Press, 1987).

5) The Perception that the Legal System Fails to Provide Timely Relief[92]

There is a general perception that the Japanese legal system fails to provide timely relief to plaintiffs. This belief is grounded both in fact and in fiction. The fact is that the civil legal system has been notorious for its failure to act quickly. Japanese newspapers refer to civil trials as proceeding at a snail's pace. News reports of decisions in famous cases show that such cases have been pending in the court system for several years. But it is also the fact that in recent years the judges in Japan have made strenuous efforts to reduce the time it takes for a case to move from filing to judgment—or at least to resolution. This difference of judgment and resolution is important as most cases in Japan are not brought to final judgment but are mediated or conciliated by the court (either formally or informally) and are resolved by settlement. And, in a high number of cases the defendant defaults and a judgment by default is entered. It is estimated that as many as 40% of cases are default cases.[93]

Beginning about a decade ago, the judicial system (especially the Tokyo District Court) began to utilize a system in which the court would hold informal preparatory meetings with counsel and/or the parties. These informal meetings had no basis in the Code of Civil Procedure but were based on German law reforms and were utilized in an effort to try to move litigation faster. To do so, the procedure (sometimes referred to as an Oral Argument with Settlement)[94] combined the usual preliminary procedures needed to expedite a case, such as part of the clarification process that made determinations regarding the admissibility of evidence and the definition of issues to be tried, with settlement negotiations. Although utilized to help narrow the issues to be tried, in reality the process was a screen behind which the court and parties could informally meet in order to get the settlement negotiation process initiated at an early stage in the litigation. The effect of this procedure was to speed up resolution and disposal of cases, primarily by bringing about settlements at an earlier stage of litigation than had previously been the case.

While recognized as a useful device to speed up litigation, the procedure had no "legal" basis and its use was questionable, as the 1920s reform of the Code had adopted the principle of Oral Argument that required public hearings in cases. When the Code of Civil Procedure was amended in 1996 (effective 1998) this

---

92 The charts contained herein are republished from and this section is based on Carl F. Goodman, Japan's New Civil Procedure Code: Has it Fostered a Rule of Law Dispute Resolution Mechanism, 29 Brooklyn Journal of International Law 511 (2004). The Brooklyn Journal of International Law has given permission for the use and copying of this material.

93 Masafumi Kodama & Jay Tyndall, Kitahama Law Office, on the web at *www.Masafumi Kodama & Jay Tyndall, Kitahama.or.jp/English/litigatn.htm* at page 6 of 14 (8/1/2000).

94 For a discussion of the history of the Preparation for Oral Argument procedure pre-Code and the Code's adoption of the procedure in Articles 168-174 see, Shozo Ota, Reform of the Civil Procedure of Japan, 49 American Journal of Comparative Law 561 (2001); Koichi Miki, Roles of Judges and Attorneys under the Non-Sanction Scheme in Japanese Civil Procedure, talk delivered at Conference on Multiple Roles and Interaction of Judges and Attorneys in Modern Civil Litigation at Chu-o University, Tokyo 6/1/03.

procedure was given a legal foundation in Articles 168 through 174 (discussed in more detail infra.) Although these articles say nothing about settlement, the real objective of the Preparation for Oral Argument procedure is to permit the parties and the court to discuss settlement out of the public light of an open public Oral Argument. This new procedure gives a legal basis to the experimental procedure that had a positive effect on speeding up resolution of cases. The consequence has been that the accelerated handling of cases experienced under the Oral Argument with Settlement procedure has been even further accelerated under the new Code. Thus, while in 1992 the average time to dispose of cases in the District Court was 10.9 months, in 2001 the time had dropped to only 8.5 months. A chart showing the decline in processing time of all cases in the District Court from 1992 to 2001 follows. Special notice should be taken of the sharp decline in months required for disposition for cases beginning in 1998, the year the new Code became effective:

Average Number of Months from Filing of Complaint to Disposition—District court

Year	All Cases Filed
1992	—
1993	10.1
1994	9.8
1995	10.1
1996	10.2
1997	10.0
1998	9.3
1999	9.2
2000	8.8
2001	8.5

When it is considered that even default judgment cases require approximately two-months of handling time, the numbers indicate that for the average case the judicial remedy is not inordinately delayed.

Even when default judgment cases are factored out, the average time for disposing of cases is not inordinately long. Thus, in cases where the testimony of two or more witnesses is taken [clearly default judgment cases have been factored out as there is no need to take testimony in a default judgment case], the average time from filing to disposition has dropped from 21.8 months in 1992 to 19.2 months in

2001. A chart showing the decline in processing time of cases involving two or more witnesses from 1992 to 2001 follows:

Average Number of Months from Filing of Complaint to Disposition—District court	
Cases Involving Testimony of Two or More Witnesses	**Year**
21.8	1992
21.2	1993
20.9	1994
21.1	1995
21.3	1996
20.8	1997
20.8	1998
20.5	1999
19.7	2000
19.2	2001

Although the average case is disposed of quickly, cases that are neither settled nor resolved through default judgment take a longer time for resolution:

Percentage of Judgment Cases Decided in One and Two Years		
Year	**Percentage of Cases Decided After One Year**	**Percentage of Cases Decided After Two Years**
1996	15.1	13.1
1997	15.0	13.4
1998	14.2	12.8
1999	14.4	13.3
2000	14.4	14.0
2001	14.8	14.7
2002	15.4	14.7

What these figures disclose is that it takes about as much time today to resolve a case that goes through trial to judgment as it did before the new Code and the New Preparation for Oral Argument Procedure came into effect. The new procedure does not appear to speed up cases that are not settled. And, when cases that are tried to judgment are appealed, the time for ultimate resolution is further extended:

Judgment Cases Appealed to High Court Number and Percentage of Cases Resolved in One, Two and Three Years				
Year	Total Cases Appealed	One Year (Number / %)	Two Years (Number / %)	Three Years (Number / %)
1996	8259	3402/41.2	1764/21.4	304/3.7
1997	8588	3554/41.4	1743/20.3	344/4.0
1998	9024	3531/39.1	1784/19.7	412/4.6
1999	9376	3338/35.6	1388/14.8	348/3.7
2000	9812	3114/31.7	1357/13.8	314/3.2
2001	9724	2955/30.4	1157/11.9	259/2.7
2002	9817	2973/30.3	1043/10.6	181/1.8

Although the average time to dispose of an average case at the District Court level is now only 8.5 months and the average time to dispose of a case at the first stage appeal level is extended by only 7.9 months, hotly contested cases take a substantially longer time to be resolved.

The number of cases appealed to the Supreme Court is steadily rising:

Filed Cases				Location of Termination of Decision		
Year	Appeal / Cert.		Cert. Granted	Appeal	Cert. Denied	Cert. Granted
1997	2741	—	—	3062	—	—
1998	2542	768	1	3040	370	0
1999	2160	1770	12	2389	1528	11
2000	2418	2106	26	2410	1820	19
2001	2323	2314	53	2298	2089	40

The time to ultimate resolution remains a problem for potential plaintiffs who have reason to believe that their adversary will litigate the case to final judgment.

Even though the "average" time to dispose of cases is steadily declining, the public's perception is that cases are as slow to be resolved today as was true in the past. Part of this perception is due to the fact that news reports of litigation deal with older cases. This is to be expected as news reports would not likely deal with cases that are settled early in the process. News reports are likely to deal with cases that are either tried to judgment or that are resolved just before judgment when the judge has indicated what the likely disposition will be if a judgment decision has to be entered. And, because many newsworthy cases are appealed and the appeal process takes additional time, by the time the news report reaches the public the case is quite old. From the litigant's point of view, the reality is that cases move faster than in the past if, but only if, there is a settlement of the case. If the case goes all the way through trial to judgment and then on to appeal the process remains slow and quite time consuming.[95]

6) The Failure of the Judicial System to Provide a Sanctions Regime to Aid in the Processing of Cases

American lawyers are familiar with a system where the judge plays less of a role than in the Japanese system. Yet the role played by the judge is powerful when the judge utilizes authority to move procedures forward. The American judge has the power to summarily punish a litigant or party for a contempt of court committed in the presence of the court. The American judge in ruling on discovery and other pretrial motions can Order a party to do something and failure of the party to obey the court's Order is contempt of the court. Such contempt can be dealt with by the court through fine, refusal to permit a party to submit evidence on an issue or even the sanction of dismissal of claims or defenses. In addition to the judge's inherent power to punish a party for failure to obey a court order (an inherent power based on the judge's equity power to punish contempt, and failure to obey an Order of the court displays a contempt for the court and its Order) the Federal Rules of Civil Procedure specifically grant the trial judge authority to sanction a party for failure to make discovery or failure to obey discovery Orders. The judge's authority to punish for failure to obey the court Order extends beyond parties to witnesses. Thus a third-person witness who refuses to produce documents when ordered by the court may be punished for contempt and may even be placed in prison until it purges itself of the contempt by making production. The judge's authority to sanction extends beyond merely sanctioning for failure to obey court Orders. Conduct in litigation that is reprehensible and is an abuse of the judicial system can lead to sanction. Thus, a court recently dismissed a 13-year-old case seeking royalty payments from Walt Disney Company in connection with "Winnie the Pooh" products after finding that there had been such abuse based on such matters as alteration of and cover up of conduct related to potential theft of

95 In April of 2004 the Supreme Court finally disposed of litigation brought by miners who contracted pneumoconiosis disease from working in mines. The court found both the mining company and the government responsible for the miner's health problems and ordered damages be paid to the miners. The case had been started in 1985, the District Court opinion was handed down in 1995, the High Court opinion in 2001 and the Supreme Court had the case for almost 3 years. By the time the decision was handed down most of the plaintiffs had died. Top Court Ends Pneumoconiosis Case, State, Mining Firm Ordered to Pay Sickened Workers, Japan Times on Line 4/28/04.

documents.[96] A system that utilizes sanctions to punish parties who fail to make discovery or otherwise follow procedural rules serves to cause parties and third persons to follow both the procedural rules and the Orders of the judge.

Japan's civil procedure is not based on a sanctions philosophy. Rather, it is based on the belief and hope that the parties and third persons will follow the rules and obey court direction or suggestion. Where a party is involved the court has a certain power by virtue of the fact that it is the ultimate decision-maker and may punish the recalcitrant party in its ultimate ruling. However, the system is not based on sanction.

Even where sanctions do exist they are weak and rarely invoked. For example, the new Code seeks to speed up the Oral Argument (Plenary Hearing) in a case by having the parties appear for Preliminary Oral Argument. The purpose of this preliminary stage (a part of the Oral Argument as distinguished from and not to be confused with the Preparation for Oral Argument) is to try to better define the issues to be tried. The rationale behind the procedure (Articles 164-167) is to get the parties to submit their arguments and theories early in the procedure rather than having the arguments and theories change as the case moves along. To the extent the plaintiff's case changes as the case advances, the defendant is chasing a moving target and the case will undoubtedly get more complicated and take more time. The same is true if the grounds for defense are continually in flux and subject to change. Through this procedure it was hoped that the theories, arguments and witnesses and other evidence could be identified early in the process and then the Oral Hearing (Plenary Hearing) could be held with a clear roadmap of the case. Such a procedure in the United States would result in a pretrial Order setting forth the arguments and contentions of the parties and the witnesses and evidence each proposes to introduce. If a party seeks to raise an argument or contention not contained in the pretrial Order the court will hold that it is precluded from doing so. In a sense, a party must "speak now or forever hold your peace." But in Japan, the Code of Civil Procedure contains no such preclusion provision. Rather, the Code provides merely that the person raising new issues must explain to the opposition why it did not raise those issues prior to the conclusion of the Preliminary Procedure. In theory the Japanese judge may have authority to reject the party's explanation and preclude the argument. In realty the court will not preclude. This follows as the judge is concerned about substantive justice, has a paternalistic attitude towards parties and counsel, is responsible for making a "correct" decision under which the party who should win does win and does not wish to punish the party for errors of counsel in failing to raise issues at the proper time. In essence there is no sanction for failure to follow the mandate of the Preliminary Procedure.

Similarly, where a non-party witness has refused to produce a document ordered by the court to be produced, the sanction is limited to a non-penal fine of 200,000yen (or the equivalent of $2,000 at a 100yen=$1 ratio).[97] In substantial cases such a minimal fine may not have the effect of getting documents produced.

96 See, Laura M. Holson, After 13 Years Judge Dismisses Case on Pooh Bear Royalties, New York Times 3/30/2004.

97 CCP Article 225.

For example a supplier may be quite prepared to pay 200,000yen rather than endanger a relationship with a major customer. And, the new Inquiry Process (to be discussed in greater length in Chapter 7 C) designed to replicate the American Interrogatory procedure relies entirely on the good faith of parties and counsel in producing answers. As a consequence the procedure has proven to be virtually worthless.

The lack of sanctions in the Japanese civil procedure regime is an anomaly. In the United States the judge is a relatively minor player in the litigation but has great power and authority to enforce her decrees; in Japan the judge is a major player in the litigation but has limited authority and power to enforce her decrees. This lack of power by the Japanese judge may be explained in several ways. For one thing neither judges nor lawyers want the judges to possess strong sanctioning power. The lawyer does not want to be the possible subject of the court's sanction and further wishes to retain its independence of the judiciary. The court similarly does not wish to get involved in subsidiary matters but, rather, wants to focus on the substance of the case not procedural disputes. For the judge the concern of getting bogged down in procedural hassles that delay the case and impinge on an already tight calendar and overworked schedule is significant. Moreover, sanctions such as preclusion can result in a decision that does not work substantive justice. Just as the exclusionary rule in criminal cases may serve to let some guilty defendants go free and thus is little used by Japanese courts, so too an exclusionary rule based on preclusion may cause the wrong party in a civil case to win the case because of a technicality. In any event, American lawyers used to a system where failure to abide by a rule or statute or Order may result in severe sanction must rethink the situation when placed in a Japanese litigation environment.

7) Counsel and the Pro Se Litigant[98]

In the United States counsel does not represent many plaintiffs in small claims litigation. The amount at issue is small and the cost of a lawyer makes the retention of counsel uneconomic. The same is true in Japan for Summary Court proceedings. In Federal District Court and in State Court proceedings where the amount in issue may warrant it, counsel typically represents parties in the United States. In the United States corporate entities must (as a general rule) be represented by counsel and cannot appear (as they can in Japan) through a non-lawyer Director or Officer. Where parties in the United States appear without counsel (pro se) the court will exercise its authority to try to assure that failure to be represented does not lead to technical errors that can prejudice the claim or defense. Thus judges will be more liberal in interpreting Complaints; Answers and other filings made by pro se litigants.

98 The charts contained herein are republished from and this section is based on Carl F. Goodman, Japan's New Civil Procedure Code: Has it Fostered a Rule of Law Dispute Resolution Mechanism, 29 Brooklyn Journal of International Law 511 (2004). The Brooklyn Journal of International Law has given permission for the use and copying of this material.

In Japan the number and percentage of parties in litigation who are not represented is significantly higher than in the United States, and as noted earlier Japanese judges generally view their role as paternalistic, whether or not counsel represents a party. In more recent years the percentage of ordinary civil cases filed in the District Court where both sides are represented by counsel has been declining as the number of cases in which neither side is represented by counsel has increased. The data discloses:

First Instance District Court—Ordinary Civil Cases—% of cases				
Year	Both sides represented	Plaintiff only represented	Defendant only represented	Neither represented
1996	42.2	35.5	3.3	19
1997	42.5	35.1	3.3	19.1
1998	40.9	34.7	3.6	20.8
1999	41.2	34.0	4.0	20.7
2000	41.3	32.9	4.4	21.4
2001	39.4	34.8	4.7	21.1

At the appeal court level, whether it be an appeal from the Summary Court to the District Court or the District Court to the High Court, counsel are more in evidence. At the High Court both sides are represented in some 75% to 78% of cases. In the year 2001, 31.5% of all cases handled by the District Court as an appeals court involved at least one party not represented by counsel. Most appellants in such cases were represented (52%). A far larger percentage of respondents were not represented.

It is unclear whether parties are not represented because of the high costs of counsel or because of the unavailability of sufficient numbers of lawyers to represent them,[99] or whether parties see no need for representation because they are prepared to rely on the judge to protect their interest (or some combination of the above). What is clear is that because such a high percentage of litigants are not represented by counsel Japanese judges are confirmed in their view that they must adopt a paternalistic attitude towards litigants. Moreover, litigants without counsel cannot be expected to understand the intricacies of procedure (even though the new Code was written in more familiar Japanese to make it easier to understand) nor can they be expected to move a case along as quickly as professional counsel does. Pro se

99 Not only are there few lawyers in Japan compared to comparable economically developed societies but the lawyers who are available tend to congregate in Tokyo and Osaka and to a lesser degree in other population/industrial centers such as Nagoya. This makes counsel virtually unavailable in remote and rural parts of Japan. This unavailability of counsel poses a problem for civil litigants but may be a matter of liberty and freedom for criminal suspects located in remote areas. To try to deal with this problem, Bar Associations in Japan have tried (with some, but minimal, success) to open offices in remote areas to provide counsel in criminal cases.

litigants cannot be expected to engage in the sort of "adversary procedure" that trained lawyers are theoretically able to handle. In such situations it can be expected that cross-examination and even direct examination will be taken over by the court—and indeed the court may take over such examinations in cases where the parties are represented. Moreover, as first level appeal courts may take new evidence and hear new arguments not presented at the initial level trial, parties may feel free to handle the case themselves at initial trial knowing that if they lose counsel will be able to reopen issues and raise new issues on appeal. Appeal courts knowing that pro se litigants cannot be expected to professionally handle cases may be more willing to hear new arguments on appeal when the party was not represented below. Because of the willingness of appeal courts to hear new evidence and new issues, it has been suggested that the entire initial trial may be a kind of "discovery process."[100]

Unlike the United States where corporations are typically required to appear in court by counsel, in Japan corporations need not have bengoshi represent them in litigation. In Japan a corporation may appear in court represented by its Representative Director[101] or under the new style of management arrangement involving independent directors, committees and corporate officers, a Representative Executive Officer.[102] The Representative Director or Executive Officer need not, indeed because of regulations of the Bar prohibiting lawyers from working for corporations as full time employees (with some exceptions), cannot be a bengoshi. Naturally the Representative Executive Officer or Representative Director may engage counsel to represent the company.

Because lawyers are frequently not used in litigation, the authority of a lawyer to represent a party is not assumed. In the United States counsel's authority is assumed through counsel's signing of the Complaint or Answer document. In Japan counsel's authority to represent a party in litigation must be separately documented

---

100 Craig P. Wagnild, Civil Law Discovery in Japan: A Comparison of Japanese and U.S. Methods of Evidence Collection in Civil Litigation, 3 Asian-Pacific Law and Policy Journal 1, 18 (2002).

101 Where a corporation (or an Agricultural Cooperative) sues a Director, a statutory auditor also has authority to represent the company in the litigation. See Case No. 545 and 546 of 2002, 57 Minshu ___ (Sup. Ct. 12/16/03) available in English through the web site of the Supreme Court of Japan.

102 In Japan there are different classes of corporate directors. The Representative Director is at the top of the director ladder and has authority to bind the corporation. Most Japanese Boards are structured with at least two classes of Directors—Managing Directors (some of whom may be Representative Directors) and Directors (none of whom will be a Representative Director). Historically board members rose from the ranks of employees and most boards were composed of heads of departments or divisions of a company and were active employees supervising such divisions. In recent years legislation has been passed to permit a more Americanized board consisting of independent or outside directors exercising management authority over senior executive officers managing departments or divisions of companies. Such legislation also permits action by committees of the board when such committees have the appropriate percentage of independent directors. Under the new style of Committee and Independent Director system corporations are beginning to create American style Executive Officers and Representative Executive Officers. For a discussion of the new style of management see, Motomi Hashimoto, Commercial Code Revisions: Promoting the Evolution of Japanese Companies (Nomura Research Institute) NRI Papers No. 48, 5/1/2002.

in writing.[103] And, authority to represent a party does not give the attorney authority to perform certain acts that must be specially authorized by the client. Thus, a special authority is required for counsel to file a counterclaim or to compromise, withdraw, abandon or consent to a claim.[104] However, where there are related claims arising out of the same dispute, some of which are in litigation and some of which are not, and where the lawyer is given authority to settle the litigation, such authority may be deemed to include the authority to settle the related claims.[105] Representation of a party at the initial stage of a case is not assumed to grant authority to represent the party on appeal and thus new authorization is required for the filing of an appeal.[106] A party is ultimately in control of its litigation even if represented by counsel and may controvert its own counsel's statement of fact in a matter.[107]

B. The Court System for the Handling of Civil Cases

As Japan is a unitary State it has a single court system governed by the court Organization Law of 1947,[108] as amended. The court structure places the Supreme Court at the top of a pyramid with 8 High Courts (having 6 branch offices) below it and 50 District Courts (with 203 branches) as the courts of general jurisdiction. The High Courts are, generally speaking, courts of appeal and hear appeals from determinations of the District Courts. The District Courts are courts of general initial jurisdiction, but they can hear appeals in civil (but not criminal) cases coming from Summary Courts. District Courts hear both civil and criminal matters as a first instance court. Below the District Courts are 405 Summary Courts with basically small claims civil and minor criminal jurisdiction. On a level with the District Courts (but not serving as an appeal court from the Summary Courts) are 50 Family Courts having 280 branch or local offices. This structure of basically three levels (District/High/Supreme) replaces the four-tiered structure of Meiji Japan.[109] Because of its special Family jurisdiction (family affairs, inheritance and juvenile justice) the Family Court is only treated in passing.

103 CPR Rule 23 (1).

104 CCP Article 55.

105 Case No. 1996 (O) No. 2177, 54 Minshu 1126 (Sup. Ct. Petty Bench, 3/24/2000) available in English through the web site of the Supreme Court of Japan.

106 CCP Article 55.

107 CCP Article 57.

108 Court Organization Law, Law No. 59, April 16, 1947. The title Court Organization Law is used throughout although the Law may also be referred to as the Court Law or the Judiciary Law.

109 For a general discussion of the organization of the courts in Japan see, Yosiyuki Noda, INTRODUCTION TO JAPANESE LAW (translated and edited by Anthony H. Angelo) (University of Tokyo Press, 1976) 126-132; Shigemitsu Dando (Translated by B.J. George Jr.) JAPANESE CRIMINAL PROCEDURE (Fred B. Rothman & Co., 1965) Section 4.08-4.16; See also, Percy R. Luney, Jr., The Judiciary: Its Organization and Status in the Parliamentary System, in JAPANESE CONSTITUTIONAL LAW (Luney & Takahashi Ed., University of Tokyo Press, 1993)123. An organizational chart discussing the court system and indicating the location of the various courts may also be found on the Web site of the Supreme Court of Japan.

The Supreme Court is located in Tokyo.[110] The court must always sit as a collegial body, although it may sit as either a Grand Bench of all 15 Justices or in Petty Benches of not less than 3 Justices (the present composition of Petty Benches is 5 Justices) each.[111] The court must sit as a Grand Bench to declare an act of the Diet or other ordinance, regulation or governmental disposition unconstitutional.[112] A Grand Bench is also required when the court finds a law constitutional (unless the court is following established Supreme Court precedent) and when the court reverses a previous decision of the Supreme Court.[113] The Supreme Court's building in Tokyo is a modern courthouse that houses the Grand Bench and the three Petty Benches as well as the main body of the judicial Secretariat. Justices of the court are required to express their judgments in a case in writing[114] although they may join the opinion of the court rather than writing separate opinions. As a consequence Justices may and do write dissenting opinions as well as concurring opinions in cases. The Supreme Court is the only court in Japan where written dissenting opinions are permitted. There is no dissenting opinion in the High Court or the District Court. Of the 15 Supreme Court Justices the court Organization Law requires that at least 10 of the Justices must have held one or two of the following positions for a period of at least ten years:

President of a High Court;

Judge (meaning a judge of the High or District Court);

Judge of the Summary Court;

Public Prosecutor;

Bengoshi; and

Professor or Assistant Professor of Law[115]

Certain other positions, including positions in Ministry of Justice and in the Supreme Court's educational branches may substitute for 5 years of the 10 years required in the said positions.[116] The placement of the above categories may be significant in reflecting the respective social/professional standing of the categories mentioned. Thus, it is probably no accident that bengoshi lawyers are listed below judges and prosecutors just as Presidents of High Courts are placed first on

110 Court Organization Law Article 6.

111 Court Organization Law Article 9.

112 Court Organization Law Article 10 (2).

113 Court Organization Law Article 10 (1) and (3).

114 Court Organization Law Article 11.

115 Court Organization Law Article 41. Professors of Law with more than 10-years experience could, prior to 2004, with the permission of the Bar Association, become practicing bengoshi without taking the Bar Examination or the Legal Research and Training Institute program. As part of the Spring 2004 judicial reform initiative the government submitted a Bill that no longer permits Professors of Law to become bengoshi without passing the Bar Examination and Institute training.

116 Court Organization Law Article 41 (2).

the list of positions. Although 10 of the Justices must meet the above requirements, the remaining five Justices need not have any judicial or legal background or education.[117] Under Article 50, Supreme Court Justices must retire at age 70.[118]

The Supreme Court judicial Secretariat administers the Judicial Branch on behalf of the Supreme Court[119] and under the authority of the Chief Justice.[120] Such administration should not (according to the Court Organization Law) interfere with the judicial independence of the individual judges.[121] Nonetheless, as noted earlier the Secretariat's authority to set salaries and transfer judges as well as its ability to make judicial assignments may have an effect on the independent judgment of individual judges.

There are eight High Courts having general appellate jurisdiction as courts of first appeal over judgments coming from the District Courts, the Family Courts and criminal appeals from the Summary Courts. Each High Court has one Chief Judge who sits in the main High Court location[122] (not in a branch office). The High Courts also have second tier (*jokoku*) appellate jurisdiction over appeals from decisions of the District Court when such court acted as a court of appeals (hearing appeals from Summary Court) rather than a trial court and also from some Summary Court determinations. In cases involving alleged violation of the Criminal Code provisions relating to insurrection, the High Court sits as a trial court[123] (with 5-judges). A 5-judge panel is also used to hear some issues under the Anti-Monopoly Law.[124] Similar to United States Circuit Courts of Appeal, the High Courts have a general appellate jurisdiction based on geographic boundaries. Thus, the eight High Courts are situated in eight geographic regions from Sapporo in the northern island of Hokkaido to Fukuoka in the southern island of Kyushu and in such population centers as Tokyo, Osaka and Nagoya. There are also High Courts located in Sendai, Takamatsu and Hiroshima. To assist the High Courts in conducting their business, there are six branch offices of the High Court. Branch offices are located in the general jurisdiction area of the High Court.

---

117 Toru Miura, Independence, Transparency and Accountability of the Judiciary in Japan, on the web at *www.unafei.or.jp/pdf/indonesia_pdf/session4.pdf* at page 35.

118 Court Organization Law Article 50.

119 The Supreme Court has a Secretary General who under the direction of the Chief Justice is responsible for administering the affairs of the judicial Secretariat. Court Organization Law Article 53.

120 Shigemitsu Dando (Translated by B.J. George Jr.) JAPANESE CRIMINAL PROCEDURE (Fred B. Rothman & Co., 1965) Section 4.14.

121 Court Organization Law Article 81.

122 Court Organization Law Article 42.

123 Court Organization Law Article 16. Penal Code Articles 77-79; see, See, Shigemitsu Dando (translated by B. J. George, Jr.) JAPANESE CRIMINAL PROCEDURE (Fred B. Rothman & Co., 1965) Section 4.18 (4).

124 Shigemitsu Dando (Translated by B.J. George Jr.) JAPANESE CRIMINAL PROCEDURE (Fred B. Rothman & Co., 1965) Section 4.15(d).

The Tokyo High Court has special jurisdiction over civil appeals in patent and software programming cases.[125] In the spring of 2004 the Japanese Cabinet acted to approve the submission of legislation to the Diet that would create a new Intellectual Property High Court similar to the Federal Circuit in the United States. The bill was enacted by the Diet on June 11, 2004. Such court will not be a separate court but, rather, will be a constituent court of the Tokyo High Court. Such court should come into existence in April 2005. The Supreme Court will designate the judges of the court. Because the objective is to create a court with specialized knowledge and competence in the intellectual property area, it is unlikely that the judges of this new court will be transferred as frequently as is presently the case for judges of the High Court. In addition to jurisdiction to hear appeals from patent and software program cases decided by the Osaka and Tokyo District courts, this new court will have jurisdiction over copyright cases appealed from any District Court.

Under the 1996 Code, the Tokyo and Osaka District courts were given concurrent jurisdiction with other courts to hear patent cases. This change was brought about in recognition of the special expertise these courts had developed in patent matters. The suggestion that these courts be given exclusive jurisdiction over such cases was rejected as too extreme.[126] Other District Courts were given authority to transfer patent cases to the Tokyo and Osaka District courts. By 1998 fully three-quarters of all patent infringement cases in Japan were pending before these two courts.[127] By the year 2000 81% of all patent infringement cases were being filed in Tokyo or Osaka. The Law Reform Council recommended that rather than be concurrent the jurisdiction of these courts in patent matters be made exclusive.[128] Under the 2003 amendments, patent cases must be brought in either the District Court for Tokyo (cases in eastern Japan) or District Court in Osaka (cases in western Japan).[129] Under the 2003 amendments jurisdiction concurrent with that of other District Courts was given to the Tokyo and Osaka District Courts for copyright and trademark cases. Such cases may be brought in the Tokyo District court when coming from eastern Japan or may be filed in Osaka when coming from western Japan.[130] Unlike patent cases, these two districts do not have exclusive jurisdiction in the trademark and copyright area. This may be a preliminary step towards exclusive jurisdiction since the same non-exclusive jurisdiction was

---

125 See, 2003 amendment to CCP Article 6 and addition of Article 6-2. The Tokyo High Court also has a special jurisdiction to hear cases involving maritime accidents under the Marine Accident Adjudication Law.

126 Yasuhei Taniguchi, The 1996 Code of Civil Procedure of Japan—A Procedure for the Coming Century? 45 American Journal of Comparative Law 767, 782 (1997).

127 John B. Pegram, Recent Developments in IP Litigation in Japan (Fish & Richardson, 2000) on the web at *www.fr.com/news/articledetail.cfm?articleid=67* at page 2 of 12.

128 Recommendations of the Justice System Reform Council—For a Justice System to Support Japan in the 21st Century (June 12,2001) on the web at *www.kantei.go.jp/foreign/policy/sihou/singikai/990612_e.html* at p. 20-21 of 90.

129 CCP Article 6 as amended in 2003.

130 CCP Article 6-2 (2003).

given to these courts for patent matters prior to the 2003 amendment, and the new Intellectual Property High Court that is to be part of the Tokyo High Court will have jurisdiction over copyright cases. This makes it likely that eventually these cases will be heard in the Tokyo and Osaka Districts to the exclusion of other District Courts. These courts can obtain expert assistance in patent matters from the National Patent Agency.

Like the Circuit Courts of Appeals in the United States that have jurisdiction over review of certain administrative agency determinations, the Tokyo High Court hears appeals from determinations of a certain few administrative agencies in Japan, most notably the Fair Trade Commission,[131] the Patent Office[132] and the Election Management Commission.[133] Unlike the United States Circuit Court that hears such appeals on the basis of the record made in the administrative agency, in Japan the High Court may, in certain situations, take additional evidence in connection with such agency appeals.[134] It has been estimated that in appeals from determinations of the Patent Office the median number of party briefs filed with the court is six. As these briefs can present both legal and factual argument, it seems clear that parties use their ability to present new evidence after the determination of an administrative agency that is subject to appeal before the Tokyo High Court.[135] The Tokyo High Court also has exclusive jurisdiction to hear appeals by lawyers challenging disciplinary action taken by the Japan Federation of Bar Associations[136] and hears appeals from refusal to grant registration to or from the rescission of the registration of or the discipline of a foreign lawyer licensed to practice as a foreign law expert in Japan.[137]

---

131 Law No. 54 of 1947, Fair Trade Commission Act ("FTCA") Section 77. In Fair Trade Commission appeal cases the court sits in a 5-judge panel.

132 Law No. 1221 of 1959. Patent Law Section 178.

133 Fair Election Act Section 217. At the time of passage of the Act, reapportionment cases were not contemplated raising the question as to whether such cases may be instituted in the District Court. The majority view is that even though not contemplated when the Act was enacted reapportionment cases must be instituted in the High Court.

134 See for example, FTCA Section 81 under which new evidence is only permitted if the party offering the evidence was not at fault for failing to introduce the evidence at the agency proceeding or the FTC was in error for failing to accept the evidence at the proceeding. Under Section 83 the High Court may refuse to take additional evidence and can remand the matter to the Agency for additional fact finding.

135 Setsuko Asami (Japanese Patent Office Examiner), Japan-U.S. Patent Infringement Litigation Comparison: A Visit to the United States Court of Appeals for the Federal Circuit (Center for Advanced Study and Research on Intellectual Property "CASRIP" University of Washington School of Law, 1999) on the web at *www.law.Washington.edu/casrip/newsletter/newsv5i3asami.htm*

136 Toshiro Nishimura, The Code of Ethics Applicable to Bengoshi (Temple University Japan) 12/1/98 on the web at *www.tuj.ac.jp/newsite/main/law/benethics.html*

137 Special Measure Law Dealing with Legal Business by Foreign Lawyers, Law No. 66 of 1986 as amended by Law No. 128 of 2003, Article 60.

Three-judge panels hear most High Court cases.[138] Where necessary the High Court may ask a District Court or Family Court judge within its geographic region to sit as a member of the court on an appeal.[139] The Court Organization Law provides that High Court judges may be appointed from persons having 10 years experience as judges, assistant judges, public prosecutors, bengoshi and professors of law (including certain judicial research and teaching positions). High officials of the Ministry of Justice may substitute Ministry experience for some of the required experience. As a practical matter, High Court judges are usually appointed from District Court judges and such appointments are promotions in the judicial civil service.

Japan has 50 District Courts. As is the case with US Districts Courts where there is at least one District in each State so too in Japan there is at least one District Court in each prefecture (Hokkaido has several District Courts). The District Courts in turn have over 200 branch offices to assist in doing the initial trial level work. Although consideration was given to the establishment of prefecture or municipal courts under the Local Autonomy Law,[140] no such courts have been established. Each District Court has a Chief Judge who sits in the prime location of the court and not in a branch office. In most District Courts the ordinary civil divisions in the headquarters office of the court (as distinguished from the branch offices) handle cases brought under the Administrative Case Litigation Law (ACLL) seeking review of administrative action. However, because of presently existing forum provisions most such ACLL cases are filed in Tokyo. In Tokyo there are three divisions of the District Court that exclusively handle administrative cases. Similarly District Courts in Osaka, Nagoya, Yokohama, Saitama, Chiba, Kyoto and Kobe have divisions that exclusively handle administrative cases. In Osaka the court has two such exclusive divisions. As discussed in greater detail in Chapter 12, the Cabinet in the spring of 2004 submitted a bill to amend the ACLL. The bill was passed at the end of the spring 2004 session of the Diet in June 2004. Under the proposal submitted, concurrent forum jurisdiction over administrative cases would be extended to the headquarters office of the District Court in the location of the High Court having jurisdiction over the plaintiff's forum (the Tokyo District Court would continue to have concurrent forum jurisdiction as it is the location of defendant's forum). This may move some administrative cases presently brought in Tokyo to other District Courts and may permit more administrative cases to be heard by ordinary District Court judges in ordinary civil divisions, as such District Courts as Hiroshima and Sendai do not have exclusive administrative divisions.

Unlike US District Courts that are courts of limited jurisdiction, Japanese District Courts are more like State trial courts that have general jurisdiction except for

---

138 Court Organization Law Article 18.

139 Court Organization Law Article 19.

140 Alfred C. Oppler, The Reform of Japan's Legal and Judicial System under Allied Occupation, 24 Washington Law Review 290, 306 (1949).

such matters as are specifically removed from the court's jurisdiction by statute.[141] Such matters include matters delegated to the Family Court or the Summary Court or cases that must be initiated in a higher court. In addition to its trial court duties the District Court hears appeals from the Summary Court. Japan recognizes the general rule that the sovereign acts of a foreign sovereign are immune from the jurisdiction of Japanese courts.[142] When hearing appeals, the District Court must sit in 3 judge panels, similar to the High Court.[143] Each panel has its own chief judge who presides over the case (referred to herein as chief judge of the panel or presiding judge).

As a general rule, the Court Organization Law provides that the District Court sits as a single judge court except when the court itself decides that a collegial court of 3-judges should hear the case or when a statute requires a collegial court.[144] Most civil cases in Japan are tried before a single judge rather than a 3-judge panel. A single judge court may permit a new judge in the first 10-year training period (an "assistant judge" or a "judge in training") to sit in on the proceedings—not as a judge but rather as part of the training of the new judge. When it sits as a 3-judge court, the court makeup is typically a presiding judge, an assistant judge (a judge with less than 10 years experience) and a third judge. Under the 1996 Code the court may assign complex litigation to 5-judge panel courts.[145] In the case of a 5-judge court, no more than 2 judges may be assistant judges.[146] Assistant judges with less than 5-years experience may not try cases on their own.[147] It used to be the rule that during the first 10-year appointment assistant judges could not try cases. Because of the shortage of judges, assistant judges with more than 5-years experience may try cases assigned to them as single judge courts. Under the 2004 judicial reform initiative judges may work for two years in a bengoshi office to gain experience. Whether this time will be counted as part of judicial training so that a judge who has served 2 years as an assistant judge in a bengoshi office and

141 Court Organization Law Article 25.

142 Japan appears to recognize the limited theory of immunity rather than the absolute theory of immunity. Under the limited theory sovereign acts (*jure imperii*) are immune whereas acts taken in a commercial or private nature (*jure gestionis*) are not immune. In Case No. 1999 (O) No. 887, 1999 (Ju) No. 741, 56 Minshu 729 (Sup. Ct. Petty Bench, 4/12/02) available in English through the web site of the Supreme Court of Japan, the Supreme Court held that the acts of the United States military in undertaking military take off and landings at a military base in Japan was a sovereign act and hence not subject to the jurisdiction of Japanese courts.

143 Court Organization Law Article 26 (3).

144 Court Organization Law Article 26.

145 CCP Article 269 (1).

146 CCP Article 269 (2).

147 There are categories of judges in inferior courts. "Assistant judges" are judges in their first 10-year appointment. This 10-year period is considered as a training period. Upon reappointment to a second 10-year term the judge becomes a full-fledged judge. Bengoshi with more than 10-years experience may be appointed as full judges without an initial assistant judge appointment. For a discussion of the judge system in Japan see, Toru Miura, Independence, Transparency and Accountability of the Judiciary in Japan, on the web at *www.unafei.or.jp/pdf/indonesia_pdf/session4.pdf* at page 35.

3 years as an assistant judge on the Bench will be allowed to try cases remains to be seen. It is unlikely that the time served in a bengoshi office will be considered as "judicial training" to enable the judge to handle cases on his/her own as the purpose of the 5-year rule is to allow the judge to receive judicial training. On the other hand, time served working for the judicial Secretariat is counted as judicial training even if the Secretariat work is not on the Bench, such as assisting in the Legal Research and Training Institute.

This organizational set up belies the collegial nature of the court and reflects the reality that the 3-judge and 5-judge set up operates as a means of dividing labor. As the assistant judge cannot decide a case on his/her own[148] and as such a judge is a trainee judge who is not going to "dissent" (there is no dissenting opinion at the District or High Court levels although there are dissenting opinions at the Supreme Court) and as the assistant judge will likely side with the more senior experienced and more respected presiding judge in the event of a disagreement between judges on the panel, the case is really in the hands of the presiding judge. This primacy of the presiding judge is highlighted by the Code of Civil Procedure, which gives various authorities to the presiding judge and provides that the authority may be used by an associate judge after such judge has conferred with the presiding judge.[149] While many provisions of the Code permit the chief judge of a panel (also referred to as the presiding judge) to take evidence or perform other acts, the associate judge on the panel may typically also perform such functions. This speeds up the judicial process. (An assistant judge with less than 5-years experience is limited in functions that he/she may perform on his/her own.) When there is a single judge then of course the single judge may perform any function the chief judge of a panel may perform.

There is a mandatory retirement age for inferior court judges. High Court and District Court judges (as well as Family Court judges) must retire at age 65.[150] High Court and District Court judges are appointed for 10-year terms of office, subject to reappointment for additional 10-year terms.[151] Judges are appointed as judges and not appointed to a specific court, as is the case in the United States. Judges may be transferred between High and District Courts during this period. Judges may not, while serving in the Judicial Branch (including when they are assigned to the Executive for a period of time) engage in private business, engage in political activity or serve in elected office, and may not hold another salaried position without the consent of the judicial Secretariat.[152] Although law sets the salary of judges,[153] the Constitution protects judges' salaries by providing that the salary of judges may not be reduced during their term of office. However, in 2003 the Su-

148 Court Organization Law Article 27.

149 CCP Article 149.

150 Court Organization Law Article 50.

151 Court Organization Law Article 40.

152 Court Organization Law Article 52.

153 Court Organization Law Article 51.

preme Court consented to a reduction of 3% in judges' salaries because of budgetary problems.[154] Although Article 48 of the Court Organization Law provides that judges cannot be transferred from one location to another without consent, the reality is that the Secretariat determines on transfer of judges and judges accept such transfers. Failure to accept transfer is viewed by the Secretariat as similar to a failure of an executive to accept transfer by his company and would substantially impair a judge's future advancement. As a general matter judges are transferred to a different locality or different court about every three years. This frequent transfer of judges means that the judge (or panel of judges) initially responsible for handling a case usually is different from the judge or panel that finally resolves the case at the District Court and frequently at the High Court level.

The judge or panel of judges that actually tried the case at the Plenary Hearing must make a decision at the District Court level. Since judges are frequently transferred, the Code of Civil Procedure requires that the parties must bring the new judge up to date on the results of previous sessions of the Plenary Hearings.[155] The statement of the status of the proceedings by the parties at a public Oral Argument session makes it unnecessary to retry matters already handled in the case. However, either party may by motion require that witnesses previously examined be reexamined when there has been a change in either a single judge handling a case or a majority of the panel trying the case.[156] This reexamination is rarely requested. As a practical matter the new judge gets up to date by reading the judicial file in the case.

As is true in the United States, judges must be impartial decision-makers of the cause before them. Where the judge has certain family relations to a party before the court, or has certain financial interests in the matter either directly or as a guarantor, or where the judge was a witness (or expert) in the case or represented a party, or participated in a determination (including an arbitration decision) in the case that is now on appeal the judge may be excused from the case. Recusal may be *sua sponte* by the court or by motion of a party. However, if a party fails to move before proceeding at the Oral Argument or Preparation for Oral Argument stage of the case then the party waives the right to seek exclusion of the judge. A similar rule applies to exclusion in criminal cases where exclusion is based on alleged bias. The basis of the waiver doctrine in both civil and criminal cases is the

154 This is reminiscent of the reduction in judges' salaries in the prewar period. The 2003 reduction was taken as part of a general government "belt-tightening" designed to control the budget deficit. To exempt judges from a belt-tightening that was seen as in the public interest would appear to be self serving and selfish on the part of the judiciary. During the prewar period the government, as part of "belt-tightening" attempted to reduce the salaries of prosecutors while exempting judges from the reduction so as to recognize judicial independence. The prosecutors objected to this discriminatory treatment and judges' salaries were reduced in line with the reduction in prosecutor salaries.

155 CCP Article 249.

156 CCP Article 249 (3).

same, namely the potential for abuse.[157] Should the facts showing a ground for recusal not be known until a later stage, then waiver is not applied until the party takes an action thereafter that would constitute waiver.[158] Motions for recusal must, as a general rule, be made in writing and must clearly state the basis for the motion.[159] A determination by the court that the judge will be excused is not subject to appeal, but a determination not to excuse the judge is immediately subject to appeal.[160] Although the challenged judge may not sit in judgment of the challenge, the judge may state a position as to the motion.[161] During the exclusion motion phase (including any appeal thereof) the main action is stayed.[162] Thus, such a motion can be used to delay proceedings. Such motions are rarely granted.

There are several hundred Summary Courts in Japan handling small claim type civil cases and minor criminal cases. Because of the small claim nature of their jurisdiction, Summary Courts are not treated in depth (except in Chapter 13) herein—except that their authority to deal with civil conciliation matters under the Civil Conciliation Law is considered in Chapter 10. Because Summary Court judges need not retire until age 70,[163] some High Court and District Court judges become Summary Court judges upon mandatory retirement.

Under legislation submitted by the Cabinet to the Diet and passed in the spring of 2004 a new Labor Tribunal will be established to hear disputes between employer and employee. 3-judge panels composed of one judge and two laypersons will preside and the court will first attempt to conciliate the dispute. (The composition of the court is interesting. Under the Civil Conciliation Law dealing with conciliation of civil disputes a conciliation panel is used, composed of a judge and two laypersons.)[164] If conciliation is unsuccessful, the court may try the matter under the same rules as are contained in the Code of Civil Procedure, except that no more than three hearing sessions will be permitted (except in unusual circumstances) before decision. If a party is dissatisfied with a determination of the new court, it may start a new action in the District Court and the filing of the new action vacates the Labor Tribunal's determination. The intent of the new court pro-

157 See, Shigemitsu Dando (Translated by B.J. George Jr.) JAPANESE CRIMINAL PROCEDURE (Fred B. Rothman & Co., 1965) Section 4.16 (2).

158 CCP Article 24. A similar rule applies in criminal procedure. Shigemitsu Dando (Translated by B.J. George Jr.) JAPANESE CRIMINAL PROCEDURE (Fred B. Rothman & Co., 1965) Section 4.16 (2).

159 Civil Procedure Rules ("CPR") Rule 10.

160 CCP Article 25. The judge challenged may not participate in the determination of whether to excuse or not. If the case is before a single District Court judge, the motion must be heard by a 3-judge panel. If the challenge is to a Summary Court judge it must be heard by the District Court having appeal authority over the Summary Court involved.

161 CPR Rule 11.

162 CCP Article 26. The exclusion motion is heard expeditiously. CPR Rule 10 requires that a preliminary showing of grounds for exclusion must be made within 3 days of the motion.

163 Court Organization Law Article 50.

164 Civil Conciliation Act Article 6.

vision is to provide a formalized structure for conciliating employee-employer disputes while retaining a right to seek more formalized judicial relief if conciliation is unsuccessful.

Because District Courts are courts of general jurisdiction, Japanese civil procedure does not have to deal with the complex federal jurisdictional questions, such as diversity, complete diversity, federal questions, etc. raised in federal litigation in the United States.[165] Japanese courts do, however, have to deal with questions of proper venue or forum. As a general matter the suit should be brought in the District of defendant's domicile (the defendant's general forum).[166] Domicile is considered to be the place where a person habitually resides. The location of a person's family register is not the place of domicile, but when moving from one domicile to another, persons are required to register their new domicile within 14 days.[167] Hence if domicile is contested such registers may be used as evidence to help establish domicile. For a company (or any other juridical person such as an association or foundation), the general domicile is considered the place where the company has its principal place of business or failing such a place the domicile of the responsible representative of the company.[168] For a non-Japanese entity the general forum for litigation is the place where it has its principal place of business or office in Japan or where its representative is located.[169]

Forum or venue based on domicile is not exclusive, and proper venue may also be based on special factors set out in the Code to cover specific situations. Thus, for example, where a suit seeks payment based on a Bill or Note it may be instituted in the place where payment was due; a tort action may be brought in the District where the tort is alleged to have been committed; a suit dealing with real property may be brought in the District where the property is located; an action based on a property right may be brought in the place of performance of the obligation; etc.[170] Because forum based on domicile and forum based on special situations are not exclusive but are concurrent, forum shopping is not uncommon in Japan.[171]

Substantive laws may provide for the appropriate venue of litigation. Thus, the Commercial Code provides that a shareholder's derivative lawsuit "shall" be

---

165 Because some matters must be brought in the High Court or Family Court or Summary Court, Japanese courts do have to deal with subject matter jurisdiction questions dealing with the exclusive jurisdiction of these courts.

166 CCP Article 4. In Case No. 1993 (O) No. 764 (Sup. Ct. Petty Bench, 6/24/96 (available in English through the web site of the Supreme Court of Japan) the Court confirmed that even in situations involving an international dispute the preferred venue is where the defendant resides and that if the defendant resides in Japan that is the preferred place of suit.

167 There is a civil penalty of 50,000 Yen for failure to make such registration.

168 CCP Article 4 (4).

169 CCP Article 4 (5).

170 CCP Article 5.

171 International Commercial Litigation in Japan, Masafumi Kodama & Jay Tyndall, Kitahama Law Office, on the web at *www.kitahama.or.jp/English/litigatn2.htm* p. 3.

brought in the District where the company has its principal office.[172] Under the Arbitration Law of 2003[173] the proper form for a suit brought under the Arbitration Law is the District Court agreed to by the parties in the Arbitration Agreement or the District Court of the District where the arbitration is to be held (provided the place of arbitration is only within the jurisdiction of a single District Court) or the District Court of the general forum of the defendant.[174]

Where the defendant has no domicile in Japan—such as a foreigner or foreign business entity—the suit may be brought in a District where property of the defendant can be attached or where the subject matter of the claim or security for the claim is located.[175]

These venue provisions apply to international litigation that is brought in Japan as long as the court finds that maintenance of the action in Japan is not contrary to accepted norms of fairness, impartiality towards the parties and ability of the court to timely resolve the matter.[176] This rule allows the court discretion to determine not to accept jurisdiction of a case (similar to the concept of *forum non convenience*) by finding that any of these factors do not apply.[177] Thus, where it would be difficult for a Japanese court to obtain necessary evidence in a case the court may decline to accept jurisdiction on the basis that to accept would be contrary to

---

172 Commercial Code Article 268 (1).

173 Arbitration Law, Law No. 138 of 2003. Although the Arbitration Law is generally applicable to arbitrations, there are special rules for certain categories of arbitrations. Thus, there are special rules for arbitration between a consumer and a business (Arbitration Law Supplementary Provisions Article 3—for example, a consumer may cancel an arbitration agreement provided the consumer is not the claimant in the arbitration proceeding and such cancellation shall be deemed to have occurred if the consumer fails to appear at an arbitration instituted by the business entity), and individual employer/employee disputes are not subject to arbitration under the Arbitration Law (Supplementary Provisions Article 4). Such employer/employee disputes would be subject to the jurisdiction of the new proposed Labor Tribunal.

174 Arbitration Law Article 5. If the suit is filed in the wrong district, the court is to transfer the case to the appropriate district.

175 CCP Article 5. Except that for ambassadors, ministers and other Japanese citizens abroad who have immunity as a consequence of the posting, the general forum of such person shall be deemed to be the Chiyoda Ward of Tokyo. CCP Article 4 (3).

176 See, Malaysian Airline System v. Michiko Goto, 35 Minshu 1224 (Sup. Ct. Petty Bench 10/16/81); and KK Tsuburaya Production v. Sompote Saengduenchai, Tokyo District Court, 1/28/99 discussed in Teruo Doi, JAPANESE COPYRIGHT LAW IN THE 21ST CENTURY 54-55 (Oceana Publications, Inc. Dobbs Ferry, NY (2001)). For a discussion of the Malaysian airlines case and the court's approach to jurisdiction in transnational litigation see also, Tasuku Matsuo, Jurisdiction in Transnational Cases in Japan, 23 International Lawyer 6 (1978); see also, Dispute Resolution in Japan on the web at *www.gsid.nagoya-u.ac.jp/project/apec/lawdb/japan/dispute/disp1-en.html* (APEC Study Center, Nagoya University) 1.1.2 (Jurisdiction in International Cases); For a discussion of the Malaysian Airlines case in the context of mirror image suits pending in the United States and Japan see, Hideyuki Kobayashi and Yoshimasa Furuta, Products Liability Act and Transnational Litigation in Japan, 34 Texas International Law Journal 93, 110-112 (1999).

177 See, Dispute Resolution in Japan on the web at *www.gsid.nagoya-u.ac.jp/project/apec/lawdb/japan/dispute/disp1-en.html* (APEC Study Center, Nagoya University) 1.3 (Non-Exercise of Jurisdiction).

the fairness requirement. This follows as it would not be fair to the parties to handle a case where the court could not get necessary evidence.[178] Similarly, where a contract is executed in Germany and relates to importation of product into Germany and Japanese law is not selected to govern the contract and the defendant had no reason to expect that a claim under the contract would be brought in Japan, the court in Japan would decline jurisdiction. Exerting jurisdiction is unfair to the defendant.[179] On the other hand, it is not inconsistent with the concept of fairness to permit a Japanese court to exercise jurisdiction over a foreign defendant even after a court of a foreign country has pending before it a suit seeking similar relief. This theory applied when the defendant was alleged to have committed a tortious act in Japan (even though defendant never entered the territory of Japan—such as by sending a letter to a party in Japan allegedly falsely accusing such party of violating a legal right) and the plaintiff has been injured in Japan.[180] Nor is it unfair to permit a Japanese husband to sue his German wife for divorce in Japan after his wife already obtained a divorce in Germany.[181] The flexibility of concepts such as fairness and extraordinary circumstances gives the court great discretion in this arena.[182]

Because forum or venue is not exclusive in these cases, venue objections may be waived and such waiver is considered as an agreement between the parties as to venue. Waiver is demonstrated by a party proceeding in the case without making a venue objection at the first opportunity.[183] Parties may also agree in writing to a proper venue—thus, contracts in Japan may have exclusive venue selection provisions[184]—and may even provide that arbitration is the exclusive

---

178 See, Hideyuki Kobayashi and Yoshimasa Furuta, Products Liability Act and Transnational Litigation in Japan, 34 Texas International Law Journal 93, 107 (1999).

179 Case No. 1993 (O) No. 1660, (Sup. Ct. Petty Bench, 11/11/97) available in English through the web site of the Supreme Court of Japan. For a discussion of the criticism of the Malaysian Airlines case and the subsequent modification of the Malaysian airlines rule in Case No. 1660 decided 11/11/97 see, Toshiyuki Kono, Enforcement of Foreign Intellectual Property Rights in Japan: Jurisdiction and Applicable Law, 6 CASRIP Publication Series: Rethinking Intellectual Property 20, 21-22 (University of Washington School of Law, 2000).

180 Case No. 2000 (O) 929, 2000 (Ju) No.780, 55 Minshu 727 (Sup. Ct. Petty Bench, 6/8/01) an English language version may be found on the web through the web site of the Supreme Court of Japan. (Court also held that to establish jurisdiction it is not necessary for plaintiff to first establish a prima facia case that the acts committed were tortious.)

181 Case No. 1993 (O) No. 764 (Sup. Ct. Petty Bench, 6/24/96) available in English through the web site of the Supreme Court of Japan.

182 See, Masaki Hamano, Comparative Studies in the Approach to Jurisdiction in Cyberspace Chapter V Japan, on the web at *www.geocities.com/SiliconValley/Bay/6201/japan/art.html* for a discussion of the basis for jurisdiction in Japan in general and a discussion of Japanese court jurisdiction in international disputes in particular. For an American approach see, Society of Lloyd's v. Ashenden, 233 F.3d 473 (7th Cir. 2000).

183 CCP Article 12.

184 CCP Article 11. See, Case No. 1970 (O) No. 297(Sup. Ct. Petty Bench, 11/28/75) an English language translation may be found through the web site of the Supreme Court of Japan.

forum.[185] Where arbitration is stated to be the exclusive forum and suit is instituted in court, the party objecting to suit must raise the arbitration agreement's forum clause by motion seeking dismissal. The court will not *sua sponte* dismiss. However, when such a motion is made the court should dismiss the action in favor of arbitration.[186] Failure to raise the arbitration clause providing for an exclusive forum through arbitration until after the defendant has already raised substantive defenses in the Oral Argument or in the Preparation for Oral Argument constitutes a waiver of the forum defense.[187]

Such forum clauses may even provide that the exclusive forum for resolution of the matter is outside Japan. To be valid such provisions must deal with a subject matter as to which the courts in Japan do NOT have exclusive jurisdiction and further the court selected must have jurisdiction over the matter under its general law and not simply because the parties selected the forum.[188] Similarly parties to commercial agreements may choose the law that will govern the agreement or any dispute arising from the agreement,[189] except that the law of a foreign country that is contrary to public order or good morals may not be applied.[190] For torts[191] and for special matters such as real property[192] and family matters,[193] etc. the parties may not select the governing law.

185 Ringling Brothers Arbitration decision, Case No. 1994 (O) No. 1848 (Sup. Ct. Petty Bench, 9/4/77) an English language translation may be found through the web site of the Supreme Court of Japan. See also, Dispute Resolution in Japan on the web at *www.gsid.nagoya-u.ac.jp/project/apec/lawdb/japan/dispute/disp1-en.html* (APEC Study Center, Nagoya University) 1.2.1 (Forum Agreements) and 1.2.2 (Arbitration Agreements) noting that the prevailing rule is that forum selection agreements should be in writing.

186 Arbitration Law Article 14 (1). If the court finds the arbitration agreement to be null and void or to have been cancelled or superceded or to otherwise be invalid or if the court finds that the arbitration agreement cannot be carried out, the court may decline to dismiss the litigation in favor of arbitration. Arbitration Law Article 14 (1) (i) and (ii).

187 See, Arbitration Law Article 14 (1)(iii); see also, Takao Tateishi, Inquisitional Approach in Dispute Resolution—A Japanese Way to Mete Out Justice, Wavelength, JSE Bulletin No. 44 (March 2002) 8, 11-13.

188 International Commercial Litigation in Japan, Masafumi Kodama & Jay Tyndall, Kitahama Law Office, on the web at *www.kitahama.or.jp/English/litigatn2.htm* p. 3.

189 Horei, Law on the Application of Laws Article 7.

190 Horei, Law on the Application of Laws Article 33.

191 Horei, Law on the Application of Laws Article 11—tort actions and claims for unjust enrichment are governed by the law of the place where the acts giving rise to the claim occurred.

192 Horei, Law on the Application of Laws Article 10—real property is governed by the law of the situs of the property.

193 See, e.g., Horei, Law on the Application of Laws Article 13 (regarding marriage), 18 (relationship of parent and child), etc.

Filing suit in an improper venue is not a jurisdiction defect that will lead to dismissal. Rather, the court transfers the case to the appropriate venue.[194] Although venue may be proper, the court on its own motion or on motion of a party may transfer the case to another court of proper venue.[195] Where a transfer motion is based on the "interests of justice," the opposing party has a right to be heard in opposition.[196] As a general rule transfer motions are to be made in writing and should clearly indicate the basis for the motion.[197] Transfer rulings are immediately subject to appeal.[198] Once a transfer determination becomes final (there is no appeal or the appeal route has been exhausted), the transferee court may not further transfer the case or refuse to take jurisdiction. The case is treated as if filed in the transferee venue.[199] Where a court has exclusive jurisdiction over a matter, such as the exclusive authority of the Tokyo and Osaka District Courts over certain patent matters,[200] the court may not transfer venue. This is so even if transfer might be considered as in the "interests of justice" or even if the parties consent to transfer.[201]

194 CCP Article 16.

195 CCP Article 17. The Code speaks of transfer to avoid delay and for reasons of fairness. This is similar to the American idea of transfer in the "interests of justice."

196 CPR Rule 8.

197 CPR Rule 7.

198 CCP Article 21.

199 CCP Article 22.

200 CCP Article 6.

201 CCP Article 20.

7

Civil Litigation[1]—Getting the Case Started

A. Pre-Filing Considerations

1) Cost-Benefit Analysis

As in all conflict situations the first consideration before filing suit is whether the problem can be resolved without the need to initiate litigation. A corollary to this concept is the question of whether some effort must be made to resolve the matter through conciliation or some other Alternative Dispute Resolution process before suit can be filed. In some administrative cases, for example, it may be necessary to exhaust administrative remedies before a suit can be instituted and in some civil situations the law may command an effort at conciliation before suit. Thus, family matters within the jurisdiction of the Family Court must generally be conciliated before litigation is permitted.[2] A challenge to a landlord's attempt to raise the rent must be conciliated before litigation may be instituted.[3]

Similarly in deciding whether to litigate it is useful to do a cost/benefit analysis of the proposed action. If the costs outweigh the potential benefits, then litigation would seem to be a poor option. Of course, some costs and some benefits may not be measured in economic terms. Thus, much Japanese litigation is initiated not because the plaintiff believes that it may recover monetary damages or that it will be made economically whole. Rather, many cases are brought in Japan for psychological reasons. Plaintiff may sue to make the defendant acknowledge its wrongful act. Some plaintiffs may seek closure through a judicial statement that plaintiff is in the right. Thus the "comfort women" cases brought by former "comfort women" appear to have been brought for reasons other than monetary relief. The

1 For an outline treatment of Japanese Civil Procedure prepared by the judicial secretariat see OUTLINE OF CIVIL LITIGATION IN JAPAN available through the web site of the Supreme Court of Japan.

2 Family Affairs Adjudication Act, Article 18.

3 1992 Amendment to Civil Conciliation Act.

amount of damages sought in such cases is typically quite modest by American standards. The plaintiffs appear to seek a formal statement that they suffered at the hands of the Japanese military and that Japan is responsible for such suffering. American lawyers are familiar with the adage that when the prospective plaintiff denies that it seeks monetary reward but instead insists that it is the "principle" that is important, what is really being said is that it is both the "principal and interest thereon" that is being sought. However, in Japan the monetary damage sought in many cases is merely a surrogate for the psychological relief plaintiff is after. In the same vein, many Japanese cases involving "hot button" or "politically charged" issues are instituted because litigation is a means of getting press coverage for the position of the plaintiff. As trials are non-continuous affairs, the press is likely to cover several hearings over a period of time thus making the plaintiff's story a public matter over an extended period of time. Some suits are brought out of frustration. Once these non-economic considerations are put aside there are genuine economic questions that should be considered before suit is instituted in Japan.

As an initial matter there is the question of filing fee. Unlike American litigation where access to the courthouse is not inhibited by the cost of entry, in Japan the cost of entry can be quite high. And, as the plaintiff seeks more monetary damages so too the cost of entry typically increases. (This is typical of civil law systems where the filing fee increases as the size of the recovery sought increases.)[4] When a Complaint is filed, the plaintiff must purchase appropriate stamps to evidence the payment of the filing fee. For a case seeking $1 Million the filing fee (at a $1=100 yen exchange rate) would be in excess of $4,000.[5] Failure to pay the filing fee will result in a court order granting a plaintiff a period of time in which the

4 For an illustration of how the filing fee in Austria acted to inhibit litigation against the Austrian Government and an art gallery to recover back paintings allegedly confiscated during the Nazi regime in the Second World War see, Republic of Austria v. Altman, Supreme Court of the United States, Case No. 03-13, 6/7/04.

5 See filing fee schedule in English in Joseph Gourneau, Practical Aspects of Litigating in Japan: An American Lawyer's Perspective on the web at *www.intl-lawyers.com/articles/jplaw/index.htm* at footnote 21; see also International Commercial Litigation in Japan, Masafumi Kodama & Jay Tyndall, Kitahama Law Office, on the web at *www.Masafumi Kodama & Jay Tyndall, Kitahama.or.jp/English/litigatn.htm* (8/1/2000) and see also, Takashi B. Yamamoto, Copyright Enforcement in Japan on the web at *www.itlaw.jp/tokyo%20seminar%202003%20re.pdf* with a filing fee schedule at p. 20; and Yasunobu Sato, Commercial Dispute Processing in Japan (Kluwer Law International, 2001) at page 151. A filing fee schedule sent to the author by the Supreme Court Secretariat in June 2004 shows the following typical fee charges:

for a suit seeking yen value	fee in yen
1,000,000	10,000
5,000,000	30,000
10,000,000	50,000
1,000,000,000	3,020,000
2,000,000,000	5,020,000

plaintiff must pay the fee[6] and upon failure to make payment the Complaint will be dismissed.[7] Filing fees in Japan can be quite high and there is evidence that plaintiffs will sometimes reduce their addendum so as to reduce the cost of filing.[8] There are separate filing fees for each level of appeal. The fee in the High Court is 1 ½ times the fee at the District Court and in the Supreme Court 2 times the District Court filing fee.

In addition to the filing fee, if counsel represents the plaintiff there is a substantial counsel fee. Counsel fees in Japan also increase as the size of damages sought increase. Counsel fees are typically divided into two parts—a) a fixed fee that is paid up front and b) a "success" fee that is typically a percentage of the recovery in the case. Unlike American contingent fees where the entire fee is contingent upon success, the fixed portion of the fee is not contingent on recovery. As it typically is paid "up front" the potential plaintiff has a substantial expense (both the fixed counsel fee and the filing fee) to gain access to the courthouse. As these fees are up front payments, the plaintiff loses any potential up side that might result from the investment of these sums during the course of litigation. Notwithstanding potential antitrust considerations,[9] the Japan Federation of Bar Associations publishes a fee schedule that is utilized by various Bar Associations throughout the country. The local Bar Association in the front of address/note/memo books prepared by the Association for its members typically reprints such fee schedule.[10] Although lawyers are not compelled to follow the fee schedule,[11] the paucity of lawyers in Japan and the relative lack of competition mean that there is little incentive not to follow the fee schedule. In situations where the lawyer may have a professional or

---

8 CCP Article 137 (1).

7 CCP Article 137 (2).

8 See, Mark D. West, The Pricing of Shareholder Derivative Actions in Japan and the United States, 88 Northwestern University Law Review 1436, 1463 (note 119) (1994). Where the amount of the claim is indeterminate and there is no relationship of the suit to specific assets the filing fee is quite modest, only about 8,400yen. This provision is not applicable to most litigation but was claimed to be applicable to derivative suits against a corporation by a shareholder. Court determinations indicating that the fee for such cases was only 8,400yen together with American pressure to open Japanese derivative litigation so as to introduce a greater measure of corporate democracy resulted in an amendment of the Commercial Code limiting filing fees for derivative litigation to only 8,400yen. Commercial Code Article 267.

9 Which may or may not be obviated by the fact that such schedules are simply "advisory" and not mandatory and that such schedules are called for by the Bengoshi-ho (Lawyer's Law) Article 33 (8), Law No. 205 of 1949.

10 Carl F. Goodman, Japan's New Civil Procedure Code: Has it Fostered a Rule of Law Dispute Resolution Mechanism, 29 Brooklyn Journal of International Law 511, 592 note 317 (2004).

11 Toshiro Nishimura, The Code of Ethics Applicable to Bengoshi (Temple University Japan) 12/1/98 on the web at *www.tuj.ac.jp/newsite/main/law/benethics.html*. The Bar Association ethical standards do not prohibit contingent fees—although they did prohibit them in the past. The Bar Associations consider it a violation of ethical standards for lawyers to take a contingent fee that is excessive. Although not prohibited, the prior practice of prohibition was based on ethical concerns (Id.) that still have some weight among lawyers. In any event with many clients and few lawyers there is no rationale for lawyer's to accept contingent fee cases except in rare situations.

political or social interest in the matter, the fee may be reduced or even waived. In any event, most attorneys use the fee schedule. Examples of the schedule show that for suits seeking approximately $500,000 the up-front portion of the fee would be about $24,900[12] (using a $1=100yen exchange rate); for suits seeking less than $3 million the attorney retainer fee up front would be 3% of the amount sought plus approximately $7,000. Accordingly, if the suit sought $2 million the up-front fee would be about $67,000.[13] Some attorneys may use a general 10% up-front fee.[14] At all events, whether the fee schedule or a 10% up-front fee is used, there is a high up-front cost to initiate serious litigation.[15] This cost must be considered in the cost benefit analysis.

Each level of the case involves a separate lawyer's fee arrangement. Accordingly, if a plaintiff is unsuccessful at the District Court and appeals to the High Court the plaintiff must pay a new additional retainer fee. This fee is typically based on the same schedule as the original retention.[16] As many cases are appealed in Japan, the plaintiff must realistically factor in a double cost for attorney's fees at double the initial retainer fee amount.

Many Japanese attorneys are committed to the civil and human rights clauses of the Constitution. The Bar Associations are committed to such clauses as is demonstrated by the Bar Association acceptance of the rule that prohibit bengoshi from being full time government employees (there is a perceived conflict of interest between government service and protecting the public's human rights vis-a-vis the government). The guidelines also limit bengoshi from becoming company officials without specific Bar Association approval[17] and then only when the attorney commits to representing the public interest when not on the job. Many attorneys are associated with interest groups such as consumer groups or environmental

---

12 See, Joseph Gourneau, Practical Aspects of Litigating in Japan: An American Lawyer's Perspective on the web at *www.intl-lawyers.com/articles/jplaw/index.htm* at footnote 14 and text associated therewith; see also Yasunobu Sato, Commercial Dispute Processing in Japan 153 (Kluwer Law International, 2001) for an English language version of an attorney fee schedule.

13 For a discussion of attorney fees in Japan see, Mark D. West, Why Shareholders Sue: The Evidence from Japan, 30 Journal of Legal Studies 351, 365-366; see also, Takashi B. Yamamoto, Copyright Enforcement in Japan on the web at *www.itlaw.jp/tokyo%20seminar%202003%20re.pdf* with an attorney's fee schedule at p. 20.

14 See, Mark D. West, The Pricing of Shareholder Derivative Actions in Japan and the United States, 88 Northwestern University Law Review 1436, 1459 (1994).

15 For a discussion of the inhibiting effect of high up front costs on litigation rates in Japan see, Nobutoshi Yamanouchi and Samuel J. Cohen, Understanding the Incidence of Litigation in Japan: A Structural Analysis, 24 International Lawyer 443, 453 (1991). The Chairman of Japan's Judicial Reform Council also noted that high court filing fees and lawyer's fees are barriers to access to Japanese Courts. See, Carol Lawson and Simon Thornley, Translation: Perceptions of the Current State of the Japanese Legal System, 4 Asian Law 76, 84 (2002).

16 Joseph Gourneau, Practical Aspects of Litigating in Japan: An American Lawyer's Perspective on the web at *www.intl-lawyers.com/articles/jplaw/index.htm*

17 The web site of the Tokyo Bar Association notes that because bengoshi in Japan were under a bureaucracy of an undemocratic government they are "always" aware of their role in protecting human rights and freedom. The Association also notes that the number of bengoshi employed by companies as in-house counsel is quite small. www.toben.or.jp/ english_welcome.html

groups. As a consequence many attorneys donate their time to handle cases that are affected with a public interest or that may have a political component.

Other costs of litigation are also quite high. Because Complaints must plead facts not merely information and belief, there theoretically should be a substantial investigation before a plaintiff can determine whether or not to sue. The lack of any effective pre- or post-filing discovery complicates investigation. As lawyer's fees are based on factors other than time, many Japanese lawyers do not perform an extensive pre-filing investigation. Counsel may try to submit a bare minimum to survive court review and then use the "pre-Oral Argument" stage of the case (discussed infra) to obtain information.[18] Of course, if the case is settled at an early stage the lawyer may not be required to do the fact finding at all. This can increase lawyer rents by enabling the lawyer to devote time that would have been taken up by fact finding to other cases. Nonetheless some investigation either by the client or counsel must be undertaken to have enough information for a valid Complaint. Where the lawyer does the work, the lawyer will want to be paid a fee before engaging in such investigation. Although there may be substantial discovery expense in the United States, the existence of a court supported mechanism for discovery of facts and a requirement that the opposing party produce damaging information moderates the costs of discovery. Such factors are not present in Japan making discovery of evidence and facts more difficult, more expensive and something lawyers have reason to postpone if possible.

In addition the Code of Civil Procedure permits a defendant sued by a plaintiff who lacks a residence or business office in Japan to make a motion for security for court costs. The court "shall," order such security to be posted except in cases where there is no dispute as to either part or all of a claim that is sufficient in amount to cover the costs of litigation. In addition, the defendant may waive the right to security by proceeding in the case without moving for security.[19] When a defendant moves for security the motion stays proceedings until the plaintiff posts the necessary security and should the security later prove inadequate the court shall enter further security orders. Where a plaintiff fails to provide security within the time set by the court, the court may dismiss the action without proceeding to the Oral Argument (Plenary Hearing) stage of the case. If security is posted prior to the entry of a dismissal order, the posting of the security cures the previous defect.[20] Security may be posted by cash or negotiable securities[21] or by posting a bond from one of several financial institutions mentioned in the Civil Procedure Rules.[22] In addition to the Code of Civil Procedure, other laws may require the posting of security for specific types of actions. Thus, the Commercial

18 This failure to make an exhaustive pre-filing investigation (based in part on lack of pre-filing discovery devices) is probably one of the reasons for substantial delay in Japanese litigation.

19 CCP Article 75.

20 CCP Article 78.

21 CCP Article 76.

22 CPR Rule 29. Where security is required by a law other than the Code of Civil Procedure, the same methods of providing security—bond, cash or negotiable securities apply.

Code provides that a defendant in a derivative lawsuit may move to require the plaintiff to post security.[23] Similarly where a creditor sues challenging a merger, the court may, on motion of the company, order the creditor to post security.[24]

Another cost of litigation is the cost in time and use benefit of resources. If the alternative to litigation is resolution—with less than full recovery—the cost of seeking to obtain full recovery becomes a cost of following the litigation alternative. This represents a true cost in Japan, as there are numerous opportunities to resolve the matter through mutual compromise and settlement.

On the benefit side of the equation there is the hoped for recovery. This recovery should be discounted to take account of the likelihood that the court will attempt to bring about a settlement of litigation and settlement means some form of compromise. In addition, the reality is that damage awards in Japan are significantly lower than awards in the United States. There is no windfall pot of gold at the end of the Japanese civil litigation rainbow. Not only are damages low[25] but there are no punitive damages. However, since damage awards in Japan generally are quite consistent, a prospective litigant can make a reasonably good estimate of what the recovery in the case would be assuming success and a final not settled/compromised judgment. As damage awards in Japan are consistent, parties are more likely to settle before litigation than is the case in the United States since each side has a reasonably good (and common) understanding of what the likely financial outcome will be. With such information in the hands of the disputing parties settlement that saves the plaintiff litigation costs and discounts the recovery so that the defendant can share in such savings is more rational than litigation.

One factor that the potential plaintiff usually need not consider is the defendant's counsel fees. This is because Japan, like the United States, typically follows the American Rule[26] for counsel fees. Under this rule each side pays its own counsel fees. However, in tort cases the fee actually paid by plaintiff to its lawyer is considered as an aspect of the damages in the case. (Courts rendering judgments in tort cases typically discount the lawyer's fee to less than plaintiff's actual cost.) Japan does have some fee shifting statutes that may need to be considered, such as the rule that permits a successful derivative lawsuit plaintiff to recover attorney's fees from the defendant. The American Rule is presently under consideration for revision in Japan. The Law Reform Council has recommended that the rule be changed to allow the winning party to collect its legal fees from the losing party. The supposed rationale for this proposed change is that it will lead to greater use

---

23 Commercial Code Article 267 (5).

24 Commercial Code Article 106 (1).

25 The Law Reform Council acknowledged the criticism that damages in Japan are not adequate but made no substantive recommendation to increase damage awards. Recommendations of the Justice System Reform Council: For a Justice System to Support Japan in the 21st Century, 6/12/01 on the web at *www.kantei.go.jp/foreign/policy/sihou/singikai/990612_e.html* 7-Expnasion of Access to the courts (4) Effective Relief for Victims.

26 Alyeska Pipeline Service Co. v. Wilderness Society, 421 U.S. 240 (1975).

of the legal system.[27] Reform of the fee system to allow plaintiffs to recover fees as part of a winning determination would open up the courthouse to additional litigation. Permitting a successful defendant to recover fees from a plaintiff would add an additional potential cost to the cost benefit analysis and would reduce the use of litigation. In the spring of 2004 the Cabinet submitted a bill to the Diet under which the court could award attorney's fees to the winner of a case if the parties at any time prior to the close of the Plenary Hearing (Oral Argument) agreed to such arrangement but the Diet failed to take action on such bill.[28]

2) Pre-Filing Factual Analysis

Before filing suit the plaintiff must analyze the facts known to the plaintiff that would support litigation. Factual analysis, investigation and discovery before filing are particularly important in Japan as the Japanese system does not countenance information and belief pleading backed up by a Rule 11 obligation of counsel. Rather, Japan follows a fact pleading system, not uncommon in civil law countries. Litigation in Japan is initiated by written Complaint (in Summary Court an oral Complaint is permitted)[29] that must contain a description of the parties, counsel and the grounds for the claim set forth.[30] Although the Code itself does not mention what papers must accompany this description of the claim, the Rules flush out the Code provision. In addition to stating the grounds for the claim, the Complaint must set forth facts on which the claim is based. It is not sufficient to allege ultimate facts but also underlying facts that need to be established to support the claim must be asserted.[31] Failure to properly plead the facts supporting the plaintiff's case can lead to dismissal before the Complaint is even served on the defendant.[32]

---

27 Recommendations of the Justice System Reform Council: For a Justice System to Support Japan in the 21st Century, 6/12/01 on the web at *www.kantei.go.jp/foreign/policy/sihou/singikai/990612_e.html* Recommendation 7. Expansion of Access to the courts b) Losing Party Responsibility for Lawyer Fees.

28 Proposed Civil Procedure Cost Act new section 28-3 (5). If the bill is enacted in substantially the same form as submitted, it remains to be seen how the courts will handle pre-dispute agreements regarding attorneys' fees. Such arrangements by contract are part of the right of parties to set their own contractual terms. If one party to the contract refused to honor the contract's term by refusing to agree to loser pays during the course of the Oral Argument, attorney's fees might still be ordered against the party in default on the grounds of breach of contract—the fees would be part (or if the defendant won the breach action all) of the damages. On the other hand, the court might find a clause in a consumer loan contract that allows the winner to recover attorney's fees as an abuse of rights or a violation of good morals (considering the relative positions of the loan company and the borrower) in violation of Civil Code Article 1. On the other hand a clause in a contract between commercial equals might be acceptable.

29 CCP Article 271.

30 CCP Article 133.

31 CPR Rule 53.

32 CCP Article 137.

Many facts that in an American proceeding would be "discovered" in pretrial procedures must be known in Japan before the Complaint can be filed. Hence, the prospective plaintiff and counsel should perform a much more demanding pre-filing investigation into the facts than would be true in the United States. Investigation is complicated by the fact that the tools available in American pretrial procedures are not available in Japan, either after filing or pre-filing. Moreover counsel do not want to spend time on pre-filing investigation because of the costs involved. Not only does the Code require fact pleading but also it requires that evidence supporting the facts on which the claim is based must be referred to in the Complaint.[33] To the extent possible the Complaint should link evidence to fact allegations. Thus, the function of the Complaint in Japan is significantly greater than the function of the Complaint in the United States. In the United States the Complaint serves a "notice" purpose consistent with the Due Process requirement of Notice and Opportunity to Defend. As it is basically a notice document, the Complaint is sufficient if it notifies the defendant that it is being sued and sets out the basis of the claim on which it must defend itself. In Japan the Complaint serves this notice function but in addition it is a part of the issue and fact (evidence) clarification process.[34] It serves an issue and fact identification function by requiring that factual allegations be made and evidence relied on be submitted. As a consequence the defendant knows what it must defend against. The court is also advised at an early stage what the significant facts of the case are. As the Answer serves a similar function, the two documents together theoretically serve to narrow the issues for the Oral Argument.[35]

To obtain pre-filing factual materials, Japanese plaintiffs and their counsel are limited to the following devices: 1) pre-filing perpetuation of testimony; 2) requests made through a Bar Association and 3) the new (2003) pre-filing Inquiry Process. Unfortunately procedures 1 and 2 are not much assistance and procedure 3 is untested. Considering the history of the model for pre-filing Inquiry—the post-filing Inquiry Process—there is no reason to believe this device will provide meaningful discovery.

Articles 234 through 242 of the Code deal with preservation of evidence. A motion to preserve evidence may be made either before litigation is commenced or

---

33 International Commercial Litigation in Japan, Masafumi Kodama & Jay Tyndall, Kitahama Law Office, on the web at *www.Masafumi Kodama & Jay Tyndall, Kitahama.or.jp/English/litigatn.htm* at page 7 of 14 (8/1/2000).

34 See, Takeshi Kojima, Japanese Civil Procedure in Comparative Law Perspective, 46 Kansas Law Review 687, 697 (1998).

35 The ALI/UNIDROIT Principles and Rules of Transnational Civil Procedure (Proposed Final Draft, 3/9/04) adopt the civil law approach to pleadings with modifications to permit some discovery. Rule 12 (Statement of Claim) requires fact pleading in the Complaint but permits the court to take into account the possibility that facts and evidence will be developed during the course of the proceedings. Similarly Rule 13 follows the same approach with the Answer and Counterclaim.

after litigation has been started.[36] If litigation has not yet been initiated, the proper court to hear such a motion is the court where the person whose testimony is sought to be preserved is located or where the person holding documents sought to be preserved is located or where a thing to be examined is located.[37] The motion must be in writing and must name the adverse party (if known or if not some indication of the likely adverse party), the facts that will be proved by the preservation, the evidence to be preserved, and the reason why the preservation of evidence is necessary.[38] Where an adverse party is designated, it may oppose the motion. If no adverse party can be designated, the court may appoint someone to represent the interests of the unknown adverse party.[39] The preservation of evidence is within the discretion of the initial trial court and the trial court's determination is not subject to appeal.[40] The preservation device is not limited to use by a potential plaintiff but may also be used by a potential defendant. The holder of the evidence to be preserved need not be a potential party but can be a potential future witness.

Because a motion to preserve evidence may be made prior to the filing of the Complaint it has the possibility of being used as a means to discover facts required to be alleged in the Complaint. Thus it can sometimes have a pre-filing discovery aspect.[41] The problem for the potential plaintiff is that the procedure is not designed to be a discovery device and the moving party must convince the court of the need to preserve the evidence. Thus the movant must make some showing as to what the evidence will or is likely to show and must make a showing that there exists a need to preserve the evidence. Preservation may be required where there is reason to believe that a witness may die or leave the country before the case is filed or the testimony can be taken.[42] But such situations are relatively rare. If the court can be convinced that evidence may be destroyed before trial then there exists a basis for preservation. The matter is entirely discretionary with the court. Such a motion may be (and has been) successfully employed in medical malpractice cases where there is concern that the medical records will be modified or destroyed unless preserved. It has also been used in commercial cases where there is concern that a part of a factory or a manufacturing process will be destroyed or that software will be removed from computers before it can be examined for its evidentiary value. The procedure may be used in cases where a witness is about to leave the country and there is concern as to whether the testimony of the witness would then become unavailable.

---

36 CCP Article 235.

37 CCP Article 235 (2).

38 CPR Rule 153.

39 CCP Article 236.

40 CCP Article 238.

41 Hiroshi Oda, JAPANESE LAW (Oxford University Press, 2nd ed. 1999) 401.

42 See, Itsuko Mori, The Difference Between U.S. Discovery and Japanese Taking of Evidence, 23 International Lawyer 3 (1978).

The device has sometimes been used to preserve (and in the process discover) evidence.[43] However, because it is not designed to be a discovery device (indeed, a proposal to expand preservation to make it a "discovery device" was specifically rejected)[44] and because of the showing that the potential plaintiff must make to obtain an order to preserve, it has limited value.[45] It has been suggested that notwithstanding the technical requirements of the rule, preservation is in fact more useful in obtaining discovery than would appear on the face of the Code requirements.[46] The preservation of evidence device was used in a recent software copying case where pursuant to a preservation order the court examined the premises of the alleged infringer and found copies of the software on numerous computers. Preservation was needed as otherwise the infringing copies could have been quickly removed from the computers thereby effectively destroying the evidence of infringement.[47] Preservation may be used to attempt to get discovery in cases like the infringement case and in many malpractice cases because the party seeking preservation knows of the existence of the evidence and is truly trying to preserve it. In the process the party may learn somewhat more but preservation lacks the discovery nature of discovering something basically unknown. Where the evidence to be preserved is not in the possession of the prospective defendant even a court Order may have limited effect in actually getting preservation since there does not appear to be any viable sanction for failure to comply. The only sanction

43 For a discussion of preservation of evidence see, Changes in Japanese Litigation Practice, new Code of Civil Procedure page 6 of 7 on the web at *www.asahi-net.or.jp/*; Craig P. Wagnild, Civil Law Discovery in Japan: A Comparison of Japanese and U.S. Methods of Evidence Collection in Civil Litigation, 3 Asian-Pacific Law and Policy Journal 1, 9-10 (2002); International Commercial Litigation in Japan, Masafumi Kodama & Jay Tyndall, Kitahama Law Office, on the web at *www.Masafumi Kodama & Jay Tyndall, Kitahama.or.jp/English/litigatn.htm* at page 7 of 14 (8/1/2000); Koji Harada, Civil Discovery Under Japanese Law, 16 Law in Japan 21, 26-28 (1983).

44 See, Takeshi Kojima, Japanese Civil Procedure in Comparative Law Perspective, 46 Kansas Law Review 687, 704 (1998).

45 Preservation of evidence also is a device available in criminal cases. Thus the Supreme Court in agreeing that a prosecutor could introduce into evidence the uncross-examined depositions of thirteen witnesses in a criminal prostitution case, all of whom were awaiting imposed deportation at the time of giving the depositions, noted that the defense lawyer had not sought to preserve the evidence of the witnesses before their deportation. Case No. 1990 (A) No. 72, 49 Keishu 741 (Sup. Ct., Petty Bench 6/20/95) available in English on the web through the web site of the Supreme Court of Japan (of particular interest is the recognition of the concurring Justice that most criminal suspects have no lawyer who could seek such preservation in a timely fashion—all Justices agreed that the issue before the court was weighing the interests of the prosecution versus the interests of the immigration authorities—the interests of the criminally accused were not part of this weighing function as long as the prosecution did not intend to take advantage of the fact that the witnesses would be unavailable at trial because of deportation.)

46 See, Kuo-Chang Huang, INTRODUCING DISCOVERY INTO CIVIL LAW 110-123 (Carolina Academic Press, 2003).

47 See, Dr. Shoichi Okuyama, Recent IP Events in Japan October 1996 on the web at *www.okuyama.com/cipa_ai.doc* page 8 of 10.

available appears to be the modest fines that can be assessed against third persons that refuse to make production ordered during litigation.[48]

Another mechanism used to obtain discovery prior to filing a case is the request for evidence through a Bar Association. Such a request is made pursuant to the Lawyer's Law.[49] The request is first sent to the requesting attorney's local Bar Association. After review the Association may send it on to the entity from which evidence is sought. The Association may also reject the request. The matter of forwarding the request is discretionary with the Bar Association. Response from the entity receiving the request is also discretionary. The law appears to reflect the former practice where an attorney was prohibited from directly seeking out and inquiring of witnesses because of concern that to do so would violate legal ethics (concern that the lawyer's questioning might skew the witness testimony). By using the intermediary of the Bar Association this ethical concern could be avoided. But with the new "adversarial" nature of litigation, lawyers may and do question third parties and conduct their own investigation prior to filing suit. Moreover, the scope of the Lawyer's Law is limited regarding the parties to whom such a request may be sent. In any event, if the third person involved were willing to disclose information it would appear that a more direct approach would reveal more useful information. On the other hand, if the third person is unwilling to cooperate, the sending of the request will not elicit a favorable response.[50]

It remains to be seen whether an approach taken in the United States to obtain evidence in advance of litigation (and during litigation as well) will take root in Japan, namely the Freedom of Information Act. In the 1980s and 1990's many Japanese municipalities and some prefectures enacted local Freedom of Information acts granting residents the ability to obtain certain documents from the local authorities. These steps by local authorities led to the passage of a National Freedom of Information Act. While more limited than the American FOIA, the Japanese law provides a potential avenue for obtaining information in the hands of government authorities prior to the filing of litigation. Many Japanese lawyers are aware of the power of a Freedom of Information Act to aid in the gathering of evi-

---

48 See, e.g., CCP Article 193 fine of 100,000yen for failure of a witness to appear or CCP Article 225 non-penal fine of 200,000yen for third person (non-party) failure to produce a document ordered to be produced. It is technically possible to refer a refusal case to the public prosecutor for prosecutorial action but such use of the criminal law to enforce a civil case "discovery" request is not a viable option.

49 Lawyers Law, Law No. 221 of 1951 Article 23-2.

50 For a discussion of the request via the Bar Association see, Craig P. Wagnild, Civil Law Discovery in Japan: A Comparison of Japanese and U.S. Methods of Evidence Collection in Civil Litigation, 3 Asian-Pacific Law and Policy Journal 1, 10-11 (2002); International Commercial Litigation in Japan, Masafumi Kodama & Jay Tyndall, Kitahama Law Office, on the web at *www.Masafumi Kodama & Jay Tyndall, Kitahama.or.jp/English/litigatn.htm* at page 7 of 14 (8/1/2000); Koji Harada, Civil Discovery Under Japanese Law, 16 Law in Japan 21, 25-26 (1983).

dence, as they are familiar with the American experience.[51] Although not provided for by the Code of Civil Procedure, there is no reason why lawyers who expect that the government is in possession of documentary evidence that could assist in a potential litigation could not use the new Freedom of Information Act to try to obtain that information. There is no prohibition against utilizing such information, once obtained, in litigation.[52]

The 2003 amendment of the Code of Civil Procedure[53] added new sections 132-2 through 8 embodying a new pre-filing Inquiry Process. The purpose of the procedure is to give a potential plaintiff a potential means of obtaining pre-filing discovery from a named presumed defendant.[54] The Inquiry procedure is modeled after the post-filing Inquiry procedure found in Article 163 of the Code. To understand the new procedure and to consider whether it has any vitality as a pre-filing discovery tool, it is necessary to understand the practice under the post-filing Inquiry procedure.

The post-filing Inquiry procedure[55] allows a party to inquire of its adversary concerning matters as to which proof may be required in the case. The inquiry must be made in writing and must contain certain identifying characteristics, i.e., the names of the inquiring party and counsel, the name of the case and the court where pending and the date of the inquiry.[56] The inquiry must contain specific questions and give the reason why inquiry is required.[57] The inquiry must make reference to Code Article 163 to demonstrate that the inquiry is made pursuant to said provision. It must state the time within which response is requested. It must contain the postal address and fax of the inquiring person.[58] Inquiries are limited to matters needed to prepare the case or proofs in the case. However, not all matters may be inquired into. Inquiries may not be general or imprecise but must be specific and particularized; they may not insult or embarrass the party sent to; they may not duplicate previous inquires; they must relate to facts and not ask for opinion; and the inquiry may not seek privileged matter (unless the party has been relieved of his privilege obligation by a person waiving the privilege). Moreover, the inquiry is improper if response requires the expenditure of significant time or

---

51 See, Toshiro M. Mochizuki, Baby Step or Giant Leap:? Parties Expanded Access to Documentary Evidence Under the New Japanese Code of Civil Procedure, 40 Harvard International Law Journal 285, 286 (1999).

52 For a discussion of passage of Japan's Freedom of Information Act see, Diet Enacts Freedom of Information Law on the web at *www.fpcj.jp/e.shiryo/jb/j9911.html* (Foreign Press Center/Japan).

53 An Act to Amend the Civil Procedure Act, Law No. 108 of 15 Heisei (7/16/2003).

54 For a discussion of the process written while the bill was in preparation see, Koichi Miki "Roles of Judges and Attorneys under the Non-Sanction Scheme in Japanese Civil Procedure" delivered at the Symposium on Multiple Roles and Interaction of Judges and Attorneys in Modern Civil Litigation held at Chuo-o University, 6/1/03 p. 18-19.

55 CCP Article 163.

56 CPR Rule 84 (2) (i-iv).

57 CPR Rule 84 (2) (v).

58 CPR Rule 84 (2) (vi-viii).

money to get the answer.[59] As it is improper to inquire as to matter that has already been the subject of a previous inquiry the Code appears to contemplate the possibility of multiple sets of inquiries.

The post-filing Inquiry procedure was modeled after the American Interrogatory procedure. However, it differs greatly from the American procedure. As an initial matter, in Japan the Inquiry Process is considered a "lawyer to lawyer" process with lawyers both asking and in theory answering inquiries. In the United States while Interrogatories are served through counsel, it is the client (party) that answers interrogatories and the lawyer who "objects" to Interrogatories. The most striking difference between the United States Interrogatory process and the post-filing Inquiry Process is the fact that in the United States responses—either answers or objections—are required to be made within a short time frame. In Japan there is no obligation to respond—at most there exists an ethical obligation on counsel to cooperate with opposing counsel in moving the case forward. In addition, there is no penalty for failure to respond or even for responses that are inaccurate. The post-filing Inquiry Process is discussed in greater detail in Chapter 8 dealing with evidentiary discovery. For purposes of understanding the new pre-filing Inquiry Process it is sufficient to note that the post-filing process has both proven to be ineffective as a discovery device and is hardly ever used and when used hardly ever results in responses that are worthwhile.[60]

The pre-filing Inquiry Process is limited by the same constraints as post-filing Inquiries namely, the inquiries must relate to matters that the requesting party may need for use in the case. The inquiry is not restricted to matters on which the requesting party has the burden of proof but may relate to defensive matter as well. The inquiry must be specific and not imprecise, cannot be insulting or embarrassing to the recipient, cannot be repetitive, may not ask for opinion, may not seek privileged or trade secret data, and response must not be too costly or take too much time.[61]

Because there is no pending litigation, there needs to be some mechanism to initiate the pre-filing Inquiry Process. Under the new Code provision, inquiry is initiated by a prospective plaintiff sending a written notice and the inquiries to a prospective defendant. The notice must advise the prospective defendant that the prospective plaintiff intends to file a lawsuit within four months and must set out the claim and a statement of facts relating to the claim. The notice need not be as detailed as a formal Complaint. The notice should set a reasonable deadline for response.[62] In the event the recipient of the notice and inquiries actually responds then the prospective defendant may serve written inquiries on the prospective plaintiff inquiring about matters relevant to potential defense of the anticipated lit-

---

59 CCP Article 163.

60 Carl F. Goodman, Japan's New Civil Procedure Code: Has it Fostered a Rule of Law Dispute Resolution Mechanism, 29 Brooklyn Journal of International Law 511, 572-574 (2004).

61 CCP Article 132-2.

62 CCP Article 132-2.

igation.[63] If the prospective defendant fails to respond, the serving party may seek court assistance. A motion may be made to a court having jurisdiction—likely the court of the prospective defendant's domicile (general forum). To make such a motion the moving party does not have to first file a lawsuit. In other words the motion is a stand-alone procedure and is not part of an existing lawsuit. In this regard it is similar to a request to preserve evidence made before the filing of an action. The fee for the filing of such a motion is quite small—only 500yen or $5.00 if the exchange rate of 100yen=$1 is used. The court may order the prospective defendant to respond to the inquiry.[64] If there are expenses involved in communicating the court's direction that response should be made, the movant will be charged those expenses—but again these expenses would be quite small in amount.

The rules of practice in connection with such a motion are yet to be written but it can be expected that they will follow the rules dealing with post-filing inquiry and pre-filing preservation of evidence. In such case it can be expected that the motion must be in writing, must identify the party to whom the inquiry was directed by name and address, must identify the inquiring party by name and address (and counsel if one is retained). The motion should likely set out the reasons why the moving party needs responses and likely the moving party will need to make a showing as to why response is appropriate. Since the party to whom the inquiry is made is known, it is likely that such party will be given notice of the motion and an opportunity to object to an order requiring response.

Assuming a motion requesting court assistance is filed, serious question exists as to whether a court Order requiring response would be "mandatory." That is, would such an order actually compel an answer? In the case of post-filing Inquiry the system is entirely voluntary in the sense that while there may be an ethical obligation on counsel to answer a fellow Bar Member's inquiries, there is no penalty for refusal to answer. It would hardly seem reasonable that there would be an obligation to answer in the situation where no litigation has yet ensued when it is not mandatory that an answer be given after litigation has started. As there is no sanction against a party to litigation that fails to answer an inquiry it hardly seems reasonable to assume that there would be some kind of sanction against a person (entity) that fails to answer and is not yet a party to litigation. Considering that even an Order to preserve evidence directed to a non-party carries with it no sanction for failure to respond, it appears likely that there would be no sanction for failure to respond to a court Order regarding pre-filing Inquiries. It is likely that its supporters see the non-sanction inquiry regime as a first step that will eventually lead to a sanction regime. Whether that proves to be the case remains to be seen.

63 CCP Article 132-3.

64 CCP Article 132-4.

Related to the question of the testimonial aspect of Inquiry, there also exists a pre-filing document request process.[65] Like the post-filing production of document process, a document request would be limited to the categories of documents specified in the Code. These include a document that the requester has a right to demand be produced—such as a corporate document that a creditor or shareholder may be entitled to under the Commercial Code; a document made for the benefit of the requester or a document made for the benefit of both parties—such as a receipt or a copy of a contract between the parties where the requester may have misplaced its copy; and the catchall provision of any other document not subject to exceptions listed in the Code. These categories and the scope of the exceptions are discussed in detail under the Oral Argument procedure section in Chapter 9 C (2).

The Code allows use of pre-filing document request to seek documents held by a "holder" of the document. A holder may be interpreted to mean some party holding a document. This could be either the party against whom litigation is contemplated or a third person. Thus the process may possibly be used to try to get documents from a third person as well as the potential defendant. If the process is interpreted to parallel to the Inquiry Process then it may be limited to a potential party since Inquiry is limited to the potential adverse party. In any event, the process must be initiated by a letter to the target of potential litigation advising that litigation is contemplated in 40 days. Theoretically the potential defendant might be able to use the process to then try to get a document from a third person to use for defensive purposes. If a third person refuses to produce the document requested, the requester may seek court assistance—although an order compelling production is not contemplated by the Code. As is the case with questions under the Inquiry Process there is no sanction for failure to produce. As a consequence, requests for production are unlikely to result in significant production. Such requests are likely to make it clear to the recipient that litigation is contemplated and may thus serve to assist in promoting conciliation proceedings and out of court settlement prior to initiation of litigation.

The new pre-filing Inquiry Process and pre-filing document request process went into effect on April 1, 2004. It will be interesting to see how the courts deal with the process.

---

65 CCP Article 132-2, etc. Potential litigants can always request that another give it documents or answer questions and no statutory procedure for such requests is necessary. What the new Code adds is the interdiction of the court to attempt to order a response or production. Pre-filing document requests were made prior to the 2003 Code. See, Takamitso Shigetomi, Asahi Engineering KK v. Dai-ichi Seiko KK, CASRIP Newsletter Winter 2003 (Center for Advanced Study and Research on Intellectual Property "CASRIP" University of Washington School of Law) *www.law.washington.edu/casrip/newsletter/newshome.html* reporting that the named plaintiff in the litigation reported on had received a pre-filing request for documents from the named defendant prior to filing suit and that the named plaintiff refused to produce relying on one of the exceptions in CCP Article 197 incorporated into document production matters by Article 220. Thereafter the named plaintiff brought a preemptive lawsuit and the named defendant counter claimed.

The reality of the post-filing Inquiry Process is that since there is no sanction for failure to respond, responses are not given in situations where to give a response would work a hardship or disadvantage on the party receiving the inquiry. As a consequence, Inquiry Process post-litigation is rarely used and rarely does it produce any useful information when it is pursued. It is unlikely that the pre-filing Inquiry procedure will have a better fate than its post-filing antecedent. In short, it is unlikely that the pre-filing Inquiry Process will lead to any useful information being obtained unless and until a sanctions regime is adopted.

Although the pre-filing Inquiry procedure is unlikely to make a substantial difference in a party's attempt to discover facts prior to litigation, it is likely to be used more frequently than the post-filing Inquiry Process. Not to obtain evidence, but rather as a means of disclosing to a potential defendant that the complainant is serious about litigation. Such a notice may have the salutary effect of inducing the recipient and sender to meet and attempt to negotiate a settlement prior to litigation being instituted. Unless and until there is a sanctions regime in place to punish a party for failure to make response to inquiries, it is unlikely that the procedure will have a significant effect on fact gathering. The sponsors of the pre-filing inquiry legislation were aware that the post-filing procedure failed to result in meaningful discovery. It is likely that the pre-filing procedure is a first step and that it will eventually be followed up with a sanctions regime. At that point in time the pre-filing process will be in place and may lead to fact-finding of consequence. For the time being it is unlikely to aid fact-finding.

3) Social and "Political" Considerations

The government's interest in judicial reform over the last several years appears to represent another of a wave of much heralded but little accomplished reform programs. The financial big bang has produced more big and less bang. Japanese financial institutions have been seized with the urge to merge (or have been compelled to do so) but Japan's financial markets are not much more open to foreign business than they were prior to the big bang. The bad debt situation of Japanese banks is as bad as it was prior to the reform. Political reform has moved forward but only at a pace that allows the LDP to remain the major power in the government. Corporate reform has resulted in some companies changing their corporate structure to adopt a more "Americanized" structure including independent directors, but corporate policy remains in the hands of inbred corporate executives who have worked their way up the corporate ladder. Little has been done in the way of corporate democracy, the engine that might actually change the corporate mentality that is the object of the reform.

Judicial reform may have a similar fate. Although the new graduate level law schools recommended by the Law Reform Council opened their doors on April 1, 2004, the fact that a substantial percentage of new law school students will be *Hogakubu* graduates does not bode well for the reform. Indeed, the decision to allow *Hogakubu* graduates the opportunity to graduate from the new schools in two years instead of three is only explainable as an effort by *Hogakubu* faculties to insulate themselves from competition from other faculties whose students may wish to go to the new graduate schools. This preference makes the *Hogakubu* a primary choice of students who wish to be bengoshi. By equating education in the *Hogakubu* with education in the new schools (by giving the *Hogakubu* graduate who passes an exam credit for one year of law school) the new schools have essentially denied the basis for their existence. Namely, that the education received in the *Hogakubu* was not of the level required for a trained professional Bar. Recently some schools have questioned whether the role of the new school should be to better train lawyers to be advocates who can think on their feet and perform the kind of role that an adversary procedure litigation system requires of them. These schools may devote more energy to teaching the students how to be good draftsmen and brief writers. This would be consistent with the training and experience of the professors who are migrating from *Hogakubu* faculties to the new law schools and consistent with the important role the Preliminary Documents (briefs) play in the clarification process. But teaching drafting and brief writing is inconsistent with the intended reform.

Nonetheless, the proposal for judicial reform does reflect a general feeling that at least in certain areas greater use of the judicial system should be encouraged. It may also reflect a view that the judicial system can perform a valuable societal function. This reality should be taken into account in making the determination of whether to litigate. The reality is, however, not generalized. The feeling that the judicial system can be of assistance to the society as a whole does not apply across the board but may be limited to certain discreet areas of jurisprudence. Thus, if the plaintiff is considering bringing a run of the mill contract action then the judicial system may not be the place to go. On the other hand, because of the recognition by both government and the population that intellectual property is the wave of the future and that Japan will be left in the van unless it has strong protection of intellectual property rights, the bringing of intellectual property litigation may now be in the public interest.[66]

Japanese judges, like the Tokugawa magistrates of old, are concerned with doing "right" as right is seen through the lens of Japanese mores and values. Thus as val-

66 See, e.g., Case No. (Ju) No. 1256, 57 Minshu 477 (Sup. Ct. Petty Bench, 4/22/03) (Available in English through the web site of the Supreme Court of Japan) (Employee inventor granted damages from employer for use of patent notwithstanding agreement to transfer and statute of limitations liberally construed in favor of inventor employee); Case No. 2001 (Gyo-hi) No. 142, 56 Minshu 348 (Sup. Ct. Petty Bench, 2/22/02) available in English through the web site of the Supreme Court of Japan (One joint owner of trademark may sue to challenge Patent Office determination annulling trademark—Tokyo High Court reversed); Case No. 2001 (Gyo-hi) No. 154, 56 Minshu 574 (Sup. Ct. Petty Bench, 3/25/02) available in English through the web site of the Supreme Court of Japan (One joint holder of patent may sue to challenge determination of Patent Office annulling patent—Tokyo High Court reversed); but see, Case No. (O) 364 of 1998, (Sup. Ct. Petty Bench, 4/11/2000) (available in English through the web site of the Supreme Court of Japan) holding that even though a patent is presumed valid unless found invalid by the Patent Office (Patent Law Sections 123(1) and 278) where the court concludes during the hearing of the case that it is highly likely that the patent will be found invalid it may reject a suit for injunction, damages, etc.

ues in Japan change the willingness of the courts to recognize the new values also changes. The prospective plaintiff is well advised to hold its finger to the wind to see the direction of change in the area in which litigation is being considered. Just as American plaintiffs are sensitive to new emerging rules of law and legal doctrines, so too Japanese plaintiffs must be sensitive to the changes in society and how those changes may affect the judicial system. As litigation that goes to judgment may take many years, it is important to try to understand what the mores and values of the society will be when the court hands down the final judgment. In this sense small "p" political concerns are important in the litigation making decision. As the drive for judicial reform is not dead and as the government comes to recognize that certain areas such as patent law need judicial underpinning, these areas will be more hospitable to plaintiffs than in the past.[67]

As the public demands change and as the courts come to recognize the need to change to meet the public demand, new areas of the law may be more promising for plaintiffs than was the case in the past. Thus, medical malpractice has recently seen a change, albeit slow, in Japan. No longer can physicians assume that their word is the only word that is relevant to an issue. Physicians today must give their patients more information than was true in the past and must allow patients more discretion to choose whether or not to undergo invasive treatment.[68] It has recently been held that a doctor was under an obligation to inform a patient of a new treatment (apparently not available through the treating physician's hospital) and to advise her of other medical facilities where such treatment could be obtained.[69] It is no longer necessary to definitively prove an actual causal relationship between malpractice and subsequent death as long as the relationship between the malpractice and death is probable.[70] As society demands more information from doctors and demands redress for medical errors, litigation of medical malpractice cases will be seen as a social good. Hence a potential malpractice plaintiff is better off

---

67 See, Tani & Abe, How to Effectively Use Recently Revised Japanese Patent Law (2002) on the web at *www.taniabe.co.jp/e/information/main-patent006.html* at page 4-5. The public interest in speeding up patent cases, in obtaining more reliable evidence in patent cases and in assessing appropriate damages in patent cases is alluded to in the report Recommendations of the Justice System Reform Council—For a Justice System to Support Japan in the 21st Century (June 12,2001) on the web at *www.kantei.go.jp/foreign/policy/sihou/singikai/990612_e.html* at p.18-22 of 90.

68 For an interesting intersection of medical malpractice and freedom of religion see, Case No. 1998 (O) Nos. 1081 and 1082 (sup. Ct. Petty Bench, 2/29/2000) (doctor liable for damages for giving patient life saving blood transfusion when patient had advised doctor in advance that blood transfusion was contrary to patient's religious beliefs and doctor had agreed not to provide transfusion)

69 Case No. 1998 (O) 576, 55 Minshu 1154 (Sup. Ct. Petty Bench, 11/27/01) available in English through the web site of the Supreme Court of Japan.

70 Case No. 1997 (O) No. 42, 54 Minshu 2574 (Sup. Ct. Petty Bench, 9/22/2000) available in English through the web site of the Supreme Court of Japan.

suing today than was the case 10-years ago—and the malpractice plaintiff 10-years from now will likely be better off than today's plaintiff.[71]

B. Filing of Litigation

All litigation systems need to divide the work of litigation into parts. There is the pre-litigation part, the decision-making "do I sue" or "do I not sue" determination. Then comes the part of the litigation in which the court gets involved. This aspect of the case can come sooner or later depending on judgments of the system of how deeply and quickly to involve the court. Thus, in the United States there are some jurisdictions where litigation is started by a plaintiff serving a summons on the defendant. The case is begun when the summons is served—not when a paper is filed in the courthouse. If the summons starts a case there may even be no need for a Complaint to accompany the summons; rather, the summons may simply advise the defendant that the plaintiff seeks certain relief because of an alleged act or failure to act by the defendant. The defendant if it wishes more information may then demand a formal Complaint. The court is not yet involved. The Complaint may be served then an Answer served in response and parties may even begin discovery with no court involvement and indeed no court file. Only when the assistance of the court is required must papers be filed, and only then does the court become formally involved. Once the court becomes involved, a litigation system must determine the extent of the court's involvement and the extent of the parties' involvement.

In the United States the federal court becomes involved reasonably early in the process as litigation is initiated by the filing of the Complaint with the court. The service of the Complaint can be made either by the private party in the suit or by using the court mechanism (i.e., the Marshall's office).

In addition, if a litigation system is to determine matters in a rational fashion it must provide the defendant with both notice of the claim being made against it and also a fair opportunity to defend against the claim. A litigation system must determine for itself how detailed it wants the notice of the claim to be and what the penalty is for failure to defend against the claim. Moreover, each system must decide how it wishes to go about giving notice. The United States has opted for a general notice policy—notice of claim rather than fact pleading—and requires response within a reasonably short time to get the process moving.

Finally a litigation system must determine what mechanisms it will provide, if any, to assist the parties in the case in gathering evidence and whether to divide

---

71 Similarly at a time when the government and society in general was concerned with overwork of employees and the effect of such overwork on their health, the Supreme Court reversed the Tokyo High Court's determination and refused to reduce damages granted to the parents of an employee whose death was attributable to suicide caused by depression resulting from overwork on the job, notwithstanding arguments that the parents could have intervened to prevent injury to their son. See, Case No. 1998 (O) Nos. 217 and 218, 54 Minshu 1155 (Sup. Ct. Petty Bench, 3/24/2000) available in English through the web site of the Supreme Court of Japan.

the fact finding and decision making process. The United States has opted for broad discovery and mechanisms that make it easy for a plaintiff to sue and then get facts to support its suit. Only after the facts have been discovered, analyzed and sifted does the decision-making stage of the case, the trial, begin.

In Japan the system has made some different choices. The court becomes involved at the very inception of the case—indeed before there is a defendant the court becomes involved in making determinations and in serving the papers. The parties are not permitted to make service. A subtle but real process of diminishing the role of the parties and accenting the role of the court is at work as soon as the plaintiff enters the courthouse with its Complaint. In addition, Japan has opted for a specific notice policy. Notice of claim is insufficient. Rather, the complaining document must be based on fact, not innuendo and must be supported by facts. Exactly how much fact will suffice is left to the discretion of the government official—the judge—who has great discretion. The system provides little in the way of fact discovery devices and gives the judge the power to decide whether or not evidence is needed. If needed, the judge determines whether evidence can be obtained from an unwilling party or third person. As the judge is the center of the litigation universe[72] with the parties and evidence revolving around the court, the fact finding and decision-making processes are not easily separated and are typically joined in one large non-continuous Plenary Hearing.

As is the case with the United States, litigation in the District Court in Japan is typically initiated by filing a Complaint with the appropriate court. The Complaint in the District Court must be filed in paper copy (at least in duplicate as there must be copies that can be served on the defendant)[73] and cannot be filed via electronic filing.[74] The Code of Civil Procedure specifically requires a District Court Complaint be in writing.[75] (Suit may be instituted orally in the Summary Court.)[76] The Complaint must contain the names of the parties and their counsel as well as a statement of the facts necessary to support the claims made in the Complaint.[77] The Rules of Civil Procedure flush out the requirements of the pleading

72 The Japanese system is typical of civil law systems in making the judge the center of the process, including giving the court responsibility for determining what evidence will be needed or what documents a party or third person must produce as well as ultimately deciding the case. With such authority goes the responsibility of deciding the case correctly. See, Geoffrey C. Hazard, Jr., Discovery and the Role of the Judge in Civil Law Jurisdictions, 73 Notre Dame Law Review 1017 (1998).

73 CPR Rule 58.

74 Koichi Miki, Procedural Law on the Threshold of a New Millennium, World Congress on Procedural Law (1999) on the web at ruessmann.jura.uni-sb.de/grotius/english/Reports/japan.htm page 3-4 of 8.

75 CCP Article 133.

76 CCP Article 271.

77 CCP Article 133.

by noting that fact pleading is required.[78] Not merely the facts that make out the basis for the claim but also the plaintiff must plead significant facts that need to be proved and that are relevant to the case.[79] The allegations of the Complaint must distinguish between facts that are the basis of the claim and facts that are related to the claim.[80] Both the ultimate facts and the evidentiary facts that lead to and support the ultimate facts must be set out. In either event facts must be pleaded with sufficient particularity to identify the basis of the claim and the relief sought and evidence to support the factual assertions must be identified in the Complaint.[81] The basic documents on which the plaintiff expects to rely should be appended to the Complaint. Since the Complaint is fact-based and contains argument relating to the facts it is not simply a notice document. The Complaint gives the plaintiff an opportunity to present the facts and arguments in support of its case in the best light. As the judge who will be "trying" the case must review the initial Complaint the plaintiff knows that the judge responsible for the case will read the Complaint carefully. The use of the Complaint to set out the plaintiff's case, both legally and factually, and to have attached to it a sheath of papers to establish the facts on which the plaintiff relies is derived from and emulates the German law practice[82] and is consistent with civil law practice. The Complaint acts as the opening round in the case and it begins the process by which the judge begins to understand the case and the evidence that is relevant to the case.

The Complaint must contain the address and fax number of the plaintiff and counsel (if one is employed).[83] In addition to setting out the claim on which the plaintiff is proceeding, the Complaint should include arguments; statements of law and factual material designed to blunt the anticipated allegations of the defendant.[84] If preservation of evidence was undertaken before the Complaint was filed, this fact must be noted along with the designation of the court issuing the preservation order and the reasons for preservation.[85] (It remains to be seen if the Rules will be amended to require that if pre-filing Inquiry or pre-filing documents were obtained that such fact also be noted. The Rules may also be amended to provide that if an Order was obtained to assist in getting pre-filing factual materials that fact and the court issuing the order should be noted in the Complaint.) Not only must the Complaint plead law, facts and reference evidence in support of the factual assertions but also it should have attached to it various items of documentary evi-

78 CPR Rule 53.

79 CPR Rule 53 (1).

80 CPR Rule 53 (2).

81 Takeshi Kojima, Japanese Civil Procedure in Comparative Law Perspective, 46 Kansas Law Review 687, 697-698 (1998).

82 John M. Townsend and Siegfried H. Elsing, Bridging the Common Law Civil Law Divide in Arbitration, on the web at *www.hugheshubbard.com/news/news_detail.asp?newsID=215* at pages 1-2 of 7 (Jan. 2002)

83 CPR Rule 53 (4).

84 CPR Rule 53 (3).

85 CPR Rule 54.

dence.[86] In theory documents that the plaintiff intends to rely on at the Oral Argument of the case and other important documents[87] should be attached. In practice documents may be relied on and produced later in the process, at the discretion of the judge. Actions relating to real property need to have copies of the appropriate register attached, as do actions dealing with personal status (in such case a copy of the relevant Family Register needs to be attached). If a suit relates to Bills or Notes then the Bills or Notes in issue should be attached to the Complaint.[88] The Complaint must set forth the relief that the plaintiff is requesting. The yen amount of relief is an important consideration as typically the filing fee is based on the amount of recovery sought. If counsel represents the plaintiff, the power of attorney or other authorizing document for counsel should be attached to the Complaint. The Complaint must have the applicable filing fee stamps attached.

The fact pleading nature of the Complaint is not new to the Japanese system. However, the 1996 Code has as one of its principal reforms the concept of moving cases along to ultimate resolution quicker than under the old Code. To that end the Rules adopted by the Supreme Court at the same time as the new Code came into effect highlight the need to set forth the relevant facts and evidence to support those factual claims. The heavy emphasis of the Code on pleading both ultimate and also related evidentiary facts and evidence is designed to make the Complaint useful in making issue and fact identification and clarification easier. In addition it is intended that the fact intensive nature of the Complaint will help to identify factual issues at an early stage of proceedings and hence move the case along quicker.[89] In this sense, the fact intensive Complaint (and fact intensive Answer) is designed to work hand in hand with the new Preparation for Oral Argument stage of the case to speed up the process of civil litigation at the trial court level.[90]

Unlike in the United States, the plaintiff cannot simply file the Complaint with the court and then serve a copy of the Complaint on the defendant. Rather, after filing the court will undertake a review of the Complaint and the documents attached thereto to determine whether the papers are in proper order and contain the proper allegations sufficient for filing. In addition the court will review the pleading to make sure that the appropriate filing fee stamps have been purchased and filing

---

86 See, International Commercial Litigation in Japan, Masafumi & Jay Tyndall, Kitahama Law Office, on the web at *www.Masafumi Kodama & Jay Tyndall, Kitahama.or.jp/English/litigatn.htm* at page 7 of 14 (8/1/2000).

87 CPR Rule 55 (2).

88 CPR Rule 55 (1).

89 Shoichi Okuyama, Izumi Sato and Alan J. Kasper, The New Code of Civil Procedure in Japan: Toward More Effective Resolution of IP Disputes Section 5.1 Specific Requirements for Complaint on the web at *www.sughrue.com/clientfiles/new_code.html*

90 See, Takeshi Kojima, Japanese Civil Procedure in Comparative Law Perspective, 46 Kansas Law Review 687, 697-698 (1998).

fee paid.[91] If the judge (the chief judge of a panel or a single judge if the matter is before a single judge) finds that the Complaint fails to adequately and properly allege the facts of the case, the judge may refuse to accept the Complaint. Refusal is undoubtedly rare considering the court's paternalistic attitude. The judge may have the court clerk return the Complaint along with a notice of what changes need to be made as well as the time period during which change may be made.[92] Failure to make the appropriate corrections within the time allotted by the court will lead to dismissal of the Complaint even before the case has been formally filed.[93] Such dismissal order is subject to immediate appeal.[94] On appeal the Complaint must be attached to the appeal documents.[95] If the District Court concludes that there is no basis in law for the asserted claims or that the facts are insufficient to make out a claim, and that the defect cannot be cured, the court may immediately dismiss the suit.[96] In essence the court has the power to *sua sponte* render what in the United States would be an order dismissing on the face of the Complaint. Unlike the United States there is no need for a motion to dismiss. Since the Complaint has not yet been served, there is no defendant to make such a motion. Before there is an adverse party to the litigation, the court begins: a) its role of examining into the legal and factual merits of the case—clarifying the case; b) its paternalistic role—advising the plaintiff of changes that may need to be made to the Complaint and c) its inquisition role by dismissing an inadequate Complaint even before any such request has been made.

A suit may consolidate several claims to the extent that they are related and may be handled in the same litigation.[97] Similarly it is possible to split a cause of action and ask for relief on only one portion of a series of disputes related to the same events. In such case relief cannot be given as to the portions of the claims or disputes that have not been made a part of the litigation. If relief as to those portions is sought, a new action must be brought.[98] The court is limited in its review of the

91 CCP Article 137.

92 CCP Article 137; CPR Rule 56.

93 CCP Article 137 (2).

94 CCP Article 137 (3).

95 CPR Rule 57.

96 CCP Article 140.

97 CCP Articles 7, 136; see, Toshiyuki Kono, Enforcement of Foreign Intellectual Property Rights in Japan: Jurisdiction and Applicable Law, 6 CASRIP Publication Series: Rethinking Intellectual Property 20, 26 (2000) (Patent holder may sue in Japan for alleged infringement of Japanese patent and can join in action alleged infringement by same defendant in a country other than Japan).

98 The concept of issue preclusion would not apply to the new action, as Japan does not recognize collateral estoppel. Similarly, the plaintiff's claim would not be barred by *res judicata* as Japan follows the general civil law rule that only claims actually litigated are given *res judicata* effect. CCP Article 114.

case to the claims made by the parties.[99] The court may not grant damages greater than the sum sought by the plaintiff in the Complaint[100] (or an amendment to the Complaint). The ability to split causes of action[101] creates issues for the plaintiff. Unless the Complaint is clear that the plaintiff is reserving rights as to other portions of the potential claim, failure to raise them in the suit can be considered as a waiver. If deemed waived, suit on such claims cannot be brought at a later date. Still, if recovery of the payments sued on is granted and the payments not considered in the case are clearly reserved, such suit may provide a good basis for settlement of such payment claims without having to pay the filing fee for the entire default. Indeed, counsel with authority to settle the lawsuit may be deemed to have authority to settle the related claims even though they are not a part of the litigation.[102] Although claims can be aggregated or split, a plaintiff has no right to sue for damages that have not yet ripened. Thus in the case involving noise pollution at Osaka Airport[103] the court awarded damages for noise pollution that preceded the case but refused to consider claims of damage for noise that was expected in the future. The Court noted that as the future events had not occurred, the defendant had no way of defending itself as to such potential events. Of course, suit for a portion of a claim does not stay the statute of limitations for the portion not sued on.[104]

The general statute of limitations for a tort action is three years from knowledge (of both the tort and the tortfeasor) or twenty years from the time the tort was committed[105] (knowledge of damage caused by the tortuous event means the time

99 CCP Article 246.

100 Outline of Civil Litigation in Japan, Supreme Court of Japan on the web through the web site of the Supreme Court of Japan at p.7.

101 See J. Mark Ramseyer and Minoru Nakazato, JAPANESE LAW (University of Chicago Press, 1999) 144 (preclusion is limited to the claims actually made by parties and does not foreclose future litigation for claims not made).

102 Case No. 1996 (O) No. 2177, 54 Minshu 1126 (Sup. Ct. Petty Bench, 3/24/2000) available in English through the web site of the Supreme Court of Japan.

103 35 Minshu 1369 (Sup. Ct. Grand Bench, 1981) an English language translation may be found in Lawrence W. Beer and Hiroshi Itoh, THE CONSTITUTIONAL CASE LAW OF JAPAN 1970-1990 (University of Washington Press, 1996) 205.

104 The question of whether claims relate back to the filing date for the Complaint is somewhat unsettled in Japan. The Complaint in an action may be amended at anytime before the close of the Oral Argument, unless the court finds that amendment would cause unreasonable delay. CCP Article 143. Where the Complaint amendment seeks to add a different claim or where a significantly different form of relief is requested (for example specific performance rather than money damages) the new relief or new claim is probably not entitled to relation back timing for statute of limitations purposes. CCP Article 147. On the other hand there is a minority view that the filing of the case tolls the statute of limitations on all related claims and therefore relation back should apply. The Supreme Court has not yet determined the issue.

105 Civil Code Article 724.

when the victim of the tort actually knows that damage has occurred[106]—and where the Complaint deals with an injury to health that changes over time, the statute runs as to matters of which the victim has knowledge when the victim acquires knowledge but for later aggravation of the injury or change in the injury the statute runs from knowledge of the change);[107] for a commercial transaction the general statute of limitations is five years[108] although for a contact action it is ten years;[109] to recover on an insurance claim the statute is two years;[110] for medical malpractice the statute of limitations is three years;[111] the general statute of limitations is ten years;[112] in a suit by an employee against an employer seeking compensation for a patent invented by the employee and taken over by the employer under an incentive policy brought under Japan's Patent Law[113] the ten-year statute of limitations is applicable and begins to run from the date set forth in the employee compensation program under which the company is entitled to obtain the patent;[114] and for judgment claims, including claims based on judicial settlement or conciliation, the term is ten years.[115]

Parties to a contract may agree to extend the statute of limitations when to do so will not violate public policy.[116] Although the statutory term to collect on a life insurance policy is two years, the insured and the insurance company issuing a life insurance policy may agree to extend the term to three years. In a case where the insurance agreement contained a three-year clause and provided that the *term begins to run from the day after the reason for payment accrued* the Supreme Court held the three-year provision valid. However, in the case before the court the decedent insured had disappeared from home and was not heard of for several years. It was unknown whether he was alive, dead or had committed suicide (an uninsured event). No claim was made. Upon investigating a different traffic death, the police found the decedent's body more than three years after his disappearance. When claim was made under the policy, the insurance company rejected the claim

106 Case No. 1996 (O) No. 2607, 56 Minshu ___ (Sup. Ct. Petty Bench, 1/29/02) available in English through the web site of the Supreme Court of Japan.

107 See, Julian Gresser, Koichiro Fujikura and Akio Morishima, ENVIRONMENTAL LAW IN JAPAN (MIT Press, 1981) 132; see also, Case No. 1667 of 1989, 48 Minshu 441 (Sup. Ct. Petty Bench, 2/22/94) available in English through the web site of the Supreme Court of Japan.

108 Commercial Code Article 522.

109 Civil Code Article 167.

110 Commercial Code Article 663.

111 Civil Code Article 170.

112 Civil Code Article 167. The general statute of limitations period (10 years) applies to an allegation that an employer breached its duty of care to its employees (a kind of hybrid tort and contract situation) see, Case No. 1989 (O) No. 1667, 48 Minshu 441 (Sup. Ct. 2/22/94).

113 Patent Law Section 35.

114 Olympus Optical Co. v. Shumpei Tanaka, Case No. Hei 13 (uke) 1256 (Sup. Ct. Petty Bench, 4/22/03) a synopsis is on the web in English at NGB Corporation, Development of Recent IP Cases, *www.ngb.co.jp/english/news/2003/200305.html*

115 Civil Code Article 174-2.

116 Civil Code Article 91.

noting that *it was made more than three-years after death* (the time when payment accrued.) The Supreme Court allowed the insurance claim. Under Article 166 (1) of the Commercial Code the first day for the running of the statute of limitations is *the day when the right asserted is capable of being exercised. T*he court found that such date was the date when the body was located confirming the fact of death. The court thus allowed the contract extension to three years but did not allow the contract limitation by which the time began to run from the date when death occurred. Instead the court utilized the statutory starting date (the date when the right could be asserted). That date was held to be the date when it was first known that decedent was dead.[117]

A suit may not be filed where a prior action for the same claim by the same party is already pending in Japan.[118] While Japan forbids the same party from having two cases pending in Japan against the same defendant seeking the same relief on the same claim,[119] there is no prohibition against filing suit in Japan when an action on the same matter is pending in a foreign court.[120] Thus, a suit may be filed in Japan even if there is a suit pending between the same parties in a foreign jurisdiction. The rationale for this rule is the interpretation of the word "court" in Article 142 of the Code of Civil Procedure. The Tokyo High Court has held that "court" in this Article means a Japanese court and not a foreign court.[121] A Japanese national defendant in litigation pending in the United States may seek a declaratory judgment in Japan against the U.S. plaintiff for a ruling that the Japanese entity has no liability to the U.S. plaintiff. If the Japanese court rules in favor of the Japanese plaintiff, the U.S. party, even if successful in the U.S. litigation, will not be able to get execution of the U.S. judgment in Japan.[122] As Japan does not recognize class actions and as a representative action only represents those who have voluntarily joined,[123] several suits may be simultaneously pending in Japan concerning the same occurrence. A different injured party may bring each suit.

---

117 Case No. 485 of 2000 (Sup. Ct. Petty Bench 12/11/03) available on the web through the web site of the Supreme Court of Japan.

118 CCP Article 142.

119 CCP Article 142.

120 Hiroshi Oda, JAPANESE LAW (Oxford University Press, 2nd ed. 1999) 448-449.

121 Hideyuki Kobayashi and Yoshimasa Furuta, Products Liability Act and Transnational Litigation in Japan, 34 Texas International Law Journal 93, 108-110 (1999).

122 For an English language discussion of precisely such a fact pattern where the Japanese courts refused execution on a Washington State judgment because of a contrary Japanese judgment rendered in a declaratory judgment case initiated against the Washington plaintiff after suit had been filed in Washington State, see Takao Sawaki, Recognition and Enforcement of Foreign Judgments in Japan, 23 International Lawyer 29, 34-35 and see, Hideyuki Kobayashi and Yoshimasa Furuta, Products Liability Act and Transnational Litigation in Japan, 34 Texas International Law Journal 93, 116 (1999). See also, Masafumi Kodama & Jay Tyndall, Kitahama Law Office, on the web at *www.Masafumi Kodama & Jay Tyndall, Kitahama.or.jp/English/litigatn.htm* at page 2 of 14 (8/1/2000). See, INTERNATIONAL EXECUTION AGAINST JUDGMENT DEBTORS (Teruo Doi—Japan) (Oceana Publications Inc., Dobbs Ferry, NY April 2001).

123 CCP Article 30.

Where there are common issues of law and fact[124] multiple party litigation is permitted in Japan.[125] Multiple party litigation is particularly useful in tort cases where there are joint tortfeasors. Under Japanese law, joint tortfeasors are jointly and severally liable for the damage caused.[126] The use of multiple defendants is a common tactic in environmental litigation seeking damages.[127]

Once the court (the term presiding judge is used herein to describe the chief judge of a panel trying a case or, where a case is heard by a single judge, the single judge trying the case) determines that the Complaint meets the requirements, the judge will set a date for the first Oral Hearing[128]—the start of the Plenary Hearings—and the court will serve the Complaint on the defendant along with a summons to appear at the first Oral Hearing. The first hearing date should be set within 30 days.[129] Where the parties agree, the court may dispense with the first hearing date and move the case directly to the Preparation for Oral Argument (informal procedure) stage.[130] The parties may also agree to a change in the date for the initial hearing.[131] Where one party seeks a delay in the date of initial hearing and the other refuses to agree the court may only grant the request on a finding of good cause.[132] This good cause requirement is a reflection of German law civil procedure, which required such a showing in an effort to avoid delay in proceedings[133] and serves the same purpose in Japan. Of course the parties may collude to delay the case by agreeing to delay. It is unlikely that such collusion would last long unless serious discussions for settlement were being held outside the influence of the court. This is also an unlikely scenario, as the parties would likely prefer court involvement in settlement discussions.

124 Where several claims or several parties are involved the rules for determining the amount at issue in the case can be complicated. Such determination is necessary as the court filing fee is based on such amount. The Code has provisions dealing with the subject. See CCP Articles 8, 9.

125 CCP Articles 38, 7.

126 Civil Code Article 719.

127 See, Chris Clarke, Update Comparative Legal Study (European Union, 2001) p. 92 noting that among the changes made by the Big Four pollution cases were easing of the rules permitting apportionment of liability to defendants who can not be shown to be directly causally related to plaintiffs' injury but contributed to the total pollution that is at the heart of the injury. See, Yokkaichi Air Pollution case, an English language report may be found at Julian Gresser, Koichiro Fujikura and Akio Morishima, ENVIRONMENTAL LAW IN JAPAN (MIT Press, 1981) 105.

128 CPR Rule 60 (1).

129 CPR Rule 60 (2). In special circumstances a date later than 30 days from filing may be set. The purpose of quick action is to get the case moving quickly.

130 CPR Rule 60 (1).

131 CCP Article 93 (3).

132 CCP Article 93 (3).

133 See, Peter Gottwald, Simplified Civil Procedure in West Germany (Comment), 31 American Journal of Comparative Law 687, 688 (1983).

Since the court is responsible for service, the Complaint must contain the necessary information to permit the court to effect service. As service is a court responsibility there is little that the plaintiff or its counsel needs know about the intricacies of the Japanese service system. However, some essentials are significant. First, service is not a private matter but is a court matter. Court officials make service.[134] Counsel, parties or process servers are not permitted to make service. Second, service is personal as a general rule, that is to say service should be made on the defendant in a personal manner. Personal service is made by delivering process to the defendant's residence, business or office[135] or any other place where the defendant may be found.[136] In some cases, service may be made by mail,[137] utilizing registered mail.[138] Where service is to be made by mail it is made by court officers and not by private parties or counsel. Where service is made abroad, it must be made through official government and government-to-government channels.[139] There are situations where service can be made through service by publication. For example, if the location of the defendant is unknown such as residence, place of business, etc. service can be made by publication.[140] In the United States service by publication typically requires broad-based publication, such as publication in a newspaper likely to reach the defendant (e.g., a paper of general circulation or for a company in a financial matter a business newspaper). Article 111 of the Rules of Civil Procedure requires that a notice be posted on the notice board at the courthouse. The notice is to the effect that the court clerk has the papers and is, in essence, ready and willing to deliver them to the defendant.[141] Such notice is reminiscent of the posting of notice of "laws" during the Tokugawa regime.[142]

As noted, service of process is accomplished through and by the court in Japan. It is important to understand that service is a court officer function. Question exists in United States courts as to whether service by mail, sent to Japan from the United States, pursuant to the Federal Rules of Civil Procedure is sufficient service on a Japanese entity. Japan and the United States are both signatories to the

134 CCP Article 98.

135 CCP Article 103.

136 CCP Article 105.

137 CCP Article 99 (1).

138 CCP Article 107.

139 CCP Article 108.

140 CCP Article 110.

141 As discussed later failure to Answer a Complaint and to appear at the initial Oral Hearing may be construed as an admission of the facts set out in the Complaint and can lead to a default judgment. However, the rule of constructive admission does not apply to cases where service is made by publication and the party fails to respond or appear. See, CCP Article 159 (3); Takeshi Kojima, Civil Procedure Reform in Japan, 11 Michigan Journal of International Law 1218, 1222 Note 15 (1990).

142 For a discussion of service of process in Japan see, Hideyuki Kobayashi and Yoshimasa Furuta, Products Liability Act and Transnational Litigation in Japan, 34 Texas International Law Journal 93, 101-103 (1999).

Hague Convention on Service of Process. Under the Convention, service is to be undertaken through the contracting parties themselves and the process for service in Japan is both time consuming and expensive. Under the Convention's formal procedures the Complaint (translated into Japanese) must be sent to Japan's Central Authority (Ministry of Justice) for service. However, the Convention also permits service by more informal means when the contracting parties consent. The issue relates to Article 10 of the Convention that provides as follows:

Provided the State of destination does not object, the present Convention shall not interfere with—

> a) the freedom to send judicial documents, by postal channels, directly to persons abroad,
>
> b) the freedom of judicial officers, officials, or other competent persons of the State of origin to effect service of judicial documents directly through the judicial officers, officials or other competent persons of the State of destination,
>
> c) the freedom of any person interested in a judicial proceeding to effect service of judicial documents directly through the judicial officers, officials or other competent persons of the State of destination.

Japan objected to subparts b) and c) of Article 10 but did not object to subpart a) when it acceded to the Convention. Does this mean that service can be made by mail? On the one hand, such an interpretation is illogical in the sense that both b) and c), which require some action by an official of the destination State, are more formal than a). If the formal procedures of b) and c) were considered insufficient by the government of Japan then surely the even more informal procedure of subpart a) would be considered insufficient. On the other, Japan did object to b) and c) but did not object to a). Whether logical or not, if subpart a) covers service of process than it would appear that an American plaintiff can avail itself of the informality of mail service under subpart a). But, subpart a) does not use the phrase "service of judicial documents" used in subparts b) and c). Rather, it uses the term to "send." Does sending judicial documents mean that service of such documents by sending them according to subpart a) is sufficient to constitute service of process? Or does "send" rather than "serve" mean that subpart a) does not relate to service of process? Just as significantly, since in Japan a party cannot serve process by sending it by mail or otherwise, is it likely that Japan did not think it needed to object to subpart a) because a) did not (indeed could not) apply to service of process? In answering this question the methods of service in Japan may be relevant. If Japan permitted service by mail by a private party it can be argued that Japan was familiar with private mail service and consented to private mail service. However, if Japan did not permit private mail service then there is a strong argument that Japan saw subpart a) as not applying to judicial service. It is the position of the government of Japan that service of process is a governmental function and that attempt to serve process in Japan (such as by mail) other than through the formal mechanisms of the Convention is an infringement of Japanese sovereignty.[143]

The authorities in the United States are divided on the issue of whether private mail service under the Federal Rules is sufficient service under the Convention.[144] Those courts that hold that service by mail accords with the Convention view the use of the term "send" as simply sloppy drafting and read it to include service. In arguing against jurisdiction an important argument is that Japan itself does not recognize private mail service and hence such service should not be considered as agreed to by it in not objecting to subpart a). Those courts that reject service by mail on a defendant in Japan draw upon the Japanese process—which requires official action—and the anomaly of permitting mail service but not permitting more formal official-to-official service of process, in concluding that Japan did not consent to service by mail.[145] If treaties are to be interpreted consistent with the intent of the Contracting Parties it seems clear that the better argument lies with those who claim that the more formal diplomatic channels method of service set out in the Convention should be applied. By agreeing that some judicial documents may be sent by mail Japan was not agreeing that *service of process* could be made by counsel in the United States sending an English language American Complaint to a party in Japan. Indeed, CCP Article 108 requiring that service of Japanese process abroad should be made through competent authorities shows that this is Japan's understanding of its agreement under the Convention. Japan has no provision that would allow either private parties or court officials to serve a foreign defendant abroad by registered mail. It is difficult to understand why it should assume that the United States or any other country has such informal procedure available to serve a Japanese not located in the United States. This is especially so when the Hague Convention does not use the phrase "service of process" when discussing sending judicial documents by mail and does use the phrase "service of process" when discussing service through official but somewhat less formal channels.

143 See, Department of State Circular, Service of Process in Japan on the web at http://travel-.state.gov/japan_service.html page 5 of 9. The circular also explains the formal mechanism to effect service in Japan through the Japanese Central Authority, i.e., the Ministry of Foreign Affairs.

144 A listing of cases pro and con may be found in the State Department circular.

145 See, e.g., Golub v. Isuzu Motors, 924 F. Supp. 324 (D. MA 1996) (service by mail insufficient—"Because Japan does not allow domestic service except through a court clerk . . . it would be at least anomalous if Japan were to allow service from abroad to be effected through the mail."); Bankston v. Toyota Motor Corp., 889 F.2d 172 (8 Cir. 1989) (citing cases pro and con but concluding mail service invalid). See, Yoshio Ohara, Judicial Assistance to be Afforded by Japan for Proceedings in the United States, 23 International Lawyer 10 (1989). For a recent discussion see, Recent Developments in the Interpretation of Article 10(A) of the Hague Convention on the Service Abroad of Judicial and Extrajudicial Documents in Civil or Commercial Matters, 24 Suffolk Transnational Law Review 387 (2001).

The law regulating the activities of foreign lawyers in Japan specifically prohibits such foreign lawyers from serving process in Japan for litigation pending abroad.[146]

After process is properly served and the first Oral Argument date set, the defendant is to file an Answer. The defendant may also use the Answer to counterclaim when the counterclaim is related to the initial Complaint (unless the subject of the counterclaim falls within the exclusive jurisdiction of another court).[147] The right to counterclaim is not limited to the Answer as would be the case in the United States. The counterclaim may be alleged at any time before the close of the case unless the court finds that the late assertion of the counterclaim would considerably delay proceedings. The Code of Civil Procedure does not directly call for a defendant to answer the Complaint before the initial Oral Argument session. The Code alludes to such an Answer by providing that a Preparatory Document should precede Oral Argument[148] and the Answer is considered a Preparatory Document. The presiding judge (in the case of a 3-judge panel or the relatively infrequent 5-judge panel in a complicated case the chief judge of the panel is the presiding judge) sets the date when the answering document is to be submitted.[149] The Answer must be submitted in a timely fashion that permits the plaintiff time to prepare a response at the initial Oral Argument.[150]

Whereas an American Answer must admit, deny or deny knowledge or information sufficient to form a belief as to plaintiff's allegations, the Japanese Answer, as in the case of the Complaint is a fact-pleading document. The written Answer must contain a specific agreement or disagreement with the facts set out in the written Complaint and must set out facts concerning the defense to the Complaint.[151] If a fact asserted in the Complaint is denied, the Answer must state the reasons for the denial. If the Answer alleges affirmative defenses, the facts (both ultimate and evidentiary) to support the defense must be alleged. As with the Complaint it is insufficient to set out factual conclusions. Evidentiary facts must be asserted. Just as important documents must be included with the Complaint, so too documents that are to be used to contest the claim must be included with the Answer. Such documents may be submitted at a later date where circumstances make it impossible to file them with the Answer.[152] Even if such documents are not submitted with the Answer it is unlikely that the judge will prohibit the defendant from relying on them during the Oral Argument. Nonetheless it is important to set out such documents, as the Answer is the defendant's first opportunity to

146 Special Measure Law Dealing with Legal Business by Foreign Lawyers, Law No. 66 of 1986 as amended by Law No. 128 of 2003 Chapter 2 Article 3 (4).

147 CCP Article 146.

148 CCP Article 161.

149 CCP Article 162.

150 CPR Rule 79 (1).

151 CPR Rule 80 (1).

152 CPR Rule 80 (2).

address the court as to why it should not be held responsible in the case. It would not be good strategy for a defendant to go to the initial Oral Argument session with the judge having only the plaintiff's arguments (as set out in the Complaint and documents attached) before the court.

The Complaint and Answer in Japan serve a much more important issue and fact narrowing function than in the United States. They are the first "briefs" and evidence presentations that the parties make and they form the basis for the court's clarification function in which the court is attempting to understand and limit the issues between the parties. The defendant may serve its Answer by fax or by delivery to the court and must also serve the plaintiff with the Answer. E-mail service is not permitted in Japan. Unlike the United States where the serving party files a certificate of service, the receiving party in Japan must acknowledge receipt.[153]

In circumstances where the plaintiff needs to respond to the Answer (such as when it contains a counterclaim) a fact pleading, with documents attached, is required.[154] Again the responding party needs to file the paper with the court and serve the opposition. If a document is referred to (but not attached) in any of the preceding documents, the opposing party is entitled to receive a copy thereof upon request.[155] At this point the "pleading stage" of the case is over and the parties are ready to enter the Trial or Plenary Hearing (Oral Argument) stage of the case.

A critical difference between Japanese "pleading" and American "pleading" is that in the United States allegations of fact are made to support notice of claim pleadings while in Japan the pleadings are fact pleadings and must detail the facts that will be proven and the evidence that will establish the claim or the defense. Documents supporting claims or defenses must be submitted with these preliminary pleadings. As Japanese procedure requires fact pleading the plaintiff must have a far greater knowledge of the facts of the case before instituting suit. A plaintiff cannot rely on information and belief to get into the courthouse where discovery then opens the door to evidence. In Japan "discovery" during trial is limited. In any event, as the Complaint must be fact-based and evidence supported, the plaintiff needs real facts to be able to gain entrance to the court process. Indeed, Article 85 of the Rules of Civil Procedure specifically mandates that the parties conduct detailed investigation of the facts prior to setting forth their allegations in pleadings. In the United States an investigation sufficient to survive a Rule 11 challenge is required prior to pleading, and pretrial discovery is completed after the pleading stage but prior to the trial stage of the case.

---

153 CPR Rule 83.

154 CPR Rule 81.

155 CPR Rule 82.

C. Inquiry Process

With the pleading stage of the case over, the parties are ready to attend the initial Oral Argument. However, the Code of Civil Procedure does not move smoothly from Preliminary Documents to the Preliminary Oral Hearing phase. Instead the Code places the new 1996 provision dealing with the Inquiry Process before the Preliminary Oral Argument and at the end of the Preliminary Document sections. This is likely recognition that the Inquiry Process is designed as a kind of American style pretrial (hence before the Preliminary Oral Argument—a part of the trial stage) procedure. Indeed, the Inquiry Process is borrowed from and is loosely copied from the Federal Rules of Civil Procedure provisions dealing with interrogatories to a party. Like the American interrogatory procedure, the Inquiry Process deals with questions that one party to litigation asks to an adversary party in an effort to discover facts. Both procedures may be instituted before the trial stage of the case begins. In Japan the post-filing Inquiry Process can be utilized at any time after the institution of the suit and thus can be used before the Plenary Hearing or Oral Argument stage of the case begins. In the United States the process can be used at any time during the pretrial stage of the case. Interrogatories in the United States are typically a first step discovery device utilized early in the case in an effort to discover the identities and locations of potential witnesses as well as the existence of potentially relevant documents and the custodian thereof. In many cases interrogatories are a form of preliminary discovery device in the sense that once the names of witnesses are discovered the next step is to depose those witnesses (take witness testimony in a lawyer's office). Similarly, once documents are identified, the next step is to request the production of those documents. Of course interrogatories can be used to discover facts. They may also be used to help define the issues in a case and obtain the opinions of experts.

In Japan the Inquiry Process has a more limited role. It can be used before the initial Oral Argument session (before the Preliminary Oral Argument) or it may be used later in the Oral Argument/Plenary Hearing stage of the case. (As noted above, under the 2003 Amendment to the Code of Civil Procedure it can be used before the initiation of litigation.) Whenever used, the process is designed to balance the interests of the inquiring party and the interests of the party to whom the inquiry is directed. Thus while the inquiring party can seek to obtain relevant information, this should not place an unreasonable burden of either time or expense on the party to whom the inquiry is directed. While the inquiring party may inquire about relevant matters, it cannot engage in a "fishing expedition." Consequently, questions must be specific—general inquiries are not permitted. The process cannot be used to insult or embarrass a party receiving questions. As the process is directed to fact matters, it cannot be used for inquiry about opinions. Of course, the process cannot be used to inquire into matters that are privileged or trade secrets.[156]

156 CCP Article 163.

Inquiry can only be directed against another party—it cannot be directed to third persons in possession of information. It is not restricted to matters as to which the inquiring party has the burden of proof and can be used by a plaintiff to inquire about potential defenses. Defendants can make inquiry of the plaintiff, as the process is not restricted to either party. Any matter that is privileged from oral testimony is excluded from the scope of the Inquiry Process. The inquiries must be directed to matter that is "needed" by the inquiring party to prepare its case or defense, including its response to the other side's case or defense. The question of whether "need" should be given a broad or a restricted definition is an interesting question that may find its way into litigation if the process ever becomes the subject of judicial sanction. (No sanction for refusal to respond is presently available.) Because there is no sanction for refusal, the issue at the moment is dormant. Should the Code be amended in the future to provide for sanction for failure to make response (and there are suggestions in Japan that such a sanctions regime should be adopted) then it is to be expected that parties will argue over the meaning of "needed." What does seem certain is that any definition of "need" will be more restricted than the American idea that material should be produced that is either admissible in evidence or could lead to admissible evidence.

When the Inquiry Process was adopted, it was considered to be a major step forward in providing parties an opportunity to discover evidence from their adversary. Although the Code provides no sanction for a party's failure to respond to an inquiry or even for a party's failure to truthfully respond to an inquiry, the procedure was expected to result in evidence being forthcoming in response to inquiries. As there are relatively few lawyers in Japan, and as all lawyers must be members of the Bar Association and its local affiliates, it was considered that professional responsibility and collegiality would result in responses. That has not proven to be the case.[157]

The problem for the Japanese lawyer who receives an inquiry under Article 163 of the Code is a question of loyalty and ethics. A lawyer has an ethical responsibility to deal with Inquiries professionally and may not simply disregard the Inquiry coming from a fellow Bar member. On the other hand there is no legal compulsion to respond to the inquiry. The lawyer has an ethical responsibility to the client and a duty not to disclose facts coming to the lawyer's attention as a consequence of representation of a client.[158] Thus if response would damage the interests of a client the lawyer is on the horns of an ethical dilemma. On the one hand, answering the Inquiry will hurt the client's interest and thus violate the duty of loyalty to the client. On the other hand, refusal to answer will run contra to the ethical responsibility to other members of the Bar. Presented with such a Hobson's choice, Japanese lawyers either do not respond to Inquiries or do not meaningfully respond "at

157 See, Shozo Ota, Reform of the Civil Procedure of Japan, 49 American Journal of Comparative Law 561, 570 (2001).

158 See, e.g., Lawyers Law Article 23 concerning privileged communication.

this time". The result is that the Inquiry Process has not been used often and when used has rarely uncovered any useful information.[159] The high hopes that were held for the Inquiry Process have simply been unrealized.[160]

The failure of the Inquiry Process is due to multiple causes. Having no sanction mechanism to back up the questions asked fatally flaws the procedure. Without any means of compelling answers and worse yet compelling truthful answers, there is no mechanism by which parties and/or their counsel may be required to participate in the Inquiry Process. The reality is that without sanction the process becomes entirely voluntary. It asks too much of a client that it *voluntarily* discloses information that would be hurtful to its case or that would support a defense to its case. It asks too much of a lawyer paid by a client and owing a duty of loyalty to that client to seek to have the client authorize such a voluntary harmful disclosure. Sanctions were not provided in the Code because of objections by both the Bench and the Bar. From the perspective of the court, judges did not want to become involved in subsidiary procedural matters that they did not see as going to the merits of the case. The judiciary is sensitive to the Bar's concerns that judges not be in a position to discipline lawyers. Sanctions such as preclusion are seen as hurting the sanctioned litigant even if the litigant is following the advice of counsel or if counsel is acting on behalf of the litigant. Preclusion is also seen as hurting the judge, who is deprived of the contentions and evidence that are precluded. The judge is responsible for deciding the matter "correctly." As Inquiry is viewed as a "lawyer to lawyer" process, the Bar saw sanction as a remedy the court could apply against the lawyer rather than against the client. The Bar opposed permitting judges such a lawyer sanctioning power. The Bench supported the Bar's opposition. In the United States where clients are responsible for interrogatory answers (lawyers sign objections to interrogatories while clients sign the answers to interrogatories), sanction for failure to make proper disclosure is usually directed at the client or the client's case, although lawyers may be hit with monetary sanctions where appropriate.

Another potential cause of the failure of the Inquiry procedure is the unfamiliarity of Japanese lawyers and judges with American style "discovery." To the extent there is any "discovery" in Japan it takes place during the Oral Argument stage of the case and is judge directed rather than lawyer directed. Inquiry Process is specifically designed to track the American Interrogatory process. But the American process is part of a broader discovery mechanism and Interrogatories are simply one of many discovery devices. To the American lawyer Interrogatories are preparatory to other discovery requests such as document production. Thus the Ameri-

159 Carl F. Goodman, Japan's New Civil Procedure Code: Has it Fostered a Rule of Law Dispute Resolution Mechanism, 29 Brooklyn Journal of International Law 511, 572-578 (2004).

160 Koichi Miki, Roles of Judges and Attorneys under the Non-Sanction Scheme in Japanese Civil Procedure, talk delivered at Conference on Multiple Roles and Interaction of Judges and Attorneys in Modern Civil Litigation at Chu-o University, Tokyo 6/1/03 p.14.

can lawyer sees the Interrogatory as one tool in a toolbox filled with discovery devices and uses Interrogatories as a starting point tool. To the Japanese lawyer and judge Inquiry is a stand-alone device as there are no other "discovery tools" available. While it is second nature to the American trial lawyer to use an Interrogatory as a stepping-stone for information to be discovered through a different device later in the case, such thought simply is not available to the Japanese lawyer as it is out of the lawyer's frame of reference. There is no other device for Inquiry to be preparatory to and the idea of using Inquiry as a preparatory device would be novel. As a practical matter Japanese lawyers do not use inquiries to achieve the same objectives as American lawyers. This need not be the case. Although there is no "discovery" in Japanese litigation there is the possibility of getting the judge to direct a party to produce documents. If judge directed production were considered as "discovery" then the Inquiry could be seen as a "discovery" preparation tool. In such case questions that seek to identify the existence of documents or the whereabouts of witnesses could be used so that if identified a future request can be made to the court for production. To date Inquiries have not been used for this purpose but they do lend themselves to this limited but valuable purpose. To make this "leap" in use of discovery Japanese lawyers should receive education at the new law schools in the techniques of discovering facts. The fact is that because the adversary process introduced by the American Occupation has atrophied over the years, Japanese lawyers are not educated, trained or experienced in how to use a basically American discovery device. This can be changed.

Inquiry is seen by Japanese lawyers as an inadequate substitute for a much more valuable and familiar device to obtain evidence, namely the judge-made request. While Inquiry is a totally voluntary process and one that is either disregarded or if not totally disregarded is given little weight by the receiving party, a request for information by the judge is not something to be trifled with. An Inquiry comes from either a party or a lawyer—both viewed with less regard than the court. If from a pro se party—in a very high percentage of cases in Japan at the District Court level at least one party is not represented—the request is likely to be ignored, as the opposing party is likely to have little regard for the opposition. If from a lawyer, the Inquiry carries some professional respect (especially if the receiving party is also represented). However, since lawyers are not the major players in litigation (the judge is the major player) the request has little weight. As a judge can penalize a party that fails to follow the court's direction[161] there is a sanction to back up an inquiry made by the court whereas no such sanction exists for an inquiry made by a party. Moreover, even if there is no "formal sanction" for failure to respond to a court "request" (as opposed to an Order), such requests are likely to be granted since the court is an authority figure in a society where author-

161 Under CCP Article 208 the court may accept a party's allegations as true when the opposing party refuses to appear for examination when ordered to do so by the court. Under CCP Article 224 the same penalty is available when a party fails to comply with an order to produce documents.

ity is generally obeyed. In addition there is pressure to respond to judicial requests because the judge is the ultimate decision-maker in the case. Parties and counsel do not wish to get on the wrong side of the judge. It is possible to join the moribund Inquiry Process with the more usual judge request procedure if the two are considered as related. Thus, lawyers may make inquiry and when the opposition refuses to respond may request in Preliminary Documents (briefs) that the court direct the opposition to respond. This will put the inquiry on the table for discussion at the clarification procedures held before the court and would enable the judge to ask the same questions as part of the court's clarification process.[162]

It has been suggested that lawyers have an obligation to clients and colleagues to respond to inquiries and that Bar Associations (that have exclusive authority over ethical violations of their members) could sanction lawyers who fail to respond to inquiries.[163] But the sword of ethical responsibility cuts in both directions as lawyers also have an obligation to clients not to volunteer matter that will have an adverse affect on the client's position.[164] Since there is no "obligation" to respond to inquiries, a lawyer might reasonably conclude that a response that disadvantages its client is inconsistent with its ethical obligation. Japanese lawyers as a whole are of the view that ethical obligations to clients trump potential obligations to collegiality of the Bar. Accordingly, Japanese lawyers do not respond if response would adversely affect the client. In some situations lawyers will postpone response until a time when they would in any event have to disclose the information.[165] Bar Associations do not sanction lawyers who fail to respond or fail to timely respond.[166] As the inquiry procedure is based on good will and voluntary action, it has become virtually moribund.

Whatever the reason, the Inquiry Process is not used as a pre-Oral Hearing post-Preliminary Document (pleading) filing discovery mechanism. Similarly, the procedure has not been used during the Oral Hearing stage. This may change as Japanese lawyers recognize that even failure to respond can be useful in persuading the judge to make the inquiry his/her own. It is unlikely that the procedure will

162 See, Ryu Takabayashi (translated by Toshiko Takenaka) Practices of Patent Litigation in Japanese Courts, (Center for Advanced Study and Research on Intellectual Property "CASRIP" University of Washington School of Law) on the web at *www.law.washington.edu/casrip/newsletter/newsv5i2jps.html*; Shozo Ota, Reform of the Civil Procedure of Japan, 49 American Journal of Comparative Law 561, 577 (2001).

163 Yasuhei Taniguchi, The 1996 Code of Civil Procedure of Japan—A Procedure for the Coming Century? 45 American Journal of Comparative Law 767, 779 (1997); Shozo Ota, Reform of the Civil Procedure of Japan, 49 American Journal of Comparative Law 561, 570 (2001).

164 Koichi Miki, Roles of Judges and Attorneys under the Non-Sanction Scheme in Japanese Civil Procedure, talk delivered at Conference on Multiple Roles and Interaction of Judges and Attorneys in Modern Civil Litigation at Chu-o University, Tokyo 6/1/03, pages 9-10.

165 See, Carl F. Goodman, Japan's New Code of Civil Procedure: Has it Fostered a Rule of Law Dispute Resolution Mechanism, 29 Brooklyn Journal of International Law 511, 573-578 (2004).

166 Shozo Ota, Reform of the Civil Procedure of Japan, 49 American Journal of Comparative Law 561, 570 (2001).

be used to actually obtain answers in the pre-filing stage as contemplated by the 2003 amendments. The procedure may however be used pre-filing to demonstrate the seriousness of a potential plaintiff's concerns. This may lead to out-of-court mediation, conciliation or settlement. It is unlikely that Inquiry will be meaningful as a "discovery" device unless and until a sanctions mechanism is adopted that exacts a penalty from a party that refuses to respond or refuses to respond adequately.

8

Civil Litigation—The "Pretrial" Phase

(The Pre-Oral Argument [Pre-Plenary Hearing] Stage)

A. General Discussion

[As Japan's civil procedure system is civil law based, it operates on the inquisition model and not the common law adversary model. In the inquisition the judge is responsible for developing the evidence and for finding the necessary facts to reach an appropriate decision. This fact-finding process is the Oral Argument or Plenary Hearing. This process is characterized by a series of meetings, consultations and evidence gathering and evidence taking sessions. In the United States a case is broken into relatively fixed parts—pretrial (when facts are discovered and issues narrowed by motion practice) and trial where the facts are presented to the decision maker so that a determination of the matter can be made. The American trial is a compact presentation of evidence leading to a determination. In the civil law such a neat division of labor is not part of the system. The "trial" in no way resembles the American trial. Rather, the "trial" is the Oral Argument or Plenary Hearing. In the Oral Argument the court must find the relevant issues in the case and must find the relevant facts to decide those issues. This issue-clarification and fact-finding take place over a series of meetings between the parties and the judge. At these meetings issues are discussed and narrowed while at the same time factual claims and the evidence to support such claims are discussed. As a consequence the evidence needed to make a correct decision is eventually decided upon. These multiple sessions are all part of the "trial" and while the Oral Argument may sound like a single event it is in reality a series of sessions between court and parties. Nonetheless in judicial theory all of these sessions are actually part of only one continuing process of Oral Argument. Hence matters raised at a late session in the Oral Argument are considered in law as if they had always been a part of the Oral Argument. This late raising of issues can and does result in substantial delay as the "playing field" for the litigation could change dramatically after several Oral Argument sessions. To deal with this problem, Japan in the 1920's followed the German law experience of the 1920's and amended its Code of Civil Procedure. The purpose of the amendment was to divide the Oral Argument stage into two parts—the Preliminary Oral Argument and the Oral Argument. In the preliminary stage the parties were to raise all their issues and evidentiary matters so that when that process ended the Oral Argument stage could proceed quickly. In theory arguments and evidentiary matter not raised in the preliminary stage could be precluded and thus excluded at the Oral Argument stage. In reality that never happened and the reform was unsuccessful in limiting delay. The same result followed in Germany. To deal with this problem Germany amended the Code of Civil Procedure again in 1977 to adopt the so-called Stuttgart model (discussed in more detail below). The purpose of this amendment was to create a new Preparation for Oral Argument stage. The objective was to clarify the issues and facts at this stage while at the same time strengthening the requirement that all issues and evidentiary matters be raised at either the Preparation or Preliminary Oral Argument stage. This in turn was supposed to permit the Oral Argument to proceed quickly and in a relatively concentrated fashion. In 1996 Japan followed with its own version of the preliminary Oral Argument procedure. Nonetheless, the fact remains that there is no concentrated compact trial in Japan. Moreover, in practice matter that is raised at a late date is nonetheless presented to the court. The Preparation for Oral Argument or Preliminary Oral Argument stage fails to resolve and/or identify all evidentiary issues.]

Under the old Code of Civil Procedure, the Oral Argument stage of the case was in theory divided into two stages. The first stage was a Preliminary Oral Argument stage designed to clarify the issues and arguments in the case. The second stage was the hearing stage ("Oral Argument") wherein the evidence in the case was taken. The lines between the stages were not fixed as the Code permitted parties to submit new arguments and new evidence even after the Preliminary stage had ended. The 1996 Amendments to the Code retained the Preliminary Oral Argument stage[1] but also added the new Proceeding Preparatory to the Plenary Hearing or Preparation for Oral Argument.[2] The concept behind both the Preliminary Oral Argument and the Preparation for Oral Argument is to confirm the issues and the evidence required to deal with those issues at a relatively early stage of the case. Thereafter the court proceeds to the formal process of taking and receiving evidence on the clarified issues. In essence the conclusion of the Preliminary Oral Argument or Preparation for Oral Argument stage should be a roadmap for the trial or hearing of evidence stage of the case. This roadmap is not fixed as rigidly as an American pretrial order. Thus, in this section we deal with the Preliminary Oral Argument and the new Proceeding Preparatory to the Plenary Hearing stage as the Pre-Oral argument (or "pretrial") stage. In a sense the end product of this stage (assuming there is no settlement) resembles a pretrial order in an American proceeding. There are however substantial differences in arriving at the final written document and also in the preclusive effect of the document.

---

1 CCP Article 164-167.

2 CCP Article 168-174.

In the United States the preliminary or pretrial stage helps define issues and evidence through such devices as discovery and motion practice. Discovery allows the parties to exhaust the avenues of evidence production and witness statements so that when a pretrial order is prepared the parties know what evidence is available and what parts of that evidence they wish to present to make their case or challenge the opposing case. Motion practice, especially the motion for summary judgment (or partial summary judgment) after discovery is concluded and motions in limine to limit evidence or issues at trial, serve to limit the evidence and arguments that can be presented at trial. Rulings by the court on such motions become a part of the record. In the event of appeal errors in such rulings become part of the basis for appeal.

Motions for summary judgment or partial summary judgment are essentially replacements for trial. These motions assert that there are no fact questions to be tried—that there is no factual dispute—as to either some or all issues in the case. The motion asserts that on the basis of facts that cannot be contested the moving party is entitled to a judgment as a matter of law. Such motions made prior to the completion of discovery are typically opposed on the basis that discovery of all the facts has not yet been made and that further discovery may disclose relevant fact issues. However, the opposing party must make a showing that there is a real reason to believe that significant relevant facts are in dispute. The mere fact that some facts may be in dispute is not determinative—the facts in dispute must effect the ultimate legal question that the motion concerns. For example, in a case alleging that defendant is attempting to monopolize an industry a significant fact question is whether the defendant has a reasonable likelihood of success in the alleged attempt. Assume that the plaintiff is a relatively small competitor in the industry and that the defendant while larger is also a relatively small competitor having a relatively small market share. Further assume that in discovery the plaintiff's Chief Executive testifies that a third company, not a party to the suit, has a dominant market share and further concedes that there is no likelihood that the defendant could drive this third company out of business. In such case while the parties may disagree as to defendant's motive and while there may be fact issues as to whether defendant priced its goods below incremental cost, the reality is that there is no factual dispute as to the pivotal fact question in the case. Namely, does defendant have a reasonable chance of monopolizing the industry? As both parties agree that defendant has no chance of achieving monopoly power (because of the existence of the third company's dominating market power) there can be no chance of success. Accordingly, as a matter of law, the court should grant summary judgment to defendant on the attempt to monopolize claim. The plaintiff may still have a trial on other issues in the Complaint and causes of action as to which there are fact issues, but there is no need to try the facts in the attempt to monopolize claim. In this way the Partial Summary Judgment Motion serves to narrow the issues for trial. Indeed, if the concession regarding the inability to drive the major competitor out of business comes early in the discovery process the Partial Summary Judgment Motion can be made earlier in the case. Partial summary judgment can limit the scope of discovery by removing discovery as to facts that deal with attempt to monopolize from the case.

In Japan neither discovery nor motion practice is utilized to narrow issues of either law or fact. The process of clarification through the Preparation for Oral Argument, Preliminary Oral Argument and Oral Argument is the means utilized. Prior to the Code amendment of 1996, issues in the case were theoretically narrowed at the Preliminary Oral Argument stage. However, this only operated in theory. As a practical matter, parties not only raised new issues during the course of the Preliminary Oral Argument stage but also raised new arguments after Preliminary Oral Argument was technically terminated. New issues were raised at the more familiar "trial" stage—or the stage where in theory the evidence in the case was actually presented. In reality certain evidence had already been presented at the Preliminary Oral Argument and/or the judge at the Preliminary stage had dispensed with the need to present evidence on certain points. Because new arguments could be raised at the Plenary Hearing (Oral Argument) stage as distinguished from the earlier Preliminary stage, the issues that were to be tried were not "tied down" and defined, as they would be in an American pretrial Order.

The 1996 Code attempted to deal with this shifting sand of arguments and theories relevant to the case. Under the new Code the parties to the litigation are to submit their factual contentions and evidence to support those facts at an early stage consistent with the course of the litigation.[3] The Code does not define when such submissions will be considered as either timely or untimely nor do the Rules contain any further illumination of the Code requirement. It does seem clear that some evidence and some contentions must be submitted at the very start of the process through the fact oriented Complaint and Answer. But this provision of the Code appears directed toward the presentation of facts and contentions at the "pre-Oral Argument" stage of the case where, as part of the clarification process, issues can be defined and factual questions isolated for trial. Thus, the Code also provides that if contentions and fact are not timely presented—whether intentionally or through gross negligence—the court may dismiss the issues or prevent the presentation of facts on issues as to which there was failure.[4] Articles 156 and 157 of the Code must be considered in conjunction with Article 167, which is contained in the chapter of the Code of Civil Procedure dealing with the Preliminary Oral Argument and Article 178, which is contained in the chapter dealing with the Preparatory Proceeding by way of Document. Under Article 167 a party who fails to present contentions and evidentiary issues regarding such contentions at the Preliminary Oral Argument stage may only present such matters at the Plenary Hearing or Oral Argument stage if it explains to the adverse party the reasons why

---

3 CCP Article 156.

4 CCP Article 157. Note the similarity of this provision with the German Code of Civil Procedure as amended in 1977 to adopt the Stuttgart model—the basis for Japan's new Preparation for Oral Argument process. See, Arthur Taylor von Mehren, Some Comparative Reflections on First Instance Civil Procedure: Recent Reforms in German Civil Procedure and in the Federal Rules, 63 Notre Dame Law Review 608, 617 (1988).

such matters could not have presented at the Preliminary stage.[5] The explanation should be in written form or, if made orally at an Oral Argument session the adverse party may demand that it also be provided in writing.[6] Article 167 applies the same rule to contentions and evidence not presented at the Written Preparatory Proceeding stage that precedes the Plenary Hearing or Oral Argument stage.

When the court orders that the Preparation for Oral Argument procedure be utilized and a party fails during such preparation stage to present contentions and evidentiary matters concerning those contentions, there must be a similar explanation of such failure.[7] Taken together these provisions disclose the intent of the Code to have the "pre-Oral Argument" stage of the case operate similarly to but not exactly the same as the pre-pretrial order stage of the American litigation. The pre-Oral Argument stage of the case would thus appear to be the time for timely presentation as required by Article 166. Question remains as to whether courts will exercise their preclusion authority to make "clarification" of issues and factual evidentiary contentions at the pre-Oral Argument stage mandatory. Finally, Article 143 of the Code, which permits amendment of the Complaint at any time prior to the conclusion of the Oral Argument (trial), as long as doing so does not cause unreasonable delay, must be considered. Unlike American procedure where the Complaint cannot be amended once the pretrial Order has been entered (except for a motion to conform the Complaint to the evidence at the end of the trial), Article 143 contemplates that in appropriate circumstances the Complaint may be amended up until the end of the trial phase (Oral Argument stage) of the case. The ability to amend means that lawyers and clients do not feel bound by their initial pleadings. The amendment rule also diminishes the utility of the pre-Oral Argument stage as a means of narrowing issues and binding parties to contentions and issues to be tried in the Oral Argument stage.

The idea of issue and fact clarification at an early stage of the case is not new to the 1996 Code. Indeed, during the period of Taisho Democracy the Code was amended to provide for an early identification of contentions and factual matter in order to speed up the process of civil litigation.[8] The procedure proved to be unsuccessful, probably because paternalistic Japanese judges refused to exercise their authority to preclude parties from raising issues and contentions not identified at the preparatory stage.[9] It is unlikely that the restating of the preclusion authority of the court in the new Code will prove any more effective than was the case under the old Code. Japanese judges are still paternalistic, even in cases

5 CCP Article 167.

6 CPR Rule 87.

7 CCP Article 174.

8 Like the new Preparation procedure adopted in the 1996 Code, the Taisho reforms followed the German reforms that had preceded them by a scant two years. For a discussion of the German Emminger Act of 1924 see, Peter Gottwald, Simplified Civil Procedure in West Germany (Comment), 31 American Journal of Comparative Law 687, 688 (1983).

9 See, Takeshi Kojima, Japanese Civil Procedure in Comparative Law Perspective, 46 Kansas Law Review 687, 690 (1998).

where parties are represented by counsel. Most importantly, Japanese judges seeking to do substantive justice in a case are not likely to preclude a party from raising issues of fact or law when such issues might be significant in arriving at the correct—just or proper—decision. Experience under the Code bears out the fact that preclusion is a rare event. If preclusion were a reasonable alternative, no new issues could be raised on appeal except in unusual circumstances. This result follows as all facts and contentions should have been raised at the trial court level. The fact is that High Courts continue to permit parties before them to raise new issues. In addition, High Courts take evidence from witnesses not presented in the District Court. Article 297 of the Code provides that the rules applicable to trial in the District Court apply to first instance appeals.[10] More directly the Code provides that in a first level appeal Articles 167 and 178, requiring explanation for failure to raise evidence and contentions at the pre-Oral Argument stage, shall apply.

Of course there are cases where the court may feel obliged to exercise its preclusion authority. Thus, the Tokyo High Court when finding for the plaintiff in a patent infringement case recently relied on Article 157 of the Code.[11] (Although Article 157 deals with proceedings at the District Court, it applies to first level appeals by way of Article 297.) The case is relevant both for what it says about the reluctance of courts to use the preclusion power and for the extreme circumstance that must be presented before the preclusion power is utilized. The action was one for patent infringement and at the District Court level the defense was that the products involved were produced under a different patent using a different manufacturing procedure. The litigation was initiated in 1990 and progressed quite slowly, in part because the defendant was uncooperative in regard to producing documents—even when documents had been requested by the court. This reluctance to produce documents may have been related to the later disclosed fact that some manufacturing records produced were altered from their original state. This was not known until plaintiff challenged some of the records during the appeal process. In any event, the trial court found that the defendant had been dilatory in proceeding and that such action was harmful to the plaintiff. Moreover it found that the defendant kept changing its arguments during the course of the trial. The District Court was asked to find against the defendant because of these dilatory practices but refused to do so. The court acknowledged that under the new Code it had authority to rule in plaintiff's favor because of these dilatory practices but nonetheless refused to do so. On appeal, after it was discovered that some records had been altered, new counsel for the defendant attempted to jettison its previous arguments and make a new submission of defensive materials and arguments. These new arguments were to be presented eleven years after the case had been

10 CCP Article 297.

11 Kissei Pharmaceutical Co., Ltd. V. Shiratori Pharmaceutical Co., Ltd, etc. Case No. Hei 12 (ne) 2645 (appeal to Supreme Court denied 6/27/03) an English language discussion of the facts and decision (by Jinzo Fujino) may be found on the web at NGB Corporation IP News from Japan, *www.ngb.co.jp/english/news/2003/200309.html*

initiated. The High Court found that this was not timely as required by the new Code. The court further found that the standard of gross negligence had been met since the correct documents had been in defendant's possession since the start of the case and were always available to it. If the court allowed a change in defense tactics at this late stage, it would result in a virtual retrial of a case that had already been pending for some eleven years. The court refused to allow such a retrial.

The Kissei/Shiratori case is an unusual case because it involved falsified records. The decision highlights the reluctance of District Courts to preclude a party even when the court is convinced that the party is acting in a dilatory fashion and even when the party has refused to timely deal with court requested document production. The willingness of the District Court to allow such practices was probably based on the court's acceptance of the defense and a belief that preclusion would result in the wrong party winning. In other words the desire of the court to see that substantive justice was achieved overrode any concern the court might have had that the defendant was proceeding in an inappropriate fashion. It is unlikely that the High Court would have used the preclusion power, were it not for the falsification of records, the eleven-year history of the case before new arguments were raised—at the High Court for the first time—and defendant's conduct of delay at the lower court level.

The 2003 Amendments of the Code seek to make the pre-Oral Argument stage more relevant for defining issues. Under new Article 147-2 the court and parties are to quickly resolve litigation. Article 147-3 gives the court authority, after consultation with the parties, to establish a schedule for clarification of issues and evidence, examination of witnesses, the completion of the Oral Argument stage of the case and the decision. Such provision appears to be modeled on the American practice of setting out a scheduling order to compel timely resolution of the pretrial stage of American litigation. Article 147-3 is primarily designed to assist the court and parties in moving along complicated cases although it is not limited to such cases. While the Amendment is designed to give courts greater authority to hasten the pace of the pre-Oral Argument stage of the case, courts already possessed the needed authority. The provision appears designed to make clear to the Judicial Branch the desire of the Legislature that cases move more quickly and that courts exercise their authority to clarify issues and evidence at an early stage of the proceedings. Nonetheless, it is likely that any such schedule would be subject to modification if the court deemed such action appropriate to allow the parties to make arguments that could lead the court to a more correct, more just, decision.

In order to assist the judge in clarifying issues in cases that involve technical expertise not available to the judge, the 2003 amendments adopt an expert commissioner system. Under the amendment judges may appoint expert commissioners who can submit written materials to assist the judge or who can appear personally at the pre-Oral Argument sessions to assist.[12] Where the expert lives far from the courthouse, the expert commissioner may participate in proceedings via telephonic communications. The purpose of utilizing expert commissioners early in the clarification process is to narrow the issues of expert disagreement and shorten the Oral Argument stage. There is no doubt that the expressed views of the expert may act as a spur to settlement by the parties as the court is likely to utilize the same expert at the Oral Argument stage of the case (should the case get that far). It is likely that the court will rely on the neutral expert appointed by the court rather than on a paid expert witness hired by the parties. Thus in a case involving expertise the views of the expert commissioner will be important both at trial (Oral Argument) and at the Preparation for Oral Argument stage. The 2003 adoption of the expert commissioner system is an expansion and modification of the expert examiner system that was already in existence in connection with patent cases tried before the Tokyo and Osaka District Courts. In these courts expert examiners are on the court payroll and were (are) assigned to patent cases based on their specialty and the expert issues that will arise in the case. The function of the examiner is to assist and educate the court as to the technical issues that arise in the case.[13]

B. Admissions, Constructive Admissions and Default Judgments

After the Complaint and the summons for the initial hearing have been served (thereby giving both the defendant and the court an understanding of the nature of the case and the basic facts and evidence involved in the litigation) the court sets a date for the initial hearing in the case. The initial hearing in a contested case is typically a formal affair designed to set the ground for the more intensive Preparation for Oral Argument stage of the case. Japanese procedure is based on the theory that all matters should be handled through Oral Argument in open court.[14] Accordingly, at the initial hearing the parties orally state their positions as set out in their "pleadings." Typically, to save time and effort, the parties or their counsel will simply refer to the pleadings and adopt the pleadings without extensive oral discussion. In some cases the court can skip the initial hearing step and move directly to the Preparation for Oral Argument (or Preparatory Proceedings by Document) stage of the case if the parties agree.[15] Since agreement of the parties is required to skip the initial hearing, the Rules permit the court to confer with the parties prior to the initial hearing date. Either the judge or a

---

12 CCP Articles 92-2 etc. Expert commissioners may also be utilized at the Oral Argument stage of the case.

13 See, Setsuko Asami (Japanese Patent Office Examiner), Japan-U.S. Patent Infringement Litigation Comparison: A Visit to the United States Court of Appeals for the Federal Circuit (Center for Advanced Study and Research on Intellectual Property "CASRIP" University of Washington School of Law, 1999) on the web at *www.law.Washington.edu/casrip/newsletter/newsv5i3asami.htm*

14 CCP Article 87.

15 CPR Rule 60.

court clerk may confer with the parties.[16] Before the Preparation for Oral Argument stage the court needs to review the Answer filed by the defendant. (The presiding judge reviewed the Complaint before allowing it to be filed and served.) This is required, as the Complaint and Answer together are the first steps in confirming the contentions and evidence that must be dealt with in the Preparation for Oral Argument stage.

While the initial hearing of the Oral Argument proceeding may be formal in nature, it is significant. If neither party appears, the court will consider the case voluntarily withdrawn. In such case either party may reactivate the case by filing a motion within one month to set a new date for Oral Argument.[17] Such withdrawal of the suit is similar to a voluntary dismissal, without prejudice.[18] If a defendant has not filed an Answer and does not appear at the first Oral Argument date (after being served with a summons—other than service by publication)[19] but the plaintiff does appear, the defendant will be deemed to have admitted the assertions of the Complaint. In such a case if the plaintiff requests a judgment, the court may immediately enter a judgment. It is estimated that as many as 40% of cases are disposed of through default judgment.[20]

Not all facts in a proceeding need to be proven by evidence. This is true both in the United States and in Japan. In the United States and Japan the parties may agree to some facts. Facts may also be admitted or otherwise not contested. In both systems the competing pleadings are the first place to look for agreement. In the United States the pleadings include the Complaint and Answer. In Japan, in addition to the pleadings other Preliminary Documents (generally in the nature of briefs required to make the ensuing court sessions meaningful) may contain admissions. These Preliminary Documents include the Answer and any Preliminary Document that the plaintiff needs to file to contest matter set out in the Answer (similar to a Reply in the United States).[21] The court may require additional Preliminary Documents (briefs) from the parties in an effort to enhance the Oral Ar-

---

16 CPR Rule 61.

17 CCP Article 263.

18 CCP Article 262. Failure of both parties to appear at the initial Oral Argument is considered as an agreement that withdrawal is appropriate. Hence it is without prejudice even if an Answer had been filed. Although a suit may be withdrawn at any time with consent of the opposing party and thus is treated as without prejudice, if the other party has filed an opposition paper or submitted an oral argument on the merits and does not consent the suit cannot be withdrawn without prejudice. CCP Article 261.

19 CCP Article 159 (3)

20 Masafumi Kodama & Jay Tyndall, Kitahama Law Office, on the web at *www.Masafumi Kodama & Jay Tyndall, Kitahama.or.jp/English/litigatn.htm* at page 6 of 14 (8/1/2000).

21 CPR Rule 81. Where the Complain not only raises the plaintiff's claims but also anticipates the defendant's Answer by containing contentions that are in the nature of defensive measures against the anticipated Answer, the Complaint is also considered a Preliminary Document and for the purpose of the defensive materials is treated as a Preliminary Document. CPR Rule 53 (3).

gument process[22] and may set time limits for the filing of such documents.[23] All of these Preliminary Documents contain legal contentions and are fact-based and evidence-supported documents. A Preliminary Document must admit or deny facts and legal positions asserted in the document to which it is responding.[24] Facts that are admitted need not be proven by evidence at the "trial" of the case.[25]

A principal function of the Preliminary Documents is to help define the issues and facts in the case. Accordingly, the documents must be served on the opposing party sufficiently in advance to assist in making the clarification process as well as the Oral Argument stage of the case meaningful. Although the court must formally serve the Complaint, the parties may serve Preliminary Documents through more informal means such as hand delivery, mail or fax. However, email service of Preliminary Documents is not acceptable.[26] As is the case in the United States, failure to refute facts may be taken as an admission of the facts involved.[27] However, Japanese procedure as to admission of fact as a consequence of failure to contest facts in the opposing document is more flexible than in the United States. Facts are not admitted if a party appears at the first hearing and orally contests the facts alleged by the opposing party. If a party fails to appear at the first oral argument but has filed a Preliminary Document contesting facts then the court may consider that the denials and assertions in the written document are being asserted at the Oral Argument.[28] A failure to appear at an Oral Argument session may have consequences for the defaulting party. Failure to contest at that hearing factual assertions made by the adversary who has appeared may be considered as a constructive admission of those assertions (unless the written Preliminary Documents or the general nature of the case disclose that the assertions are contested).[29] Failure to file a responding Answer and failure to appear at the initial Oral Argument can be taken as a constructive admission of the factual statements in the Complaint. This can lead to a default judgment in favor of the plaintiff.[30] In such situa-

---

22 For a discussion of the purpose of Preliminary Documents see, Takeshi Kojima, Japanese Civil Procedure in Comparative Law Perspective, 46 Kansas Law Review 687, 701 (1998).

23 CCP Articles 161 and 162.

24 CPR Rules 80 and 81.

25 CCP Article 179. See, Case No. 1989 (O) No. 1667, 48 Minshu 441 (Sup. Ct. 2/22/94) wherein plaintiffs stated in Oral Argument that they were not and did not intend to seek damages for physical injury but were only seeking damages for "moral pain" [moral damages]. The court held that the plaintiffs were bound by their statement.

26 Koichi Miki, Procedural Law on the Threshold of a New Millennium, World Congress on Procedural Law (1999) on the web at ruessmann.jura.uni-sb.de/grotius/english/Reports/japan.htm

27 CCP Articles 158 and 159.

28 CCP Article 158.

29 CCP Article 159. See, Craig P. Wagnild, Civil Law Discovery in Japan: A Comparison of Japanese and U.S. Methods of Evidence Collection in Civil Litigation, 3 Asian-Pacific Law and Policy Journal 1, 4 (2002) (a constructive admission may be withdrawn at a future date).

30 CCP Article 158 and 159, see also, International Commercial Litigation in Japan, Masafumi Kodama & Jay Tyndall, Kitahama Law Office, on the web at *www.Masafumi Kodama & Jay*

tion, the plaintiff is required to move for default judgment.[31] Unlike regular judgments, default judgments need not be read out to the parties in open court.[32] It has been estimated that as many as 40% of cases result in default judgments.[33]

Both Japan and the United States recognize that parties may admit facts and that such admitted facts need not be proven during the trial or at least that the evidence of the admission shall be sufficient to prove the fact at trial (Oral Hearing). The systems differ as to means of establishing admissions. Both recognize admissions through failure to contest pleaded facts (and in Japan facts that are presented in other Preliminary Documents or in open court and not contested, although this constructive admission may in some cases be withdrawn at a later date). In addition, both recognize that facts can be contested through denial of knowledge as to the truth of allegations or factual assertions.[34] However, in the United States discovery mechanisms are available to narrow the issues. Discovery may more precisely define facts that are not contested. For example, answers to interrogatories that admit factual information may be introduced into evidence (either by stipulation or an appropriate witness) to prove the admitted facts. Such answers may constitute judicial admissions on the part of the answering party. Under the Federal Rules of Civil Procedure a party may request judicial admission of facts that should not be in dispute (e.g., the authenticity of documents). If admitted the fact need not be proven. (If denied the denying party may be responsible for paying the costs associated with proving the fact denied.) These discovery devices are not available in Japan. What is available in Japan is the court's authority to direct that the parties submit further Preliminary Documents in an effort to discover admitted facts or areas of agreement.[35] The court may also meet with parties in an effort to clarify the facts and contentions in a case and through such meeting narrow the issues by obtaining admissions as to facts and evidence.[36]

Tyndall, Kitahama.or.jp/English/litigatn.htm at page 5 of 14 (8/1/2000). There is no default judgment where service has been by publication since publication is not considered as providing sufficient notice. However, if there is service by publication the court may take evidence and issue a judgment based on the evidence. See, Takeshi Kojima, Civil Procedure Reform in Japan, 11 Michigan Journal of International Law 1218, 1222 note 15 (1990).

31 CCP Article 244.

32 CCP Article 254 (1) and (2); Takeshi Kojima, Japanese Civil Procedure in Comparative Law Perspective, 46 Kansas Law Review 687, 709 (1998).

33 Masafumi Kodama & Jay Tyndall, Kitahama Law Office, on the web at *www.Masafumi Kodama & Jay Tyndall, Kitahama.or.jp/English/litigatn.htm* at page 6 of 14 (8/1/2000).

34 CCP Article 159 (2) permits a party to deny knowledge of asserted facts and such assertion constitutes a denial of the fact, is not an admission of the fact and places the factual assertion in issue.

35 CCP Article 170 (1).

36 CCP Articles 149, 151, and 165.

C. Preparation for Oral Argument

Prior to the adoption of the new Code the typical practice in a contested case was for the court to order the commencement of the Plenary Hearing or the Preliminary Plenary Hearing. The Preliminary Plenary Hearing is actually a part of the Plenary Hearing. The court had little alternative because under the old Code there was no intermediary procedure between the "pleading stages" of the case and the Oral Hearing or Plenary Hearing stage. This resulted in complications because the Plenary Hearing stage had to be held in public (except for very rare situations). It was generally recognized, especially by lawyers and judges, that a public forum was not the best forum to resolve technical issues. Such a forum was also not conducive to settlement negotiation. Both the initial hearing and the early Oral Hearing (Plenary Hearing) sessions tended to be sterile affairs with parties relying on written preliminary statements filed prior to the hearing date. Little of substance took place in the court.[37] To deal with this situation, the court and practitioners developed a private discussion procedure not contemplated by the Code. In this procedure the lawyers, parties and the court could meet and deal with technical procedural questions, clarification of issues and evidence matters. Most importantly settlement could be discussed. All of this could take place out of the glare of a public courtroom.[38] This private hearing phase of the case had no statutory basis. Nonetheless it proved to be a useful device in moving cases forward and bringing about settlements.[39] This device, variously known as "Oral Argument combined with Settlement,"[40] "Pleading Settlement Session"[41] and "Hearing and Settlement Method"[42] was based on a German experiment that proved successful and was enacted into German law in 1977 as the Stuttgart model.[43] Japanese judges, lawyers and professors of civil procedure liked the Stuttgart model, although it required

37 See, International Commercial Litigation in Japan, Masafumi Kodama & Jay Tyndall, Kitahama Law Office, on the web at *www.Masafumi Kodama & Jay Tyndall, Kitahama.or.jp/English/litigatn.htm* at page 5 of 14 (8/1/2000) describing the initial hearing as "ceremonial;" see also, Takeshi Kojima, Japanese Civil Procedure in Comparative Law Perspective, 46 Kansas Law Review 687, 697-698 (1998) describing the plenary hearing as "nominal" and formal.

38 Shozo Ota, Reform of the Civil Procedure of Japan, 49 American Journal of Comparative Law 561, 569-570 (2001).

39 Koichi Miki, Roles of Judges and Attorneys under the Non-Sanction Scheme in Japanese Civil Procedure, talk delivered at Conference on Multiple Roles and Interaction of Judges and Attorneys in Modern Civil Litigation at Chu-o University, Tokyo 6/1/03, pages 4-5.

40 Koichi Miki, Roles of Judges and Attorneys under the Non-Sanction Scheme in Japanese Civil Procedure, talk delivered at Conference on Multiple Roles and Interaction of Judges and Attorneys in Modern Civil Litigation at Chu-o University, Tokyo 6/1/03, pages 4-5.

41 Yasuhei Taniguchi, The 1996 Code of Civil Procedure of Japan—A Procedure for the Coming Century? 45 American Journal of Comparative Law 767, 771 (1997).

42 Masahisa Deguchi, Reform of Civil Procedure Law in Japan, 17 Ritsumeikan Law Review (March 2000).

43 For a discussion of the German model see, Peter Gottwald, Simplified Civil Procedure in West Germany (Comment), 31 American Journal of Comparative Law 687 (1983); William B. Fisch, Recent Developments in West German Civil Procedure, 6 Hastings International and Comparative Law Review 221 (1983); Arthur T. von Mehren, Some Comparative Reflections

some modifications to meet Japanese needs.[44] Its adoption is another illustration of the Japanese civil procedure's movement away from the Occupation inspired adversary system and back to a more German law model. The advantages of the procedure were seen as: a) its generally private nature (thereby leaving the parties greater freedom to express themselves and perhaps suggest or accept compromise positions without public exposure), b) its ability to probe facts at a time when these facts could be used to help bring about a settlement and c) through its informal setting to allow the judge to exercise the paternalistic attitude that both the court and the parties expected.[45] Although successful in moving cases faster than the previous reliance on the Preliminary Oral Argument and much more useful and successful in resolving matters by settlement (a Japanese imperative), the procedure was challenged by some as having no statutory basis. The amendment of the Code of Civil Procedure in 1996 gave the process a legal basis. It also made the process available to judges all over the country whereas the previous practice was available for use in only a few District Courts.

Although the primary hope of the Preparation for Oral Argument proceeding is the resolution of the case through settlement, the Code does not mention such objective. Nonetheless that objective is at the root of the process and the court and parties are aware that settlement may result from the process. If there is no settlement, the Code adopts the fiction that the proceeding complies with the mandate that Oral Arguments in a case be public events by requiring that the results of the Preparation for Oral Argument proceeding be announced in open court at the first Oral Argument session after the preparation proceedings are concluded.[46]

The initiation of Preparation for Oral Argument proceedings is discretionary with the court. The court makes the determination after consultation with the parties or their counsel.[47] To advance the process by having the parties prepared to discuss matters in a substantive way the Code gives the court authority to require the parties to submit further Preliminary Documents (such as briefs regarding fact questions, contentions or evidence matters) prior to the initial and subsequent meetings.[48] To assure that relevant persons are present for preparation sessions, the court may allow the attendance of persons whom it believes should be present. To assure that parties are able to negotiate with authority, the court must permit attendance by persons invited to the session by the parties—unless the court con-

---

on First Instance Civil Procedure Recent Reforms in German Civil Procedure and in the Federal Rules, 63 Notre Dame Law Review 609 (1988).

44 Takeshi Kojima, Civil Procedure Reform in Japan, 11 Michigan Journal of International Law 1218, 1220 (1990); Yasuhei Taniguchi, The 1996 Code of Civil Procedure of Japan—A Procedure for the Coming Century? 45 American Journal of Comparative Law 767, 771 (1997).

45 Koichi Miki, Roles of Judges and Attorneys under the Non-Sanction Scheme in Japanese Civil Procedure, talk delivered at Conference on Multiple Roles and Interaction of Judges and Attorneys in Modern Civil Litigation at Chu-o University, Tokyo 6/1/03, pages 4-5.

46 CCP Article 173.

47 CCP Article 168.

48 CCP Article 170 (1).

cludes that such persons would interfere with the smooth functioning of the session.[49] The judge is in charge of the Preparation proceeding. This is made clear by the authority given to the court to control the proceeding[50] and to terminate such proceedings either on motion of a party or *sua sponte*.[51] In addition the Preparation procedure incorporates various Code provisions dealing with the authority of the judge. If the parties conclude that settlement is not possible and that the Preparation procedure has accomplished all that it can and therefore should be terminated the court must close down the Preparation stage of the case.[52] Once the Preparation stage has ended, if a party wishes to advance contentions or facts not raised in the Preparation stage it must explain to the opposition why it could not have raised the matters at the Preparation sessions.[53]

The expectation of the Preparation for Oral Argument process to speed the pace of litigation is highlighted by the extensive powers granted to the court in conducting this supposedly "informal" procedure. Thus the Code grants the judge the following powers at the Preparation for Oral Argument procedure:

a) Order the submission of Preliminary Documents[54] with the provision for constructive admission in the event matters that should be contested are not;[55]

b) Make rulings regarding the evidence that can be considered;[56]

c) Examine written materials such as documents, photographs, drawings, audiotapes and videotapes and other materials that serve to communicate information;[57]

d) Order a party to appear[58] and be questioned by the court;[59]

e) Require the parties to present evidence;[60]

f) Require that a managing agent or other person assisting a party in its business make a statement before the court;[61]

---

49 CCP Article 169.

50 CCP Article 148 incorporated through Article 170 (6).

51 CCP Article 172.

52 CCP Article 172.

53 Article 174 incorporates CCP Article 167 into the Preparation stage. By incorporating Article 167, Rule 87 requiring that the explanation be given in writing (or if given at an Oral Argument session the opposing party may then demand it be given in writing) is also incorporated.

54 CCP Article 170 (1).

55 CCP Articles 158, 159 and 161 incorporated by Article 170 (6).

56 CCP Article 170 (2).

57 CCP Article 170 (2) and CCP Article 231.

58 CCP Article 151 (1) incorporated by Article 170 (6).

59 CCP Article 151 (1) incorporated by Article 170 (6).

60 CCP Article 151 (1) incorporated by Article 170 (6).

61 CCP Article 151 (1) incorporated by Article 170 (6).

g) Order parties to produce documents or other things in their possession;[62]

h) Conduct an inspection outside the court as well as consider expert opinions;[63]

i) Order investigations by various organizations such as the government, universities or private organizations;[64] and

j) In cases where a party has resorted to the Inquiry Process the court may suggest that answers be forthcoming or can question a party in an effort to get necessary answers.

By incorporating by reference virtually all of the provisions of Chapter 2 Section 1 of the Code dealing with Oral Argument and by incorporating many of the provisions dealing with Preliminary Documents and some of the Preliminary Oral Argument provisions, the Code gives primacy to the Preparation for Oral Argument procedure. The Code also gives the judge conducting such procedure great authority to both narrow issues and evidence matters as well as bring the parties to a settlement. It is apparent that the court was given such broad authority in the Preparation for Oral Argument procedure because the drafters of the Code wanted to both provide a statutory authorization for the pre-1996 practice and also expand that practice because of its favorable results.

In the Preparation for Oral Argument stage the court may actually receive documentary evidence "into evidence" thereby overtaking a portion of the Oral Argument stage of the case. However, there is no provision in the Code allowing the judge at the preparation stage to hear the testimony of witnesses (although the court can question parties as part of its clarification role). Third-person witness testimony is limited to the public Oral Argument (Plenary Hearing) process.[65]

The process itself is flexible giving the court power to make use of modern technology as well as psychology to attempt to bring about accommodation. Thus, courtrooms in Japan have been redesigned to create new "roundtable" courtrooms where Preparation for Oral Argument proceedings may be conducted. In these rooms a large round table dominates the room. The parties, their lawyers and the judge sit around the table. The round form means that all participants sit at the

62 CCP Article 151 (1) incorporated by Article 170 (6).

63 CCP Article 151 (1) incorporated by Article 170 (6).

64 CCP Article 151 (1) incorporated by Article 170 (6). Under Article 186 of the Code the court may request various organizations such as the government, foreign governments, schools, commercial organizations, etc. to perform investigations. Although Article 186 is not specifically incorporated in Article 151 (1) it is incorporated in Article 171 (3) dealing with Preparation for Argument and hence by implication is within the authority of the court to request during the Preparation stage.

65 See, e.g., Takeshi Kojima, Japanese Civil Procedure in Comparative Law Perspective, 46 Kansas Law Review 687, 773 (1998).

same level with no barriers between them.[66] Sitting around the table the participants can discuss the case and, if possible, bring about settlement. If settlement is not achieved, the participants can confirm, narrow and refine the issues that must be tried in the Oral Argument. As was true of the former procedure (and is true of the Preliminary Oral Argument and Oral Argument procedure today) the Preparation for Oral Argument procedure is neither a single session nor a series of continuous sessions. Preparation is conducted through a series of meetings separated by significant periods of time. Between meetings the parties and the court can refine what has occurred at previous sessions. The parties can gather and produce evidence requested by the court, can prepare additional Preparatory Documents (i.e., briefs) requested by the court, etc. Consistent with the pre-Code process, the court and the parties use the informal atmosphere of the roundtable courtroom to clarify issues and probe for opportunities for settlement. Through its power to order the parties to submit Preliminary Documents (briefs) dealing with contentions and with questions the court may raise as part of its clarifying role the court can convey to the parties its view of the case so as to perhaps move the parties to settlement. The court also uses its ability to address questions to the parties at the Preparation sessions (again as part of its clarifying role) to channel settlement discussions. As Japanese lawyers want the judge to make the necessary moves to bring about settlement and as judges see it as their role to try to help bring about settlement, the expression of views by the court is considered not simply appropriate but is something the parties expect.[67]

Roundtable courtrooms are equipped with modern communications equipment and in some cases video equipment so that attorneys and parties located at a distance from the courthouse may participate without having to travel to the courthouse.[68] This avoids unnecessary expense. This is particularly relevant in the Japanese context. Japanese lawyers tend to establish offices in Tokyo, Osaka and Nagoya. There are parts of the country where there are few lawyers.[69] In cases brought outside the Tokyo and Osaka and Nagoya districts, lawyers may have to travel great distances to reach the courthouse. Some cases must be brought in Tokyo or other major centers by parties located elsewhere. This may be a result of the defendant's domicile or because there may be exclusive jurisdiction in the To-

---

66 Carl F. Goodman, Japan's New Civil Procedure Code: Has it Fostered a Rule of Law Dispute Resolution Mechanism, 29 Brooklyn Journal of International Law 511, 540 (2004).

67 See, e.g., Takeshi Kojima, Civil Procedure Reform in Japan, 11 Michigan Journal of International Law 1218, 1222-1223 (1990) (noting that the judge is encouraged to use his clarifying power to express views on the case to the parties. Although Professor Kojima is discussing the pre 1996 experimental procedure, the same holds true to the 1996 Code Preparation for Oral Argument procedure).

68 Carl F. Goodman, Japan's New Civil Procedure Code: Has it Fostered a Rule of Law Dispute Resolution Mechanism, 29 Brooklyn Journal of International Law 511, 540 (2004).

69 See, Curtis J. Milhaupt and Mark D. West, Law's Dominion and the Market for Legal Elites in Japan, 34 Law & Policy in International Business 451, 460 (2003) noting that 75% of the Japanese Bar is located in Tokyo and Osaka and that in over 70 District court locations there are either no lawyers or only one lawyer.

kyo or Osaka District Court. Local attorneys situated at the plaintiff's domicile whose presence in Tokyo would be quite expensive may represent such plaintiffs. In the United States where there are requirements that local counsel be utilized—if for no other reason than lawyers are licensed by the State and a lawyer from a different state may be allowed to handle litigation only when the court grants admission for the case. In Japan lawyers are nationally admitted and can practice in all courts. For example, lawyers in Hokkaido may handle litigation in Tokyo. If a Hokkaido-based company has a patent infringement case in the Tokyo District Court it may be represented by a lawyer in Sapporo. For counsel to travel to Tokyo from Hokkaido is both time-consuming and expensive. Under previous practice lawyers had to appear personally for each session, many of which were formalities and of little if any substance. Under the new Code as long as the lawyer for one side appears at the Preparation for Oral Argument session, the lawyer for the other party may proceed via telephone or video.[70]

In the typical Preparation for Oral Argument procedure the early sessions will deal with the same type of clarification of facts, evidence and contentions process as in the Preliminary Oral Argument procedure—although in a more informal setting and out of public view. At a certain point, typically determined by the initiative of the judge, the court will likely raise the question of settlement. (Japanese judges as a rule hold to the view that lawyers and parties expect and wait for the judge to raise the issue of settlement so that the parties do not appear weak or too anxious to settle.) Even when a 3-judge collegial panel hears a case the presiding judge need not conduct the Preparation for Oral Argument stage. Rather, any member of the panel (except for an "assistant judge" during the first 10-year assignment) may perform virtually all of the functions of the court in Preparation proceedings.[71] Because the court has the power to make certain evidentiary rulings at the Preparation stage and because the court will already have been exposed to the factual contentions of the parties and evidence to support or contradict those contentions and will have reviewed some documentary evidence and perhaps interviewed parties, the court is in a reasonably good position to form a tentative opinion as to the merits of the case and the way in which a settlement should be structured. The court has leverage in dealing with the parties through its control over the Preparation for Oral Argument process. The court's ability to set the roadmap for the Oral Argument stage of the case gives the court additional leverage. This strengthens the court's hand in pressuring the parties to settle the case. Further, since the Preparation stage is not a single meeting but a series of meetings over time the informal atmosphere of the procedure and the paternalistic attitude of the court can create a good climate for resolution through compromise. Judges

70 CCP Article 170 (3); see, Koichi Miki, Procedural Law on the Threshold of a New Millennium, World Congress on Procedural Law (1999) on the web at ruessmann.jura.uni-sb.de/grotius/english/Reports/japan.htm.

71 CCP Article 171 (1). There are some exceptions. Thus, where either the presiding judge or another member of the panel seeks to question a party or order the party to present evidence (Article 149 (1)), a party may raise an objection and have it ruled on by the entire panel. CCP Article 150.

must be adept at choosing the right time to broach settlement and the right proposals to make to the parties to bring about a negotiated resolution through compromise. These are skills that are highly developed in the Japanese judiciary.

The primary objective of the new Preparation for Oral Argument stage of the case is to speed up the resolution of litigation in Japan. In this regard the procedure has been quite successful in cases where a settlement has been reached. The predecessor informal procedure on which the current procedure is based was also remarkably successful in speeding up the resolution of cases at the District Court level. Although Japanese lawyers on the whole tend to feel that the new procedure is simply a continuation of the old insofar as its effect on the pace of litigation is concerned, the statistics show otherwise. The reality is that the average time to resolve a Japanese litigation at the District Court level has dramatically improved since the adoption of the new Code and the Preparation for Oral Argument procedure. The average number of months that it takes to resolve the average case at the District Court level has declined from 10.9 months in 1992 to 8.5 months in 2001. The average number of months for the handling of a case involving testimony in court by two or more witnesses (by definition a "complicated case") has declined from 21.8 months in 1992 to 19.2 months in 2001. The following chart discloses the quickened average pace of litigation in Japan from 1992 to 2001:[72]

Average Number of Months from Filing of Complaint to Disposition—District court		
Year	All Cases Filed	Cases Involving Testimony of Two or More Witnesses
1992	10.9	21.8
1993	10.1	21.2
1994	9.8	20.9
1995	10.1	21.1
1996	10.2	21.3
1997	10.0	20.8
1998	9.3	20.8
1999	9.2	20.5
2000	8.8	19.7
2001	8.5	19.2

72 The charts contained herein are republished from and parts of this section are based on Carl F. Goodman, Japan's New Civil Procedure Code: Has it Fostered a Rule of Law Dispute Resolution Mechanism, 29 Brooklyn Journal of International Law 511 (2004). The Brooklyn Journal of International Law has given permission for the use and copying of this material.

The average rate of disposition may be misleading. Such rate does not give a true picture of the pace of litigation that is resolved through judgment. The average rate of disposition takes into account default cases as well as cases that are settled either during the preparation for Oral Argument stage or other stages of the litigation. For cases that actually go to Oral Argument and judgment at the end of the Oral Argument stage the pace of litigation is significantly slower. The data does confirm that the new Preparation for Oral Argument process does what it is supposed to do. Namely it results in more and quicker settlements than the old Preliminary Oral Argument procedure and even the experimental Oral Argument with Settlement process on which it is based.

Should the Preparation for Oral Argument procedure fail to lead to a settlement, the court may order the parties to prepare a summary of the Preparation for Oral Argument procedures.[73] The parties must orally state the results of the Preparation procedure at the Oral Argument stage. This oral presentation in open court confirms the fiction that the Preparation for Oral Argument is part of the constitutionally required public trial. Before closing the Preparation for Oral Argument stage the court should have finished its clarification process and in theory the case should be ready for trial or Oral Argument. At this point, again in theory, the contentions of the parties should be fixed, the facts that need to be proven at Oral Argument should be designated[74] and again in theory the parties should be barred from raising new contentions and fact issues. But, as discussed above, the reality is that the case may not be as fixed as appears since the court may and frequently will allow the parties to raise new or different contentions and fact issues even after the conclusion of the Preparation stage.

The Preparation for Oral Argument is the preferred method of pre-Oral Argument procedure in Japan. The main reasons for such preference are: a) its utility in confirming the contentions and facts that must be proved at Oral Argument and b) its utility in bringing about settlements at an early stage of the case thereby saving judicial resources and achieving substantive justice in a harmonious way.

D. Preliminary Oral Argument[75]

Although the Preparation for Oral Argument process is the most popular in Japan, the Code did not do away with the Preliminary Oral Argument as a pre-Oral Argument stage. Actually since the Preliminary Oral Argument is a part of the Plenary Hearing or Oral Argument it is not technically a pre-Oral Argument step. However, as the function of the procedure is to confirm the contentions, issues and facts to be tried at the Oral Hearing, it functions as a pre-Oral Argument process.

73 CCP Article 165 incorporated through Article 170 (6) and CPR Rule 86.

74 CCP Article 165 (1) incorporated through Article 170 (6) and CPR Rule 86.

75 CCP Articles 164-167.

Preliminary Oral Argument is discretionary with the court.[76] Unlike the Preparation for Oral Argument stage the court need not confer with the parties prior to sending a case for Preliminary Oral Argument. Since Preparation for Oral Argument may be terminated at any time that the parties conclude that it is not useful,[77] where the parties would prefer to have the Preliminary Oral Argument rather than Preparation procedure the court will hold Preliminary Oral Argument. It is likely that since the judiciary prefers the new Preparation procedure it would confer with the parties in virtually all cases rather than simply moving to the Preliminary Oral Argument stage.

The basic function of this stage is to engage in the clarification procedure of defining issues, contentions and facts that need to be tried in the Oral Argument stage. The rules of constructive admission discussed earlier apply at this stage just as they apply at the Preparation stage. Since this stage is actually a part of the Oral Argument or Plenary Hearing stage of the case, it must be held in open court. The court may use the roundtable courtroom typically associated with the Preparation for Oral Argument stage. Use of the roundtable courtroom might severely restrict the public viewing of the proceedings. Nonetheless the Preliminary Oral Argument would be a public hearing.

As in the case of the Preparation for Oral Argument procedure the objective of the Preliminary Oral Argument is to resolve contention issues, fact issues and evidence issues to the extent possible so that the matters that need to be tried can be clearly and concisely defined. The ultimate goal is to achieve something like the American pretrial Order so that the Oral Argument or trial stage of the case can move quickly. To this end the Code provides that parties should raise all contentions and fact issues at the Preliminary Oral Argument stage. Failure to do so will require the failing party to explain (in writing) the reasons for such failure.[78] The Code does not provide for a preclusion penalty for failure to raise issues. However, the general provision of Article 157 providing the court with authority to preclude matter not raised in a timely fashion where failure can delay procedure applies to Preliminary Oral Argument. Still, preclusion is a rarely used remedy.

The court may require the parties to prepare a document that summarizes the conclusions of the Preliminary Oral Argument (the same as the court may order in a Preparation for Oral Argument procedure). The court may also have the court clerk enter a memorandum of the facts that are in issue for the Oral Argument stage.[79] Although a single judge who is not the presiding judge may handle matters at the Preparation for Oral Argument stage, the Code contains no similar provision for the Preliminary Oral Argument. The Preliminary Oral Argument process does not contain any provision allowing the court and parties to utilize audio or video communications devices. Accordingly the attorneys (or parties when

76 CCP Article 164.

77 CCP Article 172.

78 CCP Article 167 and CPR Rule 87.

79 CPR Rule 86.

not represented) must appear in person at Preliminary Oral Argument sessions. This does not appear to be a matter of oversight or omission. Rather, the use of audio and video communication devices would be inconsistent with the formal Oral Argument publicly held nature of the procedure. By requiring counsel's appearance even for minor matters the Code may also seek to dissuade parties from insisting on Preliminary Oral Argument and push them towards the newer, more streamlined, potentially less expensive, more informal and more conducive to settlement Preparation for Oral Argument stage.

E. Preparation by Document[80]

There are some situations where it is not appropriate to require that the parties or their counsel appear at the courthouse to narrow the issues in the case. In such cases it may be more appropriate to prepare the case for trial through written means. The Preparation by Documents process is designed to deal with such cases. Here the court, after consultation with the parties, may try to narrow the issues and confirm the contentions and evidence required at trial, through written means. The thrust of the procedure is to use the Preliminary Document mechanism to clarify contentions, issues and facts that must be tried in the Oral Argument stage.[81] Although termed as a Preparatory Proceeding by Documents, to better clarify the case the Code actually permits procedures other than simple exchanges of documents. As in the case of the Preparation for Oral Argument procedure, so too in the Preparation by Document procedure the court (in this situation limited to the presiding judge) may utilize oral telephonic communication to assist in the clarification process. Unlike the Preparation for Oral Argument process, in this case neither party nor counsel for either party needs to be present at the courthouse. In other words both parties may be communicating telephonically and neither need be physically present.[82] The results of the telephonic conference may be summarized in writing by the court clerk and become a part of the court file.[83]

The presiding judge in an effort to clarify the issues and facts in the case may make inquiry of the parties and may ask them to produce evidence.[84] Either party may raise an objection to the manner in which the presiding judge is proceeding. If there is an objection the entire panel assigned to the case must rule on the objection.[85] Such objections are unlikely to be successful as the panel is likely composed of the presiding judge (senior member) and associate judge and an assistant judge. The assistant judge is unlikely to disagree with the presiding judge and the associate judge is unlikely to raise an issue with how the more senior member of

80 CCP Articles 175-178.

81 CCP Article 175.

82 CCP Article 176 (3).

83 CCP Article 176 (3); CPR Rule 91 (2).

84 CCP Article 149 (1) incorporated by Article 176 (4).

85 CCP Article 150 incorporated by Article 176(4).

the panel is proceeding. Thus such objections are unlikely to have much weight and if made are probably designed for delaying tactics rather than to achieve a substantive outcome.

The court may require the parties to prepare a summary of the clarification procedure.[86] The court may direct the court clerk to enter into the record the facts that are to be the subject of the Oral Argument.[87] At the Oral Argument the court confirms with the parties the facts that are to be the subject of the Oral Argument.[88] As the purpose of the procedure is to establish what is essentially a pretrial order for trial of the case, parties who attempt to introduce new contentions or factual issues after the procedure has ended must explain (in writing) why the matter could not have been brought up in the preparation stage.[89] Of course the sanction of Article 157 prohibiting evidence on matters not timely brought up and that can delay the case is possible (but it is unlikely to be used except in rare cases).

At any time while the action is pending, the court has the authority to call the parties together for a conference. Because these conferences are not public sessions, they cannot involve the taking of testimony or presentation of any other evidence, and the parties may not at such conferences deal with allegations or other substantive matters. Such conferences are for purposes of scheduling.

F. Summary

The 1996 Code's introduction of the Preparation for Oral Argument process as a legally authorized procedure has had a significant effect on moving cases to resolution faster than in the past. Moreover, this new procedure has become the favored mechanism to clarify contentions and fact issues for trial. This is consistent with the intent of the legislative change and with the desire of the government to expedite the course of civil litigation. The process acknowledges the historical fact that the judge is the controlling figure in the process of pre-trying issues in Japan. It acknowledges the historical tie of Japanese civil procedure to German law procedure and represents another movement away from the adversary model adopted during and because of the Occupation. It gives the judge almost all of the power that the court would have at the Oral Argument trial stage of the case, except for the taking of witness testimony and ordering third persons to produce documents. However, those powers may be used in an informal setting without the glare of public attention as only the parties and invited persons have a right to attend the procedures. It enables the judge to raise the subject of settlement at a time when the court is aware of the factual contentions as well as a good deal of the evidence and thus is in a good position to suggest an appropriate compromise.

86 CCP Article 165 incorporated by reference by Article 176 (4); CPR Rule 92.

87 CPR Rule 86.

88 CCP Article 177.

89 CCP Article 178; CPR Rule 87.

The procedure employs modern technology to reduce the costs of the pre-Oral Argument process. By creating a roundtable discussion atmosphere, the process takes heat out of contentions and enables parties to more easily come together to agree that issues are or are not in the case and, more importantly, come together to settle the dispute by compromise.

In the event the case is not settled, the Preparation for Oral Argument allows the judge to confirm the issues and facts in the case so as to narrow the scope of the Oral Argument public trial. It even has the additional potential for speeding up the trial stage since some of the evidence normally reserved for trial has already been entered at the Preparation stage. It results in more and faster compromise settlement. It is virtually entirely inquisitional in nature. Its recent incarnation may be German law in origin, but it resembles in many respects the proceeding before the Tokugawa magistrate. The magistrate in a private proceeding had the authority to press the parties to make admissions as to matter that was not in real dispute. The magistrate could request that the parties produce evidence and answer inquiries designed to identify the outstanding issues. The magistrate could define the real basis for the dispute. Once armed with facts and contentions of the parties the magistrate could seek a compromise solution.

The pre-Oral Argument process is designed to produce the equivalent of the American pretrial order roadmap for the trial—the Oral Argument or Plenary Hearing stage. However, the paternalistic attitude of Japanese judges and the desire of the court to do substantive justice—meaning that the party who should win does win—make use of a preclusion remedy illusory. Although the Code theoretically permits a court to preclude a party from introducing fact issues that were not raised in the pre-Oral Argument stage when to allow such new issues would delay proceedings, preclusion might prevent the court from understanding which party is in the right. This militates against preclusion. Moreover, the failure to raise issues at the appropriate time might be the fault of counsel (where a party is represented). In such a case it would be considered unfair to require the client to suffer for counsel's mistake. If there is no counsel, like courts elsewhere, the court is unlikely to preclude a party unlearned in the law because of a procedural error. Although the sanction exists, the reality is that the "pretrial order" (clarification of facts to be tried) in Japan lacks the preclusive authority of its American counterpart. Nonetheless the procedure is a great improvement over the Preliminary Oral Argument procedure in both narrowing issues in cases that will be tried and also in settling cases—a prime reason for the adoption of the procedures in the first place.

Since adoption of the new Preparation for Oral Argument procedure the average case is resolved much faster than in the past. Whether that is because of the legalization of the procedure or whether it is simply a continuation of the process begun when the procedure was utilized by Bench and Bar without explicit statutory authority is not significant. What is significant is that the process tends to speed up the process of pre-Oral Argument issue and fact identification and clarification. This in turn speeds up cases that eventually go to trial. It also leads to faster resolution of cases through party compromise and settlement.

Consistent with the theory that after preparation the case should be quickly "tried" at the Oral Argument stage, when the preparation stage is completed the court is to set a date for the Oral Argument. This date should not be changed lightly but only on a strong showing of necessity.[90]

90 CCP Article 93 (4).

9

Civil Litigation—The "Trial" Stage

(Oral Argument or Plenary Hearing)

The Oral Argument stage is defined herein as the stage entered after the Preparation for Oral Argument or Preliminary Oral Argument or Preparation by Document stage, although technically all of the above are part of the Oral Argument stage.[1] The Oral Argument stage of the case as so defined is the rough equivalent of the trial stage in the United States. Some aspects of the American trial have already been achieved at the "Pre-Oral Argument" stage. Notwithstanding, for American lawyers to understand the Oral Argument stage it is useful to consider it as analogous to the American trial. However, unlike the American trial the procedure is neither the compact continuous trial utilized in American trial nor is it adversarial in an American understanding of an adversary procedure.

Trials in Japan are public events. Only in cases where a unanimous court concludes that public trial will be dangerous to public order or morals may the court close the hearing. Cases involving the rights granted to the people of Japan under Article 3 of the Constitution and cases involving political offenses and rights of the press must always be held publicly.[2] The presiding judge at the trial is responsible for maintaining order and may call upon police authorities to assist in maintaining order.[3] The presiding judge may order any person who interferes with the orderly conduct of the Oral Argument to leave the courtroom. The judge may take such actions regarding spectators as is deemed necessary to maintain order.[4]

---

1 For a discussion of the lack of distinctions between pretrial and trial in civil law systems see, Geoffrey C. Hazard, Jr., Discovery and the Role of the Judge in Civil Law Jurisdictions, 73 Notre Dame Law Review 1017, 1020-1022 (1998).

2 Constitution of Japan, Article 82.

3 Court Organization Law Article 71 and 71-2.

4 Court Organization Law Article 71 (2).

The extent of the presiding judge's authority was challenged in the *Courtroom Note Taking Case.*[5] In that case an American lawyer studying in Japan attended the Oral Argument sessions of a District Court trial and attempted to take notes as to the proceedings. The presiding judge refused to permit him to take notes and his various requests for permission were either not responded to or were denied. The lawyer sued seeking damages for the court's refusal to permit him to take notes at open public Oral Argument sessions of the court. The Supreme Court first found that the taking of notes at judicial proceedings had constitutional authority behind it since the taking of notes in such cases was related to the freedom of expression guaranteed by the Japanese Constitution.[6] This constitutional right had to be balanced against the need for a quick and correct administration of justice—the reason for giving the presiding judge great discretion in matters of maintaining order in the court. The determinations of the presiding judge in this regard are entitled to great respect and under certain circumstances the presiding judge can prohibit the taking of notes. If note taking by spectators is part of a coordinated demonstration strategy, the presiding judge can prohibit it. In the note taking case the Supreme Court found that there was no rational basis for forbidding the taking of notes by the lawyer because the act of his taking notes could not reasonably be found to interfere with the administration of justice in the handling of the case. In addition the court noted that the changing times in Japan (the case was decided in 1989) made note taking an activity that should be looked on with favor by the courts. However the court also noted that in the past note taking in court was a demonstration technique. Considering that historic fact, the Supreme Court denied the lawyer monetary damages. Nonetheless, the court made it clear that in the future note taking should, except in rare cases where the note taking activity disturbed the administration of justice, be permitted.[7] Although the Supreme Court found that there was no rational basis for denying the lawyer the right to take notes in the circumstances of the case, the court made it clear that the presiding judge has great discretion in exercising the authority granted by the Court Organization Law to maintain order in the court.

A. Reforms Designed to Speed Up the Pace of Litigation

Except for the Tokugawa period, Japan's legal system has continually been plagued with issues concerning the pace at which litigation proceeds. In

---

5 Repeta v. Japan, Case No. 436 of 1988, 43 Minshu 89 (Sup. Ct. Grand Bench 3/8/89) available in English through the web site on the Supreme Court of Japan. Also available in English in Lawrence W. Beer & Hiroshi Itoh, THE CONSTITUTIONAL CASE LAW OF JAPAN, 1970-1990 (University of Washington Press, 1996) at 627. For a discussion of the Repeta case and its influence on opening court proceedings to note taking see, Lawrence W. Beer, Freedom of Expression: The Continuing Revolution, in JAPANESE CONSTITUTIONAL LAW (Luney and Takahashi Ed., University of Tokyo Press, 1993) 221, 240-241.

6 Constitution of Japan, Article 21.

7 The question may be asked who won the note taking case? The lawyer did not get the damages he sought. The court denied his claim. But since the decision note taking has been permitted in Japanese courts.

Tokugawa times this was not an issue as the governing authority was not enthusiastic about the use of the emerging judicial mechanism and litigation was disfavored. In such a situation if litigation took a long time, so much the better as the time factor served to discourage litigation and thus supported the government's policy. Delay in handling the case was significant both because it postponed resolution and also because it added to the parties' expense. As litigants could not be represented (except in rare cases such as infancy or incapacity), litigants themselves needed to travel to the site of the hearing. Typically the plaintiff would need to stay at an Inn that specialized in housing of litigants. Such Inns were located close to the government office where the Tokugawa magistrate handled cases and in addition to room and board provided advice on how to deal with litigation. Such specialized Inns tended to be expensive and thus the longer the case dragged on the higher the plaintiff's cost.[8] This cost factor dissuaded the bringing of insignificant cases. High costs also assisted the magistrate in performing his role of bringing about a settlement. High cost put pressure on the parties to settle. This was especially so for the plaintiff as he typically had to travel to the court although defendants frequently had the same problem.

In the Meiji era litigants also frequently had to stay in specialized Inns while a case was being heard. It was not until 1873 that parties could be represented. As in modern Japan many parties to litigation were not represented. In 1926 significant changes were made in the Code of Civil Procedure.[9] This reform was motivated at least in part by a desire to speed up the process of litigation.[10] Additional reforms were instituted under the American Occupation. Again part of the purpose of the reform was to speed up the process of litigation.[11] In the late 1980's both the Bar and some portions of the judiciary suggested additional reform of the Code of Civil Procedure to speed up the process of litigation.[12] The 1996 Code, the 2003

8 See, Richard W. Rabinowitz, The Historical Development of the Japanese Bar, 70 Harvard Law Review 62 (1956).

9 Law No. 61, 1926; Kenzo Takayanagi, A Century of Innovation: The Development of Japanese Law, 1868-1961 in LAW IN JAPAN (VON Mehren Ed. Harvard University Press, 1963) 32; Kohji Tanabe (assisted by John B. Hurlbut), The Process of Litigation: An Experiment With the Adversary System in LAW IN JAPAN (Arthur Taylor von Mehren Ed. Harvard University Press, 1963) 73, 99.

10 Yasuhei Taniguchi, The 1996 Code of Civil Procedure of Japan—A Procedure for the Coming Century, 45 American Journal of Comparative Law 767, 770 (1997); Takeshi Kojima, Civil Procedure Reform in Japan, 11 Michigan Journal of International Law 1218 (1990).

11 Kohji Tanabe (assisted by John B. Hurlbut), The Process of Litigation: An Experiment With the Adversary System in LAW IN JAPAN (Arthur Taylor von Mehren Ed. Harvard University Press, 1963) 73, 81-82.

12 Takeshi Kojima, Civil Procedure Reform in Japan, 11 Michigan Journal of International Law 1218, 1219 (1990).

Amendment of the Code and the 2004 judicial reform initiative are simply the latest steps taken to move litigation along faster in Japan.[13]

The American Occupation view of how to speed up the litigation process was to follow a procedure, which if it did not track the American trial process at least had some attributes of that process. The most important of these attributes from a speed standpoint was the idea of the "continuous trial." In the United States continuous trial is required because of the necessity to get the jury in and out as quickly as possible. To make the continuous trial work in the United States, extensive pre-trial procedures (under control of the lawyers) are utilized so that when the case is set for trial all of the preparatory work has been completed. If the preparation is not complete, then typically the parties are precluded from stopping the trial to do more preparation. In emergency situations the court may grant a short continuance (perhaps a day or two) to allow some unanticipated matters to be examined.

The idea of a continuous trial is inconsistent with the German law notion of civil procedure and when introduced by the Occupation was inconsistent with the Japanese system. It remained inconsistent with Japan's civil procedure norm even during the period when American ideas about procedure were on the rise in Japan. Where the idea may have relevance is in the final stages of the Oral Argument or Plenary Proceeding stage as this stage may be viewed as similar to the American trial stage. The notion of continuous trial is however completely inconsistent with the procedure undertaken "pre-Oral Argument." As noted above, the pre-Oral Argument stage of the case, whether by Preparation by Document or Preliminary Oral Argument or the new Preparation for Oral Argument procedure, is characterized by a series of meeting between the parties and the court. These meetings are prepared for in advance through the use of Preliminary Documents (in the nature of briefs). The function of the meetings is to allow the judge to confirm the issues and facts that must be the subject of the Oral Argument. The meetings also permit the parties, with the active assistance of the court, to reach a compromise settlement.

---

13 As part of the 2004 initiative the government submitted several bills to the Diet for enactment. Among those of most interest for Civil Procedure and discussed herein the following bills were enacted into law in the spring Diet session. Law establishing Labor Tribunal, Law amending the Administrative Case Litigation Law, Law permitting young judges and prosecutors to gain experience by working in a bengoshi office, Law establishing the Intellectual Property High Court, Law amending the courts law to provide greater protection to trade secrets disclosed in litigation. All of these bills were passed late in the spring 2004 session (some in the last week of the session) and the text of the bills was not available as this work was going to press. However, as all were government bills, were relatively politically acceptable to all Parties and were technical in nature it is unlikely that any significant change was made by the Diet in the bills as presented and as discussed in the text herein. No information currently available to the author indicates any change in the bills as enacted and sources in Japan indicate no knowledge of any change. The Diet also enacted the bill to allow for lay participation in major criminal cases. Some minor changes were made in this bill as initially presented and as passed. These changes deal with the issue of penalty that may be assessed against lay participants who disclose private personal information coming to their attention as a consequence of their service as "jurors." Privacy questions are a subject of political debate in Japan. The substance of the law as passed is consistent with the government bill submitted and discussed herein.

Under the Rules of Civil Procedure the parties have an obligation to make a detailed investigation of facts prior to the Oral Argument in an effort to expedite the case.[14] This rule is however not as significant as may appear on its face. Rather, it is more permissive than mandatory in the sense that its purpose is to abolish the old notion that it was unethical for lawyers to meet with potential witnesses before Oral Argument. The prohibition was based on the idea that witness testimony should be uninfluenced by counsel and should come naturally from the witness. Discussion with counsel beforehand was seen as potentially contaminating the witness testimony. The lawyer who met with a witness could be viewed as being a party to such contamination. This led to the belief that such meetings were unethical.[15] With transformation to a more adversary procedure and a procedure where witnesses should get on and off the stand as quickly as possible, interview beforehand was essential.

Without lawyer/witness contact there was no effective way for the Oral Argument stage of the case to move swiftly as witnesses who might have nothing to offer would nonetheless need to be heard. The Rule permitted screening of witnesses to avoid such needless waste of court time. Requests by counsel or a party to allow a witness to testify must detail what the witness has to say. (The judge decides whether a witness will or will not be allowed to testify but except for cases under the Administrative Case Litigation Law or Impeachment cases the judge has no authority *sua sponte* to call a witness to testify.) To gain such information, meetings between counsel and the witnesses are essential. Although such meetings were to be held prior to preliminary proceedings in court, the reality is that they were not. For various reasons including costs, lawyer time and the continuation of the relatively lax non-concentrated trial practice, meetings with potentially helpful witnesses that are undertaken early in the pre-trial process in the United States are delayed in Japan.[16]

Throughout the modern period Japanese civil procedure has attempted to create a more concentrated trial process. Some such attempts were self-generated, as was the Taisho Democracy (1926) reform of the Code of Civil Procedure. This reform followed and in some respects was modeled on the 1924 German reform of civil procedure. Other attempts were suggested by others, as was the reform undertaken during the American Occupation. At each turn the system has systemically rejected the concentrated model and fallen back to the familiar original German law model of the activist judge taking the necessary time or the necessary number of sessions to lead the attorneys and/or parties to the evidence and witnesses. The explanations for this process are many—inadequate numbers of lawyers make the

14 CPR Rule 85.

15 Kohji Tanabe (assisted by John B. Hurlbut), The Process of Litigation: An Experiment With the Adversary System in LAW IN JAPAN (Arthur Taylor von Mehren Ed. Harvard University Press, 1963) 73, 96-98.

16 Kohji Tanabe (assisted by John B. Hurlbut), The Process of Litigation: An Experiment With the Adversary System in LAW IN JAPAN (Arthur Taylor von Mehren Ed. Harvard University Press, 1963) 73, 101-105.

concentrated model impracticable, costs to counsel (which are not recouped because counsel is paid by the case not by the hour) make the model uneconomic, the large numbers of pro se litigants make the practice impossible. It may be that the lack of a discovery system in Japan makes the idea of a concentrated trial at the Oral Hearing stage unworkable. The reality is that whatever its faults, the ability to know in advance what a witness will say at trial and the ability to know in advance what documents relating to that testimony say shortens the actual trial time for witness testimony. It may be that without an effective pre-Oral Argument discovery mechanism the concept of concentrated trial cannot succeed.[17] Alternatively it may be that discovery is not essential and that an effective pre-Oral Argument process with preclusion for matters not confirmed during the process would suffice.

Although the new Preparation for Oral Argument procedure has helped to reduce the time that it takes to resolve the average case, it does not yet appear to have had the desired effect on cases that go to judgment. The Preparation for Oral Argument procedure also appears not to have reduced the time required in complicated cases, such as medical malpractice or construction engineering. Such complicated cases are on the increase in Japan. The 2003 amendments seek to have all civil litigation resolved within two years of the filing of the Complaint, a goal that surely is unattainable. The disjointed non-continuous trial process is designed in part to give parties a chance to recess to prepare further evidence or arguments. Recess is required so that arguments can be refined. Both the parties and court need the recess time to work their way to resolution of the case. This is so whether resolution comes by settlement or trial (Oral Argument). This process does not end when the pre-Oral Argument stage is completed. Because a judge must attempt to achieve settlement at all stages of the case and because the "discovery" of evidence continues during the Oral Argument stage, a disjointed trial process appears essential.

At the end of the pre-Oral Argument process, if settlement is not reached, a roadmap for the trial—the equivalent of the American Pretrial Order but without the sanction of said Order—is arrived at. Theoretically the case could then proceed to continuous Oral Argument or continuous trial. However, for that to occur two things need to be present: a) a clear picture of the witnesses who will testify and b) ability to quickly and smoothly introduce documentary evidence. Neither is present in the current procedure, although greater emphasis on consolidated witness testimony is present under the new reform. Because some of the aspects of the Oral Argument are conducted during the Preparation for Oral Argument stage, they need not be conducted again. In some cases review of documents produced by the parties at the court's suggestion are completed before the Oral Argument stage. This should speed up the Oral Argument stage.

Where the current reform has had its greatest impact in speeding up trials is at the pre-Oral Argument stage. Through the use of the more informal Preparation for

17 The Reception in Japan of the American Law and its Transformation in the Fifty Years since the End of World War II—Makoto Itoh, Civil Procedure law, 26 Law in Japan 66 (2000).

Oral Argument roundtable sessions the court is able to bring about settlement, thus shortening the time before resolution and freeing up judicial time to deal with cases that proceed to the Oral Argument stage. The second major improvement in time at the initial trial level is the court's greater emphasis on consolidating witness testimony in cases where witnesses testify.[18] The greatest impediment to speed at the Oral Argument stage is the lack of sanction and preclusion. This is based in part on the ingrained objective of the process to see that the correct party wins. To achieve this end procedure may be delayed to enable that party to present matters that otherwise might be precluded because not raised at an earlier and more appropriate time. Moreover, while speed is important the reality is that settlement is also a goal of the process and for settlement to be achieved sometimes delay is useful. Just like Tokugawa litigants, modern Japanese litigants can tire of the process and seek a way out of the morass through settlement. In addition, the mere passage of time tends to remove the "heat" that generated the litigation in the first place. The process of meeting over and over again with the court and listening to the paternalistic judge can bring the parties together to resolve their disputes.[19] In any event, the 2003 amendments seek to move the case more quickly by providing that the court shall act so as to bring cases to a timely and quick determination.[20] The amendment also gives the court discretion to consult with the parties on a scheduling plan with time limits for confirming evidence and issues (the pre-Oral Argument stage), examining witnesses, and the completion of the Oral Argument stage. The schedule may also deal with timing for the decision in the case.[21] This reform is designed to pressure the judiciary to act more quickly. The government's stated objective to complete litigation in two years places pressure on the judiciary to move cases more quickly.

B. General Considerations for Oral Argument

1) Evidentiary Matters

Viewing the Oral Argument phase of the case as equivalent to an American trial requires recognition of some of the significant differences between the trial in an adversary system and the "trial" in the Japanese system. For example, in the United States the pleadings, which are designed to define the claim being made, are fixed at pretrial and are not changed during the trial except as a motion to conform at the end of the trial may be granted. In Japan the Code is quite specific in

18 CCP Article 182; CPR Rule 100.

19 It probably goes too far to say that after enough time the parties may feel that they have a common enemy to defeat, namely delay. But, once they have reached this point the intercession of the judge to get the right terms for settlement may quickly resolve the matter. If this does not happen during the Preparation for Oral Argument stage there is still a good chance it can happen at the Oral Argument stage. And if it does not happen at Oral Argument it may happen at the Appeal stage.

20 CCP Article 147-2 (added 2003).

21 CCP Article 147-3.

permitting the parties to amend the pleadings during the course of the Oral Argument stage of the case. Amendment is permitted so long as the court does not conclude that such amendment would substantially delay the case.[22]

The Code also states that the Oral Argument proceeding is under the control of the presiding judge. This control is substantially greater and more involved than is the control of the courtroom by the judge in the United States. In controlling the case the judge in Japan may determine who can and who cannot make statements to the court.[23] The judge is the central figure in the trial and may control the flow of evidence and the method by which evidence is received as well as what evidence may or may not be received, etc. After a case has been "tried" the court may nonetheless determine that it is appropriate to open up the trial for further Oral Argument proceedings.[24] The court sets the date for Oral Argument to commence. In theory, the initial date may not be changed because a party claims that it needs more time to investigate the matter.[25] It is estimated that pre-Oral Argument Preparation proceedings are scheduled approximately three to six weeks apart.[26]

By controlling the proceeding the court also controls what evidence may be introduced during the Oral Argument stage. The judge controls the form in which evidence is received. Form may be significant since there is no hearsay rule in civil cases in Japan.[27] Many matters that are the subject of live witness testimony in the United States are introduced through affidavit in Japan. The judge decides whether witness testimony is necessary and the parties have to present the judge with formal written proffers of what the proposed witness may say.[28] The court in lieu of the oral testimony may accept such proffers[29] and attorneys for opposition parties may be stuck with the written record even though they may technically have a right to cross-examine.[30] Notwithstanding the adversarial form of trial set

---

22 CCP Article 143.

23 CCP Article 148.

24 CCP Article 153.

25 CPR Rule 64.

26 International Commercial Litigation in Japan, Masafumi Kodama & Jay Tyndall, Kitahama Law Office, on the web at *www.Masafumi Kodama & Jay Tyndall, Kitahama.or.jp/English/litigatn.htm* at page 5 of 14.

27 Koichi Miki, Procedural Law on the Threshold of a New Millennium, World Congress on Procedural Law (1999) on the web at ruessmann.jura.uni-sb.de/grotius/english/Reports/japan.htm.

28 CCP Article 180; CPR Rule 107.

29 CCP Article 205. Under the Rules the parties may object to the court accepting a written statement instead of oral examination but the reality is that in most cases this right to object is more illusory than real. As the judge is in control of the case and as the judge is the bureaucratic government presence in the court and as the judge decides whether witnesses are needed and as the judge will decide the case ultimately and will be significant in any settlement discussions, the number of cases where lawyers will object is small.

30 CCP Article 202.

out in the Code and Rules, the judge is in charge of the case through control over case management as well as control over the proceedings and evidence.[31]

As in the United States there are some matters that need not be proven at trial. In addition to admissions (discussed earlier) both systems recognize that judicial notice may be taken of certain facts. The judicial notice rule in the United States is quite limited. In Japan, on the other hand, the rule has greater latitude. Many matters that require evidentiary proof in the United States may be accepted by the court in Japan through representation by counsel and the judge's understanding that such is in fact the fact.[32] Moreover through the clarification function the judge determines what facts need be proven at trial. The court can, if it decides that evidence on a matter is unnecessary, reject evidence proffered by a party at the Oral Argument.[33] Moreover, the court may, if it determines that the taking of evidence will delay the proceedings, determine not to take the proffered evidence.[34]

The Code and the Rules are structured as if the Oral Argument is to proceed as an adversary proceeding. Thus the parties are given the right to cross-examine witnesses. Parties must submit documents in advance if they are going to use such documents on the examination of a witness[35] (except for impeachment documents as obviously counsel and the court do not want to give a witness a chance to conform testimony to obviate impeachment). In the United States cross-examination is considered an essential aspect of the adversary system. American lawyers and judges believe that the whole truth can be discovered only through effective cross-examination. If cross-examination is denied after a witness has testified on direct examination the witnesses' direct testimony should be stricken, as it has not been tested by cross-examination. In criminal cases the denial of the right to cross-examine is considered a violation of the defendant's constitutional right to confront witnesses. In short, cross-examination is a critical element of the adversary process. American lawyers are trained to be effective cross examiners; classes at law schools utilize mock trials to enable lawyers to learn the skills of both direct and cross-examination; clinics at law schools enable students in their third year to undertake direct and cross-examination of witnesses under the supervision of senior lawyers; major law firms insist that young lawyers be present at direct and cross examination of witnesses (at least at deposition) so that they can learn the examination skill.

Cross-examination is not a subject at Japanese *Hogakubu* law faculties and it is likely that it will not be a major item on the syllabus of the new law schools. Although Japanese lawyers eager to improve the standing of the profession accepted the concept of cross-examination, the reality was that post-war Japanese lawyers

31 See, Masako Kamiya, Narrowing the Avenues to Japan's Supreme Court: The Policy Implications of Japan's Code of Civil Procedure Reforms, 4 Australian Journal of Asian Law 53, 56 (2002).

32 CCP Article 179.

33 CCP Article 181 (1).

34 CCP Article 181 (2).

35 CPR Rule 102.

were untrained and unskilled at cross-examination. In this connection not much has changed in the 50+ years since the war. The system accommodated to a kind of middle ground where lawyers performed some examination into evidence before trial. The basic process remained the inquisition mode modified by some questioning by lawyers to elicit witness testimony.[36] As a consequence of this accommodation there was little incentive for law faculties to teach or lawyers to learn new skills. Since judges continued to take an active role in evidence gathering during the non-continuous trial, there was little need for lawyers to spend valuable time on fact gathering. If evidence were needed there would be time to gather it during the pre-Oral Argument or non-continuous Oral Argument stage of the case. Moreover, as Japan is a civil law system it does not give as much credence to the value of cross-examination as does a common law system. Cross-examination is, of course, the rationale behind the hearsay rule. It is only because hearsay evidence is not subject to cross-examination that hearsay evidence is, as a rule (subject to exceptions tied to reliability notions) excluded from consideration at the trial.

Even in the criminal law arena, where the liberty of the defendant is at stake and constitutional issues are presented, cross-examination and/or the exclusion of hearsay are not essential components of the criminal trial in Japan.[37] Thus the Supreme Court of Japan has held that an affidavit executed under penalty of perjury in the United States by a witness in a criminal case in Japan was made under circumstances that made it credible and thus it was admissible in a criminal trial.[38] In a criminal case where the defendant was charged with running a prostitution ring, the prosecutor took the deposition testimony (without cross-examination) of 13 foreign women at a time when the women were in custody preparatory to deportation. These depositions were submitted to the court to prove the charge of prostitution. The Supreme Court found the depositions admissible as an exception to the hearsay rule rejecting the defendant's objection that it was entitled to cross-examine. Only if there had been prosecutorial misconduct through intentionally taking advantage of the fact that the women would be deported would the depositions

36 Kohji Tanabe (assisted by John B. Hurlbut), The Process of Litigation: An Experiment With the Adversary System in LAW IN JAPAN (Arthur Taylor von Mehren Ed. Harvard University Press, 1963) 73, 101-105; The Reception in Japan of the American Law and its Transformation in the Fifty Years since the End of World War II—Makoto Ito, Civil Procedure law, 26 Law in Japan 66, 68-69 (2000).

37 Unlike the Code of Civil Procedure, the Code of Criminal Procedure has a general hearsay rule although there are many exceptions that allow hearsay into evidence. See, Case No. 1960 No. 1378, 10 Keishu 1795 (10/17/63) available in English on the web through the web site of the Supreme Court of Japan. For a discussion of the hearsay rule and exceptions to the rule in criminal cases see, Shigemitsu Dando (Translated by B. J. George Jr.) JAPANESE CRIMINAL PROCEDURE (Fred B. Rothman & Co., 1965) 198-201.

38 Case No. 1999 (A) No. 400, 54 Keishu 735 (Sup. Ct., Petty Bench 10/31/00) available in English through the web site of the Supreme Court of Japan.

be rejected.[39] Considering that a civil case does not implicate the same constitutional issues and does not concern itself with the question of individual human rights and liberty, it is natural that cross-examination and the hearsay rule would play a lesser role in the civil litigation context.

Just as the hearsay rule is not as stringently used in civil procedure in Japan so too the best evidence rule—another rule whose basic function is to protect lay jurors from being misled by unreliable evidence—is not applicable.[40]

In the United States, in a federal case when testimony of a witness in another location far from the courthouse is involved, the typical mechanism is for the party seeking the testimony to depose the witness during the pretrial stage. This involves "noticing" the deposition and having the clerk of the District Court where the witness is located issue the necessary subpoena to compel attendance. The notice is served on the opposition and the opposition counsel is "invited" to attend and cross-examine. The opposition may make a motion to have the court where the case is pending order the party seeking the testimony pay the expenses of opposition counsel to travel to the location of the deposition. Granting such a motion is discretionary with the court. The costs of the deposition are "taxable costs" to be paid by the losing party. Once the deposition is taken, it may be read into evidence at the later trial. The result is a continuous trial with no break for the taking of the unavailable witness's testimony.

Unlike the United States where the trial stage of the case takes place in one place, the Oral Argument stage of the case in Japan may take place in several places. Thus, testimony need not be taken in the court where the case is pending. The court may take evidence outside the courtroom, and if there is a panel of judges not all members of the panel need be present for such examination of evidence.[41] Indeed, since the court may assign the function of taking such evidence to a lower court, it is possible that none of the members of the panel need be present. Moreover, the examination may be assigned to a judge of a different District Court when the evidence is located in a different district.[42] Where a different court examines the evidence, that court has the responsibility for recording the evidence and transmitting it to the trial court.[43] Thus where oral testimony of a witness far from the location of the trial court is required, that testimony may be taken during

39 Case No. 1990 (A) No. 72, 49 Keishu 741 (Sup. Ct. Petty Bench, 6/20/95) available in English through the web site of the Supreme Court of Japan. It is difficult to see how the prosecutor could not have known that the women would be unavailable at trial considering that at the time of the depositions they were all in custody of the immigration authorities awaiting involuntary deportation; see also, Case No. 1960 (A) No. 1378, 17 Keishu 1795 (Sup. Ct. Petty Bench, 10/17/63) (available in English through the web site of the Supreme Court of Japan).

40 See, e.g., CPR Rule 102.

41 CCP Article 185.

42 CCP Article 185 (2). In such case the court clerk is given responsibility for making the necessary arrangements for the taking of testimony. CPR Rule 104.

43 CPR Rule 105.

the Oral Argument stage—indeed must be taken at that time since there is no pre-trial deposition possibility available. As the opposition has the right to cross-examine, the opposition may (at its own expense but as a taxable cost) travel to the location where the testimony will be taken in order to cross-examine. The court is limited in its authority to order the taking of testimony outside the court where the case is pending and may do so only when:

a) The witness has a good reason for not being able to appear at the trial court;

b) To have the witness appear at the trial court would involve either undue delay or undue expense;

c) It is necessary to examine the witness at another location to better understand the testimony (such as the location of property where the witness explains the condition of the property and it is best to do so at the situs of the property);

d) Where the parties agree.[44]

Although Oral Argument (trial) in Japan is a bifurcated affair in the sense that court sessions are not continuous, the trial itself is not bifurcated in the sense that liability and damages issues are not considered separately. Rather, such matters are considered in one Oral Argument procedure. This is similar to the process in criminal cases in Japan where the guilt and penalty phase are consolidated in one proceeding.[45]

2) Burden of Proof

The party asserting the fact at issue during the Oral Argument bears the burden of proof. So the plaintiff bears the general burden of proof to establish the claim, while the defendant has the burden of establishing the facts to support any "affirmative defenses." As a general rule, the burden on the plaintiff in Japan is more severe than in the United States. Japan does not follow the American practice wherein a 50. +% chance of success is sufficient to meet the burden of proof in a civil case. In the United States in a civil case[46] the plaintiff need prove its case by a

44 CCP Article 195.

45 In the criminal law arena this can work a serious disadvantage for the defendant as evidence that may not be "admissible" in the guilt or innocent phase but is relevant to penalty is presented to the court before a determination of guilt or innocence is made. Moreover, for the defendant to show contrition to affect the penalty phase, the defendant must show that contrition during the guilt phase. To do so works an implied if not a direct admission of guilt.

46 In a criminal case since the defendant must be found guilty beyond a reasonable doubt the United States requires a substantially higher burden of proof. Likewise in Japan the criminal burden of proof is beyond a reasonable doubt. Atsushi Nagashima (assisted by B.J. George, Jr.), The Accused and Society: The Administration of Criminal Justice in Japan in LAW IN JAPAN (Arthur Taylor von Mehren Ed. Harvard University Press, 1963) 297, 315); J. Mark Ramseyer and Minoru Nakazato, JAPANESE LAW 172 (University of Chicago Press, 1999).

mere preponderance of the evidence. In Japan the court must be convinced that the plaintiff is correct for the plaintiff to win. The Code says little about the burden of proof or how to allocate the burden. Rather, it adopts the rule that the court should be convinced by all of the evidence that an allegation is or is not true.[47] As a rule the necessity to be convinced by the evidence of a matter requires a high degree of confidence that the party is correct (a "high probability" standard). This is a higher standard of proof than a mere preponderance. It is suggested that this high probability standard is roughly equivalent of the American clear and convincing standard.[48] This places the plaintiff—who has the primary burden—at a disadvantage[49] compared to an American plaintiff. Although it is not as stringent as the beyond a reasonable doubt standard, the high probability standard is difficult to meet.[50]

Because of the more stringent burden of proof that a plaintiff must satisfy in Japan, there have been movements to alleviate the burden in cases where the public interest requires it. Thus, although in a tort action the plaintiff has the burden of establishing both causation and negligence, in the Big Four pollution cases the courts adopted a new concept of causation for pollution related injuries thereby reducing the burden of proof placed on the plaintiffs.[51] In automobile accident cases where there is personal injury the burden has been shifted from the plaintiff to the defendant who must establish that he was not negligent or that the plaintiff or a third party was the negligent party.[52] The Products Liability Law of 1995 sim-

---

PAN (Arthur Taylor von Mehren Ed. Harvard University Press, 1963) 297, 315); J. Mark Ramseyer and Minoru Nakazato, JAPANESE LAW 172 (University of Chicago Press, 1999).

47 CCP Article 247.

48 Kuo-Chang Huang, INTRODUCING DISCOVERY INTO CIVIL LAW 139-140 (Carolina Academic Press, 2003).

49 Takeshi Kojima, Japanese Civil Procedure in Comparative Law Perspective, 46 U. Kansas L. Rev. 687, 708 (1998).

50 See, Akira Negishi, Economic Law part of The Reception in Japan of the American Law and its Transformation in the Fifty Years the End of World War II, 26 Law In Japan 34, 37 (2000) taking the position that compensatory damage cases under the Anti Monopoly Law are subject to the same burden of proof as any other civil case and such burden is high making the chances of winning such a case minimal.

51 See, Frank K. Upham, LAW AND SOCIAL POLICY IN POSTWAR JAPAN (Harvard University Press, 1987); Frank K. Upham, Litigation and Moral Consciousness in Japan: An Interpretative Analysis of Four Japanese Pollution Suits, 10 Law and Society Review 579 (1976); Julian Gresser, Koichiro Fujikura and Akio Morishima, ENVIRONMENTAL LAW IN JAPAN (MIT Press, 1981) 42, 128-130; Hiroshi Oda, JAPANESE LAW 196 (Oxford University Press, 1999). See also, Chris Clarke, Update Comparative Legal Study (European Union, 2001) p. 92 dealing with the Big Four pollution Cases and p. 95 noting that strict liability is the standard under the 1972 provisions of the Water Pollution Control Act.

52 Ichiro Kato (assisted by Ben Bruce Blakeney), The Treatment of Motor Vehicle Accidents: The Impact of Technological Change on Legal Relations in LAW IN JAPAN (Arthur Taylor von Mehren Ed. Harvard University Press, 1963) 399, 406-407 (contending that this shifting of the burden of proof in auto cases creates a situation close to absolute liability in auto accident incidents).

ilarly shifts the burden by providing for liability without proof of fault.[53] Strict liability has also been established for loss caused by an accident at a nuclear energy facility.[54] (Japan is an energy poor country relying on imports of oil to fuel its economy. As a consequence nuclear energy meets a significant portion of Japan's energy needs, although public objections to nuclear plants have slowed the government's plans to increase nuclear sources in recent years). The 1999 Patent Law Amendments are designed to make it easier for a patent owner to establish infringement. Accordingly, the alleged infringer is required to justify its acts rather than the Patent holder establish that the acts constitute infringement.[55] In medical malpractice cases the doctor needs to establish that his treatment meets the professional standards in the community.[56]

In a recent case the Supreme Court of Japan held that a doctor was liable in a case where the patient suffered from cirrhosis of the liver. The treating doctor was a specialist who was aware that the patient was in the high-risk group for liver cancer, although he did not have cancer at the time of initial treatment. The doctor failed to perform recurring tests (as recommended) to determine whether cancer had developed and as a consequence when liver cancer did develop it was unknown and untreated. The patient died when a tumor burst. It was established that if the testing had been performed and the cancer detected the patient's life might have been prolonged for an indeterminate period. The doctor argued that the link between failure to perform liver cancer tests and prolongation of the patient's life had not been determined sufficiently to meet the plaintiff's burden of proof. The Supreme Court held that the causal connection did not have to be established to the extent of showing that there was no doubt as to the causal link—in other words not beyond a reasonable doubt. Rather, it was sufficient if plaintiff established a "high probability" of such a causal link. Such high probability of causation was met if the proof was such that an average person would be convinced. The length of time the patient might have lived had proper care been given could not be determined either from the evidence or as a scientific matter. But the extent of the duration of additional life was not considered by the court as an issue that affected defendant's liability. Such uncertainty was a factor to be considered in es-

---

53 Mark A. Behrens and Daniel H. Raddock, Japan's New Products Liability Law: The Citadel of Strict Liability Falls, But Access to Recovery is Limited by Formidable Barriers, 19 University of Pennsylvania Journal of International Economic Law 669, 689 (1995); see also, Jocelyn Kellam, Product Liability in the Asia Pacific (Clayton Utz) p. 7 on the web at *www.claytonutz.com/downloads/ProdLiabAsiaPac.pdf*.

54 Hiroshi Oda, JAPANESE LAW 196 (Oxford University Press, 1999).

55 See, Patent Law Section 104 (Presumption of Manufacture Using Patented Process); Dr. Shoichi Okuyama, The 1999 Amendments to the Patent Law in Japan, on the web at *www.okuyama.com/1999_amend_jp_pat_law.htm;* JPAA, Revisions of the Japanese Patent Law (January 2000) on the web at *http://knpt.com/english/news4.htm*

56 J. Mark Ramseyer and Minoru Nakazato, JAPANESE LAW 67 (University of Chicago Press, 1999).

tablishing the amount of damages due to his family.[57] In other words, the burden of proof appears to have been allocated as follows: the doctor had the burden of showing that his failure to treat was consistent with medical standards in the community—this he failed to do. The patient had to meet a high burden of showing a causal connection between the failure to treat and the injury. The patient could meet this burden through evidence that would convince the average person of such a high degree of probable linkage.[58]

Accordingly, although the burden of proof on a plaintiff is generally higher than in the United States, there are several statutes in Japan that modify the rule to permit recovery based on a lower burden of proof. This lowered standard of proof in medical malpractice cases is particularly relevant as more and more of such cases are filed in Japanese courts each year.

As in an American trial the two most important aspects of a case once it reaches the Oral Argument stage are documentary evidence and witness evidence. Accordingly the next sections deal with these topics. Documents are considered first (although the Code deals with witnesses first) because in the United States documents are seen as a foundation for witness testimony. Moreover, the reality is that documents tend to be more important in Japan than witness testimony.

C. Documentary Evidence

1) Introduction into Evidence

There is nothing extraordinary about the admission into evidence of a document in possession of a party. The document, when in the possession of the party proffering it, is simply given[59] to the court together with a sufficient number of copies to be served on the opposition. When the document is not in the possession of the party proffering it, it may be offered in evidence through a motion to require the person in possession to produce the document. The procedures for such a motion are discussed in the next section. For this section it is sufficient to note that parties have no "right" to have evidence produced by an adverse party or a third person but only such evidence as the judge believes is important for the court's decision

---

57 Case No. 1996 (O) No. 2043, 53 Minshu 235 (Sup. Ct. Petty Bench, 2/25/99) available in English through the web site of the Supreme Court of Japan.

58 The court's use of high probability is consistent with previous determinations but its holding that such high probability may be shown through evidence to convince an average person may be inconsistent with previous pronouncements. For a discussion of high probability see, Kuo-Chang Huang, INTRODUCING DISCOVERY INTO CIVIL LAW 138-143 (Carolina Academic Press, 2003).

59 CCP Article 219.

will be required to be produced.[60] If the court orders production the person in possession produces the document directly to the court.[61] Along with the document the proffering party must submit an explanatory statement showing the title and writer of the document together with a statement of the purpose of the document's introduction—i.e., the facts it is asserted to prove.[62] The basis on which it is argued that the documentary evidence proves the ultimate fact or the facts that will eventually prove the ultimate facts must be specifically stated.[63]

The proffering party may serve the document and statement directly on the opposition rather than submit copies to the court for service.[64] If the document is in a language other than Japanese the portion relied on must be translated and the translation should be served along with the document and explanatory note.[65] Note that the Rule does not require that the entire document be translated only those portion on which the offering party relies. The adverse party may contest the translation and may submit a translation of its own.[66] The court is always in control of the case and thus it has the authority to set deadlines for the submission of documentary evidence.[67] Not all documentary evidence need be presented at the Oral Argument phase of the case. Some documents may already be part of the evidentiary record because submitted at the pre-Oral Argument stage at the Preparation for Oral Argument sessions. This is inconsistent with the notion that the "trial" (Oral Argument) should be a public event as the Preparation for Oral Argument may be restricted to parties and invited persons. Nonetheless the Code specifically allows documents to be considered at the Preparation for Oral Argument stage and permits the court to make rulings concerning evidence, including documentary evidence, at the Preparation for Oral Argument stage.[68] Where documents are admitted at the Preparation for Oral Argument stage, this fact and an explanation of the documents should be stated in open court at the first Oral Argu-

---

60 This is the basic rule in civil law procedure. See, Geoffrey C. Hazard, Jr., Discovery and the Role of the Judge in Civil Law Jurisdictions, 73 Notre Dame Law Review 1017, 1019, 1024, 1025, 1026 (1998).

61 See, Toshiro M. Mochizuki, Baby Step or Giant Leap:? Parties Expanded Access to Documentary Evidence Under the New Japanese Code of Civil Procedure, 40 Harvard International Law Journal 285, 288 (1999).

62 CPR Rule 137. The explanatory note may be omitted or modified if the information therein is obvious from the document itself.

63 CCP Article 180 and CPR Rule 99.

64 CPR Rule 137 (2).

65 CPR Rule 138 (1).

66 CPR Rule 138 (2). Although not stated in the Code or Rules it appears that the adverse party may also translate portions of the document not submitted as evidence by the proponent of the document that show that the meaning sought to be given to the translated portion is inconsistent with the true meaning of the document.

67 CCP Article 162; CPR Rule 139.

68 CCP Article 170 (2) is specific in this regard and Article 170 (6) permits documents to be admitted at this earlier stage through incorporating Article 149.

ment session after the Preparation stage is completed in order to maintain the fiction that the trial is a public event.[69]

A document utilized at the trial must be authenticated. In the case of most documents presumptive authentication is based on the signature (uncommon in Japan but common on documents executed abroad or with foreign companies) or seal (*inkan*).[70] The electronic signature law of 2000 provides for authentication of documents utilizing an electronic signature rather than a seal or a signed signature.[71] The opposition party may challenge authentication by specifically stating the grounds for challenge.[72] Procedures exist for comparing handwriting or seal impressions.[73] If the challenge is made in bad faith (either intentionally or through gross negligence) the court may levy a non-penal fine against the objecting party. Although on its face the penalty provision may seem a sufficient sanction to substitute for the lack of a Request for Admission policy that would deal with authenticity questions as they relate to documents, the fine is so small that it has little meaning in big money cases. The fine may not exceed 100,000yen, which at a rate of $1=100yen would be not in excess of $1,000.[74] Since the court can waive the assessment of the fine if the objecting party later concedes the authenticity of the document,[75] the threat of a fine may be used as leverage to get an admission of authenticity. Since the imposition of a fine involves a factual determination of gross negligence or intentional conduct and since the imposition of such a fine is subject to immediate appeal,[76] use of the fine procedure may present an opportunity for a defendant to delay proceedings in a case.

Government documents that are introduced that show on their face that they were prepared by a government official in the course of his/her duties are presumed au-

---

69 CCP Article 173. This retains the fiction that the Preparation stage is part of a public proceeding in accordance with Constitution of Japan, Article 82 that requires that both trials and announcement of judgments be public events. It also preserves the concept of direct participation in the trial by the judges making the decision. CCP Article 249. While the preparation stage may be conducted by a single judge designated for that purpose, by announcing the results of the Preparation in Oral Argument all of the judges are now aware of the events and thus Article 249 is complied with. This is consistent with Article 249 (2), which uses a similar process to bring an incoming replacement judge up to date on matters in the case without having to retry the case every time there is a change of judge. Since Japanese judges typically are transferred every three years and since cases may take longer than three years from filing to decision, it is common for at least one judge to be transferred during the course of the case. Where a single judge examines a document, a record of the examination must be made for the record. CPR Rule 142.

70 CCP Article 228 (4).

71 See, Kazuhiko Yoshida, Legal Aspects of E-commerce in Japan (2001) on the web at *www.lawgazette.com.sg/2001-7/july01-feature3.htm* at page 3 of 7.

72 CPR Rule 145.

73 CCP Article 229; CPR Rule 146.

74 CCP Article 230.

75 CCP Article 230 (3).

76 CCP Article 230 (2).

thentic. If authenticity is questioned, the court may make inquiry of the government entity to determine authenticity.[77]

The rules dealing with documents are applied to modern technology methods of communicating ideas. Thus, photographs, drawings, audiotapes and videotapes, etc. are covered by the same rules to the extent that they may be applicable.[78] Accordingly the proffering party must submit an explanatory note as to the facts to be proven by photographs, tapes, etc. Since these materials do not necessarily have the same authenticating symbols (signature or seal) as documents nor does the material itself speak for itself (a tape must be played to be understood, etc.), the proffering party needs to include additional information in the explanatory statement submitted with the physical evidence. The statement must identify the date, time, and place when the tape or photographic was made.[79] If the tape is in a foreign language, either the court or adverse party may ask for a translation.[80] The same rules as are applicable to documents apply when authenticity questions are raised as to such materials.

If a challenge is made to authenticity, the authenticity should theoretically be established through testimony subject to direct and cross-examination. Before undertaking such testimony the court will request that a written proffer be made as to the testimony proposed. After discussion of the proffer with the parties (as part of clarification of whether there exists a real authenticity question) the authenticity issue may be resolved by agreement or the court may accept the proffer in place of testimony. Accepting the proffer as if it was testimony theoretically requires the opposing party's consent but considering the court's discretion to determine whether evidence is or is not required on a matter the court, if convinced, can probably compel such acquiescence.

Documents are not inadmissible simply because they contain hearsay utterances. The professional judge will give such documents such weight as they presumably deserve.

---

77 CCP Article 228 (2), (3).

78 CCP Article 231.

79 CPR Rule 148.

80 CPR Rule 149. Unlike the case of traditional documents, CPR Rule 149 does not refer to partial translation—that is translation of only the portion of the tape that is being offered as proof. It is likely that as in the case of traditional documents the party offering the tape need only translate the portion that is being offered. Where a party offers a written transcription of a tape into evidence the adverse party may request and the proffering party shall deliver a copy of the tape. CPR Rule 144.

2) "Discovery" of Documents[81]

While the rules for introduction of documents into evidence are relatively straightforward and uncontroversial, the real issues in the document area concern the ability of a party (usually the plaintiff) to obtain documents so that they may be offered into evidence. As there is no pre-filing discovery in Japan, document production from third persons must be handled at the Oral Argument stage. For parties, document production can be part of the Preparation for Oral Argument or Oral Argument stage of the case. Because the rules for filing the Complaint (discussed earlier) require fact pleading and the attachment of documents to the Complaint, this is a disadvantage to the plaintiff and distinguishes the document production rules in Japan from discovery as that term is used in the United States. In the United States the function of discovery is to enable a party to obtain documents before the party knows what the document says—in other words to discover not simply the document but the facts contained in the document. This is achieved through notice of claim pleading that does not require the pleading of facts to any great extent and open discovery that does not require the party seeking discovery to know what the documents sought actually say, only that they may be related to the case. In American practice the documents need not themselves be relevant evidence in the case but are still discoverable if they might lead to relevant evidence.[82] In Japan since the Complaint is based on fact pleading and there

81 For discussions of the requirements for production of documents under the old Code and the new Code and the reasons for the change in requirements and provisions concerning document production see, Toshiro M. Mochizuki, Baby Step or Giant Leap:? Parties Expanded Access to Documentary Evidence Under the New Japanese Code of Civil Procedure, 40 Harvard International Law Journal 285, 286 (1999); Takeshi Kojima, Japanese Civil Procedure in Comparative Law Perspective, 46 U. Kansas L. Rev. 687 (1998); Yasuhei Taniguchi, The 1996 Code of Civil Procedure of Japan—A Procedure for the Coming Century? 45 American Journal of Comparative Law 767 (1997); Shozo Ota, Reform of Civil Procedure in Japan, 49 American Journal of Comparative Law 561 (2001); Koichi Miki "Roles of Judges and Attorneys under the Non-Sanction Scheme in Japanese Civil Procedure" delivered at the Symposium on Multiple Roles and Interaction of Judges and Attorneys in Modern Civil Litigation held at Chuo-o University, 6/1/03; Koji Harada, Civil Discovery Under Japanese Law, 16 Law in Japan 21 (1983); Craig P. Wagnild, Civil Law Discovery in Japan: A Comparison of Japanese and U.S. Methods of Evidence Collection in Civil Litigation, 3 Asian-Pacific Law and Policy Journal 1 (2002); International Commercial Litigation in Japan, Masafumi Kodama & Jay Tyndall, Kitahama Law Office, on the web at *www.Masafumi Kodama & Jay Tyndall, Kitahama.or.jp/English/litigatn.htm*; Carl F. Goodman, The Somewhat Less Reluctant Litigant: Japan's Changing Views Towards Civil Litigation, 32 Law and Policy in International Business 769 (2001); Carl F. Goodman, Japan's New Civil Procedure Code: Has it Fostered a Rule of Law Dispute Resolution Mechanism, 29 Brooklyn Journal of International Law 511 (2004); Ryu Takabayashi, (translated by Toshiko Takenaka) Practices of Patent Litigation in Japanese Courts, University of Washington School of Law, on the web at *www.law.washington.edu/casrip/newsletter/newsv5i2jp2.html*.

82 The American approach to the broad scope of document discovery is not unique but is consistent with common law practice in general. The rule is premised on the 1882 English case Compagnie Financiere et Commerciale du Pacifique v. Peruvian Guano Co., 11 QBD 55 (1882) in which the court made it clear that documents should be produced that reasonably were believed to contain evidence that could either directly or indirectly assist a party in sup-

is no meaningful discovery prior to filing the Complaint,[83] the plaintiff is at a disadvantage.[84] Assuming the plaintiff clears the pleading hurdle, the 1996 Code was designed to make it somewhat easier for the plaintiff to obtain documents to support its case. The Code and Rules are, of course, parallel for plaintiff and defendant, but the reality is that in most litigation it is the defendant that knows the facts and the plaintiff that needs to discover the facts. And, in most litigation (the exceptions being cases where there is legislation shifting the burden) the plaintiff has the burden of persuasion and the burden of proof.

In the United States the discovery process is principally in the hands of the lawyers. At the start of the case the lawyers are required to make certain mandatory disclosures[85] and can later serve each other with document requests. The court only becomes involved if there is a dispute as to whether documents must be produced or whether a request is somehow inappropriate.[86] In Japan the question of document production is a matter for determination by the court. Similarly, in the United States the lawyers are in charge of document production from third persons not party to the lawsuit. Such documents can be demanded by use of a deposition and subpoena *duces tecum* requiring the third-person witness to appear for deposition and bring the requested documents to the examination. Third persons may be compensated for the cost of gathering the documents together and may object to the document request through a motion to quash. The burden of quashing is on the moving third person and is a difficult burden to meet. In Japan the question of production by a third-person non-party is a matter for the court's discretion.

---

porting its case or damaging the opposition's case. See, ALI/UNIDROIT Principles and Rules of Transnational Civil Procedure (Proposed Final Draft, 3/9/04) p. 12.

83 As noted earlier the new pre-filing Inquiry Process suffers from the same inadequacy as the post-filing Inquiry Procedure, namely lack of any meaningful sanction and consequently is unlikely to be any more successful in obtaining information than the post-filing Inquiry Process.

84 Since there is fact pleading in Japan and production of documents in Japan comes after the fact pleading, the comments of some commentators that the production of documents mechanism in Japan is the equivalent of discovery of documents in the United States should be considered in context. See, Itsuko Mori, The Difference between U.S. Discovery and Japanese Taking of Evidence, 23 International Lawyer 3 (1989).

85 The mandatory disclosure rule has been attacked by some as inconsistent with the adversary process and with requiring lawyers to violate their ethical obligations to a client by voluntarily turning over data to the adversary. (An argument similar to the argument as to why Japanese lawyers need not respond to unsanctioned inquiry requests). For a discussion challenging the notion that mandatory disclosure has benefit see, Kuo-Chang Huang, Mandatory Disclosure: A controversial Device With No Effects, 21 Pace Law Review 203 (2000).

86 Prior to the modern formulation of Rule 34 of the Federal Rules of Civil Procedure, the party seeking documents was required to make a motion for production and was required to establish a need for the documents sought to be produced. The rule was changed to take the judge out of the initial stages of document discovery and leave the issue of discovery to the lawyers, with the judge acting as a final arbiter of disputes. The change in the rule also took out the good faith showing requirement for production thereby making document discovery against a party easier to achieve. Under the old formulation the question of whether or not to order a party to produce documents to an adversary party was, like in Japan, a matter for the court.

To obtain production of documents from an adversary or third person, the party seeking the documents is required to file a motion with the court seeking the documents.[87] (Some documents are to be produced without motion. Thus, the documents that are attached to the Complaint and Answer are produced when the papers are served.) The Code provides that the motion must set out the following information:

a) A description of the title of the document;

b) The content or substance or gist of what the document has to say;

c) The person or entity in possession of the document;

d) The facts that are to be established through the use of the document as evidence; and

e) The basis on which the motion to produce is made[88](that is which of the categories of allowed document production contained in Code Article 220 does the sought document fall into).[89]

These requirements are the same as under the Code prior to 1996.[90] Under the old Code it was recognized that the moving party was under a severe disadvantage because it was difficult to know the information required unless the movant had seen the document.[91] In sum, to discover the content of a document, the applicant needed to know what the document said. This is not as incongruous as it sounds. The purpose of the production rule was not discovery but production.

Especially difficult was the requirement that the movant describe the title and the content or substance of what the document said. The theoretical basis for these requirements were a) that they identified the document requested so that the court and the party in possession could easily order and produce and b) providing the substance of the document demonstrated that there was good reason for its production. If the party seeking production did not already have possession of the document or if the document's substance was not otherwise readily available the requirement acted as a prohibition against production. To alleviate this difficulty (but not completely remove the requirement) the 1996 Amendment to the Code provides that when it is extremely difficult for the movant to identify the title and substance of a document sought (items a and b above) the movant need only sub-

---

87 CCP Article 219.

88 CCP Article 221.

89 CCP Article 220.

90 See, Nobutoshi Yamanouchi and Samuel J. Cohen, Understanding the Incidence of Litigation in Japan: A Structural Analysis, 24 International Lawyer 443, 447 (1991); Toshiro M. Mochizuki, Baby Step or Giant Leap:? Parties Expanded Access to Documentary Evidence Under the New Japanese Code of Civil Procedure, 40 Harvard International Law Journal 285, 288 (1999).

91 Hiroshi Oda, JAPANESE LAW 408 (Oxford University Press, 1999); Toshiro M. Mochizuki, Baby Step or Giant Leap:? Parties Expanded Access to Documentary Evidence Under the New Japanese Code of Civil Procedure, 40 Harvard International Law Journal 285, 288 (1999).

mit such facts as will enable identification by the person from whom the document is sought.[92] The requesting party may then move the court to order the holding party to supply the necessary information. Once such a showing of great difficulty is made, the court may request that the holder of the document provide information so that the movant's obligation can be completed.

Exactly how much of a showing of substantial difficulty a movant must make is as yet undetermined. There are two theories. Under the more restrictive theory the moving party must show a good faith effort to obtain the necessary information and failure to get results from such effort. This would be time consuming and expensive. The other, while requiring such good faith showing, would assume such showing when there is reason to believe that an effort would be time consuming, expensive and worthless. Since the purpose of the Code amendment is to loosen (to some extent) the restrictions on production courts likely will adopt the second approach.

Complications may arise as the Code merely gives the court authority to request that the holder provide the necessary information. The court is not given compulsion authority. And, like the Inquiry Process discussed previously there is no Code-specified sanction if the party refuses to follow the court's suggestion.[93] Although collegiality and Bar Association ethics concerns may not be sufficient to compel compliance with the court's request, the fact that the court is the ultimate decision-maker in the case and may draw inferences from conduct of the parties (even if the Code does not specifically give that authority), should lead to compliance. Moreover, the court has authority to order production and if the holder declines to submit the needed information the court may nonetheless order the document to be produced, using general language in the court Order to substitute for the more specific identification that would normally be required. Such an approach may be inconsistent with the actual wording of the statute but it is likely that the court would undertake such a reading if required. The problem, of course, is the lack of a sanctions regime to assist the court in carrying out evidence production functions.

Although helpful, the amendment to the Code does not throw open the gates of discovery as the movant must still make a substantial showing, such as the facts that the document will establish and the grounds on which production should be based. The chicken and egg problem still exists. There is no "discovery device" under which a movant may ask the person in possession of a document to produce documents that relate to the subject matter of the suit or even through an Inquiry ask for a description of documents that relate to the issues in dispute. The movant in Japan still requires a great deal more knowledge and information about docu-

92 CCP Article 222.

93 For a discussion see, Koichi Miki "Roles of Judges and Attorneys under the Non-Sanction Scheme in Japanese Civil Procedure" delivered at the Symposium on Multiple Roles and Interaction of Judges and Attorneys in Modern Civil Litigation held at Chuo-o University, 6/1/03, pages 10-11.

ments than a party in the United States. Where a movant has information about documents the new Code amendment does assist the movant in overcoming the procedural burdens of seeking production of the document. Anecdotal evidence from Japanese bengoshi indicates that under the new Code the procedural barriers to requests for production orders are lower than under the old Code, even if actual production has not yet been significantly loosened.[94]

Not all documents that may be relevant to the case can be obtained through production. For starters, documents that do not themselves prove facts that are in issue need not be produced. As a consequence a party cannot use one document to trace another document to trace a third document that might have evidence of facts that need to be proved. It is not sufficient that the document might lead to admissible evidence (as would be the case in the United States) but the document itself must be admissible, in the sense that it must assist in establishing the facts in the case. And, the movant must set forth the fact or facts to be proven by the document. Nor can a document be sought because the text of the document might identify a person with information that might be relevant or that might prove facts at issue. The Code retains the production rather than discovery aspect of document production. American (and Japanese) lawyers who see the amendment of the Code as adopting discovery as a goal mistake the Code's purpose.

If the movant is able to meet the requirements of the first four subparts of Code Article 221 (description, gist, possessor and facts to be established), the movant must still show that the document sought falls into one of the four categories of documents subject to production under the Code. These categories are:

a) A document in possession of and relied on by the opposing party. Thus a document that is identified in the Complaint, Answer or Preliminary Documents as a document on which the opposing party is relying must be produced by the opposing party if it is in possession of the document.

b) A document that some substantive law makes available to the movant upon request. Such documents are limited in nature. It is possible that the new Freedom of Information Act may make some government documents concerning a person available to such person on request or may even make other government documents available on request and that such documents would fall into this category. In this connection the relationship between this section of the Code and the 2001 amendment setting forth limits to the government's refusal to produce documents in its possession and requested by a party in litigation[95] will need to be better defined in the future. Some corporate documents may be available to shareholders under the corporation law and these documents would fall into this category.

94 Carl F. Goodman, Japan's New Civil Procedure Code: Has it Fostered a Rule of Law Dispute Resolution Mechanism, 29 Brooklyn Journal of International Law 511, 581 (2004).

95 See, e.g., CCP Article 223 (3), (4), (6).

c) A document that was prepared for the benefit of the requesting party or a document that was prepared as a consequence of the relationship between the parties. Thus, a receipt is prepared for the benefit of the person who delivered goods or money. If such a party has lost its copy of the receipt, it may be possible to get the person who prepared the receipt to produce its copy. Similarly a contract is prepared as a consequence of the relationship between the contracting parties and thus falls under this provision. It may be that a medical record prepared by a doctor was prepared based on the relationship of the doctor and patient or prepared for the benefit of the patient because it is necessary for treatment purposes.[96]

These three categories are the same as the categories of documents subject to production under the old Code. Under the old Code it was recognized that the limited nature of categories b) and c) made it extremely difficult for a party (especially a plaintiff) to get production of meaningful documents. As a consequence various inferior courts began to interpret the categories more loosely to permit production and to some extent discovery.[97] Thus, what benefited a party could be read much more broadly than simply those documents whose *initial* purpose was to grant the requester a benefit. Benefit could even mean a document that benefited the party in prosecuting its claim in litigation. Thus, an accident report that had been prepared for the use of the government in connection with an accident could be interpreted as created for the benefit of the plaintiff if the text of the report would benefit the plaintiff in the litigation. Many considered such an expansive view as outside the scope of the Code. It was surely outside the original intent of the Code. A document that relates to the legal relationship of the parties was also broadly interpreted to include documents that clearly were not intended by the Code.

Similarly although a medical record is prepared for the benefit of the doctor it may also be considered as prepared for the benefit of the patient. But could a medical record of the patient ever be considered as having been prepared for the benefit of a third person in litigation with the patient? One would think not. Yet some courts in Japan, in an effort to get at the truth of the matter, found that such documents containing valuable information could be construed as falling within the scope of the production rule.

As a backlash to limit this broad interpretation trend, other courts adopted the self-use doctrine. Under this doctrine a document that might otherwise fall under the judicially broadened interpretation of categories b) and c) would not be produced if it had been prepared for the sole use of the holder of the document and had never been intended to be disclosed to third parties. Such self-use documents

---

96 See, Hiroshi Oda, JAPANESE LAW 408 (Oxford University Press, 1999). On the other hand, since the medical file is not given to the patient but is retained for the use of the doctor, the record may be considered a self-use document and thus not subject to production. See discussion of the self-use document exception under the fourth category of documents subject to production under Article 220.

97 For a discussion of the inferior court efforts to broaden the production of documents requirement see, Koji Harada, Civil Discovery Under Japanese Law, 16 Law in Japan 21, 43-48 (1983).

although their production might benefit the requesting party were considered as not having been prepared for that party's benefit (as they were prepared for the sole use of the preparing party). Through use of this judicially created self-use exception the judicially created expansion of category b) and c) documents could be modified and limited. (The concept of limiting document production to prohibit the production of self-use documents can be traced back to debate over the 1866 Hanover Protocol that was incorporated into the old German Code of Civil Procedure).[98] The 1996 Code added a new catchall category of documents that were subject to production and thus the rationale behind the judicial expansion of category b) and c) was eliminated. However, the self-use exception was written into the new statute as a limitation on this new catchall category of documents subject to production but not as a limitation on category b) and c) documents. This creates the question of whether the pre-existing judge made "law" that expanded the interpretation of b) and c) remains "good law" and whether the limitation on that doctrine of expanded production (the self-use doctrine) no longer applies to b) and c) documents?[99]

From a common law point of view there exists a strong argument that the new Code, not having explicitly rejected the judge-made law that expanded the scope of b) and c) documents, has not changed the pre-existing law. Further, there is a strong argument that the new Code having specifically recognized the self-use document exception for category d) documents (to be discussed below) but not for category b) and c) documents did not intend the exception to apply to category b) and c). The common law views Codes and Code amendments as "floating" on the sea of case law that preceded them. To the extent the Code does not change that law the case law remains viable and vibrant. Thus the above arguments appear powerful to the common law. However, the civil law sees the law as being the Code. The cases that preceded the Code do not continue with vibrancy, as the cases apply solely to the specific cases decided and do not constitute law. There is no sea of law on which the Code floats—the Code is the law. Thus the real question for the civil law is what do categories b) and c) mean and for that the words of the Code are most significant. As there is a new category d) designed to meet the perceived need that the court liberalization of b) and c) was aimed at, there is no need to treat b) and c) as other than what they say. Accordingly, the "failure" of the Diet to apply the self-use doctrine to b) and c) is really not a failure at all. It is recognition that b) and c) should be narrowly interpreted as originally intended. Both the liberalizing cases and the restricting cases are to be disregarded as not affecting the true meaning of b) and c).

98 See, Koji Harada, Civil Discovery Under Japanese Law, 16 Law in Japan 21, 40-41 (1983).

99 For an interesting discussion of the history of the self-use document exception see, Mochizuki, Baby Step or Giant Leap? Parties Expanded Access to Documentary Evidence Under the New Japanese Code of Civil Procedure, 40 Harvard International Law Journal 285 (1999); Yasuhei Taniguchi, The 1996 Code of Civil Procedure of Japan—A Procedure for the Coming Century?, 45 American Journal of Comparative Law 767, 775 (1997).

The 1996 rewrite of the Code added a fourth general category:

d) Any other document that does not fall within certain specified exceptions set out in Article 220 of the Code.

On its face this fourth category appears to be a catchall that makes all documents subject to production provided they do not fall within the exceptions set forth. Indeed, it was the purpose of category d) to expand the scope of document production under the Code to make it easier to obtain documents. To date the exceptions are so great and the resulting production so small that the catchall nature of the provision may be misleading.

The exceptions to production fall into three categories as well as a general prohibition against applying the general catchall to documents possessed by the government or to government documents in the possession of former government officials. When the Code was adopted in 1996, the government wanted an exception that would give it discretion as to when and whether it would produce documents in private litigation. To compromise the matter and obtain a bill that would be acceptable to all interests, the general exception for government documents was to be resolved by legislation within two years after adoption of the Code. In 2001 the Diet enacted a general provision to deal with the question of government documents. Under the provision government-held documents are exempt from production whenever there is fear that production would disclose official secrets and would or might cause harm to the public interest. To determine whether the documents sought are exempt from production the court does not simply rely on the statement of the government. Rather, a procedure is established under which the court will receive the government's opinion as to whether the documents are protected. (If the court on its own can tell either that the documents are protected or that the applicant for production cannot meet the requirements for production the court need not get the government's opinion.) It is not sufficient for the agency with control over the documents to make conclusory statements regarding the need to protect the documents. Rather, the agency must present the grounds for its refusal to make production.[100] The court may not inquire into the reasons given by the government. However, the court may determine for itself whether the rationale given by the agency fails to reasonably establish that i) production will endanger national security, damage relations with or cause harm to dealings with a foreign power or international organization or ii) interfere with law enforcement obligations of the government such as prevention of crime or prosecution of those charged or to be charged with a crime or enforcement of criminal law or iii) otherwise interfere with matters of public safety.[101] If the government documents involved contain technological or business secrets of a third person, the government may object to production on the grounds set out above and the person whose secrets are involved may also be heard on the matter. To the limited extent that the court may review the agency's determination and rationale, the court may make

100 CCP Article 223 (3).

101 CCP Article 223 (4).

an *in camera* review of the documents themselves to see whether the reasons given by the agency are reasonable.[102]

While not a part of the Code of Civil Procedure, Japan has a new Freedom of Information Act[103] and documents may be sought under this Act. Of course, if documents have already been produced under the FOIA, it would appear unreasonable for the government to refuse to produce the same documents under the Code. Moreover, if documents are not exempt from production under the FOIA it would appear that they are not exempt under the Code of Civil Procedure. Thus, as the scope of the government's production obligations under the FOIA becomes clearer, the scope of production under the Code will be affected.

Under the FOIA documents in the possession of the government need not be produced (subject to certain exceptions) where production would violate the privacy rights of individuals.[104] Similarly documents concerning a corporation that were voluntarily given to the government in confidence on the understanding that they would not be produced are exempt from production[105] as are documents that are in the nature of trade secrets.[106] The FOIA also has exemptions that parallel those in the Code of Civil Procedure.[107] It is likely that a court would find that the Code of Civil Procedure's specific reasons for refusing to produce are not exclusive and that at least some portions of the FOIA exemptions would be sufficient to protect against production. Thus, it is likely that a document that was voluntarily given to the government under a pledge of confidentiality would not have to be produced under the Code of Civil Procedure as the government would argue that to do so would interfere with matters of public safety and good order. This follows because if parties could not rely on the government's pledge of confidentiality they will refuse to voluntarily produce documents and thus interfere with the government functions designed to protect the public.

Other FOIA exemptions may also be exemptions from production in civil litigation even though no "outside" interests are implicated and the exemptions are not repeated in the Code of Civil Procedure. For example, the FOIA exempts most internal deliberation documents where production would risk harming the frank exchange of opinions between government officials.[108] As discussed below when such internal documents are in the hands of private parties the Supreme Court of

102 CCP Article 223 (6).

103 Freedom of Information Act, Law No. 42 of 1999. (Also called "Law Concerning Access to Information Held by Administrative Organs.")

104 FOIA Article 5 (1).

105 FOIA Article 5 (2) (b).

106 FOIA Article 5 (2) (a).

107 FOIA Article 5 (3)—documents whose production would harm national security or interfere with relations with foreign powers or international organizations exempt from production—(4) documents whose production would interfere with criminal law enforcement exempt from production.

108 FOIA Article 5 (5).

Japan has indicated that they are not subject to production under the "self-use" exemption to production because there is a need to protect the frank exchange of views within a business entity.[109] The same rationale would seem to apply to a government entity and surely that would be the position of the government.

Where the litigation is a case against a government entity brought under the Administrative Case Litigation Law (ACLL)[110] there is also a question of what documents the government needs to produce. Unlike the United States where the entire administrative record is forwarded to the court handling a challenge to an administrative determination, such record is not forwarded to the court in Japan. An amendment to the ACLL proposed by the government in the spring of 2004 as part of the package of Government bills designed to deal with judicial reform[111] would permit the reviewing court to order the government agency whose decision is under review to produce materials that throw light on the reasons and the underlying facts considered by the agency in making the challenged decision. The amendment also permits the court to order production from a different government entity in possession of such documents.[112]

Non-governmental documents subject to the catchall category are not to be produced when:

The document contains matter that would subject the holder or certain relations of the holder to self-incrimination or would otherwise subject the holder or relations to injury to their good name and reputation.[113] As a rule, witnesses in Japan need not testify when to do so would subject the witness or certain relatives of the witness to potential criminal prosecution. This is an analogue to the right against self-incrimination in the Constitution. In addition, witnesses do not have to testify if to do so would subject them to litigation for libel or slander. The Code of Civil Procedure incorporates these witness testimony exemptions into the production of document rules.

The document contains privileged materials, trade secrets or official secrets.[114] Once again the production rules adopt the rules applicable to witness testimony. Privileges in Japan are somewhat broader than in the United States so the category of persons who may not divulge secrets is somewhat larger than in the United States. For example, in addition to the acknowledged privileges of doctors, lawyers and religious officials so too communications with pharmacists, midwives, patent agents and notaries are privileged in Japan. Foreign lawyers who give foreign business law advice are included in the privileged categories. If the privilege

109 Fuji Bank v. Maeda, Case No. 1999 (kyo) No. 2, 53 Minshu 1787,1695 Hanrei-Jiho 49 (Petty Bench, 11/12/99) available in English through the web site of the Supreme Court of Japan.

110 Law No. 139 of 1962 as amended.

111 Near the close of the spring 2004 Diet session the Diet passed a bill to amend the ACLL.

112 ACLL Article 23-2.

113 CCP Article 220 and CCP Article 196.

114 CCP Article 220 and CCP Article 197.

has been waived (or if the government waives the official secret) then the document can be ordered produced.[115]

However, in the case of the attorney/client privilege the attorney may be under an obligation under the Lawyers Law and the Code of Ethics of the Bar Association not to disclose a confidence even if the client waives.[116] Therefore it may be that a privileged communication contained in a document in possession of the lawyer cannot be waived—except perhaps where the client wishes to affirmatively use the communication. This incongruity in the Code and the Lawyers Law and ethical standards may be a result of the 1996 Code's effort to align document production with witness testimonial obligations. Under the court's new power to redact parts of a document it may be that the privileged portions of documents could be redacted while the non-privileged portions could be ordered produced.

The Code of Civil Procedure does not define the term trade secret. However there is a definition of trade secret in the Unfair Competition Protection Act (Section 2(4)). Under this statute, whose purpose is to provide the rules for protection of business or technical trade secrets in the commercial world, a trade secret needs to possess three characteristics: a) it must be information useful in the operation of the business; b) it must not be publicly known (or else it would not be secret and hence would not be worthy of secrecy protection); and c) the possessor of the secret must have in place a program designed to protect the secrecy of the trade secret.[117] Under the Code of Civil Procedure, it is not sufficient that the person opposing production show that the information is useful in its business and that it is not publicly known. The mere fact that technical data is contained in the document sought is not sufficient to show that it should not be produced. Rather, to rely on the trade secret exception the opposing person must also show that production could cause it harm.[118] In a decision rendered in 1973 the Osaka High Court held that a company's direct labor costs and certain other costs of production were trade secrets and need not be disclosed in a proceeding undertaken in Osaka to provide assistance to an American court.[119]

As a general matter the court records of a case in Japan are public records just as the trial itself is a public event. Any person may seek to review the records of a

115 CCP Article 197 (2).

116 Toshiro Nishimura, The Code of Ethics Applicable to Bengoshi (Temple University Japan) 12/1/98 on the web at *www.tuj.ac.jp/newsite/main/law/benethics.html* (referring to Articles 23 of the Lawyers Law and 20 of the Ethics Code) (page 4 of 6).

117 For an English language discussion of the Unfair Competition Protection Act see, Takamitso Shigetomi, Asahi Engineering KK v. Dai-ichi Seiko KK, CASRIP Newsletter Winter 2003.

118 Case No 20 of 1999, 54 Minshu 1073 (Sup. Ct. Petty Bench, 3/10/2000) available in English through the web site of the Supreme Court of Japan.

119 See, English language discussion of 737 Hanrei Jiho 49 (7/12/73) (High Court Osaka) in Yoshio Ohara, Judicial Assistance to be Afforded by Japan for Proceedings in the United States, 23 International Lawyer 10, 27 (1989).

case.[120] However, parties to the case may, by motion, seek an order limiting the disclosure of the record or portions thereof that would disclose a trade secret or would violate the privacy rights of a party.[121] The making of the motion operates as a stay of disclosure until the court rules on the motion. The person seeking disclosure may seek reconsideration of a ruling that portions of the record not be disclosed. Immediate appeal is allowed from a determination that would permit disclosure or a determination denying reconsideration of a determination prohibiting disclosure. During appeal the material at issue remains confidential.[122]

The inadequacy of procedures to protect trade secrets in Japanese litigation inhibits the bringing of trade secret and other intellectual property cases.[123] The International Chamber of Commerce identified the lack of adequate protection of trade secrets in litigation in Japan as a deterrent to enforcement of Japan's international obligations under treaties designed to protect intellectual property rights.[124] In the spring of 2004 the Cabinet approved the submittal to the Diet of proposed legislation that would enhance the protections against disclosure of trade secrets in patent infringement cases. Such a bill was enacted by the Diet on June 11, 2004 as an amendment to Court Organization Law. The law gives the court authority to close hearings in cases when trade secrets are involved and/or to exclude certain persons from attending hearings. The amendment also allows the court to prevent parties and counsel from discussing matters involved in patent cases with third persons.

If parties settle a case, the court may delete certain items, including the record of witness and party testimony, from the public record.[125] Accordingly, potentially embarrassing testimony given by a party or a witness may become the basis for a settlement in order to restrict access to such testimony.

A document prepared solely for the use of the holder (the self-use exception).

The self-use exception was added to the Code in 1996 as a counterweight to the catchall category of document production. The catchall itself was a compromise position and the compromise could only be obtained in exchange for the legislative acknowledgment of the self-use exception. Reform minded advocates of

---

120 CCP Article 91. Exception is made in cases where the Oral Argument itself was closed to the public. This is consistent, as the reasons for closing the Oral Argument stage of the case should equally apply to the record of the closed sessions. Parties and third persons with a sufficient interest in the case may also obtain copies of the record and may even obtain copies of videotapes and audiotapes entered into the record.

121 CCP Article 92; CPR Rule 34; John B. Pegram, Recent Developments in IP Litigation in Japan (Fish & Richardson, 2000) on the web at *www.fr.com/news/articledetail.cfm?articleid=67* at page 7 of 12.

122 CCP Article 92.

123 For a discussion see, Takamitso Shigetomi, Asahi Engineering KK v. Dai-ichi Seiko KK, CASRIP Newsletter Winter 2003.

124 International Chamber of Commerce Report on Implementation of TRIPS Enforcement provisions (6/17/97) on the web at *www.iccwbo.org/home/intellectual_property/tripse.asp.*

125 CPR Rule 67 (2).

change in the Code of Civil Procedure wanted to open document production broadly. These forces were inspired by American discovery and document production procedures. Potential defendants were opposed to expanding the scope of document production. These potential defendants included the powerful business community and its allies in the government. To arrive at a compromise the catch-all provision was included and the judicially created self-use exception was added to limit the scope of the catchall just as the concept had limited the judicial expansion of categories b) and c).

Prior to the 1996 Code the courts had created the self-use exception to moderate the expanded discovery permitted by some courts under categories b) and c). If a document were created solely for the use of the holder of the document then it was clear that it did not fall within the category of documents that were prepared for the benefit of the party seeking its production. Such a document also was not prepared as a consequence of the relationship between the parties. Thus, the old Code did not require the production of self-use documents. A self-use doctrine of law was developed to distinguish documents prepared for use of the party seeking production (subject to production) or documents prepared as a consequence of the relationship of the parties (subject to production) and self-use documents (not subject to production).

The history of the self-use exception raises questions as to the reach of the amendment. A broad interpretation of the amendment incorporating judge-made law on how to interpret the exception under the old Code's document production provision would make the new Code's catchall virtually meaningless. After all if the only documents that could be produced were non-self-use documents and if that category was limited to the documents that had been subject to production under the old Code and now were again specifically designated as subject to production under the 1996 Code, then there was nothing for the catchall provision to catch. The logic of giving the self-use exception a broad interpretation could result in the exception swallowing up the rule.

The Supreme Court of Japan has opted to give the exception a broad interpretation but not so broad as to completely swallow the catchall provision. Nonetheless, the broad interpretation given to the exception by the court has resulted in making the catchall provision inapplicable to most damaging documents and protecting potential defendants in most situations. Japanese lawyers and judges are well acquainted with the Supreme Court's broad interpretation of the self-use exception. Consequently judges in inferior courts apply the exception broadly and requests to produce documents today do not appear to be granted any more liberally than in pre-1996 litigation. The consequence is that there has been no significant movement in making document production more available to plaintiffs than was the case before the catchall provision was adopted, although there has been some small movement. A more recent tightening of the broad sweep originally given to the exception by the Supreme Court may result in somewhat expanded production in the future.

In the first case to reach the Supreme Court dealing with this question the heirs of a deceased borrower sued a lending company. The company had extended substantial loans to the deceased who had used the money in securities transactions that had resulted in significant losses. The deceased had no other assets with which to repay the loans. One of the deceased's heirs sued the lending company asserting that the company had violated its duty of care to potential borrowers by making the loan knowing that the deceased would be unable to pay back either the principal or interest. To establish its case, the heir sought to have the lending institution produce certain documents in the lending company's loan files. Under the bank's internal procedures before a loan could be approved various officials and employees of the lending company were required to provide written recommendations. It was these internal recommendation documents that the plaintiff sought to have produced. The Tokyo High Court found that the internal documents of the lending institution did not fall within the self-use exception and ordered that the documents be produced. The lending institution appealed to the Supreme Court, which reversed.

The Supreme Court was of the view that the internal documents of the lender were self-use documents.[126] The documents had been produced solely for the purpose of enabling the lending institution make a decision as to whether or not to grant the loan. There was never any intent or purpose of giving the documents to anyone outside the lender. Thus the document was prepared for the sole-use of the lender and could not be ordered produced. In reaching this decision, the court appears to have been motivated by two considerations: a) disclosure would violate the privacy rights of the lender's employees who had rendered opinions in the matter. Apparently the court was of the view that such employees were entitled to have their opinions kept private except for the persons or institution to which it was given. Disclosure would also violate the privacy rights of the lender, which had a right to have its documents kept private unless there was a legal provision under which the documents were not to be kept private. b) Disclosure would adversely affect the free flow of information and ideas (including opinions) within the business establishment and thereby would inhibit the company in running its business. In other words if employees and officers believed that their opinions might be available to others outside the organization they might tailor their opinions to take account of this potential disclosure. Such tailoring would deprive the business organization of the unfettered judgment of its employees. The court left open the possibility that there might be unusual circumstances allowing for disclosure. As a rule, to protect the free flow of information, ideas and opinions documents prepared in a business for the use of business executives in making decisions for the business would appear to be exempt from disclosure. It is, of course, exactly such documents that the plaintiff wishes to obtain as it is exactly

126 Fuji Bank v. Maeda, Case No. 1999 (kyo) No. 2, 53 Minshu 1787,1695 Hanrei-Jiho 49 (Petty Bench, 11/12/99) available in English through the web site of the Supreme Court of Japan. For an English language discussion and criticism of Fuji bank see, Miyuka Nishi, Protection of Corporate Internet Communications from Discovery—Comparison with Japanese Practice, on the web at *www.vsb.org/sections/cc/docs/thirdplace.doc*

such documents that likely would contain the "smoking gun" evidence that the defendant knew that its conduct was wrongful.

In a follow up case, derivative lawsuit plaintiffs sought certain internal records of the bank whose directors were being sued. The bank objected on the ground that the records being sought were prepared for the sole use of the bank and thus were self-use documents. The Supreme Court agreed.[127]

In both cases the Supreme Court could have taken a broad view of the production obligation and a narrow view of the exception. Thus, the court could have found that the documents prepared by the bank were prepared in connection with the relationship between the parties. Or the court could have found that it would have been in the best interests of both the bank and the deceased not to make a loan that could not be paid back. In such case the document could have been considered as prepared for the use of both parties—the bank in deciding whether to make the loan and the potential borrower by carrying out the good faith obligation of the bank to advise the borrower that the loan was not in his best interest. If such an interpretation had been adopted, the self-use exception would not have been applicable. Similarly in the derivative lawsuit case the court could have found that the document was created for the use of the bank and that the derivative plaintiffs were suing in the name of the bank and for the bank's benefit and thus should be entitled to the documents. A derivative recovery would have flowed directly to the party that had prepared the document. Accordingly, it could be argued either that the Director defendants should not have been entitled to rely on the exception, or that the exception did not apply when the party seeking the documents stood in the shoes of the holder for whose use the document was prepared. The court did not follow either course.[128] Rather, the Supreme Court based its determination on the policy consideration that a company and its employees had a privacy interest in the internal documents. This was buttressed by the company's right to the free open opinions and ideas of its employees unfettered by concerns that would be implicated if the documents could be later produced in litigation.

More recently the court has also shown some willingness to allow production of documents if the production will not adversely effect the holder of the docu-

127 Case No 35 of 2000, 54 Minshu 2709 (Sup. Ct. Petty Bench, 12/14/2000).

128 Japanese courts are less likely than American courts to see derivative litigation as litigation brought for the benefit of the company involved. The company has a right (absent special circumstances) to intervene in the derivative case to support the Directors being sued, disclosing the "unity" between the company and the Directors against the derivative plaintiff. Case No. 17 of 2000, 55 Minshu 30 (Sup. Ct. Petty Bench, 1/30/01) (available on the web through the web site of the Supreme Court of Japan). Moreover, the potential for *sokaiya* to enter the derivative lawsuit field as a way of extorting money from companies (See, Mark D. West, Why Shareholders Sue: The Evidence from Japan, 30 Journal of Legal Studies 351 (2001)) may make the courts in Japan less likely to see derivative suits as a public good protecting corporate democracy.

ment.[129] Thus, in a tort action where the plaintiff asserted that certain telecommunications equipment it purchased was defective and sought production of the circuitry documentation, the Supreme Court reversed the Osaka High Court's ruling that the documents were self-use documents and remanded the matter for further consideration of the question. In its decision the court adhered to the rule established in *Fuji Bank v. Maeda* but noted that in that case in addition to the documents sought having been prepared solely for the benefit of the holder, the production of the documents would disadvantage the holder in some meaningful way. In *Fuji Bank* the holder's privacy interests as well as its interest in a free flow of information and opinions from its employees would be damaged by production. In remanding the telecommunications equipment case the court noted that the lower court had made no inquiry into the question of whether the holder would suffer any disadvantage from production and required that the lower court consider that issue on remand.

The reorganization of a company may effect the question of whether a document is subject to the self-use exception. Where a credit union was failing and was taken over by another company ("Plaintiff") pursuant to authorization by the Japanese equivalent of the Federal Deposit Insurance Corporation for the purpose of collecting on loans made by the credit union that were outstanding and sued a borrower ("Defendant") the borrower set up as a defense unconscionable action by the original lender credit union. To establish that the original lender had acted improperly in interfering with the defendant's opportunity to sell property and pay off the loan, the borrower sought production of certain internal papers of the original lender. Clearly the documents were prepared internally by the credit union and clearly they were prepared for the sole use of the credit union. But, the credit union was no longer in the business of lending money because it was taken over by the Plaintiff. In such a situation the credit union has no interest in receiving unfettered advice from its employees and production of the documents could not interfere with such an interest. Accordingly the Supreme Court held that production of the document would not cause any disadvantage to the credit union. Nor would production cause any disadvantage to the present holder of the document. Production by the present holder would not inhibit advice to the holder by its employees. Under these circumstances the court found that the document should be produced.[130]

From the reported cases it does seem clear that to be subject to the self-use document exception it is not enough that the document actually be prepared for the self-use of the holder. Rather, in addition to being prepared solely for the use of the holder, production must work some disadvantage to the holder that warrants

129 Case No. 20 of 1999, 54 Minshu 1073 (Sup. Ct. Petty Bench, 3/10/2000) available in English through the web site of the Supreme Court of Japan.

130 Case No. 15 of 2001, 55 Minshu 1411 (Sup. Ct. Petty Bench, 12/7/01) a summary is available in English through the web site of the Supreme Court of Japan. Apparently the privacy interests of the credit union's employees were insufficient to support non-production. It is difficult to understand why if employees have a privacy interest in the advice given to the employer that interest disappears when the employer disappears.

not producing the document. This interpretation appears to take into account the intent of the 1996 Code to liberalize the categories of documents that are subject to production in the Oral Argument stage of the case while at the same time take into account the concerns of holders of documents that their legitimate interests should not be adversely affected. The mere fact that production of the document would disadvantage a defendant in litigation should not be sufficient to implicate the self-use exception. Similarly the fact that the document would assist the plaintiff is not sufficient to make it available to the plaintiff. The Supreme Court appears to be trying to recognize the intent of the new Code to somewhat open up document production while at the same time not expanding production beyond what industry and its government allies agreed to as part of a compromise.

The initial trial (or first instance) court's ruling on a motion to order production of a document is subject to immediate appeal.[131] The only party having standing to appeal the grant or denial of a production order is the holder of a document who has been ordered to produce or the party seeking production whose motion is denied.[132]

Another problem in the area of production that the 1996 Code was designed to deal with was the previous rule under which if any part of a document was not subject to production the entire document was not subject to production. Under this rule if a portion of the document was privileged or otherwise not properly the subject of a production order the entire document was considered as not being subject to production. Such a rule obviously worked to the disadvantage of a party seeking production and failed to carry out the purposes of the rules broadening production. It is no longer a defense to production that a part of the document is not subject to production. Under the Code the court has the authority to order that part of a document be produced by ordering production of the document except for the portions that are exempt from production.[133] In other words the court can order that portions of a document be redacted and that the remainder of the document be produced. Although on its surface this appears to be a major change that should lead to more document production—and while that may eventually become the case—the reality is that as of the summer of 2003 the redaction authority of the court had not been frequently used and was not a significant factor in production determinations.[134]

The question of whether or not the court should order the production of a document may be a fact-intensive question. Is the document a self-use document and what disadvantage would the holder suffer by production, does it contain or is it entirely a privileged communication, etc.? Where one of the parties is also the

131 CCP Article 223.

132 Case No. 36 of 1999, 54 Minshu 2743 (Sup. Ct. Petty Bench, 12/14/2000) available on the web through the web site of the Supreme Court of Japan.

133 CCP Article 223 (1).

134 Carl F. Goodman, Japan's New Civil Procedure Code: Has it Fostered a Rule of Law Dispute Resolution Mechanism, 29 Brooklyn Journal of International Law 511, 580 fn. 262 (2004).

holder of the document, the court has general authority to inquire of the party concerning the document. Where a third person is in possession of the document and the court is of the view that the document should be produced, before making its determination the court must question the holder of the document to satisfy itself that the document should be produced.[135]

To assist it in making a determination of whether the document falls into one of the categories permitting production, the court may order that the document be given to the court[136] for *in camera* examination. While the court is conducting its *in camera* review no one but the court is permitted to see the document under consideration.[137] *In camera* review is another procedure borrowed from American practice. However, in the United States the judge is typically not the finder of fact in a matter where it undertakes *in camera* review. This fact-finding function is more likely to be in the hands of the jury. Where the court is handling a case without a jury, it is likely to request that a magistrate review the document *in camera* rather than the fact-finding judge. In this way the fact-finder does not get "corrupted" by material that should not be seen. In Japan the court is the fact finder as well as the determiner of whether documents should be produced. *In camera* review by the judge who will be deciding the case creates fairness issues.

Both American and Japanese judges tend to believe that because of their professionalism they may distinguish between evidence that is properly used in making a determination and evidence that is not to be considered on the merits. The American judge handling a bench trial will accept in evidence some material that would be excluded if the case were before a jury. Nonetheless there is a tension between reviewing a document that should not be considered on the merits and making a merits decision solely on the basis of "admissible" material. Whether it is because of this tension or whether it is for other reasons, Japanese judges tend not to review documents *in camera.* As a result, *in camera* review is more illusory than real.[138]

Although the Code of Civil Procedure gives judges the authority to order the production of documents by parties and third persons, the actual workings of the Code are somewhat different. Judges tend to request that parties produce documents rather than order them to produce documents. Of course a request to a party coming from the judge may have the same coercive effect as an order but the procedure is more harmonious and less confrontational than an order. Still when an order is required the court can issue such an order.

135 CCP Article 223 (2).

136 CPR Rule 141.

137 CCP Article 223 (3).

138 Carl F. Goodman, Japan's New Civil Procedure Code: Has it Fostered a Rule of Law Dispute Resolution Mechanism, 29 Brooklyn Journal of International Law 511, 580 (2004) (subjects interviewed had heard of cases where *in camera* review was used but none had actually been involved in a case where *in camera* review was used.).

When a document is ordered produced, the holder of the document should produce either the original or an authenticated copy thereof, but the court may order that an original be produced.[139]

Unlike the Inquiry Process, the Order to Produce Documents procedure is supported by sanctions. Where a party has been ordered to produce a document and fails to do so, the court may, if it finds that the failing party does not have justification for its action, make serious inferences against that party. Among such sanctions, the court may treat the refusal to produce as an admission of the reasoning set forth by the movant. The court may accept as true the claim of the moving party as to the substance of the document and the facts the document is alleged to establish.[140] This is a potentially strong sanction and has the power to compel a party to produce. However, when the document at issue is in the possession of a third person, the sanction regime is substantially weaker. Thus, the court may levy a small (200,000yen) non-penal fine against the non-complying person or entity.[141] Such fine is not large enough to compel production where there are other interests that the non-producing party may wish to protect,[142] and it is rarely used.[143] The person assessed such a fine may immediately appeal.[144] Although small, the new Code doubled the previous 100,000yen fine.

The Code of Civil Procedure is not the only place a litigant can look for assistance in obtaining documentary evidence. Thus, substantive statutes may contain provisions requiring the production of documents. The 1999 Amendments to the Patent Law broadened a party's responsibility to produce documents in a patent case. (The Patent Law provision is incorporated into the Trademark Law and thus the broadened responsibility to produce documents applies to trademark infringement cases.)[145] The law gives the court authority (on motion of the party alleging infringement) to order the production of documents needed to prove infringement and/or to establish the damages suffered as a consequence of the infringement.[146]

139 CPR Rule 143.

140 CCP Article 229 (4); see, John B. Pegram, Recent Developments in IP Litigation in Japan (Fish & Richardson, 2000) on the web at *www.fr.com/news/articledetail.cfm?articleid=67* at page 5 of 12.

141 CCP Article 225.

142 See, e.g., Yasuhei Taniguchi, The 1996 Code of Civil Procedure of Japan—A Procedure for the Coming Century?, 45 American Journal of Comparative Law 767, 776 (1997).

143 Masafumi Kodama & Jay Tyndall, Kitahama Law Office, on the web at *www.Masafumi Kodama & Jay Tyndall, Kitahama.or.jp/English/litigatn.htm* at page 8 of 14.

144 CCP Article 229 (6).

145 Trademark Law, Law No. 127 of 1959 as amended by Law No. 220 of 12/22/99 effective 1/6/01, Article 39.

146 Patent Law Section 105 (1); see also, Recommendations of the Justice System Reform Council—For a Justice System to Support Japan in the 21st Century (June 12,2001) on the web at *www.kantei.go.jp/foreign/policy/sihou/singikai/990612_e.html* at p. 21 of 90.

The new law also requires that a party defending against an infringement action[147] produce evidence to support its conduct.[148] The production provisions of the Patent Law are designed to make it easier for plaintiffs to obtain evidence establishing a defendant's infringement. A party may refuse to produce documents that contain trade secrets or where the refusing party has any other legitimate reason for refusing production. If such grounds are asserted, the court may undertake an *in camera* review to determine whether there are secrets that need to be protected.[149] Because of the policy considerations behind the Patent Law amendments—to protect Japanese business by protecting patent rights[150]—it is likely that orders to produce will be more frequently granted in the patent law arena than in other areas. In addition, it is likely that the *in camera* procedure will be used more frequently in patent cases than in other cases. The Patent Law contains stringent penalty provisions for failure to comply with a court order to produce documents including allowing the court to accept as accurate the movant's statements of fact that the document was asserted to prove. Because the Patent Law specifically requires production of certain documents, the self-use document exception should not apply to patent cases where the documents sought fall under the Patent Law production provisions.[151]

Similarly the Copyright Act provides that on petition of the party alleging infringement the court may order production of documents needed to either prove the infringement or establish the damages suffered. The possessor of the document may raise as a defense to production the claim that there exists a justifiable reason for failing to produce. To determine whether the claim of justification is valid the court may review the document(s) *in camera*.[152] The parameters of necessity and justification are yet to be determined. An interesting question is whether the self-use document exception is justification for refusal to produce.

---

147 The Patent Law sections discussed apply to patent infringement cases brought by the patent holder or the holder of an exclusive license. Patent Law Section 105 (3).

148 Patent Law Section 104bis.

149 Patent Law 105 (2).

150 This is a change in government policy based on Japan's emergence as a major economic power. Typically countries in the early stage of development have weak patent laws and few patents issued. As they become stronger economically and as their companies become possessors of intellectual property rights that other countries may wish to take advantage of, patent laws are strengthened to take account of this new reality. Such has been the case with Japan as demonstrated by the new emphasis on patent protection including a recent movement to accept the doctrine of equivalents. See, Ryu Takabayashi, (translated by Toshiko Takenaka) Practices of Patent Litigation in Japanese Courts, University of Washington School of Law, on the web at *www.law.washington.edu/casrip/newsletter/newsv5i2jp2.html* for discussion of Japan Supreme Court decision adopting the doctrine when certain facts, discussed in the article, are present.

151 For a discussion of the 1999 Patent Law Amendments and their affect on production of evidence see, Dr. Shoichi Okuyama, The 1999 Amendments to the Patent Law in Japan, on the web at *www.okuyama.com/1999_amend_jp_pat_law.htm;* JPAA, Revisions of the Japanese Patent Law (January 2000) on the web at *http://knpt.com/english/news4.htm*.

152 Copyright Law Article 114 biz.

Similar to the Patent Law, since the substantive law itself calls for the production of such documents; the self-use exception should not apply.

Provisions similar to the Patent Law and Copyright Law are contained in other statutes dealing with Intellectual Property rights.[153]

D. Witness Testimony

A fundamental anomaly of Japanese civil procedure should be recognized. On the one hand, the Code of Civil Procedure and Rules adopt the principal of Oral Argument placing emphasis on public oral proceedings. Thus the Plenary Hearing is Oral and parties may withdraw statements and contentions made in Preliminary Documents at the Oral Argument sessions with the court. Briefs and other written statements concerning contentions and factual issues in the case are considered as *Preliminary Documents* precisely because they are preliminary to the more meaningful oral stage when the parties or counsel meet with the court to discuss the case and when evidence is formally taken. The court will attempt to use the Preliminary Documents to try to make the oral stage (whether Preliminary, Preparatory or Plenary Hearing) meaningful and great stress will be placed on the briefs to try to move the clarification process forward. Yet, the principal aspect of the Oral Argument from an American point of view is the taking of evidence. To American lawyers that means the testimony of witnesses. It is here that the Oral Argument stage of the case presents a real anomaly. The reality is that there is relatively little taking of oral evidence in the Japanese Oral Argument.

The present witness testimony system in Japan is a melding of American Occupation ideas about witness testimony and historical civil law notions of testimony taking. The original Code of Civil Procedure followed the German law model. In this model only the judge could call witnesses. Parties were prohibited from taking witness testimony, although they could ask the judge to call and examine a witness. In the 1926 reform of civil procedure the parties were given the ability to examine witnesses provided the court consented. Under the present Code the system has theoretically come full circle. The court may not on its own call witnesses and the parties have the primary responsibility to both request that witnesses be called and to examine and cross-examine.[154]

The taking of testimony is a governmental function in Japan. Testimony cannot be taken in lawyer's offices as in an American deposition[155] nor can it be taken outside the presence of the judge, unless it is taken abroad pursuant to judicial assistance in another country or through use of a Japanese government official in

153 See, Teruo Dai, JAPANESE COPYRIGHT LAW IN THE 21st CENTURY (Oceana Publications, Inc., 2001) 92-93.

154 See, The Reception in Japan of the American Law and its Transformation in the Fifty Years since the End of World War II—Makoto Itoh, Civil Procedure law, 26 Law in Japan 66, 68 (2000).

155 In unusual cases or where the parties agree the Code permits a judge to take testimony outside the court. CCP Article 195.

another country. Not only must the judge be present but also the judge is an active participant in the testimony process. The judge has the right to question witnesses both after the parties have examined and also during the examination by a party. Indeed, the court may change the order of questioning so that the first person to question a witness is the judge. Finally it is important to recognize that the judge is a gatekeeper in relation to witness testimony. The parties have no absolute right to call witnesses to testify. Parties may request that the court call the witness to testify. In support of such request the party must submit a formal proffer of proof as to the testimony and set forth reasons for taking the testimony. If the court calls the witness the court has the responsibility for getting the witness to court on the date for testimony and for this purpose the court will summons the witness to appear. If the court feels that witness testimony is not necessary it will not permit the taking of the testimony. While the court is the gatekeeper in a negative sense—it can refuse to call a witness—the court (except in an Impeachment Court case or an administrative case under the Administrative Case Litigation Law, discussed in "Chapter 12) has no authority on its own to call a non-party witness (or a non-expert commissioner under the 2003 amendment).

There are three categories of witnesses in litigation. There are the parties, third-person witnesses and experts. Expert witnesses were rarely used in Japan and it is only recently that they have been permitted. Prior to the 1996 Code experts were required to appear in court for oral examination and cross-examination. Experts could not submit testimony in written form.[156] The 1996 Code opened the possibility for greater use of expert witnesses. The Code was not very successful in increasing the use of experts for numerous reasons, the principal one being the unwillingness of experts to subject themselves to potentially embarrassing cross-examination. The 2003 amendments create a new class of expert commissioners working for the court (part-time) who can assist the court in understanding technical matters, especially in medical malpractice and construction cases. This aspect of the 2003 amendments and experts are discussed separately below.

Party witnesses may be the party itself (when the party is an individual) or a representative of the party (when the party is a juridical entity such as a corporation). third-person witnesses are witnesses to events who are not parties to the case. In Japan statistics are separately kept for cases in which parties are witnesses and cases where third persons are witnesses. Those statistics disclose that there are few witnesses in the average case in Japan. The statistics also show that the number of witnesses has been declining in recent years. This is consistent with the effort of Japanese courts to move cases along faster. Witness testimony takes more time than reading a witness statement and cross-examination may take a great deal of time if handled in a sophisticated way. Testimony of parties is also time consuming and judges anticipate that the parties will make self-serving statements that render their testimony of little value. Moreover, to the extent the judge needs

---

156 Shoichi Okuyama, Izumi Sato and Alan J. Kasper, The new Code of Civil Procedure in Japan: Toward More Effective Resolution of IP Disputes Section 5.4 Expert Opinions and Documentary Evidence on the web at *www.sughrue.com/clientfiles/new_code.html*

to find out information from a party the court may question the party as part of its clarification process. This inquiry of parties, especially if conducted in the informal atmosphere of the Preparation for Oral Argument procedure, can be more directed than actual testimony and certainly is quicker than formal testimony.

While the inquiry made of a party by the court in Preparation for Oral Argument proceedings may serve the interests of the judge, it is less certain that it serves the interests of the party. As noted earlier, taking the step of instituting litigation in Japan is a giant leap compared to the same step in the United States. Parties to the litigation may have matters they wish to inform the judge about that are not part of what interests the judge at the clarification stage or Preparation for Oral Argument or Preliminary Oral Argument stage of the case. Failure to allow the parties to give formal testimony in open court in the formal setting of a courtroom may be part of the reason why use of the judicial process is not the favored method of resolving disputes in Japan.[157]

The number of party witnesses in Japanese litigation has been in steady decline since 1996. Thus in 1996 there were approximately 49 party witnesses per 100 cases in Japan or an average of one party witness for every two cases. This meant that in at least 50% of cases (on average) neither the plaintiff nor the defendant testified and that in 75% of cases (on average) one party did not testify. By 2001 the number of party witnesses per 100 cases had dropped to approximately 38, or approximately one party witness for every three cases. On average in 60% of cases neither the plaintiff nor defendant testified.

Witnesses at the District Court Level (First Instance)[158]

Year	Third-Person Witnesses	Party Witnesses
1996	38.0	48.7
1997	35.0	44.5
1998	32.3	41.6
1999	30.4	42.3
2000	29.3	39.4
2001	28.0	37.9

157 For a discussion of the lack of use of witnesses in Japanese civil trials and the potential effect of the lack of witnesses testimony on utilization of the judicial system to resolve disputes in Japan see, Carl F. Goodman, Japan's New Civil Procedure Code: Has it Fostered a Rule of Law Dispute Resolution Mechanism, 29 Brooklyn Journal of International Law 511 (2004).

158 Carl F. Goodman, Japan's New Civil Procedure Code: Has it Fostered a Rule of Law Dispute Resolution Mechanism, 29 Brooklyn Journal of International Law 511 (2004). The Brooklyn Journal of International Law has given permission for the use and copying of this material.

The situation for third-person witnesses is even less friendly to witness testimony. In 1996 there were approximately 38 third-person witnesses testifying in each 100 cases but by 2001 the number had declined to only 28. This means that on average testimony from third-person witnesses was heard in only one of every 4 cases filed. Since a case in which a witness may testify may involve testimony by more than one witness, the reality is that significantly more than 75% of cases are determined without any witness testimony. Thus records kept by the judicial Secretariat disclose that in 2001 the percentage of cases in which no witness testified had climbed to 85.5% and that for 2002 it is estimated that the percentage had risen to 86.4%:[159]

Year	Percentage of Cases with No Witnesses
1998	83.2
1999	84.3
2000	85.0
2001	85.5
2002	86.4 (provisional data)

Of course in default judgment cases there is no witness testimony and, as noted earlier, it is estimated that 40% of cases in the District Court are default judgment cases. Even if the percentages utilized are reduced by half (assuming a 50% default rate) in over 40% of contested cases there are no witnesses. In one half of the approximately 13% of cases in which there is witness testimony, only a single witness testified. In only 0.6% of cases were there more than 5 witnesses. That parties wish to testify and that counsel wish to have witnesses testify is demonstrated by the percentage of appeal cases where the High Court allows witness testimony. In almost 10% of cases the High Court heard third-person witnesses and in a similar percentage of cases the High Court heard party witnesses. When it is considered that all of the cases coming to the High Court have passed through a pre-Oral Argument stage in which the facts at issue and the contentions have been fully explored and confirmed and that the remaining issues have been tried at the District Court, the fact that the appeals court would hear witnesses in a relatively high percentage of cases as compared to the percentage of cases at the District Court level where witnesses are orally examined throws light on two matters. First, the process of confirming the case by the District Court is not very successful in limiting new issues, new facts and/or new contentions after the pre-Oral Argument stage. Second, the District Courts are over utilizing their "gate-keeper" function of limiting evidence by overly restricting oral witness testimony.

---

159 Carl F. Goodman, Japan's New Civil Procedure Code: Has it Fostered a Rule of Law Dispute Resolution Mechanism, 29 Brooklyn Journal of International Law 511 (2004). The Brooklyn Journal of International Law has given permission for the use and copying of this material.

This lack of witness testimony leads some Japanese lawyers to believe that the judicial system does not give their clients a fair trial. This lack of witness testimony is also inconsistent with the objectives of the American Occupation and with the apparent heavy reliance on witnesses that one would assume from the structure of the Code of Civil Procedure.

The Code's basic approach to witness testimony appears consistent with the American experience. The reality is different. In theory any person may be a witness,[160] subject to limited privileges.[161] Prior to the war the privileges were quite broad and reflected the feudal concepts of loyalty and obligation. The Occupation changed the approach as part of its drive to remove the vestiges of feudalism from Japan. Thus the Code adopted a limited privilege against giving testimony rule. The first privilege is a privilege that carries out the constitutional right not to be a witness against one's self. Thus, if the answer to questions would expose the witness or certain categories of relatives to incrimination or prosecution, the witness has a right to refuse to answer. Similarly, answer is not required if the questions would expose the witness or relatives to suit for defamation or otherwise result in damage to the reputation of the witness.

The second broad category of privilege protects interests other than the interests of the witness. Here the Code provides that a witness may refuse to answer when:

> a) The witness is a public official claiming that answer to questions would expose official secrets. In such cases, if the court has not obtained permission for the witness to testify from the relevant agency then the witness may refuse to answer. This privilege applies at all levels of government. Thus, Members of the Diet may refuse to answer if testimony would disclose a public secret. In such case the court needs to obtain approval for testimony from the House of which the person is a Member. Members of the Cabinet may refuse to testify for the same reason. If a Minister refuses to testify the court may only compel testimony if the Cabinet grants permission.[162]
>
> In theory the government Agency or House or Cabinet should not refuse to allow such testimony unless the public interest or the performance of public duties would be harmed by testimony. In reality there is virtually no check on the ability of the governmental entity to refuse. In theory the court could find that the refusal to allow testimony exceeded the discretion of the agency for which the proposed witness worked (for a civil servant bureaucrat). Similarly, an excess of authority argument might theoretically be applied to the Cabinet or House of the Diet. The reality is that if the agency or House or Cabinet refuses to "waive the privilege" the official will not testify.
>
> b) The Code preserves traditional privileges based on confidential relationships. Thus a privilege extends to information gathered as a consequence of the

160 CCP Article 190.

161 CCP Article 196 and 197.

162 CCP Article 191.

following privileged relationships—attorney-client, patent agent-client, notary-client, dentist-patient, physician-patient, midwife-patient, pharmacist or pharmacy-customer, religious personage-penitent (or adherent to the religion).

If the privilege is waived, the witness can testify.[163] There exists a significant question as to whether the attorney-client privilege can be waived. Bar Association officials have taken the position that under the Lawyers Law[164] and ethical standards of the legal profession as set out by the Bar Association a lawyer is not permitted to divulge a privileged communication even if the client has released the lawyer from his obligation of secrecy.[165]

c) The final privilege prevents the disclosure of technical or professional secrets.

These privileges are the same privileges that are applicable to the refusal to present documents under Article 220 of the Code. This parallel treatment is consistent with the Code's effort to treat documents and witnesses similarly. Accordingly the privileges have been discussed in the section dealing with document production. However, there exists an additional aspect to witness testimony and privilege. This aspect relates to the question of whether the testimony of the witness will cause the witness embarrassment or otherwise adversely affect a confidential relationship that should not be disturbed. Here the power of the court to control the proceedings and to act as gatekeeper for testimony comes into play. Although it may have been the intention of the Occupation to rid the civil procedure system of the vestiges of feudalism, those vestiges remain although not in the sense of loyalty from vassal to lord. Instead the modern incarnation is in the relationship of employer-employee. In many ways the relationship of workers to company can replicate the relationships found in families.[166] There is no doubt that it would be extremely embarrassing for a company employee to testify in a manner that was damaging to the company. Moreover a company employee probably does not understand the entire company policy or position in connection with a matter in which the employee might be called as a witness. In such a case it would likely appear to the Japanese judge that it is improper to call the employee both for embarrassment reasons and because the employee does not know all the facts or factors that are relevant to testimony. Even more embarrassing would be for a company Director or senior executive to testify against the interest of the company. Considering the fiduciary nature of the relationship between the Director and the

163 CCP Article 197 (2).

164 Lawyers Law Article 23 commands that a lawyer keep secret any fact that she learned as a consequence of her business activities. It does not provide for waiver by the client.

165 Toshiro Nishimura, The Code of Ethics Applicable to Bengoshi (Temple University Japan) 12/1/98 on the web at *www.tuj.ac.jp/newsite/main/law/benethics.html* (referring to Articles 23 of the Lawyers Law and 20 of the Ethics Code) (page 4 of 6).

166 For a discussion of modern Japanese employment relationships see, V. Lee Hamilton and Joseph Sanders, EVERYDAY JUSTICE (Yale University Press, 1992) 25-30.

company, it can be argued that there exists a confidential relationship that should not be disturbed. In such case the judge is more than likely to refuse to allow such a witness to be called to testify and be embarrassed by the questioning.

The question of whether or not to permit a witness claiming a privilege to testify is a matter for determination by the court. As noted the court will be guided in part by the relationship of the witness to the testimony anticipated and whether a confidence that should remain secret (even if not specifically set out in the Code) would be jeopardized by the testimony.

The party seeking to take the testimony is required to advise the court and parties of the witness's name, make a written proffer of the testimony to be elicited and must indicate the anticipated time needed for examination.[167] Where the court agrees that testimony of the witness may be taken, the party offering the witness is required to make a good faith effort to get the witness to the courthouse at the time designated for testimony.[168] However, the obligation to summons the witness and compel appearance, like the serving of the Complaint, is a court function. Witnesses are summoned to appear on the date, time and place entered on the summons.[169] The Code and Rules provide substantial penalties for failure to appear including, arrest and production of the witness by proper authorities,[170] possible imprisonment or a non-penal fine.[171] In practice witnesses who fail to appear are rarely punished.[172] Since failure of a witness to appear is a failure of the court process to compel appearance, the party proffering the witness also is not punished. Indeed, courts would consider it improper to punish a party because a third person failed in a duty that the party could not compel.

Witness testimony is taken under oath and subject to the penalty of perjury[173]—again rarely utilized. However there are situations where a witness who does appear may refuse to take the oath. For example, a witness who voluntarily appears notwithstanding testimony may incriminate the witness or certain relatives, need not take the oath. A witness subject to a privilege against testifying may appear on the appointed date and raise the privilege by refusing to take the oath. In such case the court will determine whether the privilege is applicable.[174] An immediate appeal is available to the parties or witness from the court's ruling. Although subject to a small non-penal fine and even imprisonment, the reality is that there is little compulsion for a non-willing witness to testify.

---

167 CPR Rules 106 and 107.

168 CCP Article 109.

169 CPR Rule 108.

170 CCP Article 194; CPR Rule 111.

171 CCP Articles 192 and 193.

172 Masafumi Kodama & Jay Tyndall, Kitahama Law Office, on the web at *www.Masafumi Kodama & Jay Tyndall, Kitahama.or.jp/English/litigatn.htm* at page 8 of 13.

173 CCP Article 201.

174 CCP Article 199.

A reading of the Code discloses the American influence on witness testimony. Prior to the war, the court (as is typical in civil law inquisition systems) conducted questioning of witnesses. After the judge had completed his questions the parties could ask the court to ask additional questions and perhaps even to ask some questions themselves. However, since the judge was in charge of the case and understood where the evidence should go to make the correct party win, there was little in the way of party questioning.[175] The Occupation intended to change this inquisition model and embraced a more adversary system model.[176] The Code provides for direct examination by the party offering the witness, cross-examination by the adverse party and on permission of the presiding judge there may be redirect and recross.[177] After party examination the presiding judge (or other member of the panel after informing the presiding judge of their intention to do so) may question the witness.[178] This order of precedence was designed by the Occupation to place primacy of witness examination in the hands of the parties while allowing the court to question to clarify matters after the parties had completed their examination. This was considered as a reform in diminishing the power of the judge and making the court less paternalistic.[179] The practice was consistent with the Occupation view that civil litigation is a battle between the parties with the State, in the person of the judge, as a neutral party.

Japanese lawyers were unprepared for the kind of direct and cross-examination that the Occupation had in mind. Japanese law faculties did not sufficiently train students in the arts of examination and cross-examination (a difficult subject to teach when the professors have never been practicing lawyers, have never examined witnesses and never were taught the subject by lawyers when they went to school). Moreover, without a system for pre-Oral Argument discovery that permitted lawyers to obtain in advance the needed information concerning a witness' knowledge a party oriented questioning system was bound to fail.[180] For whatever reason, cross-examination and the adversary system of questioning witnesses was

175 Kohji Tanabe (assisted by John B. Hurlbut), The Process of Litigation: An Experiment With the Adversary System in LAW IN JAPAN (Arthur Taylor von Mehren Ed. Harvard University Press, 1963) 73, 98.

176 Alfred C. Oppler, LEGAL REFORM IN OCCUPIED JAPAN 131-132 (Princeton University Press, 1976).

177 CCP Article 202 (1) and CPR Rule 113 (1) and (2). The permissible scope of direct examination, cross-examination and redirect and recross are similar to the scope in the United States. CPR Rule 114.

178 CPR Rule 113 (4).

179 Alfred C. Oppler, LEGAL REFORM IN OCCUPIED JAPAN 130-133 (Princeton University Press, 1976).

180 See, Takeshi Kojima, Japanese Civil Procedure in Comparative Law Perspective, 46 U. Kansas L. Rev. 687, 706 (1998).

not something that was readily transplanted in Japan from the United States.[181] Judges found it necessary to intervene to move cases along and especially where pro se parties were involved to gather the needed testimony.

The 1996 Code attempts to harmonize the American style of examination and cross-examination by the parties with the necessities of a system that has neither pretrial discovery nor follows the adversary system model. The Code retains the form of the American witness examination. However, in recognition of the perceived need to have a professional adept at questioning conduct the needed examination it allows the presiding judge—after hearing the opinions of the parties—to change the order of examination even if the parties disagree.[182] Thus the presiding judge can reverse the examination roles and return to the prewar inquisition mode of court inquiry followed by party inquiry. Not only can the court reverse the role of examination to take over the initial questioning but also if it permits the parties to proceed first, the Rules provide that the presiding judge may interrupt examination at any time to ask questions of the witness.[183] The parties have the ability to object to questions through oral motion claiming that the question is outside the scope of permitted examination. (Evidentiary issues may also be raised but as there is no evidence code for civil cases and as judges sit without juries, these objections are unlikely to be received with any consideration.) The Rules require that questions be concise and asked one at a time (just as in the United States). Questions may not inquire into certain matters including: a) matter that would embarrass the witness. (Would a corporate officer be embarrassed if he had to admit that his company committed a wrong?—probably, and the question would probably not be permitted—more likely the court would not permit the taking of the officer's testimony.) b) Questions that are leading or duplicative or seek to elicit irrelevant testimony or that seek to elicit the witness's opinion (unless the witness is an expert). c) Questions that may loosely be defined as hearsay[184]—although the reality is that there is no hearsay rule. The court may rule on motions raising such matters and may *sua sponte* reject questions asked of a witness.[185] The entire panel (on objection from a party) may review the rulings of the presiding judge on the above matters. Such review is to take place immediately upon the making of the motion.[186] To protect the process the court may order any person in attendance at the Oral Argument to leave if the court feels that such person's presence is likely to effect the truthfulness of the witnesses' testimony.[187]

181 Kohji Tanabe (assisted by John B. Hurlbut), The Process of Litigation: An Experiment With the Adversary System in LAW IN JAPAN (Arthur Taylor von Mehren Ed. Harvard University Press, 1963) 73, 102.

182 CCP Article 202.

183 CPR Rule 113 (3).

184 CPR Rule 115.

185 CPR Rule 114 (2).

186 CPR Rule 117.

187 CPR Rule 121.

Witnesses are to testify to their own knowledge and orally in response to questions. Thus witnesses should not read previously prepared written testimony nor should the witness read documents in court, unless the court orders otherwise.[188]

The Code has interesting modern and experimental provisions. Modern technology is utilized so that a witness located far from the courthouse can testify without having to travel to the forum court. Unlike the United States where witness testimony is considered as a lawyer/party process, in Japan the taking of testimony is a court/governmental function. Thus a witness cannot simply appear at a lawyer's office in his home city and be hooked up by telecommunications means to an office or the court where the case is. Rather, the witness must appear at his/her local courthouse and testify and be examined by telecommunications in the courthouse. If documents are used during the examination fax transmission may be utilized.[189]

The official sovereign nature of taking testimony is important in transnational litigation. Lawyers from the United States cannot simply go to Japan and take deposition testimony even if the witness is willing to be deposed. The taking of such testimony is considered a violation of Japanese sovereignty. Rather, the taking of testimony of a willing witness must follow formal procedures that involve making a request to the United States government to utilize consular facilities in Japan for a deposition. The testimony must be taken in the Consulate (or Embassy), must be presided over by a United States Consular Officer, and must be taken under an Order of an American (State or Federal) court signed by a federal or state judge. The signature of a court clerk is insufficient, as a judge must sign the order. The signature of an Administrative Law Judge in an administrative agency is also not sufficient, as such judge is not a judge of a court. If lawyers from the United States are going to go to Japan to take the testimony they must obtain special visas for this purpose. An American lawyer in the Japan office of a law firm and in Japan under a lawful visa for a foreign lawyer need not get a special visa for taking the deposition as such action is permitted under the foreign lawyer's business visa.[190] The Japanese government views taking of testimony as a significant sovereign func-

---

188 CCP Article 203. In common law jurisdictions oral testimony, even to the extent of reading aloud portions of documents that are in evidence, was preferred to written testimony because early jurors might not be able to read. In Japan where the trier of the fact is highly educated, there is no need for a witness to read a document that the judge can read for him/her self.

189 CCP Article 204. CPR Rule 123. The use of modern telecommunications is not limited to the District Court and High Court. Even in small claims cases the Summary Court may also use such equipment. CPR Rule 226.

190 Under the Special Measure Law Dealing with Legal Business by Foreign Lawyers, Law No. 66 of 1986 as amended by Law No. 128 of 2003, foreign lawyers approved by the Justice Ministry to operate as foreign lawyers in Japan may perform legal functions limited to the expertise of the law of the country where the foreign lawyer is licensed. Such lawyer may not appear in Japanese Courts or serve process in Japan in connection with litigation pending in the lawyer's home country or express opinions about the law of any jurisdiction other than the lawyer's home jurisdiction, etc. (Chapter 2 Article 3). The handling of a deposition that is lawfully held in a United States Consulate under proper procedures would appear to fall within the scope of the lawyer's functions under the law and would thus fall within the scope of his visa.

tion and even views the informal interviewing of potential witnesses and investigation interviews of persons or entities as part of the preparation of either the filing or defense of a case as a formal function. To carry out these functions in Japan an American lawyer needs a special visa from the Japanese government.[191] These requirements are not simply formal but are considered so significant by Japanese authorities that failure to follow the rules will render a judgment issued in the American litigation ineligible for comity in Japan and hence not available to gain execution in Japan.[192]

If the parties have no objection the witness may testify by way of answering written interrogatories rather than be subjected to oral examination and cross-examination. If written interrogatories are agreed to, the opposing party may submit cross-interrogatories as a means of cross-examination.[193] Although the general rule is that witnesses should not be present in the courtroom prior to their appearance as witnesses, the presiding judge may allow such witness to be present in the courtroom.[194] One of the more interesting experimental provisions of the Code is the provision that allows more than one witness to testify at the same time.[195] When simultaneous testimony of witnesses is used, the Rules change the preferred order of questioning, and the court is expected to question before the parties.

Japanese judges are not impressed with party witnesses. As professional judges who see witnesses and parties regularly the judges are aware that parties tend to see events through biased eyes and that the testimony of a party will invariably support the party's position. Hence testimony from a party is not seen as particularly helpful. This predisposition against party testimony was displayed in the old Code of Civil Procedure through provisions that allowed party testimony but only after other testimony had been taken in the case. After other witnesses had been heard, the court could question a party witness. The objective was to use party witnesses not so much as fact witnesses to events or facts in the case but as witnesses who might help clarify or explain matters of interest to the judge and which only the parties could explain.

The new Code of Civil Procedure gives much greater importance to parties. Thus the provisions calling for party examination only at the end of the case and only

191 The requirements and the procedures to obtain the above referred to special visas as well as the steps to obtain US Government assistance and use of consular premises (and costs associated therewith) may be found in the Department of State's publication "Obtaining Evidence in Japan" on the web at *http://travel.state.gov/japan_obtaining_evidence.html*; see generally, Yoshio Ohara, Judicial Assistance to be Afforded by Japan for Proceedings in the United States, 23 International Lawyer 10 (1989).

192 See, Yoshio Ohara, Judicial Assistance to be Afforded by Japan for Proceedings in the United States, 23 International Lawyer 10, 21 (1989).

193 CCP Article 205, CPR Rule 124.

194 CCP Article 120.

195 CPR Rule 118.

when such testimony is required for decision[196] has been deleted and parties may be questioned at any time during the Oral Argument.[197] Recognizing that party witnesses may be helpful in clarifying issues and narrowing the scope of the case, the Code allows for the questioning of party witnesses at the Preparation for Oral Argument stage of the case as well as at the Oral Argument stage.[198] While the Code indicates a preference for the taking of third-person witness testimony before formal witness testimony of a party, the court may change this order of preference after discussing the matter with the parties.[199] Unlike third-person witnesses, where the initiation of examination must come from the parties and not from the court, the court may on its own motion require that parties attend and be examined.[200]

The same basic rules for testimony of a witness apply to testimony of a party with one major difference. If a party refuses to appear for examination the court, similar to its authority when a party fails to produce a document ordered produced, may consider as admitted the facts asserted by the opposition on the matters as to which the party was to be examined.[201] The Code also contains a provision for a small non-penal fine if the party gives false testimony and fails to correct the false testimony.[202] The real penalty for giving false testimony is not the small fine (which is rarely used and which is subject to immediate appeal) but rather the inferences that the court, as finder of the fact can draw from such false testimony.

While all of the aspects of the modern American adversary procedure are in place in Japan—party examination of witnesses, preference to party questioning over court inquiry, direct examination followed by cross-examination and redirect if appropriate, a preference for direct witness knowledge over hearsay, objections to questions, etc.—the trial is simply not the American trial. Japanese trials are not characterized by lawyers questioning witnesses while being interrupted by frequent objections by opposition counsel. Japanese trials do not have rulings on evidence by the judge. Nor is direct examination followed by a blistering cross-examination of the witness and then efforts at rehabilitation. As judges are

196 Takeshi Kojima, Japanese Civil Procedure in Comparative Law Perspective, 46 U. Kansas L. Rev. 687, 707 (1998).

197 Under CCP Article 149 the chief judge of a panel (and in some cases an associate judge) may question parties on any Oral Argument date.

198 CCP Articles 149 and 151 incorporated into the Preparation for Oral Argument procedure through Article 179 (6).

199 CCP Article 207 (2).

200 CCP Article 207.

201 CCP Article 208.

202 CCP Article 209.

more highly influenced by documents[203] than they are by witness recollections, most witnesses are used to authenticate documents that are then introduced in evidence. Witness testimony that is not corroborated by documents is not thought of as highly probative. Since judges may and do intervene in the questioning of fact witnesses, lawyers can be somewhat lax about their questioning of such fact witnesses and allow the court to extract what the court feels is important. Because judges decide cases without juries and there is little in the way of evidentiary rules, evidence objections are rare. As there is no contempt power to punish a witness who refuses to come to court in compliance with a subpoena there is little in the way of hostile witness testimony. Since the party proposing a witness must make a detailed proffer of the witnesses' testimony and since judges are the gatekeepers who determine whether testimony will be permitted, if the judge recommends the witness not be called but that the proffer be accepted in lieu of testimony the suggestion will likely be accepted. This is the usual practice. The judge trying the case or some substitute who is appointed when the judge is transferred to another court will read the written testimony. Oral testimony is either not necessary or the scope of the testimony will be severely limited by the court. And, as the statistics previously discussed disclose the appearance of witnesses themselves are relatively rare. While the procedure looks like the common law adversary process, the reality is that the proceeding is a civil law proceeding so that many of the adversary aspects of the procedure are little utilized and not highly thought of by the decision maker.

E. Experts

In the United States an expert is simply another witness in the case who, because of training and experience is qualified to give opinions on the subject of his/her expertise. Each side chooses (and pays) its own experts. To assure fairness each side must give copies of expert opinions to the other side sufficiently in advance to be used on pre-trial deposition examination of the expert. By the time of trial each side has typically read the opposition expert's opinion and examined the opposition expert as to her opinion. Further, each side's expert is prepared to contradict what the other side's expert had to say in the matter.

In the civil law tradition experts are supposedly neutral persons who are there to educate the court (and the parties) by giving advice in the area of their expertise. Because the judge is responsible for the taking of evidence, the court is responsible for the calling of expert witnesses. As a consequence it might be considered inappropriate for a party to compensate an expert for her testimony. When the court appoints a court expert, the parties may have the court call their own experts

203 The preference for documents over witness testimony is a common factor in civil law countries. See, John M. Townsend and Siegfried H. Elsing, Bridging the Common Law Civil Law Divide in Arbitration, on the web at *www.hugheshubbard.com/news/news_detail.asp?newsID=215* at pages 3-4 of 7 (Jan. 2002).

to contradict the court's expert. The court-paid expert is considered more neutral than an expert paid by a party to testify. Consequently, the court is likely to place greater reliance on the court-appointed witness.

Japan's system is a blend of the civil law and the adversary system with a 2003 amendment that gives the court greater authority to obtain neutral expert advice. In theory the court calls all expert witnesses to testify.[204] Parties must move to have their own expert's testimony heard. The motion must contain written statements disclosing the areas of expertise.[205] This is not substantially different from the written proffers that must be submitted for any other witness a party wishes to call. Every expert (in theory) has an obligation to give her expert testimony to the court.[206] The court, considering the written submissions of the parties as to expert testimony decides what areas of expertise are proper for expert testimony.[207] Whereas previously all experts had to give their opinions by way of oral testimony, under the new Code experts may in the discretion of the court give their opinions in writing or through oral examination.[208] Parties have the right to challenge the expert witness. If the challenge is upheld, the matter may not be appealed. Rejection of the challenge is subject to immediate appeal.[209] The court may request the assistance of the government and request that government agencies provide expert advice on a matter. Such advice may be given in writing but the court can decide to take the advice orally.[210] If the witness testifies in open court then the parties may cross-examine as to qualifications.[211] Of course, the court may examine the expert witness.

On its face the system seems relatively straightforward and represented a great advance over the previous Code in that the old Code really had little use for expert testimony. However, the expert witness system did not function well. Few experts were willing to give their time to testify in matters in court and fewer still were willing to subject themselves to questioning by the parties and/or the court as to their opinions. The consequence was a break down in the expert witness system and calls for reform. Reform was needed because many of the recently filed cases in Japan involve questions as to which expert opinion is vital. Such cases as medical malpractice and cases involving construction failures require experts who can

204 CCP Article 213.

205 CPR Rule 129.

206 CCP Article 212.

207 CPR Rule 129.

208 CCP Article 215.

209 CCP Article 214; CPR Rule 130.

210 CCP Article 218.

211 CCP Article 217.

educate the court as to the technical matters at the heart of the cases. In 2003[212] the Diet enacted a reform, which added a kind of expert commissioner system to the court system. The reform did not however change two of the more interesting and unique aspects of the previously extant expert system in Japan.

Under Rule 132, in a situation where there is more than one expert, the court may examine experts at the same time rather than taking their opinions in turn. Such a practice would permit a panel of experts to testify as to a matter. If a panel testifies, the court can question the various panel members in turn. In addition, panel members may comment on the answers and opinion of other panel members. Such a system is a great advance in the methodology of comparing and testing the different opinions of experts and has the advantage of immediacy and professional debate. Although rarely used, it is an innovation that has been used effectively in malpractice cases.[213]

The second innovation is that the Rules permit the expert to actively participate in the case to the point of permitting the expert to suggest questions for the court to present to witnesses. The Rules even permit the expert, with court permission, to question the opposing party's expert witnesses.[214] Utilization of the expert to question other experts recognizes the prevalent Japanese view that lawyers lack the necessary qualifications to effectively question experts. It further reflects a view that judges similarly lack qualifications to effectively question expert witnesses. American lawyers, on the other hand, are assumed to have the ability to be sufficiently educated by their own expert so as to be able to cross-examine the opposition's expert. Perhaps with the advent of the new law schools (April 2004) and their policy of accepting a percentage of students from faculties other than the undergraduate law faculty, Japanese lawyers and judges will come from more diverse educational backgrounds. Differing backgrounds may lead to greater confidence in the ability of the legal profession to deal with expert testimony. Such an approach is many years in the future—if at all.

The Law Reform Council recognized the difficulty encountered by parties in obtaining expert witnesses. The Council was concerned that inability to obtain expert testimony was one of the reasons for the long delay in the handling of cases requiring expertise. The Council specifically was concerned over the delay in medical malpractice cases. The Council proposed that Japan adopt an expert commissioner system under which expert commissioners are employed (in some fash-

212 Effective April 1, 2004.

213 See, Japan Times on Line 1/9/03 Doctors Debate in Court as Part of New System.

214 CPR Rule 133; John B. Pegram, Recent Developments in IP Litigation in Japan (Fish & Richardson, 2000) on the web at *www.fr.com/news/articledetail.cfm?articleid=67* at page 6 of 12. see also, Takeshi Kojima, Japanese Civil Procedure in Comparative Law Perspective, 46 U. Kansas L. Rev. 687, 707 (1998).

ion) by the courts to assist the courts in cases where expertise is required.[215] As visualized by the Council, these expert commissioners would be involved in all phases of the case—both the pre-Oral Argument and Oral Argument stages—and would be available to assist the judges in handling cases. This recommendation was accepted and took form in the 2003 amendments to the Code of Civil Procedure.[216] These amendments while adding an expert commissioner system do not do away with the previously existing expert witness system. Rather, the Council saw the expert commissioner system as working with, not instead of, the expert witness system. The expert commissioner system is a derivation and modification of the expert examiner system used by the Tokyo District Court and Osaka District Court in patent litigation. In such cases the court appoints an expert to assist the court in understanding and dealing with technical issues. Whether in the patent arena or under the 2003 system, the commissioner is to assist the court and is not to decide the case. The decision in the matter is solely for the court.

Under the 2003 amendments the court at the Oral Argument stage may, after discussion with the parties, appoint one or more expert commissioners to assist the court.[217] The appointed commissioner(s) would be able to give expert opinions to the court (and the opinion would be made available to the parties) as needed and the court could, after obtaining consent from the parties have the expert commissioner directly question witnesses or parties. Although the court technically requires party consent to permit expert commissioners to question witnesses or parties, the reality is that such consent should not be difficult to obtain. The parties are unlikely to reject a proposal of the judge especially since refusal to consent would be futile. The judge can always seek advice from the expert commissioner as to what questions to ask and after getting such advice can then ask the questions that the expert commissioner would suggest. Having the expert ask the questions is time saving and more convenient for everyone. This ability to use experts as witness examiner is consistent with the 1996 Code's provision permitting experts to question witnesses. Expert commissioners would not be full time employees of the court but would be available on a case-by-case basis and appointed to cases as needed. It is anticipated that the court will create a register of experts from whom the judges may appoint commissioners. Parties who are seek-

---

215 Recommendations of the Justice System Reform Council—For a Justice System to Support Japan in the 21st Century (June 12,2001) on the web at *www.kantei.go.jp/foreign/policy/sihou/singikai/990612_e.html* at p. 18-19, 84 of 90.

216 See CCP Articles 92-2 through 92-7 added by the 2003 amendments.

217 The expert commissioner system adopted in 2003 is consistent with the Recommendations of the Law Reform Council and is a variation of a system recommended by the then Ministry of International Trade and Industry (MITI—recently renamed so that the acronym is now METI) in a white paper written in 2000 calling for an improvement in the expert witness system as well as experts who would work as advisors or judges and might even be made members of judicial panels. Report of Corporate Legal System Study Group for Research on Economic Activity and the Judicial System (May 9, 2000) on the web at *www.meti.go.jp/english/ report/data/gCorpMaine.html.*

ing to employ expert witnesses could also use this register. A similar system already exists in patent infringement cases where the Tokyo District court and Osaka District Court may get experts to assist by borrowing such experts from the Patent Office.

Expert commissioners appointed by the court could give their opinions in the Oral Argument stage of the case either by taking the witness stand and testifying or by submitting written reports. Expert commissioners located far from the courthouse or who for some reason are unable to appear at the courthouse may communicate with the court and parties by telephone or other modern telecommunications means.[218] It is unlikely that expert commissioners will be required to testify and if they do testify it is unlikely that the court will permit any meaningful or hostile cross-examination. Since the expert commissioner system does not replace the expert witness system, parties may submit expert witnesses to disagree with the expert commissioner. The court is likely to accept the expert commissioner's view rather than the opinion of a party paid expert.[219]

In addition to recommending expert commissioners, the Law Reform Council recommended that legal professionals who are expert in technical areas but not licensed as bengoshi and hence cannot represent parties in litigation become more involved in technical litigation.[220] This suggestion has also been accepted and patent attorneys may under the supervision of bengoshi assist at patent infringement trials.

Substantive law may provide the basis for an expert report or testimony. The Copyright Law and the Patent Law each contain provisions that recognize the use of experts to calculate damages and each require the opposing party to cooperate with the expert.[221]

---

218 CCP Article 92-3.

219 For a discussion of the expert commissioner system then under discussion in Japan see, Carl F. Goodman, Japan's New Civil Procedure Code: Has it Fostered a Rule of Law Dispute Resolution Mechanism, 29 Brooklyn Journal of International Law 511, 596-598 (2004).

220 Recommendations of the Justice System Reform Council—For a Justice System to Support Japan in the 21st Century (June 12,2001) on the web at *www.kantei.go.jp/foreign/policy/sihou/singikai/990612_e.html* at p. 20-21 of 90.

221 Patent Law Section 105 bis, Copyright Law Article 114 ter.

10

Civil Litigation—Legal Principles and Conciliation

A. Relief

In Japan relief and liability are considered at the same time during the Oral Argument stage of the case. The matter of appropriate relief must be confirmed at the pre-Oral Argument stage. Relief is a matter of both substantive law and procedure. As a rule substantive law determines the relief that may be granted and sets a standard for how damages should be calculated. Procedural law on the other hand determines questions regarding proof of damages. As a rule, the law governing the contract determines damages in a contract dispute.[1] As earlier noted Japan's conflict of law rules allow the parties to choose the governing law.

Because Japan is a civil law system without American concepts of equity, the courts lack an inherent equity power and equitable relief is generally not available unless a statute provides for such relief. Some statutes do provide for injunctive relief. For example, under the Copyright Law the owner of rights whose work has been or is likely to be infringed may obtain injunctive relief.[2] Similarly the Patent Law provides that either a party owning a patent or a party with an exclusive license to use a patented product may seek an injunction against infringement.[3] However, Japanese law does not recognize the use of injunctions

---

1 See, Dispute Resolution in Japan on the web at *www.gsid.nagoya-u.ac.jp/project/apec/lawdb/japan/dispute/disp1-en.html* (APEC Study Center, Nagoya University) 1.4.2.6 (Remedies).

2 Copyright Law Section 112 (1). For a discussion of the remedies available for a violation of copyright rights see, Takashi B. Yamamoto, Copyright Enforcement in Japan on the web at *www.itlaw.jp/tokyo%20seminar%202003%20re.pdf.*; see, RIAJ wins judgment against peer-to-peer service Japan Mmo (IFPI news) on the web at *www.ifpi.org/site-content/press/20030129a.html*

3 Patent Law Section 100 (1). Both the Patent Law and Copyright Law also permit a successful plaintiff to get an Order compelling destruction of the infringing materials.

extraterritorially.[4] Thus, where a Japanese patent holder sued an alleged infringer for selling allegedly infringing products in the United States, no injunction was available. It made no difference that the alleged infringer was a Japanese entity and/or that the product involved was made in Japan. The Unfair Competition Prevention Law permits a party whose business either has been or is likely to be damaged as a consequence of unfair competition to seek an injunction.[5] Under the Civil Code, the holder of a possessory right[6] may sue to enjoin disturbance of the lawful possessory right. Injunction is also available when there is reason to believe a party intends to disturb a possessory right.[7] An action may be brought to restore possession to the lawful holder of the possessory right who has been unlawfully dispossessed.[8] Similarly, ownership of property includes not simply the right to make use of that property but also the right to prevent others from using the property. Thus an injunction may be obtained against a trespasser or a squatter on land. In defamation cases the court may, in addition to damages, require (by way of injunction) that the party responsible for the defamation take action to rehabilitate the defamed party such as by issuing and publishing an apology.[9] Courts may enjoin a threatened defamation.[10] The Civil Code also provides that a court may order specific performance.[11] Where a prohibitory injunction is entered Article 172 of the Civil Execution Act provides that a court may order the enjoined party to post security to guaranty that the party will comply with the injunction.

---

4 See, Toshiyuki Kono, Enforcement of Foreign Intellectual Property Rights in Japan: Jurisdiction and Applicable Law, 6 CASRIP Publication Series: Rethinking Intellectual Property 20, 28 (2000).

5 Unfair Competition Prevention Law Article 3 (Right to Request an Injunction). See discussion of Apple Computer Inc. v. Sotec Corporation (preliminary injunction issued under Unfair Competition law in only 28 days from initiation of litigation) at Lades & Parry LLP Intellectual Property Law Japan-Use of Unfair Competition Law to Combat "Look-Alike" Products on the web at *www.ladas.com/BULLETINS/2000/0600Bulletin/Japan_unfairCompetition.html*

6 Book 2, Chapter 2 of the Civil Code deals with Possessory Rights (see Articles 180-205).

7 Civil Code Articles 198 and 199.

8 Civil Code Article 200.

9 Civil Code Article 723.

10 An injunction that is a prior restraint on political speech that is defamatory is not a violation of the constitutional prohibition against censorship. Hoppo Journal case, Case No. 609 of 1981, 40 Minshu 872 (Sup. Ct. Grand Bench, 6/11/86) available in English through the web site of the Supreme Court of Japan; also available in English in Lawrence W. Beer & Hiroshi Itoh, THE CONSTITUTIONAL CASE LAW OF JAPAN, 1970-1990 (University of Washington Press, 1996) at 606.

11 See, e.g., Civil Code Article 414. The Civil Execution Law Article 169 provides for execution of delivery of personal property by having the execution officer take the property from the debtor and delivering the property to the judgment creditor.

The amount to be posted is determined by the court but may exceed the damages that would flow if the injunction is not carried out.[12]

Japanese lawyers have attempted to use the general provisions dealing with possessory and ownership rights to obtain injunctions in the environmental field. The theory has been that each person owns his/her own body and that such ownership includes the right to prevent others from injuring the property (body) owned. Thus, it has been argued that environmental torts that cause bodily injury, such as excessive noise that causes damage to the eardrums, invade "personal rights" in one's own body and are subject to injunctive relief. It has also been argued that environmental torts that injure the general well being of persons properly give rise to injunctive relief. The results of such arguments have been mixed.[13] Some courts, including some High Courts, recognized this personal rights theory and granted injunctions in the environmental area. Such courts even enjoined government action that adversely effected such asserted personal rights. In the *Osaka Airport case* the Supreme Court held that where action of the government was inextricably intertwined with government regulatory authority, injunction through a normal civil suit was inappropriate.[14]

Monetary damages are the principal relief granted in civil litigation. Here again guidance is found in the substantive law. The Civil Code provides that the party who tortuously violates another's right shall be responsible for compensatory damages.[15] In the normal contract breach action the plaintiff may recover ordinary damages arising from the breach, but if special circumstances either were foreseen or should have been foreseen, special damages arising from those special circumstances may also be awarded.[16] The definition of special circumstances is not completely resolved and may be fact specific, especially in tort cases. Special or unusual damages are payable in contract or tort actions only when the party responsible knew of the special circumstance and thus could foresee or should have foreseen the damages. As a consequence if one party to a contract knows that there are likely to be special circumstances in the event of breach, that party should make those circumstances known to the other. Once both parties know of the special circumstances, special circumstance damages may be awarded in the

12 For a discussion of the difficulties involved in executing on non-money judgments in Japan see, Makoto Ito, Execution of Non-Money Judgments and Means of Enforcement in Japan, 16 Hitotsubashi Journal of Law & Politics 11 (1988).

13 See, Julian Gresser, Koichiro Fujikura and Akio Morishima, ENVIRONMENTAL LAW IN JAPAN (MIT Press, 1981) 135 etc.; Hiroshi Oda, JAPANESE LAW 213-214 (2d Ed., Oxford University Press, 1999); J. Mark Ramseyer and Minoru Nakazato, JAPANESE LAW 88-89 (University of Chicago Press, 1999).

14 For a discussion of the Osaka Airport case and later developments in this area, including the government's spring 2004 initiative seeking amendment of the Administrative Case Litigation Law see Chapter 12.

15 Civil Code Article 709-710.

16 Civil Code Article 416.

event of default.[17] Where both parties are aware of the special circumstances either because the circumstances are publicly well known, were obvious, or were communicated that may be taken into account in a damage award.[18]

Liquidated damages are allowed.[19] However, where the amount involved is unconscionable or otherwise unreasonable the court may use the abuse of rights doctrine[20] to set aside the liquidated amount. A merchant who in the ordinary course of business performs acts for another that benefit that other party is entitled to reasonable compensation.[21] A party who is unjustly enriched at the expense of another through the use of that other person's property or services must recompense the injured party.[22] Where parties are joint tortfeasors, they have joint and several liability.[23] To be joint tortfeasors the parties need not act in concert and it is not necessary that each party's conduct is itself tortious. Thus, in the environmental tort area it has been held that as long as the conduct of one tortfeasor added to the pollution problem and the problem caused the plaintiff's injury each of the parties contributing to the pollution is responsible.[24] The courts apply both contributory fault in contract cases and contributory negligence in tort cases.[25] Japanese courts will from time to time use the term pain and suffering in calculating damages, and they award damages for "moral damage," which is a reasonably good surrogate for the concept of pain and suffering in personal injury cases.[26]

---

17 J. Mark Ramseyer and Minoru Nakazato, JAPANESE LAW 58-59 (University of Chicago Press, 1999); Hiroshi Oda, JAPANESE LAW 175-176 (Oxford University Press, 1999).

18 Public knowledge and/or obviousness may be particularly relevant in tort cases as it is unlikely that communication would be involved in tort. On the other hand, the physical condition of an elderly person as distinguished from a young person would be an obvious matter and might affect the damages awarded in the tort context.

19 Civil Code Article 420.

20 See, Civil Code Article 1 conditions the exercise of rights on fair dealing and prohibits an abuse of rights.

21 Commercial Code Article 512.

22 Civil Code Article 703, 704.

23 Civil Code Article 719. Parties may be joint tortfeasors even if they do not act in concert. Thus, where a doctor was guilty of malpractice in connection with treating an auto accident victim, both the doctor and the other driver at fault were joint tortfeasors. See, Case No. 168 of 1998, 55 Minshu 328 (Sup. Ct. Petty Bench, 3/13/2001) (calculating contributory damages as applied to joint tortfeasors) available in English on the web through the web site of the Supreme Court of Japan.

24 See, Yokkaichi Air Pollution Case (Tsu District Court, 7/24/72) an English language report may be found at Julian Gresser, Koichiro Fujikura and Akio Morishima, ENVIRONMENTAL LAW IN JAPAN (MIT Press, 1981) 106.

25 See, Civil Code 418 (court shall consider fault of the person suing on an obligation in determining both liability and damages); Article 722 (2) (contributory damages in tort case).

26 In case No. 168 of 1998 for example the damages assessed for the death of the deceased accident victim included approximately 24 Million Yen for lost wages and 16 Million yen for moral damage. See, Case No. 168 of 1998, 55 Minshu 328 (Sup. Ct. Petty Bench, 3/13/2001) available in English on the web through the web site of the Supreme Court of Japan.

Damages in Japan serve to compensate the victim (or survivors in the case of death) for the injury suffered. The court calculates the actual damage suffered after considering whether there are any factors that militate against those damages. Unlike the United States there is no collateral damages rule in Japan. If a third party compensates a tort victim that compensation is deducted from the damages awarded. The function of the damage award is not to reward the victim or its heirs but to restore the situation to the status quo prior to the tort. Once that status quo (in monetary terms) is achieved there are no further monetary damages to be paid. Thus, where a decedent was killed in a traffic accident and as a consequence of death his widow received pension payments that would not have been received other than because of his death, the value of such payments was an offset to the recovery allowed against the tortfeasor responsible for the death.[27]

Since damages are compensatory in nature,[28] Japanese law does not permit punitive damages. Since punitive damages impose a sanction to prevent wrongful acts from being repeated, they are considered as akin to the function of the criminal law in Japan. Punitive damages are contrary to Japanese public policy and the courts in Japan will not give comity to a punitive damages award entered by an American court.[29]

Procedural law has its impact on damages in two ways. First, the method used by individual judges to calculate damages is often a function of how the judicial bureaucracy approaches damages issues. Secondly, the procedural law may make it difficult or easy to establish the amount of damages the plaintiff has suffered. In Japan there are no jury trials so damage awards are a function of the determina-

27 See, Case No. 1749 of 1988, 47 Minshu 3039 (Sup. Ct. Grand Bench, 3/24/93) available in English on the web through the web site of the Supreme Court of Japan. (The mere acquisition of a claim against a third party is not to be set off to reduce the damages since a claim may or may not actually be recoverable in damages—but the receipt of the pension due on death was not a claim but actual receipt of a benefit and hence was set off); Case No. 434 and 435 of 1997, 53 Minshu 1211 (Sup. Ct. Petty Bench, 10/22/1999) (survivor's pension benefit received as a consequence of death of tort victim to be deducted from amount of damages recoverable from tortfeasor).

28 In an action seeking monetary relief where a foreign worker was injured on the job in Japan the Supreme Court described the function of the damage award as repairing the loss suffered and returning the plaintiff to the *status quo ante*. In calculating loss of future income the court examined into the plaintiffs potential for earnings in Japan while in Japan on a lawful visa and his potential for earnings in his home country after expiration of his visa. Needless to say his Japanese earnings lost would be greater than his home country earnings lost. But by using home country earnings rather than assuming continuous residence in Japan the damage amount while less than would be the case if assumed earnings in Japan *in futuro* were considered replaced the earnings that could be assumed lost after return from Japan. Case No. 2132 of 1993 and No. 2382 of 1996, Sup. Ct. Petty Bench 1/28/97 available in English through the web site of the Supreme Court of Japan.

29 Case No. 1762 of 1993 (Sup. Ct. Petty Bench, 7/11/97) available in English on the web through the web site of the Supreme Court of Japan. The court reiterated the function of tort damages in Japan to be to restore the plaintiff to the status quo ante and thereby to undo the disadvantage brought about by the tortuous act.

tions of judges. Damage amounts tend to be more uniform than damage awards in the United States. Japanese judges are aware of what their colleagues are awarding for damages in similar cases and the bureaucratic urge is to be consistent with the prevailing judicial approach. Thus, even where a special circumstance may exist judges tend to award the lower common denominator damage amount. This commonality—institutionalized in some situations through the existence of schedules—has the effect of making it relatively easy to settle cases. Defendants as well as plaintiffs have a reasonably good idea of the amount at issue and can structure a settlement on a common understanding of the likely damages. This is to be distinguished from the American situation where because of the wide disparity in jury awards there does not exist a common understanding of the likely damages.

Japanese damage awards are also substantially less generous to plaintiffs than American awards. Japanese judges decide the amount of damages, and through the judicial Secretariat the judges have a reasonably good idea of what other judges are awarding for similar cases. Training sessions with the Secretariat keep judges up to date on the "going rate" for certain injuries. In addition there are standardized damage schedules for automobile accident injuries as well as standardized comparative negligence calculation formula.[30] Such schedules are available for use in other cases, such as medical malpractice.[31] The phenomenon was recognized by the Law Reform Council, which recommended that studies be engaged in regarding the damages issue. The Council found no fault with the concept of placing the victim in as close to a *status quo ante* position as possible. However, the Council recommended that damages be tailored to individual cases rather than utilize standards adopted in prior cases. The Council was of the view that such prior damage awards might not be applicable to the case being decided.[32] Since damages are not seen in Japan as a tool to be used to get lawbreakers to change their ways, it is unlikely that absent special legislation dealing with damages in specific areas the amount of damages will significantly increase.

In the intellectual property area a confluence of factors has resulted in such substantive law change. Among these factors were: a) outside pressure from the United States and others, who complained that inadequate damage awards in in-

---

30 Takao Tanase, The Management of Disputes: Automobile Compensation in Japan, 24 Law & Society Review 651 (1990) Appendix 1 and 2.

31 See, Kazue Nakajima, Catherine Keyes, Tatsuo Kuroyanagi and Kozo Tatara, Medical Malpractice and Legal Resolution Systems in Japan, Journal of the American Medical Association vol. 285 No. 12. p. 1632, 1635 (3/28/01) (courts in medical malpractice cases generally reduce the award to approximately 50% of the formula used in auto accident cases). For medical malpractice cases there exists an ADR mechanism that parallels the automobile accident ADR mechanism. See, Takao Tanase, The Management of Disputes: Automobile Compensation in Japan, 24 Law & Society Review 651, 680 (1990).

32 Recommendations of the Justice System Reform Council—For a Justice System to Support Japan in the 21st Century (June 12,2001) on the web at *www.kantei.go.jp/foreign/policy/sihou/singikai/990612_e.html* at p. 30 of 90.

tellectual property cases[33] meant that foreign patents and copyright works could be ripped off with relative impunity in Japan, and b) Japan's emergence as a creator of intellectual property rights that others were now attempting to rip off. The patent and copyright law changes must be considered in the context of the proof that is required to establish damages in a Japanese proceeding.

In the typical tort action the proof of the amount of damages is not particularly difficult. There are tables dealing with issues of life expectancy and earnings over a period of years are relatively easy to calculate. The actual medical or funeral costs are available without much difficulty and judges are adept at determining what sums to award for moral (pain and suffering) injury. Loss of income, medical expenses and moral damages are all readily established as being caused by the acts of the wrongdoer. In tort cases the fees of the plaintiff's counsel are part of the damages suffered by plaintiff and are included in the calculation of the court award. Realistically the award values the attorney fee component at substantially less than the actual fee.[34]

Nonetheless in tort cases there are some factors that are unknown when awarding damages. The severity of the plaintiff's injury may be estimated by expert opinion but the actual severity may not be known until years later. The loss of income caused by the injury may turn out to be either larger or smaller than the amount calculated depending on future circumstances. Where a lump sum is awarded—and prior to the 1996 Code lump sum awards were the method of providing damages in tort cases—the plaintiff receives the full sum but may turn out to be either unduly rewarded or unfairly under compensated. The restrictions on Japan's *res judicata* rules (there is claim preclusion but only to the extent of the claims actually raised in the case) made it possible for a plaintiff to go back to court at a later date and seek additional damages. Under the new Code the court may order payments in tort actions over a period of time rather than in a lump sum. Where periodic payments are ordered *either party* may go back to court and ask for a modification based on changed circumstances that affect the damage amount.[35] The purpose of the amendment is to make the ultimate award consistent with the true facts. Since prior to the amendment the plaintiff could seek an increase in the award while the defendant was bound by *res judicata*, the amend-

---

33 See, e.g., International Chamber of Commerce Report on Implementation of TRIPS Enforcement provisions (6/17/97) on the web at *www.iccwbo.org/home/intellectual_property/tripse.asp*. Referring to the situation in Japan the Report notes that damages in infringement cases are inadequate as they only provide the same level of remuneration as would be the case under an ordinary license fee and consequently do not act as a deterrent to infringement.

34 For an international objection to this practice in cases involving protection of intellectual property rights see, International Chamber of Commerce Report on Implementation of TRIPS Enforcement provisions (6/17/97) on the web at *www.iccwbo.org/home/ intellectual_property/tripse.asp*.

35 CCP Article 117; Yasuhei Taniguchi, The 1996 Code of Civil Procedure of Japan—A Procedure for the Coming Century?, 45 American Journal of Comparative Law 767, 784 (1997); Takeshi Kojima, Japanese Civil Procedure in Comparative Law Perspective, 46 U. Kansas L. Rev. 687, 710 (1998).

ment works to the disadvantage of the plaintiff and is consistent with the view that under Japanese law damages determinations favor defendants.

Difficulty arises in commercial cases where such intangibles as lost profits must be calculated. In many cases the evidence of the value of the injury is in the hands of the wrong doer and unavailable to the plaintiff. Japan has no supplementary proceedings or deposition or request for production of documents procedure that would enable a plaintiff to gain easy access to such information. The 1996 Code recognized the issue and attempted to deal with it by providing the judge with a greater discretion than in the past to deal with damage issues. Where it is difficult for the plaintiff to prove the Yen amount of the damage the court may consider the entire Oral Argument record and make a discretionary determination of damages.[36] This is a substantial departure from the old rule that required actual proof of the various items of damage. Under the current law the court may award damages, including substantial damages even if the plaintiff cannot establish the amount of damages.[37]

This new discretion given to judges still leaves room for courts to use their discretion to render low damage awards. In the intellectual property area the newfound reliance on judicial awards to protect Japanese intellectual property rights has led to legislation whose purpose is to increase the size of awards in infringement cases. Not only the size but also the method of discovering and proving the amount of damages is affected by the changes in the Patent Law, Copyright Law and related laws.

Under the old Patent Law the party whose patent was infringed was technically entitled to damages to compensate for the loss suffered by the infringement. This is consistent with the general view that the function of damages is to place the injured party in the situation it would have been in if there had been no injury. However under the Civil Code the general rule requires a showing that damages are causally related to the acts of the wrongdoer. This causation requirement made it difficult to prove the amount of damages in patent infringement cases, and as a result most patent infringement damages resulted in plaintiff recovering the value of a license fee. Both international groups and the Japanese Patent Office urged change in the system. From a domestic point of view the inadequate damage system depreciated the value of intellectual properties that were developed in Japan. This resulted in Japanese companies downgrading their research and development

36 CCP Article 244.

37 See, Ryu Takabayashi, (translated by Toshiko Takenaka) Practice of Patent Litigation in Japanese Courts, University of Washington School of Law, on the web at *www.law.washington.edu/casrip/newsletter/newsv5i2jp2.html*; see also, Yasuhei Taniguchi, The 1996 Code of Civil Procedure of Japan—A Procedure for the Coming Century?, 45 American Journal of Comparative Law 767, 785 (1997).

activities. This was viewed as inconsistent with the national interest and stronger protection of patent rights—including higher damage awards—was suggested.[38]

In 1998 the Patent Law was amended (effective 1999).[39] The new law creates a series of damage presumptions: a) a formula method of determining damages in infringement cases wherein the profit per unit that the patent holder (or exclusive licensee) would realize is multiplied by the number of units that the holder of the patent (or exclusive licensee) could have sold had there been no infringement (calculated by the number of infringing products sold);[40] b) the amount of profit realized by the infringer shall be presumed to be the damage to the patent holder (or exclusive licensee);[41] c) a royalty fee (but the fact that the royalty fee is a measure of damages shall not exclude the court's ability to grant damages in excess of the royalty fee).[42] Although the law continues to allow a royalty fee to be used as a measure of damages, the law makes it clear that "normal" royalty fees are not contemplated. The amendment dropped the word normal from the provision dealing with royalty fees specifically to allow for higher royalty fees and higher damages. Royalty fees are not the exclusive measure of damage. Placing royalty as the last alternative demonstrates the intent of the law to provide patent holders (and exclusive licensees) with meaningful relief consistent with methods a) and b) of establishing damages. It is anticipated that the law will result in significantly higher patent infringement damage awards.

Not only the substantive measure of damages but also the means of establishing factors to increase the amount of damages have been liberalized under the new Patent Law. First the calculation formula set out above makes it easier for a plaintiff to prove damages as there are only two facts that need to be estab-

---

38 Hideao Furutani, Japanese Patent Law Amendments on the web at *www.furutani.co.jp/office/ronbun/PatentAmend.html*; CASRIP Newsletter (V413) Japan-1, The JPO's Industrial Property Committee Proposed to Increase Patent Infringement Damages on the web at *www.law.washington.edu/casrip/newsletter/newsv4i3jp1.html*.

39 Japanese business determination to protect patent rights is reflected in the recent activity of Fujitsu in suing Samsung in connection with alleged infringement of Fujitsu patent rights. See, Fujitsu Files Suit Against Samsung (Plasma Display Panel Patent Infringement Alleged), Japan Times on Line 4/8/04. Fujitsu is receiving assistance from the government in its dispute with Samsung. In the Japanese litigation Fujitsu seeks injunctive relief to prohibit the importation of the panels. Fujitsu did not apply to the court seeking provisional relief to prohibit importation during the course of the litigation pursuant to the Provisional Remedies Law. Rather Fujitsu sought Executive Branch assistance. Japanese Customs authorities have barred the importation of Samsung plasma display panels for a two-year period during the course of the litigation. See, Fujitsu Calls Foul, Customs Halts Samsung PDP Imports, Japan Times on Line, 4/22/04.

40 Patent Law Section 102 (1) Presumption Concerning Amount of Damages. This amount may be reduced if the manufacturing capacity of the patentee is insufficient to support the units calculated. Dr. Shoichi Okuyama, The 1999 Amendments to the Patent Law in Japan, on the web at *www.okuyama.com/1999_amend_jp_pat_law.htm;* JPAA, Revisions of the Japanese Patent Law (January 2000) on the web at *http://knpt.com/english/news4.htm*

41 Patent Law Section 102 (2).

42 Patent Law Section 102 (3) and (4). The court may take into consideration the failure of the defendant to have acted intentionally or with gross negligence when assessing damages.

lished—a) the number of units the infringer sold and b) plaintiff's profit per unit. As to profit per unit the plaintiff is in possession of its own data and should easily prove profit per unit. As to the number of units sold the law provides new methods of obtaining this information from the infringer. Under the new Patent Law the court may, on motion of a party, appoint an expert appraiser to assist it in determining the appropriate measure of damages. In addition the infringing party must provide information to the expert to enable the expert to calculate the proper damage amount.[43] And, the liberalized rules for document production in patent cases are extended to documents that relate to the calculation of infringement damages.[44] The Patent Law is consistent with the 1996 Code in providing that where damages are established but the amount is difficult to calculate the court may use its discretion, relying on the entire record, to set a damage amount.[45] Thus, the new law makes it easier for the court to determine the amount of damages. It also gives the court guidance to utilize the profits made by the infringer or the profits that the patent holder (or exclusive licensee) would have made but for the infringement—calculated by using the infringer's sales and the holder's cost basis. It provides that the infringer must assist a court appointed expert by giving the expert access to data that would show its profits derived from the infringement and also the number of sales of infringing units. If damages are still deemed inadequately proven, the court may nonetheless assess damages using its own discretion. Since the intent of the Patent Law is to use damages as a means of discouraging infringement and thereby encouraging research and development of products in Japan,[46] it is to be expected that significantly higher damage awards will be forthcoming in infringement cases.[47]

Not only patent law but also other areas of intellectual property law have seen changes designed to make proof of damages easier and designed to make recovery

---

43 Patent Law Section 105bis.

44 Patent Law Section 105 (3).

45 Patent Law Section 105ter.

46 The endorsement of research and development applies to company employees as well as companies. Thus under Japanese law such employees who make valuable inventions that are commercially successful are entitled to compensation from their employers notwithstanding internal company policy that limits the amount of such compensation. The amount of such awards is on the rise in Japan. In January of 2004 the Tokyo District Court rendered a 20billion Yen award for an employee whose invention had earned his employer 120billion yen. The award is on appeal. See, Nichia Deposits 10 Billion Yen in Spat over Patent Royalties, Japan Times on Line 3/7/04. However, there is concern in Japan that the granting of large awards to company employees who invent new products or services may result in companies cutting back on in-house research and development and that such laws may need to be modified to be less generous to employees or eliminated entirely. See, Kosaku Tamura, Japan Making Strategic Program for the Creation, Protection and Exploitation of Intellectual Property: Review of the Japanese Patent System (Center for Advanced Study and Research on Intellectual Property "CASRIP" University of Washington School of Law) CASRIP Newsletter Autumn 2003 on the web at *www.law.washington.edu/casrip/newsletter/newshome.html*.

47 For a general discussion of the 1999 Patent Law changes see, JPAA, Revisions of the Japanese Patent Law (January 2000) on the web at *http://knpt.com/english/news4.htm*.

of damages more meaningful. Thus, the Unfair Competition Prevention Law allows a party whose business has suffered while another has profited as a consequence of unfair competition to recover the profits earned by the wrongdoer.[48] The injured party may seek damages in excess of the profits unlawfully made[49] and under the 2004 amendments to the law the plaintiff may seek as damages the plaintiff's loss of profits. To help assess damages the law provides that a court in response to a motion may order the defendant to produce any document needed to calculate damages. The law also provides that where the defendant has a valid reason for refusing production the document need not be produced.[50] Following the lead of the recent amendments of the Code of Civil Procedure the Unfair Competition Prevention Law gives the judge discretion to assess damages even when there is no direct proof of the amount of damages.[51]

Copyright law, as was the case with patent law, assessed damages based on the Civil Code and accordingly required a showing of causation between the damages sought and defendant's wrongful act. As was true with patent infringement so too with copyright infringement the proof of damages tied to the wrongful act was difficult and resulted in insufficient assessments of damages. Under the Copyright Law as amended the profit earned by the infringer is presumed to be the appropriate loss caused to the copyright holder and consistent with the new Patent Law the Copyright Law requires the infringer to produce evidence to assist in the assessment of damages process. The law also permits a reasonable royalty.[52]

Liberalization of damage awards is reflected in a recent decision dealing with the wrongful misappropriation of trade secrets. Where it was established that the wrongdoer had misappropriated trade secrets and marketed a competing product based on such secrets, the court used a market share analysis to determine the appropriate level of damages. Finding that prior to the misappropriation the owner had an approximately 14% market share and that after the misappropriation that market share had declined to only approximately 9% the court concluded that at least part of the loss of market share was attributable to the misappropriation. The court assessed damages based on a proportion of the loss of market share.[53]

The loosening of purse strings in the intellectual property area does not mean that there will be a corresponding loosening in other areas where the governmental in-

---

48 Unfair Competition Prevention Law Article 5 (1).

49 Unfair Competition Prevention Law Article 5 (3).

50 Unfair Competition Prevention Law Article 6.

51 Masahiko Nakamura, TMI Associates (Practical Law Company) on the web at *www.plcinfo.com/scripts/article.asp?Article.asp?Article_ID=32291*. (8/20/03)

52 For a discussion of damages under the Copyright Law see, Takashi B. Yamamoto, Copyright Enforcement in Japan on the web at *www.itlaw.jp/tokyo%20seminar%202003%20re.pdf* at pages 12-16 (2003) as well as Takamitso Shigetomi, Asahi Engineering KK v. Dai-ichi Seiko KK, CASRIP Newsletter Winter 2003.

53 See, Takamitso Shigetomi, Asahi Engineering KK v. Dai-ichi Seiko KK, CASRIP Newsletter Winter 2003.

terest in higher damage awards is not as noticeable. Thus, after a court rendered a large damage award against corporate directors in a derivative litigation,[54] the government enacted legislation limiting the recovery against corporate directors. Under the new law, there is a sliding scale of recovery so that liability of Representative Directors is limited to six-years compensation, other Directors four-years compensation and Independent Directors two-years compensation.[55] To assist companies in their quest to get independent directors, a new phenomenon in Japan and one sponsored by the government,[56] companies can enter into agreements with independent directors further limiting their liability in the event of derivative litigation.[57]

Most recently the Supreme Court upheld a damage award against the government and several mining companies in a case involving the disease pneumoconiosis. The companies were found responsible for causing the miners' illness. The government was found responsible for its failure to regulate in accordance with a 1960 law dealing with pneumoconiosis. Two hundred miners were awarded 560 million yen, or an average of less than 3 million yen per miner. At an exchange rate of $1=100yen the damages awarded to each miner averaged a mere $30,000.[58]

Notwithstanding the movement towards more realistic damage awards in intellectual property cases and the liberalization of the Code of Civil Procedure to give the court greater discretion to assess damages when proof of damages is difficult, plaintiffs should not expect to see a windfall profit in intellectual property litigation in Japan. In the market share case referred to above the court did not assess damages based on the entire loss of market share that plaintiff had suffered. Instead the court assigned some part of the loss of market share to other causes and then further reduced the market share on which it would calculate damages be-

---

54 See discussion of the Daiwa Bank case in Carl F. Goodman, The Somewhat Less Reluctant Litigant: Japan's Changing Views Towards Civil Litigation, 32 Law and Policy in International Business 769, 798 (2001); Mitsuru Misawa, Daiwa Bank Scandal in New York: Its Causes, Significance and Lessons in International Society, 29 Vanderbilt Journal of Transnational Law 1023 (1996). For an English language translation of the Daiwa Bank decision see, Tsuyoshi Yamada, The Daiwa Bank Case (1999) (Summary Translation) 15 Columbia Journal of Asian Law 193 (2002).

55 See, Japan Times on Line November 30, 2001 and Japan Times on Line December 6, 2001.

56 For a discussion of the new movement to place independent directors on corporate boards in Japan and the relationship of such movement with the reduction in liability of independent directors by contract see, Motomi Hashimoto, Commercial Code Revisions: Promoting the Evolution of Japanese Companies, Nomura Research Institute, NRI Papers, No. 48 5/1/2002; See also, Hirohiko Nakahara (METI) Establishment of the "company with committees" and Corporate Governance (5/30/03) on the web at *www.rieti.go.jp/cgj/en/columns/columns_008.htm*

57 Commercial Code Article 266 Sections 7-19. For a discussion of the revision of the Commercial Code see, Motomi Hashimoto, Commercial Code Revisions: Promoting the Evolution of Japanese Companies (section entitled "Easing the Responsibilities of Directors to the Company), NRI Papers No. 48 (5/1/2002) (Nomura Research Institute).

58 See, Top Court Ends Pneumoconiosis Case, State, Mining Firm Ordered to Pay Sickened Workers, Japan Times on Line 4/28/04.

cause other wrongful acts of the same defendant could have been responsible for such loss. The government has consistently rejected calls for treble damage remedies in the intellectual property field notwithstanding such suggestion from such influential sources as the Patent Office and METI.[59] Unlike the United States where the jury can disregard the amount of monetary relief asked for in the Complaint, in Japan the court is not permitted to award damages in excess of the amount requested in the original Complaint as subsequently amended.

There are also restrictive rules that limit the availability of damages in suits brought against the government under Article 32 of the Constitution (all persons are granted access to the courts), Article 17 of the Constitution (persons may sue the State where damage has been suffered because of an illegal act of a public official), and the State Tort Liability Act.[60] Under the statute, a person who has suffered injury as a consequence of willful or negligent actions of a government official in the course of the performance of official duties may sue the government (as distinguished from the employee) for compensation. Where the government official simply made an error, compensation is not available. In the Repeta *Courtroom Note Taking Case*, the Supreme Court found that the presiding judge in the District Court was wrong for failing to permit Repeta to take notes in court. The decision makes it clear that note taking is permitted in the future. Repeta was denied monetary relief because the judge had not acted willfully or negligently. Although in error, the judge's actions might have been valid at an earlier time. In any event the action of the court in prohibiting note taking in the Repeta cases was consistent with the widely held view that such prohibition was acceptable.[61] Another example is the *Model Gun Case*[62] where the court found the government action wrongful but denied monetary relief because the officials who acted in that case were neither negligent nor did they act with malice.[63]

---

59 Not only did the government reject the treble damage award remedy suggested by the Patent Office but when a METI formed study group dealing with the Antimonopoly Law reported on that law it specifically did not deal with the issue of treble damages for violation of the law on the basis that treble damages were a means of law enforcement and deterrence and in Japan law enforcement and deterrence are not a part of the civil justice system. See, Study Group on the Antimonopoly Act Report, 11/21/03 page 24.

60 Law No. 125 of 1947. Also variously called the State Compensation Law and the State Redress Law. For a discussion of the law see, Hiroyuki Hata & Go Nakagawa & Takehisa Nakagawa, JAPAN CONSTITUTIONAL LAW Sec. 325-327 (Kluwer Law International, 2001).

61 Repeta v. Japan, Case No. 436 of 1988, 43 Minshu 89 (Sup. Ct. Grand Bench 3/8/89) available in English through the web site on the Supreme Court of Japan. Also available in English in Lawrence W. Beer & Hiroshi Itoh, THE CONSTITUTIONAL CASE LAW OF JAPAN, 1970-1990 (University of Washington Press, 1996) at 627.

62 Kondoru Kogyo K.K. v. Japan, 27 Kaminshu 499 (Tokyo District Court 8/23/76) discussed in English at Mitsuo Matsushita, The Legal Framework of Trade and Investment in Japan, 27 Harvard International Law Journal 361, 379 (1986).

63 In the United States government officials who are sued for actions undertaken in their official capacity may escape liability because of a qualified immunity theory wherein unconstitutional

In the normal civil case the winning of a judgment is only an initial step to relief. What the successful plaintiff wants is an opinion of the Judicial Branch of the government recognizing that the plaintiff is in the right and the defendant in the wrong, as well as a monetary recovery. Where a plaintiff's principal objective is a monetary recovery, the case will probably be resolved through settlement or in-court conciliation.[64] The difficult cases to settle are those where a matter of honor or dignity is at stake. Thus for the Minamata disease plaintiffs, monetary relief was not sufficient. The Minamata plaintiffs required recognition of their suffering and lack of blame as well as acceptance of responsibility by the company. If the company would not accept responsibility voluntarily then a court judgment was needed that recognized that responsibility. Even where the principal element of the litigation is frustration and the need to seek judicial relief to compel acceptance of responsibility, the plaintiff wants a sufficient monetary award to either (or both) compensate for the injury or to serve as a financial recognition of the defendant's responsibility. A piece of paper saying that Yen should be paid to plaintiff is not relief. Payment of a monetary award is what plaintiff ultimately seeks. Payment of a judgment may require execution of the judgment and assets of the defendant available to pay the judgment.

In appropriate cases in the United States—such as where there is reason to believe that a defendant in litigation will transfer assets outside the jurisdiction of the court for the purpose of making such assets unavailable to pay a judgment—the court may grant provisional remedies. Such remedies include attachment or injunction to insure that assets remain in the jurisdiction and available. So too in Japan the 1989 Civil Provisional Remedies Law permits a plaintiff to obtain a provisional remedy prior to judgment.[65] The appropriate court before which a request for a provisional remedy may be made is either the court that has jurisdiction over the main action or the District Court for the district in which the property sought to be attached (or the property that is the subject matter of the dispute) is located.[66] Provisional relief is sought by motion. The motion must be supported by a preliminary showing of likelihood of success as well as necessity for provisional relief.[67] The plaintiff has the burden of establishing both that provisional re-

---

action taken by officials may not be used as a basis for such suit if the activity was not known to be unlawful such as in a case of first instance. Japan appears to have adopted a similar approach where liability of the State as distinguished from government officials is involved.

64 In-Court conciliation is discussed in subpart B hereof.

65 Civil Provisional Remedies Law (Law No. 91 of 1989), also known as Civil Provisional Relief Act and Civil Preservation Act, Articles 20, 23, 24 and 47-57. This law was part of the old Code of Civil Procedure until 1989.

66 Civil Provisional Remedies Law Article 12.

67 Civil Provisional Remedies Law Article 13.

lief is necessary and that the plaintiff will probably succeed in the action.[68] The granting of a provisional remedy is within the sound discretion of the presiding judge,[69] who may or may not require security.[70] Denial of the request for relief is subject to immediate appeal. Such appeal must be filed within two weeks of notice that the relief has been denied.[71] Oral Argument is not necessary but the court may clarify issues before ruling on the motion and for this purpose may question witnesses (in such order as the court deems appropriate) and may hear statements from the parties.[72] Prior to 1996 a party could object to the change in order of questioning a witness but consistent with the 1996 change in the Code of Civil Procedure giving the court greater authority to determine the order of questioning this provision was removed from the Act.[73]

The conditions for the granting of a provisional attachment are concern that without such attachment it would be impossible or significantly difficult to execute after judgment.[74] The provisional attachment order must set forth the amount of security required for lifting the order. Upon filing such security the party served with the order is entitled to have the attachment lifted.[75]

Where the suit seeks specific performance relating to a specific asset, a plaintiff may obtain a provisional order to insure that the asset will be available if plaintiff is succcssful. An ordcr of provisional disposition may take any of several different forms: it can order a party to perform an act or enjoin the performance of an act, it can order that specific property be delivered, it can order sequestration of property, etc.[76] As in the case of provisional attachment the grounds for ordering provisional disposition of property are concern that intervening acts occurring during the course of the litigation will adversely affect plaintiff's rights.[77] Money security may not be filed to get a lifting of the order unless money damage is adequate relief.[78]

Provisional remedy is available even where the parties have agreed that the dispute is to be resolved via arbitration. The arbitrators have authority to issue a pro-

68 See, Practical Law Company Dispute Resolution: Japan Q&A Craig Celniker and Fuyuo Mitomi, Morrison & Foster/Ito & Mitomi—practicallaw.com: reports: Dispute Resolution: Japan.

69 Civil Provisional Remedies Law Article 15.

70 Civil Provisional Remedies Law Article 14.

71 Civil Provisional Remedies Law Article 19.

72 Civil Provisional Remedies Law Articles 3 and 9.

73 Civil Provisional Remedies Law Article 11 was removed in 1996.

74 Civil Provisional Remedies Law Article 20 (1).

75 Civil Provisional Remedies Law Article 22.

76 Civil Provisional Remedies Law Article 24.

77 Civil Provisional Remedies Law Article 23.

78 Civil Provisional Remedies Law Article 25.

visional protection order dealing with the subject matter of the dispute and may order that security be provided in connection with such an order.[79] In addition, although arbitration may be the exclusive forum for resolving the dispute, a party to the arbitration may request (either before arbitration is started or during the pendence of the arbitration proceeding) the court to issue a provisional remedy and the court may so order.[80]

After it has been served with a provisional order, a party may file objections with the court. Upon receiving the objection the court may temporarily stay the order, pending a final ruling on the issue of provisional remedy. To obtain a stay, a party must make a preliminary showing of grounds for setting aside the order and a showing that failure to set aside the order will cause irreparable injury to the party seeking relief.[81] Before making a final ruling on a provisional remedy request that has been objected to, the court must hold either an Oral Argument or an interview session with the parties. Both parties may attend such an interview session.[82] In other words, while the initial provisional order may be issued *ex parte*, a ruling on an objection requires that parties be present at proceedings concerning the ruling. At the conclusion of the hearing the court may modify, set aside or affirm its original determination to issue a provisional remedy. The court may also modify any security it previously required.[83] Property that was turned over to a party pursuant to a provisional order must be returned if the order is set aside.[84] The court may stay its order voiding the original order for two weeks to permit the filing of an appeal (and a request for relief from the appeal court).[85]

Since provisional relief may be granted prior to the institution of the main lawsuit, the party against whom a provisional order has been entered can obtain a court order requiring the institution of the main suit not later than two weeks from the date of the order. Within such two-week period the plaintiff must provide proof that the suit was filed. Failure to institute the suit (or to file proof of institution) results in an order voiding the provisional remedy. Such order must be based on motion of the party adversely affected by the provisional order.[86] Because more than one court may have concurrent jurisdiction to issue a provisional remedy, the court to

79 Arbitration Law Article 24 (1) and (2).

80 Arbitration Law Article 15. The appropriate forum court is any District Court designated as appropriate by the parties, the District Court for the district where the arbitration is pending or the District Court of the responding party's general forum. Arbitration Law Article 5.

81 Civil Provisional Remedies Law Article 27.

82 Civil Provisional Remedies Law Article 29.

83 Civil Provisional Remedies Law Article 32.

84 Civil Provisional Remedies Law Article 33.

85 Civil Provisional Remedies Law Article 34.

86 Civil Provisional Remedies Law Article 37.

which an objection has been filed may, if it deems it appropriate, transfer the matter to a more appropriate court.[87]

After a provisional remedy has taken effect, it is possible that there will be a change of circumstances that would render the relief inappropriate or unnecessary. The court that issued the provisional remedy or the court where the main action is pending may set aside the provisional remedy order when, on motion of the affected party, it finds that changed circumstances warrant such action.[88]

Any decision made in response to either an objection to or motion to set aside the provisional remedy order is subject to appeal. The court entering the order must transfer the case to the appeal court and has no authority to consider whether the appeal is properly filed or is inadequate on its face.[89] The appeal court, on motion, may stay provisional relief pending a determination of the appeal.[90]

Where the provisional remedy forbids a party from selling realty, the execution mechanism is similar to a filing of a *lis pendence* in the United States except that the registration of the order against the property prohibits the sale or disposition of the property.[91] In the event the recipient of the provisional remedy is successful in the litigation, the right to possession and ownership of the property relates back to the date of registration of the provisional order against the property.[92] If personal property is the subject of a provisional disposition and the property is nonetheless transferred to a third person, it is possible to recover the property back from such person. To recover the property the holder of the order must make a showing of knowledge by the recipient prior to receipt of the property.[93] The recipient of the property has a right to object to recovery.[94]

In the United States execution on a judgment is a government function. Execution follows immediately upon the granting of a final judgment and requires no additional judicial proceedings and no specific language in the judgment permitting execution. Execution may be postponed by the filing of an appeal. Typically such action requires the posting of an appeal bond sufficient to pay the judgment or at least a substantial portion of the judgment. Typically the judgment is filed in a county clerk's office as a lien on real estate owned by the defendant in the county. The filing creates the lien and operates as a *lis pendence* putting the world of potential purchasers or lenders on notice that there exists a lien on the property. Any

---

87 Civil Provisional Remedies Law Article 28.

88 Civil Provisional Remedies Law Article 38.

89 Civil Provisional Remedies Law Article 41.

90 Civil Provisional Remedies Law Article 42.

91 Civil Provisional Remedies Law Article 53.

92 Civil Provisional Remedies Law Article 58.

93 Civil Provisional Remedies Law Article 62.

94 Civil Provisional Remedies Law Article 63.

purchase or borrowing using the property as security occurring after the filing of the judgment against the property is subject to the prior lien of the judgment. After filing, the judgment creditor can seek to have the property foreclosed through a foreclosure proceeding handled by a local sheriff or marshal. The judgment is also given to a local marshal or sheriff who has authority to execute by seizing and selling personal property owned by the defendant. Although these officers are public servants paid a salary by the government, the official's employing department is in many cases entitled to a commission that is paid from the seized assets, i.e., from the judgment debtor itself. This system has the advantage of assuring that public servants are available to execute on judgments and gives those servants an inducement to be successful as the payment of commissions to their employing agency can have valuable fiscal effects on employee salaries and perks. Where the defendant is a large enterprise, the location of its assets may be easily known. For smaller entities (and sometimes even for large entities) location and ownership of assets may prove difficult. In the United States the judgment creditor has means available to it to try to locate the assets of the judgment debtor. Supplementary proceedings wherein the judgment creditor may take testimony of the debtor and others to try to locate assets and document discovery against the debtor and third parties such as banks, brokerage houses, etc. are available to the judgment creditor. State law provides a remedy wherein assets transferred in contemplation of the judgment—assets transferred to defraud creditors—may be transferred back to the debtor so that the judgment creditor may seize and execute on such assets. The purpose of the system is to make it as easy as possible for the judgment creditor to collect its judgment.

In the civil law system it is usual to require an execution document, in addition to the judgment, in order to execute on a judgment. Such document is typically obtained in a summary procedure before the execution court. Japan follows this system. However, the final judgment can, if it contains a provision allowing for compulsory execution, be used as the execution document. If it fails to contain language permitting compulsory execution then the judgment creditor must obtain an execution document. (Compulsory execution is used to satisfy a judgment. Provisional execution is a process whose purpose is to preserve assets so that they may be used to satisfy a judgment on which compulsory execution is permitted.)

In Japan, historically, it has been difficult to collect on judgments. As in the United States there are public officers who have the task of collecting through the sale of real estate and personal property. Bailiffs are under the supervision of the District Court and have the obligation, among other things, of handling the execution of judgments.[95] Although "public officials," bailiffs are not paid a salary from the public fisc but are paid on the basis of commissions earned by executing judg-

95 Court Organization Law Article 62.

ments.[96] As in the United States the Law on Execution of Judgments provides for the sale of real estate to pay judgments[97] and allows for the seizure[98] and sale of personal property[99] to satisfy judgments. It may be necessary in some situations to obtain additional execution documents.[100] To execute on a judgment without obtaining a separate execution document, it is necessary for the judgment to state that compulsory execution is permitted. The procedures for execution are more complicated and more time consuming than in the United States. When a second court order is required, the execution process is delayed.

The history of execution of judgments in Japan affects the ability to satisfactorily execute on a money judgment. As an historical matter, execution officers in Japan were underpaid and overworked and had difficulty collecting on judgments—a necessary step for the officer, as the officer's compensation was dependent on commissions generated from such execution sales. To assist them in their task, execution officers were permitted to hire assistants. This led to the hiring of assistants who used strong-arm tactics to get judgment debtors to pay. As in the case of *sokaiya* (corporate gangsters who engage in extortion tactics against companies as a price of maintaining order at corporate annual meetings) these assistants discovered that there were additional ways of obtaining money as part of the collection process. If real estate was sold at auction to collect the judgment debt, the strong-arm assistants could earn more by buying the building themselves at a low price—either by scaring off other potential buyers or by allowing tenants to remain in the building thereby decreasing its value—and then, after purchase, using strong-arm tactics to empty the building thus raising its value once they were in possession. Various practices were engaged in to keep prices low in order to generate profits that were not available to the judgment creditor or the judgment debtor.[101] Such assistants could also place their own "employees" in possession as tenants in the building and then demand extortion rates to empty the building so that it had value. In either case the judgment creditor had difficulty in collecting while the judgment debtor was disposed of its property. Execution on personal property as well as realty was hampered by fictitious claims by fictitious creditors who demanded payment to discharge their "claims." This corruption led to

96 Bailiff Law, Law No. 111 of 1966, Article 8 (3). But under Article 21 the Bailiff may receive public funds to maintain a minimum income.

97 See, e.g., Civil Execution Law (Law No. 4, 1979 as amended) Article 43.

98 Civil Execution Law Article 122-124.

99 Civil Execution Law Article 134.

100 See Civil Execution Law (Law No. 4, 1979) Article 22 where the documents on which execution may be had are listed. See also articles 26-28 for attachment of execution clauses to documents on which execution can be made. Execution can then be made but only when the obligor is properly served. Article 29. In cases where it is necessary to obtain an execution clause in a document, the debtor may file objections and execution may then be stayed by the court until a decision is made on whether to issue the execution clause. Article 32.

101 See, Akira Ishikawa, Civil Execution Procedure in Japan, 5 Keio Law Review 47, 51 (1985).

changes in the law. Execution officers were closely supervised by the judicial system and were prohibited from hiring assistants. But the damage had already been done. Like *sokaiya* simply passing laws to outlaw the former practice did not result in the practice disappearing. As a consequence difficulties remain even though the law has been changed to make execution easier than in the past.[102]

Not only do criminal activities hamper the effort to collect on judgments but also there is little effective way to discover the whereabouts of a debtor's assets when the debtor has engaged in activity designed to hide assets from a creditor. Even if property has to be registered and thus there is the possibility of tracing ownership via official registers, there may be difficulty in proceeding against the property. The named register owner is presumed to be the owner and has rights to prevent execution against "its" property.[103] Where movable property (personal property) that does not require registration is involved, it may be even more difficult to locate assets. There is no supplementary proceeding as in the United States.

When the debtor is in possession of personal property, the bailiff of the court may seize the property after an execution document has been issued.[104] Where the debtor's property is in the possession of a third party, an additional collection action may be required. Traditionally banks have been reluctant to assist creditors who claim a right to execute on property owned by debtors and in the possession of banks. Although the Civil Execution Law permits third parties in possession of personal property assets of judgment debtors to voluntarily turn such assets over to the court bailiff so that the property may be sold to pay the judgment,[105] banks have refused to cooperate. To recover against such assets creditors may have to institute action under the Civil Execution Law. The Civil Execution Law allows an action for collection of movable property (personal property) to be brought against a third party possessor when the debtor has a right to demand possession.[106] Once such an order has been obtained, it must be served on both the third party possessor and the judgment debtor. Seven days after such service the possessor of the order may demand that the property be given to the court bailiff so that the property can be sold to pay the judgment.[107] In 1999 the Supreme Court held that the execution procedures mentioned applied to safe deposit boxes (and the property contained in such boxes) held under lease in a bank. This ruling

---

102 For a discussion of the history of execution in Japan and difficulties in collecting on judgments see, Frank G. Bennett, Jr., Civil Execution in Japan: The Legal Economics of Perfect Honesty (9/21/01) available on the web at www.nomolog.nagoya-u.ac.jp/~bennett/pubs/enforcenew.pdf.

103 See, Civil Execution Law Article 38, which provides that a party who has ownership rights in property that is sought to be executed against may institute suit to prevent execution.

104 Civil Execution Law Article 123.

105 Civil Execution Law Article 124.

106 Civil Execution Law Article 157.

107 Civil Execution Law Article 163.

should prove a great help to creditors who seek to execute on property of a debtor held by a bank in a safe deposit box. In a supplemental opinion one of the Justices of the Supreme Court urged banks to change their policy and cooperate with the bailiff and judgment creditors.[108]

In a White Paper issued by MITI (now METI) in 2000, MITI acknowledged the difficulties encountered by creditors in executing on judgments. MITI recommended measures that would prevent concealment of property to avoid enforcement and execution. MITI suggested a system requiring debtors to list their property. Under MITI's proposal third persons could be employed to locate the property of debtors. Neither seems likely to remedy the problem. Debtors who are secreting assets to prevent execution are unlikely to report the existence of such secreted assets. Third parties, unless armed with judicial tools to locate assets are unlikely to have more information about a debtor's assets than the creditor or the creditor's lawyer.[109] The Civil Execution Law nonetheless now contains provisions that permit the bailiff to investigate into the location of certain assets of the debtor.[110] The court has a general authority to examine judgment debtors and in the process may ask about the location of assets.[111]

MITI also suggested that the existing debt collection system under which credit agencies can use the services of so-called "servicers" to collect on debts prior to litigation[112] be expanded to judgment debts.[113] Legalizing the efforts of "servicers" to collect on judgments would appear to bring Japan's judgment collection system full circle. It is likely that if the "servicer" proposal were adopted organized crime organizations, which are already utilized by some judgment creditors to collect judgments, would enter and dominate the field. This could breed corruption but also might be a means by which present unregulated activities of gangsters could be brought within the law and regulated.

---

108 Case No. 556 of 1996 (Sup. Ct. Petty Bench, 11/29/1999) available in English through the web site of the Supreme Court of Japan. The Supplemental Opinion of Justice Kitagawa sets out the argument that banks are not liable to their safe deposit box customers when they voluntarily cooperate with provisional execution orders in favor of judgment creditors. Among the reasons given is that such cooperation is a socially justifiable act. In the opinion Justice Kitagawa urges banks to change their policy.

109 Organized crime operatives might have more information or at least have effective methods for obtaining such information.

110 Civil Execution Law Article 57.

111 Civil Execution Law Article 5.

112 Prior to February 1999 only lawyers could provide debt collection services. However to assist financial institutions a new law effective in February 1999 created the "servicer" occupation. The purpose of the law was to make it easier to collect on nonpaying loans. Debt collection companies perform services for financial institutions seeking to collect on a limited category of bad debts such as bank loans, credit card debt, etc.

113 Report of Legal System Study Group for Research on Economic Activity and the Judicial System, MITI White Paper 5/9/2000 at P. 5-6 of 9. Available on the web at www.meti.go.jp/english/report/data/gCorpMaine.html

The Law Reform Council in its 2001 Report specifically recognized that effective execution to satisfy judgments remained a problem in Japan. The Council identified cost as an impediment to successful execution especially in the case of small money judgments. In addition the Council identified lack of personnel to collect judgments and lack of information concerning the location of assets available for execution as problems that needed legislative action. As to real property execution the Council noted that tenants in buildings pursuant to short-term leases could effectively obstruct execution sales, as could "illegal occupants."[114]

In January of 2003 the Justice Ministry introduced legislation to make it easier to evict short-term lessees in situations where property was to be sold to collect on a debtor's unpaid obligation. Prior to the legislation short-term tenants could remain in property being sold on execution sale for as long as three years. This obviously had an adverse effect on the judgment creditor's ability to collect. Under the legislation short-term tenants can be evicted after only three-months of its sale at auction.[115] The legislation was enacted to be effective no later than August 2004.[116] Under the legislation the purchaser of property at an execution sale can force short-term tenants out in only a few months from purchase. The legislation also permits a prospective buyer of such property to get a court order permitting an inspection of the property in order to enable the potential buyer to make a more informed judgment about what price to pay. Such inspection, while it may disclose defects, is likely to result in higher prices, as the buyer has more assurance as to what it is getting and need not hold back for fear of unknown excessive repair and rehabilitation costs. The legislation also permits creditors (including judgment creditors) who are contemplating foreclosure on real property to seek and obtain a court order requiring the debtor to disclose the whereabouts of assets. There is however no effective sanctions regime if the debtor fails to comply with such an order.[117]

The 2003 legislation is obviously a help to judgment creditors anxious to collect on their judgment. However, it is far from a panacea. The likelihood is that gangsters who previously used short-term leases to extract profits from execution sales will continue to view such sales as a means for extracting profits. Intimidation and other methods are likely to continue and perhaps additional strong-arm tactics will be employed to continue to gain profits from such sales. Previous efforts, such as amendments to the Civil Execution law in 1996 and 1998, were not successful in making execution of judgments significantly easier. The new legislation does not provide an effective means to discover the location of a debtor's assets nor does the new legislation make it easier for a judgment creditor to simply execute without procedural complications.

---

114 Recommendations of the Justice System Reform Council—For a Justice System to Support Japan in the 21st Century (June 12,2001) on the web at *www.kantei.go.jp/foreign/policy/sihou/singikai/990612_e.html* at p. 25-26 of 90.

115 Japan Times on Line, Justice Council Looks to Smooth Tenant Evictions 1/29/03.

116 Civil Preservation Law Article 25-2.

117 Civil Execution Law Article 64-2. See, Asahi Koma Law Offices Amendments to the Civil Code and Civil Execution Law of Japan 11/1/03 on the web at www.asianlegalonline.com/asia/list_regional_updates.cfm?country=japan.

Japan is not a party to multilateral treaties dealing with execution of foreign judgments but is a party to a number of multilateral and bilateral agreements dealing with recognition of and execution based on a foreign arbitration award, including the treaty of Friendship, Commerce and Navigation between Japan and the United States as well as the New York Convention. Japanese law does provide for recognition of foreign judgments under certain conditions discussed below. If these conditions are met, execution may be had on a foreign judgment. Where a foreign judgment deals with a family law matter, such as foreign divorce decree involving Japanese nationals, recognition of the judgment may be extra-judicial in that the Registrar for the Family Register system may simply accept the foreign judgment and enter the divorce in the Family Register.[118] This registration gives effect to the foreign decree.[119]

To collect on a foreign judgment, the judgment creditor must first obtain an execution document in Japan.[120] To obtain such a document the foreign judgment creditor must institute a suit in Japan in the District Court of the defendant's domicile (defendant's general forum).[121] The Japanese court will not look into the merits of the foreign judgment and typically the judgment will be given the same kind of effect in Japan as it has in the foreign jurisdiction.[122] Thus where a California judgment did not provide for interest to run on the amount of the judgment until paid but where California law provided for such interest as a matter of course, the Su-

118 In Japan there are several methods for obtaining a divorce. There is judicial divorce where a court enters a divorce decree in a contested divorce situation. There is divorce via conciliation obtained through conciliation before the Family Court. And there is consensual divorce wherein the parties simply enter the fact of their divorce in the Family Register. See Family Register Law Article 76. When there is a judicial divorce that fact is also entered in the Family Register. See Article 77. Where divorce is entered in the Register the divorced parties' names are reentered in the Register as they were prior to the marriage. Article 19. Prior to the Occupation judicial divorce was restricted to limited categories of cases and the law greatly favored the husband. The provisions regarding divorce were changed during the Occupation. Under the new law judicial divorce is available if there is sufficient reason for one party to the marriage to end the marriage because of a marriage breakdown. This provision raised the issue of whether the party responsible for the marriage breakdown could take advantage of the provision and seek a judicial divorce when the innocent party objected to divorce. In 1987 the Grand Bench of the Supreme Court overruled prior precedent and held that the responsible party could obtain a judicial divorce. See, Case No. 260 of 1986, 41 Minshu 1423 (Sup. Ct. Grand Bench, 9/2/87) available on the web through the web site of the Supreme Court of Japan.

119 See, e.g., Takao Sawaki, Recognition and Enforcement of Foreign Judgments in Japan, 23 International Lawyer 29 (1989). Japan is a signatory to the Convention on Civil Liability for Oil Pollution Damage. This convention has certain provisions dealing with international recognition of damage awards.

120 Civil Execution Law Article 22 (6). For a discussion of execution based on foreign judgments see, INTERNATIONAL EXECUTION AGAINST JUDGMENT DEBTORS (Teruo Doi—Japan) (Oceana Publications, Inc., Dobbs Ferry, NY, April 2001).

121 Civil Execution Law Article 24 (1).

122 Question exists as to whether the Japanese court may look into facts that occurred subsequent to the obtaining of the judgment. For example if after the judgment was entered it was satisfied in the foreign jurisdiction this fact should be available to the Japanese court. Similarly, if there was an agreed modification of the judgment this fact should be available to the court.

preme Court of Japan allowed an execution document to be issued in the amount of the California judgment with interest.[123] Similarly, where the law of Hong Kong provided for the automatic granting of interest such interest calculation was entitled to recognition in Japan even if not specifically provided for in the Hong Kong judgment.[124]

If the defendant has no general forum, suit can be instituted in the District where property subject to execution is located.[125] The judgment must be a final judgment and the judgment creditor has the obligation of proving the final character of the judgment.[126] Where effect is given to the foreign judgment, the court should issue an execution document without reexamining the merits of the case.[127] When an execution document is issued, it must state that it is based on a foreign final judgment.[128]

To be eligible for recognition in Japan a foreign judgment must satisfy four statutory conditions:[129]

The foreign court must have had jurisdiction in the matter and neither Japanese law nor a treaty should exist that prohibit the exercise of that jurisdiction. For example, if the matter concerns a case in which the court in Japan (or some country other than the forum that issued the judgment at issue) has exclusive jurisdiction then the Japanese court will not recognize the foreign judgment.

The defendant was properly served with notice of the action (other than service by publication) or had actually appeared in the case. If the defendant was served by

---

123 Case No. 1761 of 1993, 51 Minshu 2530 (Sup. Ct. Petty Bench, 7/11/97) available in English on the web through the web site of the Supreme Court of Japan. The Supreme Court of Japan allowed enforcement of the compensatory damages aspect of a California judgment while denying enforcement to the punitive damages awarded. The court noted that an execution document could be awarded on the basis of the California judgment and that the court could not examine into the merits of the compensatory award. Since the judgment was to be given the same effect as in California and since interest on the judgment runs as a matter of general course in California, interest would be permitted in Japan. To deny interest in Japan would be to give the California award less recognition than it would have in California.

124 Case No. 1838 of 1994 (Sup. Ct. Petty Bench, 4/28/98) available in English through the web site of the Supreme Court of Japan.

125 Civil Execution Law Article 24 (1).

126 Civil Execution Law Article 24 (3).

127 Civil Execution Law Article 24 (2).

128 Civil Execution Law Article 24 (4).

129 CCP Article 106; See generally, Dispute Resolution in Japan—Recognition and Enforcement of Foreign Judgments at www.gsid.nagoya-u.ac.jp/project.apec/lawdb/japan/dispute/disp2-en.html#2.1.2; see also, Thomas S. Mackey, Litigation Involving Damages to U.S. Plaintiffs Caused by Private Corporate Japanese Defendants, 5 Transnational Lawyer 131, 172-178 (1992). Although the statute lists four conditions these conditions have been further refined by commentators as follows: 1) foreign court issuance, 2) the judgment is a civil judgment, 3) finality, 4) proper jurisdiction in the court entering the judgment, 5) proper notice given to the debtor, 6) no violation of Japanese public policy and 7) reciprocity. See, Hideyuki Kobayashi and Yoshimasa Furuta, Products Liability Act and Transnational Litigation in Japan, 34 Texas International Law Journal 93, 113 (1999).

publication and actually received notice of the action through the publication the judgment is still not entitled to recognition in Japan, unless the defendant actually appeared in the action.[130]

Both the procedures leading to the judgment and the substance of the judgment do not violate Japanese public policy.[131]

The jurisdiction whose judgment is being enforced grants reciprocity to Japanese judgments. For United States judgments this is typically a question of State law as State law typically controls whether foreign judgments will be granted comity in the jurisdiction.[132]

The name of the final determination is not of consequence. As long as the final determination is rendered by a foreign court and finally decides a matter of private law between parties who have been given procedural protections it will be considered a final judgment. If a foreign court "Order" meets the above requirements, it is entitled to recognition whether denominated an Order, Judgment, Ruling, etc. Accordingly, where a final judgment was entered in favor of a plaintiff in Hong Kong and then later, in accordance with Hong Kong law, an Order awarding the successful party costs was entered, the court in Japan recognized both the judgment and the Order for costs.[133]

In determining whether the foreign court entering the final judgment had jurisdiction in the matter (item a above) treaties between Japan and the foreign jurisdiction should be examined. However, a treaty that describes what jurisdiction is appropriate would be rare. In order to determine jurisdiction, the Japanese courts are to be guided by reason and the concept that the parties have had a fair, just and speedy procedure. This is the same standard that Japanese courts use to determine domestic jurisdiction in transnational cases.[134] The concept of territorial jurisdiction is given primacy. If the foreign court's jurisdiction rule is similar to the juris-

---

130 See, Hideyuki Kobayashi and Yoshimasa Furuta, Products Liability Act and Transnational Litigation in Japan, 34 Texas International Law Journal 93, 115 (1999).

131 See, Takao Sawaki, Recognition and Enforcement of Foreign Judgments in Japan, 23 International Lawyer 29, 33 (1989) discussing a 1983 Supreme Court of Japan decision holding that the public policy exception applies to both substantive and procedural matters.

132 Judgments from such major commercial States as New York and California and from the nation's capital in Washington DC have qualified for reciprocity status. Hiroshi Oda JAPANESE LAW (2d Ed., Oxford University Press, 1999) 451-452.

133 Case No. 1838 of 1994 (Sup. Ct. Petty Bench, 4/28/98) available in English through the web site of the Supreme Court of Japan.

134 Malaysian Airline System v. Michiko Goto, 35 Minshu 1224 (Sup. Ct. Petty Bench 10/16/81); and KK Tsuburaya Production v. Sompote Saengduenchai, Tokyo District Court, 1/28/99 discussed in Teruo Doi, JAPANESE COPYRIGHT LAW IN THE 21st CENTURY 54-55 (Oceana Publications, Inc. Dobbs Ferry, NY (2001)). See also, Case No. 1993 (O) No. 1660, (Sup. Ct. Petty Bench, 11/11/97) available in English through the web site of the Supreme Court of Japan. For a discussion of the criticism of the Malaysian Airlines case and the subsequent modification of the Malaysian airlines rule in Case No. 1660 decided 11/11/97 see, Toshiyuki Kono, Enforcement of Foreign Intellectual Property Rights in Japan: Jurisdiction and Applicable Law, 6 CASRIP Publication Series: Rethinking Intellectual Property 20, 21-22 (University of Washington School of Law, 2000).

diction rules of the Code of Civil Procedure Japan will recognize the jurisdiction of the foreign court.[135] Japanese forum rules are typically based on presence and Japan does not have a general long-arm statute. Accordingly, where jurisdiction over a Japanese entity not present in the American jurisdiction has been obtained via an American long-arm jurisdictional statute there is a substantial question as to whether the Japanese court will grant recognition to the American judgment.[136] On the other hand, Japanese courts have accepted jurisdiction in a domestic litigation where the defendant was a foreigner who sent a letter into Japan from abroad, which was alleged to have caused a tortious injury to a Japanese national in Japan. The defendant never was present in Japan.[137] Question also exists as to whether Japanese courts will give effect to an American judgment in a case where jurisdiction was obtained through personal service on a defendant who was simply passing through the United States (so-called "tag jurisdiction"). Although such assertion of jurisdiction is constitutional,[138] its fairness is subject to serious question, and there is question as to whether American courts would recognize a foreign judgment where jurisdiction is based on tag jurisdiction.[139] Both jurisdictional fairness and reciprocity objections could be raised to an attempt to recognize a United States judgment based on tag jurisdiction. Where an American judgment is based on the extra-territorial application of United States law to activities occurring outside the United States significant question exists as to whether Japan would recognize the American judgment. This is especially so if the American application of the law were to activity in Japan that was not considered as improper under Japanese law.[140]

---

135 Case No. 1838 of 1994 (Sup. Ct. Petty Bench, 4/28/98) available in English through the web site of the Supreme Court of Japan giving recognition to a Hong Kong judgment and Orders related thereto entered prior to the turn over of Hong Kong to China.

136 See, Hideyuki Kobayashi and Yoshimasa Furuta, Products Liability Act and Transnational Litigation in Japan, 34 Texas International Law Journal 93, 114 (1999) discussing the decision of the Osaka High Court refusing to recognize a Minnesota judgment against a Japanese national where the jurisdiction was obtained under a long-arm statute. See INTERNATIONAL EXECUTION AGAINST JUDGMENT DEBTORS (Teruo Doi—Japan) (Oceana Publications, Inc., Dobbs Ferry, NY, April 2001) discussing Japanese cases refusing to recognize foreign judgments where jurisdiction of the foreign court was based on the foreign country being the place of performance of a contract obligation but noting that the new Code of Civil Procedure Article 5 now permits jurisdiction in Japan based on the place of performance where the action involves a property right. See also, Takao Sawaki, Recognition and Enforcement of Foreign Judgments in Japan, 23 International Lawyer 29, 33 (1989) suggesting that where the plaintiff is in a superior financial position to the defendant long-arm jurisdiction might be against Japanese public policy.

137 Case No. 2000 (O) 929, 2000 (Ju) No.780, 55 Minshu 727 (Sup. Ct. Petty Bench, 6/8/01) an English language version may be found on the web through the web site of the Supreme Court of Japan.

138 Burnham v. Superior Court, 495 U.S. 604 (1990).

139 See, American Law Institute, International Jurisdiction and Judgments Project, Proposed Foreign Judgments Recognition and Enforcement Act (Revised) Tentative Draft No. 2 (4/13/04) at Reporters' Notes to Section 6 note 1 p. 78.

140 Extra-territorial application of United States law is most common in the anti-trust context. In June 2004 the Supreme Court of the United States limited the extra-territorial application of American anti-trust law by holding that foreign (non-United States) plaintiffs who had pur-

Although forum is generally based on residence, suit may be brought against a person who has no domicile in Japan by setting venue in a District where the defendant has property subject to attachment.[141] The property need not have any relationship to the subject matter of the action. A Japanese judgment based on such "quasi in rem" jurisdiction might be denied effect in the United States.[142]

A Japanese court will not enforce a foreign judgment for punitive damages because the granting of punitive damages is inconsistent with Japanese public policy. While the punitive award will not be given effect in Japan, the portion of the judgment awarding compensatory damages will be recognized if the other conditions for recognition are met. Enforcement of laws in Japan is deemed a sovereign function of the administrative arm of government and the grant of punitive damages is an attempt to enforce law through private litigation activity of private parties. By parity of reasoning, a treble damage award would not be entitled to enforcement. The taking of testimony in litigation is considered a sovereign act. Similarly, the judge (a government function) is responsible for development of the evidence in a case. Accordingly, failure to follow the formal requirements for the taking of testimony by deposition in Japan (use of the Embassy or Consulate, obtaining the proper visa, etc.) or the failure to obtain the proper visa before interviewing potential witnesses is grounds for the Japanese court to refuse recognition. Failure to serve the summons and Complaint in the American litigation on a Japanese defendant through the government to government formal methodology of the Hague Convention (such as serving by mail under the Federal Rules of Civil Procedure) will lead to refusal to recognize the judgment.[143]

---

chased agricultural pharmaceutical products outside the United States could not sue in the United States for alleged cartel activity by the sellers of the products purchased. Among the companies sued were Japanese and other non-United States entities. The court returned the case to a lower court to consider the plaintiff's argument that the activity involved had an effect on United States commerce by raising the price of the products sold in the United States—an issue not previously considered by the lower court. However, the Court's rhetorical question as to why American law should trump Japan's determination on how to protect Japanese customers (or any other foreign country's determination of how to protect their own consumers) would be equally applicable to an attempt to get recognition of an American judgment issued in favor of Japanese consumers who purchased product in Japan under a regime not considered unlawful in Japan but considered unlawful in the United States whether or not that regime had an effect on American consumers. See, Hoffman-La Roche et al v. Empagran (6/14/04).

141 CCP Article 5 (iv).

142 See, ALI, International Jurisdiction and Judgments Project Proposed Foreign Judgments Recognition and Enforcement Act, Tentative Draft No. 2 (4/13/04) Section 6 (a)(i). See also, Shaffer v. Heitner, 433 US 186 (1977).

143 Case No. 1838 of 1994 (Sup. Ct. Petty Bench, 4/28/98) available in English through the web site of the Supreme Court of Japan. In the cited case the foreign court entered a final judgment entitled to recognition in Japan. Thereafter a motion was made in the case for an Order allowing costs related to the action. The motion was not served in accordance with the Hague Convention but was delivered by a lawyer in Japan. The Supreme Court upheld the general rule that such service is improper and that a judgment based thereon is not entitled to recognition. However, in the circumstances of the case—where the matter related to a motion made after a final judgment and where the defendant (an Indian national in Japan) contested the motion in Hong Kong, the court gave the Order for costs entered based on the motion recognition.

If the Japanese defendant in an American litigation has prosecuted a Japanese declaratory judgment action against the American plaintiff and received a declaration that there is no liability then the Japanese court will not recognize the contrary American judgment.[144] It has been suggested[145] that an American injunction issued in an area where Japanese law permits a Japanese court to issue an injunction might be entitled to recognition under Code of Civil Procedure Article 118. However, as Japanese injunctions are not applicable to conduct outside of Japan,[146] it is likely that American injunctions having extraterritorial effect (e.g., effect in Japan) would not be recognized in Japan, as they would probably fail the reciprocity test. The court in Japan will not retry the case when a foreign judgment has been properly issued. The court may, however, look behind the judgment to determine the basis for the decision and may examine the underlying transaction in order to determine whether the transaction and/or the basis for the decision violates Japanese public policy. To violate public policy it is not sufficient to show that the underlying transaction would have been illegal under Japanese law.[147] The underlying transaction must itself violate public policy by being in contravention of Japanese mores and prevailing views of morality.[148]

Similarly, to collect on an arbitration award the creditor must obtain an execution judgment.[149] For domestic awards, the Arbitration Law provides that an arbitration award has the same effect as a final judgment.[150] To obtain compulsory execution, the holder of the award must obtain a court authorization for execution.[151] The appropriate court for such an order is either the District Court agreed to by the parties, the District Court of the debtor's general domicile, the District Court

---

144 Takao Sawaki, Recognition and Enforcement of Foreign Judgments in Japan, 23 International Lawyer 29, 34 (1989); Hideyuki Kobayashi and Yoshimasa Furuta, Products Liability Act and Transnational Litigation in Japan, 34 Texas International Law Journal 93, 108-109 (1999).

145 Thomas S. Mackey, Litigation Involving Damages to U.S. Plaintiffs Caused by Private Corporate Japanese Defendants, 5 Transnational Lawyer 131, 177 (1992).

146 See, Toshiyuki Kono, Enforcement of Foreign Intellectual Property Rights in Japan: Jurisdiction and Applicable Law, 6 CASRIP Publication Series: Rethinking Intellectual Property 20, 28 (2000).

147 Takao Sawaki, Recognition and Enforcement of Foreign Judgments in Japan, 23 International Lawyer 29, 33 (1989) (foreign judgment recognized although underlying transaction failed to conform to Japan Foreign Exchange Control Act). For an analogous American decision recognizing a Mexican judgment based on a loan agreement that would be considered usurious under Texas law see, Southwest Livestock and Trucking Co. v. Hargrove, 169 F.3d 317 (5th Cir. 1999).

148 Hideyuki Kobayashi and Yoshimasa Furuta, Products Liability Act and Transnational Litigation in Japan, 34 Texas International Law Journal 93, 116 (1999). United States law is to the same effect. See, Loucks v. Standard Oil Co., 224 N.Y. 99, 111 (1918) (Cardozo, J.).

149 Civil Execution Law Article 22. For a discussion of recognition of and execution based on a foreign arbitration award see, INTERNATIONAL EXECUTION AGAINST JUDGMENT DEBTORS (Teruo Doi—Japan) (Oceana Publications, Inc., 2001) [discussing cases where enforcement under the New York Convention was permitted].

150 Arbitration Law Article 45.

151 Arbitration Law Article 46 (1).

where the arbitration took place[152] or the District Court having jurisdiction over the claim arbitrated or where the debtor's assets subject to seizure are located.[153] The Arbitration Law requires that the court issue an execution document when an application supported by a true copy of the award is made unless the statutory grounds for refusal to recognize an award are present. Those grounds are: invalidity of the arbitration agreement based on lack of capacity, invalidity of the agreement for some other reason, lack of proper notice of the arbitration, inability to present a case in opposition during the arbitration, the award deals with matter outside the scope of the arbitrator's authority, the composition of the arbitration panel was inconsistent with the requirements of the law of the place of arbitration or the arbitration award is not final under the law of the place where the arbitration took place or has been reversed or suspended by a court in the country where the award was entered.[154] As to all of these items the party opposing execution bears the burden of proof.[155] In addition, the court may refuse to issue an execution document when the claims adjudicated in the arbitration may not properly be the subject of arbitration under Japanese law or the award is contrary to public policy or good morals of Japan.[156]

An execution document is also required to get compulsory execution based on a foreign arbitration award. As Japan is a party to the New York Convention on the Recognition and Enforcement of Foreign Arbitral Awards[157] obtaining such an execution document for a foreign arbitral award is not significantly more difficult than obtaining such a document for a domestic award. It has been suggested that there is only one reported case in Japan where a court refused to issue an execution document when requested to do so under the New York Convention.[158] While the New York Convention permits a country to refuse to give effect to a foreign arbitration award when to do so would violate public policy, the courts in Japan take a restrictive view of public policy in the arbitration context. If the parties have agreed that a law outside Japan governs the arbitration and the arbitration award has not been challenged under procedures available under that foreign law, the court will not permit an argument that the award violates public policy be-

152 Arbitration Law Article 46 (4) incorporating Article 5.

153 Arbitration Law Article 46 (4).

154 Arbitration Law Article 45 (2) (i)-(vii).

155 Arbitration Law Article 46 (8).

156 Arbitration Law Article 45 (2) (viii) and (ix).

157 Japan joined the Convention June 20, 1961. Japan is also a party to the Convention on the Execution of Foreign Arbitral Awards having acceded thereto on July 11, 1952.

158 See, Takao Tateishi, The Enforcement of Foreign Arbitral Awards in Japan, on the web at *www.Jseinc.org/en/bulletin/bulletin40/vol40-enforcement.pdf.*

cause had it been a Japanese award an action to set-aside would lie under the Japanese Arbitration Act.[159]

Because Japan is a party to the New York Convention, arbitration awards issued in a Japanese arbitration are entitled to New York Convention enforceability in countries that are signatories to the Convention.

B. In-Court Conciliation[160]

Conciliation is the government's preferred method of resolving disputes. Conciliation as an integral part of the judicial system[161] was required during the Second World War. It was supported and expanded during the pre-war years through a series of laws in the 1920s and 30s that required conciliation in lieu of litigation. The original Code of Civil Procedure (1891) contained provisions for in-court conciliation (as does the present Code). At the same time as the French designed Civil Code was promulgated bringing Japan into the modern Western legal world, conciliation was adopted (1875) as a step that could be taken prior to instituting

---

159 See, discussion of Nagoya District Court judgment enforcing an American Arbitration Award in the face of such a challenge reported in Takao Tateishi, The Enforcement of Foreign Arbitral Awards in Japan, on the web at *www.Jseinc.org/en/bulletin/bulletin40/vol40-enforcement.pdf.*

160 For a discussion of in-court conciliation in Japan see, Rieko Nishikawa, Alternative Dispute Resolution in Japan, on the web *www.iadb.org/int/jn/English/support_files/Nishikawa_law_paper_nov.pdf*; Norihiko Maeda, ADR in Japan (Japan Commercial Arbitration Association) on the web at *www.jcaa.or.jp/jcaa-j/jigyou/textadrinjapan.html*; Dispute Resolution in Japan on the web at *www.gsid.nagoya-u.ac.jp/project/apec/lawdb/japan/dispute/disp1-en.html* (APEC Study Center, Nagoya University); Kazuo Iwasaki, Reconciliation of Commercial Disputes in Japan on the web at *www.gsid.nagoya-u.ac/project/apec/lawdb/japan/dispute/adren.html*; Yasunobu Sato, Commercial Dispute Processing in Japan 283-298 (Kluwer Law International, 2001); Toshio Sawada, Conciliation—Japan's Experience—Prospects of Success in International Transactions, 5 American Review of International Arbitration, 162 (1994); Takesi Kojima and Yasuhei Taniguchi, Japanese National Report on Access to Justice Part 1 in ACCESS TO JUSTICE, A WORLD SURVEY VOLUME I (Cappelletti and Garth Ed., Sijthopff and Noordhoff, 1978) at 689, 717-727; Takeshi Kojima, The Representation of Collective and Public Interests in Civil Litigation in ACCESS TO JUSTICE, A WORLD SURVEY VOLUME I (Cappelletti and Garth Ed., Sijthopff and Noordhoff, 1978) at 735, 740-741; Tetsuya Obuchi, Role of the court in the Process of informal Dispute Resolution in Japan: Traditional and Modern Aspects, With Special Emphasis on In-Court Compromise, 20 Law in Japan 74 (1987).

161 Conciliation is discussed herein as part of the civil procedure system or as an alternative method of resolving disputes between private parties. However, conciliation or mediation by the government is also used as a form of administrative regulation in Japan. Thus, Administrative Guidance—a process wherein the government "advises" parties as to the government's policy on a subject and "urges" parties to follow such guidance is a form of conciliation, especially when it involves several private parties whose interests may be different. Although the statute law states that guidance can only be employed when parties voluntary accept guidance and further that government agencies may not punish or discipline a party for failure to abide by guidance, the reality is that in Japan guidance is almost always followed. See, Carl F. Goodman, THE RULE OF LAW IN JAPAN: A COMPARATIVE ANALYSIS (Kluwer Law International, 2003) 335-348; Michael Young, Judicial Review of Administrative Guidance: Governmentally Encouraged Consensual Dispute Resolution in Japan, 84 Columbia Law Review 923 (1984). For a discussion of Administrative Guidance and judicial review see Chapter 12.

litigation. Conciliation was the preferred method of dispute resolution during the Tokugawa period. Many times the Tokugawa magistrate acted more as a conciliator rather than a decision-maker in the sense of the modern judge. Moreover, there was a formalized procedure wherein parties to a dispute before the magistrate (or the magistrate himself) could bring in a third person to try to conciliate the dispute. Notwithstanding the American Occupation's objective of establishing an adversary style litigation system as the prime means of resolving legal disputes, a comprehensive Civil Conciliation Act was passed in 1951.[162]

As we enter the 21st century, the Judicial Reform Council has called for expansion and strengthening of Alternative Dispute Resolution. The Council has suggested that such strengthening is needed to make ADR equally attractive as litigation.[163] The Council has proposed a common institutional base for all forms of ADR. Among the forms of ADR discussed by the Council is conciliation undertaken by the court system. The Council recommends liaison officers who promote cooperation between the various institutions engaged in conciliation and ADR functions including the various Ministries, private organizations and the court system. A study group under the Council was established and set March of 2004 as the target date for a comprehensive law to carry out the Council's recommendation. As many of the proposals of the Council have been accepted and have found their way into legislation, it is expected that the government will, in the not too distant future, propose legislation to carry out this recommendation. Although the government submitted several bills dealing with judicial procedure to the Diet in March 2004 (enacted by the Diet prior to the close of its spring 2004 session),[164] a Bill to carry out coordination and creation of a single institutional base for ADR was not included in the package. The history of conciliation as a means

162 For discussions of the pre-contemporary history of conciliation in Japanese law see, Yasuhei Taniguchi Mediation in Japan and Mediation's Cross-Cultural Viability, Biennial IFCAI Conference (10/24/97) at p. 3-4 of 9 on the web at *http://arbiter.wipo.int/events/conferences/1997/october/taniguchi.html*; Takao Tateishi, Mediation as Pre-Stage to Arbitration—is it the way Ahead of ADR in Japan on the web at *www.jseinc.org/en/bulletin/bulletin41/med_arb_scheme.pdf.*

163 Recommendations of the Justice System Reform Council—For a Justice System to Support Japan in the 21st Century (June 12,2001) on the web at *www.kantei.go.jp/foreign/policy/sihou/singikai/990612_e.html* at p. 31-34 of 90.

164 As part of the 2004 initiative the government submitted several bills to the Diet for enactment. Among those of most interest for Civil Procedure and discussed herein the following bills were enacted into law in the spring Diet session. Law establishing Labor Tribunal, Law amending the Administrative Case Litigation Law, Law permitting young judges and prosecutors to gain experience by working in a bengoshi office, Law establishing the Intellectual Property High Court, Law amending the courts law to provide greater protection to trade secrets disclosed in litigation. All of these bills were passed late in the spring 2004 session (some in the last week of the session) and the text of the bills was not available as this work was going to press. However, as all were government bills, were relatively politically acceptable to all Parties and were technical in nature it is unlikely that any significant change was made by the Diet in the bills as presented and as discussed in the text herein. No information currently available to the author indicates any change in the Bills as enacted and sources in Japan indicate no knowledge of any change. The Diet also enacted the Bill to allow for lay participation in major criminal cases. Some minor changes were made in this Bill as initially presented and as passed. These changes deal

of resolving disputes indicates that each time Japan moves in the direction of strengthening the judicial system as a dispute resolution measure it also adopts ADR conciliation laws to parallel (and perhaps replace?) judicial development.[165] It is anticipated that a comprehensive ADR law will soon be enacted.[166]

Conciliation may affect litigation in several different respects. Thus, parties to a dispute may conciliate before institution of litigation. In the event such conciliation is successful the question arises as to how to make the agreed upon resolution binding on the parties. The Civil Code provides that such a resolution has the effect of a contract[167] and thus it forms a new contractual relation between the parties. However, contract law in Japan is not as "fixed" as contract law in the United States, and the parties, having already experienced one dispute, may want to make the resolution of that dispute more binding than the typical contract. The Civil Code attempts to do this through Article 696, which gives the conciliated dispute resolution contract stronger evidentiary value than a typical contract. The conciliated settlement works a novation in which the conciliated settlement takes the place of the old agreement, and renders inadmissible evidence that tends to show that the conciliated resolution was improper.[168]

The conciliation settlement is itself a contract with no special rights or conditions, except for its novation character. If a party fails to comply with its terms, such as a failure to make a payment agreed to, the parties are again in dispute mode. The agreement itself is not subject to compulsory execution. On the other hand, where the agreement calls for the payment of money a notarized conciliated settlement, which states that the agreement is subject to compulsory execution has the same effect as a judgment and is subject to execution.[169]

The parties may prefer to go directly to court to make their conciliated agreement a formal judgment subject to compulsory execution rather than use the notarization process.[170] Under Article 275 of the Code either party to the conciliation settlement may institute a suit in Summary Court and by motion seek to make the

---

with the issue of penalty that may be assessed against lay participants who disclose private personal information coming to their attention as a consequence of their service as "jurors." Privacy questions are a subject of political debate in Japan. The substance of the law as passed is consistent with the government Bill submitted and discussed herein.

165 See, Meryll Dean, JAPANESE LEGAL SYSTEM (2 ed., Cavendish Publishing Limited, 2002) 359.

166 See, Kazuhiko Yamamoto, The ADR Basic Law 11th SOFTIC International Symposium (11/15/2002) for a discussion of matters to be considered in such a basic law.

167 Civil Code Article 695.

168 Civil Code Article 696, see, Rieko Nishikawa, Alternative Dispute Resolution in Japan, on the web *www.iadb.org/int/jn/English/support_files/Nishikawa_law_paper_nov.pdf.*

169 Civil Execution Law (Law No 4 of 1979 as amended) Article 22 (5).

170 Notarization is quite expensive in Japan. It may be less expensive to make the conciliation settlement a judgment than to get it notarized.

settlement a matter of court record.[171] Because the parties have agreed to the settlement prior to filing suit, the court clerk may enter the compromise in the record without the intercession of a judge.[172] Once the settlement becomes a matter of court record, it has the same effect as a judgment.[173]

If the conciliation is held under the auspices of the Japan Commercial Arbitration Association, the Association will agree to initiate Arbitration immediately upon conclusion of the conciliation naming the conciliators as arbitrators and making the conciliated agreement an Arbitration Award. Since Japan is a signatory to the New York Convention on Arbitration Awards, this award should be available for conversion into a judgment in other signatory countries. In addition the Arbitration Award would have binding effect in Japan.[174]

A party to a dispute may institute, by motion, a proceeding in the Summary Court seeking a conciliation of the dispute. The court will set a date for a compromise session and will attempt to conciliate the matter. However the matter will be terminated if either party to the dispute fails to appear on such date.[175] It has been estimated that approximately 300,000 mediation/conciliation cases were filed in Summary Court in 1998 and, of these, mediation/conciliation was successful in some 48% of cases.[176]

There are basically three types of court involved conciliation: A) direct involvement of the judge during pending litigation, B) creation of a court conciliation by separate action of the parties and C) creation of court conciliation during a pending litigation. The basic procedures utilized by the conciliators in cases B and C are similar. In situation B there is no pending litigation before a party to a dispute requests conciliation. As conciliation can be time consuming, the statute of limitations is tolled during the period of the conciliation provided litigation is instituted within 2 weeks of notice that conciliation has been terminated. If suit is instituted in the 2-week period the case is deemed initiated when the conciliation request was made.[177]

---

171 The filing fees for initiating a conciliation matter before the Summary Court are substantially less than the fees for instituting a normal civil action.

172 CPR Rule 169.

173 CCP Article 267; Civil Execution Act Article 22 (7).

174 Arbitration Law Article 45 provides that arbitration awards have the same effect as a final judgment, but that to get compulsory execution of such an award the holder of the award must get a court order permitting execution. Article 46. See, Dispute Resolution in Japan on the web at *www.gsid.nagoya-u.ac.jp/project/apec/lawdb/japan/dispute/disp1-en.html* (APEC Study Center, Nagoya University).

175 CCP Article 275.

176 Rieko Nishikawa, Judges and ADR in Japan (Keio University) on the web at www.iadb.org/mif/v2/speeches/nishikawa.html.

177 Civil Conciliation Act Article 19.

A) The court in a pending litigation may, at any time in the litigation, try to bring about a settlement.[178] Either the chief judge of a panel or a panel member may seek to bring about a compromise settlement of a case. Typically the court utilizes the new Preparation for Oral Argument procedure to suggest settlement to the parties. An American judge generally would not be personally involved in the settlement negotiations for fear of being influenced by the positions stated by the parties in a confidential procedure. (The judge might suggest that a magistrate meet with the parties for settlement negotiation purposes.) The Japanese judge is an active player in the settlement process. Because the judge can seek to compromise the case at any point, the settlement process may be ongoing with the pre-Oral Argument procedures and during the Oral Argument stage of the case. It is not unusual for the court to suggest the terms of a settlement to the parties. In Japan a decision in a case is reached when the court determines it is ready to decide the matter.[179] It is not unusual for the court to advise the parties of the likely determination in order to get the parties to agree to settlement. Parties are entitled to notice of the date when the decision in a case will be rendered. This allows the parties to be present in court to hear the decision.[180] The Code contemplates judgment in a case within two months of the close of Oral Argument. The court may extend the date.[181] The case may be settled during the period between notice and the end of Oral Argument or announcement of the court's decision. The court when giving notice and/or announcing that Oral Argument is concluded may suggest settlement terms to the parties. The court has authority to reopen Oral Argument.[182] If the parties need more time to consider or negotiate after Oral Argument is closed, the court may reopen and reschedule Oral Argument to assist in the settlement process. Because execution in Japan is typically more complicated than in the Untied States and because it may be difficult to track down assets to pay a judgment, settlement that provides for immediate payment may be preferred over a significantly larger judgment by a successful plaintiff. Indeed, since settlement may be attempted at any stage of the case, cases pending on appeal to the High Court may also involve judicial intercession to try to bring about settlement.

Parties may give the court authority to resolve the case through mediation/conciliation.[183] The authority must be set forth in a written motion that specifically states the parties will abide by the court's determination. In such a situation the court becomes, in effect, an arbitration body and its proposed compromise settlement becomes binding on the parties. However, either party may, before the judge has given the compromise determination, withdraw the authority of the court to com-

178 CCP Article 89.

179 CCP Article 243.

180 CPR Rule 156.

181 CCP Article 251.

182 CCP Article 153.

183 CCP Article 265.

promise the matter.[184] As arbitration is not looked on as favorably in Japan as is conciliation (probably for the same reasons that litigation is not favored over settlement and conciliation)[185] this arbitration role is sparingly used.

In utilizing its authority to try to bring the parties to a compromise settlement, the court typically meets with the parties. The settlement can be made a part of the record in the Plenary Proceeding or Oral Argument. The court may submit its proposal for settlement terms to the parties in writing and a party may agree in writing to the terms. The court's written terms must advise the party receiving it of the effect of written acceptance.[186] Written acceptance is not sufficient in and of itself to conclude a settlement. The court must take steps to determine that the party accepting in writing intends to accept the compromise.[187] Such intentional acceptance taken together with the other party's appearance at and agreement to the settlement terms at the Oral Argument results in a judicial compromise of the case.[188]

B) C)—Both of these processes involve conciliation before a panel established by the court. The difference is that in case B) the application is made before there is a pending lawsuit between the parties and in case C) there is a pending litigation and the application for conciliation may be made by a party or by the court *sua sponte*.[189] When the court acts *sua sponte* it must nonetheless get the consent of the parties. Such consent is obviously important, as conciliation with parties who are unwilling participants is unlikely to achieve results. It has been estimated that as many as 95% of the civil conciliation cases in Tokyo District Court in 1996 were cases referred to conciliation by the court itself.[190] It is argued that judges who do not use conciliation to resolve disputes receive less important assignments that are damaging to career advancement.[191] Conciliation has a positive effect on judicial statistics because it resolves cases without the time that is necessary to try a case, write an opinion, and then await the results of a first level appeal.[192]

---

184 CCP Article 265 (4).

185 See, Robert Bennet Lubic, International Commercial Arbitration in Japan: Background and Suggestions, 2 American Review of International Arbitration 87 (1991).

186 CPR Rule 163.

187 CPR Rule 163 (2).

188 CCP Article 264.

189 The idea of the court assisting the parties in the quest for a settlement through a non-binding conciliation proceeding is supported by The ALI/UNIDROIT draft Principles and Rules of Transnational Civil Procedure that provides that courts "should" facilitate ADR during court proceedings. ALI Council Draft No. 2 (9/29/03) Principle 24.2.

190 Norihiko Maeda, ADR in Japan (Japan Commercial Arbitration Association) on the web at *www.jcaa.or.jp/jcaa-j/jigyou/textadrinjapan.html*

191 Percy R. Luney, Jr., The Judiciary: Its Organization and Status in the Parliamentary System, in JAPANESE CONSTITUTIONAL LAW (Luney & Takahashi Ed., University of Tokyo Press, 1993)123, 140.

192 See, Tomoyuki Ohta and Tadao Hozumi (translated by Peter Figdor) Compromise in the Course of Litigation, 6 Law in Japan 97, 105 (1973).

When conciliation takes place in a pending litigation, the court may stay the litigation to permit the conciliation to move forward. When there is no pending litigation, either party to a civil dispute may ask the Summary Court to conciliate the matter.[193] The appropriate Summary Court is the court where the defendant (the opposition party to the party seeking conciliation) has its domicile—the same as the general forum rule for the District Court. If the plaintiff has sought conciliation from the wrong court, the court may transfer the case to the appropriate court.[194] Parties may, by agreement, choose the forum court for the conciliation.[195]

When a case is sent to in-court conciliation, a conciliation commission is established. Typically such commission is composed of three conciliators, only one of who is a judge.[196] Sometimes a judge will handle the conciliation[197] but typically there are two laypersons on the commission and if a party insists there must be two laypersons.[198] The court, not the parties, selects the commission members.[199] The court must select commissioners from a list on file with the court. The Supreme Court designates the list of commissioners. Conciliation commissioners must meet qualifications set by statute law. Commissioners must be bengoshi or persons whose expertise or whose background makes them adept at settlement of disputes. Above all, conciliators are required to be persons of good character. Although the non-judicial members of the conciliation commission should have expertise useful in resolving matters, that expertise need not relate directly to the nature of the dispute submitted for conciliation. The persons on the list are considered part time government employees during the period when they perform duties as commissioners.[200] Approximately 12,000 people are on such lists.[201]

Once established, the litigation effectively moves to the conciliation commission. The commission sets the dates for meetings and schedules its own activities. Commission meetings are closed to the public. Unlike American conciliation where the parties would negotiate under the eye of the conciliator or discuss matters privately with the conciliator but would not "try the case" before the conciliator, the conciliation commission has the power to call witnesses and to take testimony as well as examine documentary evidence. In other words, the commission may hold a mini-trial in private in an effort to better understand the case so

193 Civil Conciliation Act Article 2.

194 Civil Conciliation Act Article 4.

195 Civil Conciliation Act Article 3.

196 Civil Conciliation Act Article 6.

197 Civil Conciliation Act Article 5.

198 Civil Conciliation Act Article 5(2).

199 Civil Conciliation Act Article 7 (2).

200 Civil Conciliation Act Article 8 (2).

201 The Japanese Legal System, The Secretariat of the Justice System Reform Council, July 1999 Chapter VI page 13 of 15 on the web at *www.kantei.go.jp/foreign/policy/sihou/singikai/990620_e.html;* Toru Miura, Independence, Transparency and Accountability of the Judiciary in Japan, on the web at *www.unafei.or.jp/pdf/indonesia_pdf/session4.pdf* at page 45.

that settlement suggestions are realistic. The commission has the right to issue a summons and can even levy a non-penal fine on parties or witnesses who fail to appear in compliance with a summons.[202] The conciliation commission will require that the parties (even if represented by counsel) personally appear before the commission in an effort to assure that the real parties in interest attempt to resolve the matter. The purpose of holding hearings and examining evidence is not judicial in nature, as the function of the commissioners is not to come up with a judicial type solution. The testimony or evidence reviewed is not considered as part of the Oral Argument record in the case. Compromise, concession and a solution that fits reason and the circumstance in which the parties find themselves govern conciliation.[203] Although the commission has the authority to direct retention of the status quo during the conciliation process, the direction is neither binding nor self-executing.[204]

The function of the judge on the commission is to assure the parties that any compromise settlement they reach will not be unfair to either side. The basic idea is that the lay members of the commission, being experienced and practical persons will suggest reasonable approaches to resolution. Because of the judge's stature and the respect given to judges in Japan, if the judge were too deeply involved in the substance of the committee's work, the procedure would devolve into a normal settlement role of the judge. On the other hand, because of the respect given to the judge, parties to conciliation have confidence that the conciliated result is fair and just.[205]

The parties may reach a compromise agreement through discussion outside the presence of the conciliators. If the parties reach such a conciliated settlement, the conciliation commission must determine whether to approve the settlement.[206] At this stage the judge plays a significant role by reviewing the settlement for purposes of legality and in assuring the parties that there has not been over reaching by one side or the other. In assuring fairness the role of the judge is similar to the paternalistic role that judges in Japan have traditionally had. It is not unlike the role of a Federal District Court Judge in approving the settlement of a class action or derivative lawsuit—but without the formality assigned to such role in the United States. Fairness does not mean that the result reached is in accordance with legal requirements or that the settlement reflects what a court would rule as a matter of law. Since conciliation is to be governed not by the strict rule of law but rather by a reasoned decision based on the circumstances of the case and entered into in a spirit of compromise,[207] it is this reasonableness that governs the question of fairness. The parties may reach a compromise agreement outside the concilia-

202 Civil Conciliation Act Article 34.

203 Civil Conciliation Act Article 1.

204 Civil Conciliation Act Article 12.

205 See, e.g., Rieko Nishikawa, Judges and ADR in Japan (Keio University) on the web at www.iadb.org/mif/v2/speeches/nishikawa.html at page 5 of 8.

206 Civil Conciliation Act Article 14.

207 Civil Conciliation Act Article 1. Article 1 specifically refers to concessions by the parties, reason and existing circumstances as the basis on which the Act is premised.

tion proceeding and may then bring it to the conciliators as their agreement. If the agreement is deemed by the conciliation commission to be proper under the circumstances, the agreement will be approved and then may be treated as a judicial compromise with the effect of a court judgment.[208]

The major differences between an in-court conciliation process in Japan and a conciliation in the United States are: a) the court is actively involved in the conciliation process and indeed may set the process in motion by ordering conciliation in a pending litigation,[209] b) the conciliation commission may take testimony and examine into the facts of the case on its own,[210] and c) the conciliation process is not walled off from the judge. Indeed, the judge "trying" the case will likely be the judge on the conciliation commission. This makes the trial judge familiar with the conciliation proceedings.[211] If no conciliated settlement is reached, the conciliators will recommend to the court an appropriate settlement.[212] In the United States if there is conciliation during the progress of a lawsuit the judge might stay proceedings to give the conciliation a chance of success. It is unlikely that American conciliators would hear witnesses or effectively try the facts of the case—although they will listen to each party's version of the facts and arguments. In the United States conciliation would be private. Not only would conciliation take place outside the public view but also the judge would not ask and the conciliator would not inform the court what the conciliator thinks is an appropriate resolution. In Japan if conciliation is unsuccessful, the court can seek advice from the conciliators regarding an appropriate settlement.

If there is no agreed settlement, the court may *sua sponte* enter a ruling that is effectively a settlement of the case.[213] (Such a ruling would take into account the settlement that the commission thought was appropriate.) The parties have two weeks from notification by the court of the entry of such settlement to object.[214] If no objection is filed, the matter is settled in accordance with the court's ruling and the settlement is then as effective as a judicial compromise[215](i.e., it is as effective as a court judgment). If objection is filed, the settlement is null and void and the parties go back to the *status quo ante*[216] with a huge qualification. The qualification is that the court knows what the commission thinks is an appropriate settlement and the parties are aware of the court's view of what is a fair resolution of the matter.

---

208 Civil Conciliation Act Article 16.

209 Civil Conciliation Act Article 20.

210 Civil Conciliation Act Article 8. The Act gives this responsibility to the lay members of the conciliation commission.

211 International Commercial Litigation in Japan, Masafumi Kodama & Jay Tyndall, Katahama Law Office, on the web at *www.Masafumi Kodama & Jay Tyndall, Katahama.or.jp/English/litigatn.htm* at page 5 of 13.

212 Civil Conciliation Act Article 17.

213 Civil Conciliation Act Article 17.

214 Civil Conciliation Act Article 18.

215 Civil Conciliation Act Article 18(3).

216 Civil Conciliation Act Article 18 (2).

In a commercial dispute the parties may give the conciliation committee authority to resolve the matter. When the committee has such authority, it may make a determination that differs from an agreement reached by the parties. The committee's use of this authority is rare. It is exercised when the committee is of the view the agreement is inappropriate. The agreement to give this, essentially, arbitration authority to the conciliation commission must be in writing.[217]

The Law Reform Council report appears to suggest that efforts are needed to support conciliation in Japan because of conciliation's alleged declining popularity. The reality is that conciliation remains not just an alternative to litigation but an alternative that is used more frequently than litigation. Even when the judicial system is called upon to assist in resolving disputes, conciliation is an important part of the judicial function. Nonetheless the popularity of conciliation suits is on the decline. Statistical data shows that in 1964 there were approximately 95,000 conciliation cases filed, in 1974 the number rose to 111,500,[218] by 1995 the number had reached 130,000. Figures after 1995 are skewed because of the large number of conciliation cases dealing with debt restructuring counted thereafter but not available prior to that date. Nonetheless the number of commercial conciliation cases remains relatively constant—1995 = 12,628; 2000 = 13,342; 2001 = 11,350.[219] Of course these figures represent cases for conciliation filed with the court and do not take into account the cases already in litigation where a party seeks or the court *sua sponte* sends a case to a conciliation commission. Historically, approximately one half of cases filed that seek conciliation are successfully conciliated. The success rate for commercial cases is lower. The recent legislation creating a new Labor Tribunal shows continuing government support of conciliation. The Labor Tribunal is modeled after conciliation commissions. As is the case with conciliation commissions the Labor Tribunal will have one judge and two expert conciliators. Conciliation is required before the Labor Tribunal undertakes a judicial role.

It has been suggested that conciliation has been the Japanese government's response to various new claims that have been presented under new circumstances.[220] Conciliation was the response when the government sought greater power over labor management and other industrial matters in the period between the wars and it was the response when the government attempted to regain control over the pollution debate in Japan in the 1970s. It was the government's response to health related failures of both government and private industry (both the pharmaceutical industry and the medical services industry), the response to demands for greater freedoms and rights for women in the marketplace and has been the

217 Civil Arbitration Act Article 31.

218 Takesi Kojima and Yasuhei Taniguchi, Japanese National Report on Access to Justice Part 1 in ACCESS TO JUSTICE, A WORLD SURVEY VOLUME I (Cappelletti and Garth Ed., Sijthopff and Noordhoff, 1978) at 689.

219 These statistics may be found on the web at *www.stat.go.jp/english/data/nenkan/zuhyou/y2511000.*

220 For an interesting discussion of the conflict between ADR and litigation from an historic prospective see, Meryll Dean, JAPANESE LEGAL SYSTEM (2 ed., Cavendish Publishing Limited, 2002) 358-359. Dean notes that the resort to conciliation was a response to landlord tenant disputes in the 1920s and again in the 1960s and 70s in connection with pollution matters.

government's continuing response to family matters. All of these are matters where the government bureaucracy has sought to either retain/or control changes in customary norms or to remain in control of evolving issues. In the United States such evolving matters are typically the source of litigation. It remains to be seen whether the Law Reform Council's suggestions for strengthening ADR are utilized to provide claimants with an alternate means of obtaining adequate relief or whether they are used to strengthen the hand of bureaucrats by displacing or at least limiting claimants' access to the independent judiciary.

C. Complicated Cases and Continuous Hearing

In recent years Japan has seen an increase in litigation that involves complicated issues and that may require testimony from several witnesses. Such cases as construction disputes involving large construction projects and technical engineering facts and medical malpractice cases involving complicated medical information are examples of such cases. Because generalist judges and small-firm general practitioner lawyers do not possess the technical skills to deal with the technical issues involved in these complicated cases, the judicial system faces challenges in dealing with such cases. The American practice of expert witness examination is time consuming and expensive. Moreover, there is difficulty in finding experts willing to testify in Japan.[221] To deal with these issues several steps have been taken. First, by opening the new law schools (opened April 2004) to graduates of undergraduate faculties other than law it is hoped that lawyers and judges will have a broader technical education than is presently the case. By adopting the new expert commissioner system discussed above the courts are attempting to make expert advice available through neutral experts whose reports can guide the court. While helpful these steps do not deal with the issue of how to deal with the multiple witnesses that may be needed in such cases. Nor do these steps assist in scheduling the case in such a way as to resolve issues quickly.

The increase in medical malpractice cases is particularly large. In recent years Japanese consumers of medical services have had available sources of information previously available only to the medical profession. Thus the World Wide Web has made medical information available to patients who are concerned about their treatment. Not only information but also mores concerning the role of the physician and the right of the patient are undergoing change in Japan. No longer can it be taken for granted that a doctor knows what is best for the patient and thus need not consult the patient about treatment options. Rather, the doctrine of informed consent is beginning to take hold in Japan.[222] An older population needing more medical help from a profession with more sophisticated means at its disposal and

221 See, Mainichi Daily News, Slow Malpractice Suits Under the Knife 3/29/00 on the web at *www.maincihi.co.jp/english/news/archive/200003/20news01.html* reporting that doctors do not wish to appear as witnesses because of the way they are treated on the stand and because they do not wish to testify against other doctors.

222 See, e.g., Yutaka Tejima, Recent Developments in the Informed Consent Law in Japan, 36 Kobe University Law Review 45 (2002).

with more doctors as potential targets for medical malpractice claims may lead to more claims.[223] There is an alternative dispute resolution mechanism available to doctors (and their patients) who are members of and have malpractice insurance through the Japan Medical Association (JMA). Under this claims procedure doctors are bound to accept the decision of the claims resolution mechanism while patients are free to reject the determination and seek a remedy in court.[224] Nonetheless Japanese patients are more and more exercising their legal rights by seeking compensation for medical errors from the courts. As a consequence the number of medical malpractice cases is on the rise. In the ten-year period from 1992 to 2001 the number of new medical malpractice cases filed has increased 2 1/2 fold from 371 new cases a year to 805 new cases a year. Cases are being brought at a rate that exceeds the disposition rate for such cases. The backlog of medical malpractice cases has increased 50% since 1992. The statistics show:[225]

Year	New Cases Filed	Bac log
1992	371	1, 257
1993	442	1,352
1994	505	1,465
1995	484	1,523
1996	572	1,595
1997	593	1,661
1998	622	1,699
1999	663	1,793
2000	775	1,878
2001	805	1,968

Not only has there been an increase in the number of malpractice cases brought and pending, but also the reality is that such cases take longer to try than the average case. This has the effect of skewing the statistics and making the Judicial Branch look worse than the judicial Secretariat would like. As a consequence the courts are seeking methods to deal with the problem. Three procedural devices are available for assistance in dealing with such cases.

223 See, Kazue Nakajima, Catherine Keyes, Tatsuo Kuroyanagi and Kozo Tatara, Medical Malpractice and Legal Resolution Systems in Japan, Journal of the American Medical Association vol. 285 No. 12. P. 1632 (3/28/01).

224 For a discussion of how the JMA program works see, Kazue Nakajima, Catherine Keyes, Tatsuo Kuroyanagi and Kozo Tatara, Medical Malpractice and Legal Resolution Systems in Japan, Journal of the American Medical Association vol. 285 No. 12. P. 1632 (3/28/01).

225 Carl F. Goodman, Japan's New Civil Procedure Code: Has it Fostered a Rule of Law Dispute Resolution Mechanism, 29 Brooklyn Journal of International Law 511 (2004). The Brooklyn Journal of International Law has given permission for the use and copying of this material.

First, recent legislation strengthens the Code of Civil Procedure to give the courts authority to adopt the equivalent of a scheduling order early in the case.[226] Such a scheduling order should be the result of a conference between the court and the parties.[227] This movement brings the Japanese system for dealing with complicated cases closer to the German law system. In Germany there is court ordered scheduling and preclusion where a party fails to meet schedules and such failure adversely affects the pace of the case. To avoid preclusion in such circumstance the party must show justification for failure.[228] Of course the court has always had the authority to schedule matters on a "fast track" through its inherent authority over the procedure. The new law gives impetus to scheduling orders. Under the law the court may use the scheduling order as a means to expedite the pre-Oral Argument stage of the case as well as the Oral Argument stage. Such orders can be used in all complex litigation. The idea of a scheduling order type of procedure was under discussion for many years prior to amendment of the Code. Use of a scheduling order was recommended in 2000 by the then Ministry of International Trade and Development (MITI now changed to METI).[229]

The new provision calls for discussion between the court and the parties in the creation of a scheduling order. Not only should the order deal with pre-Oral Argument time limits but also it should deal with oral testimony of witnesses and should set a final date for the completion of the Oral Argument. The court may reject arguments and/or facts presented in an untimely basis on a finding that to accept such matters at a late date will result in significantly throwing off the schedule and that there is no good reason for the late submission.[230] This ability to sanction parties by refusing to hear arguments or facts is similar to the authority

---

226 CCP Article 147-3.

227 CPR Rule 165.

228 For a discussion of the German model see, Peter Gottwald, Simplified Civil Procedure in West Germany (Comment), 31 American Journal of Comparative Law 687 (1983); William B. Fisch, Recent Developments in West German Civil Procedure, 6 Hastings International and Comparative Law Review 221 (1983); Arthur T. von Mehren, Some Comparative Reflections on First Instance Civil Procedure Recent Reforms in German Civil Procedure and in the Federal Rules, 63 Notre Dame Law Review 609 (1988).

229 See, Report of Corporate Legal System Study Group for Research on Economic Activity and the Judicial System on the web at *www.meti.go.jp/english/report/data/gCorpMaine.html*. METI suggested both a "proceeding plan" and improvement in the system for expert information in court proceedings.

230 Professor Miki notes that the introduction of the concepts of significant effect on the scheduling order and the use of a "considerable" rather than "imperative" reason were intentional and designed to mitigate the sanction effect of the law. See, Koichi Miki "Roles of Judges and Attorneys under the Non-Sanction Scheme in Japanese Civil Procedure" delivered at the Symposium on Multiple Roles and Interaction of Judges and Attorneys in Modern Civil Litigation held at Chuo-o University, 6/1/03 p. 17. Miki suggests that the sanction authority under the new provision will meet the same fate as the sanction authority already held by the court—namely lack of use.

already possessed (but little used) by the court.[231] While such authority may be given to the court, it is likely that it will be sparing used. Nonetheless, the legislation indicates that society, through its elected representatives, wants faster processing of complex cases and thus it can be expected that the judicial system will respond with faster processing.

How the court will reconcile faster processing with its paternalistic attitude (the desire to see that the party that should win in fact does win), its history of clarification, and the general civil law notion that even though the Oral Argument (Plenary Hearing) stage of the case is conducted in disparate sessions all sessions are treated as one Oral Argument and thus evidence should be allowed at any point in the process, remains to be seen. Since the 2004 amendment appears designed to bring the 1996 Code closer to the German Stuttgart model it will be interesting to see if Japanese judges will look to German law scholars and court opinions in interpreting the scope of the new amendment.[232] As the judge in the case will likely change (because of Japan's policy of transferring judges every three years) and the new judge will need to get up to speed on all of the old judge's cases, the scheduling order established by the original judge may not fit the new judge's schedule. Further, since evidence and arguments that were not raised below may be raised on appeal, it seems unfair and counterproductive to preclude a party from presentation at the trial level when presentation may then be permitted at the appeal level.[233] One advantage of the drive for more concentrated proceedings in complicated cases is that such cases will likely involve parties represented by counsel. To some extent the ability to move cases faster under the new system will be dependent on the ability (and willingness) of bengoshi graduating from the new law schools. It is hoped that these graduates will have better lawyering skills to move cases along faster. As the liberalization of the Lawyers Law allowing for larger law firms takes hold, lawyers may be better able to gather evidence and prepare for cases than is true with today's small law firms with limited person power. Of course, what is lacking from the drive to move cases faster and to concentrate the Oral Hearing into something resembling an American trial is discovery. Without effective discovery prior to the Oral Argument stage of the case, the Oral Argument will still have to devote some time and effort (meaning several sessions

231 See, e.g., CCP Articles 157(1) and 167.

232 For an informative look at the German approach as of 1988 see, Arthur T. von Mehren, Some Comparative Reflections on First Instance Civil Procedure Recent Reforms in German Civil Procedure and in the Federal Rules, 63 Notre Dame Law Review 609, 614-620 (1988).

233 See, Peter Gottwald, Simplified Civil Procedure in West Germany (Comment), 31 American Journal of Comparative Law 687, 698 (1983) for the proposition that under the German approach to the Stuttgart model a party failing to meet the court set deadlines for argument and facts in the lower court is unlikely to be able to introduce such arguments or facts on appeal although the possibility is not entirely out of the question. See also, Arthur T. von Mehren, Some Comparative Reflections on First Instance Civil Procedure Recent Reforms in German Civil Procedure and in the Federal Rules, 63 Notre Dame Law Review 609 (1988) for the proposition that in Germany where the court sets a deadline for the parties and the parties fail to comply, delay is not usually excused.

between the judge and the bengoshi) to the questions of production of documents and testimony of witnesses.

Second, the Code of Civil Procedure emphasizes the authority of the court to take continuous testimony in a case. The court has had that authority ever since 1956 when the Rules of Civil Procedure called for concentrated taking of testimony.[234] However, the 1996 Code has a specific provision that directs the court to take concentrated testimony to the extent that such concentrated proceeding is possible.[235] Notwithstanding the prior existence of the authority, the reality was that as the American style of Civil Procedure declined and the German law style became more acceptable, continuous testimony was rarely used. The new emphasis on speed of resolution has caused a revitalization of the continuous testimony process. Not only do courts now have the power in statute rather than rule, but also the courts have gotten the message and are exercising the power to hold continuous hearings. Litigation attorneys are also supporting the use of such hearings in complicated cases. Thus, the old practice of having a witness testify on direct examination on one day with cross-examination a month or two later is no longer considered acceptable. This is especially so in time consuming technical and/or otherwise complicated cases. Not only are witnesses being examined and cross-examined on the same day but also courts are now more likely to hear testimony of several witnesses in the case on the same day. Courts even schedule two or more days back-to-back for hearing oral testimony. Even questions of convenience or lack of availability of a witness can be handled to permit concentrated evidence taking. Under the Code, when the parties agree, the court can accept witness testimony in writing thereby avoiding delay to meet the witness's time schedule.

The prospects are good for greater use of more concentrated hearings. The government has accepted the idea of criminal procedures that permit a 9-judge panel in some serious criminal cases. As six of the nine members of the panel will be lay citizens, the rules for such cases require greater use of concentrated hearings to accommodate the needs of these lay judges. Just as the model of concentrated hearing in jury trials in the United States has resulted in utilization of concentrated hearings in all trials, it is likely that this reform will have some spin off effects on civil cases in Japan. In addition, the new reforms, be they the Preparation for Oral Argument procedure or the new scheduling order authority, are based on German law models[236] rather than American models (although scheduling orders are a staple of American trial practice). As such they do not have any "taint" from an "imposed" system. Instead the reforms reflect what Japanese legal scholars look on as the more traditional modern Japanese system (i.e., the prewar system with German law roots). They are consistent with the trend since the Occupation of mov-

234 See, Takeshi Kojima, Civil Procedure Reform in Japan, 11 Michigan Journal of International Law 1218, 1227 (1990); see also Yasunobu Sato, Commercial Dispute Processing in Japan 158 n.109 (Kluwer Law International, 2001).

235 CCP Article 182.

236 See, e.g., Peter Gottwald, Simplified Civil Procedure in West Germany (Comment), 31 American Journal of Comparative Law 687 (1983).

ing away from American models of procedure to German law models. As a consequence there is a greater chance that they will serve to expedite the handling of complicated cases.[237]

Third, the new Code permits complicated cases to be heard by 5-judge panels.[238] As each panel member can take testimony, the increase in the size of the panel should speed up the process of taking witness testimony.[239] There is no reason why different panel members in different courtrooms cannot examine witnesses at the same time. The Code contemplates such a practice. This may create a burden for counsel. As Japanese lawyers begin to associate in larger firms this burden should be alleviated. In addition, complicated cases may involve several parties on each side. In such cases the lawyers may designate a lead counsel to handle communications between the lawyers and between the lawyers and the court.[240] This recognition of multiple counsel in complicated cases leads to the natural conclusion that the lawyers can designate one of their number to handle witness testimony in room A while another attends witness testimony in room B.[241]

D. Representative or Appointed Party Actions

The class action idea is based on a concept that all members of the class share a common interest in the result and that the right asserted is common to all class members. To civil law lawyers the idea of the class action is rooted in a theory of a group right that is alleged by the class representative on behalf of the group. Civil law as a rule does not recognize or acknowledge "group" as distinguished from

237 It is of interest that the new procedural rules (the 1996 Code and its 21st Century amendments) have German law roots in their pre-Oral Argument stage. The 1926 Amendment of the Japanese Code of Civil Procedure set up the Preliminary Oral Argument stage as a form of "pretrial" stage and also was supposed to separate the preliminary stage from the Oral Argument stage to allow for a more concentrated "trial." Preclusion was also a possibility under the Old 1926 Code. This followed by two years the 1924 amendment to the German Code of Civil Procedure that had adopted a similar process of dividing the "pretrial" and "trial" stages. See, Peter Gottwald, Simplified Civil Procedure in West Germany (Comment), 31 American Journal of Comparative Law 687, 688 (1983). Neither the German nor the Japanese approach achieved its objective of speeding up the Oral Argument process. The German solution was the Stuttgart model and change in the Code to adopt the experiment as law. The initial Japanese solution was to adopt a more Americanized procedure and when Japan moved back to its German law procedural roots appears to be a variation of the Stuttgart experiment with corresponding change in the German civil procedure through two Code provisions—Preparation for Oral Argument and scheduling.

238 CCP Article 269.

239 CCP Article 268.

240 CPR Rule 166.

241 See, Yasuhei Taniguchi, The 1996 Code of Civil Procedure of Japan—A Procedure for the Coming Century, 45 American Journal of Comparative Law 767, 786 (1997).

individual rights. As a consequence the notion of class action is difficult for civil law societies to accept[242]. For Japan, whose history is rooted in notions of group identity and rejection of individual rights, it would seem that the psychological barriers to class action that may exist in other civil law societies should be more easily overcome. The reality is that the rejection of class action in Japan probably has less to do with legal theory and more to do with industry objection to the class action idea. This objection is probably based on industry's understanding that class actions have resulted in substantial damage awards in the United States. Industry also knows that the class action device can be abused to obtain large legal fees from big corporations while class members receive little or no recovery. The abuses of the class action mechanism are well known in Japan.[243]

Japan has no class action. Discussions about class actions and whether they should be made a part of Japanese civil procedure date back to at least the 1970s.[244] The debate concerning the issue of class actions was taken up again in the drafting of the 1996 amendments to the Code of Civil Procedure. The class action concept was rejected. As a compromise the "representative action" mechanism was strengthened. Whether representative actions in the consumer field and other fields where class actions would be the norm in the United States will be classified as complicated cases and benefit from the expanded (5-judge panel) court process remains to be seen. In part the answer may depend on how commonplace such actions become and whether they are in fact complicated cases.

Japan's representative action (also known as the appointed party system)[245] is a break from the German law origins of the civil procedure system. Rather, the representative action has its roots in the English equity courts.[246] In a representative action multiple plaintiffs may select one or a small group of their number to represent the entire group of plaintiffs.[247] Although a small group of representatives may represent all of the members of the group, all of the members of the group must individually join the action. In other words there may be 500 individual

---

242 Antonio Gidi, Class Actions in Brazil—A Model for Civil Law Countries, 51 American Journal of Comparative Law 311, 344-347 (2003)

243 See, e.g., Comment of the Japan Business Federation on the OECD Principles of Corporate Governance Draft Revised Text (January 2004) (2/5/04) on the web at *www.keidanren.or.jp/english/policy/2004/014.html* p4 of 7 referring to misuse of class actions in the United States.

244 See, Takeshi Kojima, The Representation of Collective and Public Interests in Civil Litigation in ACCESS TO JUSTICE, A WORLD SURVEY VOLUME I (Cappelletti and Garth Ed., Sijthopff and Noordhoff, 1978) at 735.

245 See, Takeshi Kojima, Japanese Civil Procedure in Comparative Law Perspective, 46 U. Kansas L. Rev. 687, 711 (1998). Keidanren also refers to the system as the "appointed party system." See, Comment of the Japan Business Federation on the OECD Principles of Corporate Governance Draft Revised Text (January 2004) (2/5/04) on the web at *www.keidanren.or.jp/english/policy/2004/014.html* p. 4 of 7.

246 Takeshi Kojima, Japanese Civil Procedure in Comparative Law Perspective, 46 U. Kansas L. Rev. 687, 711 (1998); Yasuhei Taniguchi, The 1996 Code of Civil Procedure of Japan—A Procedure for the Coming Century, 45 American Journal of Comparative Law 767, 770 (1997.

247 CCP Article 30.

plaintiffs who designate a group of say 5 plaintiffs to represent them all. Individuals or entities that have interests in common with the plaintiffs are entitled to a recovery only if they are named plaintiffs in the action. Membership in the "class" whose interests may be exactly the same as the individual plaintiffs does not qualify as being affected by the decision. To be represented by the representative plaintiffs, an entity or person must join the case as a plaintiff.

Prior to the 1996 Code Japan recognized representative suits. However prior to the new Code to be a party to such an action the plaintiffs had to be named at the time the suit was instituted. A party similarly situated with plaintiffs could not join the suit after the filing of the initial Complaint. This had the effect of substantially restricting the size of the "class" or "group" represented by the representative plaintiffs. The 1996 Code changed this by permitting joinder after suit has been filed.[248] Where a new party appoints the previous representative to represent the new party, the representative may amend the Complaint to present the new party's claim. Such amendment may be made at any time before the completion of the Oral Argument.[249]

Many people in Japan consider the representative action to be Japan's version of the class action. Unlike the class action a "class member" seeking to join a representative suit must opt into the case by actually becoming a plaintiff and appointing the representative plaintiff its representative. The opt in requirement serves to limit the number of class members represented in the suit. In the United States class members are automatically members of the suit unless they take the affirmative step of opting out. Since "class members" must opt into the representative suit, questions are raised regarding how to inform "class members" that there is a suit pending and that they have a right to opt in. The matter is complicated because of ethical considerations. Can Japanese lawyers who represent a representative plaintiff in a lawsuit take out advertisements in newspapers to invite others to join the action? Is this a violation of ethical standards dealing with lawyer advertising? How is the public to know that the information set forth in the advertisement is accurate? Who is to pay for the advertisement? Problems similar to these arise in the United States in connection with notices published in class action and bankruptcy cases.

To avoid "appearance" ethical issues and to provide some guaranty of accuracy, the court can review notices and undertake the responsibility for approving the filing of the notice in the paper. Such a solution was suggested while the 1996 Code was being drafted. The suggestion was rejected. One reason for rejection was objection by the Bench. The question remains, are there restrictions that prohibit Japanese lawyers from publishing such notices in an attempt to increase the size of the represented group?

---

248 CCP Article 30 (3). See, Shoichi Okuyama, Izumi Sato and Alan J. Kasper, The new Code of Civil Procedure in Japan: Toward More Effective Resolution of IP Disputes Section 4.1 Parties on the web at *www.sughrue.com/clientfiles/new_code.html*.

249 CCP Article 144.

Among Japanese lawyers there appear to be a variety of opinions on the subject. Whether such advertising is or is not prohibited, many Japanese lawyers view the idea of publishing a notice to entice parties to join a lawsuit as distasteful. Many lawyers believe publication should be avoided. To others the issue is not whether the notice can be published but, rather, whether the lawyer should be required to pay for the advertisement. Still others believe that if the issue in the case is significant the lawyer can get the message across through interviews with the press and other public relations activities.[250] In any event, subsequent to amendment of the Code the representative action has been utilized in some consumer protection cases. Representative action has the potential for greater use in pollution and product liability cases—both areas where the injury alleged probably affects a large class of individuals. With the advent of Japanese awareness of privacy rights and the vulnerability of private data to be abused or compromised by breakdowns in security of web sites and other computer accessible data bases, the representative action may be a means for consumers whose private data has been compromised to sue the web site that failed to properly safeguard the private data.[251] It is unlikely that the representative action will cause as much difficulty for Japanese industry and generate the type of significant recoveries and legal fees as the American class action.

Although the representative action has usually been discussed as an alternative for the class action, the representative action has potential uses that are unrelated to class actions. The action permits one party to represent several plaintiffs with shared interests in a single litigation. This can be useful where the plaintiffs are united in some fashion but each has a separate cause of action. In the patent law area where intellectual property rights are owned/shared by parent and subsidiary company the representative action that joins the parent and subsidiary in a single suit may be a useful device.[252]

---

250 See, Carl F. Goodman, Japan's New Civil Procedure Code: Has it Fostered a Rule of Law Dispute Resolution Mechanism, 29 Brooklyn Journal of International Law 511, 591-592 (2004).

251 Responding to an alleged leak of data, Softbank in Japan offered to pay all customers 500yen in the nature of apology money. Three customers rejected the 500yen payment and have sued in Osaka District Court seeking 100,000 yen each in compensation. See, Japan Times online 2/28/04 Softbank offer 500yen to Yahoo BB users; Mainhichi Daily News interactive 5/17/04 Internet Customers sue Yahoo BB Operator Over Info Leak. It remains to be seen whether this case will turn into a "representative action" and whether other customers whose data was allegedly compromised will seek to opt into the case. In any event, the litigation demonstrates an area where the representative action might be used as a class action would be used in the United States.

252 See, Study on the Utilization of Intellectual Property Rights in a Business Group, IIP Bulletin 2002, 134 at 139-140 on the web at www.iip.or.jp/e/summary/pdf/detail2001/e13_12.pdf.

E. Determination at the First Instance Court

Only the court may render a judgment. A single judge of a collegial court cannot render a judgment.[253] A judgment by a collegial court of first instance is rendered by unanimous decision. There is no dissenting opinion[254] in inferior courts. The judges in conference may have disagreements among themselves, as each must follow only conscience and the law.[255] Deliberations of a collegial court are private and not opened to the public.[256] As is true with so much of Japanese society, the objective of the panel is to reach a consensus decision.

A final judgment in a case is given when the court handling the matter believes that it is ready to deliver the judgment. The time for delivery is in the hands of the panel (or in the case of a single judge court the single judge).[257] In recent legislation the Diet has made it clear that it is the government's policy that all civil and criminal cases should be finally decided (at the first level) within two years of commencement of the case. However this is a policy statement that has no binding effect on the court system. The policy will have an effect on the judiciary. The judicial Secretariat will attempt to move litigation faster than in the past. The Supreme Court (not to be outdone by the politicians) has stated that it has an even more aggressive plan for faster decisions. In any event the objective of these plans, whether it be two years or one year, is still far in the future.

Where part of a case is ready for final judgment, the court may render a final judgment as to that part.[258] The Code sets as a guideline the proposition that final judgments be rendered within two months of the closing of the Oral Argument.[259] The court has discretion in extending this time period and can even decide to reopen the Oral Argument after having announced its closure.[260]

Consistent with the idea that court proceedings are public events and consistent with the philosophy that matters in court are orally stated, the court publicly announces its final judgments through the presiding judge.[261] Because the parties have a right to be present when the judgment in their case is announced (but are

---

253 CCP Article 123.

254 See, Percy R. Luney, Jr., The Judiciary: Its Organization and Status in the Parliamentary System, in JAPANESE CONSTITUTIONAL LAW (Luney & Takahashi Ed., University of Tokyo Press, 1993)123, 131.

255 Constitution of Japan Article 76.

256 Court Organization Law Article 75.

257 CCP Article 243.

258 CCP Article 243 (2).

259 CCP Article 251.

260 CCP Article 153.

261 CPR Rule 155. The presiding judge need not read the entire decision of the court but may summarize the reasoning of the court.

not required to be present)[262] the court tells the parties the date when the judgment will be announced.[263] The announcement of the judgment day is also useful to the court in its settlement "coercion" role. It is not unusual for a judge who is closing Oral Argument and setting the date for judgment to also suggest a settlement to the parties. The judge may even informally advise the parties of the likely terms of the decision. By informing the parties of the date when judgment will be rendered and by advising them of what judgment to expect, the court can use the period between announcement and judgment to try to bring about settlement.[264] Indeed, to coerce a settlement the court may inform a recalcitrant defendant that if it fails to accept the settlement proposed by the court it can expect an even more unfavorable judgment.[265] Similarly, a stubborn plaintiff may be told to expect a less favorable judgment.

An interesting example of the court's use of its authority to suggest settlement terms is the *S.M.O.N. case*. A series of lawsuits were brought against the government of Japan and against the manufacturers of the pharmaceutical drug that was later identified as causing S.M.O.N. disease. After various proceedings in the case the court entered an "opinion"—not a binding decision in the matter but, rather, a statement of the views of the court. In the "opinion" the court indicated that both the manufacturer and the government bore responsibility for the injury caused to S.M.O.N. patients. The court then, rather than entering a judgment in the matter, sets forth its proposals for a settlement of the case. Under the court's proposal a schedule of damage payments is provided. Payments are based on the severity of the disease and such factors as whether the patient is a wage earner providing the major source of income for a family. The proposal even includes the suggested attorney fee that should be allowed and added to the payments. In short the proposed settlement has all of the terms and conditions that one would expect to find in a judgment deciding the case. The court refrained from entering a judgment. The court proposed the settlement to the parties. The parties eventually accepted.[266]

Although it may seem that settlement at this late date does not serve the judiciary's objective of saving judicial time, in reality it is quite useful as a time saving measure. First, as a rule judgments should be written and should state, among other things, the actual decision, the facts underlying the decision and the court's rea-

262 CCP Article 251 (2).

263 CPR Rule 156. The notice of date of judgment may be given by the court clerk.

264 Tetsuya Obuchi, Role of the Court in the Process of informal Dispute Resolution in Japan: Traditional and Modern Aspects, With Special Emphasis on In-Court Compromise, 20 Law in Japan 74 (1987).

265 International Commercial Litigation in Japan, Masafumi Kodama & Jay Tyndall, Kitahama Law Office, on the web at *www.Masafumi Kodama & Jay Tyndall, Kitahama.or.jp/English/litigatn.htm* at page 5 of 13.

266 See, Proposals for Settlement and Accompanying Opinions translated by Seiichi Yoshikawa, The Judge's Power to Propose Terms For settlement: The S.M.O.N. Case, 11 Law in Japan 76 (1978).

soning.[267] Unlike in the United States, Japanese judges do not have law clerks who are graduates of law schools. Such clerks are knowledgeable of the law and can and do help the judges by preparing first drafts of decisions. Japanese judges must write the decision themselves. Settlement prior to judgment relieves the court of this onerous and time-consuming function. Even if the judge writes a tentative opinion or an opinion to be used for settlement discussion purposes, such an opinion need not be as detailed and reasoned as the actual opinion in a judgment case. Second, if the matter is settled there will be no appeal. A first level appeal is a right in Japan and the appeal process is time consuming. By having the parties settle prior to judgment the time of the appeal court is saved. This is a benefit to the judicial system and is viewed favorably by the judicial Secretariat. If the parties are aware of the probable determination of the first level court, they can better determine whether to settle and at what cost. For the winning party there is reason to accept a discount from the presumed judgment. Acceptance means immediate payment. Acceptance avoids a time consuming and potentially expensive appeal and a potentially difficult execution of judgment problem.[268] For the losing party there is the chance to settle at a discount that takes into account the possibility of reversal on appeal and the time consuming and expensive proposition of the appeal. With greater knowledge of the likely result at the initial level trial the parties can make a more informed judgment as to settlement.

Certain judgments need not be announced orally and need not be contained in formal judgment documents prepared by the court. For example, the court immediately on default may announce default judgments.[269] Judgments are not required when the court *orders* a case dismissed for failure to pay the filing fee or correct a defect that the presiding judge has identified in review of the initial Complaint prior to service. Nor is judgment required where the plaintiff has failed to pay for the summons to be served on the defendant after being so ordered by the court.[270]

A formal written judgment must be signed by the judge. If there is a collegial court the panel of judges rendering the decision must sign the judgment[271] (there are no dissents in inferior courts). The judgment is given to the court clerk who then serves authenticated copies on the parties.[272] The rendering court has one week to amend its judgment for errors of law and may do so without granting the parties an opportunity to be heard as to the amendment/correction.[273] Clerical errors may be corrected at any time.[274]

267 CCP Article 253.

268 Shunko Muto, Concerning Trial Leadership in Civil Litigation: Focusing the Judge's Inquiry and Compromise, 12 Law in Japan 23 (1979).

269 CCP Article 254; CPR Rule 155 (3).

270 See CCP Articles 137, 141.

271 CPR Rule 157.

272 CCP Article 255; CPR Rule 158, 159.

273 CCP Article 256; CPR Rule 160.

274 CCP Article 257.

Although the Code says that a judgment has effect from the date of its pronouncement[275] this can be misleading as an appeal as of right may be filed within two weeks of service of the judgment on the appealing party.[276] A judgment does not become final and binding until the expiration of the appeal period or determination of the final appeal.[277] Further, if the judgment calls for the losing party to make a series of payments over time the Code permits the parties to come back to the court that entered the judgment to seek a modification based on changed circumstances affecting the calculation of the damage amount.[278] In such a recalculation proceeding the parties can rely on a change in wage level or even a change in the nature and extent of the injury to the plaintiff if such change affects the computation of damages. Any change authorized by the court has prospective effect only and cannot affect payments already made under the old schedule.[279] While this new amendment to the Code takes reality into account, it has two effects that are less than helpful. First, the only party hurt by the procedure is the injured plaintiff. This follows because under the prior law the plaintiff could always go back to court to seek additional damages based on new factors. Such suit was permitted because of Japan's limited *res judicata* rule. New factors not resolved in the initial litigation are not barred by *res judicata*. *Res judicata* only applies to the claims actually litigated. Under the amendment the losing party may also seek a modification of the damage award. Second, while injecting reality into the damage process the new procedure rejects one of the principal reasons for the *res judicata* doctrine. Namely to bring an end to the litigation and end the dispute between the parties. This process sometimes referred to as pacification[280] is not carried forward if the parties to the case can re-litigate the damage issue over and over again as alleged changed circumstances arise.

Final judgments (those that are not appealed or those that have survived appeal) are entitled to *res judicata* effect between the parties to the litigation (and those in privity with them).[281] However, *res judicata* only applies to matters that are actually determined in the case.[282] Japan does not follow a collateral estoppel rule[283] nor does it permit *res judicata* effect to be given to claims not raised in the case but that could have been raised. The refusal to give preclusive effect to claims that

275 CCP Article 250.

276 CCP Article 285.

277 CCP Article 116.

278 CCP Article 117 (1).

279 CCP Article 117.

280 See, Harald Koch & Frank Diedrich, CIVIL PROCEDURE IN GERMANY (Kluwer Law International, 1998) sec. 136-137 for the two exceptions to *res judicata* pacification doctrine that are permitted under German law—irregularities such as criminal conduct in the awarding of the first judgment and public policy where carrying out the first judgment would violate public policy.

281 CCP Article 115.

282 CCP Article 114.

283 Hideo Tanaka, THE JAPANESE LEGAL SYSTEM 151 (University of Tokyo Press, 1976).

might have been but were not raised is consistent with the general civil law concept of preclusion and is not unique to Japan. It is also consistent with the Code of Civil Procedure's requirement that the court can only decide claims raised by the parties.[284] In this regard Japan differs from the American view of preclusion.[285] The Japanese rule is consistent with civil law concepts of preclusion[286] and finds favor with the suggested Principles for Transnational Litigation being considered by the American Law Institute ("ALI"). The ALI draft would permit collateral estoppel (issue preclusion) in cases where the party urging preclusion had relied on a previous judicial finding in its dealings with the opposing party. While considerably narrower than the common law approach to preclusion, the ALI Principle is closer to the civil law rule under which such preclusion may be achieved not through preclusion rules but through use of the civil law concept of good faith and the prohibition against an abuse of rights.[287] In Japan the rule may actually be broader than the ALI discussion draft. Because of the highly bureaucratic nature of the Japanese judiciary and because of the judge's role in clarifying issues and determining what facts need and what facts do not need to be proven at the Oral Argument, the Japanese rule may actually be closer to the American rule than to other civil law systems. It would be rare that the judge in case 2 would not discover what had happened in case 1 and rarer still for the judge to disagree with the first determination. Japanese decisions do not have binding effect on future cases. Nonetheless Japanese judges have a good idea of what their colleagues are doing and what the judicial Secretariat expects.

Where a judgment is a partial judgment, that part of the case not decided continues in the court of first instance.

There are a limited number of situations where even a final binding judgment can be reopened for appeal:

a) Where the court's composition was improper (for example where a 3-judge panel included 2 judges in their first 5-year assignment);

b) A judge who participated in the judgment was prohibited from doing so as a matter of law;

c) The legal representative of the party or the bengoshi for the party was not properly authorized to represent the party;

d) A judge who participated in the decision committed a crime such as bribery in connection with the case;

---

284 CCP Article 246.

285 See, Allen v. McCurry, 449 U.S. 90 (1980); Restatement (Second) Judgments Section 24 (1) (1982).

286 See, e.g., Antonio Gidi, Class Actions in Brazil—A Model for Civil Law Countries, 51 American Journal of Comparative Law 311, 385 (2003); see also, Harald Koch & Frank Diedrich, CIVIL PROCEDURE IN GERMANY (Kluwer Law International, 1998) sec. 134.

287 See, ALI/UNIDROIT Principles and Rules of Transnational Civil Procedure Council Draft No. 2 (9/29/03) Principle 28.3.

e) A party either consented to a point or failed to raise an issue because of the criminal conduct of a third party (for example intimidation of a party by an organized crime organization);

f) It is discovered (after judgment) that a relevant document in a case was forged or otherwise altered;

g) Perjury in the giving of relevant evidence (this can include the perjury of the interpreter where an interpreter was required);

h) If the judgment in the civil case was based on a prior criminal judgment or administrative disposition and the prior act has been reversed or significantly changed;

i) Major factors that could have affected the decision were not taken into consideration;

j) The judgment is inconsistent with a previously rendered judgment.[288]

Where the grounds for setting aside the prior judgment are based on misconduct (items d-g) the case charging such misconduct must have resulted in a conviction (or non-penal fine) that is final and conclusive. If no such case has been brought the reason for failure to do so must be unrelated to evidentiary problems (such as the statute of limitations).[289] Because the first level appeal in Japan is considered as a continuation of the trial, if there has been a first level appeal, the initial court's judgment may not be set aside.[290] Instead the appeal would have to be made against the decision of the appeal court. Thus, if a judge on the initial trial panel took a bribe but the case was appealed and the High Court reached the same determination, the High Court's ruling could not be set aside and the judgment would be final and not subject to retrial. Except for a claim that there was a defect in a representative's authority (item c above) or that the judgment is inconsistent with a previous final and binding judgment (item j above) all other claims for retrial are barred after five years from entry of the final judgment.[291] Any motion for retrial must be made within 30 days of acquiring knowledge of the defect relied on.[292] A petition for retrial must be in writing. The judgment appealed from must be attached to the petition.[293] The petition must list the names of the parties and their legal representatives, a clear statement that retrial is sought and must set forth the grounds for retrial.[294]

---

288 CCP Article 338 (1).

289 CCP Article 338 (2).

290 CCP Article 338 (3).

291 CCP Article 342 (2 and 3).

292 CCP Article 342 (1 and 3).

293 CPR Rule 211.

294 CCP Article 343.

Retrial is a rare procedure and it is not designed to take the place of normal appeal. The court to which the petition is directed (the court whose judgment is being challenged in the retrial petition) may dismiss the retrial petition by ruling without a trial if the court concludes that the petition is without merit or otherwise improper.[295] An immediate appeal from such a ruling is available. An immediate appeal is also available if the court determines it should grant a retrial.[296] The court should not grant a retrial without first interviewing the party who was successful at the trial being challenged.[297]

When a retrial is held, the new trial is limited solely to the points that caused a retrial to be ordered. In other words, retrial does not open the case to retrial of all issues in the case but solely to the issues that are the basis for the retrial.[298] If the court concludes that the judgment initially entered was proper, it must dismiss the retrial petition. However, if it concludes that the original judgment was improper, it will enter such further decision as to the court appears proper.[299]

The principles that govern the court's decision-making process in making its judgment are set out in Article 247. Broadly speaking the determination of a case is left to the good sense and judgment of the court relying on all of the evidence heard. The court must be convinced of a fact for the court to decide the fact question in favor of a party. This is a higher standard than the American preponderance of the evidence standard but not as stringent as beyond a reasonable doubt. It is somewhat analogous to clear and convincing. As noted in Chapter 9, while the standards for meeting the burden of proof imposed on a plaintiff in the Japanese system are greater than in the United States, there are many situations where the standard has been reduced to meet social needs. The most significant of such situations are pollution litigation (where the standard was reduced by the courts) and automobile accident cases where the standard was reduced by the Diet. In any event, the judge has great discretion in rendering rulings as to the facts. In the United States facts decided by the trial court are entitled to deference (and in jury trials great deference as the fact finding of the jury in a civil case is constitutionally protected and cannot be overturned lightly).[300] In Japan the facts are fair game for review at the first level appeal. This follows because the first level appeal is viewed as a continuation of the trial. In theory the judge or panel of judges that

295 CCP Article 345.

296 CCP Article 347, CCP Article 346 (1).

297 CCP Article 346 (2).

298 CCP Article 348.

299 CCP Article 348.

300 A criminal jury's finding of not guilty in the United States cannot be reviewed as to do so would constitute double jeopardy. In Japan the prosecutor may appeal from a lower court's determination that the defendant is not guilty. Such appeal is considered part of the original case and thus not subject to the double jeopardy clause in the Japanese Constitution.

tried the case must be the same judges who decide the case.[301] In reality since Japanese judges are frequently transferred from court to court and location to location, the judge or panel of judges initially assigned to a case will change before decision. To avoid retrial the Code permits an oral statement to the new judge of a summary of important matters that preceded appointment to the case. Where a single judge is transferred or where a majority of a panel has been transferred after witness testimony has been taken, either party may, in theory, request that the new judge(s) rehear the witness's testimony.[302]

The successful party is entitled to recover court costs, except that the court may in special circumstances involving abuse charge the costs against the winning party.[303] The court may *sua sponte* render a determination as to the appropriate costs. The winning party may make a written motion to have costs imposed.[304] In most cases such costs are relatively low except that a successful plaintiff may recover the filing fee (which can be quite high for a high money damage case) as part of the court costs.[305] Where the winning party has made a motion for assessment of court costs, the court clerk rather than the judge can assess the appropriate costs.[306] Giving this authority to the clerk recognizes the professionalism of court clerks in Japan and relieves the judges from this time consuming task so that they can focus on more important aspects of the litigation. As a general rule the parties pay their own attorney's fees except that in tort cases the plaintiff's attorney's fee is considered as part of the damages suffered. In tort cases the court will typically assess a reasonable fee (perhaps 10-20% of the recovery) that is actually less than what the plaintiff pays. In stockholder derivative cases the successful plaintiff is also entitled to reasonable attorney's fees. The American Rule for attorney's fees is under attack in Japan.

Cases may, of course, be disposed of without reaching a judgment. A plaintiff may voluntarily withdraw the case. If the opposing party has answered or opposed the claim in Oral Argument its consent is required for the withdrawal to be without prejudice.[307] The most frequent method of resolution without judgment is acceptance of a compromise arrived at either separately between the parties or through the court's intervention (either by the judge's suggestion of a settlement or

---

301 CCP Article 249.

302 CCP Article 249.

303 CCP Article 61 sets out the general rule. CCP Articles 62 (unnecessary costs due to a party's actions) and 63 (costs due to a party's dilatory actions may be charged against the dilatory party even if the winner). Where there is a partial victory the court may split the costs or may impose the costs on one party.

304 CCP Articles 67, 258; CPR Rule 161.

305 Takashi B. Yamamoto, Copyright Enforcement in Japan on the web at *www.itlaw.jp/tokyo%20seminar%202003%20re.pdf at p. 20.*

306 CCP Article 71. This is a new (1996) provision in the Code.

307 CCP Article 261, 262, 263.

through the use of a conciliation commission).[308] Claims may also be abandoned.[309] The entry into the court record of the abandonment or compromise of a claim has the same effect as a judgment entered by the court after Oral Argument.[310] If the parties fail to make any provision regarding court costs in their compromise each party bears its own costs.[311] The parties to a compromise may determine which party bears the court costs and leave it to the court clerk to determine the amount of costs to be assessed.[312] In any situation where the court clerk determines the amount of the costs, a party may file a written objection within one week. If such an objection is filed, the court itself will fix the costs.[313]

308 CCP Article 264, 265.

309 CCP Article 266.

310 CCP Article 267.

311 CCP Article 68.

312 CCP Article 72.

313 CCP Article 71, 72. CPR Rule 24.

11

Judicial Process in Japan—Appeal

A. First level Appeal (*Koso* Appeal) or Continuation of the Trial at the Appeal Level and Kokoku Appeal

Both Japan and the United States have basically a three-tier court system.[1] Each is headed by a Supreme Court below which there is a regional court of appeals—a Circuit Court of Appeals in the United States and a High Court in Japan. Below the appeal court is a general jurisdiction court of first instance with offices throughout the country. Each country has some other courts that, like the Bankruptcy Court in the United States or the Summary Court in Japan, are typically situated below the entry-level court of general jurisdiction. In each system there is an assumption that a losing party has a right to appeal the determination of the entry-level court to the next level. In each system the appeal level court is collegial in character. In each system the losing party at the entry-level has a relatively short period of time in which to decide whether to file an appeal. Beyond these fundamentals the two systems are significantly different. They may be the same structurally, but in function and purpose they share nothing in common. In process they are also fundamentally different.

In the American federal system the District Court is the basic trial level court. The basic function of the District Court is to try the facts in the matter and compile a factual record. With this record in hand and with the facts in the matter fixed by this record, the District Court can make its decision. If dissatisfied the losing party may appeal to the Circuit Court of Appeals. The District Court's decision as to the fact is made by the jury in a jury trial and by the judge in a case tried without a jury. Factual determinations made by a jury have constitutional protection against

1 Because of its Federalism character the classifications of courts in the United States varies from State to State. Some states may have only one level of appeal. Some states may still retain the difference between courts of equity and courts of law at the entry-level court. But fundamentally the States have systems similar to the federal system described above although they may have only two levels instead of three.

against change at the appeal level, except for cases where the jury clearly made an error. Factual determinations of a judge have less weight before the appeal court but nonetheless have substantial weight. Weight is given in part because the trial judge has the advantage of seeing the witnesses in the witness box. Such personal view of witnesses makes determinations regarding credibility more reliable than credibility determinations based on a cold record. Of course District Courts decide cases based on facts and law. Most cases decided at the District Court level are not appealed. But the basic function of the District Court (when a case is appealed) is a factual function. When appealed the District Court's determination of legal matters is not given great weight. The District Court creates the factual record. It is on this record that all appeals are taken.

In a system designed for trial by jury, the establishment of the record in the court of first instance is essential. To retry the fact questions on appeal is to make the jury function virtually meaningless. To protect the jury trial right the facts found by the jury based on the record are the facts for the case forevermore. If the judge erred in allowing the jury to consider certain evidence that was inadmissible and if such error was not inconsequential but could have effected the jury's findings, the court has committed an error of law. The appeal court is not permitted to decide for itself how the jury would have decided if the case had been properly tried. The function of the court is to remand the case for a new trial so that a new, appropriate fact record can be created. The Circuit Court of Appeals is a court of law (not of fact). The function of the appeal court is to supervise the District Court and correct errors of law made by the District Court. If a party failed to present evidence at the trial court that would have changed the decision that is not a matter for consideration by the appeal court.

Sitting on top of the federal structure is the Supreme Court. It too is a court of law (although it has a rare first instance authority). Unlike the Circuit Court of Appeals it is not the function of the Supreme Court to correct errors made by the court from which it takes appeals. The function of the Supreme Court is to settle the law of the United States so that the law applied by the federal courts is applied uniformly throughout the country. Thus, many cases that are brought to the Court but are rejected without a hearing may be cases where the appeals court committed an error. The Court does not search out errors made by the court below to correct them. Rather, the Court principally takes cases where two Circuit Courts are in disagreement as to the law. In addition the Court will hear cases where the legal issue is of such great public moment that the Court feels it should be resolved at this point in time rather than waiting to see what the Circuit Courts may do with the issue. Whereas there is a first level right to appeal there is virtually no right to appeal to the second level—the Supreme Court. Rather, the Supreme Court is in control of its own docket and decides what cases it will hear and when.

Because the Circuit Court of Appeals and the Supreme Court are not in the fact-finding business (that is the function of the District Court) the arguments before these courts are fundamentally arguments as to the law. The factual record made in the District Court follows the case on appeal and legal issues are addressed to this factual record. Consequently, appeals are basically matters of brief writing and oral argument directed to question of law. Typically the appellant files a brief, the appellee responds and a short reply brief is permitted. Court rules establish the maximum length cf the respective briefs. If a party files a brief in excess of the maximum permitted, the court clerk will either return the brief or simply tear off the excess pages. After the case has been briefed, the case will be set for oral argument. Oral argument is limited to a fixed time period. The Supreme Court typically allows each side 30 minutes. In unusual circumstances the Court grants additional time. The argument is typically a spirited question and answer session with the Court asking for explanation of legal arguments or seeking answers to legal questions raised by the judges. The lawyer who comes prepared to read a 30-minute speech is soon off base and answering the judge's questions not delivering his prepared text. After oral argument the Court takes the matter under advisement and eventually issues its decision. In the Supreme Court cases heard during the court's term, which begins on the first Monday in October, are usually resolved before the end of June of the same term.

In Japan the function of the District Court is NOT to establish the record. Rather, it is the function of the District Court to begin the trial process. What this means is that the first level appeal is not what the American lawyer would typically consider as an appeal. Rather, it is a continuation of the trial. The appeal court may take additional and new evidence and indeed the parties may raise new issues not considered by the court below. The function of the first level appeal court is not to supervise the trial court and correct any errors that court may have made. The function of the appeal court is the same function as the trial court—to see that the party who should win does win. The first level appeal court is not even a "court of errors" in the sense that it corrects errors made by the initial court. Appeal is a chance for a second bite of the apple. A new trial may be had as to issues not fully tried at the first trial. Issues not raised at the first trial may be raised on appeal. Issues improperly tried at the first trial may be retried. Although there is a record created in the District Court, appeal is not on the basis of that record. The consequences of this distinction between American and Japanese practice are enormous. Cases on first level appeal may involve new witnesses. The appeal court may receive new evidence. The appeal is not limited to questions of law. Questions of law and questions of fact may be considered by the appeal court. Appeal is not exclusively on the basis of legal arguments. Because of the fundamentally different function of the appeal court the time to resolve appeals in Japan is substantially greater than in the United States. This is especially so if the appeal court receives new evidence. Whereas the facts are fixed when the parties leave the United States District Court, the facts have not yet been fixed when the parties leave the District Court in Japan. Whereas the trial is over when the parties rest in the United States District Court, the trial is not yet over after the District Court in Japan renders its decision.[2]

As a general rule the first level appeal is considered as a continuation of the trial. Although appeal is not considered lightly—because of the additional costs—it is considered frequently and is undertaken frequently in Japan.[3] A party contemplating litigation must consider the reality that the case will probably be tried twice. The additional costs can be considerable, as there will be a second attorney's fee and a second filing fee (typically 1½ times the initial filing fee).

The first level appeal from a judgment is known as a *koso* appeal. *Koso* appeals from District Court (and Family Court) judgments are taken to the High Court.[4] *Koso* appeals from judgments of the Summary Court that are subject to appeal are taken to the District Court.[5] Appeal is permitted of certain "rulings" made in the course of first level trial. Such appeals are called *kokoku* appeals. *Kokoku* appeals are permitted when the Code specifically allows such appeal. For example, when a challenge to a judge under Code Article 24 is denied, the Code permits an immediate *kokoku* appeal. An immediate *kokoku* appeal must be filed within one week of service of notice of the ruling being challenged.[6] Where there are multiple parties to a case and a determination is made that is subject to *kokoku* appeal the time limit within which to appeal may create complicated questions. Complications can arise if notice of the determination is served on the parties at different times. In theory each party has one week from service in which to appeal. There may, however, be factors that warrant allowing *kokoku* appeal by any party adversely affected within the time permitted for appeal by the last served party. In a case involving distribution of an estate the Supreme Court recognized the general rule under which each party entitled to make an immediate *kokoku* appeal has only one week from service on that party to file an appeal. The one-week period begins to run for each party on the date each party is served. Nonetheless, the court allowed

---

2 The concept of taking new evidence or rehearing old evidence at the first level of appeal is taken from the German procedure where, as long as it will not unduly delay the appeal, new evidence and new arguments may be submitted on appeal. Harald Koch & Frank Diedrich, CIVIL PROCEDURE IN GERMANY (Kluwer Law International, 1998) sec. 157. This is a common feature of civil law systems. See, ALI/UNIDROIT Principles and Rules of Transnational Civil Procedure, Proposed Final Draft (3/9/04) 8.

3 Akira Mikazuki, Judicial System reprint in Hideo Tanaka, THE JAPANESE LEGAL SYSTEM 444, 465-468 (University of Tokyo Press, 1976).

4 The Court Organization Law Article 15 gives the High Court jurisdiction over first level appeals (civil and criminal) from the District Court (sitting as the first level trial court not as an appeal court from the Summary Court) and from the Family Court. The High Court also has *koso* appeal authority over certain criminal cases tried by the Summary Court.

5 Court Organization Law Article 24 (3). The Summary Court has a new small claims authority to handle small claim cases (300,00yen or less) in a one-day trial. Such cases may be appealed to the Summary Court that rendered the determination but may not be appealed to a higher court. CPR Rules 222; CCP Article 377. See Chapter 13.

6 CCP Article 332; under the Law for Determination of Family Affairs, Article 14 immediate *kokoku* appeal may be had within two-weeks of notice of the determination subject to immediate *kokoku* appeal.

a party to make an immediate *kokoku* appeal when appeal was filed outside that time period but within the one-week after service on the last served successor of the decedent. The basis for the decision was the general understanding of parties before the Family Court and advice given to the appellant by the court clerk that appeal could be filed up to the expiration date of the last served successor.[7]

Unlike *koso* appeals, some *kokoku* appeals may be made to the Supreme Court.[8] *Kokoku* appeals to the Supreme Court are permitted where the decision of the High Court on a *kokoku* appeal is asserted to be unconstitutional or where the High Court specially certifies the case to the Supreme Court.[9]

The procedure for *kokoku* appeal to the Supreme Court where the High Court certifies a question to the Supreme Court is new and of interest.[10] To qualify for certification the issue must meet certain conditions: a) the question is constitutional in nature, or b) the ruling is inconsistent with previous Supreme Court authority (or if there is no intervening Supreme Court determination a determination of the prewar Great Court of Judicature) or c) the High Court considers the issue of such moment for judicial proceedings that it should be immediately resolved by the Supreme Court.[11] The party seeking *kokoku* appeal must move the High Court for certification. This new procedure may be useful in resolving potential different approaches by High Courts in connection with procedural matters. As a consequence the new procedure may bring a needed uniformity to procedures nationwide.[12] In this sense the new provision adopts an approach similar to the Supreme Court of the United States disagreement among the circuits approach. On the other hand, the new procedure is inconsistent with the idea of giving the Supreme Court authority over its own docket. If the High Court certifies the question, the Supreme Court of Japan must accept the certification.

The *kokoku* appeal is filed with the court whose ruling is being challenged. This gives the judge (or if the ruling of a single judge on a panel is the subject of the *kokoku* appeal the entire panel) an opportunity to reconsider and reverse the ruling. If the Code permits an immediate *kokoku* appeal, the challenged ruling is automatically stayed during the time of the appeal.[13] Where a *kokoku* appeal is permitted although an immediate *kokoku* appeal is not provided, the reviewing court has discretion to stay the ruling.[14] Because there are situations where the case cannot proceed without a determination of the *kokoku* appeal—such as a rul-

7 See case No. 21 of 2003, 57 Minshu 10 (Sup. Ct. Petty Bench 11/13 /03) available through the web site of the Supreme Court of Japan.

8 Court Organization Law Article 7 (2).

9 CCP Article 336.

10 CCP Article 337.

11 CCP Article 330.

12 Takeshi Kojima, Japanese Civil Procedure in Comparative Law Perspective, 46 U. Kansas L. Rev. 687, 717 (1998).

13 CCP Article 334 (1).

14 CCP Article 334 (2).

ing denying a challenge to the judge hearing the original case—*kokoku* appeal may be utilized as a tactical device to delay a proceeding. Although a *kokoku* appeal may be a first level appeal, because it deals with rulings rather than judgments some *kokoku* appeals are not subject to Oral Argument. The court may require the appellant or other persons to appear and be questioned by the court concerning the appeal.[15]

The principal appeal process is appeal from the judgment in a case. The appeal period in Japan is very short. The appellant party must file the appeal no later than two weeks after being served with the judgment being appealed. Since the judgment in the case must be announced in open court and the judgment document served thereafter, it is possible to file a *koso* appeal even before the judgment document has been served.[16] On the other hand a party who believes that it will lose a case has no right to file a *koso* appeal until there is a judgment. Thus, if the first instance court makes known its probable judgment in an effort to get the parties to compromise and settle, the "losing party" has no right to immediately file a *koso* appeal. The reason for this rule is that as no judgment has been announced, there is no judgment to appeal from. As in the United States only the losing party may appeal. A party who wins but is dissatisfied with the court's reasoning cannot appeal, as it is the judgment that is appealed from not the reasoning behind the judgment.

The "notice of appeal" (to use the American term) is filed with the court whose judgment is being challenged. It must contain the following items of information: the names of the parties and their counsel (if any), identification of the judgment being appealed and a clear statement that first level appeal is being taken against said judgment.[17] Like the Complaint in the court of first instance, a judge of the court that will hear the appeal reviews the *koso* appeal document to determine whether the "notice of appeal" meets technical requirements. The review also considers whether the filing fee has been paid and the stamps attached to the appeal document.[18] The court is responsible for serving the *koso* appeal on the appellee. The appellant may be required to pay the costs of a summons ordering a party to appear (this is similar to the process with the initial Complaint). If stamps have not been attached or the summons fee prepaid as ordered, the appeal is dismissed by ruling.[19] As in the case of an order to dismiss a Complaint that fails to contain the necessary stamps (or where the plaintiff fails to prepay the summons fee when ordered to do so) dismissal of an appeal for these reasons is subject to *kokoku* appeal.[20] Both the first level trial court and the appeal court review the "notice of appeal" to determine whether appeal is obviously inappropriate and upon such

15 CCP Article 335.

16 CCP Article 285.

17 CCP Article 286.

18 CCP Article 288.

19 CCP Articles 288, 289, 291.

20 CPR Rule 176, Rule 57 and CCP Article 291 (2).

review either court may dismiss the appeal.[21] Once the presiding judge of the *koso* appeal court accepts the appeal, the judge will set the date for the first Oral Hearing. Typically it will be several months before such hearing is held. The clerk of the initial trial court needs time to assemble the file and deliver it to the *koso* appeal court. In addition time is needed for the court to schedule the first hearing date.

The notice of appeal need contain only a cursory amount of information to enable the appeal court to know who the parties are, what judgment is being appealed and that the appellee actually means to appeal the cause. However, because the presiding judge of the panel hearing the appeal (all appeals are heard by panels) will review the notice of appeal document, appellees take this opportunity to make a good first impression. As a result, the appeal document typically takes on the flavor of a first brief (Preliminary Document) setting forth the appellant's position. Because the appeal is a continuation of the trial and thus involves both questions of fact and law, the document setting out the reasons for appeal deals with both fact and law issues and contentions. Indeed, since the appeal is not limited to the factual record made below, the grounds for appeal may deal with facts never considered by or presented to the first level trial court. If the appellant fails to adequately address the reasons for reversal in the appeal document, it still has 50 days from filing the appeal to file a Preliminary Document setting forth reasons.[22] The presiding judge then sets the date for a responding brief by the appellee.[23] These briefs serve the same function in the appeal court as such briefs would serve in the initial trial court. Namely, they are the beginning documents for the court to use in its clarification process.

The clerk of the first instance court has the obligation to send the record of the entire case to the clerk of the appeals court.[24] Although the appeal is not "on the record" as would be the case in the United States, the record is important. All of the evidentiary matter taken in the court below is now a part of the appeal record as if taken in the appeal court. It is not necessary to retry the entire case and recall witnesses or authenticate documents. All of the trial work done below is before the appeal court.[25] In addition the appeal court is aware, through the record, of the actions taken by the parties below. Thus such important information as the attitude of the parties to in-court conciliation will be in the record as will the fact as to whether conciliation has been held. This may influence the appeals court as it too has the power to send the case to conciliation. Most importantly the court will know whether a party has been dilatory in its actions below. If for example a party failed to timely raise contentions before the close of the Preparation for Oral Ar-

21 CCP Articles 286, 290. Where the court of first instance makes such a ruling it is subject to *kokoku* appeal.

22 CPR Rule 182.

23 CPR Rule 183.

24 CPR Rule 174.

25 CCP Article 298.

gument stage that will be in the record as will the party's explanation for failure. This may be of importance to the court if the same party attempts on appeal to raise issues that were not raised in a timely fashion at the original trial. The record below becomes a part of the record before the appeal court but it is not the sole record for the court.

As the appeal process is really a continuation of the trial the appeal court may take testimony of witnesses, may receive new evidence not presented below and may even hear evidence of facts or occurrences that happened since the rendering of the original judgment. Similarly the appealing party is not restricted to the arguments, claims and contentions made below. The appellant is not restricted to the defenses raised below. However, a new counterclaim can only be made if the appellant consents.[26] In a representative action, new parties can be added and their claims considered at the appeal level only if the opposition consents.[27] The case is simply opened for a new trial—with some of the work having already been done at the first level. If deemed important the appeal court can recall a witness who testified at the first level and have the witness re-examined. On the *koso* appeal, a party may not argue that the court of first instance lacked jurisdiction except where the lack of jurisdiction is alleged to arise because there is a different court that had exclusive jurisdiction over the matter.[28]

All of the procedures discussed in Chapters 8 and 9 relating to the pre-Oral Argument stage of the case and the Oral Argument stage of the case are incorporated by reference into the procedures before the *koso* appeal court.[29] Thus the appeal court will meet with the parties to discuss such matters as the scheduling of Preliminary Documents (briefs), amendment of the claim in the case (including the question of adding additional parties and claims in a representative action), and the filing of a counterclaim. As was the case in the first instance court, failure of a party to meet the time schedule set by the court requires explanation.[30] The provision for making Inquiry is applicable at first level appeal. The court may set Preparation for Oral Argument sessions for discussions with the parties and the court will engage (as did the lower court) in clarifying the contentions, issues, facts and evidence in the case. The parties may request and the court may order the production of documents, the court may seek the assistance of an expert commissioner, etc. During the Preparation stage the court at the appeal level may utilize the same round table meeting procedures and the same electronic communications media as was the case in first instance. In other words virtually every thing procedurally is the same as had been the case below.

---

26 CCP Article 300.

27 CCP Article 300 (3). A party's arguing the merits of the counterclaim or additional claim presented in the representative action can evidence consent.

28 CCP Article 299.

29 CPR Rules 179, 180, 181.

30 CCP Article 301.

As a practical matter the effect of holding new pre-Oral Argument steps means that parties are again subject to the requirement to make timely presentation of their contentions and factual allegations. To the common law lawyer this appears confusing. If the issues were not raised at the first stage of the case, the common law lawyer sees the raising of the issues on appeal as untimely. Since appeal is a continuation of the trial process, this is not confusing to the Japanese litigant. Indeed, the Diet specifically rejected a strongly worded preclusion section modeled after the German law preclusion (on appeal) provisions. Instead the Diet opted for a much more limited provision even when dealing with scheduling under the new complicated case procedure.[31] As Japanese judges are looking to achieve substantive justice, preclusion that would prohibit an important contention or fact would be counterintuitive and out of step with the function of the judge and the court. Of course, in truly inappropriate cases—such as the case where the party seeking to raise a totally new defense had doctored records and based its original defense on those falsified records only to admit the doctoring some nine years later when it sought to change the basis for its defense—the court can apply its preclusion power under Code Article 157. Although the appeal court may preclude new issues relying on Article 157 of the Code, it is not without significance that Book 3 of the Code (the Book dealing with appeal) specifically incorporates Articles 167 and 178 into the rules applicable on appeal. Articles 167 and 178 merely require an explanation for late action.[32] This represents an intentional choice made by the drafters. This choice discloses the preference of the Code for explanation rather than preclusion.

As the evidence shows that many parties who are not represented at the initial trial level are represented at the appeal level, it is reasonable for the courts to expect new issues of both fact and law to be presented on appeal. As Japanese parties have come to expect a second round of trial—perhaps this is why so many are not represented at the initial trial stage—it would be unfair to deny those parties an opportunity to present their best facts and arguments at the appeal (lawyer represented) stage. To prohibit a party from presenting important arguments would mean that the court is deprived of those arguments when it is making its decision. Such a situation is inconsistent with the civil law view that it is the role of the judge (not the parties) to discover the relevant facts. It is also inconsistent with the judge's role in rendering a correct decision. It would be inconsistent with the Japanese judiciary's view that it is its function to do substantive justice and it would run counter to a long history of paternalistic Japanese judges.

---

31 Koichi Miki "Roles of Judges and Attorneys under the Non-Sanction Scheme in Japanese Civil Procedure" delivered at the Symposium on Multiple Roles and Interaction of Judges and Attorneys in Modern Civil Litigation held at Chuo-o University, 6/1/03 p. 17.

32 See, Yasuhei Taniguchi, The 1996 Code of Civil Procedure of Japan—A Procedure for the Coming Century?, 45 American Journal of Comparative Law 767, 789 (1997).

Moreover, as appellants are successful in approximately 25% of all appeals,[33] there appears to be good reason for High Courts to carefully consider new contentions and evidence at the *koso* appeal level.

On the other hand, it is clear that it was the intent of the 1996 Code and the 2003 provisions to speed up the appeal process by reducing the appeal as a means for retrying the entire case. The Code attempts to utilize two methods to achieve this end: a) reducing the *de novo* aspects of evidence taking at the High Court level to be consistent with the concept of early "clarification" of issues and facts so that the trial is unhampered by pretrial matters. b) Utilizing the new procedures of scheduling and Preparation for Oral Argument at the High Court level to more quickly handle cases. To achieve its goal of speeding up the *koso* appeal process the Code must rely on the High Court judges. There is evidence that High Courts in Japan are using the new Code to move cases more quickly than previously. Thus there has been a sharp drop in the number of witnesses heard at the appeal level. This drop is noticeable at both the High Court level and at the District Court level when the District Court sits as the *koso* appeal court hearing appeals from judgments of the Summary Court. For example, the number of third-person witnesses heard at the *koso* appeal level at the High Court has declined by almost 50% since 1996. The same is true of the number of party witnesses heard by the appeals court. The statistics show that the number of party and third-person witnesses heard per 100 cases in the High Court has declined from 37 witnesses in 1996 to 19.7 witnesses in 2001:[34]

Percentage of Cases Where the High Court Received New Evidence in Normal Civil Cases on Appeal

Year	Third-Person Witness	Party Witness	Court Expert	Other
1996	19.0	18.0	1.4	0.6
1997	16.3	15.8	1.4	0.4
1998	15.4	14.9	1.4	0.4
1999	13.8	12.6	1.3	0.3
2000	11.4	9.7	1.2	0.3
2001	10.0	9.7	0.9	0.2

It is not clear whether this decline is caused by the High Courts seeking to actively reduce the number of witnesses heard because the courts are trying to reduce the

33 Masafumi Kodama & Jay Tyndall, Kitahama Law Office, on the web at *www.Masafumi Kodama & Jay Tyndall, Kitahama.or.jp/English/litigatn.htm* at page 6 of 13.

34 Carl F. Goodman, Japan's New Civil Procedure Code: Has it Fostered a Rule of Law Dispute Resolution Mechanism, 29 Brooklyn Journal of International Law 511 (2004). The Brooklyn Journal of International Law has given permission for the use and copying of this material.

de novo aspects of the appeal process or whether the decline in number of witnesses at the High Court is simply a reflection of the desire of all courts to reduce the number of witnesses so as to reduce the time taken in hearing witness testimony. Thus, there was also a sharp decline in witness testimony heard at the District Court when the District Court was acting as the initial trial court. What is clear is that in addition to hearing fewer live witnesses on appeal the High Courts have cut the average time it takes to hear a *koso* appeal from 11.3 months in 1992 to 7.9 months in 2001:[35]

Average Disposition Time (months) at District court and High Court		
Year	**District court**	**High Court**
1992	10.9	11.3
1993	10.1	11.2
1994	9.8	10.9
1995	10.1	10.6
1996	10.2	9.9
1997	10.0	9.9
1998	9.3	9.8
1999	9.2	9.0
2000	8.8	8.4
2001	8.5	7.9

Even though the courts have reduced the time for hearing the average appeal, the fact remains that only about 30% of all cases that were determined by District Court judgments and appealed were decided by the High Court in one year or less. What is more troubling is that more than 50% of *koso* appeal cases require more than two years for resolution at the High Court level.[36] Appeal cases lasting more than 5 years are not uncommon.[37] It is apparent that in a significant number of cases High Court appeal of judgments results in substantial delay. While such delay is inconsistent with the judicial system's stated intention of resolving cases quickly, it does act as a spur to plaintiffs to settle cases at the District Court level. The ability of the High Court to speed up the process of appeal in individual cases

35 Carl F. Goodman, Japan's New Civil Procedure Code: Has it Fostered a Rule of Law Dispute Resolution Mechanism, 29 Brooklyn Journal of International Law 511 (2004). The Brooklyn Journal of International Law has given permission for the use and copying of this material.

36 Carl F. Goodman, Japan's New Civil Procedure Code: Has it Fostered a Rule of Law Dispute Resolution Mechanism, 29 Brooklyn Journal of International Law 511 (2004).

37 Masafumi Kodama & Jay Tyndall, Kitahama Law Office, on the web at *www.Masafumi Kodama & Jay Tyndall, Kitahama.or.jp/English/litigatn.htm* at page 6 of 13.

may be seen by defendants as a spur to settle. The High Court will have before it the entire record of proceedings below. As a result the court will know, especially in cases where an in-court conciliation commission was utilized and the court entered a proposed settlement that the defendant rejected, if the defendant was the party refusing to agree to a reasonable settlement. Thus, the slow pace of resolution of High Court appeals from judgment cases may assist the more speedy resolution of cases at the District Court level through compromise. Further, as Japanese judges have the right to propose settlement at any stage of the case including *koso* appeal[38] and as in-court conciliation can proceed while a case is pending on *koso* appeal, the slow pace of dispositions at the High Court level also acts as a spur to settlement of appeal cases. It has been estimated that almost 35% of all *koso* appeal cases are resolved through settlement.[39]

The speed at which cases are decided at the High Court is entirely in the hands of the High Court judges who have discretion as to how much new evidence and what new contentions and arguments will be permitted. The Code gives the court authority to reject contentions and arguments not timely made and for which there is no acceptable explanation. As all arguments and evidentiary matters should have been discussed at the Preparation for Oral Argument stage at the District Court, the pace of appeals can most powerfully be affected by the interpretation the High Courts place on their preclusion authority. To date it does not appear that the High Courts are using the preclusion authority to consistently accelerate High Court appeals of contentious matters.

The appeal results in taking away the finality of the lower court's judgment and that judgment is no longer binding on the losing party.[40] In effect, the filing of the appeal stays execution on the judgment. If the initial level court in a case involving monetary relief has entered an order permitting provisional execution on property needed to satisfy the judgment, the appeal does not operate as a stay and provisional execution to ensure that the judgment will be paid (as distinguished from compulsory execution under which the judgment is paid) may be had. The appeal court may also, on written motion, decide that compulsory execution should be allowed and a security bond posted.[41] The court of first instance has discretion in determining whether the winning party should be compelled to post security as a condition of provisional execution.[42] The first instance court may enter a judgment and refuse to grant the winning party provisional execution. When provisional execution is permitted that fact and the determination regarding secu-

38 CCP Article 89.

39 Masafumi Kodama & Jay Tyndall, Kitahama Law Office, on the web at *www.Masafumi Kodama & Jay Tyndall, Kitahama.or.jp/English/litigatn.htm* at page 6 of 13.

40 CCP Article 116.

41 CCP Article 398; CPR Rule 239.

42 CCP Article 259.

rity must be contained in the judgment issued by the court.[43] Provisional executions are utilized in cases seeking money damages and are used for the same reasons as provisional attachments in the United States, namely to protect assets available for execution from being dissipated or hidden. While provisional attachment comes at the start of a case, provisional execution comes at the end of the first stage of the trial (as the *koso* appeal is actual stage two of the trial). Provisional execution is designed to prevent the *koso* appeal process from becoming a means for avoiding payment of a judgment. Since the first instance court has decided the matter based on the Oral Argument, it is typical in money damages cases for the court to enter a judgment containing a provisional execution.

The *koso* appeal court also has the authority to issue provisional execution orders. The entire court record comes to the appeals court, including those parts of the record dealing with portions of the case that might not be the subject of the judgment issued. To protect assets in connection with the parts of the case not yet decided, the *koso* appeals court is given specific authority to enter a provisional execution order.[44] In this way appeal from a partial judgment cannot be used to buy time to secrete assets that otherwise could be used to satisfy potential future judgments in the same case. If an order for provisional execution has been entered as part of the initial judgment, the appellant may ask the *koso* appeal court to lift the provisional execution. If such a request is made, the *koso* appeal court will likely require the posting of security—the equivalent of an appeal bond in the United States. The amount of the security may be quite high if the damages awarded are high such as may be the case in modern patent cases. Thus, a company that was ordered to pay its employee 20billion yen for remuneration for a patented discovery was required by the *koso* appeal court to post a bond of 10billion yen.[45]

Just as the appellant may go beyond the arguments it made below in seeking a reversal, so too the appellee and the *koso* appeal court may raise issues that were not the basis for the lower court's decision. Thus, the appeal court may find that the lower court was entirely wrong in its findings of fact and in its legal reasoning and still affirm the judgment. Such affirmation may be based on the new facts found by the appeal court and/or different legal reasoning leading the court to conclude that the winning party below still deserves to win.[46] On the other hand, the court may not go beyond the four corners of the portion of the judgment appealed from in its decision. In other words if the appellant only appealed from part of the judgment, the court on appeal may not reverse the portion of the judgment not ap-

---

43 CCP Article 259 (4). If there is no provision contained in the judgment the winning party may move the court to modify its judgment or the court may *sua sponte* modify its judgment to contain such a provision.

44 CCP Article 294.

45 See, Nichia Deposits 10 Billion Yen in Spat over Patent Royalties, Japan Times on Line 3/7/04.

46 CCP Article 302.

pealed.[47] Nor, as a general rule, can the court enter an award that is worse for the appellant than the judgment below unless the appellee has taken a cross appeal. This is consistent with the general philosophy that the parties are in charge of the scope of the case[48] even though the court may be in charge of the procedures in the case. The court may consider certain matters *sua sponte* such as questions concerning the authority of the lower court to have determined the case in the first instance. If the appeals court reverses the lower court (and this happens in almost ¼ of the cases) it may remand the case to the lower court for further proceedings or, if remand is not required it may enter its own judgment in the case.[49] Most cases do not require remand. In the United States, remand is more usual because the appeal court has no authority to take evidence. Thus, if the court below made an error that related to evidence or made an error of law that requires new or additional evidence to be taken that can only be done in the United States via remand. Since the *koso* appeal is really a continuation of the trial in most cases there is no need to send the case back to the first instance trial court. All the necessary evidence can be taken in the appeal court. Where a case is remanded on procedural grounds, the procedural rulings of the appeal court act as law of the case on the remand.[50] If the judgment below is reversed because the court of first instance had no jurisdiction over the matter but another court in Japan had the exclusive jurisdiction, the appeal court should remand the case to the court having jurisdiction.[51]

Because the *koso* appeal operates as a stay of execution (except if provisional execution is permitted—and even then it is usual for the *koso* appeal court to lift the provisional execution if the losing party posts adequate security) and because the *koso* appeal may take several years to complete, there is the potential for abuse of the appeal process to delay the inevitable. To avoid such abuse of the *koso* appeal process the Code provides that when the appeals court dismisses a *koso* appeal it may, should it decide that the purpose of the appeal was simply delay, require the appellant to pay up to 10 times the *koso* appeal filing fee.[52] Such a penalty is considered as a nonpenal fine and is subject to collection by the public prosecutor.[53] The levying of such a nonpenal fine is extraordinary and is not permitted if any part of the appeal is granted or the matter is reversed on the merits. Moreover, if the case moves to a further appeal level (*jokoku* appeal) the *jokoku* appeals court may affirm the decision but reverse the fine.[54] (In the case of a matter initiated in the District Court the *jokoku* appeal court would be the Supreme Court while for a case that was started in the Summary Court it would be the High Court.) The fine

47 CCP Article 304.

48 CCP Article 246.

49 CCP Article 307, 308.

50 CCP Article 325 (3).

51 CCP Article 309.

52 CCP Article 303.

53 CCP Article 189.

54 CCP Article 303 (4).

is automatically reversed if the *jokoku* appeals court reverses the decision of the *koso* appeals court. To protect against dissipation of assets in the event that a *jokoku* appeal is taken, the *koso* appeals court may include in its judgment a provisional execution.[55]

As the provisions of Chapter 4 of the Code dealing with Judgment are made applicable to *koso* appeals, the requirements for announcing a judgment in open court and advising the parties as to when judgment will be announced are applicable to *koso* appeal. This, of course, gives the appeal court the same opportunity as is given the initial trial level court to attempt to use the proposed decision as a means of obtaining a settlement in the case. Moreover, the same principles regarding burden of proof and the same freedom to make its determinations on the merits from the totality of the record are applicable on appeal.

The completion of the *koso* appeal by a final order (rather than a remand) effectively ends the "trial" of the case. If the *koso* appeal court renders a judgment in the matter either by dismissing the appeal or reversing and entering its own final judgment, the fact-finding phase of the case is complete. Like District Courts, the High Court decides cases on a consensus basis. The judges of the court are required to sign the opinion of the court and while there may be disagreements when the panel is deliberating the matter, there is no dissenting opinion.

Not all Summary Court cases that are appealed go to the District Court, and not all District Court cases that are appealed go to the High Court. There is a procedure under which the parties to the case may decide to skip the *koso* appeal process entirely and move the case directly to the *jokoku* appeal. This is known as a "jumping appeal."[56] In such case the "trial" phase of the case is completed when the court of first instance renders its judgment since facts are not at issue in the *jokoku* appeal procedure.[57] In addition, the new one-day speedy trial process for small claim matters pending at the Summary Court precludes appeal.

B. *Jokoku* Appeal or Appeal as to Matters of Law

The second stage appeal, the *jokoku* appeal, is more comfortable for American lawyers. This is an appeal on the record made below and is an appeal that is limited to legal matter. The *jokoku* appeal court does not review factual matter—this was the job of the trial courts through the initial trial and the continuation of the trial at the *koso* appeal level. Indeed, the *jokoku* appeal court is bound by the facts found below and cannot go behind those facts. The *jokoku* court may not make new factual findings.[58] As this is a second stage appeal, it may be: a) an appeal to the High Court from a judgment of the District Court sitting as the *koso* appeal

55 CCP Article 310.

56 CCP Article 281; see, Hiroyuki Hata & Go Nakagawa & Takehisa Nakagawa, JAPAN CONSTITUTIONAL LAW Sec. 137 (Kluwer Law International, 2001).

57 CCP Article 321.

58 CCP Article 321.

court from a determination of the Summary Court, or b) an appeal to the Supreme Court from a High Court sitting as *koso* appeal court from a District Court judgment. *Jokoku* appeal may in limited situations be a first level appeal. When the High Court is sitting as the court of first instance in an insurrection case or hearing an appeal from a determination of the Fair Trade Commission, appeal from the High Court decision is *jokoku* appeal. Panels of three judges hear appeals to the High Court. When there is a shortage of judges, a District Court judge may be assigned to a High Court panel. Except in rare cases where it meets as a Grand Bench, the Supreme Court hears cases in panels of five Justices. Supreme Court panels do not have a revolving membership—the same five Justices make up the panel and a new panel is not created for each case being heard. Grand Bench determinations are quite unusual and involve serious constitutional issues. Not all constitutional issues are considered worthy of Grand Bench determination. There has been only one Grand Bench argument in the past year.

For many years there have been complaints that the Supreme Court of Japan is overworked and that its caseload is out of control. It has been urged that this is one of the reasons that some opinions of the court appear rushed and may not be as reasoned as litigants or professors of law might prefer. Furthermore, the right of many appellants to appeal to the Supreme Court resulted in delay in appeal cases. In an effort to resolve this problem, a party's right to appeal has been narrowed. In addition a form of certiorari appeal by permission has been added.

The right to take a *jokoku* appeal to the Supreme Court has been narrowed to cases where:

a) Constitutional questions are raised;

b) Certain procedural issues that affect the validity of the decision have been raised. These procedural issues are: improper composition of the court, improper participation in the decision-making by a judge not permitted to be involved in the case, the court lacked jurisdiction because another court had exclusive jurisdiction over the matter or no court had jurisdiction over the matter, the lawyer who appeared for the party in the case was not authorized to conduct the Oral Argument, the Oral Argument was held but not in public, and the judgment appealed from either has no reasoning given for the decision or if reasons are given they are inconsistent or contradictory.[59]

For a *jokoku* appeal to the High Court from a District court determination when the District Court sits as an appeal court there is a third basis for *jokoku* appeal. This basis is that the decision of the District Court was based on an incorrect understanding of the law.[60] In either event the decision of the *jokoku* appeal court is to be based on law and not fact. The Oral Argument stage of the case (the fact finding stage of the case) ended with the *koso* appeal.

---

59 CCP Article 312 (1), (2). See, Masako Kamiya, Narrowing the Avenues to Japan's Supreme Court, 4 Australian Journal of Asian Law 53, 57 (2002) (appeal as of right restricted to misinterpretation or violation of constitution and serious procedural defects.)

60 CCP Article 312 (3).

For cases that do not fall into the categories where appeal to the Supreme Court as of right is permitted, the appellant is entitled to petition the Supreme Court for permission to appeal. Petitions for discretionary *jokoku* appeal to the Supreme Court are based on either of two grounds:

a) The decision is inconsistent with a previous precedent of the Supreme Court or its prewar predecessor The Great Court of Judicature or, if there is no highest court precedent on the issue the decision is inconsistent with a previous High Court precedent where the High Court acted as an appeal court;

b) The court should exercise its discretion to hear the matter because of the legal importance of the issue.[61]

The Code of Civil Procedure does not define the term important. Such definition is left up to the court. However, the Ministry of Justice is of the view that such matters as cases of first impression, overruling precedent that is considered no longer applicable and correcting interpretations of law by the lower courts are all within the definition of important matters.[62] This approach of the Ministry is consistent with its historical approach to the court's jurisdiction and its objections to limiting the court's role to important issues rather than acting as a court of errors. Should the court accept this interpretation there appears to be little to separate the present certiorari system from the old as of right appeal system, except that appeals now must be made by motion. How the court will interpret its authority remains to be seen. It is likely that the court will be less liberal in accepting appeals than the Ministry suggests. The Ministry's approach notably fails to take into account a factor that would be high on the Supreme Court of the United States' list of important elements—how the decision below affects the public interest particularly where an action of the government is being challenged. The reason for this omission may be the refusal to acknowledge that it is the role of the Judicial Branch to become involved in matters that affect the public interest or the administration of laws by the government. Rather, the Ministry approach seeks to cabin the court's role to simply interpreting statutes and the Constitution without considering giving weight to questions of public policy and public interest. The idea that the court should exercise its discretion to hear cases of first impression is inconsistent with the approach of the Supreme Court of the United States to certiorari review. In the United States the court would avoid hearing cases of first impression to allow the Circuit Courts time to explore the various issues of first impression. Only when a disagreement between the circuits was presented or where the court felt the issue was of such importance and the Circuit Courts might be in error would the court step in. Merely being a matter of first impression is grounds for rejection rather than acceptance of certiorari review in the United States.

The American influence can be seen in the basis for discretionary *jokoku* appeal to the Supreme Court. By specifying that one ground for granting review is that the

61 CCP Article 318 (1).

62 See, Masako Kamiya, Narrowing the Avenues to Japan's Supreme Court, 4 Australian Journal of Asian Law 53, 64-65 (2002) referring to the handbook prepared by the Ministry of Justice.

decision being challenged is inconsistent with another High Court ruling (and there is no Supreme Court precedent on the matter) the Code appears to be pointing the court in the direction of taking discretionary appeals when it is necessary to do so to make the law in Japan common throughout the eight High Court jurisdictions. In essence this aspect of the Code says that discretionary appeal should be permitted when there is a disagreement among the High Courts (analogous to a disagreement among the circuits in the United States). This same rationale permeates the ability of the High Court to certify a *kokoku* appeal to the Supreme Court. A bit of common law philosophy can be seen in the Code.

A decision of the Supreme Court, like all other judgments, binds only the parties to the action in front of the court. The civil law does not recognize *starie decisis* and hence the court's reasoning is, in theory, not controlling on the lower courts in future cases. On the other hand the strong hand of the judicial Secretariat as the arm of the Supreme Court is at work to make the law throughout Japan uniform (not simply the law but as discussed earlier even the question of what damages to award). By directing the Supreme Court to give consideration to issues where there is a disagreement among the High Courts the Code is in essence directing the High Courts to follow the Supreme Court's precedent—as if it were *starie decisis*. This same philosophy is seen in the Code's permitting discretionary appeal because the decision being appealed is inconsistent with highest court precedent. In this regard the 1996 Code is moving the Supreme Court's jurisprudence more in line with the American view that an appeal court should exercise supervisory authority over the lower court and seek to make the law in the country uniform. Such a philosophy is basically inconsistent with the previous notion that the appeal court is a court of errors whose function is to correct errors made by lower courts. Here the view is not that appeal should be permitted because the court below made a wrong decision but, rather, it is being exercised to assure that all of the courts follow the same law. This approach has not met with uniform approval. The idea that the Supreme Court of Japan is a court of errors has strong supporters in Japan. These supporters argue that the American approach adopted in the 1996 Code is inconsistent with the Rule of Law on the theory that the Rule of Law requires that "correct" or "just" decisions be made in all cases.[63] On the other hand, even critics of the loss of the right to appeal based on error recognize that a court

63 See, Masako Kamiya, Narrowing the Avenues to Japan's Supreme Court, 4 Australian Journal of Asian Law 53, 64 (2002). It is suggested that this represents a misunderstanding of the Rule of Law concept. The idea behind the Rule of Law is not that a just result is assured in each and every case. Indeed, the Rule of Law has little to do with "just" results. Rather, the central idea behind the Rule of Law as applied to relations between individuals and non-government entities is that a consistent rule whose parameters are known ahead of time is applied to the voluntary relationship established between the parties through, for example, their contract. In some cases the end result may appear to be "unjust" because of a change in circumstance but the function of the Rule of Law is not to do justice but to enable parties to enter into voluntary relationships with a relatively clear understanding of what they are agreeing to. Justice enters the picture where the government is implicated and here the function of the Rule of Law is to carry forward the concepts of Justice enshrined in the Constitution and assure that government does not infringe on rights of the public. By insisting on a "just" result in each and every case be-

whose docket is so crowded that it cannot devote the time needed for adjudication of cases before it, cannot do justice for all litigants.[64] The Code appears to represent a compromise between those who sought to restrict Supreme Court authority and those who sought to retain the two levels of appeal as of right extant before the 1996 amendment to the Code.

Japan's Supreme Court retains some of its court of error functions. The court of error function of the High Court sitting as a *jokoku* appeal court is specifically recognized by the Code through Article 312 (3). This Article permits appeal on the ground that an error of law influenced the decision. That same basis for appeal is not contained in the Supreme Court's authority and is not even contained in the reasons why the Supreme Court may grant discretionary appeal. However the Supreme Court can grant discretionary appeal whenever it believes a case presents an important legal question. This broad authority makes it possible for the Supreme Court to remain a court of errors when a legal error affects the judgment—as set out in the Justice Ministry approach. The court of error function when fact issues have been incorrectly decided below appears to have been completely removed from the Supreme Court's jurisdiction.[65]

It was the hope of the reformers that this limitation on the Supreme Court's appeal as of right jurisdiction and the grant of an American style certiorari jurisdiction would limit the number of cases brought to the court. The purpose of the amendment was to relieve the court of its heavy workload leading to more reasoned opinions on more important matters. Limiting appeal as of right would also speed up the process of final decision-making in civil cases by reducing the number of cases appealed. As the number of cases appealed to the Supreme Court declined, the number of cases finally decided at the High Court level would increase, meaning a greater number of cases would be finally resolved at an earlier stage. In addition by reducing the cases heard by the court the court could decide more cases faster.

However, the reform does not appear to have achieved its desired objective. Although the court's Rules require that the grounds for appeal and grounds for requesting discretionary appeal must be specifically[66] and separately stated, the Rules allow both to be submitted in a single appeal document.[67] (Where both are in the same document, the document must disclose that both an appeal and motion

---

tween non-government entities the Rule of Law may in fact be damaged as the rules to govern the consensual conduct of the parties may be deemed different by a court seeking to do "justice" than the rules whose shadow the parties acted under.

64 Masako Kamiya, Narrowing the Avenues to Japan's Supreme Court, 4 Australian Journal of Asian Law 53, 65 (2002).

65 Article 321 makes facts found below, even when there has been a jumping appeal and thus no second trial at the *koso* appeal level, binding on the court. In the jumping appeal situation the court is specifically restricted so that it may not reverse based on an error in fact finding. (CCP Article 321 (2)). It would seem that such rule must also apply to regular appeals.

66 See, CPR Rule 190 and 192.

67 CPR Rule 188.

for permission to appeal are contained therein.) Since both the appeal and motion need to be filed in the same 14 days from service of the judgment time period there is no reason to file separate documents. When filing the appeal the appellant must pay the filing fee (two times the filing fee for the original Complaint) as well as an estimate of the costs of serving the appeal documents.[68] Parties that file an appeal to the court now typically join with their appeal documents a petition seeking discretionary appeal in the event the court finds the matter is not subject to appeal as of right. A judge of the court whose decision is being appealed will review the appeal papers and if there is a defect in the appeal the judge will order correction. Failure to make the ordered correction leads to a dismissal of the appeal.[69] The rules dealing with service of the appeal as of right document and the motion for discretionary appeal document are the same. By making all of the procedural steps for appeal as of right and discretionary appeal identical and by making the fees for each the same there are economies of scale for the appellant in simply filing one appeal document raising both appeal as of right and discretionary appeal motion. There is no additional cost and little to lose by joining both in one document.[70]

Not only are more appeals being filed with the Supreme Court since the Code restricted the court's appeal jurisdiction but also the court itself appears to be undermining its own authority to control its docket. While the docket of the Supreme Court of the United States is declining each year so that only about 100 cases are heard on Certiorari each year, in Japan the number of petitions for discretionary review that are granted appears to be rising each year:[71]

Year	Filed Cases		Cert. Granted	Location of Termination of Decision		
	Appeal / cert.			Appeal granted	cert. denied	cert. granted
1997	2741	—	—	3062	—	—
1998	2542	768	1	3040	370	0
1999	2160	1770	12	2389	1528	11
2000	2418	2106	26	2410	1820	19
2001	2323	2314	53	2298	2089	40

68 CPR Rule 187. Rule 199 incorporates Rule 187 by reference in situations where a motion for permission to appeal is filed.

69 CCP Article 318 and Articles 314, 313, 288, and 137 incorporated by reference.

70 For a discussion of the technical steps involved in both appeal and motion for discretionary appeal see, Masako Kamiya, Narrowing the Avenues to Japan's Supreme Court, 4 Australian Journal of Asian Law 53, 57 (2002).

71 Carl F. Goodman, Japan's New Civil Procedure Code: Has it Fostered a Rule of Law Dispute Resolution Mechanism, 29 Brooklyn Journal of International Law 511 (2004). The Brooklyn Journal of International Law has given permission for the use and copying of this material.

The above discloses that Japanese lawyers are more prone to file appeals and requests for certiorari today than they were prior to the 1996 reforms. Thus in 1997 (before the effective date of the Code) there were 2741 civil appeals filed while in 2001 the court had to consider 2314 requests for discretionary appeals as well as 2323 cases where attorneys filed civil appeal cases. (Moderating this rise is the fact that some appeal cases are also discretionary certiorari cases. Such cases are double counted in the court's figures.) It is true that the court rejected most of the discretionary appeal cases but the trend for granting certiorari review is clearly on the upswing. The court granted twice as many petitions for discretionary review in 2001 than it did in 2000. While it granted certiorari in only approximately ½ the number of cases that the Supreme Court of the United States hears in a year the Supreme Court of Japan also has appeal as of right jurisdiction.

Although the average number of months it takes to dispose of a case filed with the Supreme Court has been declining, the reality is that the time for the Supreme Court to decide a case on the merits has probably not changed significantly. The statistics show:[72]

Disposition of Civil Cases in the Supreme Court—Number of Months	
Year	**Average Number of Months Pending**
1992	7.6
1993	9.3
1994	7.7
1995	7.0
1996	8.7
1997	9.5
1998	8.1
1999	6.6
2000	5.4
2001	5.3

Half of the court's workload was determining whether to deny certiorari review. Denial of certiorari cases should be resolved very quickly. In the United States such cases are usually not even considered as an initial matter by the Justices themselves.

72 Carl F. Goodman, Japan's New Civil Procedure Code: Has it Fostered a Rule of Law Dispute Resolution Mechanism, 29 Brooklyn Journal of International Law 511 (2004). The Brooklyn Journal of International Law has given permission for the use and copying of this material.

How the Supreme Court will eventually determine to function under its certiorari jurisdiction is uncertain and is likely to change if certiorari type motions inundate the court. It appears that the present system is to give consideration to all motions as if the motion carried its own weight in determining whether the issue presented was worthy of Court consideration. It appears as if the motion is assigned to a panel as would any appeal to the Supreme Court and motions are then assigned to individual Justices who make an initial determination as to whether or not the matter is worthy of Court consideration. Of course the individual Justices use the assistance of the judges assigned to the judicial Secretariat who perform many of the research functions performed by law clerks for the Justices in the United States. Unlike clerks for Justices in the United States, the legal assistants at the judicial Secretariat are full time judges on assignment to the Secretariat. These judges do not work for the individual Justices and are not assigned to individual Justices but, rather, work for the Secretariat itself. How much influence these judges actually have on the determination of whether or not to accept a case for discretionary review will be worked out over time.

After the initial Justice reviews the matter, a memorandum of some type is prepared so that the other Justices on the panel can understand the reasoning of the assigned Justice. The matter then goes to the other members of the panel for decision on whether to hear the appeal. If certiorari review is denied, the matter can be dismissed by order as distinguished from a judgment. The procedures for an order determination are simplified as compared to procedures for judgment. Thus a determination to deny a motion for discretionary appeal need not go through the formal stages of a judgment such as a written opinion announced in open court. Denial of a motion for discretionary appeal does not involve the briefing schedule required for an appeal as of right or a case in which discretionary appeal is granted.[73] The court's average time for handling cases has not declined by 50% as would be expected considering that denial of discretionary review occupied about half of the court's dispositions. It thus appears that the average time for the Supreme Court to resolve a civil appeal that falls within its jurisdiction has not declined. There do not appear to be reliable statistics comparing how long cases that do not fall within the court's jurisdiction but where appeal is nonetheless filed take to resolve. Nor are there statistics comparing such time with the time required prior to the 1996 reform.

Another factor to be determined and worked out over time is how "paternalistic" the Supreme Court will be in handling motions for discretionary appeal. For example, if a party fails to make an argument for exercise of discretion that the Justice reviewing the matter considers relevant, will the court nonetheless be in a position to accept the motion? While it appears that the *issues* the parties raise in the motion bind parties and the court, this does not mean that the court is bound by the *arguments* made for the grant of the motion. Will the court exercise discre-

73 Masako Kamiya, Narrowing the Avenues to Japan's Supreme Court, 4 Australian Journal of Asian Law 53, 59 (2002).

tion as in the United States to accept part of the motion and deny other parts? In other words will the court reject certain issues even if the court feels acceptance of the issues could change the result but the court feels the issues are not important from an overall law defining perspective and yet accept other issues in the same case that the court feels are sufficiently important to be heard? The main question is whether the views of the Justice Ministry (acceptance of which would keep the court bound into its court of errors role) will influence the court's approach to motions for discretionary appeal.

After the case has been orally argued to the Supreme Court the court will consider the matter and ultimately deliver its decision. Oral argument of the appeal in Japan is a rather sterile procedure with parties basically reading their briefs to the court and the court passively listening. Oral argument is not required in cases before the court. The decision may be to dismiss the appeal or to grant relief via reversing the judgment below (either in whole or in part).[74] When a judgment below is reversed, the usual recourse is to remand the matter to the inferior court,[75] however a judge who had previously heard the case below may not hear the case on remand.[76] If a judgment below is quashed and the matter remanded, any factual conclusions or legal rulings made by the Supreme Court bind the remand court.[77]

The denial of an appeal in Japan can be either because the appeal does not fall within the scope of the court's appeal jurisdiction or because it does fall within the court's jurisdiction but the court is not disposed to reverse the lower court. In dismissing an appeal the Supreme Court (as was the case with the High Court) is not bound by the arguments or reasoning of the court whose determination is on review. Thus the Supreme Court may disagree with the lower court's legal reasoning and nonetheless dismiss the appeal based on a different legal analysis that reaches the same result.[78] Judgments of the court must be publicly delivered. The parties are informed when the judgment will be delivered and the decision is given in open court on the scheduled date.[79]

Of course the speed within which the Supreme Court can handle civil appeals is also dependent on the workload the court has from criminal cases. If the court is "flooded" with criminal appeals this will have as great an inhibiting effect on quick resolution of civil cases as if the court is "flooded" with civil appeals. Here

---

74 CCP Article 326.

75 CCP Article 325. The Supreme Court may also remand the case to another inferior court of the same level as the court from which the judgment appealed from came. (325(2)).

76 CCP Article 325 (4).

77 CCP Article 325 (3).

78 CCP Article 302 incorporated by reference via Article 313.

79 Masako Kamiya, Narrowing the Avenues to Japan's Supreme Court, 4 Australian Journal of Asian Law 53, 59 (2002).

too the court's caseload has been increasing in recent years.[80] The Code of Criminal Procedure allows for more appeals as of right than the Code of Civil Procedure. Thus, while certiorari is the basis for appeal of a civil case where there is a claim that the decision below is inconsistent with a prior Supreme Court decision, such inconsistency gives rise to a right to appeal in a criminal case.

When the Supreme Court exercises its discretion and decides to hear a discretionary appeal, it must set forth the grounds on which it will hear the appeal.[81] Whether it is hearing the case pursuant to its discretionary authority or whether the case is an appeal as of right, the Supreme Court is limited in its review to the grounds set forth by the appellant. (The same rule applies where the *jokoku* appeal court is the High Court.)

Although the general rule is that a party may only get one *jokoku* appeal review, the fact that the High Court is sometimes the *jokoku* appeal court (hearing cases that started in the Summary Court) means that there may be unusual situations where the Supreme Court may hear *jokoku* appeals from the High Court sitting as a *jokoku* appeal court. These cases are limited to questions of unconstitutionality.[82]

Because the Supreme Court's authority is broadest when questions of constitutionality are raised, such questions are frequently raised in appeals to the court even though there are really no constitutional issues presented. As discussed earlier the court has found a law to be unconstitutional in only six cases. In addition, all courts in Japan are "case or controversy" courts that can only hear justiciable questions brought to the court by a party with judicial standing. The standing requirement in Japan is more strictly construed than in the United States. The court, as a case or controversy court, is limited to rendering judicial decisions rather than giving advisory opinions. Nonetheless the reality is that on issues of great moment in Japan where action of the government is challenged on constitutional grounds the court has frequently denied that a party has standing or has denied that there is a justiciable question and then has proceeded to discuss the substantive legal issue at great length, indicating the permissibility of the government's action. This has been particularly noticeable in the Article 9 "Renunciation of War" context.[83] The reason for this approach would appear to be the court's recognition that both the

---

80 Carl F. Goodman, Japan's New Civil Procedure Code: Has it Fostered a Rule of Law Dispute Resolution Mechanism, 29 Brooklyn Journal of International Law 511, 557 (2004).

81 CPR Rule 200.

82 CCP Article 327.

83 See, e.g., Sunakawa Case, Sakata v. Japan, Case No. 710 of 1959, 13 Keishu 3225 (Sup. Ct. Grand Bench, 12/16/59) available in English through the web site of the Supreme Court of Japan also available in English in John M. Maki, COURT AND CONSTITUTION IN JAPAN (University of Washington Press, 1964) 298—political question doctrine applicable but Court nonetheless discusses legality of government's action and indicates that such action is legally acceptable; Hyakuri Air Base, Ishizuka v. Japan, Case No. 164 and 165 of 1982 (Sup. Ct. Petty Bench, 6/20/89) available in English through the web site of the Supreme Court of Japan—Article 9 not applicable to private parties, but government right to build air base is not contrary to public mores.

public and the political system look to the court for guidance on issues that are law related even if the court cannot directly affect the determination.

Unlike determinations of inferior courts, Justices of the Supreme Court may write dissenting opinions. The writing of dissenting opinions is a relatively new phenomenon in Japan. Dissenting opinions were part of the American Occupation reform. In a country where harmony and consensus are the rule, the Supreme Court's use of the dissenting opinion is a sharp break with tradition—although the caustic dissents that are seen in the United States are not seen in Japan.

12

Administrative Litigation

To the American lawyer, litigation between the citizen and the government falls into either of two categories: a) criminal litigation instituted by the government to enforce the norms of the criminal law, or b) civil litigation either instituted by government to enforce its rights as a normal party or to enforce non-criminal law or instituted by the citizen against the government. Litigation by the citizen to prevent the government from taking some action or to compel the government to take some action is viewed as civil litigation and falls within the authority of the normal civil courts. In the civil law tradition the thinking is different.

To the civil law lawyer there are also two forms of litigation, private and public law matters. The normal civil case between persons or entities involves private law. Where the government is a party involved in private law activity then the matter is a private law matter. Where the government is prosecuting a violation of public law such as the criminal law or where the subject matter of the suit is public administration of the law it is a matter of public law. In many civil law countries a special Administrative Court handles litigation involving "public law" issues between the citizen and the government. It is the function of the Administrative Court to oversee the operations of administrative agencies to the extent that such agencies operate within the law and do not exceed the powers given to them by the law. An independent Administrative Court with a tradition of legal oversight—such as the French administrative judicial system—can effectively cabin the natural bureaucratic impulse to exceed the limits of power that may be seen as hamstringing the bureaucratic desire to do good. Such a court also is a useful device to allow outside judgment on interpretation and intent of the law. It can correct errors made by those too close to the administrative process and too closely identified with government policy.

The United States has shied away from a separate Administrative Court and indeed has stayed away from specialized courts in most areas. The exceptions can be counted on the fingers of one hand. The exceptions include the old Court of Claims to handle normal civil damage cases against the government (but even there the District Courts had jurisdiction over many civil damage cases against the government so that the court of Claims did not exercise exclusive jurisdiction in the area). More recently special "courts" have been established to deal with international trade and customs matters. The greatest break with the tradition of generalist courts was the recent creation of the Court of Appeals for the Federal Circuit. The Federal Circuit has non-geographic jurisdiction over patent matters and certain questions involving government employees. The more traditional administrative law case, the suit by the citizen challenging the actions of the government or seeking to overturn a decision of a government agency, is heard as a normal civil case by the normal civil courts.

Japan at the time of the Meiji Restoration decided to follow the more traditional civil law approach and created a special Administrative Court. Unlike the French approach the approach of the Meiji oligarchs was not to create an independent body that could control administrative agencies that acted unlawfully by overturning their determinations and decisions. Instead the oligarchs created a dependent body that could place its seal of approval on bureaucratic action. It was a principal objective of the Occupation legal reforms to undo the Meiji system and replace it with the American system. To achieve this end the Administrative Court was abolished and the Constitution specifically prohibited the creation of special courts. In theory, actions of the government were to be subject to judicial review by the ordinary courts. Administrative power was to be cabined by the judicial system. The Administrative Case Litigation Law[1] ("ACLL") was to provide the special legal framework for administrative litigation. With certain exceptions discussed later, after the case was started in accordance with the ACLL normal civil procedure was to control. The Occupation's goal to create an effective system of judicial oversight over government action was a failure. In its 2001 Report the Law Reform Council noted the important role of a judicial system in serving as a check on administrative action by the government and urged a searching review of the existing system. The Council noted several problems with the existing system:

a) The present system fails in its primary function of reviewing administrative action because of the primacy the system gives to the agency in conflicts with citizens—this primacy is based on numerous factors that have in common a trust in the bureaucracy and creation of procedures to protect bureaucratic action from judicial review;

b) The present system has no means for dealing with modern problems because it is based on a structure that centers on reviewing administrative decisions affecting individual parties and does not deal with modern administrative actions that are far removed from such things as granting or denying licenses but rather deal with more general issues such as whether government action in an area is required and if so what action should be taken;

---

1 Law No. 139 of May 16, 1962. The ACLL replaced and abolished the former law dealing with administrative cases that had been promulgated under the American Occupation in 1948.

c) The court system itself is not properly structured to handle administrative litigation.[2]

In the spring of 2004 the government sent a bill to the Diet to reform the ACLL. Near the close of the spring 2004 Diet session (June 11, 2004) the Diet passed a bill to amend the ACLL.

The bill attempts to address some of the issues raised by the Law Reform Council, but it is suggested that it represents too little too late. While the bill will provide some relief, it will likely be a case of form over substance with little changing in the way of judicial oversight over the way in which government actually regulates in Japan. This is to be expected—it is not likely that the bureaucracy (which has responsibility of working with others in connection with proposing changes in the law) will suggest a legal regime that will effectively oversee the actions of the bureaucracy. Real reform in the administrative law area will only come when legislation is proposed by those outside the government and is considered by Japan's political elite without the assistance of the entrenched bureaucracy.

The main problem with the Administrative Case Litigation Law is what it fails to address. The Act begins by stating that unless there is a special procedural law governing, the ACLL governs administrative litigation.[3] Consistent with precedent established by the prewar judiciary this means that ordinary civil litigation to challenge government action is not permitted unless there exists a special law permitting challenge. On the other hand, where substantive law provides a specific remedy in damages for government action normal civil procedure rather than the ACLL applies. When government action causes injury to a party through negligence or intentional action of government officials, the injured party can institute a normal civil action under the State Compensation Law (also known as the State Tort Liability Act and/or State Redress Law). Such suit seeking monetary damages follows the usual procedures of the Code of Civil Procedure. Indeed, the right to seek such compensation is a constitutional right. Article 17 of the Constitution guarantees individuals the right to sue "for redress as provided by law" when the individual is damaged by illegal act of a public official. The State Compensation Law allowing damage suit carries out this constitutional right. Such litigation can be used to obtain monetary damages in situations where an injury recognized by the State Compensation Law is involved. The action can also be used to obtain a judicial determination that the government has acted wrongfully. However, such litigation cannot stop or reverse the wrongful government action. In other words such litigation cannot enjoin unlawful government action or reverse a government determination.

The ACLL and the State Compensation Law and/or tort principles can be utilized in a single litigation. For example, if the government withdraws a license required

2 Recommendations of the Justice System Reform Council—For a Justice System to Support Japan in the 21st Century (June 12,2001) on the web at *www.kantei.go.jp/foreign/policy/sihou/singikai/990612_e.html* at p. 34 of 90.

3 ACLL Article 1.

by a business, the business may sue under the ACLL seeking to have the withdrawal decision reversed. The business may also seek damages for the losses suffered during the period when the license was improperly withdrawn. The ACLL permits the joinder of both claims in one litigation.[4] Because the ACLL is plaintiff unfriendly, many cases challenging government actions are brought under the State Compensation Law. Although plaintiffs may obtain damages and satisfaction of knowing that the court has found that the government action was wrongful, such a suit cannot reverse the government determination. Only monetary relief is available to the plaintiff in such a case.

That is not to say that inventive Japanese lawyers have not attempted to use the tort law and the ability of the courts to temporarily stop action of private parties in an attempt to obtain injunctive relief against government action. Such attempts have at times been successful but the controlling law is that the normal process of the civil courts cannot be used to challenge government administrative action. This is the antithesis of what the Occupation had in mind and is a throw back to the prewar Administrative Court jurisprudence—put in the clothing of the ACLL.[5]

The principal arena for attempting to utilize the normal civil procedure to obtain relief against government action alleged to be in excess of government power has been in the environmental area. There are probably two reasons for this: i) failure to cleanup the environment or action that will lead to degradation of the environment will likely have a direct effect on individuals that is a harm recognized by tort law and further that action causing pollution damage can be considered an abuse of right, so that there exists a basis for seeking relief from the ordinary civil judicial system. ii) Ever since the Big Four pollution cases, the public and the courts (especially the lower courts) have been sensitized to the need for protection of the environment. In any event, private parties have used the abuse of rights/tort doctrine to sue in pollution situations. Inferior courts have used their power to temporarily freeze (and in rare cases to alter) the status quo in litigation (provisional disposition)[6] and their power to enforce a property owner's rights in its own property to effectively enjoin private pollution activity. To find a means to provide relief in many of the pollution cases, lower courts held that the same type of rights inherent in property ownership applied to a person's own body and hence to the person's health and general well being. This "personal right" became the basis for several lower court determinations providing injunctive relief in the environmental law area. In the wake of the Big Four pollution cases the courts also began to use the same theories to grant injunctive relief against administrative action in the environmental area that conflicted with court understanding of required

4 ACLL Article 13.

5 For a discussion of the difficulties involved in obtaining an administrative suspension under the ACLL see, Jody Chafee, Administrative Suspension: A Snapshot of Equitable Jurisprudence in Japan on the web through Senrei.com.

6 Civil Preservation Act, Law No. 91 of 1989 Articles 23 and 24 (previously part of the Code of Civil Procedure). This act is also known as the Civil Provisional Remedies Law or the Civil Provisional Relief Act.

norms. In the *Osaka Airport Noise Pollution case*, the Supreme Court of Japan considered the reach of such judicial intervention under the normal civil action (as distinguished from the ACLL) process.

Residents of Osaka who lived near the airport sued seeking both damages for noise pollution and an injunction to prevent night flights in and out of the airport. The inferior courts found that the level of noise pollution in the area near the airport exceeded the level permissible under the standards set by the Environmental Agency acting under authority of the Basic Law for Environmental Pollution Control. Not only was the noise level high but it was continuous and particularly bad at night when accompanied by the sight of the jet aircraft with lights on descending for landing. The injury to the residents was unavoidable because the noise levels were so high that residents could not reduce their injury by becoming accustomed to the noise. Not only was there excessive noise but also the court found that there was pollution from aircraft exhaust fumes. The noise was so great that roof tiles in the area were loosened as a consequence of the sound waves. The High Court found that the residents suffered physical injury to their health through hearing loss. The court found other physical disabilities and found that such health injuries were caused, at least in part, by the aircraft noise.

The government built the airport involved. Airport operations were under the authority of the Minister of Transportation although the named defendant was the government of Japan. The Minister argued that an injunction could not be issued because the case was a normal civil case and not litigation under the ACLL. In essence the Minister argued that decisions concerning operating the airport were a matter of administrative discretion and could not be challenged in a normal civil action seeking a request for injunction. There was no serious dispute but that damages could be sought under the State Compensation Law. The High Court disagreed. First, the court found that while matters between the Minister and the users of the airport might be matters of administrative discretion, the dispute between the Minister and the residents was not about discretion. Rather, this dispute was more closely related to normal civil case questions dealing with private rights (that is the "personal right" mentioned above) than to the Minister's public authority to tell users of the airport how to operate. Accordingly the court felt that there was no need to proceed under the ACLL but that the court had authority to issue an injunction prohibiting flights at certain late night hours.

Second, the Minister was not being asked or enjoined to undertake a specific action but, rather, was being enjoined from permitting the late night flights from continuing. In other words the court was of the view that no mandatory injunction requiring the Minister to undertake a specific action was requested. Instead a normal civil injunction was being issued. How the Minister proceeded to get compliance was within his discretion.

Third, relying on the conclusion that the case concerned merely private law issues between the operator of the airport and third persons in the vicinity of the airport, the court was of the view that a balancing of interests under private law was all that was called for. The court insisted that it was not displacing the judgment and discretion of the Minister and thus the judiciary was not interfering with rights of the Executive Department and there was no separation of powers violation.

Finally the court confronted the claim that as this was in essence a suit under the ACLL the plaintiff's injunction claim should be dismissed because the plaintiffs lacked standing to sue under the ACLL. The High Court recognized this as a crucial question in the case. Crucial not only for the Airport case but potentially for other litigation involving the right of a court in a normal civil case to render an injunction against public action that affected rights of citizens who had no standing under the ACLL to bring suit but who were injured and thus had a cause of action under the Civil Code. The High Court held that the plaintiffs had standing to sue.[7] The High Court reasoned that if it accepted the government's argument it would be effectively closing the courthouse door to citizens with a valid cause of action for damages—citizens who were injured in fact by government action—but who needed injunctive relief to solve their problem. To hold as the government sought would, in the High Court's view, effectively mean that whenever a suit involved government action normal civil judicial proceedings (at least where injunction was concerned) was prohibited. In the view of the High Court this was not only unreasonable but raised constitutional issues, as it would mean that the judiciary could not deal with administrative matters. Finding that it had authority to deal with the injunction request, the court proceeded to consider whether injunction should issue.

The High Court found that the Constitution protects an undefined category of personal rights. Analogizing to rights to privacy clearly recognized by substantive law such as defamation law, the court found that the residents living close to the airport had rights to physical safety as well as freedom from mental anguish. Constitution Articles 13 ("right to life, liberty and the pursuit of happiness") and 25 ("minimum standards of wholesome and cultured living") were referred to as con-

7 Several years later, in the Niigata Airport case a similar standing question was raised. In the Niigata litigation the plaintiffs were also residents near an airport. The Minister had given an airline a license to operate flights from the airport to Korea. Residents sued under the ACLL seeking to have the determination to grant the license over turned. The High Court held that *if* the plaintiffs were claiming that the excessive noise from the aircraft operated under the license was injurious to their health then they would have standing to challenge the issuance of the license under the ACLL but denied the plaintiffs relief on other grounds. The Supreme Court affirmed the High Courts ruling and in doing so indicated that the High Court's determination that plaintiffs had standing was correct. The basis for denial of relief was the fact that the plaintiffs were not grounding their case on high noise levels causing them injury but, rather, were arguing that the passengers on the allowed flights would commit acts at their destination that were inconsistent with Japanese public policy. This public policy question (unlike the question of personal health) did not violate any of plaintiffs' legal rights. As a consequence the plaintiffs were not entitled to relief under the ACLL. Niigata Airport Case, 2/17/89. Exactly what the effect of the Niigata Airport case is on the question of standing in Noise Pollution and other personal rights cases is difficult to judge. The Supreme Court did not reverse the High Court's reasoning or ruling on the personal rights standing question—on the other hand the plaintiffs were denied relief and it can be argued that there was no need to decide if they had standing based on personal right since that was not the basis of their claim.

firming the court's view. In short the plaintiffs had a right not to be subjected to the kind of continuous and especially nighttime trauma created by flights into and out of the airport. While money damages could partly compensate for the loss of such rights, the court found money damages inadequate to fully compensate the plaintiffs. Not only was injunctive relief appropriate but the court extended by one hour (from 9 PM to 7 AM) the injunction that the District Court had entered. In the face of the Minister's argument that the hour between 9 PM and 10 PM was important for business travelers and international travelers the court noted that fault lay with the Minister for allowing construction of the additional runway that was the cause of most of the trouble. The Minister was also to blame for allowing jet traffic knowing of the injuries to the plaintiffs.

The government appealed to the Supreme Court. Initially a Petty Bench panel that sought to get the parties to agree to a compromise settlement heard the matter. The government refused and the case was sent to the Grand Bench. The High Court's decision had been rendered in November 1975. The Supreme Court decision was entered in December of 1981 more than six years later.

The Supreme Court recognized from the start that the injunction request while phrased in private right terms actually involved a matter of public law, namely the administration of the Transportation Ministry's authority concerning the airport. The court noted that the Minister had two authorities—a) the normal ministerial authority to regulate air transport and b) the typically private law type authority to manage a facility. In regard to the second authority the court noted that this authority was also tinged with a public purpose as the operation of the airport was necessary for international traffic and in general carried out a public purpose. The management of the Osaka (and Narita) airport was inextricably intertwined with the general administration of air transport. To give the plaintiffs the relief they requested would inevitably require the Minister to exercise his governmental authority over aviation matters. Whether such relief could be obtained under the ACLL was not before the Supreme Court. What was before the court was whether such relief could be obtained in an ordinary civil suit. As to this question the Supreme Court responded in the negative and reversed the injunction granted below.

The Supreme Court's opinion while only dealing with an airport and with a question where the airport management and the governmental regulatory power were united has far greater impact. First, it was precisely because the government through the Minister (or the Government Corporation under the Minister's supervision) was operating the airport that an injunction might be sought. If the airport were operated by a private entity the entity's defense would have been that it was required to keep the airport open at night so that international flights could come in because the Minister had ordered or directed it to do so. In such a case the plaintiff's recourse would have been limited to trying to overturn the Minister's direction to the airport. Such an attempt would clearly implicate the ACLL rather than an ordinary civil action. In other words the basis for seeking an injunction was that government action—public law action—was not implicated because the government was privately acting by operating the airport. In essence the plaintiffs argued we are just suing a private party what has that to do with the government? The court's answer was that the government's authority to control and manage air transport matter was inextricably intertwined with the government's operation of the airport. Second, the court cut through the legal underbrush to get to the real basis of the Complaint. Namely, the Minister's decision to open a second runway and to open the airport to jet traffic. These decisions were the root cause of plaintiffs' injuries and these decisions were public law matters. As such if subject to challenge at all they needed to be challenged under the ACLL. But no ACLL case had been brought. Instead a normal civil suit had been instituted. This rationale was equally applicable to other government decision-making such as constructing a highway near residences. The *Osaka Airport case* acts as a break on the authority of the courts to issue injunctions against government action through normal civil suit. Objectors must rely on the ACLL.[8]

The *Osaka Airport case* discloses the failure of the Occupation to achieve its goals in the administrative law arena. The idea that the normal court system could handle challenges to administrative action assumed that the normal relief that civil courts grant would be applicable to cases challenging government action. The *Osaka Airport case* makes it clear that that is not the case.

The normal civil courts are restricted in the relief they may grant in normal civil cases against government. The method by which Japan handles "review" of administrative decisions is also inconsistent with assumptions made by the Occupation. Although there is no Administrative Court as such, the reality is that there is a separate administrative branch in many District Courts that handles ACLL cases. ACLL cases brought in Tokyo—where most ACLL cases are brought—as well as in Osaka, Nagoya, Yokohama, Saitama, Chiba, Kyoto and Kobe are assigned to special administrative divisions and are not heard by civil judges arbitrarily chosen to hear such cases. There is a kind of Administrative Court within the normal court system.

Some have read the Supreme Court's 1995 decision in the *National Route 43 Highway* case as limiting the reach of the *Osaka Airport case.* In the *Highway case* residents near a major expressway sought a reduction in both air pollution and noise from the Highway. The residents sought an injunction restricting the use of the Highway. Plaintiffs brought a normal civil suit seeking injunctive relief relying on the personal rights theory. The High Court acknowledged that in an appropriate case injunctive relief could be obtained but ruled against the injunction request on the merits. The High Court did allow the plaintiffs monetary damages.

---

8 For a discussion of the development of civil injunctive relief from actions involving government regulatory action prior to the Osaka Airport case and for an English language translation of the District and High Court opinions in the Osaka Airport case see, Julian Gresser, Koichiro Fujikura and Akio Morishima, ENVIRONMENTAL LAW IN JAPAN (MIT Press, 1981) 149-196. For an English language version of the Osaka Airport case at the Supreme Court level, 35 Minshu 1369 (Sup. Ct. Grand Bench, 12/16/81) see, Lawrence W. Beer & Hiroshi Itoh, THE CONSTITUTIONAL CASE LAW OF JAPAN, 1970-1990 (University of Washington Press, 1996) at 205.

On appeal the Supreme Court affirmed the decision of the High Court. The Supreme Court made no mention of the *Osaka Airport case*. While it can be argued that the Highway case (and perhaps the *Niigata Airport case*) reflects a loosening of the Osaka Airport rule, the fact is that the Supreme Court has never granted an injunction against government action in a normal civil case.

Further, the Occupation's assumption that in reviewing administrative action the courts would apply a standard similar to the standard applied in other civil litigation has not proven to be the case. Japanese courts have applied a "rule of free discretion" to agency determinations that shelters most agency decisions in the technical and/or policy areas from substantive review. While questions of "law" are technically subject to judicial inquiry, questions of discretion are not. Discretion implicates many areas that would be subject to review in a United States court.[9] The question of discretion is in many instances a question of statutory interpretation and as Japanese bureaucrats draft most statutes they do so in a way that gives the bureaucracy wide discretion. Courts then looking at challenges to the bureaucratic action are confronted with a statute that broadly delegates discretionary authority. Although the form of administrative law may be American, the substance remains German law and to a great extent prewar. The result has been that the court system has not been performing a check and balance function when dealing with administrative action of the government. This was the source of the basic complaint of the Judicial Reform Council and the basis underlying its calls for Reform of the Justice System to reform how administrative cases are dealt with.

Although the ACLL provides for four different types of administrative suits, only one is of interest herein. A unique form of taxpayer suit is permitted under the law. Unlike the United States where taxpayer suits are not permitted, the ACLL specifically permits such suits if they seek to have money returned to the public fisc.[10] In such a suit a resident would sue a local government official—in his/her personal capacity—seeking to have the official return public funds allegedly improperly spent. Under the 2002 amendment to the ACLL suit is brought against the local government agency rather than the allegedly offending official and if the resident is successful the agency has the responsibility of recovering the monies from the official. The agency must request payment within 60 days of the successful suit by the resident. If the official refuses to pay, the government entity must institute suit for recovery.[11] The resident/plaintiff in such a suit may not seek to recover money damages on its own account but can only obtain a return of funds to the government entity. Many of the freedom of religion cases fall into this category of suit.

9 For a discussion of the doctrine of free discretion see, Itsuo Sonobe, Comparative Administrative Law: Trends and Features in Administrative Law Studies (Japan) 19 Law in Japan 40 (1986) translated by Kevin Hansen, from 1 Gendai gyoseiho taikei, I. Ogawa, H. Shione, I. Sonobe, eds., 121-146 (1983).

10 ACLL Article 5. See also, Local Autonomy Law Articles 242-2, 242-3 (amended 2002).

11 Local Autonomy Law Article 242-3(1) and (2).

In such cases a resident will seek to have public funds spent for a religious purpose repaid to the local government entity.

A second category of suit is a suit between private individuals where one of the parties relies on administrative action in asserting its position.[12] Although basically a suit between private parties, the litigation may implicate the legality of administrative action since one party may assert that the right asserted by the other based on public law is itself improper and unlawful. In such a case a government entity is permitted to intervene in the action.[13] When such a situation arises, the ACLL calls for giving the government entity whose determination may be at issue notice of the litigation.[14] The ACLL also permits suit between private parties where one of the parties claims a right based on administrative action. The other party may sue challenging the right on the grounds that the administrative action upon which the asserted right is based was void *ab initio*.[15] Such suits are rare.[16]

A third category of suit involves resolution of disputes between government agencies or between levels of government.[17] The *Okinawa Governor Mandamus case* in which the National Government sued the Prefectural Governor to require him to sign leases for American air bases on Okinawa was such a case.[18]

The main administrative law case is a suit wherein a party seeks to challenge governmental action.[19] Such suits may fall into four categories: a) suits to overturn a disposition, b) suits to overturn a decision made by an administrative agency appeal body, c) suits to affirm the existence of or non-existence of a government de-

12 ACLL Article 4. For example, a landowner whose property is taken for a public purpose such as the laying of an electric power transmission line may sue the power company seeking greater compensation for the taking than was allowed by the government agency.

13 ACLL Article 23. The ACLL makes intervention discretionary with the court but if the position of the government is being challenged it is clear that intervention will be permitted. See also Article 45.

14 ACLL Article 39.

15 ACLL Article 45.

16 This type of suit was used during the Occupation to challenge aspects of the Occupation's agricultural land reform policy as it was carried out by local government entities.

17 ACLL Article 6.

18 See, Okinawa Governor Mandamus Case, Case No. 90 of 1996 (Sup. Ct. Grand Bench, 8/28/96) available on the web through the web site of the Supreme Court of Japan.

19 ACLL Article 3. For a discussion of the various types of litigation permitted by the ACLL see, Hiroyuki Hata & Go Nakagawa & Takehisa Nakagawa, JAPAN CONSTITUTIONAL LAW Sec. 362-367 (Kluwer Law International, 2001). Professor Hata notes that there is an additional type of Administrative Litigation not provided for in the ACLL itself but which the ACLL contemplates may be brought where another law specifically provides for court review. Professor Hata uses as an example the challenge to the validity of an election under the Public Officer's Election Act. It was on the basis of this law that the various apportionment cases that reached the Supreme Court were filed. (See Hata, etc. Section 368). There are special provisions in the authorizing laws of certain agencies that permit judicial review of administrative action such as the review of determinations of the Fair Trade Commission and the Patent Office. Such review is in the High Court in Tokyo and not in the District Court. Suits under the ACLL are in the District Court.

termination, and d) suits to declare that the failure of the government to act in a matter is itself unlawful. Suits to overturn a disposition made by a government agency are the most frequent. Suits to overturn a disposition are the cases of most interest because they implicate the judicial review power of the court where agency action is involved.

The ACLL is a default statute in the sense that the Code of Civil Procedure handles all matters concerning administrative cases that are not specifically dealt with in the law by default.[20] Thus, the filing of a Complaint in an administrative case follows the procedure of a normal Complaint. This means that the normal jurisdiction/venue rules apply. The venue for most national government cases (with the exception of tax cases) would thus be in Tokyo where the Minister or head of the agency whose action is challenged is resident. However if it can be shown that local officials were sufficiently involved in the challenged decision-making the suit may be instituted elsewhere.[21] The venue requirements have meant that it is sometimes difficult for parties located far from Tokyo to institute administrative litigation. This was one of the problems confronted in the prewar era when cases before the Administrative Court had to be filed in Tokyo, the only place where the court met. To meet the objections to this limitation on filing suits, the government in the spring of 2004 introduced legislation (enacted at the close of the Diet session) providing for concurrent jurisdiction in the Tokyo District Court (the residence of the defendant) and in the District Court located in the same place where the High Court having authority over the District Court of the plaintiff's residence has its principal office. Thus, for example, a resident of a district in the Tohoku (northeast) section of the country could bring an action in the Tokyo District court or the District Court in Sendai. Sendai would be permitted because Sendai is the location of the High Court with jurisdiction over the District Courts in Tohoku. Similarly a resident of the Chyugoku region could file in either Tokyo District Court or Hiroshima District Court. The effect of this legislation is to permit suits in Tokyo or depending on where the plaintiff resides any one of the other seven locations of High Courts.

When a suit under the ACLL is brought under present provisions of the ACLL, the question of what division of the civil division of the District Court should handle the case is brought into question. In Tokyo there are three special divisions that handle ACLL cases. The judges of these divisions do not handle other civil cases. Special divisions also exist in Osaka (2 divisions) and in Nagoya, Yokohama, Saitama, Chiba, Kyoto, and Kobe (each with one division). If suit were brought in Hiroshima or Sendai (for example) under the 2004 revision then it would be assigned to an ordinary civil division that handles ordinary civil cases as

20 ACLL Article 7.

21 ACLL Article 12 (3); for a case holding that the substantial involvement of the Wakayama Governor's office in the denial of a national pension request was sufficient to permit venue in Wakayama when denial of the request was at issue see, Case No. 2 of 2000, 55 Minshu 149 (Sup. Ct. Petty Bench, 2/27/01) available on the web through the web site of the Supreme Court of Japan.

well as ACLL cases. Thus the revision could affect the judges who hear ACLL cases outside of the Districts where special administrative divisions exist.

Another problem confronted by a plaintiff in an administrative case is the short statute of limitations set by the ACLL. The ACLL provides that a suit must be instituted within three months of knowledge of the challenged disposition.[22] The government's spring 2004 bill would change this to a six-month statute of limitations and would allow suits after the expiration of such six-month period if good cause for the delay existed. The amendment does not define good cause.

Under the ACLL the suit challenging government action is not filed against the government but, rather, is filed against the government official responsible (such as a Minister or Prefecture Governor or city Mayor) or the Agency.[23] This creates complications, as sometimes the plaintiff is unaware of the correct official or agency to sue. Under the 2004 amendment suit can be instituted against the National Government or a prefecture or other local government or public entity thus resolving this issue.

Under the government's 2004 initiative two new categories of suit are permitted under new subsection 6 of Article 3 of the ACLL. First, the plaintiff can seek to compel an agency to act in a regulatory fashion when it has failed to take action. Prior law did not permit such relief.[24] Secondly, a plaintiff may seek an order requiring the agency to enter a favorable determination in a situation where the applicant has applied for some form of government benefit (such as a social security payment or a license) and the agency has failed to act.[25] Under prior law, in this situation the applicant could only seek a declaration that the agency must act in a reasonable time. Under the 2004 amendment the court may order the agency to grant the relief requested. The court has authority when granting relief to the plaintiff to either order the specific terms of the agency action or may order the agency to grant plaintiff relief while permitting the agency to determine the specifics of that relief. For example in a social security payment case the court could order that the agency make the payment but permit the agency to calculate the payment rather than have the court make the calculation. The new provision opens the possibility for suit *before* a determination has been made and permits suit to compel a specific determination. Under prior law the only relief allowable was a declaration that the agency must act on an application. Alternatively suit may be brought seeking reversal of agency action but only *after* a determination has been made by the agency.

Another new section (37-2) restricts the use of the new subsection 6.1 suit seeking regulatory action to cases where the plaintiff can show that there is no other ade-

---

22 ACLL Article 14.

23 ACLL Article 11.

24 ACLL Article 6.1. Some commentators have argued that such relief was always available under the ACLL but the courts have not granted such relief.

25 ACLL Article 6.2.

quate remedy and that agency inaction may cause serious loss to the plaintiff. The court may only order the agency to issue a disposition when a statute or other legally binding rule requires that a disposition be entered or when the failure to act is an abuse of discretion.

New subsection 6.2 allows two different types of relief—an order compelling the agency to generally take affirmative action on plaintiff's application and an order directing the agency to take a specific action (including the reversal of an action already taken by the agency). Such relief requested by the plaintiff must be joined with a request for the type of declaratory relief presently available under the ACLL. In other words both declaratory and "active" relief must be sought. The court will then determine what form of relief to grant. As an historical matter the grant of declaratory relief has not always been followed by administrative action consistent with the declaratory judgment.[26] Under the new initiative the court may grant the same relief that is presently available. This obviously represents a compromise between competing interests that wanted, on the one hand to reform and change the law and those who, on the other, wanted to leave the law as is. The ultimate compromise appears to allow parties to seek the new form of relief but require parties to join such request with a request for the old form of relief and leave it to the court to determine on a case by case basis what relief to grant.

In a case asserting an agency failure to act, such failure must meet two conditions. First, it must relate to an application for a disposition or an appeal within the agency (both of which must be based on statute or legally binding legislative type rule). Second, a reasonable period of time must have passed without agency action. Relief can only be granted if the court finds that the agency's inaction is unlawful or an abuse of discretion. A reasonable period of time is undefined.

In the case of a request for an order to require that the agency enter a determination in plaintiff's favor where the agency has already acted to deny plaintiff's request, the suit must specifically ask that the court reverse the agency action. The standard of review is that the agency disposition is: a) unlawful, b) the statute or legally binding rule requires that the agency grant the relief requested at the agency level, or c) the determination is an abuse of discretion.

While proposed new subsection 6 would allow actions seeking two different types of relief—regulatory relief and relief seeking a benefit—the standard of review to be used by the court in either case is the same. Namely, did the agency abuse its discretion or is the agency action (or inaction) clearly contrary to authorizing law or binding rule.

It remains to be seen what judicial gloss is placed on such an action—how much weight will the court give to the doctrine of free discretion when considering whether the agency has abused its discretion in either failing to issue a disposition or denying the relief the plaintiff seeks.

---

26 See, Makoto Ito, Execution of Non-Money Judgments and Means of Enforcement in Japan, 16 Hitotsubashi Journal of Law & Politics 11, 20-22 (1988).

New subsection 7 of Article 3 allows an injunction action to prevent an administrative agency from taking an action when it is asserted the agency has no legal authority to so act. This is a potentially significant change in the law, as it would permit injunctive relief in situations where previously the court had no power to intervene. Although new subsection 7 allows a plaintiff to seek such relief, the new subsection does not change the standards under which the court would review such a request.

New Section 37-4 (1) limits the subsection 7 suit to cases where the plaintiff has no other available remedy and the agency is threatening to take action that will inflict a "grave" loss on plaintiff. "Grave" loss is undefined except that in determining whether there is a "grave" loss the court must consider such things as the difficulty of recovering damages to compensate for the loss, as well as the nature and extent of the loss threatened. Damages to compensate for loss may be a stumbling block to effective control of unlawful administrative action. Recently a Tokyo District Court found that the government decision to build a highly controversial beltway highway around Tokyo was improper and had failed to take into account relevant factors such as noise levels. The District Court found both the administrative determination to build the road and the expropriation of land for the road illegal.[27] Plaintiffs then sought an injunction to prevent continuing work on the road. Notwithstanding the ruling that the road was improperly approved and that the expropriation of land to build the road was unlawful, the District Court refused to issue an injunction finding that plaintiffs could be compensated for their loss by monetary compensation. There was thus no irreparable injury.[28] It appears that the new law would not change this determination as the loss to plaintiffs can be compensated in monetary terms and hence would not be a "grave" loss.

New Section 37-4 (3) also provides that only a person with a statutorily protected interest may seek to restrain an agency from acting. However, new subsection 37-4 (4) makes it clear that in determining whether a party has a statutorily protected interest the broadened standing rule of new Section 9 (2) discussed below should be applied. This rule means that a plaintiff need not show that the statute that grants the plaintiff a legal interest is the statute under which the agency is acting. The standard to be used by the court in determining whether an agency has acted unlawfully is, as in the cases above, whether it has abused its discretion or whether its action is clearly contrary to statute or legally binding rule. (Section 37-4 (5)).

Abuse of discretion and/or acting in excess of an agency's discretion is the typical standard of review in administrative cases.[29] As in all civil cases, the burden of proof is on the plaintiff to establish that the agency abused its discretion. A mere

---

27 The determination of the District Court is subject to debate. The same judge had found the road unlawfully approved in an earlier case that was overturned by the Tokyo High Court and the High Court's determination was affirmed by the Supreme Court.

28 Follow up Beltway Ruling Snubs Land Claim, Japan Times on Line 4/27/04.

29 ACLL Article 30.

preponderance of the evidence is not sufficient. The court must be convinced of the abuse of discretion. Since abuse of discretion may be a legal rather than a factual issue the difference in burden of proof between Japan's rule and the American preponderance rule may not be as great in this area of law as it is in the typical civil case. What is different is the definition of abuse of discretion. In the United States an abuse of discretion exists if the court concludes that the agency action was irrational. To make such a determination the court may take a hard look at the rationale given by the agency. This rationale is measured against fact and logic. In Japan bureaucrats are given more discretion than in the United States. This is especially true in areas involving policy or technical information. The definition of a policy or technical matter is also viewed more liberally in Japan.[30]

If the courts continue to defer to administrative action as they have in the past the fact that a plaintiff may be able to ask for an injunction may have little meaning. What a plaintiff wants is not simply a right to seek an injunction but a reasonable chance of getting an injunction. Still, the only purpose that one can find for such a change in the law is to allow such injunctions to be granted. Accordingly, the courts should regard the change as a suggestion that they get more involved in cases alleging that an agency proposes to undertake an action that it has no right to undertake. This intent must be weighed against the new 37-4 (5) that again refers to abusc of discretion. There are conflicting signs in the new legislation but that probably reflects the conflicts in the committee drafting the legislation. To reach a consensus that all could coalesce around the new law appears to both liberalize the old law and restate the old law. In this way all views are accommodated. To some extent this is reminiscent of the approach the Code of Civil Procedure takes to production of documents where the old Code provisions were retained verbatim and a new provision was added that appears to open discovery to any other document. To accommodate those who did not want to open documentary discovery the self-use exception was written into the Code to bring the legislation close to where it was before there was any legislation. Just as it has taken several years for the court to begin to loosen the self-use exception so that damage as well as self-use must be shown, so too it will likely take several years to get an understanding of the meaning of the new provisions in the ACLL.

A new Section 37-5 is added to the ACLL that would give the court authority to issue temporary injunctions when a suit to prohibit an agency from granting a disposition is instituted. To qualify for preliminary injunctive relief the court must find: a) an action for a permanent injunction (37-4) is pending, b) there is a need for immediate relief to prevent irreparable injury that would follow if the disposition were entered, and c) the plaintiff is likely to succeed on the merits. Even if these showings are made, temporary injunction cannot be granted if the court

30 There are of course exceptions to the rule. In nuclear power reactor citing the potential catastrophic accident and loss of life is so great that the courts have loosened both the standing requirements (a loosening that now appears to be spreading to other areas through the 2004 initiative) and the abuse of discretion standard bordering on holding the government to showing that the agency's determination was correct.

finds that grant would have a grave impact on the public interest. It is to be expected that the public interest exception to granting temporary injunctive relief will act as a restraint on court allowance of such orders. Similarly the new law would permit the issuance of a temporary mandatory injunction in rare cases based on the same factors mentioned for prohibitory injunction. The same public interest exception is applicable. It is unlikely that the courts will grant many temporary mandatory injunctions.

Although the new provisions permitting the court to order the agency to make a disposition are contrary to the general rule that only a disposition can be reviewed under the ACLL, it does not seem likely that the new provisions will substantially change the doctrine of *shobunsai*. Under this doctrine there must be a disposition for the court to have something to review. It is true that the court can now order the agency to make a disposition but, as a general rule, it does not appear that substantive review can be had unless and until there is a *shobun* or disposition. The general rule that a case under the ACLL must challenge the exercise of public power in a way that deals with rights of members or a member of the public appears unchanged except for the situation where an agency is ordered to make a decision. This is a big exception in that one of the problems with *shobunsai* is that an agency can delay making a decision that will affect an individual's rights until a point in time when it may be too late to get a court to reverse the agency determination. Although it may be easy to stop the construction of a bridge prior to any construction work, once the roads on each side of the waterway have been completed and the only thing remaining to tie them together is the bridge, it is unlikely that any court will reverse the determination to build the bridge. If bridge opponents must wait until the decision to build the bridge is made and cannot sue when the decision to build the roads leading to the bridge are made, then the practical effect is to deny any relief. By permitting the court to order the agency to make the decision on whether or not to build the bridge at an early stage, it may be possible to give the court an opportunity to hear a challenge to the construction of the bridge.

Nonetheless the doctrine of *shobunsai* appears otherwise to be secure. The importance of this is that only an exercise of agency power through a determination about a matter is subject to review. Accordingly if an agency does not make a decision but simply suggests a course of action there has been no *shobun* and accordingly there is nothing to review. As most of Japanese administration takes place through Administrative Guidance rather than dispositions, this leaves a huge hole in administrative matters subject to review.

Administrative Guidance is, as its name implies, the use of suggestion (guidance) to administer. Unlike the United States most Japanese administrative agencies lack the compulsory weapons of American agencies. There is usually no cease and desist authority and although some agencies have substantive rule making authority, most administrative action occurs at a more informal level. Japanese agencies tend to administer through cooperative dialogue between administrators and the administered. The new Administrative Procedure Law ("APL") (which has virtually no procedures dealing with Administrative Guidance) defines guidance as suggestion as to policy or practice that the agency wants to carryout that is voluntarily followed by the administered entity.[31] Guidance ceases to be guidance when it becomes compulsory. Since by definition guidance cannot be compulsory it cannot be a disposition. Since it is not a disposition, guidance is not subject to review under the ACLL.[32] Yet it is the way administrators in Japan actually function.[33]

Administrative Guidance is ubiquitous in Japan. Although technically not mandatory, the reality is that guidance is in most instances either perceived as mandatory or is actually mandatory. The nature of Japanese society and especially the respect given to government officials is such that for all practical purposes guidance is almost always followed. Moreover, considering the historic power of the bureaucracy it is not too much to suggest that even though the Administrative Procedure Law is clear in prohibiting an agency from punishing an entity that fails to follow guidance, regulated entities may reasonably fear that refusal to follow guidance could have negative consequences for the entity. Such reasonable concern may well lead some companies to adhere to guidance. Moreover, the thinking person knows that although the APL may reject the notion of punishment for failure to follow guidance, it says nothing about whether a competitor who follows guidance may receive some benefit. Bureaucracies have policies and memories of their own and the relatively low or mid level official of today whose guidance has been rejected may be the powerful bureaucrat of the future who recalls the incident. This is not to suggest that such a person would let the past failure to achieve a goal affect future determinations, but still the official may consider the entity that refused to follow guidance in the past as "unreliable" and not worthy of benefits or sincere consideration in the future. Whatever the reason the fact is that Administrative Guidance is typically followed in Japan.

---

31 Administrative Procedure Law Article 2 (6).

32 For a discussion of Administrative Guidance see, Carl F. Goodman, THE RULE OF LAW IN JAPAN: A COMPARATIVE ANALYSIS 335-348 (Kluwer Law International, 2003); Michael K. Young, Judicial Review of Administrative Guidance: Governmentally Encouraged Consensual Dispute Resolution in Japan, 84 Columbia Law Review 923 (1984); Tom Ginsburg, Dismantling the "Developmental State"? Administrative Procedure Reform in Japan and Korea, 49 American Journal of Comparative Law 585, 593-594 (2001); Takehisa Nakagawa, Administrative Guidance: A Tentative Model of How Japanese Lawyers Understand It, 32 Kobe University Law Review 1 (1998); Meryll Dean, Administrative Guidance in Japanese Law: A Threat to the Rule of Law, 1991 Journal of Business Law 398; Wolfgang Pape, Gyosei Shido and the Antimonopoly Law, 15 Law in Japan 12 (1982); Russell Allen Yoemans, Administrative Guidance: A Peregrine View, 19 Law in Japan 125 (1986); Mitsuo Matsushita, The Legal Framework of Trade and Investment in Japan, 27 Harvard International Law Journal 361 (1986); Muneyuki Shindo, Administrative Guidance, 20 Japanese Economic Studies 69-87 (1992). For the view that guidance is followed, in part, because of concern over possible negative reaction by government officials see, A Lawyers Guide to Japan, Asahi Law Office Tokyo, March 2004 on the web at www.lexmundi.com/images/lexmundi/pdf/guide-japan04.pdf.

33 It is not without interest that guidance is the basic tool for administrative action in Japan and the law that controls administrative procedure provides no procedure (as procedure is understood by the American administrative lawyer) for guidance and the law that controls litigation to challenge administrative action provides no method of challenging guidance.

Not only is guidance followed but also all segments of the society understand that guidance is how administrators administer and is how things get done. Nonetheless the law appears to be of two minds about guidance. The District court in the *Daiwa Bank case* rejected the argument made by Daiwa officials that they should not be held responsible for failure to advise American authorities of the Bank's inappropriate actions because the bank had simply been following the guidance of the Ministry of Finance. The court was of the view that if the bank followed advice from Ministry officials, the bank was responsible for such action as it was under no compulsion to follow the advice[34] and the Directors were required to manage the business on their own responsibility rather than allowing the Ministry to run operations.[35] In the *Oil Cartel case* the Ministry of International Trade and Industry (MITI now known as METI) had been closely associated with the activities of the oil companies. The claim of the companies that they were acting lawfully because they were following MITI guidance received a mixed reception by the court. As the companies had come up with the cartel plan on their own and simply received MITI guidance after they had proposed the plan to MITI, they could not rely on guidance as a defense. MITI's more direct involvement in the cartel's production limits plan was permitted as a defense.[36] In the case where NHK (the nationally owned media stations company in Japan) sought guidance as to whether to broadcast certain material and followed that guidance by not broadcasting, the Supreme Court found that government censorship was not involved. The rationale was that the action by NHK was voluntary and not compelled by government.[37]

In the opinion accompanying the Tokyo District court's suggested settlement in the *S.M.O.N. case*[38] the court rejected the notion that the government had played no role in the distribution of the pharmaceutical drug that was responsible for the nervous disorder that caused the injuries to the plaintiffs. The court pointed out the inherent contradiction of the government's contention that it is not responsible

---

34 See, Mitsuru Misawa, Daiwa Bank Scandal in New York: Its Causes, Significance and Lessons in the International Society, 29 Vanderbilt Journal of Transnational Law 1023 (1996) for a discussion of the supposed meetings between the Ministry and Daiwa.

35 See English language summary translation of Daiwa Bank decision at Tsuyoshi Yamada, The Daiwa Bank Case (1999) (Summary Translation) 15 Columbia Journal of Asian Law 193, 210-211 (2002).

36 See, Japan v. Idemitsu Kosan, et. Al., 985 Hanrei Jiho 3 (Tokyo High Court, 9/26/80) (partial translation in English available at Yukio Yanagida, Daniel H. Foote, Edward Stokes Johnson Jr., J. Mark Ramseyer and Hugh T. Scogin, Jr., LAW AND INVESTMENT IN JAPAN 141-147 (Harvard University Press, 1994).

37 NHK Censorship case, Case No. 800 of 1986 (Sup. Ct., Petty Bench 4/17/90) an English translation is available through the web site of the Supreme Court of Japan.

38 The Judge's Power to Propose Terms for Settlement: The S.M.O.N. Case, (translated by Seiichi Yoshikawa) opinion of Judge Kabe.

for what entities do when entities follow Administrative Guidance. The government sought to argue that as entities have no obligation to follow guidance the fact that an entity followed the guidance has nothing to do with the government and cannot be the basis for government responsibility. At the same time the government conceded that it used guidance to respond to new situations that require government attention but for which there was as yet no legislation. The court acknowledged that guidance has the actual effect of regulating. The court found the government's position contradictory because on the one hand the government acknowledged that it regulated through guidance and hence did not require legislation while on the other it attempted to deny any responsibility for its guidance.

What is perhaps most significant about the *NHK, Oil Cartel, Daiwa Bank* and *S.M.O.N.* situations is that in all of them the Administrative Guidance given was not questioned—it was followed. Although guidance is not universally followed,[39] the reality is that failure to follow guidance is the exception rather than the rule.[40] Whatever gloss is placed on Administrative Guidance it is how Japanese government administrators administer.[41] Whether characterized as voluntary or as compulsory guidance is followed and it is not subject to judicial review under the ACLL,[42] although a damage remedy may sometimes be available.[43]

---

39 See, e.g., the Hiroshima Pharmacy case, Sumiyoshi v. Hiroshima, Case No. 120 of 1968, 29 Minshu 572 (Sup. Ct., Grand Bench 4/30/75) available in English translation on the web through the web site of the Supreme Court of Japan and also in Lawrence W. Beer & Hiroshi Itoh, THE CONSTITUTIONAL CASE LAW OF JAPAN, 1970-1990 (University of Washington Press, 1996) at 188.

40 For a discussion of the changing role of Administrative Guidance in the regulation of the Financial Services industry see, Regulation and Compliance in Japanese Financial Institutions, 14 Columbia Journal of Asian Law 327, 346, 365-367 (2001).

41 For an interesting discussion of guidance and how it has supplanted the criminal law provisions applicable to pollution see, Julian Gresser, Koichiro Fujikura and Akio Morishima, ENVIRONMENTAL LAW IN JAPAN (MIT Press, 1981) 261.

42 See, e.g., Meryll Dean, JAPANESE LEGAL SYSTEM (2 ed., Cavendish Publishing Limited, 2002) 138-141.

43 Under Japanese criminal procedure law when a suspect has privately retained counsel the prosecutor designates the time, place and length of meetings that can be held between counsel and the suspect. The prosecutor has wide discretion in determining when meetings can be held as meetings can be prohibited at a time when the prosecutor is interviewing the subject or even when preparations for the interview are being undertaken. A defense counsel upset with the designation made by the prosecutor cannot seek relief under the ACLLbut can sue for damages on the theory that the prosecutor interfered with counsel's right to properly represent the client. Such damage suit is a kind of review of the administrative action but it hardly gives either counsel or the client what is most needed—a chance to meet to formulate a defense on a time schedule that is best for the suspect. Money damages given to the lawyer (and small damages at that) may serve to show that the prosecutor acted in an improper fashion and may have moral satisfaction value but it is surely not a substitute for judicial review of the prosecutor's designation determination. On the other hand money damages may not be available when Administrative Guidance to a third person is implicated. Thus when the Ministry of Education gave "non-binding" suggestions for changes in text-books such action was not found to implicate the State Compensation Law and thus no money damages could be sought against the Minister

Most regulation in the United States is undertaken through the issuance of rules and regulations adopted by federal agencies under the "informal" notice and comment rule making provisions of the Administrative Procedure Act. These rules are ubiquitous and cover such diverse actions as OHSA "standards" regulating safety and health conditions in the workplace, or EPA rules regulating effluents released into the air or water, or Federal Communications Commission rules concerning use of the broadcast airwaves, etc. There is of course some granting of licenses and some agencies such as the National Labor Relations Board use adjudication to regulate relations between labor and management. The essence of regulation in the United States (at least at the federal level) is rule and regulation. Dispositions on the other hand rarely deal with matters that in the United States are dealt with by regulations and rules. Dispositions tend to deal with the grant or refusal to grant a license—important in some cases but a minor aspect of the over all administrative regulatory function of government. Excluding Administrative Guidance from coverage of the law that permits challenge to administrative action is like excluding rules and regulations in the United States from judicial review by the courts.

In rejecting a challenge to Administrative Guidance that permitted the construction of a shopping center in the face of objection by local merchants who would be injured by the center's competition, the court found that there was nothing to review and in any event the merchants had no standing. The rationale for both holdings was the same. The agency proceeded through guidance. Since guidance was not compulsory, it could not have a binding effect on the shopping center operator. Accordingly, whatever action the operator took could not be attributed to the government and thus a legal interest of the merchants could not have been injured by government action. In essence there was no *shobun*—no government determination—without a *shobun* the government could not injure a legal right. Whether one wants to characterize the court's decision as one denying plaintiffs standing (no legal right injured) or whether it is characterized as a lack of a *shobun* (no government disposition) the fact remains the same. The government achieved its administrative end and there was no judicial review available.[44]

Approximately 90 to 95% of all suits filed under the ACLL deal with a party seeking to set aside a disposition (decision granting or denying relief or otherwise de-

---

when the suggestions were followed and the text books were revised. However, when the Minister gave binding instructions that textbooks delete reference to Military Unit 731 because there was asserted to be no reliable evidence concerning such unit, monetary damages were available since such assertion was inconsistent with prevailing academic opinion and inconsistent with textbook screening standards. See Case No. 1119 of 1994, 51 Minshu 2921 (Sup. Ct. Petty Bench, 8/29/97) a summary of the decision is available in English through the web site of the Supreme Court of Japan.

44 See, Frank K. Upham, Privatizing Regulation: The Implementation of the Large -Scale Retail Stores Law, in POLITICAL DYNAMICS IN CONTEMPORARY JAPAN (Garry D. Allison and Yasunori Sone Ed., Cornell University Press 1993) REPRINTED IN PART IN Yukio Yanagida, Daniel H. Foote, Edward Stokes Johnson Jr., J. Mark Ramseyer and Hugh T. Scogin, Jr., LAW AND INVESTMENT IN JAPAN 129-133 (Harvard University Press, 1994). The Large-Scale Retail Sales Law was abolished as part of a deregulatory plan by law No. 91 of 1998 effective 2000.

ciding a matter) made by an administrative agency. Under the ACLL only a party with standing to sue can bring such an action.[45] Standing jurisprudence has been one of the biggest stumbling blocks to successful litigation of ACLL cases.[46] Under United States law plaintiffs in administrative suits must also have standing to sue. Under American law standing is given a broad sweep so that a party to an administrative proceeding generally has standing to challenge the results of that proceeding even if otherwise the party would lack sufficient personal interest to have standing. Besides this "private attorney general" standing, standing can exist when a party has injury in fact and falls within the general class of interests protected by the statute under which the agency is acting. Thus an American plaintiff in an administrative case need not show that its legally protected interest is being invaded. That is to say the plaintiff need not point to a statute and say "under that law I have a right that is being violated by the agency's determination." It is enough to say "the law under which the agency is acting protects the environment and my interest in the environment is implicated in this case and I will be hurt if the decision is allowed to stand."

In Japan the rules for standing to sue in an administrative case are substantially more restricting. To have standing the plaintiff must have a "legal interest" in the matter and not a "reflex interest." Mere injury in fact is not sufficient as the injury in fact may result from a "reflex" action. If the agency decision hurts all hikers, the fact that plaintiff is a hiker does not provide standing to sue in Japan. Rather, plaintiff must point to a statute that says that as a hiker plaintiff has a legal right that the agency action is injuring. If the agency makes a determination that affects the public in general, the fact that such action may have a particularly damaging effect on plaintiff is not sufficient to give plaintiff standing. Plaintiff's injury is not to a legal interest but the injury is simply a reflex of the agency's decision. Even if plaintiff has a legal interest that is going to be affected by the agency's final decision, until that decision is taken all plaintiff can say is that it *will* have an injury not that it has an injury. Thus, if a road is in the planning stage the fact that as planned the road will cut through plaintiff's land (a legal interest would be damaged as plaintiff has a legal interest in the use of its own land) is not sufficient to give plaintiff standing. Only when the plan is actually put into effect does plaintiff have a sufficient legal injury for standing. Until the agency starts proceedings to take a section of plaintiff's farmland to build the road plaintiff has no standing to challenge the road construction project. Of course, by the time the government gets around to taking the land it may be too late for a court to intervene as the road may already be constructed on both sides of the land and without plaintiff's land the road would be useless. In such a case no court will leave the two ends of the road going nowhere while plaintiff challenges the right to take its piece.

---

45 ACLL Article 9.

46 See, V. Lee Hamilton and Joseph Sanders, EVERYDAY JUSTICE (Yale University Press, 1992) 35-36; see also, Tom Ginsburg, Dismantling the "Developmental State"? Administrative Procedure Reform in Japan and Korea, 49 American Journal of Comparative Law 585, 595-596 (2001).

Similarly if there is a law that is designed to protect small business interests by requiring that large department stores in the neighborhood open later than small stores and close earlier than small stores a small store owner would have standing to challenge an agency determination to permit a large department store to open early and close late. If plaintiff is a resident of the community concerned that there will be excessive traffic late at night because of the store's late hours, plaintiff has no standing to sue as plaintiff has no legal interest. Even if there is a traffic control law that provides that there should be less traffic at night for various reasons this does not give plaintiff standing because that law gives individuals no specific legal rights that are disturbed by the agency determination. An interest shared in common by all citizens is a reflex interest and not a legal interest. Injury in fact to a specific plaintiff in common with all in the community is not a basis for standing when that injury comes from an agency decision that affects all in common with all others.[47] Where an agency does not take formal action but adopts policies that guide the administrated as to how to proceed, such guiding advice is not grounds for standing even if the reality is that such guidance changes the playing field that statutes appear to set out to govern situations. Since Administrative Guidance is by definition non-binding (although followed) it cannot give rise to standing to sue as no legal interest can be adversely affected by guidance.[48]

Under a classical application of the rule a resident could not challenge agency action that permitted excessive night time traffic in his/her neighborhood even if there were a pollution control law that seeks to restrict night time traffic because of atmospheric changes that cause more pollution at night. This is also true even if the resident is an asthmatic. The rationale is that the resident would not have standing as no *legal* right (as distinguished from health) is being adversely affected by the agency determination. But such a rule is too harsh in extreme situations. Thus if the government licenses the construction of a nuclear plant under a law that deals with the construction design of the plant, residents in the zone where an accident at the plant could have fatal results would seem to have interests that are different from the average person and the public in general. That special interest should be protected. Under classical application of the standing requirement residents have no legal interest in the design of the plant and thus no standing to challenge the design approval. On the other hand the purpose of a design law is to protect against catastrophic accident, and accordingly it would seem reasonable to allow people who could be killed by such an accident an opportunity to challenge the approval of the design. In such severe situation the courts have loosened the standing rule and have permitted persons in danger of life

---

47 See, Frank K. Upham, After Minamata: Current Prospects and Problems in Japanese Environmental Litigation, 8 Ecology Law Quarterly 213 (1979).

48 For a discussion of the connection between restrictive rules on standing, necessity for a disposition and Administrative Guidance see, Frank K. Upham, Privatizing Regulation: The Implementation of the Large Scale Retail Stores Law, POLITICAL DYNAMICS IN CONTEMPORARY JAPAN (Gary D. Allison, & Yosunori Stone Ed. Cornell University Press, 1993).

threatening injury to challenge government licensing of nuclear facilities.[49] Such persons are within the zone of interests that the design law protects even if the design law gives *them* no legal rights that are being affected by the design approval. There is debate on how far this loosening goes and whether it is limited to life threatening or similarly potentially devastating situations. In any event, the doctrine of standing and the specific requirement that a legal interest of the plaintiff is injured by the agency disposition has been a major impediment to administrative litigation.

In the *Niigata Airport case* of 1989 the Supreme Court appeared to have supported a loosening of the standing requirement. The Supreme Court refused to grant plaintiffs relief in that case finding that no legal interest had been damaged. The reasoning of the court is interesting. The plaintiffs argued that the permit to allow additional flights to Korea would lead to passengers engaging in conduct (while in Korea) that violated good morals. The court found that such argument did not demonstrate interference with a legal right of the residents who were suing. The court implied that *if* the argument had been based on the flights affecting the resident's health (from excess noise vibrations) then standing might be proper. The Supreme Court appeared to retreat from this broadening approach in the *Route 6 Ring Road case* of 1999 by requiring the plaintiffs who were challenging a highway project actually own land affected by the project.

In 2001 the Supreme Court held that where a law has as its intent the protection of a specific interest of individuals as distinguished from the public interest in general then such individuals have standing to challenge government-licensing action that may adversely affect the statutorily protected interest. Thus where it was proposed to build golf courses upriver of plaintiffs' land and where the river had flooded in the past and where the Forestry Law had as its purpose the protection of downstream land owners whose property could be adversely affected by land slides or other disasters if Forest Preserve land was permitted to be used for development, such downstream owners had standing to challenge the grant of a development permit that permitted the development of the golf courses. However, owners of trees in the development area and farmers who used the waters from the river for their farms were not specifically intended to be protected by the Forestry Law and thus had no standing.[50]

In December of 2003 the Tokyo High Court rejected an attempt by residents living near the Odakyu Rail Line to challenge the government's approval of a plan to place an extension of the line overhead rather than underground. The residents had argued that the overhead line would cause excessive noise and that the government had failed to consider the advantages of an underground line over the overhead line. The Tokyo District Court had held that plaintiff residents who had property within the construction site and those with property near the site had

49 See, 46 Minshu No. 6, 571 (Sup. Ct. 9/22/1992).

50 Case No 180 of 1996, 55 Minshu 283 (Sup. Ct. Petty Bench, 3/13/01) available in English through the web site of the Supreme Court of Japan.

standing and had reversed the government's approval of the project. The High Court reversed finding that the residents without property inside the construction site had no standing to sue as they did not own any land being used for the project. Accordingly no legal right was being affected.[51]

The ACLL standing requirement and the requirement that a legal interest be damaged are statutory in nature. Article 9 of the ACLL specifically requires that a legal interest of the party suing be injured. The government's 2004 initiative to amend the ACLL does not change the wording of the present Article 9 but it does add a new Article 9 subdivision 2 whose purpose would appear to be to loosen the legal interest doctrine. This provision would allow a reviewing court to consider statutes other than the statute under which the agency is acting to determine whether a legal interest has been injured. Indeed, it appears that the new legislation intends to apply the doctrine of the nuclear power plant standing ruling to all administrative action and not simply cases of potential catastrophic accident with potential loss of life.

Under the amendment, in determining whether a party has standing the court can look beyond the named parties in a disposition and in doing so should take into consideration a) the language of any statute or rule involved in the disposition, b) the purpose of the statute or rule. In other words the court is not limited to a literal reading of the language of the rule. The court should consider the purpose of the statute or rule in determining whether there is injury to a party's legal interest. In making standing to sue determinations courts should not only consider the specific statute or rule under which the agency is acting but also other statutes that have a common purpose. Moreover, in making a standing determination the degree of injury suffered by the plaintiff and the strength of the interest affected should be considered. The legislation is a compromise between those who wished to open standing to all cases of injury in fact as long as the plaintiff was within the zone of interests protected by the law under which the agency was acting and those who wished to keep standing requirements strict. As a consequence the legislation keeps the legal interest test but seems to try to define that test by use of the zone of interest notion that is common to American administrative lawyers. There is of course a clash between legal interest and zone of interest. Those who have a legal interest that the statute protects are clearly within the coverage of the statute while those within the zone of interest are outside the legal interests granted by the statute but inside the zone of interests that the statute attempts to deal with. On the other hand the legislation would appear to be applying the loosened standing to sue requirements of the nuclear plant citing case to other administrative cases. It remains to be seen whether the new approach will substantially modify the stringent standing to sue rule of present administrative litigation.

---

51 For a discussion of the Odakyu decision and of the standing requirement's adverse effect on judicial review of agency action in general see, High Court backs Elevated Odakyu Line, Japan Times on Line 12/19/2003; see also, Editorial, Forfeiting the Watchdog Role, Japan Times on Line 12/22/03.

As a rule a plaintiff in Japan is not compelled to exhaust administrative remedies.[52] However, in some cases the substantive statute dealing with agency action requires exhaustion. In such a case the plaintiff is required to exhaust.[53] However, it is not always easy to know whether exhaustion is required. The new amendments require that an agency issuing a disposition advise the parties: a) who is the proper party to be sued in the event that litigation is commenced to challenge the disposition, b) the deadline for timely filing litigation, and c) whether exhaustion of administrative remedies is required.

In the United States the agency taking an administrative action must prepare an administrative record that is sent to the court. The court reviews the case "on the record" created in the agency. In Japan the agency typically does not prepare such a formal record. In any event, review of administrative action—like review of the first instance court—is not "on the record." This has many ramifications that are unusual to the American lawyer dealing with administrative cases. For one thing the agency is not bound by the reasons it gave for its action in the first instance. Unlike the United States where the agency wins or loses based on the rationale it gave when it made its regulatory decision, in Japan the agency can raise new rationales to justify its action when it is challenged before the court. It is not sufficient for the party challenging administrative action to show that the reasons given for the action were irrational, were arbitrary or were capricious. Assuming all of the above the agency may simply change tactics and raise other reasons for its actions. If the court finds such post hoc reasons justify the action then the government wins.

Moreover, the government is not limited to the record made in the agency. At the court appeal level the parties may introduce new evidence to support their positions. Once a suit is properly filed under the ACLL the basic procedure of the case is the same as for any other civil case. The procedures of the Code of Civil Procedure are utilized except where there is a specific governing provision of the ACLL. Under those procedures there is to be clarification, Preparation for Oral

52 Although exhaustion is not usually required, administrative appeals are permitted in most cases where a *shobun* has been denied. See, Administrative Complaint Investigation Law (Law No. 160, 9/15/62 as amended). Article 4 of the Law lists 11 categories of cases where administrative appeal is not permitted. In addition to those categories that would be expected—e.g., acts of the Diet, final judicial decisions, etc.—there are other more controversial categories such as a disposition by a public prosecutor, or a decision dealing with school children or a disposition regarding entry or departure of aliens or dispositions dealing with nationality, etc. A party who seeks an investigation into a administrative decision or who seeks reversal of the decision from the agency itself cannot suffer a worse decision on the basis of the investigation or appeal. Article 40 (5) and 47 (3). Where an investigation by an entity other than the deciding agency concludes that the decision of the agency was either illegal or erroneous the investigating agency may nonetheless permit the illegal decision to remain in effect if overturning the decision would be inconsistent with the public interest. In making this determination the investigating agency in addition to considering the effect on the public also considers the damages suffered by the aggrieved party and the extent to which such damages may be offset by compensation. Article 40 (6).

53 ACLL Article 8.

Argument or other pre-Oral Argument procedures and the Oral Argument with the introduction of evidence. This is not just a theoretical right. Evidence is taken at the District and High Courts when there is an administrative appeal. For example, in 2001 the High Court received new witness testimony evidence in approximately 17% of all administrative cases before the High Courts. This was a decline from approximately 30% of cases where new evidence was heard by the High Court in administrative cases in 1996:[54]

Percentage of Cases Where the High Court Received New Evidence in Administrative Cases

Year	Third-Person Witness	Party Witness	Court Expert	Other
1996	19.4	10.1	—	0.9
1997	25.5	10.6	0.2	0.5
1998	16.1	7.2	—	2.0
1999	15.6	5.1	0.4	—
2000	10.0	3.6	0.4	0.1
2001	13.7	3.2	0.5	0.5

One of the governing principles of the ACLL dealing with procedure is Article 24. Under Article 24 the court has the authority *ex officio* (on its own motion) to take the testimony of witnesses and examine other evidence. The prewar Code of Civil Procedure gave the courts this same *ex officio* authority as part of the inquisition nature of civil procedure. It was the objective of the Occupation to make the civil procedure more "democratic" by taking this power away from the court and giving responsibility for litigation to the parties. By removing the *ex officio* authority of the court the Occupation believed it was preserving the court's neutrality. As it has worked out, in the normal civil case the parties have the responsibility of suggesting witnesses—the court cannot *ex officio* call a witness[55]—and the parties typically first examine the witnesses—the court can change the order of examination and the court may examine after the parties. How much the removal of the *ex officio* authority has meant is debatable. What is not debatable is that the prewar form of judge as active participant through *ex officio* authority to examine evidence has been retained in administrative litigation. Such a provision might work to the benefit of a pro se litigant with little experience in judicial affairs. However, in a bureaucratic society such as Japan where both the administrative agency

54 Carl F. Goodman, Japan's New Civil Procedure Code: Has it Fostered a Rule of Law Dispute Resolution Mechanism, 29 Brooklyn Journal of International Law 511 (2004). The Brooklyn Journal of International Law has given permission for the use and copying of this material.

55 In addition to the special provisions of the ACLL allowing the court *ex officio* to take evidence, the Law on Procedures for Resolution of Personal Status permits the court to take evidence *ex officio* if the court believes that such evidence will assist in preserving the marital status of the parties. Article 14.

whose action is being challenged and the judiciary are bureaucratic organs and where bureaucrats are highly regarded, such authority by the court is more likely to work to the benefit of the government. Indeed the close affinity of the administrative and judicial arms of the government is highlighted by the fact that judicial officials (judges) are regularly assigned to work in administrative bodies while retaining their position as judges.

The government's 2004 initiative would make the ACLL consistent with the new Patent Law and the amended Code of Civil Procedure in providing greater access to government documents. Since the challenge to administrative disposition is not based on the record made in the agency, the challenger may have no understanding of what the real reasons were for the administrative action. Indeed, it is possible that the reasons given by the agency for its actions are not the actual reasons for the action. The actual reasons can be hidden because the agency need not support its position by supporting the publicly stated rationale. To enable the challenger to better understand the government's rationale and to enable the court to better understand the true facts behind the agency's determination, the 2004 initiative requires that on motion of the challenger the court can order the agency to produce the agency documents that disclose the reasons for the agency action. The court may also order production of documents disclosing the facts behind the agency determination.[56]

The ACLL contains a provision that permits a reviewing court to temporarily suspend the applicability of a disposition where a suit to set aside the disposition is pending. This temporary suspension authority is similar to a Temporary Restraining Order ("TRO") in the United States. Under the old law, to obtain such a temporary suspension the plaintiff had to show that failure to grant suspension would result in irreparable injury.[57] The 2004 amendments change the law by replacing the requirement for irreparable injury with a requirement that the injury be shown to be "serious". "Serious" is not defined but it would appear that a lesser standard than the old irreparable injury standard is to be followed. As is true in other injunction type situations the court may not issue the temporary suspension if issuance *could* seriously affect the public welfare.

The temporary suspension authority gives rise to one of the more unusual features of Japanese procedure—the Prime Minister's Objection. Temporary suspension authority is rarely utilized and when it is used it usually is directed at a disposition that has almost immediate effect and where failure to suspend will result in the subject matter of the litigation being overtaken by events. For example, the revocation of a permit to protest in a public park on a specific date. If the revocation occurs shortly before the date set, there is no reasonable expectation that the disposition can be effectively reviewed since by the time the court has an opportunity to proceed to the merits of the case the date will have passed. In such a case the applicant may seek a temporary suspension of the disposition revoking the per-

56 ACLL Article 23-2.

57 CCP Article 25.

mit.[58] If the government considers the planned demonstration to be dangerous to public safety, the ACLL contains a safety valve in Article 27. Article 27 is not limited to the situation presented but by its terms is applicable to any request by a party for a temporary suspension.

Under Article 27 when a party requests a temporary suspension from the court, the Prime Minister may set forth an objection to temporary suspension. Although objection by the Prime Minister may seem overkill, it is not particularly troubling to permit the head of the Executive Branch to state a position on whether a court should temporarily suspend a determination of the Executive Branch. What is unique—and troubling—is the effect of the Prime Minister's objection. Under the statute the court is compelled to recognize the Prime Minister's objection and deny the request for suspension or cancel the suspension if already granted. In essence the law makes the Prime Minister's objection binding on the Judicial Branch. Although the Prime Minister must explain the grounds for the objection and must state the Prime Minister's conclusion that failure to suspend will result in serious adverse effect to the public welfare, the court is not permitted to go behind the reasons and conclusion. The court is obligated to accept the Prime Minister's objection and to act in accord with the objection. As an attempt to give some political review to the action of the Prime Minister, the ACLL requires the Prime Minister to report on his conduct to the next session of the Diet. The report to the Diet adds some political accountability to the Prime Minister's action. However, the report fails to deal with the main defect in the Prime Minister's objection system, i.e., its violation of the separation of powers and the constitutionally mandated independence of the judiciary. In essence the Prime Minister has the power to reverse a temporary suspension issued by a court. Moreover, the system gives one side of the litigation a right to determine at least the temporary outcome of the litigation. Where the temporary outcome can oust the court of meaningful jurisdiction because the matter has become moot, it gives the government the power to ultimately decide a case challenging government action. Although calling for reform of the Administrative Case Litigation Law and recommending that the judicial system be made a true check to balance the power of the Executive, the Law Reform Council did not recommend any change in the Prime Minister's objection.

The ACLL has another provision that is unusual and has the effect of protecting the government administration from effective judicial control. This is the authorization of a "circumstance decision."[59] A circumstance decision is a decision in which the court effectively holds that agency action was unlawful but where the court nonetheless, because of the circumstances of the case, refuses to reverse the agency action. In theory the circumstance decision is similar to an equity court's refusal to grant an injunction where the requesting party shows that it has a right but where the court in balancing the equities finds that grant of the injunction

58 Temporary suspension would not apply to denial of a permit.

59 ACLL Article 31.

would be so detrimental to the public interest that no injunction should be issued. However, a circumstance decision takes into account all of the circumstances—not simply the public interest—and although it finds the agency action unlawful it nonetheless permits that unlawful action to take effect. In the past, the inability to sue until there has been a *shobun* has meant that many situations have developed where the government through postponing the *shobun* until it was too late for effective action to be taken to undo the *shobun* has prevented a plaintiff from obtaining effective relief. Even if the court ultimately concluded that plaintiff was in the right the circumstances that were changed during the delay prevent relief (other than monetary damages). By delaying the *shobun* and then by delaying the course of the trial—while all the while building the dam or the highway or the power plant—the agency ultimately presents the court with a fait accompli and argues for and obtains a circumstance decision. The "successful" challenger is left with a moral victory and an action for damages, but the government gets its project. Thus, where an administrative agency improperly concluded that land could be expropriated to construct a dam and after the dam's construction it was determined that the agency acted improperly the court could allow the dam to remain in place because a determination to tear down the dam could have devastating effects on people living downstream.[60] The circumstance decision has been used by the Supreme Court in apportionment cases in refusing to reverse unlawful elections even though the Public Office Election Law specifically excludes action under ACLL Article 31.[61] Nonetheless the Supreme Court, arguing by analogy to the circumstance decision, held that to overturn the election would be too harmful to the public.[62]

Although the 2004 initiative is helpful in dealing with certain historical problems faced by plaintiffs in challenging administrative action it surely does not go as far as the Law Reform Council has suggested. The new initiative would allow the court in administrative cases to issue injunctions but it does not change the law as stated in the *Osaka Airport case* that the normal civil action cannot be used to obtain an injunction where highly political governmental regulatory authority is challenged. The initiative should liberalize the rules for standing to sue by making it easier for plaintiffs to show that they have an interest that is sufficient to give them standing but it does not change the rule that a "legal interest" is required. The initiative does however give the court the opportunity to broaden the interpretation of legal interest. The new initiative will enable plaintiffs to compel the government to act on an application earlier than was formerly the case. As a

60 See, e.g., Kayano v. Hokkaido Expropriation Committee (Nibutani Dam Case), 1598 Hanrei Jiho 33, 938 Hanrei Taimuzu 75, Sapporo District Court 3/27/97. For an English language version, see, 38 Int'l Legal Materials 394.

61 Public Office Election Law Article 219(1) (Law No. 100 of 1950).

62 *Kurokawa v. Chiba Election Commission* 30 Minshu 223, case No. 1974 (Gyo-Tsu) No. 75 (Sup. Ct. Grand Bench, 4/30/76) available on the web in English on the web site of the Supreme Court of Japan, Judgments of the Supreme Court, also in Lawrence W. Beer & Hiroshi Itoh, THE CONSTITUTIONAL CASE LAW OF JAPAN, 1970-1990 (University of Washington Press, 1996) at 355.

consequence this might allow the courts to review actions that otherwise would be not subject to review because time would have made the issue either moot or would have rendered affirmation of the government action the only rational action. All these changes are useful and move in the direction sought by the Law Reform Council. However, the use of the judiciary as a check to balance the power of the bureaucracy cannot be achieved when Administrative Guidance, the real vehicle for regulation in Japan, is not subject to judicial review under the ACLL. Making the ability to sue easier in the perhaps 10% of instances where parties might wish to challenge government action is simply tinkering at the edges. The real engine of regulation, the real mechanism behind bureaucratic administration of the economy, commerce, workplace relations, communications policy, etc., is Administrative Guidance and the requirement for a *shobun*, the need to show a government disposition, effectively insulates Administrative Guidance from any possible check from the Judicial Branch. In addition, the 2004 initiative does nothing to deal with the substantive rules under which the courts review agency dispositions. The prewar German administrative law doctrine of free discretion under which bureaucratic action that is deemed to be discretionary is given such deference as to make it almost immune from review stands in the way of effective judicial review of agency determinations in many situations.[63] To achieve the goals sought by the Judicial Reform Council a significant overhaul of the ACLL is required. In light of the 2004 reform it is likely that any attempt in the near future will meet with the objection that reform has already been undertaken and it is time to move on to different issues.

---

63 The High Court's decision in the Odakyu Railway case is a recent example of the problem. Even assuming the plaintiffs had standing the High Court would have reversed the District Court and upheld the agency because at the time of the agency decision there were no noise standards in effect and hence the agency's determination that there was not too great a noise level could not be found as in excess of the agency's discretion. But six years later, when the suit was at the High Court there were in fact noise standards and apparently the agency's determination was inconsistent with the noise standards. An American court would look at the standards in effect at the time of decision and require the agency to disclose how its determination was consistent with the standards that would be applied to the future construction project. The High Court disregarded current standards and looked at the agency's determination in a vacuum finding no standards at the time of decision and hence no action in excess of discretion. Editorial, Forfeiting the Watchdog Role, Japan Times on Line 12/22/03. Further, the Odakyu case demonstrates how the judicial system's built in time delays insure effective government immunity from judicial review. The plan for the rail line was adopted in 1993 and the government approval at issue was issued in 1994. The District Court held the approval granted for the line unlawful in 2001. The government appealed in October 2001. The High Court's decision was two years in the making and during this entire period the rail line at issue was being constructed. Even if the Supreme Court hears the case it is unlikely that the court would render a decision until after March 2005—by which time the project will have been completed. Clearly the plaintiffs can get no effective relief because even if the Supreme Court were inclined to reverse the High Court the best that could be expected is a circumstance decision. See, High Court backs Elevated Odakyu Line, Japan Times on Line 12/19/2003 for a listing of the dates referred to.

13

Summary Courts and Special Cases

Just as American State court systems provide special forums for small claims matters and have special procedures for certain cases that are not deemed to require the complicated procedural rules of the typical case, so too Japan's judicial system and Code of Civil Procedure have special provisions to deal with such cases.

A. Summary Court and Small Claims Matters

The Summary Court is established at a level below the District Court. In civil cases, in addition to handling conciliation cases discussed earlier in Chapter 10,[1] it is similar to a small claims court in that it handles cases involving claims that do not exceed 1,400,000yen.[2] In addition to the typical procedure applicable to most cases, the Summary Court has a special "one-day" procedure for the handling of cases involving less than 300,000yen.

There are 438 Summary Courts scattered throughout Japan. Summary Court judges may serve until the age of 70.[3] As a consequence some District Court judges upon reaching the mandatory retirement age of 65 will move to the Summary Court. To qualify as a Summary Court judge a person need not have judicial

---

1 Where the parties have settled a matter prior to coming to Summary Court but wish to have the settlement become a judicial determination (so that it can more easily be the subject of compulsory execution without having to pay the fees of a Notary to Notarize the settlement) there is no ceiling on the amount of claim involved.

2 Court Organization Law Article 33 (1). The jurisdictional limit used to be 900,000yen but the limit was recently raised to 1,400,000yen. Law No. 128 of 2003. See also, A Lawyers Guide to Japan, Asahi Law Office Tokyo, March 2004 on the web at *www.lexmundi.com/images/lexmundi/pdf/guide-japan04.pdf*.

3 Court Organization Law Article 50.

experience. Most Summary Court judges have had experience as court clerks.[4] Unlike the District Court where cases may be handled by a panel of judges, a single judge handles all Summary Court cases.[5]

As is the case with small claims courts in the United States, procedures in the Summary Courts are simplified. The Complaint in Summary Court does not need to be in writing but can be stated orally[6]. In addition the statement of the case need not be as detailed as in District Court.[7] Although the principle of Oral Argument applies to Summary Court cases, Preparatory Documents such as in the District Court need not precede the Oral Argument[8] although briefs may be utilized. Where a writing is utilized and is served on the opposition party, failure of the opposing party to appear may constitute a default, unless the party not appearing has filed a writing contesting the claims or defenses.[9] A defendant in a Summary Court matter may file a counterclaim that exceeds the jurisdictional limits of the Summary Court. In such situation the case is transferred to the District Court.[10]

Witnesses may appear in Summary Court and parties may testify. The court may require that a witness, an expert or a party submit a statement in writing in place of oral testimony.[11] If a written statement is used, the opposition party may submit written questions to the witness.[12]

To assist the parties in resolving the matter and to aid the court by providing a practical approach to the case Summary Court judges may make use of laypersons—Judicial Commissioners[13]—who, upon permission of the court may directly question parties or witnesses.[14]

Consistent with the more informal nature of Summary Court cases, the records of the case may be expunged if the judge deems it appropriate[15] and opinions and de-

---

4 Toru Miura, Independence, Transparency and Accountability of the Judiciary in Japan, on the web at *www.unafei.or.jp/pdf/indonesia_pdf/session4.pdf* at page 36.

5 Court Organization Law Article 35.

6 CCP Article 271.

7 CCP Article 272.

8 CCP Article 276.

9 CCP Article 158 incorporated into Summary Court procedures by Article 277.

10 CCP Article 274; CPR Rule 168.

11 CCP Article 278; CPR Rule 171.

12 CPR Rule 124 incorporated by Rule 171.

13 CCP Article 279.

14 CPR Rule 172.

15 CPR Rule 170.

cisions in Summary Court matters need not be as detailed and complete as in the District Court.[16]

Parties may be represented by counsel in Summary Court cases. However, because of the high cost of counsel and the small claim nature of Summary Court litigation, representation is not typical or economical. Summary Court litigants do however sometimes obtain the out of court assistance of Judicial Scriveners. Upon the recommendation of the Law Reform Council Judicial Scriveners are now permitted to represent parties in small matters before the Summary Court.

Decisions of Summary Court in typical small claim cases may be appealed to a 3-judge panel of the District Court. This first level appeal is a continuation of the trial. Thus the District Court may take the testimony of witnesses on appeal of Summary Court cases. As has been the case with appeals to the High Court from District Court determinations so too in appeal to the District Court the number of witnesses heard on appeal has been declining since the adoption of the new Code. Third-person witnesses heard on such appeals declined by 50% from 16 per 100 cases in 1996 to only 7.2 per 100 cases in 2001. Party witnesses declined from almost 21 per 100 cases in 1996 to only 13 per 100 cases in 2001. Where cases are appealed to the District Court the parties tend to use counsel, although in 2001 in some 31.5% of appealed cases neither side was represented.

The new "one-day" trial procedure is an innovation of the 1996 Code. The procedure applies to cases where the amount in dispute is 300,000yen or less. The plaintiff may at the time of initiating the case request that small claims—"one-day"—procedures be utilized.[17] To avoid small claims matters brought by debt collectors clogging up the one-day trial procedure, a party may only apply for one-day trial ten times in any one year before any particular Summary Court.[18] The defendant has the option of demanding that normal Summary Court procedures be followed but must do so prior to making any presentation at Oral Argument.[19] The defendant can exercise this option in writing prior to appearing for the Oral Hearing or orally at the hearing.[20] If the defendant exercises the option to have the matter heard by ordinary procedure, the clerk must immediately advise the plaintiff[21] unless the option is exercised orally and the plaintiff is present and thus obtains notice through hearing the objection to the one-day pro-

16 CCP Article 280.

17 CCP Article 368.

18 CCP Article 368, CPR Rule 223. The plaintiff must certify that it has not used the procedure more than 10 times in any one year in the Summary Court involved and if the certification is not accurate the plaintiff may be fined a non penal fine of 100,000yen. CCP Article 381.

19 CCP Article 373.

20 CPR Rule 228.

21 CPR Rule 228 (2).

cedure.[22] To assure that the defendant understands the rules of the one-day trial procedure the clerk of the Summary Court must, at the same time as the defendant is summoned to appear in the case, provide the defendant with an explanation of the procedure.[23] The judge, prior to the start of the proceedings must explain to the defendant: 1) the defendant's right to require that ordinary procedure be used; 2) the fact that under the one-day procedure the court will only consider evidence that is available at the time and 3) that there is no right to appeal from a final judgment in the matter although the judgment may be subject to review by the Summary Court under normal procedure if an application is filed within two weeks of the judgment.[24] The judge also has the obligation to determine that the claim is both within the jurisdictional limits of the one-day procedure and that the matter is appropriate for a one-day trial.[25] If the judge determines that the matter not be heard by the one-day procedure, the clerk must notify the parties to this effect.[26] A default may not be taken on a one-day trial case if the defendant has been served by publication—in such a case the matter must be handled as a normal Summary Court proceeding.[27]

Except for special circumstances (determined by the court) the court is to complete the case within one-day and render its decision immediately after hearing the case on the single day.[28] Testimony is taken immediately. The court may use audio telecommunications equipment to take the testimony of witnesses not present in the courthouse.[29] Because of the immediacy of witness testimony there is no need to file written statements concerning testimony.[30] The court may require a party to personally appear even if the party appears by a representative (bengoshi or Legal Scrivener).[31]

In a one-day trial the court may frame an order so as to provide some protection to a losing defendant. This represents a reason why a defendant may not object to the one-day trial procedure. Thus, the court has authority (and the plaintiff cannot appeal from the court's exercise of its authority) to spread the payment of the

---

22 CPR Rule 228 (2).

23 CPR Rule 222 (1).

24 CPR Rule 222 (2).

25 CCP Article 373 (3).

26 CPR Rule 228 (3).

27 CCP Article 373 (3) 3.

28 CCP Article 370, 374.

29 CPR Rule 226.

30 CPR Rule 225.

31 CPR Rule 224.

judgment out over a three-year period and to waive the payment of pre-suit delinquency charges as long as the payment schedule is maintained.[32]

A losing party has no right of appeal to a higher court. The losing party may, within two weeks of the decision, file an *objection* to the determination.[33] If objection is filed, the matter is returned to the Summary Court for proceeding as if the matter had been an ordinary case.[34] The court retains discretionary authority to order a payment schedule in lieu of immediate payment and may still waive pre-filing delinquency payments.[35] Neither party may appeal the final determination of the Summary Court.[36]

The new Code was enacted in 1996 and came into effect in 1998. One year later, in February 1999, the Tokyo Maritime Arbitration Commission (TOMAC) of the Japan Shipping Exchange (JSE) adopted a new set of rules to permit small claims arbitration before the JSE. These rules apply to claims where the amount at issue is 5,000,000yen or less and where there is no counterclaim exceeding that sum. It is likely that the JSE recognized that just as small claim litigation needed a faster route for resolution so too small claim arbitration had a future. Of course, the definition of "small claim" differs greatly. Nonetheless, the coincidence of timing between the effective date of the new small claims jurisdiction of the Summary Court and the adoption of small claims arbitration by the JSE is not likely to have been coincidental. This is especially so as the JSE rules provide for a one-day hearing (exceptional circumstances excepted—as is the case with the new one-day small claim process in Summary Court). In addition, like the Summary Court small claims process the JSE allows the arbitrator to provide for installment payments over a three-year period without interest. Failure to make an installment payment not only accelerates all payments but also subjects the payments already made to interest charges that would otherwise have been waived if installment payments were timely made.[37]

B. Bills and Notes / Payment Demand

In some states of the United States it is possible to initiate an action to recover on the basis of a Bill or Note by Motion for Summary Judgment in lieu of Complaint. The rationale behind this process is that there are really no fact questions once it is

32 CCP Article 375.

33 CCP Article 378.

34 CCP Article 379.

35 CCP Article 379 (2).

36 CCP Article 380.

37 For a discussion of the JSE small claims arbitration rules see, Toshio Matsumoto (Executive Director JSE) Rapid and Cost-effective Arbitration Procedure for Small Claims Launched by TOMAC, JSE Bulletin No. 38 on the web at www.jseinc.org/en/bulletin/bulletin38/matsumo.htm.

established that the Bill or Note was executed and the defendant has failed to make payment when timely demanded. In such situation it is deemed that a speedy recovery by the creditor holding the Bill or Note is appropriate.

So too in Japan an action on a Bill or Note may be filed (depending on the amount at issue the case is filed in either the District or Summary Court) and the plaintiff can demand expedited procedure. To get the special procedure the plaintiff must specifically request such procedure.[38] When such an action is filed, the defendant is not permitted to counterclaim.[39] The presiding judge will set an early date for Oral Argument and the defendant will be summoned and advised of the expedited procedure, including the fact that it is expected that Oral Argument will be concluded on the date specified.[40] The summons in the case must inform the defendant that a written Answer is due on a specified date. The summons must also inform the defendant that failure to contest the allegations at the date set for Oral Argument will lead to a judgment in favor of the plaintiff without further Oral Argument sessions.[41] It is possible to delay the date for Oral Argument and have it rescheduled, but in such case the rescheduled date must be within 15 days of the originally scheduled date.[42] This shows the court's determination to deal with such cases expeditiously and not permit undue delay.

At the Oral Argument there is not supposed to be any oral testimony and evidence is to be taken solely by documents.[43] The court may, however, *sua sponte*, determine to take some evidence.[44] In addition, where either the authenticity and/or presentment of the instrument is in issue the testimony of the parties (not third-person witnesses) may be taken as to these issues.[45] The only real issues to be considered at the Oral Argument are: a) the authenticity of the instrument, b) whether demand was properly made, and c) whether the defendant has failed to make payment. If judgment is entered in favor of the plaintiff the defendant may not appeal[46] but may (within two weeks of judgment) file an objection with the court.[47] Objection has the effect of moving the case to an ordinary proceeding of the court in which pending (either Summary Court or District Court).[48] The court may reject the objection if, on its face, it appears that there is no ground for objec-

---

38 CCP Article 350(2).

39 CCP Article 351.

40 CPR Rule 213 (1) and (2), CPR Rule 214.

41 CCP Article 354, CPR Rule 213 (3).

42 CPR Rule 215.

43 CCP Article 352.

44 CCP Article 352 (5).

45 CCP Article 352 (3).

46 CCP Article 356.

47 CCP Article 357.

48 CCP Article 361.

tion.[49] As a judgment has been entered, after an objection takes the case to an ordinary proceeding the defendant must take steps to attempt to stay execution or execution will be made. To do this, the defendant will typically need to provide security so that if the objection case is lost payment will be guaranteed.[50]

If an action has been filed as a special procedure for a case involving Bills and Notes and such procedure is not appropriate, the plaintiff has the option of transferring the case to the normal procedure without the defendant's consent so long as plaintiff acts prior to the close of the Oral Argument.[51] In such case, the court must advise the defendant of the transfer.[52] This does not change the date set for Oral Argument.[53] A defendant may not rely on the belief that the case filed as a special Bills and Notes case does not qualify and thereby refuse to respond to the case. If the defendant takes such action and the plaintiff at the Oral Argument requests transfer to an ordinary case, the court may conclude the Oral Argument and enter a judgment.[54]

Another special procedure involves creditor collection matters where it is assumed that no factual dispute exists and that judgment should be entered without extended procedures. This procedure deals with obligations to pay money or to deliver negotiable instruments. A motion can be made to the court clerk requesting the clerk to issue a demand for payment notice to the debtor. The proper clerk is the clerk of the Summary Court in the District where the debtor has its general domicile. The motion may also be made to the clerk of the Summary Court for the District where a Note or check is payable. Where the demand relates to the debtor's business, the motion may be made to the clerk of the Summary Court in the District where debtor's place of business is located.[55] If it appears that the motion is well founded the clerk issues the demand for payment. There is no need to question the debtor before issuing the demand and such questioning is not allowed.[56] If the face of the motion shows that the procedure is not appropriate the clerk should deny the motion.[57] The purported debtor has two weeks within which to challenge the demand for payment. If challenge is not made in such time then the demand becomes subject to provisional execution.[58] The demand must be

49 CCP Article 359.

50 CCP Article 398 (1) 4.

51 CCP Article 353.

52 CCP Article 353 (3).

53 CCP Article 353 (4).

54 CCP Article 354.

55 CCP Article 383.

56 CCP Article 386.

57 CCP Article 385.

58 CCP Article 387, 391.

served on the purported debtor but it cannot be served by publication.[59] If the debtor has been served with a demand for payment with a declaration of provisional execution (thus a period of two weeks will have expired from the date the demand was issued, and during this two weeks no challenge to the demand was filed) and has failed to object within a second two weeks or the objection has been made but dismissed by the court and such dismissal has been made final and conclusive, the demand shall have the same effect as a final conclusive judgment and will be subject to compulsory execution.[60]

Although instituted in Summary Court the demand for payment may be in amount in excess of the Summary Court's typical jurisdiction limits. If an objection to demand is filed and the objection appears sufficient to raise an issue then the Summary Court will either retain the case if within its jurisdictional limits or transfer the case to the appropriate District Court.[61] In such case, the filing of the motion for demand for payment shall be deemed for statute of limitations purposes to be the date when the action was commenced.[62] The purpose of the demand procedure is to deal with creditor collection matters where there is no dispute but that the monetary claim is due. If there is a dispute the existence of that dispute will be raised by challenge or objection. Once the existence of dispute is known, the case will take on the character of a contested litigation in either the District or Summary Court.

59 CCP Article 382, 388.

60 CCP Article 396.

61 CCP Article 397 (3).

62 CCP Article 397 (3).

14

American Litigation Involving Japanese Entities and Japanese Litigation Involving American Entities

A. General

To a great extent the practice of international and transnational law is the art of understanding language and culture. The foreign client to whom English is a second language is never fully comfortable in understanding what is transpiring in this alien tongue and requires assistance in understanding nuance and technical terms. Words that seem to have a clear meaning to the native English speaker, such as "right" may have a different meaning to one whose language has borrowed the word from another without either accepting or fully understanding the baggage inherent in the term. Layered on this is the baggage that culture in the borrowing society places on the term. The end result may be a perfect misunderstanding of what is being said by a party with a complete understanding of the words. Similarly, familiarity with a legal system and its associated baggage can lead to lack of understanding of another's legal system. This can arise because of ingrained assumptions regarding concepts of law. Where concepts appear to be the same or where the concepts use the same words or where one system has borrowed heavily from another the potential for misunderstanding is greatest. To better understand the client's perspective, it is necessary to understand the client's frame of reference. To understand American litigation involving Japanese entities, it is necessary to understand the Japanese perspective about litigation. In this context it is useful to understand the Japanese litigation system and the differences that the Japanese and American litigation systems place on words that appear to be the same and concepts that appear to be the same—but are not. Accordingly, to the American practitioner involved in either representing or suing a Japanese entity an understanding of the Japanese system and the Japanese approach to litigation is not simply useful it is essential.

Language is of course a major factor in understanding and avoiding misunderstanding. The transnational lawyer quickly learns never to advise his client in mandatory terms such as "You must understand that from his perspective. . . ."

Why MUST I understand? Is this a command? What is compelling me to do this? What is the penalty for failure to carry out this command? Sometimes we lose sight of the fact that words that appear to mean the same thing have different meanings because the context in which they are used is different. Context, when dealing with legal issues, includes the legal system that is familiar to the client.

A Japanese client is likely to view what occurs in United States litigation through eyes that translate events into a Japanese litigation. Thus, in American litigation courts have come to utilize voluntary conciliation as a means of trying to get parties to settle litigation before trial. In some jurisdictions the process is formalized, in others judges will ask the lawyers whether they think a conciliator would be helpful. To the American client the voluntary nature of the process is clear. To the Japanese client the matter may be confusing. It is the role of the lawyer to explain the voluntary, non-binding and confidential nature of the process to the client in a way that is understandable. To do this is it important to understand how the American process differs from the Japanese process. For example, the Japanese client may not appreciate that conciliation is being undertaken outside the judicial system or that when the federal judge refers the parties to the magistrate to try to conciliate or mediate that the process is secret from the judge. In the United States the magistrate would never think of suggesting to the judge that party P or D was not willing to compromise. The magistrate would never suggest that negotiations fell apart because of the unreasonable attitude of a specific party. The conciliation process in the United States court is entirely confidential. Parties and the court would consider it a violation of ethical standards to relay information to the judge other than we succeeded and there is no need to go to trial or we didn't so let's set a trial date. An American lawyer may not realize that explanation is required. Only by understanding that judge recommended (ordered) conciliation in Japan is different from conciliation in the United States does the need to explain that conciliation does not mean "conciliation" arise.

Moreover, in the conciliation process the magistrate or a third party lawyer may suggest to a party that it might wish to consider a certain proposal. In the American litigation system this is merely an effort by the third party to see if it is possible to bridge the gap between the parties. Such a suggestion is not a statement that the conciliator or more importantly that the court feels the proposal is reasonable. To a Japanese client such a proposal may appear to be what it would be in Japan, namely the recommendation of the court. Consequently the client may feel that failure to react positively might prejudice the case if the case is tried to judgment. Unless the American lawyer is sensitive to this nuance brought on by the client's understanding of litigation in Japan, serious disadvantage can result.

Similar considerations affect the procedure of the trial. Thus, a Japanese client understanding that the Japanese Inquiry Process is based on the American Interrogatory procedure may believe that the same rules apply to Interrogatories as apply to Inquiries. Nothing could be further from the truth. The Japanese client has no reason to doubt the similarity and hence no reason to raise the question of difference. The American lawyer on the other hand may not know that there is an Inquiry

Process in Japan. The American lawyer may not appreciate that the client is bringing to the Interrogatory procedure assumptions about Interrogatories that are not accurate. It is the obligation of the American counsel to understand the differences and make sure that the client is informed of the differences and the consequences that could flow from treating mandatory Interrogatories as if they were non-mandatory Inquiries.

It is now commonplace to generalize that Japanese clients do not like to litigate. This homily is based on a partial understanding of cultural values and the relative paucity of litigation in Japan. As is true of most generalizations there is a kernel of truth in the statement. As most generalizations it must be understood in context and when the context of comparative lack of litigation is understood the statement loses some of its force. Thus, the relative lack of litigation in Japan may have more to do with institutional barriers to plaintiff success than with social/cultural norms that rejects confrontation. The relative lack of litigation may be a reflection of the numerous alternative dispute resolution mechanisms available in Japan that make it unnecessary and in many cases economically inefficient to litigate. Perhaps the potential Japanese plaintiff would be willing to litigate in the United States if the lawyer explained the difference in function and hence the incentives of litigation in the American legal system. Perhaps the lawyer would be less likely to recommend litigation to the Japanese client if the lawyer better understood the Japanese executive's distrust of depositions and unwillingness to testify either by deposition or in open court. The sword has two edges and to explain the true situation to the Japanese client it is necessary to understand the client's perspective.

The frequently made assumption that Japanese companies will settle anything to avoid litigating is incorrect. Experience shows that Japanese companies will endeavor to settle disputes before they evolve into actual litigation. They will negotiate in good faith in an effort to reach a reasonable compromise and may even try to find a compromise that will create a new mutually beneficial relationship. Once the gauntlet of litigation has been thrown down the Japanese client can be as aggressive as any other entity that feels itself attacked. Indeed, perhaps because the effort to resolve disputes before they ripen into litigation is so intense once there is litigation a Japanese client might be more aggressive in protecting its interests. Japanese commentators share the experience of all out conflict once litigation has begun as compared to willingness to compromise prior to the start of litigation.[1]

The difference may be in timing and the circumstance of the case. Some Japanese executives—typically graduates of the *Hogakubu* law faculty—have internalized the Japanese litigation system with its high costs for filing litigation, high up front costs for counsel, long delays in process, unavailability of realistic discovery devices and low damage awards. These factors may lead these executives to shun the role of plaintiff in American litigation. At the same time, news stories about American jury awards, punitive damages and broad excursions into company files

1 See, Yasuhei Taniguchi in Mediation in Japan and Mediation's Cross-cultural Viability, Biennial IFCAI Conference (10/24/97) at p. 3 of 9.

and depositions of company executives—all unavailable in Japan—may lead Japanese companies to try to avoid becoming either defendants or plaintiffs. Better understanding how the client sees actual and potential litigation is a great help when it comes to explaining the realities of American litigation to a foreign client.

Recognition that the Japanese client may think it can keep documents in its file secret even after litigation has been initiated because such documents are secret in Japan is the first step in being able to adequately advise the client as to the reality of American discovery. Recognition that the files of an American subsidiary are American documents and thus subject to the power of the American court is essential in evaluating litigation. Understanding that American courts view discovery as a personal obligation of a party and thus within the control of the American court when the party is subject to the jurisdiction of the American court can help avoid misunderstandings about discovery obligations. It may be second nature to American lawyers that Interrogatories in the United States must be answered and that there are severe sanctions for failure to answer or failure to answer truthfully. To the American lawyer it goes without saying that the client must answer accurately and timely. But Inquiries in Japan do not need to be answered and there exists no sanction for failure to respond in a timely fashion. Thus it does not go without saying that American Interrogatories need to be approached differently from Japanese Inquiries. Unless the American lawyer understands or at least operates on the understanding that to the Japanese client an American Interrogatory may appear to be the same as a Japanese Inquiry, the lawyer may fail in his/her obligation to the client. Japan has a no sanctions regime governing such matters as inquiries while the United States has a sanctions regime governing all discovery. It is incumbent on counsel to adequately explain to the Japanese client the full scope and reach of the sanctioning power of the American judge and the necessity to make full and timely discovery. Japanese clients must be closely counseled about the potential penalties in the American system. When counsel understands the differences in the Japanese and American systems more meaningful and more understandable counseling is available. Explanations that take into account the client's preconceived notions have more meaning to the client. In this regard the court's authority to enforce its orders via contempt is unavailable in Japan and there is no reason to believe that a Japanese client would even ask about the possibility since there is no reason for the client to even consider the question. The contempt power is not easily understood by persons with little familiarity with the equity system and the authority of the equity court. Contempt is simply outside the frame of reference of many Japanese clients. Only by understanding that lack of commonality can the lawyer and the client occupy common ground so that the client can understand the American system.

B. Checklist of Differences

Some aspects of the Japanese system must be understood to properly represent a client in the United States considering suit against a Japanese entity. In such a case service by mail that might be appropriate against an American defendant may not be appropriate in Japan. Similarly, the American client sued in Japan needs to understand some of the differences between the two systems.

Of course some Japanese entities have been doing business in the United States for so long that they are fully Americanized when it comes to the American legal system. Their experiences in American courtrooms may mean that they know more about the American system than they do about the Japanese system. For the client who may not be sophisticated about American procedure, or for the client that may think it is sophisticated about the United States judicial system and its workings but is not, for the Japanese executives in Tokyo who have never been exposed to the American system and for American clients who are unfamiliar with the Japanese system a short checklist may be in order. As starters counsel might want to consider:

a) In the United States filing fees are low and many plaintiffs have no out of pocket expenses for the litigation as the case may be on a contingent fee—meaning that the pressure to settle may be more on the lawyer than the client. In Japan costs to sue are high and legal fees are similarly high—contingent fees are virtually unknown—since part of the lawyer's fee in Japan is paid "up front" there is money out of pocket to the plaintiff as soon as the suit starts. However, pressure to settle may also be strong for the lawyer as the bengoshi has been paid the up front portion of the fee immediately and typically will not receive higher fees for working longer hours;

a.1) As a rule, Japanese lawyers are not paid on an hourly basis for litigation (although this is changing especially where international litigation is involved). Japanese clients may not be familiar with the American hourly rate system and thus may be suspicious that the American lawyer is padding the hours or avoiding settlement talks to increase fees. The American fee system should be carefully explained. Bills should be clearly written to avoid confusion over billing;

b) In Japan there are formalized and institutionalized alternative dispute resolution mechanisms available to resolve many disputes that in the United States can only be resolved by the court. Before going to litigation the availability of such mechanisms should be explored as they may provide a better (for both sides), quicker and less expensive avenue of dispute resolution. Because Japanese damage awards are more predictable than American awards (there is no jury to be concerned about and judges generally are well informed of what their colleagues are doing in the damages area and try to stay in the same range as their colleagues) settlement without trial may be more economical and involve less costs than litigation;

c) There is no "shame" in the United States in being a party to litigation and few if any potential plaintiffs avoid litigation out of social stigma concerns. In Japan the potential plaintiff may be obsessed with concern about how the community in general and the groups of which the potential plaintiff is a part may feel about litigation. There may be concern that being a plaintiff will hold the party up to scorn, ridicule and charges of selfishness;

d) If following procedural rules will result in a miscarriage of justice i.e., the wrong party winning the case, Japanese courts may give the procedural rule less importance than would be the case in the United States;

e) The Complaint in the United States is notice of claim pleading and can be based on information and belief. While there needs to be some exploration into facts to support a good faith belief in the claim there does not need to be an exhaustive examination into the facts before filing suit. In Japan the Complaint is based on fact pleading. As a consequence the Complaint must plead both ultimate facts and evidentiary facts. Documents to support the claim should be attached to the Complaint. This requires a much more exhaustive exploration into the facts before a Complaint is filed in Japan. Because of post-filing discovery problems, to be successful the plaintiff must have a relatively complete case before filing the Complaint;

f) Service of process in the United States may be performed by private parties and can be made by certified mail. Service of process in Japan is a governmental function and is made by the court. The Japanese view of the Hague Convention does not permit service by mail on a Japanese defendant through informal means such as certified mail. There is a division of authority on the issue in American courts. If an American court obtains jurisdiction over a Japanese defendant by a means not recognized by Japan, any judgment obtained will not be granted comity and execution in Japan;

g) Discovery in the United States is very extensive and will likely involve an exploration in the files and records of the defendant. The relevant files of the plaintiff can also be discovered. Officials of both parties will likely be examined at a deposition where oral testimony will be recorded. Such testimony may be used at trial. Depositions taken in a lawyer's office are unknown in Japan and document "discovery" is substantially limited;

g.1) Taking of testimony and assembling the evidence in a case in Japan is viewed as a sovereign function. It is an act by a public official, namely the judge. As a consequence American lawyers cannot simply travel to Japan to interview prospective witnesses or investigate facts in litigation. Nor can depositions be taken in the office of an American lawyer practicing as a foreign law expert in Japan. There are complex formalities that must be followed including obtaining a special visa for these purposes. Depositions can only be taken pursuant to government-to-government agreement and in the United States Embassy or Consulate. Failure to follow these procedures may not only result in difficulties for the lawyer while in Japan but will result in any judgment obtained in the United States being denied recognition in Japan;

h) America has no "self-use" document exception to discovery—in Japan documents created solely for the use of a party and whose production would injure an interest of the preparing party are not subject to production;

i) Discovery is a "right" in the United States. The lawyers and parties engage in discovery. The judge only becomes involved in discovery when the lawyers cannot resolve disputes. In Japan there is no discovery although document production may be obtained through court order. During the Oral Argument (Plenary Hearing) (including the Preliminary Oral Argument and Preparation for Oral Argument stages) the judge can direct that a party produce documents. Production is in the discretion of the judge and there are limits on what documents a judge can order produced. The most significant limit is that self-use documents will not be ordered produced if production will in some way harm the party for whose use the document was prepared. (Harm would result if an ongoing business enterprise had to disclose advice and/or recommendations received from staff as this would inhibit ongoing frank discussions within the enterprise.) Production of meaningful documents is significantly less likely in Japan than in the United States;

i.1) Documents in the files of an American subsidiary or American branch of a Japanese company will be treated by an American court as American documents. Such documents are subject to American rules concerning discovery. Where an American court has *in personum* jurisdiction over a Japanese entity the American court will exercise authority over documents of that entity wherever located. American courts will not apply the self-use document exception even if the document is located in Japan;

j) Parties are required to truthfully answer American Interrogatories. Answer must be made within a relatively short period of time. The client answers the Interrogatories (the lawyer can help draft answers) and the lawyer signs objections to questions. In Japan there is no requirement to answer Inquiries from the opposition. Although lawyers may have an ethical obligation to answer there is no sanction for failure to answer. Most lawyers do not answer questions that could hurt their client's case. The non-sanction regime for Inquiries applies to both pre-filing and post-filing Inquiries;

k) Witnesses and parties in the United States have few privileges to enable them to avoid answering questions at discovery or trial. Although the Code of Civil Procedure appears to have few privileges, the reality is that witnesses and parties in Japan have much greater access to privilege than in the United States. Questions whose answers may prove embarrassing to an entity or person with whom the witness has a relationship or answers that could harm a protected relationship may be ruled out of order because of a kind of modified "privilege." American courts will apply American privilege rules to testimony of executives and/or employees of Japanese entities that are party to American litigation;

l) Trial in the United States is divided into two and sometimes three distinct parts: pre-trial for discovery, trial and damages. The pre-trial is typically the longest stage and may last for a year or more. Trial proceeds day to day until completed and is typically a relatively continuous quick hearing process. In Japan the "trial" consists of the entire Oral Argument or Plenary Hearing. The court sets the first Oral Argument session when the court serves the Complaint in the action. The Oral Argument stage can take several years. There is no separate "trial" stage in the case. The court may utilize a semi-private Preparation for Oral Argument procedure in an attempt to resolve some issues. Most importantly this procedure is used in an attempt to quickly settle the case. The court may send the case to in-court conciliation;

m) American trials are characterized by oral testimony of witnesses who are vigorously cross-examined. As a general rule lawyers decide who will be the witnesses in the case. The judge's gatekeeper function as to witnesses is limited. The judge is a gatekeeper concerning expert witness testimony. In the United States there are strict rules of evidence that are enforced through lawyer objections to questions and immediate judicial rulings as to admissibility. Japanese procedure calls on the lawyers to submit proffers of proof concerning witness testimony. Judges may not on their own call witnesses (except in administrative law cases under the ACLL and in Impeachment trials). However, judges perform the gatekeeper function of deciding whether a party designated witness may be called to give oral testimony. Proffers are very detailed in Japan. Judges frequently prefer to accept either the proffer or a written statement instead of oral witness testimony. Oral testimony is the exception rather than the rule in Japan, although the Code may create a different impression;

n) Third-person witness testimony is rarely used in Japan (except in some of the more recent types of litigation such as medical malpractice and building construction cases). Party testimony also is not favored by judges who view parties as self-interested and hence not helpful witnesses. On the other hand, parties and their representatives may be questioned by the court in more informal sessions such as the Preparation for Oral Argument sessions;

o) The judge in the United States will be a relatively minor player in the trial/pre-trial process and will not suggest a settlement to the parties (although the judge will be pleased if the parties settle the case). The American judge does not consider it a duty to protect the rights of either party (except perhaps for a pro se party). The American system places protection of party rights in the lawyer representing the party. American judges are not part of a civil service bureaucracy. Whether judges resolve cases by settlement or judgment after trial has no effect on their position, status or salary. In Japan the judge has a paternalistic attitude towards parties (and lawyers). The judge is concerned with protecting the rights of the parties. The judge has an obligation to see that a substantively correct decision is reached. The judge is an active participant in the case and controls the hearing, witness testimony, production of documentary evidence, etc. Unlike the American judge the Japanese judge sees it as his/her duty to bring about a settlement in the case. Settlement is in the judge's interest as a civil service judicial Secretariat closely monitors judges and one factor considered by the bureaucracy is the judge's record in getting parties to settle. The judge may actively suggest settlement terms to the parties and may try to compel settlement by explaining what decision will be reached if the parties fail to settle;

p) Conciliation is functionally different in Japan than in the United States. In Japan the judge may be directly involved in the conciliation process; a conciliation commission may have authority to recommend a settlement to the parties; if the parties do not agree the commission may suggest that the judge adopt its recommendation as the decision in the case. The judge is the decision-maker in regard to questions of law and fact and will use the position of judge to obtain a settlement. In the United States the judge is removed from the conciliation process. The judge will not be informed of the workings of the process but simply will be advised whether an agreement was reached. The American judge will facilitate party negotiation but will probably not suggest a settlement as the judge wishes to remain a neutral party with no interest in the result;

p.1) "In-Court" conciliation in the United States is a private affair although it may take place under a court suggestion, in the courthouse or even with the assistance of the magistrate or a judge not handling the case. The negotiations are private. The judge determining the case will not be made privy to the settlement talks. The conciliator will not suggest a course of action to the judge. The judge will not attempt to compel a settlement if the parties cannot agree. A party who does not agree to settle will not be "blamed" by the court for failure of negotiations. In Japan the process is not confidential in that the court may participate in the conciliation process. If the court does not participate, the conciliation commission may advise the judge handling the case as to an appropriate settlement;

q) Lawyers are in charge of the litigation in the United States. Lawyers do the discovery of facts, decide what witnesses to depose and call at trial, actively question and cross-examine witnesses and make frequent exceptions during the course of trial to try to prevent adverse information that is not properly admissible at trial from being presented to the trier of fact (either a jury of lay people or a judge trying a case without a jury). Lawyers in Japan have a much more restricted and subdued role. Lawyers may ask for document production but production is in the control of the judge and limited in scope. Lawyers may suggest witnesses but the calling of witnesses is a judicial function. Lawyers may question witnesses but rarely are proficient at the task of direct or cross-examination. The judge may be a more effective questioner. The judge is a more active questioner than in the United States. The judge decides what witnesses and evidence will be considered in the case;

r) American trial is characterized by Oral Examination of witnesses in open court. The examination is governed by rules of evidence that are quite technical and are designed to assure that only relevant facts are presented to the decision-maker (typically an untrained jury). The same procedures that govern fact witnesses govern expert witnesses except that experts are qualified to give opinions. In addition the American judge is supposed to act as a gatekeeper to assure that the expertise involved is consistent with generally accepted professional standards. In Japan there are few witnesses in the typical trial. Judges may accept written witness statements in lieu of oral testimony. Because a professional judge presumed to better understand what evidence is relevant tries the case there are few rules of evidence and little in the way of evidentiary objections. While expert witnesses can testify, the use of experts is more restricted in Japan as many experts refuse to testify out of concern about being treated badly on cross-examination. A new expert commissioner system has been established and expert commissioners can give their expert views either orally in open court or through written testimony. Expert commissioners will be able to question witnesses—including party experts. Courts are likely to place greater weight on the opinion of an expert commissioner than on a party-paid expert witness;

s) Japanese Oral Argument [Plenary Proceeding or Plenary Hearing] is dominated by the judge's "clarification" obligation. Clarification means more than simply clarifying a statement to make it more understandable. Clarification means clarifying the issues and facts and in doing so narrowing and deciding some of the issues and facts. In carrying out this obligation the judge plays a very active inquisitional role and may order parties to appear in court to answer questions and produce evidence. American judges play a "clarification" role only when responding to a motion by a party. Typically a case does not get "clarified" (indeed there is no attempt to clarify the case) until after discovery is completed and the pre-trial order setting the road map for the trial is prepared;

t) American judges and juries are severely limited as to what facts not introduced into evidence they may consider. Only notorious or historical facts or facts agreed to by the parties need not be proven at the trial. In Japan the judge has greater discretion to take "judicial notice" of facts. Some facts that need to be proven in the United States do not need to be proven in Japan. Japanese judges are presumed to know the mores and customs of Japanese society. Facts as to mores of society are typically not presented at trial;

u) In the United States the plaintiff needs to establish its civil case by a mere preponderance (50%+) of the evidence. In Japan the judge uses a free evaluation of evidence methodology under which the court must be convinced that the plaintiff is correct. This is a more stringent standard than the American preponderance rule. In some areas the law shifts the burden. Burden is shifted, for example, in automobile accident cases and the burden has been dramatically lightened in environmental cases;

v) Japanese judges and lawyers are overworked. Judges want to avoid writing decisions or have their cases appealed. Decision writing and appeal use up judicial resources and time. Even at the end stages of a District Court Plenary Hearing the judge will try to get the parties to settle. The judge may give parties an outline of the probable decision in the case. Judges may point out (and if judges do not point it out counsel should be aware) that execution and collection on a judgment in Japan are not as easy as in the United States. Parties in Japan may be more successful in hiding assets from a judgment creditor than is true in the United States. Settlement that includes a payment at time of settlement may be more valuable than a judgment for a greater amount, which might take longer to collect on (or that might not be collectable). Although there is no guarantee of collection in the United States there are procedures available in the United States that help a lawyer locate assets and trace the path of assets that may have been owned by the judgment debtor. Collection is easier in the United States than in Japan and takes less time than in Japan;

w) On appeal in the United States the parties are bound by the record made in the trial court. New evidence is not admissible at the appeal level. Arguments not raised in the lower court usually cannot be raised on appeal. Appeal is based on legal issues including the question of whether the trial judge committed errors in making legal rulings during the course of the trial. In Japan the first level appeal is not restricted to the record made below. Parties can, with permission of the court, raise new issues and can present new evidence on appeal. The first level appeal (*koso* appeal) is considered a continuation of the trial. Appeal can be a lengthy affair in Japan. In the United States, because appeal involves only legal questions, appeal tends to be a relatively quick process;

x) Most parties in litigation in the United States are represented by counsel. In Japan at the trial level many parties are not represented by counsel. However, once the case moves to appeal most parties (especially appellants) are represented by counsel. Because the first level appeal is in many ways a continuation of the trial, when counsel appears for the first time at appeal the case will be tried in the appeal court;

y) Appeal courts in Japan are as active as are trial courts in trying to get the parties to reach an amicable settlement. Appeal courts will devote resources to attempt to get the parties to settle;

z) The Japanese lawyer is one of the brightest of the brightest having passed a test that most American lawyers could not pass (even if given in English). The lawyer is one of a very few to be able to gain bengoshi status. The bengoshi is highly educated and smart. However, as a general rule the lawyer's *legal* training is not up to American standards and it should not be expected that most lawyers are able to do in litigation what an American lawyer regularly does in litigation. Inability to conduct effective cross-examination is a prime example of the difference in training and experience of Japanese and American lawyers;

aa) Precedent in Japan is not as important as precedent in the United States. Japan is a civil law society. Decisions of upper courts are only binding on lower courts in the case in which rendered. On the other hand, Japanese judges as bureaucrats do not wish to make mistakes that can hurt their career opportunities. Judges in Japan are very well tuned in to what their senior judges are doing and will not want to "step out of line" on matters that are already a part of established law;

bb) Japanese judges are highly educated, very bright, of the highest integrity and take their job as jurist very seriously. Unlike American judges most have never practiced law and have little first hand appreciation of the feelings and emotions of clients. The judge will attempt to protect the client from mistakes that could prejudice a virtuous case and will even attempt to protect the client from the client's lawyer if the judge feels the lawyer is making mistakes;

cc) As a consequence of being part of a civil service in a country that has a high regard for the bureaucracy, the judge has a greater respect for the government and the position taken by the government in litigation than would an American judge. It is exceedingly difficult—and surely substantially more difficult—for a plaintiff to win litigation against the government, especially a case seeking to overturn governmental action, than is true in American litigation.

dd) Litigation seeking to reverse an administrative disposition in Japan is much more difficult to win than in the United States. The Japanese approach to standing to sue is more restrictive than the American approach. Even the 2004 initiative to amend the Administrative Case Litigation Law is unlikely to greatly expand standing. The Japanese approach to administrative discretion gives Japanese bureaucrats much greater leeway in exercising discretion than their American counterparts. Japanese judges are more solicitous to the views of the bureaucracy as to what is appropriate government policy than American judges are of American administrative officials. This solicitude is more pronounced where a question of changing administrative action is involved than where a plaintiff seeks money damages;

ee) The Administrative Case Litigation Law governing administrative law cases has a relatively short statute of limitations (even after the amendment proposed by the government in the 2004 initiative that will extend the statute to six months). The ACLL also has some provisions that are quite unusual when compared to American practice. Among these are the provision allowing the court *sua sponte* to call and question witnesses; the circumstance decision pursuant to which the court may find the administrative action being challenged unlawful but nonetheless permit the action to stand on the theory that to overturn the action would harm the public; and the Prime Minister's objection to a provisional remedy. The ACLL allows for suit to overturn administrative determinations (a *shobun*). However, most Japanese administrative action is undertaken informally through the process of Administrative Guidance. Guidance is, in theory, voluntary and thus there is no government decision that is subject to judicial review. The reality is that guidance is followed and there is good reason for the administered in Japan to follow guidance even though the written law may state that failure to follow guidance cannot lead to penalty. American clients doing business in Japan are well advised in many cases to seek guidance in advance and in all cases to take Administrative Guidance seriously;

ff) Monetary damages in Japan are significantly less generous than in the United States. There is no collateral damages rule and payment from a third party to compensate for damage suffered will be offset against the damages sought in an action. In the intellectual property area there have been recent changes reflecting a change in national policy. Under these changes damages are both easier to prove and are becoming more generous in the patent, copyright and other intellectual property areas;

gg) It is easier to sue Japanese public officials for negligent or intentional misconduct than it is to sue American officials. This route is typically taken when it is considered ineffective to attempt to challenge administrative action under the ACLL. However, only money damages can be collected in such suits. There exists a kind of "qualified immunity" under which the government is not responsible if the action of government officials and/or employees is simply mistaken or erroneous rather than negligent or intentional;

hh) Although cases may be tried to a collegial court in Japan the important judge to convince (at least at the District Court level) is the chief judge of the panel. The assistant judge is a judge in training and will not want to buck higher authority, and in a dispute between the chief judge of the panel and the other judge in the panel the chief judge of the panel will likely win. At the appeal level this division is less apparent. Nonetheless it is important to win the vote of the presiding or chief judge. In America all judges are equal and when arguing a case to a panel it is not seniority but temperament, division of opinion among the judges and reputation of the judges that is important;

ii) In Japan it is important to remember that the judge is a part of the government bureaucracy and is attempting to resolve cases in a way that is both fair and in accord with the bureaucratic agenda. The first items on that agenda are speed of determination and a fair resolution of the matter. The judicial bureaucracy supports compromise settlement as a means of achieving both these objectives;

jj) In Japan a matter may not be finally resolved even after a final judgment has been entered. Japan's rules for preclusion are different from those in the United States. There is no collateral estoppel rule and *res judicata* applies to the specific *res* that is adjudicated. Claims that are related and might have been raised in the suit but were not are not resolved by the decision—although counsel having authority to settle the suit that has been brought may have implied authority to settle the claims that are related but not raised in the litigation. In the United States there is a collateral estoppel rule. *Res judicata* has a broader reach than in Japan and applies to matters that are related and could have been raised in the litigation. This difference must be considered when drafting settlement documents;

kk) Foreign judgments are usually entitled to comity in Japan if the granting jurisdiction gives reciprocity to Japanese judgments, the rendering court had jurisdiction, the defendant was properly served (not by publication) and the judgment does not violate Japanese public policy. The reciprocity requirement applies to the jurisdiction granting the judgment. In the United States most judgments are granted by State courts. Thus reciprocity questions may involve issues of State law. Punitive damage awards violate Japanese public policy. Failure to take the necessary formal steps regarding witness testimony and even witness interviews in Japan may place an American judgment in violation of Japanese public policy. A judgment for a Japanese defendant in a declaratory judgment action may render an American judgment unavailable for execution in Japan;

ll) Japan is a signatory (along with the United States) of the New York Convention. Accordingly, Japan recognizes foreign arbitration awards from other signatory nations. Similarly the United States recognizes arbitration awards granted in a Japanese arbitration;

mm) There is no class action in Japan. The representative action may allow others similarly situated to join in the litigation and be added as parties even after the litigation is in progress. A party similarly situated must take the affirmative step of seeking entry to the case and must be added as a party in order to receive the benefits of a judgment. To Japanese clients the American class action could easily be confused with the representative action (indeed some may even refer to the representative action as Japan's class action). Such a misunderstanding could well lead to a misunderstanding of the extent of exposure and potential liability—especially where a jury is entitled to determine damages or where punitive damages (also unknown in Japan) may be involved.

nn) First level appeal in Japan (*koso* appeal) is not based on the record made at the initial trial level as is the case in the United States. Rather, first level appeal is a continuation of the trial at the appeal court level. Thus new evidence may be submitted, the Preparation for Oral Argument or Preliminary Oral Argument stage is engaged in at the appeal level, new arguments may be raised on appeal. Although the Code of Civil Procedure provides for the possibility of preclusion if issues are not properly raised at the proper time, the reality is that preclusion is rarely invoked.

oo) Counsel must obtain a new authorization to represent the party on appeal in Japan. Appeal involves a new filing fee as well as a new up-front payment of counsel fees. Cases may be pending on appeal in Japan for several years. Unlike the Supreme Court of the United States that typically decides all cases argued during the Term by the end of June of the Term, the Supreme Court of Japan may take several years before deciding a case.

pp) It is more time consuming and more difficult to execute on judgments in Japan than is true of judgments in the United States. Whereas in the United States parties have discovery devices available in Supplementary Proceedings to attempt to locate assets or transfer of assets by judgment debtors, such devices are not available in Japan.

15

Justice and Civil Procedure in Japan

In the lobby of the Supreme Court of Japan there is a small bronze statue of Justice. As in the United States she holds the scales of justice in her hand. But unlike the statue of Justice that one would find in the United States she is not blind. Rather, Justice can see the parties whose cause she must weigh in the balance. Moreover, her face is the face of the Buddha of compassion. As well as "right" compassion may thus tip the scales of justice. This statue tells us much about justice in Japan—at least civil justice.

Blind justice need not see the parties before her. The law treats all equally and looking upon the parties may allow considerations other than the facts and the law to govern the decision. Of course justice must be tempered with compassion but compassion is not permitted to override the rights of the parties as established in the law. It is more significant to blind justice that society (the sum total of all who have or who may have disputes in the future) has an understandable system of rules to govern personal and commercial intercourse than that a specific party in a specific situation for whom one may feel great compassion win a case. Of course the rules must be based on fundamental principles such as those contained in the United States Constitution—due process of law, equal protection of the laws and the fundamental freedoms spelt out in that document. With these fundamental freedoms as a basic foundation for the legal system, American law permits the parties to enter into relationships with a reasonably good understanding of what the legal principles are that are to govern that relationship. As a rule, those principles govern even if the circumstances of the parties should change during the course of their relationship. To blind Justice bad law (providing it is not so bad as to violate the basic principles of the system) is better than no law or at least law so flexible that its parameters and application to situations is unknown or unknowable.

Justice that sees all with the eyes of compassion informs us that individual instances of right are at least as important as a system that grants predictability and places primary responsibility on individuals in society. It is not the function of blind Justice to search out the facts of the matter and protect a party from ineffective counsel. Compassionate Justice seeing how a matter is developing in the court has an obligation to protect clients from mistakes of counsel. Compassionate Justice has an obligation to seek out the true facts to assure a correct decision.

To some Japanese lawyers, professors, judges and theorists the American system is strange indeed. The highest appeal court does not have a primary function of correcting the wrongs of the lower court and does not seek out cases where the lower court made an error. Certiorari may be denied because the lower court decision is correct. On the other hand, denial of certiorari does not mean that the lower court decision is correct. Certiorari is usually denied because the issue is not one that the court wishes to hear at this time. Usually certiorari is denied because there is no conflict between the circuits. To the Japanese commentator the inquisitional system, where the judge is required to seek out the true facts and arrive at substantive justice even if this means the waiving of certain procedural niceties, may be preferred to the American adversarial system.[1] Nonetheless the civil procedure system in Japan does not provide for a classical inquisition system. The judge does not have the authority to *ex officio* call witnesses. The judge may only call such witnesses as the parties may request. Nonetheless the court does have authority as part of its clarification obligation to point the parties in the correct direction. Once a party suggests a witness, the court may examine the witness. The court may change the order of examination to assure that all of the facts are properly brought out in the Oral Argument.

But does the Japanese court's more broad ranging authority to investigate into facts and its paternalistic attitude towards the parties and above all its desire to see that the party who should win does in fact win mean that a litigant in Japan will get more justice than in the United States? From the common law adversarial system lawyer's perspective the inquisition system fails to achieve greater justice than the adversarial system. Recall that in Japan's drive to be free from the unequal treaties imposed on it by the Western powers the British objected because Japan had decided to follow the route of becoming a civil law country. To the British representatives in Japan, Consular Jurisdiction was better than permitting British citizens to be subjected to the inquisition of the civil law. To the adversary system lawyer the inquisition falls short as the real party in interest, the parties to the case and their champions (their lawyers), must stand aside and permit a civil servant bureaucrat with no personal stake in the outcome to control investigation and also decide the matter. To the American common law lawyer the adversary system, which gives the responsibility for developing both the facts and the legal contentions to the parties who have the most to win and lose, stands a much better chance of arriving at a just decision.

---

1 For an interesting exposition of this position in the context of arbitration see, Takeo Tateishi, Inquisitional Approach in Dispute Resolution—A Japanese Way to Mete Out Justice, Wave Length JSE Bulletin No. 44, p 8 (Japan Shipping Exchange, March 2002).

It is suggested that the issue of Justice and Civil Procedure in Japan is not dependent on the inquisition versus adversary nature of the two systems. Rather, the question of whether the Japanese civil litigation system provides justice or at least as much justice as it could provide resides elsewhere. It resides in how the system actually operates. As in the dispute between inquisition advocates and adversarial advocates the answer may depend on how one views the problem and what part of the problem is being considered.

The single most driving force in litigation in Japan today may be the need to resolve cases more quickly. It is undoubtedly true that justice delayed is justice denied. The sword of speed cuts both ways. It is also true that to achieve speed shortcuts are taken that stand in the way of achieving real justice. Speed may lead parties to the belief that they have been denied justice. If the cost of speed is an inadequate procedure to determine the facts or a procedure that appears inadequate to the parties and their champions then there are flaws in the system that need to be addressed.

The drive to speed up the litigation process has been accompanied by a reduction in the use of live witness testimony in Japanese litigation. Not only third-person witnesses but also party witnesses have been on the decline in recent years as the pace of litigation has quickened and as the average case is decided more quickly. The inability of many parties to have an opportunity to tell their side of the case at the formal Oral Argument stage of the procedure may lead to a belief that justice cannot be obtained in the courts and that other means of resolving disputes should be sought. Lawyers, unable to present oral witnesses to support their client's position and unable to cross-examine the written witness statements of the opposition may see the system as failing to provide an appropriate degree of justice. Cross-examination may have more meaning to the common law advocate than to the civil law *bengoshi* but the Code of Civil Procedure adopts the cross examination model. Such model can only have meaning if there are live witnesses to cross-examine.

Speed also affects the manner of resolving cases. There is a commonality of interests in Japan between the courts, the bengoshi and possibly the parties to resolve cases through voluntary settlement. The resolution of cases through settlement is a positive for any judicial system. To the extent the parties are satisfied with the settled result the system promotes justice. Nonetheless, question remains as to whether the push for settlement in some cases is so strong that parties either are or feel compelled to settle. Thus the practice of letting the parties know in advance what the court is likely to decide while holding out the possibility that failure to settle upon terms reflecting the court's approach will result in some penalty is inconsistent with justice. Compelling parties to conciliate in an effort to reach a settlement can greatly aid the process of finding a just decision especially when the conciliators are chosen for their practical approach to problem solving rather than a strict legal approach to issues. Justice problems are presented when conciliators can report to the ultimate decision-maker regarding what has occurred during the conciliation process and/or when the trial judge is conciliator and decision-maker.

Such problems are more likely when career judges are rated, promoted, assigned, etc. at least in part based on their ability to bring about conciliated settlements than when such factor is left out of the career enhancing equation.

Speed can be attained by requiring parties and their counsel to be responsible for their acts. Failure to raise issues at the Preparation for Oral Argument stage of the case (or the Preliminary Oral Argument stage) could in reality be the basis for refusal to allow the issue or evidence to be raised at a later date. Closer attention to the modern German system and its restrictions on abuse of the late raised issue question might be helpful and is consistent with Japan's movement back to German law principles of civil procedure. If the new law schools are able to produce better trained and better practically equipped lawyers then these legal professionals should be made to shoulder more of the responsibility for cases. Judges can utilize their traditional paternalistic role for pro se cases and for cases where there is reason to believe that the counsel is failing to properly represent the client. In cases where a party is represented, counsel should shoulder more of the burden of putting the case together and presenting it in a timely fashion. That burden should include the burden of timely presentation of issues and facts. In this way the Oral Argument stage of the case can move in a relatively compact way after completion of the Preparation for Oral Argument or Preliminary Oral Argument stage. In some few cases this may result in judgments that may appear to be inconsistent with the idea of justice. However, the over all effect on the system should be to speed up litigation, to compel lawyers to provide better representation leading to all parties receiving better justice from the system. As an initial step the courts should presume that new arguments are not allowed at the first level appeal. This presumption may be overcome when the party was not represented below or where there is a showing of extraordinary reasons for the failure. If the court were to announce its intentions by way of a Rule strengthening the timely presentation provisions of the Code and making clear that the court is serious about application of the Rule in future cases then parties and bengoshi would be placed on notice. Considering the high intellectual quality of Japan's bengoshi corps bengoshi would react to the new Rule with timely activities.

Surely at the first level and second level appeal level there is no need for cases to take as long as they presently take. Legislation giving the Supreme Court control over its docket by further reducing the grounds for appeal as of right is inconsistent with the view that the court is a court of errors. The numbers of appeals coming to the Supreme Court call for a reexamination of the court's role. It is suggested that the function of the court should more closely resemble that of the Supreme Court of the United States. A Supreme Court of errors cannot reasonably handle the workload of appeals that come to it from such a broad base. Granting the Supreme Court the discretionary authority to take appeals along with having the court announce some of the principles for its certiorari function and rejecting the court of errors approach of the Ministry of Justice will make the court more efficient and effective. Such a system permits the Supreme Court to use its court of errors function in cases where the error is so grave as to require correction. Such a system would enable the court to handle the truly significant cases that need highest court consideration. In any event, adoption of such a discretionary role, if the discretion is exercised to significantly decrease the court's workload, will not only result in faster handling of cases in the Supreme Court but also will result in more cases being resolved at the High Court level. Such change could significantly reduce the time of civil litigation.

The true resolution of the speed of litigation issue is not legislation that points the courts in the direction of deciding cases at the first instance within a fixed time period (two years). An increase in the size of the corps of judges and better use of the judge corps are more appropriate. A recent cost-benefit analysis of the effect of increasing the number of judges available to handle civil suits at the District Court shows both that the number of civil trials is proportional to the number of judges and that increasing the corps of judges would have benefits for the Japanese society. The analysis shows that substantial benefits to the Japanese economy and welfare would flow from an increase in the pool of judges to try civil cases.[2]

Recent graduates from the new law schools who have passed the Bar Examination and have passed through the Legal Research and Training Institute should be considered for employment in the Judicial Branch as law clerks. Such law clerks might be hired for two-years as in the American system. Such clerks could be assigned to court panels leading to mentoring of such clerks by senior judges. The clerks could free up time of judges by providing legal research activities presently performed by judges. Other work performed by judges such as first drafts of opinions, orders, etc. could be performed by law clerks. Not only would such clerks help the judicial system but also the clerks themselves would become better bengoshi knowing how the court system works from the inside. This in turn would lead to better, more competent representation. Understanding the system from the inside could assist in the process of a change over to a system where lawyers take more responsibility for cases and judges take less responsibility. A clerk system might bring Bench and Bar closer together. Clerks will eventually become practicing lawyers and likely remain in contact with mentoring judges.[3]

---

2 Tomio Kinoshita, A Cost-Benefit Analysis of Enlarging the Japanese Judicial System, in 20 Contemporary Economic Policy 179-192 (Western Economic Association International, April 2002) (concluding that the Japanese judicial system should be increased by at least two-fold and that such doubling will increase net social benefits to Japanese society by over 900 billion yen.)

3 Law clerks would not supplant the present system where such District Courts as the Tokyo and Osaka District Court utilize the services of Legal Research Officials. Such officials help in cases where specialized knowledge is required—such as patent cases—and need not be lawyers. See, The Japanese Justice System, The Secretariat of the Justice System Reform Council, July 1999 page 2 of 15 on the web www.kantei.go.jp/foreign/policy/sihou/singikai/990620_e.html.

The Lawyers Law[4] should be amended and Bar Associations should recognize a class of bengoshi who work full time for the administrative arm of government. When such bengoshi leave government service they should be permitted to enter into the private practice having already been recognized as bengoshi. The government, like any client, is entitled to representation and there is no reason why the government cannot have its own lawyer or lawyers on staff. Indeed, since bengoshi have historically had an independent streak, having in-house government bengoshi who can leave the government at any time and set up shop as private practitioners could lead to more independence by government officials who are responsible for giving legal advice and better advice and decision making concerning legal questions by the government. The Bar and the Executive Branch might structure a system that provides for a corps of bengoshi whose career advancement is separated from the control of the agency for whom the bengoshi work. To resolve issues affecting the career advancement and/or discipline of bengoshi working in the government, a committee composed of members of the Bar could be established. Judges who presently serve in the Executive Branch can then be returned to the Judicial Branch advancing three objectives: a) freeing the Judicial Branch from a separation of powers problem, b) obviating a real or a perceived public relations and independence problem, and c) making more judges available to handle cases.

Class actions while viewed positively in the United States by consumer and plaintiff advocates are not an essential element of a system that provides justice to the parties. The defendant is also entitled to justice and question exists as to whether an American style class action system with little recovery to individual plaintiffs, large expense to business and potentially excessive profits to lawyers is either in the public interest or the interest of the legal system and justice in general. There may be problems that are so small that litigation is not the way to get results. Cost benefit analysis may show that the costs to the economy and society may outweigh the benefits to individual plaintiffs in certain class action scenarios. Certainly class actions that result in multimillion-dollar awards to counsel and coupons or other virtually worthless consideration to the plaintiff class along with expenses to the national economy through the costs of the litigation are not serving the interests of justice. On the other hand, class actions that obtain real systemic relief or that result in real damage awards to persons who have actually been victims of wrongful action are a positive and certainly have a place in a system that seeks to do justice. The representative action, while probably in need of some modification to make notice of the case and ability to join easier and less expensive, may represent a useful middle ground between the class action and no action at all.

Inadequate damages provided by courts in Japan raises a justice issue. Japan has begun the process of assessing the inadequacy of its damages system. Reforms

4 Lawyers Law Article 30 prohibits a lawyer from assuming a full time government position with exceptions listed in the law. None of the exceptions would allow for in-house government counsel.

undertaken to assist the Japanese economy and to assist major companies in protecting their intellectual property rights should result in more realistic damage awards in intellectual property cases. No change has been made in damage awards that favor individuals who have been damaged by large commercial interests. The Judicial Branch has the power to slowly ratchet up damage awards so that plaintiffs receive realistic compensation for injuries while at the same time avoiding the abuses and bounty nature of some American litigation.

The lack of a sanctions regime to support the pre-filing and post-filing Inquiry Process and the lack of sanctions to enforce the timeliness aspects of the Preparation for Oral Argument system inhibit the justice aspects of the Japanese judicial system. The recent change in the Inquiry Process allowing inquiries before the filing of litigation is potentially a major step towards increasing justice. As presently structured the Inquiry Process is inadequate and virtually useless. Permitting some form of discovery pre-filing is a potential breakthrough in relieving plaintiffs from the almost impossible burden many of them face of submitting enough facts at the start of a case to support a fact-based Complaint system. It is possible that within a few years the system will adopt a sanctions regime so that parties are compelled to provide answers to questions. If such a sanctions regime is put in place and proves successful it may pave the way for a limited post-filing discovery system. Such discovery need not be (and it is suggested should not be) as broad and as free as the American system. Some realistic means of obtaining relevant evidence that aids the judge in understanding the case would serve the public interest, would mobilize bengoshi to use their talents to discover evidence and would increase the level of justice.

The extensive use of the self-use exception to document production also has an inhibiting effect on civil justice. The Supreme Court's recent decisions reinforcing the idea that injury as well as self-use of the preparing entity is required for the application of the rule should allow inferior courts to order production of more documents. Open discussion within an organization is an important value worthy of protection. At the same time factual material (as opposed to opinions or advice) contained in self-use documents that disclose wrongdoing on the part of the entity should be available to plaintiffs. Such information should certainly be available in cases where the public interest is served by either disclosing the wrong doing or providing damages to the injured party. Pollution cases, consumer fraud cases or cases involving a dangerous product are situations where liberalization is particularly important. If the facts in internal documents show that management callously disregarded known defects and thereby caused injury to the plaintiff the court is entitled to use such information in rendering a just decision.

Perhaps the greatest challenge for the civil procedure system is how it handles cases where the government is a party and the interests of the government and the governed clash. The present inability to use the justice system as part of a system of checks and balances against the power of the bureaucracy is a significant justice issue. Similarly the inability to use the civil procedure system to effectively challenge legislation on constitutional grounds is a justice issue. Of course litigation challenging legislation may be brought. The Supreme Court may ultimately decide such litigation. But that begs the question of whether the civil procedure system allows for effective use of the Constitution as a brake on legislative or executive action. As long as judges serve in the Executive Branch and give the Executive advice as to the constitutionality of laws and as long as such assigned judges (as well as bureaucrats serving in the same capacity) are elevated to the Supreme Court there seems little likelihood that the Supreme Court will find many laws unconstitutional. Such a holding would certainly cause fellow judges (and perhaps the judicial system as a whole) to lose face.

The deference that the Supreme Court grants to Legislative or Executive action is so great that although decisions note that for abuse of discretion the court may intervene the reality is the court does not find such abuse of discretion. The court needs to reassess its role not as a part of the government but as an independent watchdog over the legislature and the Executive Branch and as a guardian of the people. After 50 years it may be time for the Supreme Court to assert itself as an equal branch of government. Recognition that the Diet is the highest organ of state power is not inconsistent with recognition that the power given to the Diet is restricted by the Constitution. The Constitution designates the Supreme Court as the organ that decides what is and what is not constitutional under its power of judicial review. Failure on the part of the court to utilize its judicial review power may result in the court losing that power as calls for "reform" heard in the form of a new Constitutional Court are given more credence. Such a court is unlikely to solve the problem. Indeed, insular judges appointed by the political branches of government for the sole purpose of ruling on the constitutionality of acts of those branches are less likely to hold the government to account than are generalist judges hearing a wide variety of cases.

The judicial bureaucracy's deference to the administrative bureaucracy also needs to be rethought. To truly perform a justice granting role the court system must protect the rights of the governed against the governors. The Judicial Branch, if it is to do justice, must be an effective check that can balance the power of the administrators in government. So long as the courts utilize restrictive doctrines of standing and the necessity of a determination (*shobunsai*) and so long as the doctrine of free discretion continues to guide review of administrative action the court will be failing in an important aspect of its justice responsibility. As long as Administrative Guidance, the real vehicle for government administration in Japan, is outside the reach of the judicial power justice cannot be fully administered by Japan's courts. The 2004 initiative at Administrative Case Litigation Law reform falls short of the recommendations of the Law Reform Council.

The problem with the pace of judicial reform in Japan is not that there are not enough lawyers nor is it that lawyers are not sufficiently trained. (Although more and better-trained lawyers are needed and the advances of the last few years are helpful.) The concept of the new law schools is movement in the correct direction even if the advantage given to *Hogakubu* graduates entering the schools might be viewed as inconsistent with the reform. Part of the problem is that there are not enough judges. The failure to institute a sanctions regime for either evidence production or failures to raise issues at the appropriate time means that previous efforts at reform have little effect on actual cases. Just as the Roman Law system was characterized by the notion that all roads lead to Rome so too in Japan all roads lead to conciliation. While conciliation is an important aspect of dispute resolution, it should not displace the rights of the litigants including the right to have their dispute decided by the judicial system. The existence of a strong litigation system is not only important to the parties who wish to use litigation to resolve disputes but litigation in court is essential to the growth of a vibrant legal system. The input of adverse parties through contests in court helps the law grow and adjust to new situations and problems. Evolution of the law is too important to be left to government bureaucrats who are removed from everyday life. Litigation between parties with real disputes arising out of real life situations is essential to the orderly evolution of the legal system.[5]

In the next round of judicial reform the government can, when it acts on the Judicial Reform Council's recommendations dealing with alternative dispute resolution, foster a friendly competition between the judicial system and ADR. It remains to be seen whether the government follows that path and consequently strengthens both the ADR and judicial dispute resolution systems. If the government acts to strengthen ADR at the expense of judicial litigation it will do a disservice to justice in Japan.

Although American common law lawyers may have a bias against an inquisition system or indeed any system that fails to provide American style discovery, it is well to remember that the American system is the exception and not the rule. The civil law system is more common than the common law system and discovery on the American model is unusual even for common law systems. Further, the American system has spawned its own set of abuses that result in excessive damage awards that may be adversely affecting the public interest, a litigation culture that threatens some of the medical and scientific advances made and that could possibly be made in the future, trial by threat that could lead to settlement under fear rather than legal rights of the parties, etc. Any objective observer would need to admit that the asbestos mess in American courts calls for a solution other than more of the same. American courts are not free of the charge of unreasonable delay in the handling of civil cases. Civil cases filed in federal District Courts that have a significantly large backlog of criminal (principally drug) cases that take precedence over civil cases because of Speedy Trial Act requirements may take many years before coming to trial. It is not uncommon for automobile accident cases in some State court systems to take 4 or 5 or even more years before coming to trial. Such long delay, as is the case with delay in Japan, obviously accommodates a settlement system where monetary compensation if not as large as antici-

5 See, Takao Tanase, The Management of Disputes: Automobile Compensation in Japan, 24 Law & Society Review 651, 685-687 (1990).

pated at least is received earlier than would be the case if litigation took its normal time.

As for non-governmental disputes between private parties the situation in Japan today may not be so different from what it was in Tokugawa times.[6] Today's magistrate (judge) seems to prefer the role of conciliator to decision-maker. Settlement of cases brought to the court is the desired result. An up or down right or wrong decision by the judge is considered failure of the system. Not only do judges see themselves as carrying out a mediation/conciliation role but also there are numerous alternatives to the judicial system where mediation and conciliation can be carried out cheaper and faster. Each step in Japan's history of shoring up and supporting the legal system as a mechanism to resolve disputes through the use of the Code of Civil Procedure appears to have been met by a corollary move to strengthen alternative means of resolving disputes outside the legal system. The present drive to reform the legal system is no exception. As a rule parties in Japan receive justice from these alternatives to the courts. As these alternatives are more frequently used than the courts it may be that justice exists outside of and perhaps with little consideration of the Code of Civil Procedure. On the other hand the courts and the alternative dispute resolution mechanisms that exist in Japan might view each other as in a friendly competition with potential litigants as the customers for their services. Just as settlement is undertaken in Japan under the shadow of the law so too resolution of disputes in the court may take place in the shadow of ADR alternatives. If this is the case than every advance that makes one system more responsive to the needs to do justice and that provides the tools to assist in the quest for justice may have a positive spin-off effect requiring the other to match and seek to surpass that advance. [The Summary Court's small claim one-day hearing/decision process appears to have spawned a one-day hearing/decision arbitration process for relatively small commercial claims.]

To date the government's view of the judicial system as a dispute resolution mechanism appears to be to talk the talk of reform. But failure to turn talk into walk (action) may more accurately reflect a view that regards the system as more of a hindrance than a primary means of resolving disputes.[7] (Reforms in the intellectual property arena may be heralding a change—but it is likely that this is a case of special circumstance where the judicial system is assisting Japanese industry in warding off challenges to its research and development advances.) Perhaps it is

6 Writing in 1987 Judge Obuchi noted that the justice system in Japan harmonizes the foreign/imported Western system and the traditional Japanese system of conciliation and settlement through use of in-court compromise. Judge Obuchi concludes that the current Japanese system is not that dissimilar from the tradition system of Tokugawa times. See, Tetsuya Obuchi, Role of the court in the Process of Informal Dispute Resolution in Japan: Traditional and Modern Aspects, With Special Emphasis on In-Court Compromise, 20 Law in Japan 74, 100 (1987).

7 Professor Upham has pointed out that adjudication has been rejected by Japan's political elite in favor of some form of direct negotiation such as mediation or conciliation. Frank K. Upham, Visions of Justice in Postwar Japan: A Preliminary Inquiry in LAW IN EAST AND WEST (Waseda University Press, Tokyo 1988) 145, 161-165.

fear on the part of the bureaucracy that a strong viable judicial system will lead to use of that system as a law enforcement mechanism rather than allowing the bureaucracy to set the agenda and pace of enforcement. Perhaps it is simply a matter of culture and history. It may be a view that matters should be resolved in a non-hostile non-adversarial fashion.

The conservative approach of the LDP appears to prefer "old Japan values" and "old Japan dispute resolution" mechanisms to more modern—borrowed—approaches. In 1961 speaking at the conference that provided the materials for LAW IN JAPAN, Professor von Mehren noted that while traditional forms of dispute resolution in Japan may not be applicable to modern Japanese society resolution of disputes by the Judicial Branch of government was in a transitional phase and not yet accepted by Japanese society.[8] The transition period appears to be continuing forty years later and the knee jerk reaction of relying on ADR does not appear to have abated, with calls for modernizing and strengthening ADR paralleling reform of the judicial system and the Code of Civil Procedure. Just as cooperation and agreement were necessities and, if need be, forced necessities of the Tokugawa village, it may be that Japanese governments from Meiji times to modern times see it as their obligation to strengthen cooperation and agreement even if individual rights and the judicial system may suffer in the process. Whatever the reasons, it appears that each time the judicial system is strengthened, countermeasures are taken to insure that ADR remains the first line of dispute resolution in Japan.

Justice, whether through the courts or through ADR is not blind in Japan—but she could use some help in making the judicial system more receptive to damage claims and some procedures that aid the plaintiff in seeking justice. Above all, Justice requires a legal system that acts as an effective check on the powers of the other branches of government. It is in this arena that the Japanese system is at its weakest and requires dramatic improvement before (as recommended by the Law Reform Council) the Rule of Law permeates all aspects of Japanese society and before the public can receive the kind of Justice the Constitution contemplates.

8 LAW IN JAPAN (Arthur Taylor von Mehren Ed., Harvard University Press, 1963) 191.

Statutory Index

Administrative Case Litigation Law (ACLL)

Arbitration Law

Civil Code

Civil Conciliation Act

Civil Execution Law

Civil Procedure Code (CCP)

Civil Procedure Rules (CPR)

Civil Provisional Remedies Law

(Civil Provisional Relief Act Civil Preservation Act)

Commercial Code

Constitution of Japan

Copyright Act

Court Organization Law

Impeachment Law

Patent Law

Subject Index